Revision Checklist

Considering Your Whole Essay–Chapter 3

Using the <u>FACT</u> acronym, ask yourself these questions:

❑ Does my essay <u>F</u>IT together, presenting a central point for a specific audience? Does my thesis statement accurately reflect the content of my essay, or have I included material that has no bearing on the main point?

❑ Have I included all the material my reader will need to grasp my meaning, or do I need to <u>A</u>DD information or examples?

❑ Have I included material that fits the thesis but needs to be <u>C</u>UT because it is uninteresting, uninformative, or repetitious?

❑ Does a <u>T</u>EST of my organization show that the writing flows smoothly, with clear transitions between the various ideas?

Strengthening Paragraph Structure and Development–Chapter 14

❑ Does each paragraph have only one central idea?

❑ Is the idea stated in a topic sentence or clearly implied?

❑ Does the topic sentence help to develop the thesis statement?

❑ Does each paragraph contain enough supporting detail?

❑ Is each paragraph appropriately organized?

❑ Is the relationship between successive sentences clear?

❑ Is each paragraph clearly and smoothly related to those that precede and follow it?

❑ Does the introduction arouse interest and set the appropriate tone?

❑ Does the conclusion reflect the content of the essay and provide a sense of completeness?

Sharpening Sentences and Words–Chapters 15 and 16

❑ Are my sentences clearly and effectively constructed?

❑ Have I varied the pattern and length of my sentences?

❑ Do I know the meanings of the words I use?

❑ Do I explain meanings my reader may not know?

❑ Have I used the appropriate tone and level of diction?

❑ Does/would figurative language enhance my style?

❑ Have I avoided wordiness, euphemisms, clichés, mixed metaphors, and sexist language?

Editing the Draft–Handbook

❑ Have I inspected my writing for the types of errors listed in the editing symbols on the last page of the book?

STRATEGIES FOR SUCCESSFUL WRITING

A Rhetoric, Research Guide, Reader, and Handbook

SIXTH EDITION

James A. Reinking

Andrew W. Hart

Robert von der Osten

All of Ferris State University

Prentice Hall

Upper Saddle River, New Jersey 07458

Library of Congress Cataloging-in-Publication Data

Reinking, James A.
   Strategies for successful writing: a rhetoric, research guide, reader, and handbook /
James A. Reinking, Andrew W. Hart, Robert von der Osten.—6th ed.
   p. cm.
   Includes bibliographical references and index.
   ISBN 0-13-040673-2
   1. English language—Rhetoric—Handbooks, manuals, etc.   2. English
language—Grammar—Handbooks, manuals, etc.   3. Report writing—Handbooks, manuals,
etc.   4. College readers.   I. Hart, Andrew W.   II. Osten, Richard von der.
PE1408.R426   2001
808′.0427—dc21

2001024617

This edition is for little Stone Michael ("the Bink"),
whose infectious smile and endearing actions
always reinforce what's truly important.

Editor in Chief, English: *Leah Jewell*
Acquisitions Editor: *Corey Good*
Editorial Assistant: *Jennifer Collins*
VP/Director of Production/Manufacturing: *Barbara Kittle*
Director of Marketing: *Beth Gillet Mejia*
Senior Marketing Manager: *Brandy Dawson*
Senior Managing Editor: *Mary Rottino*
Production Editor: *Alison Gnerre*
Production Assistant: *Elizabeth Best*
Prepress and Manufacturing Manager: *Nick Sklitsis*
Prepress and Manufacturing Buyer: *Mary Ann Gloriande*

Creative Design Director: *Leslie Osher*
Art Director: *Maria Lange*
Interior and Cover Design: *Maria Lange*
Director, Image Resource Center: *Melinda Reo*
Photo Research Supervisor: *Beth Boyd*
Image Permissions Supervisor: *Kay Dellosa*
Permissions Coordinator: *Carolyn Gauntt*
Photo Researcher: *Diane Austin*
Line Art Manager: *Guy Ruggiero*
Illustrators: *Karen Noferi, Mirella Signoretto*

ACKNOWLEDGMENTS
Margaret Abbott, "Heritage," from *Matched Pair,* Condor Press, Dexter, MO, 1963.
(Acknowledgments continue on page 729, which constitutes an extension of the copyright page.)

© 2002, 1999, 1996, 1993, 1991, 1988 by Pearson Education, Inc.
Upper Saddle River, New Jersey 07458

Printed in the United States of America
10 9 8 7 6 5 4 3 2 1

ISBN 0-13-045292-0

PRENTICE-HALL INTERNATIONAL (UK) LIMITED, *London*
PRENTICE-HALL OF AUSTRALIA PTY. LIMITED, *Sydney*
PRENTICE-HALL CANADA, INC., *Toronto*
PRENTICE-HALL HISPANOAMERICANA, S.A., *Mexico*
PRENTICE-HALL OF INDIA PRIVATE LIMITED, *New Delhi*
PRENTICE-HALL OF JAPAN, INC., *Tokyo*
PEARSON EDUCATION ASIA PTE. LTD., *Singapore*
EDITORA PRENTICE-HALL DO BRASIL, LTDA., *Rio de Janeiro*

Contents

• •

v

Thematic Table of Contents

■ Handbook   607

Preface

The sixth edition of *Strategies for Successful Writing: A Rhetoric, Research Guide, Reader, and Handbook* is a comprehensive textbook that offers ample material for a full-year composition course. Instructors teaching a one-term course can make selections from Chapters 1–16, from whatever types of specialized writing suit the needs of their students, and from appropriate essays in the reader.

Because we strongly believe that an effective composition textbook should address the student directly, we have aimed for a style that is conversational yet clear and concise. We believe that our style invites students into the book, lessens their apprehensions about writing, and provides a model for their own prose. This style complements our strong student-based approach to writing, and together they help create a text that genuinely meets student needs.

■ Changes in the Sixth Edition

The enthusiastic response to the five previous editions both by teachers and students has been most gratifying. The sixth edition retains the many popular features of the previous ones and incorporates a number of improvements, suggested by users and reviewers, that should considerably enhance the utility of the text. Among these changes the following are noteworthy.

- Twelve of the essays in the Reader, over one-fourth of the total, are new. These additions significantly broaden the Reader's scope, increase its coverage of contemporary subjects, and expand its discussion potential.

- Discussions of writing and ethics now accompany Chapter 1, the chapters that explain the individual writing strategies, and the chapters on writing about literature, the library research paper, and primary research papers. These discussions address ethical issues pertinent to writing each type of paper.

- The individual-sentence exercises in the Handbook are all new.

- The writing strategy chapters now include updated and expanded suggestions for writing.

- The library research chapters now include guidelines for evaluating Internet material and also expanded and updated guidelines for online documentation.

- The Business Letters and Résumés chapter now includes sections on memorandums and e-mail, along with an updated form of the résumé.

- Assorted updates and additions throughout the text, too numerous to mention individually, should help make the text even more effective.

■ The Rhetoric

In addition to these improvements, the text offers many other noteworthy features. The Rhetoric consists of nineteen chapters, grouped into four parts. The first part includes three chapters. Chapter 1 introduces students to the purposes of writing; the need for audience awareness, which includes a discussion of discourse communities; and the qualities of good writing. Chapter 2 looks at the planning and drafting stages. Chapter 3 takes students through the various revision stages, starting with a systematic procedure for revising the whole essay and then moving to pointers for revising its component parts. Sets of checklists pose key questions for students to consider. Chapters 2 and 3 are unified by an unfolding case history that includes the first draft of a student paper, the initial revision marked with changes, and the final version. Notes in the margin highlight key features of the finished paper. Students can relate the sequence of events to their own projects as they work through the various stages. Both chapters offer suggestions for using a word processor, and Chapter 3 explains peer evaluation of drafts, collaborative writing, and maintaining and reviewing a portfolio.

The ten chapters in the second part (Chapters 4–13) feature the various strategies, or modes, used to develop papers. These strategies, which follow a general progression from less to more complex, are presented as natural ways of thinking, as problem-solving strategies, and therefore as effective ways of organizing writing. A separate chapter is devoted to each strategy. This part concludes with a chapter on mixing the writing strategies, which explains and shows that writers frequently use these patterns in assorted combinations for various purposes. Planning and writing guidelines are presented for problem/solution and evaluation reports, two common types that rely on a combination of strategies.

Except for Chapter 13, the discussion in each chapter follows a similar approach, first explaining the key elements of the strategy; next pointing out typical classroom and on-the-job applications to show students its practicality; and then providing specific planning, drafting, and revising guidelines. Practical heuristic questions are also posed. A complete student essay, accompanied by questions, follows the discussion section. These essays represent realistic, achievable goals and spur student confidence, while the questions reinforce the general principles of good writing and underscore the points we make in our discussions. Twenty carefully chosen writing suggestions follow the questions in most chapters. All chapters conclude with a section entitled "The Critical Edge." These sections, intended for above-average students, explain and illustrate how they can advance their writing purpose by synthesizing material from various sources. Synthesis, of course, helps students develop and hone their critical reading and thinking skills. Furthermore, the *Annotated Instructor's Edition* includes suggestions for using the Reader essays and writing strategies to build assignments around themes.

In the third part, we shift from full-length essays to the elements that make them up. Chapter 14 first discusses paragraph unity; it then takes up the topic sentence, adequate development, organization, coherence, and finally introductory, transitional, and concluding paragraphs. Throughout this chapter, as elsewhere, carefully selected examples and exercises form an integral part of the instruction.

Chapter 15 focuses on various strategies for creating effective sentences. Such strategies as coordinating and subordinating ideas and using parallelism help students to increase the versatility of their writing. The concluding section offers practical advice on crafting and arranging sentences so that they work together harmoniously. Some instructors may wish to discuss the chapters on paragraphs and sentences in connection with revision.

Chapter 16, designed to help students improve their writing style, deals with words and their effects. We distinguish between abstract and concrete words as well as between specific and general terms, and we also discuss the dictionary and thesaurus. Levels of diction—formal, informal, and technical—and how to use them are explained, as are tone, various types of figurative language, and irony. The chapter concludes by pointing out how to recognize and avoid wordiness, euphemisms, clichés, mixed metaphors, and sexist language.

The fourth and final part of the Rhetoric concentrates on three specialized types of college and on-the-job writing. Chapter 17 offers practical advice on studying for exams, assessing test questions, and writing essay answers. To facilitate student comprehension, we analyze both good and poor answers to the same exam question and provide an exercise that requires students to perform similar analyses.

Chapter 18 uses Stephen Crane's "The Bride Comes to Yellow Sky" as a springboard for its discussion. The chapter focuses on plot, point of view, character, setting, symbols, irony, and theme—the elements students will most likely be asked to write about. For each element, we first present basic features and then offer writing guidelines. Diverse examples illustrate these elements. The chapter ends with sections that detail the development of a student paper and explain how to include the views of others when writing about literature.

Like other parts of the text, Chapter 19 speaks to a practical reality by reminding students that the value of writing extends beyond the English classroom. Example letters address a variety of practical situations—for example, applying for a summer job.

■ The Research Guide

The Research Guide consists of three chapters. Chapter 20 is a thorough and practical guide to writing library research papers. A sample pacing schedule not only encourages students to plan their work and meet their deadlines but also enables them to track their progress. As in Chapters 2 and 3, a progressive case history gradually evolves into an annotated student paper, which includes the results of a personal inverview, thus demonstrating that primary research can reinforce secondary research.

Chapter 21 details and illustrates the correct formats for bibliographical references and in-text citations for both the MLA and APA systems of documentation. Guidelines are based on the 1994 edition of the *Publication Manual of the APA* and current online updates as well as the 1999 edition of *The MLA Style*

Manual. The chapter also explains how to handle the various types of quotations and how to avoid plagiarism. Our detailed treatment in Chapters 20 and 21 should make supplemental handouts or a separate research paper guide unnecessary.

Chapter 22 offers an in-depth discussion of interview, questionnaire, and direct-observation reports. After pointing out the nature, usefulness, and requirements of primary research, we explain how to plan and write each report, concluding with an annotated student model that illustrates the guidelines.

■ The Reader

The Reader, sequenced to follow the order of the strategies as presented in the Rhetoric, expands the utility of the text by providing a collection of forty-four carefully selected professional models that illustrate the various writing strategies and display a wide variety of styles, tones, and subject matter. These essays, together with the nine student models that accompany the various strategy chapters, should make a separate reader unnecessary.

The Reader section opens with a unit entitled "Strategies for Successful Reading." In it, we discuss how to read for different purposes—for information/evaluation, to critique—and explain how students can use their reading to improve their writing as well as how they can synthesize information from various sources. Several of the guidelines are applied to a professional essay. Instructors can, of course, assign this unit at any point during the term.

Each of the essays clearly illustrates the designated pattern, each has been thoroughly class tested for student interest, and each provides a springboard for a stimulating discussion. In making our selections we have aimed for balance and variety:

1. Some are popular classics by acknowledged prose masters; some, anthologized for the first time, are by fresh, new writers.
2. Some are straightforward and simple, some challenging and complex.
3. Some adopt a humorous, lighthearted approach; some a serious, thoughtful one.
4. Some take a liberal stance, some a conservative one; and some address ethnic, gender, and cultural diversity.
5. A few are rather lengthy; most are relatively brief.

The first essay in each strategy section is annotated in the margin to show which features of the strategy are included. These annotations not only facilitate student understanding but also help link the Rhetoric and Reader into an organic whole. A brief biographical note about the author and a photograph, when available, precede each selection, and stimulating questions designed to enhance student understanding of structure and strategy follow it. In addition, a segment entitled "Toward Key Insights" poses one or more broadbased questions prompted by the essay's content. Answering these questions, either in discussion or writing, should help students gain a deeper understanding of important is-sues. Finally, we include a writing assignment suggested by the essay's topic.

■ The Handbook

The comprehensive Handbook, which features tab indexing on each page for easy access to all material, consists of five parts: "Sentence Elements," "Editing to Correct Sentence Errors," "Editing to Correct Faulty Punctuation and Me-chanics," "Spelling," and "Glossary of Word Usage." Explanations skirt un-needed grammatical terminology and are reinforced by sets of sentence exer-cises in the first three sections. The section on "Sentence Elements" explains how students can use these elements to improve their writing skills. We also in-clude connected-discourse exercises—unfolding narratives that engage and re-tain student interest and therefore facilitate learning—in the "Sentence Er-rors" and "Puncuation and Mechanics" sections. Extra sets of twenty-item exercises that parallel those in the Handbook are available upon request to in-structors who adopt the book. The "Spelling" unit presents four useful spelling rules and an extensive list of commonly misspelled words. The "Glossary of Word Usage" offers similarly comprehensive coverage of troublesome usages. Instructors can use the Handbook either as a reference guide or as a basis for class discussion.

■ Supplementary Material for Instructors and Students

The *Annotated Instructor's Edition* (0-13-041734-3) consists of the entire student edition as well as strong instructional support. The material in the margins of the text consists of background information on particular aspects of writing; key insights into how students view writing projects and why they experience diffi-culties; case studies that raise ethical issues for student discussion; answers to all discussion questions and to appropriate exercises in the text; supplementary ex-ercises; teaching strategies and classroom activities that instructors may want to consider; and Reader/Theme strategies that show how to use the Reader to build writing assignments based on themes.

The *Teaching Composition with Strategies for Successful Writing*, Sixth Edition, (0-13-041731-9) supplement offers various suggestions for teaching first-year composition, a sample syllabus for a sequence of two fifteen-week semesters, numerous guidelines for responding to student writing, and a detailed set of grading standards. In addition, it contains an extra set of twenty-item exercises that parallel those in the Handbook section of *Strategies*. The exercises can be used either in the classroom or as assignments.

The companion Web site for *Strategies for Successful Writing*, Sixth Edition, can be accessed at www.prenhall.com/reinking. The site includes lecture notes, self-check quizzes, additional writing models, bulletin board/chat topics, critical thinking questions, and essay questions. WEB CT and Blackboard courses for *Strategies* are complete online courses that include all of the con-tent from the Web site as well as additional material for students and instructors. These courses are available at a discounted price for instructors who adopt *Strategies.*

The online service www.turnitin.com allows teachers to check if students are copying their assignments from the Internet and is now free to professors using *Strategies for Successful Writing,* Sixth Edition. In addition to helping teachers easily identify instances of Web-based student plagiarism, Turnitin.com also offers a digital archiving system and an online peer review service. Professors set up a "drop box" at the Turnitin.com Web site where their students submit papers. This online service then cross-references each submission with millions of possible online sources. Within 24 hours, teachers receive a customized color-coded "Originality Report," complete with live links to suspect Internet locations, for each submitted paper. Professors can access the Turnitin.com site free through the faculty resources section of the Reinking Web site at www.prenhall. com/reinking.

The following supplements are free when instructors order any Prentice Hall English textbook. Contact your local representative for details.

- *The New American Webster Handy College Dictionary,* Third Edition

  This dictionary provides more than 115,000 definitions. It includes phrases, slang, scientific terms, advice on usage and grammar, notes on etymology, foreign words and phrases, and a word gazetteer.
  ISBN: 0-13-032870-7

- *English on the Internet 2001: Evaluating Online Sources*

  Explains how to access online sources, indicates the most useful English sites, notes popular search engines, and includes a glossary of terms and the latest MLA documentation guidelines for electronic sources.
  ISBN: 0-13-022073-6

- *Guide to Research and Documentation: Prentice Hall Resources for Writing* by Kirk G. Rasmussen

  This useful paperback booklet provides students with research and documentation guidelines and is designed for ease of use and portability. It features the most recent information on MLA, APA, CBE, and CM formats and also covers the research process. ISBN: 0-13-081627-2

- *Model Student Essays* by Mark Gallaher

  This anthology features 25 student essays collected from around the country, which are organized into three broad writing categories: writing to explore a personal experience, writing to explain or inform, and writing to argue a position.ISBN: 0-13-645516-6

- *The Writer's Guide Series* (new)

  Provides students and instructors with in-depth coverage of relevant topics, which allows instructors to convey information based on their course structure and students' needs.
  Writer's Guide to Document & Web Design ISBN: 0-13-018929-4
  Writer's Guide to WAC & Oral Presentations ISBN: 0-13-018931-6
  Writer's Guide to Writing About Literature ISBN: 0-13-018932-4

■ Acknowledgments

Like all textbook writers, we are indebted to many people. Our colleagues at Ferris State University and elsewhere, too numerous to mention, have assisted us in several ways: critiquing the manuscript; testing approaches, essays, and exercises in their classrooms; and suggesting writing models for the text. In addition, we would like to thank our reviewers, whose many suggestions have greatly improved our text: Elizabeth S. Bruton, Catawba Valley Community College; Judith A. Burnham, Tulsa Community College; Annie Lou Burns, Meridian Community College; Dallie B. Clark, Eastfield College; Donna Thomsen, Johnson & Wales University; and Stephen Wilhoit, University of Dayton.

Special thanks are also due to the outstanding team at Prentice Hall, whose editorial expertise, genial guidance, and promotional efforts have been vital to this project: Phil Miller, President of Humanities and Social Sciences Division, who first saw the potential in our approach, proposed the Annotated Instructor's Edition, and suggested and supported many other improvements; Leah Jewell, Editor in Chief for English, and Corey Good, Acquisitions Editor, whose efficiency, knowledge, and understanding of authors' concerns have enhanced our pleasure in preparing this edition; Alison Gnerre, our Production Editor, whom we specifically requested for this edition because she is, quite simply, the best in the business; Julie Sullivan, who did a superb job of copy editing; and Brandy Dawson, whose marketing expertise will help our book find its way.

Finally, we'd like to thank Brian Franke for his valuable contribution to the section on the Internet and Norma Reinking for her conscientious proofreading of the entire manuscript.

J.A.R.
A.W.H.
R.v.d.O.

To the Student

No matter what career you choose, your ability to communicate clearly and effectively will directly affect your success. In the classroom, your instructor will often evaluate your mastery of a subject in part by the papers and examinations you write. Prospective employers will make judgments about your qualifications and decide whether to offer you an interview on the basis of your job application letter and résumé. On the job, you will be expected to write clear, accurate reports, memorandums, and letters.

There is nothing mysterious about successful writing. It does not require a special talent, nor does it depend on inspiration. It is simply a skill, and like any other skill, it involves procedures that can be learned. Once you understand them, the more you practice the easier the writing becomes.

Strategies for Successful Writing will help you become a successful writer. And after you graduate it can serve as a useful on-the-job reference if writing problems occur. The first three chapters explore the fundamentals of writing and the general steps in planning, drafting, and revising papers. The next ten explain the basic writing strategies as well as papers that mix them. The following three chapters zero in on paragraphs, sentences, and writing style, and the final six turn to specialized writing—essay examinations, papers about literature, business correspondence, library research papers, and papers based on your own original research results. The book concludes with a Reader and, if you are using the complete version of the text, a Handbook.

From time to time you have probably had the unpleasant experience of using textbooks that seemed to be written for instructors rather than students. In preparing this book, we have tried never to forget that *you* are buying, reading, and using it. As a result, we have written the text with your needs in mind. The book uses simple, everyday language and presents directions in an easy-to-follow format. The chapters on writing strategies provide examples of student essays that supplement the professional essays in the Reader. These student examples represent realistic, achievable goals. When you compare them to the professional examples, you'll see that students can indeed do excellent work. We are confident that by learning to apply the principles in this text, you will write well too.

Here's wishing you success!

Rhetoric

1

Writing: A First Look

Why write? Hasn't the tempest of technology swept all of us into a brave new electronic world? Aren't e-mail, voice mail, cellular phones—all the magical devices of our new electronic estate—fast dooming ordinary writing? Not long ago, some people thought and said so, but events haven't supported those predictions. Although electronic devices have made some writing unnecessary, the written word flourishes both on campus and in the world of work. Furthermore, there's every evidence that writing will become even more important in the future.

Writing offers very real advantages to both writers and readers:

1. It gives writers time to reflect on and research what they want to communicate and then lets them shape and reshape the material to their satisfaction.
2. It makes communication more precise and effective.
3. It provides a permanent record of thoughts, actions, and decisions.
4. It saves the reader's time; we absorb information more swiftly when we read it than when we hear it.

Many people will expect you to write for them. College instructors ask you to write reports, research papers, and essay exams. Job hunting usually requires you to write application letters. And once you're hired, writing will probably figure in your duties. You might be asked to discuss the capabilities of new computer equipment, report on a conference you attended, or explain the advantages of new safety procedures to supervisors or staff. Perhaps you'll propose that your organization install a new security system, conduct a market survey, or develop an alternative traffic flow pattern. The ability to write will help you earn better grades, land the job you want, and advance in your career.

Furthermore, writing ability yields personal benefits. You might need to defend a medical reimbursement claim that you filed with your health insurer, request clarification of an inadequate or ambiguous set of directions, or document a demand for replacement of a faulty product. Skill in writing will help you handle these matters.

As you can see, we usually write in response to a situation. This situation often determines the purpose and audience of our paper as well as its content, style, and organization. We don't, then, write in isolation but rather to communicate with others who have an interest in our message. To do an effective job, you will need to understand the different situations that can prompt a piece of writing and respond accordingly.

■ The Purposes of Writing

Whenever you write, some clear purpose should guide your efforts. If you don't know why you're writing, neither will your reader. Fulfilling an assignment doesn't qualify as a real writing purpose, although it may well be what sends you to your desk. Faced with a close deadline for a research paper or report, you may tell yourself, "I'm doing this because I have to." An authentic purpose, however, requires you to answer this question: What do I want this piece of writing to do for both my reader and me?

Purpose, as you might expect, grows out of the writing situation. You explore the consequences of the greenhouse effect in a report for your science instructor. You write an editorial for the college newspaper to air your frustration over inadequate campus parking. You propose that your organization replace an outdated piece of equipment with a state-of-the-art model. Clearly, your purpose stems from the writing situation.

Here are four common *general writing purposes,* two or more of which often join forces in a single piece:

To Inform Presenting information is one of the most common writing purposes. The boating enthusiast who tells landlubber classmates how to handle a skiff plays the role of teacher, as does the researcher who summarizes the results of an investigation for co-workers. Some professional writers carve careers out of writing articles and books that fill gaps in the public's knowledge of timely topics. Instructors often ask you to write exams and papers so that they can gauge how well you have mastered the course material.

To Persuade You probably have strong views on many issues, and these feelings may sometimes impel you to try swaying your reader. In a letter to the editor, you might attack a proposal to establish a nearby chemical waste dump. Or, alarmed by a sharp jump in state unemployment, you might write to your state senator and argue for a new job-training program.

To Express Yourself   Creative writing includes personal essays, fiction, plays, and poetry, as well as journals and diaries. But self-expression has a place in other kinds of writing too. Almost everything you write offers you a chance to display your mastery of words and to enliven your prose with vivid images and fresh turns of phrase.

To Entertain   Some writing merely entertains; some writing couples entertainment with a more serious purpose. A lighthearted approach can help your reader absorb dull or difficult material. Satire lets you expose the shortcomings of individuals, ideas, and institutions by poking fun at them. An intention to entertain can add savor to many kinds of writing.

Besides having one or more *general purposes*, each writing project has its own *specific purpose*. Consider the difference in the papers you could write about solar homes. You might explain how readers could build one, argue that readers should buy one, express the advantages of solar homes to urge Congress to enact a tax credit for them, or satirize the solar home craze so that readers might reevaluate their plans to buy one.

Having a specific purpose assists you at every stage of the writing process. It helps you define your audience; select the details, language, and approach that best suit their needs; and avoid going off in directions that won't interest them. The following example from the newspaper *USA Today* has a clear and specific purpose.

We'll Trash *USA Today*, Too

J. Winston Porter

1   What will you do with *USA Today* after you finish reading it? If you're like most of us, you'll put the paper out with the garbage and it'll end up buried in a landfill. Over 80% of all household and commercial garbage ends up this way, and this is a problem.

2   The USA is relentlessly producing more and more trash, and we are rapidly running out of landfill space. At the same time, new landfills and incinerators are encountering local opposition. Before we are truly wallowing in waste, we need to declare a war on garbage.

3   The first battle we need to win is for public acceptance of a strategy that includes reducing the amount of waste generated and increasing the amount recycled. EPA is pushing a national goal of recycling 25% of all garbage within the next four years. But waste reduction and recycling aren't enough to stem the tide of trash that threatens to engulf us. We will continue to need safe landfilling of some garbage and incineration, preferably with energy recovery, as another option. EPA and the states are working to strengthen environmental controls on these facilities. The appropriate mix of waste reduction and recycling, landfilling and incineration should be "custom designed" by states and localities.

4   How can we all do our part? To begin with, we must recognize that we all contribute to the garbage problem. Next, we should cooperate in efforts to reduce the

amount of trash requiring disposal. Finally, we must adopt new attitudes about disposal, because there will always be trash to be handled. This means that instead of simply opposing any new disposal facilities, citizens should assist in choosing the best options.

5   Recycling is the cornerstone of a sound waste-management strategy. We all have special responsibilities to make recycling work. Individuals must be willing to participate in local programs. Local governments should plan programs and operate required facilities. States should do statewide planning and enforce their own laws and regulations. Industry should step up its recycling efforts. The federal government should provide national leadership, research and information-sharing as well as develop certain underlying regulations.

6   No one segment of society can, alone, lead us to victory in the war on garbage. Instead, we need a coordinated national effort to confront the solid-waste issue head-on.

From USA *Today*

Porter hints at his purpose in the first paragraph by noting that the disposal of garbage in landfills poses a problem. The last sentence of paragraph 2 states the purpose clearly. The remaining paragraphs name the strategies that he recommends to wage war on garbage and explain how individuals, government, and industry can all contribute. Everything Porter has written relates to his purpose.

Now examine the next paragraph, which does *not* have a firmly fixed specific purpose:

```
Community is a sea in which people swim unconsciously, like
fish. We fail to recognize our neighbors as fellow humans, and
they show the same lack of fellow feeling for us. A complete
lack of concern for one another is evident in today's complex
society. What is community? Is it a plant? A building? A place?
A state of being? Knowing what it is, we can see if such a place
exists. To know community, one must realize who he or she is.
Identity of a person is the first step in establishing a commu-
nity.
```

This student writer can't decide what aspect of community to tackle. The opening sentence attempts a definition, but the next two veer onto the shortcomings of the modern community. Notice how aimlessly the thoughts drift. The vague leadoff sentence asserts "Community is a sea . . . ," but the later question "What is community?" contradicts this opening. Also, if community is a plant, a building, or a place, why must we realize who we are in order to know it? This contradictory and illogical paragraph reveals a writer groping for a purpose.

The paragraph, however, isn't a wasted effort. These musings offer several possibilities. By developing the first sentence, the writer might show some interesting similarities between community and a sea so that instead of taking community for granted, readers can see it in a new light. By pursuing the idea in the second and third sentences, the writer might show the callous nature of modern society to encourage readers to act more humanely. The last two sentences might lead to a statement on the relationship between individual and community in order to overcome the common view that the two are in conflict. A specific purpose can sometimes emerge from preliminary jottings.

■ The Audience for Your Writing

Everything you write is aimed at some audience—a person or group you want to reach. The ultimate purpose of all writing is to have an effect on a reader (even if that reader is you), and therefore purpose and audience are closely linked. Our discussion on pages 3–4 makes this point clear by noting that your purpose can be to inform *someone* of something, to persuade *someone* to believe or do something, to express feelings or insights to *someone*, or to entertain *someone*. Any of these objectives requires that you *be able to define* that someone, the audience for your writing.

Writing operates on a delayed-action fuse, detonating its ideas in the readers' minds at a later time and place. Sometimes problems follow. In face-to-face conversations, you can observe your listeners' reactions, and whenever you note signs of hostility, boredom, or puzzlement, you can alter your tone, offer some examples, or ask a question. You can also use gestures and facial expressions to emphasize what you're saying. When you write, however, the words on the page carry your message. Once written work has left your hands, it's on its own. You can't call it back to clear up a misunderstanding or satisfy a disgruntled reader.

Establishing rapport with your audience is easy when you're writing for your friends or someone else you know a great deal about. You can then judge the likely response to what you say. Often, though, you'll be writing for people you know only casually or not at all: employers, customers, fellow townsfolk, and the like. In such situations, you'll need to assess your audience before starting to write and/or later in the writing process.

A good way to size up your readers is to develop an audience profile. This profile will emerge gradually as you answer the following questions:

1. What are the educational level, age, social class, and economic status of the audience I want to reach?
2. Why will this audience read my writing? To gain information? Learn my views on a controversial issue? Enjoy my creative flair? Be entertained?
3. What attitudes, needs, and expectations do they have?
4. How are they likely to respond to what I say? Can I expect them to be neutral? Opposed? Friendly?
5. How much do they know about my topic? (Your answer here will help you gauge whether you're saying too little or too much.)
6. What kind of language will communicate with them most effectively? (See "Level of Diction" in Chapter 16.)

College writing assignments sometimes ask you to envision a reader who is intelligent but lacking specialized knowledge, receptive but unwilling to put up with boring or trite material. Or perhaps you'll be assigned, or choose, to write for a certain age group or one with particular interests. At other times, you'll be asked to write for a specialized audience—one with some expertise in your topic. This difference will affect what you say to each audience and how you say it.

The Effect of Audience on Your Writing

Let's see how audience can shape a paper. Suppose you are explaining how to take a certain type of X-ray. If your audience is a group of lay readers who have never had an X-ray, you might note at the outset that taking one is much like taking an ordinary photograph. Then you might explain the basic process, including the positioning of the patient and the equipment, comment on the safety and reliability of the procedure, and note how much time it takes. You probably would use few technical terms. If, however, you were writing for radiology students, you might emphasize exposure factors, film size, and required views. This audience would understand technical terms and want a detailed explanation of the procedure. You could speak to these readers as colleagues who appreciate precise information.

Audience shapes all types of writing in similar fashion, even your personal writing. Assume you've recently become engaged, and to share your news you write two letters: one to your minister, the other to your best friend back home. You can imagine the differences in details, language, and general tone of each letter. Further, think how inappropriate it would be if you accidentally sent the letter intended for one to the other. Without doubt, different readers call for different approaches.

Discourse Communities

Professionals often write as members of specific communities. For example, biologists with similar interests often exchange information about their research. The members of a community share goals, values, concerns, background information, and expectations, and this fact in turn affects how they write. Because such writing is closely tied to the interests of the community, professional articles often start with a section linking their content to previous research projects and articles. Often, too, custom dictates what information must be included, the pattern of organization, and the style the paper should follow. Throughout college, you will discover that part of learning to write is becoming familiar with the values and customs of different discourse communities. To do this, you'll need to read carefully in your major field, acquainting yourself with its current issues and concerns and learning how to write about them. Ask yourself these questions as you start reading in any professional area:

1. What are the major concerns and questions in this field?
2. What seems to be common knowledge?
3. To what works do writers regularly refer?
4. How do those in the field go about answering questions?
5. What methods do they follow?
6. Which kinds of knowledge are acceptable? Which are not?

7. What values seem to guide the field?

8. What kinds of information must writers include in papers?

9. How are different writing projects organized?

10. What conventions do writers follow?

We all, of course, belong to many different communities. Furthermore, a community can involve competing groups, conflicting values, differing kinds of writing projects, and varying approaches to writing. But as part of your growth as a writer and professional, you'll need to understand the goals and rules of any community you enter.

EXERCISE   *The three excerpts below deal with the same subject—antigens—but each explanation is geared to a different audience. Read the passages carefully; then answer the following questions:*

1. What audience does each author address? How do you know?

2. Identify ways in which each author appeals to a specific audience.

1. The human body is quick to recognize foreign chemicals that enter it. "Foes" must be attacked or otherwise got rid of. The most common of these foes are chemical materials from viruses, bacteria, and other microscopic organisms. Such chemicals, when recognized by the body, are called *antigens*. To combat them, the body produces its own chemicals, protein molecules called *antibodies*. Each kind of antigen causes the production of a specific kind of antibody. Antibodies appear in the body fluids such as blood and lymph and in the body's cells.
   L. D. Hamilton, "Antibodies and Antigens," *The New Book of Knowledge*

2. [An] *antigen* [is a] foreign substance that, when introduced into the body, is capable of inducing the formation of antibodies and of reacting specifically in a detectable manner with the induced antibodies. For each antigen there is a specific antibody, the physical and chemical structure of which is produced in response to the physical and chemical structure of the antigen. Antigens comprise virtually all proteins that are foreign to the host, including those contained in bacteria, viruses, protozoa, helminths, foods, snake venoms, egg white, serum components, red blood cells, and other cells and tissues of various species, including man. Polysaccharides and lipids may also act as antigens when coupled to proteins.
   "Antigen," *Encyclopaedia Britannica*

3. The substance which stimulates the body to produce antibodies is designated antigen (antibody stimulator). . . .
   Most complete antigens are protein molecules containing aromatic amino acids, and are large in molecular weight and size. However, it has been demonstrated that other macromolecules, such as pure polysaccharides, polynucleotides, and lipids, may serve as complete antigens.
   However, certain other materials, incapable of stimulating antibody formation by themselves can, in association with a protein or other carrier, stimulate antibody formation and are the antigenic determinants. These determinants are referred to as *incomplete antigens* or *haptens* and they are able to react with antibodies which were produced by the determinant-protein complex.

However, before an antigen can stimulate the production of antibodies, it must be soluble in the body fluids, must reach certain tissues in an unaltered form, and must be, in general, foreign to the body tissues. Protein taken by mouth loses its specific foreign-protein characteristics when digested in the alimentary tract. It reaches the tissues of the body as amino acids or other altered digested products of protein. Consequently, it no longer meets the requirements for antigenic behavior.

Orville Wyss and Curtis Eklund, *Microorganisms and Man*

Just as you would not dial a telephone number at random and then expect to carry on a meaningful conversation, so you should not expect to communicate effectively without a specific audience in mind.

One other note: as you shape your paper, it is important that the writing please you as well as your audience—that it satisfy your sense of what good writing is and what the writing task requires. You are, after all, your own first reader.

■ The Qualities of Good Writing

Three qualities—fresh thinking, a sense of style, and effective organization—help to ensure that a piece of prose will meet your reader's expectations.

Fresh Thinking   You don't have to astound your readers with something never before discussed in print. Genuinely unique ideas and information are scarce commodities. You can, however, freshen your writing by exploring personal insights and perceptions. Using your own special slant, you might show a connection between seemingly unrelated items, as does a writer who likens office "paper pushers" to different kinds of animals. Keep the expression of your ideas credible, however; farfetched notions spawn skepticism.

Sense of Style   Readers don't expect you to display the stylistic flair of Maya Angelou or E. B. White. Indeed, such writing would impair the neutral tone needed in certain kinds of writing, such as technical reports and legal documents. Readers *do*, however, expect you to write in a clear style. And if you strengthen it with vivid, forceful words, readers will absorb your points with even greater interest. The chapters ahead show you how to use language in ways that project your own views and personality. Chapters 15 and 16, in particular, will help you develop a sense of style, as will the many readings throughout the book.

Effective Organization   A paper should have a beginning, a middle, and an end, that is, an introduction, a body, and a conclusion. The introduction sparks interest and acquaints the reader with what is to come. The body delivers the main message and exhibits a clear connection between ideas so that the reader can easily follow your thoughts. The conclusion ends the discussion so the reader feels satisfied rather than suddenly cut off. Overall, your paper should follow a pattern that is suited to its content. Organizational patterns, or strategies of development, are the subject of Chapters 4–13. Pages 211–17 discuss introductions and conclusions.

Freshness, style, and organization are weighted differently in different kinds of writing. A writer who drafts a proposal to pave a city's streets will probably attach less importance to fresh thinking than to clear writing and careful organization. On the other hand, fresh thinking can be very important in a description of an autumn forest scene. You will learn more about these qualities throughout this book.

■ Writing and Ethics

Think for a minute about how you would react to the following situation. You decide to vacation at a resort after reading a brochure that stressed its white-sand beach, scenic trails, fine dining, and peaceful atmosphere. When you arrive, you find the beach overgrown with weeds, the trails littered and the view unappealing, and the restaurant a greasy-spoon cafeteria. Worse, whenever you go outside, swarms of vicious black flies attack you. Wouldn't you feel cheated? Closer to home, think how you'd react if you decided to attend a college because of its distinguished faculty members only to discover upon arrival that they rarely teach on campus. The college counts on their reputations to attract students even though they are usually unavailable. Hasn't the college done something unethical?

As these examples show, good writing is also ethical writing. Like you, readers expect that what they read will be dependable information. Few if any would bother with a piece of writing that they realized was intended to deceive. A good test of the ethics of your writing is whether you would read your own work and act on the basis of it. Would you feel comfortable with it, or would you feel cheated, manipulated, deceived, or harmed in some way? By learning and practicing the principles of ethical writing, you will help ensure that your writing meets the standards your readers expect.

The Principles of Ethical Writing

- Writing perceived as truthful should *be* truthful. Granted, a writer may use humorous exaggeration to make us laugh, and some sales pitches may stretch the truth a bit in order to entice buyers. ("Try Nu-Glo toothpaste and add sparkle to your life.") But most readers recognize and discount such embellishments which, unlike major distortions, harm nobody. Deliberate, serious falsehoods, however, may harm not only the reader but sometimes the writer as well. Angered by the misrepresentations in the vacation brochure, you would certainly warn your friends against the resort and might even take some legal action against it.

- Writing meant to be perceived as truthful should tell the whole truth, omitting nothing the reader needs to know in order to make informed decisions. The text should not be deliberately incomplete so as to mislead. Suppose that a university's recruitment brochures stress that 97 percent of its students get jobs upon graduation. What the brochures don't say is that only 55 percent of the jobs are in the graduates' chosen fields despite strong employer demand for graduates in those areas. Clearly these brochures are deceptive, perhaps attracting students who would otherwise choose schools with better placement records.

■ Writing should not present itself as something different from what it is. It would be unethical for a drug company's advertising department or agency to prepare, in the form of an article, an advertisement for a hair-loss treatment (their own, of course) and pass off the article as an impartial news story.

■ Writing should be clear to the reader. All of us know the frustration of trying to read a crucial regulation that is impossible to comprehend. A person who writes instructions so unclear that they result in harmful mistakes is partially responsible for the consequences. Readers have a right to expect understandable, accurate information. Thus, it would be deceptive for a group of state legislators to call a proposed bill the Public Education Enhancement Act when it would in fact bar teachers from belonging to unions.

■ Writing should not intend to harm the reader. Certainly it is fair to point out the advantages of a product or service that readers might not need. Most people understand the nature of this type of advertising. But think how unethical it would be for a writer to encourage readers to follow a diet that the writer knew was not only ineffective but harmful. Think of the harm a writer might cause by attempting, deliberately, to persuade readers to try crack cocaine.

2

Planning and Drafting Your Paper

Many students believe that good essays are dashed off in a burst of inspiration by born writers. Students themselves often boast that they cranked out their top-notch papers in an hour or so of spare time. Perhaps. But for most of us, writing is a process that takes time and work. Better writers are not born with their gift but learn through informed practice how to incorporate their ideas into a paper.

Although successful writers can often describe how they go about their work, writing is a flexible process. No one order guarantees success, and no one approach works for every writer. Some writers establish their purpose and draft a plan for carrying it out at the start of every project. Others begin with a tentative purpose or plan and discover their final direction as they write. As a project proceeds, the writer is likely to leapfrog backward and forward one or more times rather than to proceed in an orderly, straightforward sequence. Partway through a first draft, for instance, a writer may think of a new point to present, then pause and jot down the details needed to develop it. Similarly, part of the conclusion may come to mind as the writer is gathering the details for supporting a key idea.

Regardless of how it unfolds, the writing process consists of the following stages. Advancing through each stage will guide you if you have no plan or if you've run into snags with your approach. Once you're familiar with these stages, you can combine or rearrange them as needed.

Understanding the assignment
Zeroing in on a topic
Gathering information
Organizing the information
Developing a thesis statement
Writing the first draft

■ Understanding the Assignment

Instructors differ in making writing assignments. Some specify the topic; some give you several topics to choose from; and still others offer you a free choice. Likewise, some instructors dictate the length and format of the essay, whereas others don't. Whatever the case, be sure you understand the assignment before you go any further.

Think of it this way: If your boss asked you to report on ways of improving the working conditions in your office and you turned in a report on improving worker benefits, would you expect the boss's approval? Following directions is crucial, so if you have any questions about the assignment, ask your instructor to clear them up right then. Don't be timid; it's much better to ask for directions than to receive a low grade for failing to follow them.

Once you understand the assignment, consider the project *yours*. If you are asked to describe a favorite vacation spot for a local newspaper, here is your chance to inform others about a place special to you. By asking yourself what the assignment allows you to accomplish, you can find your purpose.

■ Zeroing in on a Topic

A subject is a broad discussion area: sports, college life, culture, and the like. A topic is one small segment of a subject, for example, testing athletes for drug use, Nirvana College's academic probation policy, the Web surfing phenomenon. If you choose your own topic, pick one narrow enough so that you can develop it properly within any length limitation. Avoid sprawling, slippery issues that lead to a string of trite generalities.

In addition, choose a familiar topic or one you can learn enough about in the time available. Avoid overworked topics such as arguments about open visitation in dormitories or the legal drinking age, which generally repeat the same old points. Instead, select a topic that lets you draw upon your unique experiences and insights and offer a fresh perspective to your reader.

Strategies for Finding a Topic

Whenever your instructor assigns a general subject, you'll need to stake out a limited topic suitable for your paper. If you're lucky, the right one will come to mind immediately. More often, though, you'll need to resort to some special strategy. Here are six proven strategies that many writers use. Not all of them will work for everyone, so experiment to find those that produce a topic for you.

Tapping Your Personal Resources   Personal experience furnishes a rich storehouse of writing material. Over the years, you've packed your mind with memories of family gatherings, school activities, movies, concerts, plays, parties, jobs, books you've read, TV programs, dates, discussions, arguments, and so on. All these experiences can provide suitable topics. Suppose you've been asked to write about some aspect of education. Recalling the difficulties you had last term at registration, you might argue for better registration procedures. Or if you're a hopeless TV addict who must write on some advertising topic, why not analyze video advertising techniques?

Anything you've read in magazines or journals, newspapers, novels, short stories, or textbooks can also trigger a topic. Dan Greenburg's "Sound and Fury," pp. 436–38, in which a potentially explosive situation is defused, might suggest a paper on some dangerous encounter in your past. An article reviewing the career of a well-known politician might stir thoughts of a friend's experience in running for the student council. Possibilities crowd our lives, waiting for us to recognize and seize them.

EXERCISE   *Select five of the subjects listed below. Tapping your personal resources, name one topic suggested by each. For each topic, list three questions that you might answer in a paper.*

Life on a city street	Some aspect of nature
A particular field of work	Contemporary forms of dancing
Some branch of the federal bureaucracy	Youth gangs
Concern for some aspect of the environment	Fashions in clothing
Saving money	Trendiness
Home ownership	Human rights
Schools in your town	Public transportation
Leisure activities	Childhood fears
The two-income family	A new scientific discovery
A best-selling book	A religious experience

Keeping a Journal   Many writers, not comfortable relying on their memories, record their experiences in a journal—a private gathering of entries accumulated over a period of time. Journal keeping provides an abundance of possible writing topics as well as valuable writing practice.

The hallmark of the journal entry is the freedom to explore thoughts, feelings, responses, attitudes, and beliefs. In your own private domain you can express your views without reservation, without concern for "doing it right." *You* control the content and length of the entry without being held to a specified topic or number of words. Furthermore, depending on your instructor's preference, you usually don't have to worry about correct spelling or grammar. Journal writing does not represent a finished product but rather an exploration.

A few simple guidelines ensure effective journal entries:

1. Write in any kind of notebook that appeals to you; the content, not the package, is the important thing.
2. Write on a regular basis—at least five times a week if possible. In any event don't write by fits and starts, cramming two weeks' entries into one sitting.
3. Write for ten to twenty minutes, longer if you have more to say. Don't aim for uniform entry length, for example, three paragraphs or a page and a half. Simply explore your reactions to the happenings in your life or to what you have read, heard in class, or seen on television. The length will take care of itself.

Let's examine a typical journal entry by Sam, a first-year composition student.

Last week went back to my hometown for the first time since my family moved away and while there dropped by the street where I spent my first twelve years. Visit left me feeling very depressed. Family home still there, but its paint peeling and front porch sagging. Sign next to the porch said house now occupied by Acme Realtors. While we lived there, front yard lush green and bordered by beds of irises. Now an oil-spattered parking lot. All the other houses on our side of the street gone, replaced by a row of dumpy buildings housing dry cleaner, bowling alley, hamburger joint, shoe repair shop, laundromat. All of them dingy and rundown looking, even though only a few years old.

Other side of the street in no better shape. Directly across from our house a used-car dealership with rows of junky looking cars. No trace left of the Little League park that used to be there. Had lots of fun playing baseball and learned meaning of sportsmanship. To left of the dealership my old grade school, now boarded and abandoned. Wonder about my fifth-grade teacher Mrs. Wynick. Is she still teaching? Still able to make learning a game, not a chore? Other side of dealership the worst sight of all. Grimy looking plant of some sort pouring foul smelling smoke into the air from a discolored stack. Smoke made me cough.

Don't think I'll revisit my old street again.

This journal entry could spawn several essays. Sam might explore the causes of residential deterioration, define sportsmanship, explain how Mrs. Wynick made learning a game, or argue for stricter pollution control laws.

EXERCISE   *Write journal entries over the next week or two for some of the following items that interest you. If you have trouble finding a suitable topic for a paper, review the entries for possibilities.*

Pleasant or unpleasant conversations	Cultural or sporting events
Developing relationships	College life: myth vs. reality
Single or married life	Public figures—politicians; movie,
Parents	rock, or sports stars
Financial or occupational considerations	World trouble spots
Ideas gained through reading	Courses you are taking

Sorting Out a Subject   All of us sort things. We do it whenever we tackle the laundry, clear away a sinkful of dishes, or tidy up a basement or garage. Let's see how we might handle a cluttered basement. To start off, we'd probably sort the contents according to type: books in one spot, clothing in a second, toys in a third. That done, chances are we'd do still more sorting, separating children's books from adults' and stuffed animals from games. As we looked over and handled the different items, long-buried, bittersweet memories might start flooding from our subconscious: memories of an uncle, now dead, who sent this old adventure novel . . . of our parents' pride when they saw their child had learned to ride that now battered bicycle . . . of the dance that marked the debut of the evening gown over there.

Sorting out a subject follows a similar scenario. First, we break our broad subject into categories and subcategories, then allow our minds to roam over the different items and see what topics we can turn up. The chart on page 17 shows what one student found when she explored the general topic of public transportation.

As you'll discover for yourself, some subjects yield more topics than others; some, no topics at all.

EXERCISE   *Select two of the following subjects, then subdivide those two into five topics.*

Advertising	Movies	The space program
Dwellings	Occupations	Sports
Fashions	Popular music	Television programs
Magazines	Social classes	Vacations

Asking Questions   Often, working your way through these basic questions will lead you to a manageable topic:

1. Can I define my subject?

2. Does it break into categories?

3. If so, what comparisons can I make among these categories?

Results of Sorting Out the Subject Public Transportation

Land			Water		Air	
Buses	Taxis	Trains	Seagoing	Lake, River	Airplanes	Helicopters
County bus services for the handicapped	Rights of passengers	The Orient Express, the Twentieth Century Limited	The Titanic	Barge cruises	Airline deregulation	Air taxis
Bus tours	Preventing crimes against drivers	Monorails	Luxury liners		Overbooking flights	Cargo
Jitney buses		Preventing subway crimes	Theme Cruises		Making air travel safer	
Improving bus terminals		Guardian Angels	Modern sea pirates		Coping with hijacking	
Designing buses to accommodate the handicapped		Amtrak	Traveling by freighter		Causes and prevention of jet lag	
		Japan's high-speed trains	The impact of overseas flights on ship travel		Development of the stealth bomber	
		Deterioration of railroad track beds			Noise pollution around airports	

4. If my subject is divided into parts, how do they work together?
5. Does my subject have uses? What are they?
6. What are some examples of my subject?
7. What are the causes or origins of my subject?
8. What impact has my subject had?

Let's convert these general questions into specific questions about telescopes, a broad general subject:

1. What is a telescope?
2. What are the different kinds of telescopes?
3. How are they alike? How do they differ?
4. What are the parts of each kind of telescope, and how do they work together?
5. What are telescopes used for?
6. What are some well-known telescopes?
7. Who invented the telescope?
8. What impact have telescopes had on human life and knowledge?

Each of these questions offers a starting point for a suitably focused essay. Question 3 might launch a paper comparing reflecting and refracting telescopes; question 6 might be answered in a paper about the Hubble Space Telescope and the problems experienced with it.

EXERCISE   *Select two of the following subjects. Create general questions, then convert them into specific questions. Finally, suggest two essay topics for each of your two subjects.*

Astrology	Games	Shopping malls
Books	Microorganisms	Stars
Colleges	Plays	Television
Emotions	Religions	Warships

Freewriting   The freewriting strategy snares thoughts as they race through your mind, yielding a set of sentences that you then look over for writing ideas. To begin, turn your pen loose and write for about five minutes on your general subject. Put down everything that comes into your head, without worrying about grammar, spelling, or punctuation. What you produce is for your eyes alone. If the thought flow becomes blocked, write "I'm stuck, I'm stuck . . ." until you break the mental logjam. When your writing time is up, go through your sentences one by one and extract potential topic material. If you draw a blank, write for another five minutes and look again.

The following example shows the product of one freewriting session. Jim's instructor had assigned a two- or three-page paper on some sports-related topic; and since Jim had been a member of his high school tennis team, his thoughts naturally turned toward this sport.

Sports. If that's my subject, I'd better do something on tennis. I've played enough of it. But what can I say that would be interesting? It's very popular, lots of people watch it on TV. Maybe I could write about the major tennis tournaments. I'm stuck. I'm stuck. Maybe court surfaces. That sounds dull. I'm stuck. Well, what about tennis equipment, clothing, scoring? Maybe my reader is thinking about taking up the game. What do I like about tennis? The strategy, playing the net, when to use a topspin or a backspin stroke, different serves. I'm stuck. I'm stuck. Maybe I could suggest how to play a better game of singles. I used to be number one. I can still remember Coach harping on those three C's, conditioning, concentration, consistency. I'm stuck. I'm stuck. Then there's the matter of special shots like lobs, volleys, and overheads. But that stuff is for the pros.

This example suggests at least three papers. For the beginning player, Jim could focus on equipment and scoring. For the intermediate player, he might write on conditioning, concentration, and consistency; for the advanced player, on special shots.

Brainstorming   Brainstorming, a close cousin of freewriting, captures fleeting ideas in words, fragments, and sometimes sentences, rather than in a series of sentences. Brainstorming garners ideas faster than the other strategies do. But unless you move immediately to the next stage of writing, you may lose track of what some of your fragmentary jottings mean.

To compare the results of freewriting and brainstorming a topic, we've converted our freewriting example into this list, which typifies the results of brainstorming:

Popularity of tennis	Equipment
Major tournaments	Clothing
Court surfaces	Scoring
Doubles strategy	Conditioning
Singles strategy	Concentration
Playing the net	Consistency
Topspin	Special shots--lobs, drop volleys,
Backspin	overheads
Different serves	

EXERCISE   *Return to the five subjects you selected for the exercise on page 14. Freewrite or brainstorm for five minutes on each one; then choose a topic suitable for a two- or three-page essay. State your topic, intended audience, and purpose.*

Narrowing a familiar subject may yield not only a topic but also the main divisions for a paper on it. Jim's freewriting session uncovered several possible tennis topics as well as a way of approaching each: by focusing on lobs, drop volleys, and overheads when writing about special shots, for example. Ordinarily, though, the main divisions will emerge only after you have gathered material to develop your topic.

Identifying Your Audience and Purpose

You can identify your purpose and audience at several different stages in the writing process. Sometimes both are set by the assignment and guide your selection of a topic. For example, you might be asked to write the college president to recommend improvements in the school's registration system. At other times, you may have to write a draft before you can determine either. Usually, though, the selection of audience and purpose goes hand in hand with determining a topic. Think of the different types of information Jim would gather if he wrote for (1) beginning players to offer advice on improving their game, (2) tennis buffs to point out refinements of the game, (3) a physics professor to show the physical forces controlling the behavior of tennis balls in flight.

CASE HISTORY

Now that you're familiar with some narrowing strategies, let's examine the first segment of a case history that shows how one student handles a writing assignment. This segment illustrates the use of a narrowing strategy to find a topic. Later segments focus on the remaining stages of the writing process.

George's writing class has been talking and reading about the importance people attach to their recreation and the many forms it can take. His instructor asks the class to write a three- or four-page paper on some aspect of recreation. To begin, George uses the sorting strategy and comes up with two major categories of topics: those based primarily on reading and those based on personal experience. Under the first category, he includes legalized casino gambling, vacationing in national parks, and collecting baseball cards; under the second he lists his hobby of coin collecting, his interest in playing bridge, and the recreational possibilities of his hometown, Mt. Pleasant. Because he has only marginal interest in the topics in the first category, he rules all of them out. After weighing the possibilities of the items in the second category, he concludes that Mt. Pleasant offers the most potential and elects to pursue that topic for a high school audience.

This case history continues on page 23.

■ Gathering Information

Once you have a topic, you'll need things to say about it. This supporting material can include facts, ideas, examples, observations, sensory impressions, memories, and the like. Without the proper backup, papers lack force, vividness, and interest and may confuse or mislead readers. The more support you can gather, the easier it will be for you to write a draft. Time spent gathering information is never wasted.

Strategies for Gathering Information

If you are writing on a familiar topic, much of your supporting material may come from your own head. Brainstorming is the best way to retrieve it. With unfamiliar topics, brainstorming won't work. Instead, you'll have to do some background reading. Whatever the topic, familiar or unfamiliar, talking with friends, parents, neighbors, or people knowledgeable about the topic can also produce useful ideas.

Brainstorming   Brainstorming a topic, like brainstorming a subject, yields a set of words, fragments, and occasionally sentences that will furnish ideas for the paper. Assume that Jim, the student who explored the subject of tennis, wants to show how conditioning, concentration, and consistent play can improve one's game. His brainstorming list might look like this:

```
keeping ball in play          courtside distractions
don't try foolish shots        temper distractions
placing ball so opponent       don't continually drive ball
   runs                           with power
staying in good condition      two-on-one drill
   yourself                    lobbing ball over opponent's head
running                        returning a down-the-line passing
jogging                           shot
skipping rope                  don't try spectacular overheads
   keeps you on your toes      chance for opponent to make
keeping your mind only on         mistake
   the game                    game of percentages
personal distractions          games are lost, not won
```

You can see how some thoughts have led to others. For example, the first jotting, "keeping ball in play," leads naturally to the next one, "don't try foolish shots." "Placing ball so opponent runs" leads to "staying in good condition yourself," which in turn leads to ways of staying in condition and so forth.

Branching is a helpful and convenient extension of brainstorming that allows you to add details to any item in your list. Here's how you might use this technique to approach "courtside distractions":

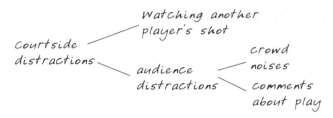

Don't worry if your brainstorming notes look chaotic and if some seem irrelevant. Sometimes the most unlikely material turns out to be the freshest and most interesting. As you organize and write your paper, you'll probably combine, modify, and omit some of the notes, as well as add others.

| **EXERCISE**   *Prepare a brainstorming sheet of supporting details for one of the topics you developed for the exercise on page 18.*

Reading   When you have to grapple with an unfamiliar topic, look in the library for material to develop it. Before going there, however, turn to Chapter 20, "The Library Research Paper," and review the guidelines under the headings "Computerized Card Catalog" and "Periodical Indexes." (If your library uses a conventional card catalog, review the guidelines in that part of the chapter.) These sections tell you how to unearth promising references to investigate. Once you have a list of references, start searching for the books or articles. Look through each one you find and jot down any information that looks useful, either as direct quotations or in your own words.

Whenever you use a direct quotation or rephrased material in your paper, you must give proper credit to the source. If you don't, you are guilty of plagiarism, a serious offense that can result in a failing grade for the course or even expulsion from college. See "Handling Quotations" and "Avoiding Plagiarism" in Chapter 21.

Talking with Others   You can expand the pool of ideas gained through brainstorming or reading by talking with some of the people around you. Imagine you're writing a paper about a taxpayers' revolt in your state. After checking the leading state newspapers at the library, you find that most of the discontent centers on property taxes. You then decide to supplement what you've read by asking questions about the tax situation in your town.

Your parents and neighbors tell you that property taxes have jumped 50 percent in the last two years. The local tax assessor tells you that assessed valuations have risen sharply and that state law requires property taxes to keep pace. She also notes that this situation is causing some people on fixed incomes to lose their homes. A city council member explains that part of the added revenue is being used to repair city streets, build a new library wing, and buy more fire-fighting equipment. The rest is going to the schools. School officials tell you they're using their extra funds to offer more vocational courses and to expand the program for learning-disabled students. As you can see, asking questions can broaden your perspective and provide information that will help you to write a more worthwhile paper.

CASE HISTORY (Continued from page 20)

After choosing to write about the recreational possibilities of his hometown, George brainstorms to gather appropriate material. The result is a twenty-item list. After checking it over, George decides that three items—the local chamber-music orchestra, little theater, and barbershop quartet—would hold little interest for his teenage audience, and he drops them. The remaining items are as follows:

End-of-the-World parties	crazy activities of party-goers
crowded streets	Mt. Pleasant Mall
Cold Water Lake	Embers Restaurant
Lake Isabella Dam	Holiday Inn
Island Park activities	Nelson Park Zoo
live bands	Mt. Pleasant Speedway
baseball games	mall parking
small gatherings	Boomer's Nightclub
Mt. Pleasant Meadows	

This case history continues on page 25.

■ Organizing the Information

If you have ever listened to a rambling speaker spill out ideas in no particular order, you probably found it hard to pay attention to the speech, let alone make sense of it. So, too, with disorganized writing. A garbled listing of ideas serves no one; an orderly presentation highlights your ideas and helps communication succeed.

Your topic determines the approach you take. In narrating a personal experience, such as a mishap-riddled vacation, you'd probably trace the events in the order they occurred. In describing a process, say caulking a bathtub, you'd take the reader step by step through the procedure. To describe a hillside view near your home, you might work from left to right. Or you could first paint a word picture of some striking central feature and then fan out in either direction. Other topics dictate other patterns, such as comparison and contrast, cause and effect, and illustration. Chapters 4–12 describe the basic patterns in detail.

You can best organize long pieces of writing, such as library research papers, by following a formal outline. (See "Organizing and Outlining," in Chapter 20.) For shorter papers, however, a simple, informal system of *flexible notes* will do nicely.

The Flexible Notes System

To create a set of flexible notes, write each of your key points at the top of a separate sheet of paper. If you have a thesis statement (see page 26), refer to it for your key points. Next, list under each heading the supporting details that go with that heading. Drop any details that don't fit and expand any points that need more support. When your sheets are finished, arrange them in the order you expect to follow in your essay. The notes for the tennis paper might look like this:

Conditioning

```
staying in good condition        two-on-one drill
   yourself                      lobbing ball over opponent's head
running                          returning a down-the-line passing
jogging                             shot
skipping rope keeps you on
   your toes
```

Concentration

```
keeping your mind only on the game
overcome distractions: personal, courtside, temper
```

Consistency

```
keeping ball in play
don't try foolish shots
placing ball so opponent runs
don't continually drive ball with power
don't try spectacular overheads
chance for opponent to make mistake
game of percentages
games are lost, not won
```

Since conditioning, concentration, and consistency are simultaneous concerns, this listing arranges them according to their probable importance—starting with the least important.

Now you're ready to draft a plan showing how many paragraphs you'll have in each part of the essay and what each paragraph will cover. Sometimes the number of details will suggest one paragraph; other times you'll need a paragraph block—two or more paragraphs. Here's a plan for the tennis essay:

Conditioning

```
staying in good condition yourself   ⎫
running                              ⎪  Off-the-court
jogging                              ⎬     conditioning
skipping rope keeps you on your toes ⎪
two-on-one drill                     ⎭
lobbing ball over opponent's head    ⎫  On-the-court
returning a down-the-line passing shot ⎭   conditioning
```

Concentration

```
keeping your mind only on the game
overcome distractions: personal, courtside, temper
```

Consistency

keeping ball in play
don't try foolish shots
placing ball so opponent runs   } Placing shots
don't continually drive ball with power
don't try spectacular overheads

chance for opponent to make mistake
game of percentages   } Playing percentages
games are lost, not won

These groupings suggest two paragraphs about conditioning, one about concentration, and two about consistency.

EXERCISE   *Organize into flexible notes the supporting details that you prepared for the exercise on page 22. Arrange your note pages in a logical sequence and draft a plan showing the number and content of the paragraphs in each section.*

CASE HISTORY (Continued from page 23)

A careful look at his brainstorming list shows George that its items fall into six categories: parties, swimming, parks, shopping, racing, and dining. After sorting the items into these categories, he draws up the following paragraph-by-paragraph plan:

Parties

End-of-World parties   One paragraph on partying
crowded streets
crazy antics of party-goers

Swimming

Cold Water Lake   One paragraph on each
Lake Isabella Dam   swimming spot

Parks

Island Park activities   One paragraph on each park
  live bands
  baseball games
  small gatherings
Nelson Park Zoo

Shopping

Mt. Pleasant Mall plenty   One paragraph on shopping
  of parking

Racing

Mt. Pleasant Meadows   One paragraph on each racing
Mt. Pleasant Speedway   spot

Dining

Embers Restaurant   One paragraph on each dining
Holiday Inn   spot
Boomer's Nightclub

This case history continues on page 28.

■ Developing a Thesis Statement

A thesis statement presents the main idea of a piece of writing, usually in one sentence. The thesis statement points you in a specific direction, helping you to stay on track and out of tempting byways. In addition, it tells your reader what to expect.

Thesis statements can emerge at several points in the writing process. If an instructor assigns a controversial topic on which you hold strong views, the statement may pop into your head right away. At other times it may develop as you narrow a subject to a topic. Occasionally, you even have to write a preliminary draft to determine your main idea. Usually, though, the thesis statement emerges after you've gathered and examined your supporting information.

As you examine your information, search for the central point and the key points that back it up; then use these to develop your thesis statement. Converting the topic to a question may help you to uncover backup ideas and write a thesis statement. For example:

Topic:	The commercial advantages of computerized data storage systems.
Question:	What advantages do computerized data storage systems offer business?
Thesis statement:	Computerized data storage systems offer business enormous storage capacity, cheap, instant data transmission almost anywhere, and significantly increased profit.

The thesis statement stems from the specifics the student unearthed while answering the question.

Requirements of a Good Thesis Statement

Unless intended for a lengthy paper, a thesis statement *focuses on just one central point or issue*. Suppose you prepare the following thesis statement for a two- or three-page paper:

Centerville College should re-examine its policies on open

admissions, vocational programs, and aid to students.

This sprawling statement would commit you to grapple with three separate issues. At best, you could make only a few general remarks about each one.

To correct matters, consider each issue carefully in light of how much it interests you and how much you know about it. Then make your choice and draft a narrower statement. The following thesis statement would do nicely for a brief paper. It shows clearly that the writer will focus on *just one issue:*

> Because of the rising demand among high school graduates for
> job-related training, Centerville College should expand its
> vocational offerings.

A good thesis statement also *tailors the scope of the issue to the length of the paper.* No writer could deal adequately with "Many first-year college students face crucial adjustment problems" in two or three pages. The idea is too broad to yield more than a smattering of poorly supported general statements. Paring it down to "Free time is a responsibility that challenges many first-year college students," however, results in an idea that could probably be developed adequately.

A good thesis statement further provides *an accurate forecast of what's to come.* If you plan to discuss the effects of overeating, don't say, "Overeating stems from deep-seated psychological factors and the easy availability of convenience foods." Such a statement, incorrectly suggesting that the paper will focus on causes, would only mislead and confuse your reader. On the other hand, "Overeating leads to obesity, which can cause or complicate several serious health problems" accurately represents what's to follow.

Finally, a good thesis statement is *precise, often previewing the organization of the paper.* Assertions built on fuzzy, catchall words like *fascinating, bad, meaningful,* or *interesting,* or statements like "My paper is about . . ." tell neither writer nor reader what's going on. To illustrate:

- New York is a fascinating city.

- My paper is about no-fault divorce.

These examples raise a host of questions. Why does the writer find New York fascinating? Because of its skyscrapers? Its night life? Its theaters? Its restaurants? Its museums? Its shops? Its inhabitants? And what about no-fault divorce? Will the writer attack it, defend it, trace its history, suggest ways of improving it? To find out, we must journey through the paper, hoping to find our way without a road-map sentence.

Now look at the rewritten versions of those faulty thesis statements:

- New York's art museums offer visitors an opportunity to view
  a wide variety of great paintings.

- Compared to traditional divorce, no-fault divorce is less
  expensive, promotes fairer settlements, and reflects a more
  realistic view of the causes of marital breakdown.

These statements tell the reader not only what points the writer will make but also the order they will follow.

Omission of Thesis Statement

Not all papers have explicit thesis statements. Narratives and descriptions, for example, often merely support some point that is unstated but nevertheless clear, and professional writers sometimes imply their thesis rather than state it openly. Nonetheless, a core idea underlies and controls all effective writing.

Changing Your Thesis Statement

Unlike diamonds, thesis statements aren't necessarily forever. Before your paper is in final form, you may need to change your thesis statement several times. If you draft the thesis statement during the narrowing stage, you might change it to reflect what you uncovered while gathering information. Or you might amend it after writing the first draft so that it reflects your additions and deletions.

Tentative or final, formulated early or late, the thesis statement serves as a beacon that spotlights your purpose.

CASE HISTORY (Continued from page 26)

His paragraph-by-paragraph plan completed, George now drafts a thesis statement that names all categories:

    Mt. Pleasant offers parties, great swimming spots, pleasant
    parks, racetracks, fine dining, and excellent shopping.

After carefully examining this initial effort, he realizes that three of the categories could be lumped together under the umbrella category "recreation spots." He alters the statement to read as follows:

    Mt. Pleasant offers parties, great recreation spots, fine
    dining, and excellent shopping.

This case history continues on pages 30–32.

EXERCISE

A. Write a thesis statement for the flexible notes that you developed for the exercise on page 25.

B. Reread "Requirements of a Good Thesis Statement"; then explain why each of the following does or does not qualify as an effective thesis statement for a two- or three-page essay.

1. My paper discusses the problem of employee absenteeism in American industry.

2. Living on a small island offers three advantages: isolation from city problems, the opportunity to know your neighbors, and the chance to go fishing whenever you want.

3. Although I don't know much about running a college, I know that Acme College is not run well.

4. Increasing federal outlays for education will help us construct needed school buildings and create a better-trained workforce.

5. Many people, wanting simpler and slower-paced lives, have abandoned high-paying executive positions for lower-paying, less stressful jobs.

6. Vacationing in Britain is a nice way to spend a summer.

7. Extending Middletown's intracity transit system will save consumers money, reduce pollution, and increase city revenues.

8. Most cable TV companies provide subscribers with several specialized-program channels.

■ Writing the First Draft

Now on to the first draft of your essay. The writing should go rather quickly. After all, you have a topic you're qualified to write about, a thesis statement that indicates your purpose, enough information to develop it, and a written plan to follow.

But sometimes when you sit down to write, the words won't come; and all you can do is doodle or stare at the blank page. Perhaps the introduction is the problem. Many writers are terrified by the thought of the opening paragraph. They want to get off to a good start but can't figure out how to begin. If this happens to you, additional brainstorming or freewriting can make you more comfortable and may suggest an opening. Keep in mind that any lead-in you write now can be changed later. If these suggestions don't solve your problem, skip the introduction for the time being. Once you have drafted the body of the paper, an effective opening should come more easily.

Here are some general suggestions for writing a first draft:

1. Stack your thesis statement, flexible notes, and written plan in front of you. They will start you thinking.

2. Skip every other line (double-space) and leave wide margins. Then you'll have room to revise later.

3. Write quickly; capture the drift of your thoughts. Concentrate on content and organization. Get your main points and supporting details on paper in the right sequence. Don't spend time correcting grammatical or punctuation errors, improving your language, or making the writing flow smoothly. You might lose your train of thought and end up doodling or staring again.

4. Take breaks at logical dividing points, for example, when you finish discussing a key point. Before you start to write again, scan what you've written.

Now for some specific suggestions that will help you with the actual writing:

1. Rewrite your thesis statement at the top of your first page to break the ice and build momentum.

2. Write your first paragraph, introducing your essay and stating your thesis. If you get stuck here, move on to the rest of the paper.

3. Follow your plan as you write. Begin with your first main point and work on each section in turn.

4. Look over the supporting details listed under the first heading in your flexible notes. Write a topic sentence stating the central idea of the paragraph.

5. Turn the details into sentences; use one or more sentences to explain each one. Add other related details, facts, or examples if they occur to you.

6. When you move from one paragraph to the next, try to provide a transitional word or sentence that connects each paragraph.

7. Write your last paragraph, ending your essay in an appropriate fashion. If you get stuck, set your conclusion aside and return to it later.

Writing a draft isn't always so systematic. If you are inspired, you may want to abandon your plans and simply use your first draft to explore ideas. You can always revise, so don't be overly concerned if you get off track. You might uncover some of your best material during this type of search.

EXERCISE   *Using the plan you prepared for the exercise on page 25, write the first draft of an essay.*

CASE HISTORY (Continued from page 28)

George now uses his thesis statement and paragraph-by-paragraph plan to write the following draft. Notice the slight changes in the thesis statement wording and in paragraphing, a common occurrence at this writing stage. Without question, this draft needs extensive revision. We'll return to it early in the next chapter to discuss the necessary changes.

Mt. Pleasant

Welcome to Mt. Pleasant, the home of Central Michigan University and the oil capital of this state. You have chosen the right town to visit because there are so many things for a high school student here. There are parties, great recreation spots, fine places to dine, and even excellent shopping.

I am sure you have all heard of Mt. Pleasant's famous "End-of-the-World Parties," which have been featured in nationwide news stories. These parties are a riot, both literally and figuratively. At the end of the school year, all the CMU students gather on fraternity row to celebrate the start of summer. For blocks and blocks, the streets are filled to overflowing with people pushing their way along with drinks in their hands to yet another bash. It is probably one of the rowdiest parties you could attend. People do all kinds of crazy things including climbing on rooftops and burning couches in the street. There was even one party-goer who stripped naked. That's what I call rowdy.

If you are not into partying, maybe a mellow day on the beach would do you some good. There is a beautiful lake called Cold Water Lake that has crystal clear water and a scenic beach. This beach is the "hit spot" on a sunny day, so you will want to be there.

If you're out for some wet-n-wild swimming fun, then Lake Isabella Dam is the place for you. It is a huge slippery slide about a hundred yards long pitched at a 160-degree angle. One could spend all day there and not get bored of sliding away.

After swimming, you could go to Island Park in the center of town. This park is unique because it is surrounded by a river that flows around it; it is Mt. Pleasant's own Island of Paradise. There are many activities at the park including live bands, small gatherings, and baseball games. This park is the main hangout for teens in Mt. Pleasant. For the children, there is also Nelson Park, which has a small zoo with bear, deer, badger, and many other kinds of North American wildlife.

If you are a person who likes to shop, then you will want to visit the Mt. Pleasant Mall at the edge of town. It has all the convenience stores necessary for a fulfilling day of shopping. There is always plenty of parking.

Mt. Pleasant also has places for those of you who like to gamble. Mt. Pleasant Meadows has fun-filled, action-packed horse races all weekend long. There is also a concession stand and a bar. The Meadows is just waiting for you to bet and win big.

> If you like horse racing, then you might also enjoy the car racing at Mt. Pleasant Speedway. On Fridays there is a high-speed stock car race all night long. So come see the fast cars, bright lights, and the excitement of racing waiting for you.
>
> Let's not forget about the fine dining Mt. Pleasant has to offer. There is an elegant restaurant called The Embers that matches all the fine cuisine in the world. There is also a Holiday Inn which hosts a class A restaurant and nightclub. The club is called Boomers and presents well-known comedians to entertain you throughout the night.
>
> Mt. Pleasant has much to offer you: fine dining, excitement, and relaxation. Why not come and see for yourself.
>
> *This essay will be revised in the next chapter.*

■ Planning and Drafting with a Word Processor

Using a computer and word-processing software allows you to compose, save what you write, insert new material, delete unwanted material, move sections around, and when you are ready, print out copies. If you can use your college's equipment and software, read the manual for your unit to discover its capabilities before you attempt to compose with it. Trying to write a paper while simultaneously learning about a word-processing program is a fast route to frustration.

Many word-processing programs can help you plan and draft an essay as well as revise and edit it. You can brainstorm or freewrite, entering words, phrases, and ideas as they come to mind. Do this for about ten minutes and then print out a copy to comb for promising bits and pieces.

If you approach a topic through the set of questions on pages 16 and 18, convert them into specific questions related to the broad subject area, and then enter them and your answers to them into your document. If you don't find a topic in the answers, brainstorm or freewrite further.

When you draft, experiment with your ideas by trying out new arrangements of material. If your writing stalls, note the spot with an asterisk or other marker so that you can easily find it later with a search command; then continue to write. Always save each draft in a file, if not in hard copy. You may want to use parts of an early draft in a later version.

Revising and Editing Your Paper

All of us at one time or another have said something careless to a friend, date, or mate and then spent the rest of the night regretting our words. In contrast, when we write we can make sure we say exactly what we mean. Good writers don't express themselves perfectly on the first try, but they do work hard at revising their initial efforts.

Just what is revision? Don't confuse it with proofreading or editing, the final stage of the writing process, where you carefully inspect your word choice, spelling, grammar, and punctuation. Revision is much more drastic, often involving an upheaval of your draft as you change its content and organization in order to communicate more effectively.

Most of what you read, including this book, has been considerably altered and improved as the writers progressed through early drafts. This fact shouldn't surprise you. After all, a rough copy is merely a first attempt to jot down some ideas in essay form. No matter how well you gather and organize your material, you can't predict the outcome until you've prepared a draft. Sometimes only touch-up changes are required. More often though, despite your efforts, this version will be incomplete, unclear in places, possibly disorganized. You might even discover an entirely different idea, focus, or approach buried within it. During revision you keep changing things—your focus, approach to the topic, supporting material, and thesis statement—until the results satisfy you.

Inexperienced writers often mistakenly view initial drafts as nearly finished products rather than as experiments to alter, or even scrap, if need be. As a result, they often approach revision with the wrong attitude. To revise successfully, you need to control your ego and your fear and become your own first critical reader. Set aside natural feelings of accomplishment ("After all, I've put a great deal of thought into this") and dread ("Actually, I'm afraid of what I'll find if I look too closely"). Instead, recognize that revision offers an opportunity to upgrade your strong features and strengthen your weak ones.

■ Preparing to Revise

To distance yourself from your writing and sharpen your critical eye, set your first draft aside for at least a half day, longer if time permits. When you return to it, gear up for revision by jotting down your intended purpose and audience before you read your paper. These notations will help keep your changes on track. In addition, note any further ideas that have occurred to you.

The right attitude is vital to effective revision. Far too many students hastily skim their essays to reassure themselves that "Everything sounds O.K." Avoid such a quick-fix approach. If your draft appears fine on first reading, probe it again with a more critical eye. Try putting yourself in your reader's place. Will your description of a favorite getaway spot be clear to someone who has never seen it? Will your letter home asking for money really convince parents who might think they've already given you too much? Remember: If you aren't critical now, anticipating confusion and objections, your reader certainly will be later.

Read your essay at least three times, once for each of these reasons:

To improve the development of the essay as a whole
To strengthen paragraph structure and development
To sharpen sentences and words

When you finish reading your paper for content, make a final, meticulous sweep to search for errors and problems that mar your writing. Use the Personal Revision Checklist on the inside back cover of this book to note your own special weaknesses, perhaps some problem with punctuation or a failure to provide specific support. Later chapters discuss paragraphs, sentences, and words in detail. Check these chapters for more information about the points introduced here.

■ Considering the Whole Essay

If you inspect your draft only sentence by sentence, you can easily overlook how its parts work together. A better approach is to step back and view the overall essay rather than its separate parts, asking questions such as "Does the beginning mesh with the end?" "Does the essay wander?" "Has anything been left out?" In this way you can gauge how part relates to part and to the whole. Use the acronym *FACT* to guide this stage of your revision.

F. Ask yourself first whether the whole essay *FITS* together, presenting a central point for a specific audience. Have you delivered what the thesis statement promises? First drafts often include paragraphs, or even large sections, that have little bearing on the main point. Some drafts contain the kernels of several different essays. Furthermore, one section of a draft might be geared to one audience (parents, for example) and another section to an entirely different audience (students, perhaps). As you read each part, verify its connection to your purpose and audience. Don't hesitate to chop out sections that don't fit, redo stray parts so they accord with your central idea, or alter your thesis statement to reflect better your supporting material. Occasionally, you might even expand one small, fertile section of your draft into an entirely new essay.

A. Whenever we write first drafts, we unwittingly leave out essential material. As we revise, we need to identify and fill these gaps. Ask yourself: "Where will the reader need more information or examples to understand my message?" Then *ADD* the appropriate sentences, paragraphs, or even pages.

C. First drafts often contain material that fits the thesis but doesn't contribute to the essay. Writing quickly, we tend to repeat ourselves, include uninteresting or uninformative examples, and crank out whole paragraphs when one clear sentence would suffice. As you revise, *CUT* away this clutter with a free hand. Such paring can be painful, especially if you're left with a skimpy text, but your message will emerge with much greater clarity. As you've probably guessed, revising a draft often requires both adding and cutting.

T. Carefully *TEST* the organization of your essay. The text should flow smoothly from point to point with clear transitions between the various ideas. Test the organization by outlining your major and minor points, then checking the results for logic and completeness. Alternatively, read the draft and note its progression. Look for spots where you can clarify connections between words and thus help your readers.

Chapters 4–12 explain nine different writing strategies, each concluding with revision questions geared specifically to that strategy. Use these questions, together with the *FACT* of revision, to help you revise more effectively.

CASE HISTORY (Continued from page 32)

Now let's apply the *FACT* approach to the first draft of George's Mt. Pleasant essay, which you read on pages 30–32. As we indicated there, the draft needs extensive work.

FIT. Much of George's draft doesn't fit his high school audience. Most of these students won't care about Mt. Pleasant being the oil capital of Michigan, won't be able to attend "End-of-the-World Parties" (which some will find distasteful), and won't have money for fine dining or nightclubs, even assuming they would be admitted. How then to proceed? George has two choices: target his intended audience more accurately or change it entirely. Either decision requires drastic revisions.

ADD. Assuming George keeps his high school audience, he needs to expand the essay at several points. As things stand, he offers only skimpy details about the water activities and never indicates where the different attractions are located or why the mall is appealing. These shortcomings must be corrected and other attractions introduced and discussed—for example, affordable places for teens to eat. Another audience would of course require different additions.

CUT. With cutting as with adding, audience determines what parts of the essay go and what parts stay. For high schoolers, George should drop any mention of Mt. Pleasant's oil status, "End-of-the-World Parties," and nightclubs. Similarly, fine dining has no place in the essay except perhaps as something reserved for special occasions. For a different audience, some of the sections mentioned under ADD might be deleted.

TEST. The introduction suggests that the essay will first discuss parties, then recreation spots and places to dine, and finally places to shop. However, the body reverses the order of the last two, and the conclusion summarizes these features in a different order. Such false signals only confuse a reader. George also errs in opening with "End-of-the-World Parties," which could cause some readers to react negatively. The essay does flow well from point to point, although too many paragraphs begin with "If you."

Without question, George's essay requires considerable work, whatever audience he chooses. After weighing his choices, he elects to stay with teenagers and zero in on Mt. Pleasant as a summer fun spot.

This case history continues on page 37.

As you read your own essay, note on a separate sheet of paper problems to solve, ideas to add, and changes to try. When you mark the actual essay, make your job easier by using these simple techniques:

1. To delete something, cross it out lightly; you may decide to resurrect it later.
2. To add a section of text, place a letter *(A, B, C, D)* at the appropriate spot and write the new material on a separate sheet, keyed to the letter. Make changes within sections by crossing out what you don't want and writing the replacement above it or nearby.
3. To rearrange the organization, draw arrows showing where you want things to go, or cut up your draft and rearrange the sections by taping them on new sheets of paper. Use whatever method works best for you.

When you finish revising your draft, you might want to team up with one or more classmates and read one another's work critically. The fresh eye you bring to the task can uncover shortcomings that would otherwise go unnoticed. Pages 50–57 discuss peer editing in detail.

"NOW THAT WE'VE BOILED YOUR PAPER DOWN TO THE
RELEVANT MATERIAL, I THINK YOU'RE READY TO RE-WRITE."

Reprinted by permission of Richard N. Bibler.

EXERCISE *List George's other options for revising this draft; then indicate the necessary changes if he had decided to write for readers between the ages of thirty-five and forty-five.*

EXERCISE *Use the* FACT *acronym to revise the draft you prepared for the exercise on page 30.*

CASE HISTORY (Continued from page 36)

After setting his draft aside for a couple of days, George revises it carefully. The original draft, showing deleted material, some added information, and a series of letters that mark where other new material should go, appears on pages 38 and 40. The other new material, keyed to the letters on the draft, appears on facing pages. Although this draft is not perfect, George's revisions have considerably improved the paper. He does, however, have more to do. (The final, polished version of the essay appears on pages 46–48.)

Mt. Pleasant

Welcome to Mt. Pleasant, the home of Central Michigan University and the oil capital of this state. You have chosen the right town to visit because there are so many things for a high school student here. There are parties, great recreation spots, fine places to dine, and even excellent shopping. (A)

I am sure you have all heard of Mt. Pleasant's famous "End-of-the-World Parties," which have been featured in nationwide news stories. These parties are a riot, both literally and figuratively. At the end of the school year, all the CMU students gather on fraternity row to celebrate the start of summer. For blocks and blocks, the streets are filled to overflowing with people pushing their way along with drinks in their hands to yet another bash. It is probably one of the rowdiest parties you could attend. People do all kinds of crazy things including climbing on rooftops and burning couches in the street. There was even one party-goer who stripped naked. That's what I call rowdy.

If you ~~are not into partying, maybe a mellow day on the beach would do you some good. There~~ *like to swim or just lie on the beach, just a few miles west of Mt. Pleasant off Beal City Road* is a beautiful ~~lake called~~ Cold Water Lake ~~that has~~ *with its* crystal clear water and a scenic beach. *surrounded by hills and woods* This beach is the "hit spot" on a sunny day. ~~so you will want to be there.~~ *You can always find a volleyball game to join; or you can simply throw around a frisbee, do some boy or girl watching, or just bask in the sun. The swimming, of course, is great.*

If you're out for some wet-n-wild swimming fun, then Lake Isabella Dam *, just down the road from Cold Water Lake,* is the place for you. ~~It is~~ *The dam forms* a huge slippery slide about a hundred yards long pitched at a 160-degree angle. ~~One could~~ *You can* spend ~~all~~ *a whole* day there and not get bored of sliding away. (B)

If you want to stay closer to town, ~~After swimming,~~ you ~~could~~ *can* go to Island Park in the center *off main street* of town. This park is unique because it is surrounded by a river that flows around it; it is Mt. Pleasant's

A. If you get tired of driving out to the same old Lake
Michigan beach this summer, you might think about giving
Mt. Pleasant a try for something different. The Mt. Pleasant
area offers swimming, canoeing, and hiking; a chance to get
together with other teens; horse and auto racing; a college
campus to wander around; movies, museums, video games, and
shopping for rainy days; and lots of places to eat. What more
can you ask for?

B. Canoeing can be great fun. Near the Mt. Pleasant area there
are a number of scenic rivers that are a delight to canoe.
There is the Chippewa River, the Cold Water River, the north
and south branches of the Salt River, and further to the west
the exciting white-water Pine River. Near or on each river are
places that rent canoes at a reasonable rate and even provide
you with transportation from your destination back to your
cars.

   For those of you who like to hike, Deerfield Park, a few
miles west of town on M-20, provides twenty-five miles of
nature trails. These secluded trails that meander through a
natural forest and gentle, rolling hills can be a great
place to take someone special for a quiet stroll. You will be
sure to spot a variety of birds as well as squirrels, raccoons, and chipmunks. If you are really lucky, you might
even spot a deer or two. Closer to town, on Harris Street,
Mission Creek Woodland Park offers sixty acres of forest
trails, a creek, and picnicking area.

C. For those of you who will be going to college in a few
years, you might want to take the time to wander around the
Central Michigan University campus and try college on for

own Island of Paradise. There are many activities at the park

including live bands, small gatherings, and baseball games.

This park is the main hangout for teens in Mt. Pleasant, so you will ~~For~~ always find something to do. If you want a break, nearby is ~~the children, there is~~ also Nelson Park, which has a small zoo

with bear, deer, badger, and many other kinds of North

American wildlife.

~~If you are a person who likes to shop, then you will~~

~~want to visit the Mt. Pleasant Mall at the edge of town. It has~~

~~all the convenience stores necessary for a fulfilling day of~~ C

~~shoping. There is always plenty of parking.~~

If you are looking for something different, on Mission Road north of M-20 ~~Mt. Pleasant~~ also ~~has places for those of you who like~~ ~~to gamble.~~ Mt. Pleasant Meadows has fun-filled, action-packed For only $2.00, you can enjoy the suspense of cheering your favorite to victory. horse races all weekend long. There is also a concession

stand ~~and a bar. The Meadows is just waiting for you to bet and~~

~~win big.~~

~~If you like horse racing, then~~ You might also enjoy the

car racing at Mt. Pleasant Speedway. On Fridays there ~~is a~~ are
                                                      s
high-speed stock car race all night long. So come see the fast

cars, bright lights, and the excitement of racing waiting for

you.   D

Let's not forget about the fine dining Mt. Pleasant has

to offer. There is an elegant restaurant called The Embers E

that matches all the fine cuisine in the world. There is also

a Holiday Inn which hosts a class A restaurant and nightclub.

The club is called Boomers and presents well-known comedians

to entertain you throughout the night.
                                         swimming, hiking, parks, racing. It
Mt. Pleasant has much to offer you: ~~fine dining,~~
is a fun alternative to whatever you are doing this summer.
~~excitement, and relaxation.~~ Why not come and see for

yourself.

size. Its ivy-covered brick buildings and tree-lined walkways give you the feel of real college life. When summer semester is in session, you might also want to stroll through a few buildings, look around the library, and visit the bookstore. If you stop to watch students bustle to class, you could be watching your own future.

D. On rainy days, there is still a lot to do in Mt. Pleasant. There are several multiscreen movie theaters that give you a choice of the most recent releases. You can also engage in a little time travel at the Center for Cultural and Natural History in Rowe Hall on the CMU campus. This museum includes lumbering tools, Civil War artifacts, a variety of household items from different historical periods, and an exhibit of wildlife, including the remains of a mastodon. You can play video games at the Royal Oasis Family Amusement Center in the campus mall on Mission Street. Or you can spend some time shopping.

E. Because Mt. Pleasant is a college town, there are a number of great cheap places to eat. The McDonald's on Mission Street is the wildest place to get a Big Mac you will ever see. With fancy chrome palm trees and glossy plastic cutouts of people having a great time, it is like an Art Deco scene. You have to see it to believe it. There are, of course, all the great fast-food places and pizza shops. If you are interested in taking a date to some place special and don't mind spending a little money in the process, you might try The Embers, a restaurant rated as "one of Michigan's finest." When you are looking for a place to eat in Mt. Pleasant, you have many great choices.

This case history continues on page 46.

■ Strengthening Paragraph Structure and Development

Once you finish considering the essay as a whole, examine your paragraphs one by one, applying the *FACT* approach that you used for the whole paper. Make sure each paragraph *FITS* the paper's major focus and develops a single central idea. If a paragraph needs more support or examples, *ADD* whatever is necessary. If a paragraph contains ineffective or unhelpful material, *CUT* it. *TEST* the flow of ideas from paragraph to paragraph and clarify connections, both between and within paragraphs, as necessary. Ask the basic questions in the checklist that follows about each paragraph, and make any needed revisions.

REVISION CHECKLIST FOR PARAGRAPHS

- Does the paragraph have one, and only one, central idea?
- Does the central idea help to develop the thesis statement?
- Does each statement within the paragraph help to develop the central idea?
- Does the paragraph need additional explanations, examples, or supporting details?
- Would cutting some material make the paragraph stronger?
- Would reorganization make the ideas easier to follow?
- Can the connections between successive sentences be improved?
- Is each paragraph clearly and smoothly related to those that precede and follow it?

Don't expect to escape making any changes; some readjustments will undoubtedly be needed. Certain paragraphs may be stripped down or deleted, others beefed up, still others reorganized or repositioned. Chapter 14 contains more information on writing effective paragraphs.

EXERCISE   *Here are three sample student paragraphs. Evaluate each according to the Revision Checklist for Paragraphs and suggest any necessary changes.*

1.   I can remember so many times when my father had said that he was coming to pick me up for a day or two. I was excited as a young boy could be at the thought of seeing my father. With all the excitement and anticipation raging inside of me, I would wait on the front porch. Minutes would seem like hours as I would wait impatiently.

2.   Going to high school for the first time, I couldn't decide if I should try out for the cheerleading team or wait a year. Since

I had time and had been on other squads, I decided "why not?" I had nothing to lose but a lot to gain. Tryouts were not as hard as I thought, but I just knew I had to be on the squad. The tryout consisted of learning the routine they made up, making up your own routine, doing splits, and making a chant. Yet although these things were not that hard, I still was not sure whether I would make the team or not. The time came for the judges to make their decisions on who made the squad. Totaling the votes, they handed the results to the coach. She gave her speech that all coaches give. We were all good, but only a few could be picked for the team. As she started to read the names, I got hot. When she called my name, I was more than happy.

3. For hours we had been waiting under the overhang of an abandoned hut. None of us had thought to bring ponchos on our short hike through the woods. Soon it would be dark. Earlier in the day it had been a perfectly clear day. We all agreed that we didn't want to stand here all night in the dark, so we decided to make a dash for it.

■ Sharpening Sentences and Words

Next, turn your attention to sentences and words. You can improve your writing considerably by finding and correcting sentences that convey the wrong meaning or are stylistically deficient in some way. Consider, for example, the following sentences:

> Just Mary was picked to write the report.
> Mary was just picked to write the report.
> Mary was picked to write just the report.

The first sentence says that no one except Mary will write the report; the second says that she was recently picked for the job; and the third says that she will write nothing else. Clearly, each of these sentences expresses a different meaning.

Now let's look at a second set of sentences:

> Personally, I am of the opinion that the results of our membership drive will prove to be pleasing to all of us.
> I believe the results of our membership drive will please all of us.

The wordiness of the first sentence slows the reader's pace and makes it harder to grasp the writer's meaning. The second sentence, by contrast, is much easier to grasp.

Like your sentences, your words should also convey your thoughts precisely and clearly. Words are, after all, your chief means of communicating with your reader. Examine the first draft and revised version of the following paragraph, which describe the early morning actions of the writer's roommate. The underlined words identify points of revision.

First Draft

Coffee cup in hand, she <u>moves</u> toward the bathroom. The coffee spills <u>noisily</u> on the tile floor as she <u>reaches</u> for the light switch and <u>turns</u> it on. After <u>looking</u> briefly at the face in the mirror, she <u>walks</u> toward the bathtub.

Revised Version

Coffee cup in hand, she <u>stumbles</u> toward the bathroom. The coffee she spills on the tile floor makes <u>a slapping sound</u> as she <u>gropes</u> for the light switch and <u>flips</u> it on. After <u>squinting</u> briefly at the face in the mirror, she <u>shuffles</u> toward the bathtub.

Note that the words in the first draft are general and imprecise. Exactly how does she move? With a limp? With a strut? With a spring in her step? And what does "noisily" mean? A thud? A roar? A sharp crack? The reader has no way of knowing. Recognizing this fact, the student revised her paragraph, substituting vivid, specific words. As a result, the reader can visualize the actions more sharply.

Don't confuse vivid, specific words with "jawbreaker words"—those that are complex and pretentious. (Most likely all of the words in the revised version are in your vocabulary.) Words should promote communication, not block it.

Reading your draft aloud will force you to slow down, and you will often hear yourself stumble over problem sections. You'll be more likely to uncover errors such as missing words, excessive repetition, clumsy sentences, and sentence fragments. Be honest in your evaluation; don't read in virtues that aren't there or that exaggerate the writing quality.

REVISION CHECKLIST FOR SENTENCES

- What sentences are not clearly expressed or logically constructed?
- What sentences seem awkward, excessively convoluted, or lacking in punch?
- What words require explanation or substitution because the reader may not know them?
- Where does my writing become wordy or use vague terms?
- Where have I carelessly omitted words or mistakenly used the wrong word?

Chapters 15 and 16 discuss sentences and words in detail.

| **EXERCISE**   *Reread exercise paragraph 1 on page 42 and revise the sentence struc-ture and word choice to create a more effective paragraph.*

■ Proofreading Your Draft

After revising your draft, proofread or edit it to correct errors in grammar, punctuation, and spelling. Since we often overlook our own errors simply because we know what we meant, proofreading can be difficult. Inch through your draft deliberately, moving your finger along slowly under every word. Repeat this procedure several times, looking first for errors in grammar, then for sentence errors and problems in punctuation and mechanics, and finally for mistakes in spelling. Be especially alert for problems that have plagued your writing in the past.

Effective proofreading calls for you to assume a detective role and probe for errors that weaken your writing. If you accept the challenge, you will certainly improve the quality of your finished work.

■ Writing the Introduction and Conclusion

If you've put off writing your introduction, do it now. Generally, short papers begin with a single paragraph that includes the previously drafted thesis statement, which sometimes needs to be rephrased so that it meshes smoothly with the rest of the paragraph. The introduction acquaints the reader with your topic; it should clearly signal your intention as well as spark the reader's interest. Pages 211–13 discuss and illustrate effective introductions.

The conclusion wraps up your discussion. Generally a single paragraph in short papers, a good ending summarizes or supports the paper's main idea. Pages 214–17 discuss and illustrate effective conclusions.

■ Selecting a Title

All essays require titles. Unless a good title unexpectedly surfaces while you are writing, wait until you finish the paper before choosing one. Since the reader must see the connection between what the title promises and what the essay delivers, a good title must be both accurate and specific.

Titling the Mt. Pleasant essay "Shopping in Mt. Pleasant" would mislead the reader, as shopping is mentioned only briefly. A specific title suggests the essay's focus rather than just its topic. For example, "Teenage Fun in Mt. Pleasant" is clearer and more precise than simply "Mt. Pleasant." The essay is geared to teenage activities, not a description of the city as a whole.

To engage your reader's interest, you might try your hand at a clever or catchy title, but don't get so carried away with creativity that you forget to relate the title to the paper's content. Here are some examples of common and clever titles:

Common: "Handling a Hangover"
   Clever: "The Mourning After"

Common: "Selecting the Proper Neckwear"
   Clever: "How to Ring Your Neck"

Use a clever title only if its wit or humor doesn't clash with the overall purpose and tone of the paper.

CASE HISTORY (Concluded)

After carefully proofreading and fine-tuning the second draft of his Mt. Pleasant essay, George prepares the final version, which follows. Margin notes highlight key changes. Compare the revised and final versions to see how these changes have improved the essay.

General title made specific

Slightly rearranged listing reflects organization of essay

First sentence rephrased and divided into two to avoid repeated "If you" paragraph openings and lessen awkwardness

Last sentence reworded to lessen awkwardness

Teenage Fun in Mt. Pleasant

If you get tired of driving out to the same old Lake Michigan beach this summer, you might think about trying Mt. Pleasant for something different. The Mt. Pleasant area offers swimming, canoeing, and hiking; a city park where you can socialize with other teens; a college campus to wander around; horse and auto racing; movies, a museum, video games, and shopping for a rainy day; and many places to eat. What more can you ask?

For swimming or merely lying on the beach, you can't beat Cold Water Lake, just a few miles west of Mt. Pleasant off Beal City Road. This lake boasts crystal clear water and a scenic beach surrounded by hills and woods. Here you can always find a volleyball game to join, throw a frisbee around, do some boy or girl watching, or bask in the sun. The swimming, of course, is great.

If you prefer some wet-and-wild swimming fun, then Lake Isabella Dam, a short drive down the road from Cold Water Lake, is the place for you. The dam forms a slippery slide about a hundred yards long that is pitched at a 160-degree angle. You can spend a whole day there and not get bored with sliding.

Canoeing can be wonderful fun, and the Mt. Pleasant area offers a number of rivers that will delight anyone who likes this activity. If you prefer calm-water canoeing, you can try the Chippewa River, the Cold Water River, or the north or south branches of the Salt River. If your taste runs to the exciting white-water variety, you will find the Pine River made to order. Near or on each river are places that rent canoes at reasonable rates and even provide you with transportation from your destination back to your car.

For anyone who likes to hike, Deerfield Park, a few miles west of town on M-20, provides twenty-five miles of nature trails. These secluded trails that meander through a natural forest and gentle, rolling hills can be a fine place to take someone special for a quiet stroll. You will no doubt see a variety of birds as well as squirrels, raccoons, and chipmunks. If you're really lucky, you might spot a deer or two. Closer to town, on Harris Street, Mission Creek Woodland Park offers sixty acres of forest trails, a creek, and a picnicking area.

Island Park, located in the Pine River just off Main Street, offers you a chance to meet other teenagers without going out of town. Here you can listen to live bands, play or watch baseball games, have picnics, or just get together and talk. This park is the main hangout for Mt. Pleasant teens, so you should have no trouble making new friends. Nearby is Nelson Park, which has a small zoo where you can see deer, bear, badger, and many other kinds of wildlife.

Planning to attend college? If you are, then you might want to spend some time wandering around the Central Michigan University campus and giving it a close look. Strolling past ivy-covered buildings and along tree-lined walkways will give you the feel of real college life. When summer semester is in session, you might also want to walk through a few buildings, look around the library, and visit the bookstore. If you stop to watch students bustle to class, you could be watching your own future.

Paragraph rewritten to liven and add variety to phrasing

"fine place" substituted because "great" overused in essay. "see" substituted to avoid using "spot" twice

Paragraph rewritten to avoid "If you" opening, liven and tighten phrasing. Opportunity to make friends added.

Opening reworded to eliminate cliché and liven phrasing

First two sentences reworded and combined to avoid "If you" opening and tighten phrasing

Third sentence made smoother

Final sentence replaced to strengthen ending

First two sentences rewritten to liven phrasing

Final sentence: types of shopping added

Word "cheap" omitted; Embers restaurant expensive; "wildest" replaced with "most striking" for more accuracy

Other fast-food restaurants named

Details about Embers added

Weak ending sentence replaced with stronger one

Conclusion changed to reiterate audience

To sample something different, pay a visit to Mt. Pleasant Meadows on Mission Road north of M-20 some weekend and enjoy the fun-filled, action-packed horse races you'll find there. For just two dollars, you can enjoy the thrill of cheering your favorite to victory. The Mt. Pleasant Speedway offers you the chance to sample a second kind of racing. Each Friday the speedway puts on a nightlong program of high-speed stock car races. Fast horses or fast cars--either ensures you an evening of high excitement.

On rainy days, you can still find much to do in Mt. Pleasant. Several multiscreen movie theaters give you a choice of the most recent releases. You can also do a little time traveling at the Center for Cultural and Natural History in Rowe Hall on the college campus. This museum includes lumbering tools, Civil War artifacts, a variety of household items from different historical periods, and an exhibit of wildlife, including the remains of a mastodon. You can play video games at the Royal Oasis Family Amusement Center in the campus mall on Mission Street. Or you can spend some time shopping for clothing, books, CDs, or gifts in the many mall stores.

Mt. Pleasant has a wide range of great eating places. The McDonald's on Mission Street is the most striking place that you will probably ever see to get a Big Mac. With fancy chrome palm trees and glossy plastic cutouts of people having a good time, it resembles an Art Deco movie set. There are, of course, many other fast-food places such as Arby's, Burger King, Taco Bell, KFC, Wendy's, Hot N Now, and Little Caesar's. If you are interested in taking a date to some place special and don't mind spending the money to do it, you might try The Embers, a restaurant rated as "one of Michigan's finest." There you'll find cloth napkins and tablecloths, soft lights, and a menu offering an outstanding selection of meat and seafood. Your date will be sure to like it.

Mt. Pleasant offers enough diversions to satisfy any teenager. Why not come and investigate for yourself?

It is crucial that you view revision not as a hasty touch-up job or as a quick sweep through your draft just prior to handing it in. Instead, revision should be an ongoing process that often involves an upheaval of major sections as you see your draft through your reader's eyes and strive to write as well as you can. Only when you reach that summit have you finished revising.

■ Revising with a Word Processor

Many writers prefer the advantages of revising on a word processor. All word-processing programs allow you to write over unwanted sections of your draft, add new information, delete useless material, and move parts of the text around. Learn all the commands of your particular program and experiment to see exactly what your options are. The following practical tips will improve your efficiency:

1. Always keep a backup copy of everything. Accidentally erasing a file or losing your work to an electrical power surge is not uncommon. In addition, save copies of your earlier drafts, either as printouts or on disk; selected parts may prove useful later, and new papers sometimes sprout from old drafts. You can either save each draft under variations of your file name—"COPY A," "COPY B," "COPY C"—or keep deleted sections in specially labeled files.

2. Jot down helpful ideas or comments in your text as you revise. Enclose them with a special symbol, such as < >, and either save them in a separate file or delete them later if they serve no purpose.

3. If you struggle with a section of the text, write two or three versions and then pick your favorite. You might even open a new file, experiment freely, and then use the best version in your draft.

4. Don't allow the program to control how you revise. The easy-to-use, gentle-touch keyboards can lull you into a lapse of judgment and cause you to forget whether your words are worth writing. Pages of worthless material could pile up. Furthermore, don't be tempted to do what the commands make easiest: fiddle endlessly with sentences and words, never develop the essay as a whole, and move blocks of writing around indiscriminately. Avoid being electronically bewitched and make only those additions and changes that improve your writing.

5. Always revise using a printout. If you use just the computer, you are limited to only one screen at a time. A printed page has a different look. In addition, a printout allows you to compare several pages at once: You can see, for example, how the second paragraph might be more effective if repositioned as paragraph 5.

6. When you finish revising, check the coherence of your draft. The writing must flow smoothly at the points where you have added, deleted, or moved sections of text. In addition, altered sentences must be clearly written and logically constructed. You can best check the essay's flow with a printout.

7. Proofreading with a word processor poses certain dangers. For example, a spelling check function can't judge whether you used the wrong word (*form* instead of *from*) or confused identical sounding but differently spelled words (*their, there, they're*). Furthermore, the unit will sometimes flag words that are not misspelled but are simply not in the computer's list. In addition, there are few good programs to check grammar or punctuation. *You* are still the ultimate proofreader.

■ Peer Evaluation of Drafts

At various points in the writing process, your instructor may ask you and your classmates to read and respond to one another's papers. Peer response often proves useful because even the best writers cannot always predict how their readers will react to their writing. For example, magazine articles designed to reduce the fear of AIDS have, in some cases, increased anxiety about the disease. Furthermore, we often have difficulty seeing the problems with our own drafts because so much hard work has gone into them. What seems clear and effective to us can be confusing or boring to our readers. Comments from our peers can frequently launch a more effective essay.

Just as the responses of others help you, so will your responses help them. You don't have the close, involved relationship with your peers' writing that you do with your own. Therefore, you can gauge their drafts objectively. This type of critical evaluation will eventually heighten your awareness of your own writing strengths and weaknesses. And knowing how to read your own work critically is one of the most important writing skills you can develop.

Responding to Your Peers' Drafts

Responding to someone else's writing is easier than you might imagine. It's not your job to spell out how to make the draft more effective, how to organize it, what to include, and what language to use. The writer must make these decisions. Your job is to *identify* problems, *not solve* them. You can do that best by responding honestly to the draft.

Some responses are more helpful than others. You don't help the writer by casually observing that the draft "looks O.K." Such a response doesn't point to problem areas; rather it suggests that you didn't read the paper carefully and critically. Wouldn't you inform a friend who was wearing clothes that looked terrible *why* they looked terrible? The same attitude should prevail about the writing of others, something that makes a statement just as clothes do. Nor is a vague comment such as "The introduction is uninteresting" helpful. Point out *why* it is uninteresting. For instance, you might note that "The introduction doesn't interest me in the paper because it is very technical, and I get lost. I ask myself why I should read on." Below are two more examples of ineffective responses and their more effective counterparts.

Ineffective

The paper was confusing.

Effective

Paragraphs 2, 3, and 4 confused me.
You jumped around too much. First you
wrote about your experience on the first
day of college, then you went on to how
much you enjoyed junior high school, and
finally you wrote about what you want to do
for a career. I don't see how these ideas
relate or why they are in the order that they are.

Ineffective

More examples would help.

Effective

When you indicate that college is a scary place, I
get no real idea of why or how. What are the
things that you think make college scary?
I would like some examples.

Here are some steps to follow when responding to someone else's draft. First, read the essay from beginning to end without interruption. On a separate sheet of paper, indicate what you consider to be the main idea. The writer can then see whether the intended message has come through. Next, identify the biggest problem and the biggest strength. Writers need both negative and positive comments. Finally, reread the paper and write either specific responses to each paragraph or your responses to general questions such as the ones that follow. In either case, don't comment on spelling or grammar unless it really inhibits your reading.

<table>
<tr><td>

PEER RESPONSE CHECKLIST

- What is the main point of this essay?
- What is the biggest problem?
- What is the biggest strength?
- What material doesn't seem to fit the main point or the audience?
- What questions has the author not answered?
- Where should more details or examples be added? Why?
- At what point does the paper fail to hold my interest? Why?
- Where is the organization confusing?
- Where is the writing unclear or vague?

</td></tr>
</table>

As you learn the various strategies for successful writing, new concerns will arise. Questions geared to these concerns appear in the revision section that concludes the discussion of each strategy.

An Example of Peer Response

The following is the first draft of a student essay and a partial peer response to it. The response features three of the nine general questions and also comments on one paragraph. Before you read the response, try evaluating this essay yourself and then compare your reactions to those of the other student.

Captive Breeding in Zoos

1   This paper is about captive breeding. Today, humans hinder nature's species' right to survive. We are making it hard for over one hundred species of animals to continue to exist. But captive breeding in the world's zoos may be just what the doctor ordered. This rescue attempt is a complex and difficult undertaking. Captive breeding of endangered species is complicated by the special social and physical requirements of individual species.

2   There are many social problems that have to be solved for the successful reproduction of endangered species in zoos. Mating is one of the most important of these problems. One propagation "must" for many felines, pandas, and pygmy hippopotamuses is the complete separation of sexes until they're "ready." Leland Stowe says that cheetahs almost never get together unless they can't see or smell each other ahead of time. When females exhibit a certain behavior, they bring on the male.

Male-female compatibility is a social problem. Great   3
apes seem to be as particular as people in choosing mates.
Stowe tells about an orangutan that turned a cold shoulder on
the females in the National Zoo located in Washington, D.C.
Then they shipped him to a zoo in Colorado. There, he took up
with one of the females. The curator of the zoo, William Zan-
ten, says he's "been siring offspring ever since."

Social factors hurt care of infant primates. Sheldon   4
Campbell talks about this in <u>Smithsonian</u> magazine. He writes
about the problems of breeding golden marmosets. These are
monkeys that live in Brazil. The scientists found that cap-
tive-born parents neglected their young. Sometimes they
even killed them. The problem was due to the fact that the
marmosets had no experience living in a family situation.
They didn't know what to do. Emily Hahn writes about gorillas in <u>The New Yorker</u>. She says that those raised by humans
make poor mothers. Those raised by dutiful mothers make good
parents.

The second important stumbling block to successful cap-   5
tive breeding is physical problems. Ignorance of dietary
needs can be bad. Stowe talks about the captive breeding of
gorillas and says that when this breeding was first getting
started, infants exhibited a very high mortality rate. Then
the babies were given iron and meat protein, the latter rich
in vitamin B-12. They were sprinkled on bananas, and the
bananas were fed to the babies. The survival rate markedly
improved.

Animals can be bred more easily if they are in an envi-   6
ronment that duplicates that animal's natural habitat.
Hooved and horned animals are an easy job because of the similarity in terrain and climate of their natural habitats to
zoo habitats. Polar bears are a lot tougher. Mothers want to
be let alone until their cubs are up and about. Because of
this fact, the bears often kill their babies. Stowe says
they solved this problem by building replicas of arctic ice
caves. The mothers and cubs are left alone until they emerge
from the cave. John Perry, Director of the National Zoo,
said this:

> The world is our zoo--a zoo that must be well managed,
> its resources carefully husbanded, for these are the
> only resources it can ever have. We have appointed our-
> selves the keepers of this zoo, but we cannot live out-
> side its gates. We are of it. Our lives are inextricably
> intertwined with the lives of all that live within. Their
> fate will be ours.

Our endangered species can survive only by nature's implacable test--sustained births by second and third generations.
It will take decades to reach such a verdict of success. Thus
we can see that captive breeding is beset by many problems.

What is the main point of this essay?

*I think this paper is saying that the only chance for
endangered species is that they reproduce in zoos
but that it is hard to get them to breed in captivity.*

What is the biggest problem?

*I can't see how the paragraphs connect to the main part of
the paper or to each other. They seem disconnected. What
does "Male-female compatibility is a social problem"
have to do with the problem of reproduction or with the
previous paragraph on mating? Also, there are a number
of very unclear statements that leave me with many
questions. How are we making it hard for over a hundred
species to exist? What do you mean when you say
"Almost never get together," "bring on the male,"
"took up with," and "an easy job?"*

What is the biggest strength?

*I hadn't thought much about this question, so it was
something new for me. I liked the examples about
specific animals and the problems that they have
in captivity. I especially liked the fact that the
writer gave me several problems that occur when
animals are bred in captivity. The writer didn't
oversimplify.*

Response to paragraph 4

Do social factors always hurt the care of infant primates? Your statement seems too general. Shouldn't you combine some of your sentences? The first six sentences seem to abruptly jump from one point to the next; the writing is not smooth. How did you get from marmosets to gorillas? The jump confuses me. Also, were the dutiful mothers humans or gorillas?

Acting upon Your Peers' Responses

Sometimes you need strong nerves to act upon a peer response. You can easily become defensive or discount your reader's comments as foolish. Remember, however, that as a writer you are trying to communicate with your readers, and that means taking seriously the problems they identify. Of course, you decide which responses are appropriate, but even an inappropriate criticism sometimes sets off a train of thought that leads to good ideas for revision.

Examine the revised version of the captive breeding essay that follows and note how some of the peer responses have been taken into account. Clear transition sentences link paragraphs to the thesis statement and to each other. Vague statements identified in the earlier draft have been clarified. In paragraph 4 the writer connects the discussion of the marmosets to that of the gorillas by changing the order of the two sentences that precede the final one and combining them, thereby identifying poor parenting as the key problem with both kinds of primates. Finally, she indicates what she means by "dutiful mother."

As you read this version, carefully examine the margin notes, which highlight key features of the revision.

Captive Breeding: Difficult but Necessary	Title: specific and accurate
Today, as in the past, humans encroach upon the basic right of nature's species to survive. Through ignorance, oversight, and technological developments, we are threatening the survival of over one hundred animal species. Until their environments can be safeguarded against harmful human intrusion, the last chance for the threatened species may be captive breeding in zoos. But this rescue attempt is a complex and difficult undertaking. <u>In particular, each species presents social and physical problems that must be solved if breeding is to succeed</u>.	Introduction: arresting statement Thesis statement and statement of organization

1

Topic sentence with link to thesis statement	2 Among the social problems that complicate successful reproduction, mating problems loom especially large. For instance, the male and female of many feline species must be kept completely separated until both animals are ready to mate. Leland Stowe, writing in National Wildlife magazine,
Specific details: problems with cheetahs	notes that cheetahs almost never mate unless kept where the one cannot see or smell the other. Once the female shows signs of receptivity, a male is placed in her cage, and mating then occurs.
Mention of other species with mating problems	Pandas and pygmy hippopotamuses show the same behavior.
Topic sentence, with link to preceding paragraph. Linking device	3 A related social problem with certain species is male-female compatibility. Great apes, for instance, seem to be as particular as human beings in choosing mates. Stowe
Specific example: problem with particular orangutan	relates an amusing case of a male orangutan that totally spurned the females in the Washington, D.C., National Zoo. Shipped to a zoo in Colorado, he succumbed to the charms of a new face and has, according to curator William Zanten, "been siring offspring ever since."
Topic sentence, with link to preceding paragraph	4 Social factors can also imperil proper care of infant primates. In a Smithsonian magazine article, Sheldon Campbell talks about the problems scientists encountered in try-
Specific details: problems with marmosets	ing to breed golden marmosets, a species of Brazilian monkey. Early attempts failed because the captive-born parents neglected and sometimes accidentally killed their babies. Observation showed that the problem occurred because the marmosets had no experience living in a family situation--they simply didn't know how to handle their offspring.
Mention of other species with rearing problems	Gorillas reared by humans may also make poor mothers, reports Emily Hahn in The New Yorker.
Linking device	On the other hand, those reared by dutiful mothers, whether human or gorilla, are usually good parents themselves.
Transition sentence: signals switch to discussing physical problems	5 Physical problems rival social problems as stumbling blocks to successful captive breeding.
Topic sentence, with link to transition sentence	Ignorance of a species' dietary needs, for instance, can have disastrous consequences.
Specific details: problems with gorillas	Early in the captive breeding of gorillas, infants exhibited a very high mortality rate, Stowe notes. Then meat protein and iron, the former rich in vitamin B-12,

were sprinkled on bananas and fed to the babies. <u>As a result</u>, the survival rate markedly improved.

| | Linking device |

An <u>environment that duplicates a species' natural habitat favors easy propagation</u>. Hooved and horned animals present few breeding problems because the zoo habitats are similar in terrain and climate to their natural habitats. Polar bears, <u>on the other hand</u>, present difficult problems. Unless the mothers have complete privacy until the cubs can get around, they often kill the babies. To prevent this from happening, Stowe says, zoos now construct replicas of arctic ice caves and leave mothers and cubs completely alone until the new family emerges from the cave.

| 6 | Topic sentence |

| | Linking device |

In his book <u>The World's a Zoo</u>, John Perry, director of the National Zoo, has spoken of the need to save our endangered species:

| 7 | Conclusion: quotation plus statement reinforcing idea that captive breeding presents difficulties |

> The world is our zoo--a zoo that must be well managed, its resources carefully husbanded, for these are the only resources it can ever have. We have appointed ourselves the keepers of this zoo, but we cannot live outside its gates. We are of it. Our lives are inextricably intertwined with the lives of all that live within. Their fate will be ours.

The difficulty, unfortunately, is as great as the urgency of this problem. Only sustained births by second- and third-generation captive animals can ensure the survival of our endangered species. And it will take decades to achieve the necessary success.

8

■ Collaborative Writing

In many careers you'll have to work as part of a group to produce a single document. Recognizing this fact, many instructors assign collaborative writing projects. Writing as part of a group offers some advantages and poses some challenges. You can draw on many different perspectives and areas of expertise, split up the work, and enjoy the feedback of a built-in peer group. On the other hand, you must also coordinate several efforts, resolve conflicts over the direction of the project, deal with people who may not do their fair share, and integrate different styles of writing.

Even though you write as part of a group, the final product should read as though it were written by one person. Therefore, take great pains to ensure that the paper doesn't resemble a patchwork quilt. You can help achieve this goal by following the principles of good writing discussed throughout this book. Here are some suggestions for successful collaborative work:

1. Select a leader with strong organizational skills.
2. Make sure each person has every other group member's phone number.
3. Analyze the project and develop a work plan with clearly stated deadlines for each step of the project.
4. Assign tasks on the basis of people's interests and expertise.
5. Schedule regular meetings to gauge each person's progress.
6. Encourage ideas and feedback from all members at each meeting.
7. If each member will develop a part of the paper, submit each one's contribution to the other members of the group for peer evaluation.
8. To ensure that the finished product is written in one style and fits together as a whole, give each member's draft to one person and ask him or her to write a complete draft.
9. Allow plenty of time to review the draft so necessary changes can be made.

Collaborative writing provides an opportunity to learn a great deal from other students. Problems can arise, however, if one or more group members don't do their work or skip meetings entirely. This irresponsibility compromises everyone's grade. The group should insist that all members participate, and the leader should immediately contact anyone who misses a meeting. If a serious problem develops despite these efforts, contact your instructor.

Collaboration Using E-Mail

Increasing numbers of college students are using e-mail to collaborate on writing projects. E-mail allows you to exchange material and comments at every stage of the writing process. To illustrate, you can share

1. brainstorming ideas developed during the search for a writing topic
2. brainstorming ideas developed during the search for supporting information
3. tentative thesis statements or any general statement that will shape the document
4. individual sections of the writing project
5. copies of the entire original draft.

Whenever you use e-mail for collaborative writing, it's a good idea to designate a project leader who will ensure that all members participate and who will receive and distribute all materials. Your instructor may request copies of the e-mail exchanges in order to follow your work.

■ Maintaining and Reviewing a Portfolio

A portfolio is an organized collection of your writing, usually kept in a three-ring binder or folder. It's a good idea to retain all your work for each class, including the assignment sheet, your prewriting, and all your drafts. Organize this material either in the order the papers were completed or by type of assignment.

Why assemble a portfolio? Not only can a portfolio be a source of ideas for future writing, but it also allows you to review the progress of your current papers. In addition, should any confusion arise about a grade or an assignment, the contents of your portfolio can quickly clarify matters.

Some instructors will require you to maintain a portfolio. They will probably specify both what is to be included and how it is to be organized. They may use the portfolio to help you gain a better understanding of your strengths and weaknesses as measured by the series of papers. Furthermore, portfolios give your instructor a complete picture of all your work. Some departments collect student portfolios to assess their writing program; by reviewing student progress, instructors can determine what adjustments will make the program even more effective.

You can review your own portfolio to gain a better understanding of your writing capabilities. Answer these questions as you look over your materials:

1. With what assignments or topics was I most successful? Why?

2. What assignments or topics gave me the most problems? Why?

3. How has my prewriting changed? How can I make it more effective?

4. How has my planning changed? How can I make it more effective?

5. What makes my best writing good? How does this writing differ from my other work?

6. What are the problem areas in my weakest writing? How does this writing differ from my other work?

7. Did I use the checklists in the front of this text to revise my papers? Do I make significant changes on my own, in response to peer evaluation, or in response to my instructor's comments? If not, why not? What kinds of changes do I make? What changes would improve the quality of my work?

8. What organizational patterns have I used? Which ones have been effective? Why? Which ones have given me trouble? Why?

9. What kinds of introductions have I used? What other options do I have?

10. What kinds of grammar or spelling errors mar my writing? (Focus on these errors in future proofreading.)

4

Narration: Relating Events

> Clicking off the evening news and padding toward bed, Heloise suddenly glimpsed, out of the corner of her eye, a shadow stretching across the living room floor from under the drawn curtains.
>
> "Wh–who's there?"
>
> No response.
>
> Edging backward toward the phone, her eyes riveted on the shadow, she stammered, "I–I don't have any money."
>
> Still no answer.
>
> Reaching the phone, she gripped the receiver and started to lift it from its cradle. Just then . . .

Just now you've glimpsed the start of a *narrative*. A narrative relates a series of events. The events may be real—as in histories, biographies, or news stories—or imaginary, as in short stories and novels. The narrative urge stirs in all of us, and like everyone else, you have responded almost from the time you began to talk. As a child, you probably swapped many stories with your friends, recounting an exciting visit to a circus or amusement park or an unusually funny experience with your pet. Today you may tell a friend about the odd happening in your biology laboratory or on the job.

Many classroom and on-the-job writing occasions call for narratives. Your English instructor might want you to trace the development of some literary character. Your history instructor might have you recap the events leading to a major war, your sociology instructor have you relate your unfolding relations with a stepparent or someone else, your psychology instructor ask you to report on society's changing attitudes toward the treatment of insanity. At work, a police officer may record the events leading to an arrest, a scientist recount the development of a research project, a nurse report on a patient's changing attitudes toward surgery, and a department manager prepare a brief history of an employee's work problems.

■ Purpose

A narrative, like any other kind of writing, makes a point or has a purpose. The point can either be stated or left unstated, but it always shapes the writing.

Some narratives simply tell what happened or establish an interesting or useful fact. The reporter who writes about a heated city council meeting or a lively congressional committee hearing usually wants only to set facts before the public.

Most narratives, however, go beyond merely reciting events. Writers of history and biography delve into the motives underlying the events and lives they portray, while narratives of personal experience offer lessons and insights. In the following conclusion to a narrative about an encounter with a would-be mugger, the writer offers an observation on self-respect.

> I kept my self-respect, even at the cost of dirtying my fists with violence, and I feel that I understand the Irish and the Cypriots, the Israelis and the Palestinians, all those who seem to us to fight senseless wars for senseless reasons, better than before. For what respect does one keep for oneself if one isn't in the last resort ready to fight and say, "You punk!"?
>
> Harry Fairlie, "A Victim Fights Back"

■ Action

Action plays a central role in any narrative. Other writing often only suggests action, leaving readers to imagine it for themselves:

> A hundred thousand people were killed by the atomic bomb, and these six were among the survivors. They still wonder why they lived when so many others died. Each of them counts many small items of chance or volition—a step taken in time, a decision to go indoors, catching one streetcar instead of the next—that spared him. And now each knows that in the act of survival he lived a dozen lives and saw more death than he ever thought he would see. At the time, none of them knew anything.
>
> John Hersey, *Hiroshima*

This passage suggests a great deal of action—the flash of an exploding bomb, the collapse of buildings, screaming people fleeing the scorching devastation—but *it does not present the action*. Narration, however, re-creates action:

> When I pulled the trigger I did not hear the bang or feel the kick—one never does when a shot goes home—but I heard the devilish roar of glee that went up from the crowd. In that instant, in too short a time, one would have thought, even for the bullet to get there, a mysterious, terrible change had come over the elephant. He neither stirred nor fell, but every line of his body had altered. He looked suddenly stricken, shrunken, immensely old, as though the frightful impact of the bullet had paralyzed him without knocking him down. At last, after what seemed a long time—it might have been five seconds, I dare say—he sagged flabbily to his knees. His mouth slobbered. An enormous senility seemed to have set-

tled upon him. One could have imagined him thousands of years old. I fired again into the same spot. At the second shot he did not collapse but climbed with desperate slowness to his feet and stood weakly upright, with legs sagging and head drooping. I fired a third time. That was the shot that did for him. You could see the agony of it jolt his whole body and knock the last remnant of strength from his legs. But in falling he seemed for a moment to rise, for as his hind legs collapsed beneath him he seemed to tower upward like a huge rock toppling, his trunk reaching skywards like a tree. He trumpeted, for the first and only time. And then down he came, his belly towards me, with a crash that seemed to shake the ground even where I lay.

George Orwell, "Shooting an Elephant"

Orwell's account offers a stark, vivid replay of the slaying, leaving nothing significant for the reader to infer.

A few words of caution are in order here. Action entails not only exotic events such as the theft of mass-destruction weapons, then the ransom demand, then the recovery of the weapons and the pursuit of the villains. A wide variety of more normal events also qualify as action: a long, patient wait that comes to nothing, an unexpected kiss after some friendly assistance, a disappointing gift that signals a failed relationship. Furthermore, the narrative action must all relate to the main point—not merely chronicle a series of events.

■ Conflict

The events in our lives and our world are often shaped by conflicts that need to be resolved. It should not be surprising then that conflict and its resolution, if any, are crucial to a narrative since they motivate and often structure the action. Some conflicts pit one individual against another or against a group, such as a union, company, or religious body. In others, the conflict may involve either an individual and nature or two clashing impulses in one person's head. Read the following student paragraph and note how common sense and fear struggle within the writer, who has experienced a sharp, stabbing pain in his side:

> Common sense and fear waged war in my mind. The first argued that a pain so intense was nothing to fool with, that it might indicate a serious or even life-threatening condition. Dr. Montz would be able to identify the problem and deal with it before it worsened. But what if it was already serious? What if I needed emergency surgery? I didn't want anyone cutting into me. "Now wait a minute," I said. "It's probably nothing serious. Most aches and pains aren't. I'll see the doctor, maybe get some pills, and the problem will clear up overnight. But what if he finds something major, and I have to spend the night in the hospital getting ready for surgery or recovering from it? I think I'll just ignore the pain."

Luis Rodriguez

■ Point of View

Narrative writers may adopt either a first-person or third-person point of view. In first-person narratives, one of the participants tells what happened, whereas with third-person narration the storyteller stays completely out of the tale. Narratives you write about yourself use the first person, as do autobiographies. Biographies and histories use the third person, and fiction embraces both points of view.

In first-person narration, pronouns such as *I, me, mine, we,* and *ours* identify the storyteller. With the third person, the narrator remains unmentioned, and the characters are identified by nouns and such pronouns as *he, she, him,* and *her.* These two paragraphs illustrate the difference:

First-Person Narration

We would go to the well and wash in the ice-cold, clear water, grease our legs with equally cold stiff Vaseline, then tiptoe into the house. We wiped the dust from our toes and settled down for schoolwork, cornbread, clabbered milk, prayers and bed, always in that order. Momma was famous for pulling the quilts off after we had fallen asleep to examine our feet. If they weren't clean enough for her, she took the switch . . . and woke up the offender with a few aptly placed burning reminders.

Maya Angelou, "Momma's Encounter"

As this example shows, first-person narrators may refer to other characters in the narrative by using nouns and third-person pronouns:

Third-Person Narration

In the depths of the city walk the assorted human creatures who do not suspect the fate that hangs over them. A young woman sweeps happily from store to store, pushing a baby carriage along. Businessmen stride purposefully into their office buildings. A young black sulks down the sidewalks of his tenement, and an old woman tugs her shopping basket across a busy thoroughfare. The old woman is not happy: she has seen better days. Days of parks and fountains, of roses and grass, still stir in her memory. Reaching the other side, she stops and strains her neck upward, past the doorways, past the rows and rows of mirror glass, until her eyes rest on the brilliant blue sky so far away. She looks intently at the sky for a few minutes, noting every cloud that rolls past. And the jet plane. She follows the plane with her deep-socketed eyes and for some unexplainable reason suspects danger. She brings her gaze back to earth and walks away as the jet releases a large cloud of brownish-yellow gas. The gas hangs ominously in the air for a while, as if want-

ing to give humankind just a few more seconds. Then the cloud
slowly descends to the surface, dissipating as it goes. By the
time it reaches the glittering megalopolis, it is a colorless,
odorless blanket of death.

Richard Latta

EXERCISE   *Identify the point of view in each of the following excerpts:*

1.   The bus screeched to a stop, and Pat stepped out of it and
onto the sidewalk. Night enveloped the city, and a slight driz-
zle fell around her as she made her way to Al's office. Turning
the corner, she stepped into the dark entryway. The reception-
ist had gone home, so she proceeded directly to the office. She
knocked on the door and entered. Al, standing behind his desk
and looking out the window, turned toward her with a startled
look on his face.

Jennifer Webber

2.   It had really begun back in the Charlestown Prison, when Bimbi first made
me feel envy of his store of knowledge. Bimbi had always taken charge of any conversation he was in, and I had tried to emulate him. But every book I picked up
had few sentences which didn't contain anywhere from one to nearly all of the
words that might as well have been in Chinese. When I just skipped those words,
of course, I really ended up with little idea of what the book said. So I had come
to the Norfolk Prison Colony still going through only book-reading motions. Pretty
soon, I would have quit even these motions, unless I had received the motivation
that I did.

Malcolm X, *The Autobiography of Malcolm X*

■ Key Events

Any narrative includes many separate events, enough to swamp your narrative
boat if you try to pack them all in. Suppose you wish to write about your recent
attack of appendicitis in order to make a point about heeding early warnings of
an oncoming illness. Your list of events might look like this:

Awakened	Drove to work	Took coffee break
Showered	Parked in employee	Visited bathroom
Experienced acute	lot	Experienced more
but passing pain	Entered building	prolonged pain in
in abdomen	Greeted fellow	abdomen
Dressed	employees	Walked to cafeteria
Ate breakfast	Began morning's work	Ate lunch
Opened garage door	Felt nauseated	Returned to work
Started car	Met with boss	

| Began afternoon's work | Was rushed to hospital | Had emergency operation |
| Collapsed at work station | Underwent diagnostic tests | |

A narrative that included all, or even most, of these events would be bloated and ineffective. To avoid this outcome, identify and build your narrative around its key events—those that bear directly on your purpose. Include just enough secondary events to keep the narrative flowing smoothly, but treat them in sketchy fashion. The pain and nausea certainly qualify as key events. Here's how you might present the first attack of pain:

> My first sign of trouble came shortly after I stepped out of
> the shower. I had just finished toweling when a sharp pain in my
> lower right side sent me staggering into the bedroom, where I
> collapsed onto an easy chair in the corner. Biting my lip to
> hide my groans, I sat twisting in agony as the pain gradually
> ebbed, leaving me gray faced, sweat drenched, and shaken. What,
> I asked myself, had been the trouble? Was it ulcers? Was it a
> gallbladder attack? Did I have stomach cancer?

This passage convinces, not just tells, the reader that an attack has occurred. Its details vividly convey the nature of the attack as well as the reactions of the victim. As in any good narrative, the reader shares the experience of the writer, and the two communicate.

■ Dialogue

Dialogue, or conversation, animates many narratives, livening the action and helping draw the reader into the story. Written conversation, however, doesn't duplicate real talk. In speaking with friends, we repeat ourselves, throw in irrelevant comments, use slang, lose our train of thought, and overuse expressions like *you know, uh,* and *well.* Dialogue that reproduced real talk would weaken any narrative.

Good dialogue resembles real conversation without copying it. It features simple words and short sentences while avoiding the over-repetition of phrases like *she said* and *he replied.* If the conversation unfolds smoothly, the speaker's identity will be clear. To heighten the sense of reality, the writer may use an occasional sentence fragment, slang expression, pause, and the like, as in this passage:

> Mom was waiting for me when I entered the house.
>
> "Your friends. They've been talking to you again. Trying to
> persuade you to change your mind about not going into baseball.
> Honey, I wish you'd listen to them. You're a terrific ballplayer.

```
Just look at all the trophies and awards you've . . ." She paused.
"Joe's mother called me this morning and asked if you were playing
in the game on Saturday. Davey, I wish you would. You haven't
played for two weeks. Please. I want you to. For me. It would be so
good for you to go and--and do what you've always . . ."
    "O.K., Mom, I'll play," I said. "But remember, it's just for
you."
```

Diane Pickett

Note the mother's use of the slang expression "terrific" and of sentence fragments like "your friends" and "for me" as well as the shift in her train of thought and the repetition of "and." These strategies lend an air of realism to the mother's words.

Besides making your dialogue realistic, be sure that you also punctuate it correctly. Here are some key guidelines: Each shift from one speaker to another requires a new paragraph. When an expression like *he said* interrupts a single quoted sentence, set it off with commas. When such an expression comes between two complete quoted sentences, put a period after the expression and capitalize the first word of the second sentence. Position commas and periods that come at the end of direct quotations inside the quotation marks. Our example illustrates most of these guidelines.

■ Ethical Issues

Think how you'd react to a supervisor who wrote a narrative about the development of a new product which exaggerated his role and minimized your crucial contribution to the result. The report might cost you the opportunity for a promotion. Think of your response if you were surfing the Internet and came across a narrative about your first date that used your actual name and cast you in an unfavorable light. At the very least you would find it embarrassing. As you mull over any narrative you write, you'll want to think about several ethical issues, especially if you're depicting an actual event.

- Have I provided a truthful account that participants will recognize and accept? Deliberate falsification of someone's behavior that tarnishes that person's reputation is libel and could result in legal action.

- Would the narrative expose any participants to possible danger if it became public? Do I need to change any names in order to protect people from potential harm? Say your narrative includes someone who cooperates behind the scenes with authorities to help solve a case of cybervandalism. You should probably give that person a fictitious name.

- Does the narrative encourage unethical behavior? For example, extolling the delights of smoking marijuana for a teenage audience is clearly unethical.

These guidelines don't rule out exaggerated, humorous, or painfully truthful narratives. As with any kind of writing, however, narratives can impact the lives of people; as ethical writers we need to consider the possible consequences of our work.

■ Writing a Narrative

Planning and Drafting the Narrative

Most of the narratives you write for your composition class will relate a personal experience and therefore use the first person. On occasion, though, you may write about someone else and therefore use the third person. In either case make sure the experience you pick illustrates some point. A paper that indicates only how you violated a friend's confidence may meander along to little purpose. But if that paper is shaped by some point you wish to make—for instance, that you gained insight into the obligations of friendship—the topic can be worthwhile. To get started, do some guided brainstorming, asking yourself these questions:

> What experience in my life or that of someone I know would be worth narrating?
> What point does this experience illustrate? (Try to state the point in one or two sentences.)
> What people were involved and what parts did they play?

When you have pinpointed a topic, use further brainstorming to garner supporting material. Here are some helpful questions:

> What background information is necessary to understand the events?
> What action should I include?
> What is the nature of the conflict? Was it resolved? If so, how?
> Which events play key roles, which are secondary, and which should go unmentioned?
> Is any dialogue necessary?

Before you start to write, develop a plot outline showing the significant events in your narrative. For each one, jot down what you saw, heard, or did, and what you thought or felt.

Use the opening of your paper to set the stage for what follows. You might tell when and where the action occurred, provide helpful background information, note the incident that activated the chain of events, or identify the problem from which the action grew. If you state your main point directly, do it here or in the conclusion.

The body of the narrative should move the action forward until a turning point is about to be reached. Build the body around your key events. To avoid stranding your reader, use time signals whenever the development of the action might be unclear. Words, phrases, and clauses like *now, next, finally, after an hour,* and *when I returned* help the reader understand the sequence of events. Don't get carried away, though; a paper loaded with time signals makes the sequence seem more important than the events themselves. Finally, think about how you can best use conflict and dialogue to heighten narrative interest.

The conclusion should tie up any loose ends, settle any unresolved conflicts, and lend an air of completion to the narrative. Effective strategies to think about include introducing a surprise twist, offering a reflective summary of the events, noting your reaction to them, or discussing the aftermath of the affair.

Revising the Narrative

As you revise, follow the guidelines in Chapter 3, and in addition ask yourself these questions:

Have I made the point, stated or unstated, that I intended?

Does all of the action relate to the main point?

Is the conflict handled appropriately?

Have I included all of the key events that relate to my purpose? Given each the right emphasis? Used time indicators where needed?

Is my point of view appropriate?

Does my dialogue ring true?

Have I considered appropriate ethical issues?

EXAMPLE STUDENT ESSAY OF NARRATION

The Beach Bum

Gail Bartlett

1   Pete Miller was his name. I met him that summer on the beach of Sanford Lake. I was lying on my extra-large towel, letting the hot sun soak the water droplets off my body, when some clumsy fool flopped by and flipped sand all over me. Jerking up, an angry glare on my face, I was ready to scream at the clod when my mouth opened wide in surprise. This fox was tall with jet-black hair and sky-blue eyes. The summer sun had tanned his body to a golden brown that made me envious as I compared it to my own vague coloring. It was clearly evident that he had spent most of his summer on this beach. Immediately my anger evaporated, and a smile came to my face. In a flirting tone I joked, "Hey, Bud, watch where you're kicking that sand."

2   He grinned back and said, "Come on out in the water, and I'll help you wash it off, unless, of course, you want it left on. I can see you've already discovered it helps for a deep tan. Ha!"

I decided I had nothing to lose and hopped off my towel.   3
As we raced to the water, I could sense him glancing at me,
and I knew at once that he had intentionally tripped in the
sand only to get my attention. This pleased me but made me
even more self-conscious than usual. Not many guys noticed
me, and I never was quite sure how to act.

For the rest of the afternoon, we swam in the warm water.   4
Never before would I have wasted a good tanning sun like that
day's to play in the water, but for some reason I felt this
day was different. He must have been all alone, for I didn't
meet any of his friends. It was only the two of us, and I was
very grateful, for I knew I would not be so much at ease if
there were others around. To my amazement, he asked me out
for the next night to go to a bonfire he and his buddies were
having farther down the beach. I accepted hesitantly, as I
had dated only a few times before.

With great pains I tried to decide what I should wear.   5
Wanting to impress him, I didn't wear my usual jeans and
grubby sweatshirt. Instead I chose my new plaid slacks and
halter top, which were not at all comfortable. While nervously waiting for him, I dabbed on a little extra perfume
and a few extra swishes of blusher. The doorbell rang, and
instantaneously I was on my feet and at the door. The introduction to my parents wasn't exactly what I would describe
as smooth, and I certainly was not at ease.

We arrived at the fire about 9:00 P.M., and already twen-   6
ty of his friends had gathered. They were just beginning to
pass the beer, and when he handed me one I accepted for fear
of disappointing him if I said no. It was not normal for me
to drink, and I didn't feel myself at all. I became afraid of
what his friends would think of me. They were laughing and
telling jokes, but, not wanting to say something that would
embarrass him, I sat silent. When asked a question by his
closest friend, I could only shake my head in answer. The
first hour went by quickly, for my date stayed by my side and
tried in vain to include me in the conversation. I could not
force myself to act normally. It was as though I were being
rated, and I wanted a high score so badly I would not allow

my true personality to show through for fear of not fitting
in and being rejected. I felt as if I were going to suffocate. It was hard for me to hold back my laughter as the
jokes grew increasingly funny. Only a timid giggle would I
let escape my lips. My date became discouraged--I now can
see why--but at that time the reason puzzled me. He left me
to talk to a girl on the other side of the fire who was casually telling a joke. She spoke freely and with the confidence I wished I had. He enjoyed her easy manner, and so did
many of the others. I could tell this by the way they were
attracted to her side of the fire. Everyone was having a
jolly time, and there I sat, suppressing myself in fear.
Finally the guy I had wanted so much to impress returned and
asked in a cold tone, "Are you about ready to go?"

7   I answered with disappointment. "I am, if you are."

8   We slowly trudged to the car, making trite comments along
the way. On the way home I wanted so badly to tell him that I
was not usually so quiet and shy. I wanted to tell him how
much fun I really could be and that I had acted as I had only
because I was afraid he or his friends would think me odd or
different in some way. But instead of saying all this, I only
sat in a quiet closet, drawing myself farther into the corner with every mile.

9   As I climbed into bed, I was angry with myself and vowed
that I would never be that way again. I would force myself to
be natural, no matter what anyone thought. It seemed certain
that I would never be given another chance with this fox. Two
weeks passed without my seeing or hearing a word from him.
Every day I sat and daydreamed of what could have happened
that night had I been myself and a little more at ease.
Things could have worked out so nicely for me.

10   Two weeks later, after I had given up all hope, I
answered the ringing phone one night with a bored hello. Lo
and behold, it was the beach bum! My nerves shook and my eyes
watered as I told him I would be happy to go to a skating
party with him that weekend. Hanging up the phone, I
released an exultant scream and ran to my room to think in

quiet. This time I was not going to wear anything but my usual jeans, and I would act the way I felt.

Through my upstairs bedroom window, I watched him slowly   11
advance to the door, and I could feel that this was going to be the night I wanted so badly. We left the house, and I glanced quickly over at him with a confident smile as we strolled down the sidewalk. The skating rink was crowded, and I recognized most of the people there as his friends whom I had met before. I was surprised at how much friendlier they were to me than at our previous meeting. It was all because I wore a smile and not only listened to them talk but also offered a few quips of my own. When one of the guys skated up beside me and put his arm around me, I didn't look at the floor and shy away as I had done before but returned his warm-ness by putting my arm around him. My date seemed to enjoy my company and stayed near me the whole evening, glancing at me every now and then in disbelief that I could be the girl he had taken out two weeks before. We laughed and joked the night away, and things went much more smoothly than the last time.

While returning to my home he said, "I had a wonderful   12
time tonight and would like to see you again sometime. You're really a lot more fun than I thought you were. Why were you so quiet at the bonfire?"

Slyly I answered, "Oh, was I quiet that night?" With a   13
grin and a look from the corner of his eye, he squeezed my hand. To myself I said, "How much better it is to be yourself and act the way you feel rather than to try to please oth-ers." It had seemed such a hard ordeal to get the others to like and accept me in the beginning, but now I realized that it hadn't been their fault at all--only mine.

DISCUSSION QUESTIONS

1. Identify the point of view of the narrative.
2. List the words, phrases, and clauses that serve as time signals. What has the writer accomplished by using them?
3. This narrative spans about two weeks. At what points has the writer omitted events? Why?
4. What sentence states the point of the narrative? Why is it positioned where it is?

SUGGESTIONS FOR WRITING

1. **Write a personal narrative about an experience that**

   a. altered either your opinion of a friend or acquaintance or your views about some important matter;

   b. taught you a lesson or something about human nature;

   c. caused you great sorrow or joy;

   d. exposed you to the danger of serious injury or death;

   e. acquainted you with some previously unrecognized facet of your character or personality; or

   f. brought about a significant change in your way of life.

Keep in mind all the key narrative elements: purpose, action, conflict, point of view, key events, and dialogue.

2. **A** *maxim* **is a concise statement of a generally recognized truth. Noting the key elements above, write a personal narrative that illustrates one of the following maxims or another that your instructor approves:**

   a. A little learning is a dangerous thing.

   b. The more things change, the more they stay the same.

   c. It's an ill wind that blows no good.

   d. Don't judge a book by its cover.

   e. The road to hell is paved with good intentions.

   f. Pride goeth before a fall.

   g. The long way around is the short way home.

   h. Sometimes too much of a good thing can be wonderful.

   i. Sometimes good intentions have unexpected consequences.

   j. You'll catch more flies with honey than with vinegar.

The Critical Edge

Sometimes writers create narratives by weaving together information from different sources. When developing a narrative about some childhood experience, you might supplement your own recollections by asking relatives and friends to supply details that you've forgotten or clear up points that have become hazy. A police officer investigating an accident questions witnesses, examines physical evidence, and uses the findings to draft an accurate report. A historian writing a biography draws upon public documents, newspaper accounts, diaries, notes of other investigators, and—depending on when the subject lived—other material such as newsreels, TV clips, and interviews in order to create a balanced portrait.

   Integrating material from several sources into a coherent piece of writing is called *synthesis*. When you synthesize, you reflect on ideas you have found in various sources, establish on your own the connections among those ideas, and then determine how the ideas and connections can advance the purpose of your writing. Thus, synthesis features independent thinking in which *you* evaluate, select, and use the material of others—which, of course, must be properly documented—to further your own purpose. Although synthesis can be challenging and does call for judgment on your part, following an effective procedure can help ensure success. Start by jotting down the main points of information from your sources and identifying where those points agree. Sometimes accounts of the same event differ. A friend's memory of your childhood experience may differ markedly from your own. A police officer may find that two witnesses disagree about how an accident happened. A historian may discover that public documents and newspapers offer different motives for an action by a biographical subject. When you encounter this type of contradiction, you'll need to weigh each position carefully in order to determine the most believable account. Then, as in developing any narrative, arrange your material in a pattern that helps make your point.

Let's say, for example, that you're narrating the history of a suburban housing development for low-income families built on land that was formerly owned by a nearby chemical plant and later was found to be contaminated by toxic chemicals. Company officials admit that wastes were buried there but insist that the chemicals were properly contained and posed absolutely no health threat. After stating the company's position, you present the findings of government investigators who analyzed soil samples from the site. These findings revealed that the containers were corroded and leaking and that the wastes included chemicals that attack the nervous system, as well as highly toxic herbicides designed for chemical warfare operations. You conclude that the company is responsible for the serious health problems that now plague the people living in the housing development. Note how the strategy of presenting the company's position early in the narrative lends added force to the point that shapes your writing—company accountability for the health of the housing development's residents.*

SUGGESTIONS FOR WRITING

1. Review a number of articles in your school or local newspaper to develop a sense of journalistic style. Then interview several people about a recent event on campus or at the place you live and write a narrative that reports the event and draws on the interviews.

2. Read "Momma's Encounter" (page 439), "For My Indian Daughter" (page 443), and "Black Men and Public Space" (page 536) and then write a narrative that relates a particular minority experience and incorporates material from any of the three essays.

3. Take notes from several different newspaper accounts of an important or controversial event and write an account of the event that includes your notes.

*Because synthesis involves using several sources, including information from published ones, it is important to read the sections on card catalogs and periodical indexes in Chapter 20 and those on handling quotations and avoiding plagiarism in Chapter 21. As always, follow your instructor's guidelines for documenting sources.

chapter 5

● ●

Description: Presenting Impressions

The sound of hot dogs sizzling on a grease-spattered grill gave way to the whirling buzz of a cotton-candy machine. Fascinated, we watched as the white cardboard cone was slowly transformed into a pink, fluffy cloud. Despite their fiberglass appearance, the sticky puffs dissolved on my tongue into a sugar-like sweetness. Soon our faces and hands were gummed with a sticky mess.

You are there. Seeing, hearing, touching, tasting. This is one student writer's *description* of a small segment of a county fair. Effective description creates sharply etched word pictures of objects, persons, scenes, events, or situations. Sensory impressions—reflecting sight, sound, taste, smell, and touch—form the backbone of descriptive writing. Often, they build toward one dominant impression that the writer wants to evoke.

The human mind is not merely a logical thinking machine. Because of our emotional makeup, we react with shock to a photo of a battered victim of child abuse. We feel stirrings of nostalgia upon hearing a song from our past. We smile with satisfaction when quenching our summer thirst with tart sips from a tall, frosted drink. Responses like these, as much as the ability to think rationally, help define the human makeup.

Many occasions call for description. Your chemistry instructor might ask you to characterize the appearance and odor of a series of substances prepared in the laboratory; your art instructor might want you to describe a painting;

your hospitality management instructor might have you portray an appealing banquet room. On the job, a realtor might write a glowing advertisement to sell a house, a nurse describe the postoperative status of a surgical incision, and a journalist describe the eruption of a volcano. All are attempts to capture the world through description.

■ Purpose

Sometimes description stands alone; sometimes it enriches other writing. It appears in histories and biographies, fiction and poetry, journalism and advertising, and occasionally even in technical writing. Some descriptions merely create images and mood, as when a writer paints a word picture of a boggy, fog-shrouded moor. But description can also stimulate understanding or lead to action. A historian may juxtapose the splendor of French court life with the wretchedness of a Paris slum to help explain the French Revolution. And everyone knows the persuasive power of advertising's descriptive enticements.

Description will provide effective backup for the writing you do in your composition classes, helping you to drive home your points vividly.

■ Sensory Impressions

Precise sensory impressions begin with close physical or mental observation. If you can reexamine your subject, do it. If not, recall it to mind; then capture its features with appropriate words. When you can't find the right words, try a comparison. Ask yourself what your subject (or part of it) might be likened to. Does it smell like a rotten egg? A ripe cantaloupe? Burning rubber? Does it sound like a high sigh? A soft rustle? To come across, the comparison must be accurate and familiar. If the reader has never smelled a rotten egg, the point is lost.

Here is a passage marked by particularly vivid sight impressions:

> After our meal we went for a stroll across the plateau. The day was already drawing to a close as we sat down upon a ledge of rock near the lip of the western precipice. From where we sat, as though perched high upon a cloud, we looked out into a gigantic void. Far below, the stream we had crossed that afternoon was a pencil-thin trickle of silver barely visible in the gloaming. Across it, on the other side, the red hills rose one upon another in gentle folds, fading into the distance where the purple thumblike mountains of Adua and Yeha stretched against the sky like a twisting serpent. As we sat, the sun sank fast, and the heavens in the western sky began to glow. It was a coppery fire at first, the orange streaked with aquamarine; but rapidly the firmament expanded into an explosion of red and orange that burst across the sky sending tongues of flame through the feathery clouds to the very limits of the heavens. When the flames had reached their zenith, a great quantity of storks came flying from the south. They circled above us once, their slender bodies sleek and black against the orange sky. Then, gathering together, they flew off into the setting sun, leaving us alone in peace to contemplate. One of the monks who sat with us, hushed by the intensity of the moment, muttered a prayer. The sun died beyond the hills; and the fire withdrew.
>
> Robert Dick-Read, *Sanamu: Adventures in Search of African Art*

At first, the western sky glows with "a coppery fire," which then expands into "an explosion of red and orange" that sends "tongues of flame" heavenward and then withdraws as the sun disappears. Comparisons strengthen the visual impression: the "pencil-thin" stream, the "thumblike" mountains stretching across the sky "like a twisting serpent." The familiar pencil, thumb, and serpent help us to visualize the unfamiliar landscape.

Most descriptions blend several sense impressions rather than focusing on just one. In the following excerpt, Mark Twain, reminiscing about his uncle's farm, includes all five. As you read it, note which impressions are most effective.

> As I have said, I spent some part of every year at the farm until I was twelve or thirteen years old. The life which I led there with my cousins was full of charm, and so is the memory of it yet. I can call back the solemn twilight and mystery of the deep woods, the earthy smells, the faint odors of the wild flowers, the sheen of rain-washed foliage, the rattling clatter of drops when the wind shook the trees, the far-off hammering of woodpeckers and the muffled drumming of wood pheasants in the remoteness of the forest, the snapshot glimpses of disturbed wild creatures scurrying through the grass—I can call it all back and make it as real as it ever was, and as blessed. I can call back the prairie, and its loneliness and peace, and a vast hawk hanging motionless in the sky, with his wings spread wide and the blue of the vault showing through the fringe of their end feathers. I can see the woods in their autumn dress, the oaks purple, the hickories washed with gold, the maples and the sumachs luminous with crimson fires, and I can hear the rustle made by the fallen leaves as we plowed through them. I can see the blue clusters of wild grapes hanging among the foliage of the saplings, and I remember the taste of them and the smell. I know how the wild blackberries looked, and how they tasted, and the same with the pawpaws, the hazelnuts, and the persimmons; and I can feel the thumping rain, upon my head, of hickory nuts and walnuts when we were out in the frosty dawn to scramble for them with the pigs, and the gusts of wind loosed them and sent them down. I know the stain of blackberries, and how pretty it is, and I know the stain of walnut hulls, and how little it minds soap and water, also what grudged experience it had of either of them. I know the taste of maple sap, and when to gather it, and how to arrange the troughs and the delivery tubes, and how to boil down the juice, and how to hook the sugar after it is made, also how much better hooked sugar tastes than any that is honestly come by, let bigots say what they will.
>
> Mark Twain, *Autobiography*

EXERCISE   *Spend some time in an environment such as one of the following. Concentrate on one sense at a time. Begin by observing what you see; then jot down the precise impressions you receive. Now do the same for impressions of touch, taste, smell, and sound.*

1. The woods in the early morning
2. A city intersection
3. A restaurant or cafeteria
4. A scenic spot under a full moon
5. A storm
6. A pool or other recreation area

7. A crowded classroom or hallway

8. A construction site

9. A park or playground

10. A holiday gathering

■ Dominant Impression

Skillful writers select and express sensory perceptions in order to create a *dominant impression*—an overall mood or feeling such as joy, anger, terror, or distaste. This impression may be identified or left unnamed for the reader to deduce. Whatever the choice, a verbal picture of a storm about to strike, for example, might be crafted to evoke feelings of fear by describing sinister masses of slaty clouds, cannon salvos of thunder, blinding lightning flashes, and viciously swirling wind-caught dust.

The following paragraph establishes a sense of security as the dominant impression:

> A marvelous stillness pervaded the world, and the stars together with the serenity of their rays seemed to shed upon the earth the assurance of everlasting security. The young moon recurved, and shining low in the west, was like a slender shaving thrown up from a bar of gold, and the Arabian Sea, smooth and cool to the eye like a sheet of ice, extended its perfect level to the perfect circle of a dark horizon. The propeller turned without a check, as though its beat had been part of the scheme of a safe universe; and on each side of the *Patna* two folds of water, permanent and sombre on the unwrinkled shimmer, enclosed within their straight and diverging ridges a few white swirls of foam bursting in a low hiss, a few wavelets, a few ripples, a few undulations that, left behind, agitated the surface of the sea for an instant after the passage of the ship, subsided splashing gently, calmed down at last into the circular stillness of water and sky with the black speck of the moving hull remaining everlastingly in its centre.
>
> Joseph Conrad, *Lord Jim*

The first sentence directly identifies the impression, "security," to which the "stillness" and the "serenity" contribute. Other details also do their part: the "smooth" sea, the "perfect circle" of the horizon, the "safe universe," the quick calming of the water, and the moving hull "everlastingly" in the center of water and sky.

EXERCISE   *Select one of the following topics and write a paragraph that evokes a particular dominant impression. Omit any details that run counter to your aim.*

1. A multi-alarm fire

2. A repair facility (automobile, appliance, and so on)

3. A laboratory

4. Some aspect of summer in a particular place

5. A religious service

6. A doctor's or dentist's office

7. A dark street

8. A parade or other celebration

9. Some landmark on your college campus

10. A municipal night court or small-claims court

■ Vantage Point

You may write a description from either a fixed or a moving vantage point. A fixed observer remains in one place and reports only what can be perceived from there. Here is how Marilyn Kluger describes the Thanksgiving morning sounds she remembers hearing from her bed as a child:

> On the last Thursday in November, I could stay in bed only until the night chill left the house, hearing first the clash of the heavy grates in the huge black iron range, with its flowery scrolls and nickled decorations, as Mother shook down the ashes. Then, in their proper sequence, came the sounds of the fire being made—the rustle of newspaper, the snap of kindling, the rush of smoke up the chimney when Mother opened the damper, slid the regulator wide open, and struck a match to the kerosene-soaked corncobs that started a quick hot fire. I listened for the bang of the cast-iron lid dropping back into place and for the tick of the stovepipes as fierce flames sent up their heat, then the sound of the lid being lifted again as Mother fed more dry wood and lumps of coal to the greedy new fire. The duties of the kitchen on Thanksgiving were a thousand-fold, and I could tell that Mother was bustling about with a quicker step than usual.
>
> Marilyn Kluger, "A Time of Plenty"

A moving observer views things from a number of positions, signaling changes in location with phrases such as "moving through the turnstile" and "as I walked around the corner." Below, H. L. Mencken takes us with him as he observes from a moving express train.

> On a Winter day some years ago, coming out of Pittsburgh on one of the expresses of the Pennsylvania Railroad, I rolled eastward for an hour through the coal and steel towns of Westmoreland county. It was familiar ground; boy and man, I had been through it often before. But somehow I had never quite sensed its appalling desolation. Here was the very heart of industrial America, the center of its most lucrative and characteristic activity, the boast and pride of the richest and grandest nation ever seen on earth—and here was a scene so dreadfully hideous, so intolerably bleak and forlorn that it reduced the whole aspiration of man to a macabre and depressing joke. Here was wealth beyond computation, almost beyond imagination—and here were human habitations so abominable that they would have disgraced a race of alley cats.
>
> I am not speaking of mere filth. One expects steel towns to be dirty. What I allude to is the unbroken and agonizing ugliness, the sheer revolting monstrousness, of every house in sight. From East Liberty to Greensburg, a distance of twenty-five miles, there was not one in sight from the train that did not insult and lacerate the eye. Some were so bad, and they were among the most pretentious—churches, stores, warehouses, and the like—that they were downright startling; one blinked before them as one blinks before a man with his face shot away. A few linger in memory, horrible even there: a crazy little church just west of Jeannette, set like a

dormer-window on the side of a bare, leprous hill; the headquarters of the Veterans of Foreign Wars at another forlorn town, a steel stadium like a huge rat-trap somewhere further down the line. But most of all I recall the general effect—of hideousness without a break. There was not a single decent house within eye-range from the Pittsburgh suburbs to the Greensburg yards. There was not one that was not misshapen, and there was not one that was not shabby.

H. L. Mencken, "The Libido for the Ugly"

The phrase "on one of the expresses of the Pennsylvania Railroad" signals that Mencken will be a moving observer, and "From East Liberty to Greensburg" pinpoints the extent of his journey. "West of Jeannette," "another forlorn town," and "somewhere further down the line" specify the positions from which he views the church, the headquarters of the veterans' organization, and the stadium.

Whatever your vantage point, fixed or moving, report only what would be apparent to someone on the scene. If you describe how a distant mountain looks from a balcony, don't suddenly leap to a description of a mountain flower; you couldn't see it from your vantage point.

EXERCISE

1. **Writing as a fixed observer, describe in a paragraph your impressions of one of the following. Be sure to indicate your vantage point.**

   a. A post office lobby two weeks before Christmas

   b. The scene following a traffic accident

   c. A classroom when the bell rings

   d. A campus lounge

   e. An office

   f. The entrance to some building

2. **Writing as a moving observer, describe in a paragraph or two your impressions as you do one of the following things. Clearly signal your movements to the reader.**

   a. Walk from one class to another

   b. Shop in a supermarket or clothing store

   c. Walk from your home to the corner

   d. Cross a long bridge

   e. Water-ski

   f. Go through a ticket line and enter a theater, auditorium, or sports arena

■ Selection of Details

Effective description depends as much on exclusion as on inclusion. Don't try to pack every possible detail into your paper by providing an inventory of, for example, a room's contents or a natural setting's elements. Such an approach shows only that you can see, not write. Instead, select details that deliberately point toward the mood or feeling you intend to create. Read the following student description of nighttime skiing:

> The glowing orb of the moon, shedding its pale, silvery
> radiance on the ski slope, seemed to cast a spell. Crystal iri-
> descence of powdered snow twinkled in the night. Shadows cast by
> the skiers appeared as mysterious silhouettes darting in and
> out among snow-covered trees. The gentle breeze combing through
> the branches created a lulling musical chant that drifted into
> my head, taking control. Delicate snowflakes danced by, kissed
> me on the face, and seemed to beckon me up the hill.
>
> Sue Mutch

This writer evokes a sense of enchantment by noting the "pale, silvery radi-ance" of the moon, the "crystal iridescence" of the snow, the "mysterious silhou-ettes" of the skiers, and the "lulling musical chant" of the wind. She ignores such details as the boisterous snatches of conversation among the skiers, the crunch of ski poles digging into the snow, and the creaking towline moving to the top of the slope. Mentioning these things would detract from the desired mood.

■ Arrangement of Details

Description, like any other writing, must have a clear pattern of organization to guide the reader and help you fulfill your purpose. Often some spatial arrange-ment works nicely. You might, for example, move systematically from top to bot-tom, left to right, front to back, nearby to far away, or the reverse of these pat-terns. To describe Saturday afternoon at the football game, you might start with the crowded parking lot; move into the bustling stadium; and finally zoom in on the sights, sounds, and smells of the playing field. Or if you wanted to highlight the surroundings rather than the central event, the order could be reversed. Going another route, you might start with some striking central feature and then branch out to the things around it. To capture the center of a mall, you might first describe its ornate fountain illuminated with flashing, multicolored lights, shift to the reflection of the lights on the skylight above, and end by por-traying the surrounding store fronts.

Sometimes a description follows a time sequence. A writer might, for ex-ample, portray the changes in a woodland setting as winter gives way to spring and spring, in turn, yields to summer.

■ Ethical Issues

Imagine a police description of an auto accident that misstated the length of a car's skid marks or failed to note the icy patches of road at the scene. It might cost a blameless driver a heavy fine and a steep increase in auto insurance pre-miums. Imagine your disappointment and anger if you booked a weekend at a distant resort only to find it situated on an algae-covered pond instead of the beautiful lake described in the brochure. Imagine your irritation if a going-out-of-business sale described as "fabulous" turned out to offer only 10 percent price reductions. Clearly, inaccurate descriptions can create a wide range of undesirable consequences. Ask and answer these questions about your description.

- Would readers find my writing credible if they were at the scene?

- Are readers given adequate clues so that they will recognize any deliberate exaggeration?

- Will the description deceive readers in a harmful way?

You have an ethical obligation to present a reasonably accurate portrayal of your topic.

■ Writing a Description

Planning and Drafting the Description

If you're choosing your own topic, always select one that is familiar. Don't describe the inside of a restaurant kitchen or Old Faithful geyser in Yellowstone National Park if you've never seen either one. Instead, opt for some place where you've actually worked or a locale you've recently visited. If you keep a journal, thumb through it for possible leads.

For each potential topic that surfaces, ask yourself the following questions. They will direct your attention to matters you'll need to address.

What do I want to accomplish by writing this description? Create one or more impressions? Help the reader understand something? Persuade the reader to act?
Who is my audience and why would this topic interest them?
What dominant impression will I develop?

To help gather and organize support for your topic, pose these additional questions:

What details should I include?
What sensory impressions are associated with each detail? (Jot down any words that you feel will best convey the impressions.)
How does each detail contribute to the dominant impression?
What sequence should I follow in presenting my impressions? (Map out the sequence, setting up a 1-2-3 listing or possibly a paragraph-by-paragraph plan.)

After brainstorming a list of potential details, you might use branching (see pages 21–22) to start accumulating sensory impressions. Page 82 illustrates how student writer Kim Swiger used branching to obtain and group the sensory impressions for a paragraph describing the sounds of her kitchen at breakfast time. Note that her grouping provided Swiger with the pattern used to organize her paragraph. Thus, the paragraph begins with stove-related sounds, moves to sounds associated with coffee-making and cooking, and ends with the mixing of orange juice.

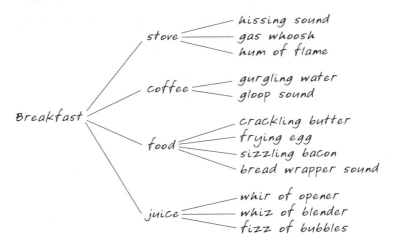

Begin your paper with an introduction that eases the reader into your topic. You might, for example, provide a historical overview, ask a provocative question, or snare the reader's attention with an arresting statement.

Develop each major feature in one or more paragraphs. Present each feature in the order you've mapped out. To ensure that the reader follows your thoughts, clearly signal any shifts in vantage point or time. As you write, aim for vivid, original language. We've all encountered writers who tell us that raindrops "pitter-patter," clouds are "fleecy white," and the sun is "a ball of fire." Such stale, worn-out language does nothing to sharpen our vision of the rain, the clouds, or the sun. The Swiger paragraph avoids this pitfall.

> Sure signs of a new day are the sounds in the kitchen as breakfast is prepared. The high sigh of the gas just before it whooshes into flame and settles into a whispering hum blends with the gurgling of the water for the morning coffee. Soon the gloop, gloop, gloop of the coffee sets up a perky beat. Then in mingles the crackle of creamy butter on a hot skillet and the shush of an egg added to the pan. Ribbons of bacon start to sizzle in the spitting grease. The soft rustle of plastic as bread is removed from its wrapper contributes to the medley. The can opener whirs, and the orange juice concentrate drops with a splat into the blender, which whizzes together the orange cylinder and splashed-in water. For minutes after the blender stops, bubbles of various sizes fizz.
>
> Kim Burson Swiger

You are there in the kitchen, hearing the carefully selected and freshly described sounds.

A word of caution about making your writing vivid. Some students are tempted to enhance their descriptions by stringing together a chain of adjectives without considering the effect on a reader. Think how you'd react if told that

A dented, cylindrical, silver-gray, foul-smelling, overloaded trash can sat in the alley.

As you can see, more than the garbage can is overloaded here. Resist the temptation to inject similar sentences into your description. Carefully examine your adjectives and eliminate those that don't advance your purpose.

End your paper by pulling your material together in some way. If you've created an impression or mood, you might offer your reaction to it. If you want your reader to understand something, you might spell your message out. If you wish to persuade, you might urge some action.

Revising the Description

As you revise, apply the guidelines in Chapter 3 and ask the following questions:

Have I written with a clear sense of purpose and audience in mind?

Have I conveyed how my topic looks, sounds, feels, tastes, or smells? Would comparisons or more precise descriptive terms help convey my perceptions?

Have I evoked one dominant impression? Can I strengthen this impression by adding certain selected details? By eliminating details that detract from the impression?

Have I used an appropriate vantage point? If the observer is moving, have I signaled changes in location? Have I included only details that would be visible to the observer?

Have I arranged my details in an order appropriate to the topic?

Have I considered appropriate ethical issues?

EXAMPLE STUDENT ESSAY OF DESCRIPTION

The Big One

Rebecca Mutch

With a final crack of a bat and a lofting fly ball, baseball ended for the year. The last swirl of water gurgling down
the drain of the community pool marked the end of its season.
These closings marked the beginning of another event, the
county fair. This season I was elected to take my little
brother on a ride--"the big one," in his words.

1

2   Once again I found myself in the familiar grass lot bordering the fairground. The fair itself was completely surrounded by a fence. No one could see what was inside. The only clues were carried in the wind. Muffled echoes of carnies hawking their games, excited squeals of children, and blaring carnival tunes, frequently punctuated by sharp, crackling static, blended with the tantalizing fragrance of popcorn, the spicy aroma of pizza, and the sweet molasses smell of caramel corn.

3   As we entered the main gate and handed our tickets to the men whose baskets already overflowed with torn stubs, my eyes immediately confirmed what my ears and nose had already reported. In one step we had gone from a semiquiet and relaxed world into an ever-revolving one. Dazzling lights, blinking out of control, seemed to flirt with anyone and everyone. Children, their white T-shirts covered with splotches of chocolate and mustard, dashed ahead of their parents and returned shortly, screaming about the giant bear that waited ahead. The distant, shuffling crowds appeared as moving shadows, their features blurred.

4   The little tug on my sleeve reminded me of that big ride that waited ahead. The path up the midway, packed with a cushion of sawdust, was strewn with empty popcorn boxes, scraps of papers, and crumpled cigarette packages.

5   Game booths and food huts, their pennants whipping and snapping in the wind, dotted the path on both sides and formed two long serpent-like strings of pleasure. BB's clinked against tin objects in the shooting gallery. Hawkers with greased hands and pudgy fingers tried to lure suckers toward their gaudy booths. A backboard thudded and a hoop clanked as still another young man tried to win the enormous purple teddy bear that smiled down mockingly from its perch above. The sound of hot dogs sizzling on a grease-spattered grill gave way to the whirling buzz of a cotton-candy machine. Fascinated, we watched as the white cardboard cone was slowly transformed into a pink, fluffy cloud. Despite their fiberglass appearance, the sticky puffs dissolved on my tongue into a sugar-like sweetness. Soon our faces and hands were gummed with a sticky mess.

We scuffled along with the rhythm of the crowd and before   6
long arrived at those metallic contraptions of nuts and
bolts--the rides. The sounds of metal clanging and banging
filled the air. Sparks shot out from where the metal pieces
slapped together. Swirling and whirling, these pieces
caught the reflection of the neon lights and, together with
the sparks, produced a world of spectrum colors.

This was it. The Ferris wheel stood towering before us.   7
As the seat gently swayed, we waited for the ride to begin.
The motor belched and then slowly started to turn; goose
bumps formed on my brother's bare arms, and his eyes grew
larger as the ride picked up speed. The fairground was soon a
kaleidoscope of fantastic images and colors. The wind
whipped through my hair and snapped it back, stinging my
face at times. Both of us were screaming uncontrollably.
Suddenly, with no apparent slowdown, the ride was over, and
we made our way dizzily to the car.

My brother talked about the big one for weeks. For me it   8
brought back many fond memories and let me, just for an
evening, be a child again.

DISCUSSION QUESTIONS

1. This description features a moving observer. Where are the writer's movements indicated?
2. Point out details that appeal to each of the five senses.
3. Reread paragraph 7. Identify perceptual observations used to describe the Ferris wheel ride.
4. How is the essay organized? Given its purpose, why is this pattern effective?

SUGGESTIONS FOR WRITING   *Choose one of the following topics or another that your instructor approves for a properly focused essay of description. Create a dominant impression by using carefully chosen, well-organized details observed from an appropriate vantage point. Try to write so that the reader actually experiences your description.*

1. Holiday shopping
2. A concert of some type
3. An exercise class
4. A crafts class
5. An amusement park, a miniature or full-sized golf course, or some other type of recreational facility

6. A juice bar or coffee shop

7. A pet store or zoo

8. The lobby of a theater

9. A professional wrestling performance

10. A shopping center or minimart

11. A fast-food restaurant

12. Some type of party

13. An outdoor place of special importance to you

14. A Thanksgiving dinner

15. A reunion of some type

16. A NASCAR race

17. A video game arcade

18. An advertisement

19. A scene of environmental damage

20. A historical building or site

The Critical Edge

Most of us know that any two people are likely to see and describe the same object, place, or event differently. A motorist whose car broke down in the desert would note the impossible distances, the barrenness, the absence of human life, the blazing sun. A biologist who was well-supplied with food and water would see a rich ecosystem with a wide variety of plant life and an interesting population of insects and animals. Each would produce a different description that served a different purpose. The motorist would emphasize the grueling heat and desolation to establish the danger of the situation. The biologist would provide a detailed description of the plants, insects, and animals to advance scientific understanding of the area.

As a writer, you may occasionally need to synthesize (see pages 72–73) information supplied by others when creating your own description. Suppose that you're writing a paper about the old growth forests of Oregon. You may read a naturalist's description of the ancient, rare species of trees and how the forest provides a habitat for much unique wildlife. You might also read a lumber industry study indicating that the trees are an important economic resource. You might even uncover an account by an early explorer that captures the emotions aroused by the discovery of the forest.

Armed with these and other descriptions, you could create a composite picture that captures all the different perspectives. You might start by offering the views of the Native American forest dwellers, then detail the towering majesty of the trees and the abundance of game as reported by early explorers. Next, you might turn to the accounts of early farmers, who regarded the forest as an obstacle to be cleared away, and continue by presenting the view of the forest as a lumber resource, perhaps including a description of a depleted lumbering site. To end the paper, you might note how contemporary conservationists view what remains of the forest. Collectively, this information would offer a stark portrayal of the near-total destruction of a splendid natural resource and by implication argue for preserving what is left. While this kind of writing task seems daunting, you can simplify it if you take up one perspective at a time.

Because different people are likely to see and describe the same object, place, or event differently, it's important to look critically at any description you consider for your paper. When you finish reading, ask yourself what features might have been omitted and what another slant on the material might have yielded. To illustrate, in "Once More to the Lake" E. B. White describes early morning fishing as follows: "We went fishing the first morning. I felt the same damp moss covering the worms in the bait can, and saw the dragonfly alight on the tip of my rod as it hovered a few inches from the surface of the water." (See paragraph 5, page 000.) If White had found fishing repugnant, he could just as easily have described the worms squiggling in the can as if they were afraid of the hook, the slimy feel of his hands after baiting the hook, the swarm of mosquitoes around his face, and the tangle in his line. Clearly, description demands choices. Different impressions and varying emphases can be selected. And like any other writer, you should carefully consider the details and slant of any description you write.*

SUGGESTIONS FOR WRITING

1. Select a famous U.S. landmark, such as the Grand Canyon, and read several writers' descriptions of it. After taking notes, write a description that includes their differing perspectives.

2. Rewrite a shortened version of an essay such as "Once More to the Lake" by building on the original details to create a different emphasis.

3. Interview several students to learn their impressions of your campus and weave those impressions into a descriptive essay.

---

*Because this type of paper includes information from published sources, it is important to read the sections on card catalogs and periodical indexes in Chapter 20 and those on handling quotations and avoiding plagiarism in Chapter 21. As always, follow your instructor's guidelines for documenting sources.

chapter
6

• •

Process Analysis: Explaining How

"Hey Bill, I'd like you to take a look at Mr. Gorgerise's car. He's really fuming. Says the engine's burning too much oil, running rough, and getting poor mileage. Check it out and see what you can find."

Bill begins by removing the spark plugs, hooking a remote-control starter to the starter in the car, and grounding the ignition to prevent the car's starting accidentally. Next, he fits a compression pressure gauge into the spark plug hole by cylinder number one, starts the engine, and reads and records the pressure; then he does the same for each of the other cylinders. Finally, he compares the readings with one another and the automaker's engine specs. The verdict? An excessively worn engine that needs rebuilding. Bill has carried out a *process,* just one among many that fill his workdays.

As we pursue our affairs, we perform processes almost constantly, ranging from such daily rituals as brewing a pot of coffee and flossing our teeth to taking a picture, taping a compact disc, preparing for a date, or replacing a light switch. Often we share our special technique for doing something—for example, making chicken cacciatore—by passing it on to a friend.

Many popular publications feature process analyses that help readers to sew zippers in garments, build catamarans, live within their means, and improve their wok technique. Process analysis also frequently helps you meet the writing demands of your courses. A political science instructor may ask you to explain how your state's governor won nomination, or a biology instructor may want an explanation of how bees find their way back to the hive. Another instructor may call for directions relating to some process in your field—for example, analyzing a chemical compound, taking fingerprints, or obtaining a blood sample.

On the job, a greenhouse crew leader may provide summer employees with directions for planting various kinds of shrubs and flowers. A technical writer may prepare a list of steps for workers to follow when unloading a particular solvent from a tank car. A sanitation department technician may write a brochure telling city residents how to get paper, glass, and metal trash ready for recycling.

As these examples show, a process can be nontechnical, historical, scientific, natural, or technical.

■ Kinds of Process Analysis Papers

Process papers fall into two categories: those intended for readers who will perform the process and those intended to explain the process for nonperformers. Papers in either category can range from highly technical and sophisticated to nonspecialized and simple.

Processes for Readers Who Will Perform Them   The audience for these papers may be technical and professional personnel who need the information to carry out a work-related task or individuals who want to perform the process for themselves.

A how-to-do-it paper must include everything the reader needs to know in order to ensure a successful outcome. Its directions take the form of polite commands, often addressing readers directly as "you." This approach helps involve readers in the explanation and emphasizes that the directions must, not merely should, be followed. Here is an illustration:

> To prepare a bacterial smear for staining, first use an inoculating loop to place a drop of distilled water on a clean glass microscope slide. Next, pass the loop and the opening of the tube containing the bacterial culture to be examined through a Bunsen burner flame to sterilize them. From the tube, remove a small bit of culture with the loop, and rub the loop in the drop of water on the slide until the water covers an area one and one-half inches long and approximately the width of the slide. Next, reflame the opening of the culture tube to prevent contamination of the culture, and then plug it shut. Allow the smear to air dry, and then pass the slide, smear side up, through the flame of the burner until it is warm to the touch. The dried smear should have a cloudy, milky-white appearance.
>
> Darryl Williams

Processes for Readers Who Won't Perform Them   These kinds of papers may tell how some process is or was performed or how it occurs or occurred. A paper might, for instance, detail the stages of grief, the procedure involved in an operation, the role of speech in the development of children's thinking, or the sequence involved in shutting down a nuclear reactor. These papers serve many purposes—for example, to satisfy popular curiosity; to point out the importance, difficulty, or danger of a process; or to cast a process in a favorable or unfavorable light. Even though the writers of such papers often explain their topic in considerable detail, they do not intend to provide enough information for readers to carry out the process.

Papers of this sort present the needed information without using polite commands. Sometimes a noun, a pronoun like *I, we, he, she,* or *it,* or a noun–pronoun combination identifies the performer(s). At other times, the performer remains unidentified. Three examples follow.

Pronouns Identify Performer

Thus, when I now approach a stack of three two-inch cinder blocks to attempt a breaking feat, I do not set myself to "try hard," or to summon up all my strength. Instead I relax, sinking my awareness into my belly and legs, feeling my connection with the ground. I breathe deeply, mentally directing the breath through my torso, legs, and arms. I imagine a line of force coming up from the ground through my legs, down one arm, and out through the stone slabs, and down again into the ground, penetrating to the center of the earth. I do not focus any attention on the objects to be broken. Although when I am lifting or holding them in a normal state of consciousness the blocks seem tremendously dense, heavy, and hard, in the course of my one- or two-minute preparation their reality seems to change, as indeed the reality of the whole situation changes. . . . When I make my final approach to the bricks, if I regard them at all they seem light, airy, and friendly; they do not have the insistent inner drive in them that I do.

Don Ethan Miller, "A State of Grace: Understanding the Martial Arts"

Noun-Pronoun Combination Identifies Performers

Termites are even more extraordinary in the way they seem to accumulate intelligence as they gather together. Two or three termites in a chamber will begin to pick up pellets and move them from place to place, but nothing comes of it; nothing is built. As more join in, they seem to reach a critical mass, a quorum, and the thinking begins. They place pellets atop pellets, then throw up columns and beautiful, curving, symmetrical arches, and the crystalline architecture of vaulted chambers is created. It is not known how they communicate with each other, how the chains of termites building one column know when to turn toward the crew on the adjacent column, or how, when the time comes, they manage the flawless joining of the arches. The stimuli that set them off at the outset, building collectively instead of shifting things about, may be pheromones released when they reach committee size. They react as if alarmed. They become agitated, excited, and then they begin working, like artists.

Lewis Thomas, "Societies as Organisms"

Performer Unidentified

The analyzer was adjusted so the scale read zero and was connected to the short sampling tube, which had previously been inserted into the smokestack. The sample was taken by depressing the bulb the requisite number of times, and the results were then read and recorded. The procedure was repeated, this time using the long sampling tube and sampling through the fire door.

Charles Finnie

EXERCISE

1. Examine your favorite newspaper or magazine for examples of process analysis. Bring them to class for group discussion of which kind each represents and the writer's purpose.

2. Examine science textbooks and professional journals for more complex examples of process analysis. Bring your examples to class and discuss how they differ from simple instructions.

■ Ethical Issues

Unclear, misleading, incomplete, or erroneous instructions written for someone to follow can spawn a wide range of unwanted consequences. Often frustration and lost time are the only results. Sometimes, though, the fallout is more serious, as in the case of a lab explosion. And in extreme cases, the outcome can be potentially catastrophic, as when an accident occurs in a nuclear power plant. As writers, we have an ethical obligation to write clear and complete instructions. To help you do this, ask and answer the following questions when you're writing a process that the reader will perform.

- Have I used clear and unambiguous language so that the reader will not encounter unnecessary frustration and inconvenience?

- Have I clearly indicated any requirements such as time needed or additional supplies that will have to be purchased?

- Have I clearly warned readers about any possible harm they could face?

■ Writing a Process Analysis

Planning and Drafting the Process Analysis

As always, when the choice is yours, select a familiar topic. If you're not the outdoor type and prefer a Holiday Inn to the north woods, don't try to explain how to plan a camp-out. Muddled, inaccurate, and inadequate information will result. On the other hand, if you've pitched many a tent, you might want to share your technique with your readers.

Finding a suitable topic should be easy. But if you do hit a snag, turn to the strategies on pages 14–20. In any event, answer the following questions for each potential choice:

Will the reader find the process important, interesting, or useful?

Should I provide directions for the reader to follow, explain how the process takes place, or explain how others perform it?

Can I explain the process adequately within any assigned length?

Processes for Readers Who Will Perform Them   If you will develop a process for readers to follow, ponder this second set of questions to help you accumulate the details you'll need:

> What separate actions make up the process? (Be especially careful not to omit any action that is obvious to you but wouldn't be to your reader. Such an oversight can ruin your reader's chances of success.)
>
> What is the reason for each action?
>
> What warnings will the reader need in order to perform the process properly and safely?

When you have your answers, record them in a chart similar to this one:

Action	Reason for Action	Warning
First action	First reason	First warning
Second action	Second reason	Second warning

Sometimes a reason will be so obvious no mention is necessary, and many actions won't require warnings. When you've completed the chart, review it carefully and supply any missing information. If necessary, make a revised chart.

Once you've listed the actions, group related ones together to form steps, the major subdivisions of the procedure. The following actions constitute the first step—getting the fire going—of a paper explaining how to grill hamburgers:

remove grill rack	light briquets
stack charcoal briquets	spread out briquets

EXERCISE

1. **Develop a complete list of the actions involved in one of the following processes; then arrange them in an appropriate order.**

   a. Baking bread

   b. Assembling or repairing some common household device

   c. Carrying out a process related to sports

   d. Breaking a bad habit

   e. Building a fire in a fireplace

   f. Accessing the Internet

2. **Examine your favorite newspaper or magazine for examples of process analysis. Bring them to class for group discussion of how they illustrate step-by-step directions.**

Start your paper by identifying the process and arousing your reader's interest. You might, for example, note the importance of the process, its usefulness, or the ease of carrying it out. Include a list of the items needed to do the work, and note any special conditions required for a successful outcome. The paper explaining how to grill hamburgers might begin as follows:

> Grilling hamburgers on an outdoor charcoal grill is a simple
> process that almost anyone can master. Before starting, you

will need a clean grill, charcoal briquets, charcoal lighter fluid and matches, hamburger meat, a plate, a spatula, and some water to put out any flames caused by fat drippings. The sizzling, tasty patties you will have when you finish are a treat that almost everyone will enjoy.

DISCUSSION QUESTION   *How does the writer try to induce the reader to perform the process?*

Use the body of the paper to describe the process in detail, presenting each step in one or more paragraphs so that each is distinct and easily grasped. If you've ever muttered under your breath as you struggled to assemble something that came with fuzzy or inadequate directions, you know the importance of presenting steps clearly, accurately, and fully. Therefore, think carefully and include everything the reader needs to know. Note the reason for any action unless the reason is obvious. Flag with a cautionary warning any difficult or dangerous step or one that will result in undesirable consequences if not carried out. If two steps must be performed simultaneously, tell the reader at the start of the first one. In some places, you may want to tell readers what to expect if they have completed the instructions properly. Feedback lets readers know they are on track or that they need to redo something.

Let's see how the first step of the hamburger-grilling paper might unfold:

The first step is to get the fire going. Remove the grill rack and stack about twenty charcoal briquets in a pyramid shape in the center of the grill. Stacking allows the briquets to burn off one another and thus produces a hotter fire. Next, squirt charcoal lighter fluid over the briquets. Wait about five minutes so that the fluid has time to soak into the charcoal. Then toss in a lighted match. The flame will burn for a few minutes before it goes out. When this happens, allow the briquets to sit for another fifteen minutes so that the charcoal can start to burn. Once the burning starts, do not squirt on any more lighter fluid. A flame could quickly follow the stream back into the can, causing it to explode. As the briquets begin to turn from pitch black to ash white, spread them out with a stick so that they barely touch one another. Air can then circulate and produce a hot, even fire, the type that makes grilling a success.

DISCUSSION QUESTIONS

1. At what points has the writer provided reasons for doing things?
2. Where has the writer included a warning?

Some processes can unfold in *only one order.* When you shoot a free throw in basketball, for example, you step up to the line and receive the ball before lining up the shot, and you line up the shot before releasing the ball. Other processes can be carried out in an *order of choice.* When you grill hamburgers, you can make the patties either before or after you light the charcoal. If you have an option, use the order that has worked best for you.

End your paper with a few brief remarks that provide some perspective on the process. A summary of the steps often works best for longer, multistep processes. Other popular choices include evaluating the results of the process or discussing its importance. The paper on hamburger grilling notes the results.

> Once the patties are cooked the way you like them, remove them from the grill and place them on buns. Now you are ready to enjoy a mouthwatering treat that you will long remember.
>
> E. M. Pryzblyo

Processes for Readers Who Won't Perform Them   Like how-to-do-it processes, those intended for nondoers require you to determine the steps, or for natural processes the stages, that are involved and the function of each before you start to write. In addition, since this type of essay will not enable readers to perform the process, think carefully about why you're presenting the information and let that purpose guide your writing. If, for instance, you're trying to persuade readers that the use of rabbits in tests of the effects of cosmetics should be discontinued, the choices you make in developing your steps should reflect that purpose.

To arouse your reader's interest, you might, among other possible options, begin with a historical overview or a brief summary of the whole process, or you could note its importance. The following introduction to an essay on the aging of stars provides a brief historical perspective:

> Peering through their still-crude telescopes, eighteenth-century astronomers discovered a new kind of object in the night sky that appeared neither as the pinprick of light from a distant star nor as the clearly defined disk of a planet but rather as a mottled, cloudy disk. They christened these objects planetary nebulas, or planetary clouds. . . . Modern astronomers recognize planetary nebulas as the fossil wreckage of dying stars ripped apart by powerful winds. . . .

Because the reader will not perform the process, supply only enough details in the body of the paper to provide an intelligent idea of what the procedure entails. Make sure the reader knows the function of each step or stage and how it fits into the overall process. Present each in one or more paragraphs with clear transitions between the steps or stages. The following excerpt points out the changes that occur as a young star, a red giant, begins the aging process:

> As the bloated star ages, this extended outer atmosphere cools and contracts, then soaks up more energy from the star and again puffs out: with each successive cycle of expansion and contraction the atmosphere puffs out a little farther. Like a

massive piston, these pulsations drive the red giant's atmosphere into space in a dense wind that blows with speeds up to 15 miles per second. In as little as 10,000 years some red giants lose an entire sun's worth of matter this way. Eventually this slow wind strips the star down close to its fusion core.

As with processes aimed at performers, end your paper with a few remarks that offer some perspective. You might, for example, evaluate the results of the process, assess its importance, or point out future consequences. The ending of the essay on star aging illustrates the last option:

> The cloud of unanswered questions surrounding planetaries should not obscure the real insight astronomers have recently gained into the extraordinary death of ordinary stars. In a particularly happy marriage of theory and observation, astronomers have discovered our own sun's fate. With the interacting stellar winds model, they can confidently predict the weather about 5 billion years from now; very hot, with *really* strong gusts from the east.
>
> Adam Frank, "Winds of Change"

Revising the Process Analysis

To revise, follow the guidelines in Chapter 3 and pose these questions:

- Have I written consistently for someone who will perform the process or someone who will merely follow it?
- If my paper is intended for performers, have I included every necessary action? Explained any purpose that is unclear? Warned about any steps that are dangerous or might be performed improperly?
- Are my steps presented in an appropriate order? Developed in sufficient detail?
- Have I considered appropriate ethical issues?

EXAMPLE STUDENT ESSAY OF PROCESS ANALYSIS

The ABC's of CPR

Kathy Petroski

A heart attack, choking, or an electric shock--any of these can stop a person's breathing. The victim, however, need not always die. Many lives that would otherwise be lost can be saved simply by applying the ABC's of CPR--cardiopulmonary resuscitation. Although presence of mind is essential, CPR requires no special equipment. Here's how it is performed. When you are certain that the victim's breathing and pulse have stopped, start CPR immediately. If breathing and circulation aren't restored within five minutes, irreversible brain damage occurs.

2   <u>A</u> stands for opening the airway. Lay the victim in a supine (face up) position on a firm surface. Then tilt the head as far back as possible by gently lifting the chin with one hand. In an unconscious person, the tongue falls to the back of the throat and blocks the air passages. Hyperextending the head in this fashion pulls the tongue from that position, thus allowing air to pass. At the same time tilt the forehead back with the other hand until the chin points straight upward. The relaxed jaw muscles will then tighten, opening the air passage to the lungs. Remove your hand from the forehead and, using your first two fingers, check the mouth for food, dentures, vomitus, or a foreign object. Remove any obstruction with a sweeping motion. These measures may cause the patient to start breathing spontaneously. If they do not, mouth-to-mouth resuscitation must be started.

3   <u>B</u> stands for breathing. Position one hand on the forehead and pinch the victim's nostrils shut with the index finger and thumb of your other hand. Open your mouth, and place it over the victim's mouth so that a tight seal is formed. Such contact allows air to reach and expand the lungs. If the seal is incomplete, you will hear your own breath escaping. Deliver two quick, full breaths without allowing the victim's lungs to deflate completely between breaths; then remove your mouth and allow him or her to exhale passively. At this point, check the carotid pulse to determine whether the heart is beating. To do so, place the tips of your index and middle fingers laterally into the groove between the trachea (windpipe) and the muscles at the side of the neck. If no pulse is evident, artificial circulation must be started.

4   <u>C</u> means circulation. Locate the lower end of the sternum (breastbone), and move upward approximately the width of two fingers. At this point, firmly apply the heel of one hand, positioning the fingers at right angles to the length of the body and keeping them slanted upward. If the hand is posi-

tioned any higher or lower on the sternum, serious internal injuries in the abdomen or chest are possible. Now place the heel of your second hand on top of your first. The fingers may be interlaced or interlocked, but they must not touch the chest, or the force of your compressions may fracture ribs.

Keeping your elbows straight and pushing down from the shoulders, apply firm, heavy pressure until the sternum is depressed approximately one and one-half to two inches. Rock forward and backward in a rhythmic fashion, exerting pressure with the weight of your body. This action squeezes the heart against the immobile spine with enough pressure to pump blood from the left ventricle of the heart into general circulation. Compress the chest, and then immediately release the pressure, fifteen times. Do not, at any point in the cycle, remove your hands from the chest wall. Counting the compressions aloud will help develop a systematic cycle, which is essential for success. When the fifteen have been completed, pinch the nose as described above, seal the victim's mouth with your own, and deliver two quick breaths of air. Then compress the chest an additional fifteen times. Alternate respiration and compression steps, timing yourself so as to deliver approximately eighty compressions per minute. 5

At various intervals, quickly check the effectiveness of your CPR technique. Lift the eyelids and notice if the pupils are constricted--a key sign that the brain is receiving enough oxygen. In addition, if the bluish color of the victim is decreasing and spontaneous breathing and movement are increasing, the victim has responded favorably. 6

To maximize the chances for survival, do not interrupt this technique for more than five or ten seconds. Continue the ABC's of CPR until competent medical help or life-support equipment arrives. 7

DISCUSSION QUESTIONS

1. How does the writer use the letters *A*, *B*, and *C* from the CPR technique in this paper?
2. How does the opening paragraph prepare the reader for what follows?

3. Where does the essay indicate the purposes of actions?
4. What order has the writer used? Explain why this order is a good choice.
5. Is the writer merely explaining how the process is carried out, or does she intend for the reader to follow the directions? Defend your answer.

SUGGESTIONS FOR WRITING   *Write a process analysis on one of the topics below or one approved by your instructor. The paper may provide instructions for the reader to follow, tell how a process is performed, or describe how a process develops. Prepare a complete list of steps, arrange them in an appropriate order, and follow them as you write the body of your essay.*

1. A natural process, such as erosion, that you observe or research
2. Overcoming some particular phobia
3. The stages in a technical process such as paper production
4. The stages in a student's adjustment to college
5. Dealing with the bite of a poisonous snake
6. Preparing for a romantic picnic in the park, on the beach, or some other place
7. Using a particular computer program
8. Celebrating a special occasion
9. Carrying out a process related to your hobby
10. Placing an order over the Internet
11. Studying for an examination
12. Performing a process required by your job
13. Performing a process required by one of your classes
14. Breaking a bad habit
15. Performing a weight-training program
16. Throwing a successful party
17. The stages in some type of storm
18. The stages in a developing friendship
19. The steps in pledging a fraternity or sorority
20. The stages in becoming independent

The Critical Edge

Is there only one way to study effectively, develop a marketing campaign, or cope with a demanding supervisor? No, of course not. As you've already learned, not all processes unfold in a single, predetermined order. The writing process itself illustrates this point.

If you were to think about how you write and talk with other students about their writing processes, you would learn that different writing occasions call for different approaches. When you write a letter to a good friend, you probably spend little or no time on preliminaries but start putting your thoughts on paper as they occur to you. By contrast, other kinds of correspondence, such as inquiry and claim letters, require careful planning, drafting, and perhaps rewriting.

Sometimes the same writing occasion may allow for differing procedures. If you're writing an essay for your English class, you might brainstorm for ideas, develop a detailed outline, rough out a bare-bones draft, and add details as you revise. In talking to other students with the same assignment, you might find that they prefer to write a much longer draft and then whittle it down. Still other students might do very little brainstorming or outlining but a great deal of revising, often making major changes in several drafts. Research papers present a more complex challenge, requiring that the student find and read source material, take notes, and document sources properly. Here again variations are possible: One student might prepare the list of works cited before writing the final draft, while another might perform this task last.

If you decided to synthesize (see pages 72–73) your findings about student writing practices, you would, of course, need to organize your material in some fashion. Perhaps you might focus on the differences that distinguish one writing occasion from another. You could develop each occasion in a separate section by presenting the practices followed by most students while ignoring any variations. A second possibility would be to report different practices used for the same writing occasion, first considering the most common practice and then describing the variations. The result might be likened to a cookbook that gives different recipes for the same dish.

Some important processes have been disputed in print, and if you wanted to investigate them you would need to consult written sources rather than talk to others. Informed disagreements exist about how the human species originated, how language developed, and how children mature. Police officers debate the best way to handle drunks, management experts the best way to motivate employees. When you investigate such controversies, determine which view is supported by the best evidence and seems most reasonable. Then, as a writer, you can present the accounts in an appropriate order and perhaps indicate which one you think merits acceptance.*

SUGGESTIONS FOR WRITING

1. Interview several students about the stages they experienced in a developing friendship and write a paper that discusses these stages. Note any discrepancies in the accounts provided by different students.

2. Research the writing process as presented in several first-year composition textbooks; after pointing out how they differ, indicate which process you prefer and why.

3. Research a controversial process, such as the extinction of the dinosaurs. After presenting different theories about the process, explain which one seems most plausible and why.

---

*If you'll rely on information obtained through interviews, read pages 406–10 in Chapter 22. If you'll rely on published sources, read the sections on card catalogs and periodical indexes in Chapter 20 and those on handling quotations and avoiding plagiarism in Chapter 21. As always, follow your instructor's guidelines for documenting sources.

7

Illustration: Making Yourself Clear

"It doesn't pay to fight City Hall. For example, my friend Josie . . ."

"Many intelligent people lack common sense. Take Dr. Brandon . . ."

"Top-notch women tennis players are among the biggest moneymakers in sports. Last year, for instance, Martina Hingis . . ."

"Predicting the weather is far from an exact science. Two winters ago, a surprise snowstorm . . ."

Have you ever noticed how often people use *illustrations* (examples) to clarify general statements?

Ordinary conversations teem with "for example . . ." and "for instance . . . ," often in response to a furrowed brow or puzzled look. A local character, Hank Cassidy, might serve as the perfect example of a "good old boy" or Chicago's Waterower Plaza illustrate a vertical shopping mall. But illustration is not limited to concrete items. Teachers, researchers, and writers often present an abstract principle or natural law, then supply concrete examples that bring it down to earth. An economics instructor might illustrate compound interest by an example showing how much $100 earning 5 percent interest would appreciate in ten years. Examples can also persuade, as when advertisers trot out typical satisfied users of their products to induce us to buy.

Many classroom writing assignments can benefit from the use of illustration. A business student writing a paper on effective management can provide a better grasp of the topic by including examples of successful managers and how they operate. A paper defining democracy for a political science course will be more effective if it offers examples of several democratic governments. An explanation of irony for a literature course will gain force and clarity through examples taken from stories and poems. Illustration plays a similarly important role in work-related writing. A teacher wanting a bigger student-counseling staff might cite students who need help but can't get it. An advertising copywriter urging that new copiers be bought might mention different instances of copier breakdown and the resulting delays in customer service. A union steward wanting a better company safety program might call attention to several recent accidents.

The old saying that a picture is worth a thousand words best explains the popularity of illustration. The concrete is always easier to grasp than the abstract, and examples add flavor and clarity to what might otherwise be flat and vague.

■ Selecting Appropriate Examples

Make sure that your examples stay on target, that is, actually support your general statement and do not veer off into an intriguing side issue. For instance, if you're making the point that the lyrics in a rock group's latest album are not in good taste, don't inject comments on the fast lifestyle of one of its members. Instead, provide examples of lyrics that support your claim, chosen from different songs in the album to head off objections that your examples aren't representative.

Furthermore, see that your examples display all the chief features of whatever you're illustrating. Don't offer Hank Cassidy as an example of a typical good old boy unless he fits the general mold by being a fun-loving, easy-going beer guzzler who likes to hang out with other men. Alternatively, consider this example of a hacker, a compulsive computer programmer:

> Bob Shaw, a 15-year-old high-school student, is a case in point. Bob was temporarily pulled off the computers at school when he began failing his other courses. But instead of hitting the books, he continues to sulk outside the computer center, peering longingly through the glass door at the consoles within.
>
> Pale and drawn, his brown hair unkempt, Bob speaks only in monosyllables, avoiding eye contact. In answer to questions about friends, hobbies, school, he merely shrugs or mumbles a few words aimed at his sneakered feet. But when the conversation turns to the subject of computers, he brightens—and blurts out a few full sentences about the computer he's building and the projects he plans.
>
> Dina Ingber, "Computer Addicts"

Clearly, Shaw fits Ingber's description of hackers as programmers who have "a drive so consuming it overshadows nearly every other part of their lives and forms the focal point of their existence."

■ Number of Examples

How many examples will you need? One long one, several fairly brief ones, or a large number of very short ones? Look to your topic for the answer. To illustrate the point that a good nurse must be compassionate, conscientious, and competent, your best bet would probably be one example, since one person must possess all these traits.

When dealing with trends, however, you'll need several examples. To show that parents have been raising children more and more permissively over the last half century, at least three examples are called for: one family from around 1955, a second from about 1980, and a third from the present time. Sometimes topics that do not involve trends require more than one example, as when you demonstrate the sharp differences between Japanese and American attitudes toward work.

Finally, some topics require a whole series of examples. If you were contending that many everyday expressions have their origins in the world of gambling, you'd need many examples to demonstrate your point.

EXERCISE

1. **Choose one of the following topic sentences. Select an appropriate example and write the rest of the paragraph.**

   a. Sometimes a minor incident drastically changes a person's life.

   b. _____'s name exactly suits (her/his) personality.

   c. I still get embarrassed when I remember _____.

   d. Not all education goes on in the classroom.

   e. I learned the value of _____ the hard way.

2. **Explain why you would use one extended illustration, several shorter ones, or a whole series of examples to develop each of the following statements. Suggest appropriate illustrations.**

   a. Many parents I know think for their children.

   b. The hamburger isn't what it used to be.

   c. The ideal pet is small, quiet, and affectionate.

   d. Different college students view their responsibilities differently.

   e. The hotels in Gotham City run the gamut from sumptuous to seedy.

   f. Modern English includes any number of words taken directly from foreign languages.

■ Organizing the Examples

A single extended example often assumes the narrative form, presenting a series of events in time sequence. One person's unfolding experience might show that "doing your thing" doesn't always work out for the best. Sets of examples that trace trends also rely on time sequence, moving either forward or backward. This arrangement would work well for the paper on the growing permissiveness in child rearing.

On the other hand, a paper showing that different individuals exhibit some characteristic to different extents would logically be organized by order of climax (from the least to the greatest extent) or perhaps the reverse order. To demonstrate how salesclerks differ in their attitudes toward customers, you might first describe a hostile clerk, then a pleasant one, and finally an outstandingly courteous and helpful one.

Sometimes any arrangement will work equally well. Suppose you're showing that Americans are taking various precautions to ward off heart attacks. Although you might move from a person who exercises to one who diets and finally to one who practices relaxation techniques, no special order is preferable.

Large numbers of examples might first be grouped into categories and the categories then arranged in a suitable order. For example, the expressions from the world of gambling could be grouped according to types of gambling: cards, dice, horse racing, and the like. Depending upon the specific categories, one arrangement may or may not be preferable to another.

■ Ethical Issues

In writing an illustration, we try to show readers something truthful about our understanding of the world. They wouldn't read what we've written if they suspected we were unusually careless in our thinking or knew we were trying to deceive them. Deception may stem from prejudice, which causes people to distort examples. For instance, parents trying to talk their teenager out of a career in acting will probably cite only examples of failed or struggling performers who have miserable lives, and they will fail to mention many successful performers. Such a distortion isn't fair to the acting profession or the teenager. Some distortions can be outright lies. In the past debate about welfare, some commentators wrote about people who lived like millionaires while on welfare. It turned out the examples were falsified, and no real instances of such massive abuse could be found. To help avoid ethical pitfalls, ask and answer the following questions.

- Have I given adequate thought to the point I'll make and the examples I'll use?

- Are the examples supporting my point truthful, or are they slanted to deceive the reader?

- Could my illustrations have harmful consequences? Do they stereotype an individual or group? Harm someone's reputation unjustly?

- Will my examples promote desirable or undesirable behavior?

■ Writing an Illustration

Planning and Drafting the Illustration

Assertions, unfamiliar topics, abstract principles, natural laws—as we've seen, all of these can form the foundation for your paper. If you have a choice, you should experience little difficulty finding something suitable. After all, you've observed and experienced many things—for example, how people can be TV junkies and the ways students manage the stresses of college life. As always, the strategies on pages 14–20 can help generate some possibilities, which you can then evaluate by asking these questions:

Exactly what point am I trying to make? (Write it down in precise terms.)

Why do I want to make this point? To show how bad something is? To encourage something? To scare people into or away from something?

Who is my prospective audience?

Should I use one extended example, or will I need more? Why?

Once you've picked your topic, ask yourself, "What example(s) will work best with my audience?" Then brainstorm each one for supporting details. Use a chart patterned after the one below to help you.

Example 1	**Example 2**	**Example 3**
First supporting detail	First supporting detail	First supporting detail
Second supporting detail	Second supporting detail	Second supporting detail

Review your details carefully and add any new ones you think of; then make a new chart and re-enter the details into it, arranged in the order you intend to present them.

Your introduction should identify your topic and draw your reader into the paper. If you're illustrating a personal belief, you might indicate how you developed it. If you're trying to scare the reader into or away from something, you might open with an arresting statement.

Present your examples in the body of your paper, keeping your purpose firmly in mind as you plan your organization. If you have many brief examples, perhaps group them into related categories for discussion. The paper on expressions from gambling, for instance, might devote one paragraph each to terms from the worlds of cards, dice, and horse racing. If you're dealing with a few relatively brief examples—say to show a trend—put each in its own paragraph. For a single extended example, use the entire body of the paper, suitably paragraphed. Thus, an extended example of someone with an eccentric lifestyle might include paragraphs on mode of dress, living accommodations, and public behavior.

Conclude in whatever way seems most appropriate. You might express a hope or recommendation that the reader implement or avoid something, or you might issue a personal challenge that grows out of the point you've illustrated.

Revising the Illustration

Think about the following questions and the general guidelines in Chapter 3 as you revise your paper:

Exactly what idea am I trying to put across? Have I used the examples that best typify it?

Do my examples illuminate my idea without introducing irrelevant material?

Are my examples interesting?

Have I used an appropriate number of examples?

Have I organized my paper effectively?

Have I considered appropriate ethical issues?

EXAMPLE STUDENT ESSAY OF ILLUSTRATION

A Lesson from Nature

Mike Braendle

As I was growing up, my parents often passed along little   1
maximlike sayings to me. Most of these have since slipped my
mind, but I still remember the exact words of my father's
favorite: "The door to success is labeled Push." Although for a
while these were just words to me, I came to understand their
true meaning as I observed the struggles of a crayfish while I
was fishing one day.

There it lay, trapped in the small plastic compartment of   2
my steel tackle box, which was sitting on the bank of the
river. The sun had been shining for some time, and the plastic of the compartment surrounding the crayfish intensified
the heat. In fact, the heat had become so great that the skin
covering the small hard-shelled body was beginning to wrin-
kle. Nevertheless, the pinching claws continually groped
about, trying to find something to grasp, some means of
escape. The hard and heavy shell, acting like an anchor,
burdened the crayfish greatly. The two small eyes, always
moving, searched wildly for some way out, but found none.
The segmented tail, as large as the rest of the body, was
constantly pushing, trying to hoist the heavy body over the
edge of the compartment.

The eyes at last fell upon a possibility for escape: The   3
back wall of the compartment was slightly lower than the
other three walls. Sensing an advantage, the crayfish seemed
to labor more deliberately. The tail, pushing vigorously,
tried to lift the heavy shell out of the plastic compartment. As the tail struggled, the claws slashed savagely back
and forth, searching for something to grab.

Finally, after some time and struggle, the crayfish   4
grasped the back wall. As it pulled, with every muscle
straining, the hard shell edged up and over the wall of the

compartment. Stopping abruptly and gazing at its surroundings, the crayfish tried to orient itself. Off to one side in another compartment lay a strange-looking creature, unmoving. The crayfish did not recognize this odd-shaped thing as a fishing lure, but it did sense that the creature, with its bright metallic tint and protruding hooks, was not alive.

5   It took only a moment for the determined crustacean to figure out which way to go. It moved, as if driven by instinct, across this compartment and then others, occasionally getting caught on a protruding hook. These hooks slowed its progress, scratching grooves and gouges in the hard shell.

6   As the crayfish moved steadily toward the edge of the box, the thought of cold water seemed to excite it. It moved faster, more deliberately now. When reaching the edge of the box, it stopped for a moment, as if pondering what to do next. Then, defiantly, it flopped over the edge, landing on its hard shell. It stayed on its back for some time but then turned over and dragged itself to the water.

7   The crayfish lay there for a long time, soaking in the cool and refreshing river. Then with a powerful flap of its tail, it disappeared into the depths. Here, where there was no threat of drying out, it could and probably would recuperate from this tiring experience.

DISCUSSION QUESTIONS

1. What general statement does this essay illustrate?
2. Why is one extended illustration effective here?
3. Explain the organization of the essay and why it is appropriate.
4. In paragraph 2, the writer says the crayfish "continually groped" and "searched wildly" with its tail "constantly pushing." How do these descriptions relate to the writer's purpose?
5. Point out specific sentences in paragraphs 3 and 4 that seem particularly effective in engaging the reader's interest.
6. Would a concluding paragraph that restated the main idea make this essay more effective? Why or why not?

SUGGESTIONS FOR WRITING   *Use one of the ideas on the next page or another that your instructor approves for your illustration essay. Select appropriate examples, determine how many you will use, and decide how you will organize them.*

1. "I don't have enough time" is a common complaint of many people today.

2. Many people appear obsessed with exercise (or diet).

3. Incivility has become quite common in public places.

4. Racial and ethnic minorities are becoming increasingly prominent in

    _____ .

5. Dedication is the secret of success for many athletes (or use any other field or occupation).

6. People have many strange remedies for hangovers.

7. Sometimes actions can have unintended consequences.

8. A good nurse must be compassionate, conscientious, and competent (or use another occupation with appropriate characteristics).

9. Campus gambling assumes various forms.

10. Many intelligent people lack common sense.

11. Sleep deprivation is causing problems for many young people.

12. Talk show hosts often leave much to be desired (or stimulate listeners to think).

13. "Doing your own thing" does not always work out for the best.

14. _____ is the most (or least) effective teacher I have ever had.

15. Not to decide is to decide.

16. How we react to circumstances, not the circumstances themselves, often makes us unhappy.

17. Today's college student is _____ .

18. Sometimes we need to take risks.

19. Wanting more than we need can be destructive.

20. Many people become obsessed with appearance.

The Critical Edge

When we write an illustration paper, we don't always draw our examples from personal experience. As we reflect on a topic, we may talk with other people and read various source materials to broaden our understanding. We explore differing perspectives and determine the connections between them en route to arriving at our own views and insights. Take, for instance, the topic of racism in America. "For My Indian Daughter" (page 443), "Momma's Encounter" (page 439), and "Black Men and Public Space" (pages 536–39) offer poignant illustrations of how racism affects people's personal lives. Reading these essays, drawing upon your own observations, and perhaps questioning minority students could lead you to an important insight: for example, that racism can have personal effects that are very different from the more widely discussed kinds of institutional discrimination. You might then synthesize (see pages 72–73) others' illustrations and your own to produce a paper that presents this insight.

　　Sometimes illustrations don't reflect reality. An author trying to make the point that many college students are irresponsible might offer examples of students who skip classes, fail to hand in assignments, and party constantly. These examples, however, overlook the many students who hold part-time jobs while taking a full load of classes, participate in professional organizations, and function successfully as spouses, and even parents, while earning good grades. Because published material can paint an inaccurate picture, develop the habit of judging the examples you read in the light of what your knowledge, further investigation, and other sources reveal. Critical thinking is one of the most important skills a writer can cultivate.*

SUGGESTIONS FOR WRITING

1. Examine the Reader essays on racism cited above. Then, drawing upon examples from the essays and perhaps the observations of minority students you know, write a paper presenting your own conclusions about the personal effects of racism.

2. Read several issues of a magazine such as *Sports Illustrated* or *Working Woman* and determine what the articles suggest about American life. Then write an essay that illustrates your conclusions and incorporates relevant material from the articles.

3. Martin Gottfried, author of "Rambos of the Road," concludes by noting, "It seems to me that it is a new America we see on the road now. It has the mentality of a hoodlum and the backbone of a coward" (page 480). Write an essay that includes both your own illustrations and one or more of Gottfried's and that agrees or disagrees with his assessment.

---

*Because this type of paper draws upon published information, it is important to read the sections on card catalogs and periodical indexes in Chapter 20 and those on handling quotations and avoiding plagiarism in Chapter 21. As always, follow your instructor's guidelines for documenting sources.

Classification: Grouping into Categories

*H*elp Wanted, *Situations Wanted, Real Estate, Personal.* Do these terms look familiar? They do if you've ever scanned the classified ads of the newspaper. Ads are grouped into categories, and each category is then subdivided. The people who assemble this layout are *classifying.* Figure 8.1 (see page 110) shows the main divisions of a typical classified ad section and a further breakdown of one of them.

As this figure indicates, grouping allows the people who handle ads to divide entries according to a logical scheme and helps readers find what they are looking for. Imagine the difficulty of checking the real estate ads if all the entries were run in the order the ads were placed.

Our minds naturally sort information into categories. Within a few weeks after their birth, infants can tell the faces of family members from those of outsiders. Toddlers learn to distinguish between cats, dogs, and rabbits. In both cases the classification rests solely on physical differences. As we mature we start classifying in more abstract ways, and by adulthood we are constantly sorting things into categories: dates or mates, eating places, oddballs, friends, investments, jobs, political views.

Classification also helps writers and readers come to grips with large or complex topics. It breaks a broad topic into categories according to some specific principle, presents the distinctive features of each category, and shows

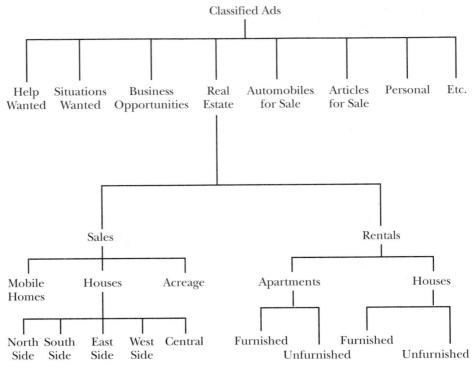

Figure 8.1

how the features vary among categories. Segmenting the topic simplifies the discussion by presenting the information in small, neatly sorted piles rather than in one jumbled and confusing heap.

Furthermore, classification helps people make choices. Identifying which groups of consumers—students, accountants, small-business owners—are most likely to buy some new product allows the manufacturer to advertise in appropriate media. Knowing the engine size, maneuverability, seating capacity, and gas mileage of typical subcompact, compact, and intermediate-size cars helps customers decide which one to buy. Examining the features of term, whole-life, and endowment insurance enables prospective buyers to select the policy that best suits their needs.

Because classification plays such an important part in our lives, it is a useful writing tool in many situations. Your accounting instructor may ask you to categorize accounting procedures for retail businesses. In a computer class, you may classify computer languages and then specify appropriate applications for each grouping. For an industrial hygiene class, you might categorize different types of respiratory protective equipment and indicate when each type is used. On the job, a state health department employee may prepare a brochure grouping illegal drugs into categories based on their effects. The communications director of an investment firm might write a customer letter categorizing investments according to their degree of risk. An employee of a textbook publisher might prepare a catalog grouping new books by field of study.

■ Selecting Categories

People classify in different ways for different purposes, which generally reflect their interests. A clothing designer might classify people according to their fashion sense, a representative of the National Organization for Women according to their views on women's rights, and the Secretary of Labor according to their occupations. A college's director of housing might classify students according to their type of residence, the dean of students according to their behavior problems, and the financial aid officer according to their sources of income.

When you write a classification paper, choose a principle of classification that's suited not only to your purpose but also to your audience. To illustrate, if you're writing for students, don't classify instructors according to their manner of dress, body build, or cars they drive. These breakdowns probably wouldn't interest most students and certainly wouldn't serve their needs. Instead, develop a more useful principle of classification—perhaps by teaching styles, concern for students, or grading policies.

Sometimes it's helpful or necessary to divide one or more categories into subcategories. If you do, use just one principle of classification for each level. Both levels in Figure 8.2 meet this test because each reflects a single principle: place of origin for the first, number of cylinders for the second.

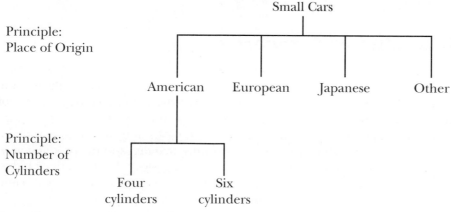

Figure 8.2   Proper Classification of Small Cars

Now examine Figure 8.3. This classification is *improper* because it groups cars in two ways—by place of origin and by kind—making it possible for one car

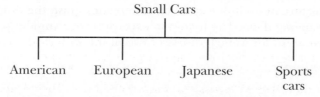

Figure 8.3   Improper Classification of Small Cars

to end up in two different categories. For example, the German Porsche is both a European car and a sports car. When categories overlap in this way, confusion reigns and nothing is clarified.

EXERCISE

1. **How would each of the following people be most likely to classify the families in Anytown, USA?**

   a. The bishop of the Roman Catholic diocese in which the city is located

   b. The state senator who represents the city

   c. A field worker for the NAACP

   d. The director of the local credit bureau

2. **The following lists contain overlapping categories. Identify the inconsistent item in each list and explain why it is faulty.**

Nurses	Pictures	Electorate in Midville
Surgical nurses	Oil paintings	Republicans
Psychiatric nurses	Magazine illustrations	Democrats
Emergency room nurses	Lithographs	Nonvoters
Terminal care nurses	Watercolors	Independents
Night nurses	Etchings	

■ Number of Categories

Some classification papers discuss every category included within the topic. Others discuss only selected categories. Circumstances and purpose dictate the scope of the discussion. Suppose you work for the commerce department of your state and are asked to write a report that classifies the major nonservice industries in a certain city and assesses their strengths and weaknesses. Your investigation shows that food processing, furniture making, and the production of auto parts account for over 95 percent of all nonservice jobs. Two minor industries, printing and toy making, provide the rest of the jobs. Given these circumstances, you'd probably focus on the first three industries, mentioning the others only in passing. But if printing and toy making were significant industries, they too would require detailed discussion.

■ Developing Categories

Develop every category you include with specific, informative details that provide a clear picture of each one and help the reader grasp the distinctions and relationships among them. The following excerpt from a student paper classifying public restrooms for women discusses two of the writer's three categories:

Luxurious restrooms are found in top-drawer business establishments such as fancy department stores, chic boutiques, and the better restaurants. This aristocrat of public facilities usu-

"SEE ME TOMORROW—I'M BUSY GRADING FINALS NOW."

Reprinted by permission of Richard N. Bibler.

ally disdains the term <u>restroom</u>, masquerading instead under the
alias of <u>lounge</u> or <u>powder room</u>. Upon entering its plush environs,
the user is captivated by its elegance. Thick carpet reaches up to
cushion tired feet, wood paneled or brocade velvet walls beckon
invitingly, and dimly twinkling chandeliers or wall sconces
soothe the eyes. Narrow little divans and gold-and-velvet tables
add to the restful, welcoming atmosphere, and the latest issues of
upscale magazines like <u>Vogue</u>, <u>The New Yorker</u>, and <u>Vanity Fair</u>
entice resters into their pages. Mirrors in carved frames,
designer lavatories with richly ornamented faucets, and creamy
scented soap go hand in hand with the attendant who quietly dis-
penses thick, white towels as soft as suede. Her detached air
deserts her only when she sneaks a furtive glance toward the silver tip dish as the patron passes it on the way out.

The adequate restroom offers utility without the swankiness
of its lavish cousin. Typically located in a large shopping mall
or mass-market department store, it is a stark world of hard,
unadorned surfaces--tile floors, tile walls, and harshly glaring fluorescent lights recessed in the ceiling. For those who

wish to rest, there is a garishly colored Naugahyde couch and next to it a battered metal or wood table holding a few tattered copies of <u>Family Circle</u>, <u>People</u>, <u>Reader's Digest</u>, and similar publications. The mirrors have steel frames, the lavatories, set in a formica counter, have plain chrome faucets, and the soap dispenser emits a thin stream of unscented liquid. Paper toweling pulled from a wall-mounted metal holder replaces the cloth article, and no maid stands by to offer her help or to exact tips from departing visitors.

Student Unknown

The concrete details in these paragraphs effectively characterize each category and clearly distinguish between them. Imagine how vague and indistinct the categories would be without these details.

■ Ethical Issues

Classification can seem quite innocent, and yet it can cause great harm. In India, an entire group numbering millions of people was once classified as "untouchables" and so was denied the jobs and rights of other citizens. Although political progress has considerably improved the lot of these people, discrimination still hobbles their lives. In this country, many high school students have suffered the sting of being classified as "nerds" or "geeks." Clearly you'll have to evaluate the appropriateness and consequences of your classification scheme. To avoid problems, ask and answer these questions:

- Is my classification called for by the situation? It may be appropriate to classify students in a school environment according to their reading skills, but classifying factory workers in this fashion may well be inappropriate and unfair to the people involved.

- Have I avoided the use of damaging classifications? We resent stereotyping because it unjustly reduces us to some distorted general idea. No one is simply a "hillbilly" or a "jock."

- Have I applied my classification without resorting to overgeneralization? In a paper classifying student drinkers, it would be a mistake, and even harmful, to imply that all college students drink excessively.

- Could my classification promote harmful behavior? When classifying the behavior patterns of young urban dwellers, it would be unethical to present favorably the lifestyle of a group that uses hard drugs and engages in disruptive behavior at sporting events.

We are ethically responsible for the classification systems that we use in our writing. Always examine the one you use for suitability, fairness, and potential harm.

■ Writing a Classification

Planning and Drafting the Classification

Many topics that interest you are potential candidates for classification. If you're selecting your own topic, you might explain different kinds of rock music to novices, take a humorous look at different types of teachers, or, in a more serious vein, identify different types of discrimination. As always, use one or more of the narrowing strategies on pages 14–20 to help stimulate your thinking. As possibilities come to mind, examine each one in light of these questions:

What purpose will this classification serve?
Who is my audience and what will interest them?
What are the categories of this topic?
What features distinguish my categories from one another?

Next, determine whether you'll discuss every category or only selected ones, and then set up a classification chart similar to the one following.

Category 1	**Category 2**	**Category 3**
First distinguishing feature	First distinguishing feature	First distinguishing feature
Second distinguishing feature	Second distinguishing feature	Second distinguishing feature

Such a chart helps you see the relationships among categories and provides a starting point for developing your specific details. Proceed by jotting down the details that come to mind for each distinguishing feature of every category. Then prepare a second chart with the distinguishing features and details arranged in the order you want to present them.

Begin your paper by identifying your topic and capturing your reader's attention in some way. A paper classifying hair dyes might point out their growing popularity among both men and women. One classifying snobs might offer an anecdote showing how far snobbery can go. Or you could cite a personal experience that relates to your topic. As always, circumstances dictate your choice.

In the body discuss your categories in whatever order best suits your purpose. Order of climax—least important, more important, most important—often works well. Or perhaps your topic will suggest arranging the categories by behavior, income, education, or physical characteristics. Whatever your arrangement, signal it clearly to your reader. Don't merely start the discussions of your categories by saying first . . . , second . . . , another . . . , next . . . , and the like. These words offer no hint of the rationale behind your order.

In addition, make sure the arrangement of material within the categories follows a consistent pattern. Recall the two categories of restrooms discussed on pages 112–14. In each case, after noting where the restroom can be found, the writer discusses its floor, walls, and lighting, moves to the furniture, and ends by discussing the lavatories, soap, and toweling.

The strategies for ending a classification paper are as varied as those for starting it. A paper on hair dyes might conclude by predicting their continued popularity. One on snobs might end with your recommendations for dealing with them. In other cases, you might express a hope of some kind or advise your reader to do something.

Revising the Classification

Revise your paper by following the guidelines in Chapter 3 as well as by pondering these questions:

Does my classification have a clear sense of purpose and audience?
Does my principle of classification accord with my purpose?
Do any of my categories overlap?
Have I chosen an appropriate number of categories?
Are these categories developed with sufficient details?
Are the categories and details arranged in an effective order?
Have I considered appropriate ethical issues?

EXAMPLE STUDENT ESSAY OF CLASSIFICATION

Undesirable Produce Market Customers

Clarence DeLong

1   You will find almost as large a variety of customers at a produce market as you will find fruits and vegetables. Undesirable produce market customers fall into three main categories--those who squeeze the fruit, those who complain constantly, and those who try to cheat the market--and when you meet them all in one day, you have one big headache. Perhaps you will recognize these people as I describe them.

2   "Sammy Squeezer" is the least annoying of these undesirables. He wants to make sure that everything he buys is "just right." He pokes his thumbs into the top of a cantaloupe. If they penetrate very deeply, he won't buy this particular specimen, considering it to be overripe. He squeezes the peaches, plums, nectarines, and any other fruit he can get his hands on. After ten of these people squeeze one piece of fruit, it will surely be soft, even if it wasn't

originally. Moving on to the corn, Sammy carefully peels
back the husk to examine the kernels inside. If they don't
suit him, he doesn't bother to fold the husk back to protect
the kernels; he simply tosses the ear back into the basket.
The problems he creates for the employees are primarily
physical--removing the damaged items after he leaves.

A more annoying customer is "Betty Bitcher." She is never   3
satisfied with the quality of the produce: The bananas are
too green, the lettuce has brown spots, the berries are too
ripe, and the potatoes have green spots. Sometimes you wonder if Betty would have been satisfied with the fruit grown
in the Garden of Eden.

The produce has no monopoly on her complaints, however.   4
Betty also finds fault with the service she receives from
the employees. Talking to other customers or directly to the
clerks, she can be heard saying such things as "Why is this
the only place I ever have to wait in line? They must have
trouble getting good help here." Even as she leaves the market, which is none too soon, she must make one last complaint: "You mean I have to carry my own potatoes to the
car?" The problems she creates for the employees are primarily mental--she can make your nerves quite active.

Perhaps the most annoying customer of all is "Charlie   5
Cheater." You have to keep your eye on him constantly
because he knows all the tricks of cheating. He will add
berries to an already full basket. He will take 6/79¢
oranges and tell you they're the 6/59¢ ones. He will put
expensive grapes in the bottom of a sack and add cheaper
ones on top. Then he'll tell you that they are all the
cheaper variety. Likewise, he will put expensive nectarines
in a sack, place a few cheaper peaches on top, and try to
pass them all off as peaches. If he is caught, he usually
says, "I don't know how that happened. My little girl (or
boy) must have put them in there." The child usually looks
dumbfounded.

The problem Charlie creates for the market is twofold: 6
financial and legal. If you don't catch him, your profits

suffer. If you do catch him, you almost have to prosecute, usually for amounts of only a dollar or two, or you'll have every Charlie in town at your door.

7   Did you recognize any of these customers? If you didn't and would like to see some of them in action, stop in at Steve's Produce Market. That's where I work, and that's where I meet them.

DISCUSSION QUESTIONS

1. What is the writer's purpose in developing this classification? Where does he state it?
2. In what order has he arranged his categories? Refer to the essay when answering.
3. Demonstrate that the writer has avoided overlapping categories.
4. How do you know he hasn't discussed every category of undesirable customers?

SUGGESTIONS FOR WRITING   *Write a classification paper on one of the topics below or one approved by your instructor. Determine your purpose and audience, select appropriate categories, decide how many you'll discuss, develop them with specific details, and arrange them in an effective order.*

1. College teachers (or college pressures)
2. Pet owners (or types of pets)
3. Herbal remedies
4. Kinds of extreme sports
5. Churchgoers
6. Computer languages
7. Patrons of singles bars
8. Reasons for surfing the Internet
9. Talk show hosts
10. Sports announcers (or fans)
11. Television judges (or sitcoms or discussion groups)
12. Alternative medicines
13. Laundromat users
14. People waiting in line
15. Bores
16. Dangerous males (or females)
17. Web pages
18. Advertisements
19. Cheating (or lies)
20. Leaders

The Critical Edge

Classification provides an effective tool for organizing material into categories. But you won't always rely exclusively on your own knowledge or experience to determine or develop categories. At times you'll supplement what you bring to a writing assignment with information gained through outside reading.

Suppose that for an introductory business course, you're asked to prepare a paper that explores major types of investments.

You realize that some research will be necessary. After consulting a number of books and magazines, you conclude that stocks, bonds, and real estate represent the three main categories of investments and that each category can be divided into several subcategories. Bonds, for example, can be grouped according to issuer: corporate, municipal, and U.S. Treasury securities.

At this point, you recognize that the strategy of classification would work well for this assignment. Reading further, you learn about the financial risks, rewards, and tax consequences associated with ownership. For example, U.S. Treasury securities offer the greatest safety, while corporate and municipal bonds, as well as stocks and real estate, entail varying degrees of risk depending on the financial condition of the issuer and the state of the economy. Similarly, the income from the different categories and subcategories of investments is subject to different kinds and levels of taxation. Thus, income from municipal bonds is generally tax free, income from U.S. Treasury securities is exempt from state and local taxes, and income from other kinds of investments does not enjoy such exemptions.

After assimilating the information you've gathered, you could synthesize (see pages 72–73) the views expressed in your sources as well as your own ideas about investments. You might organize your categories and subcategories according to probable degree of risk, starting with the least risky investment and ending with the most risky. For your conclusion you might offer purchase recommendations for different groups of investors such as young workers, wealthy older investors, and retirees.

Before using the material of others in your writing, examine its merits. Do some sources seem more convincing than others? Why? Do any recommendations stem from self-interest? For example, a writer who seems overly enthusiastic about one type of investment may be associated with an organization that markets it. Are any sources overloaded with material irrelevant to your purpose? Which sources offer the most detail? Asking and answering questions such as these will help you write a more informed paper.*

SUGGESTIONS FOR WRITING

1. Examine the Reader essays on women's issues or health and then write a paper that draws upon these sources and classifies their content.

2. Read several authors' views on success and then write a paper that draws on these sources and classifies their content.

3. Reflect on the Reader essays that you've studied and then write a paper that presents an appropriate classification system for them, perhaps based on the writers' levels of diction, tone, or reliance on authorities.

*Because you'll rely on published sources, it is important to read the sections on card catalogs and periodical indexes in Chapter 20 and those on handling quotations and avoiding plagiarism in Chapter 21 before you start to write. As always, follow your instructor's guidelines for documenting sources.

chapter
9

· ·

Comparison: Showing Relationships

Which candidate for senator should get my vote, Ken Conwell or Jerry Mander?
Let me know whether this new shipment of nylon thread meets specs.
Doesn't this tune remind you of an Anne Murray song?
How does high school in Australia stack up against high school in this country?

Everyone makes *comparisons,* not just once in a while but day after day. When we compare, we examine two or more items for likenesses, differences, or both.

Comparison often helps us choose between alternatives. Some issues are trivial: whether to plunk the first quarter into Star Wars or Space Ace, whether to order pizza or a sub sandwich. But comparison also influences our more important decisions. We weigh majoring in chemistry against majoring in physics, buying against renting, working for Microsoft against working for IBM. An instructor may ask us to write a paper comparing the features of two word-processing systems. An employer may have us weigh two proposals for decreasing employee absenteeism and write a report recommending one of them.

Comparison also acquaints us with unfamiliar things. To help American readers understand the English sport of rugby, a sportswriter might compare its field, team, rules, and scoring system with those for football. To teach students about France's government, a political science textbook might discuss the makeup and election of its parliament and the method of picking its president and premier, using our own government as a backdrop.

Both your classes and your job will call for comparison writing. Your humanities instructor may ask you to compare baroque and classical music and their contributions to later musical developments. Your psychology instructor may want you to compare two different types of psychoses and assess the legal and medical ramifications of each. Your biology instructor may have you consider how the features of two different kinds of body cells enable them to perform their functions. Comparisons in the workplace are common because they help people make decisions. An office manager may compare several phone systems to determine which one the company should install, a nurse assess the condition of a patient before and after a new medicine is given, an insurance agent point out the features of two insurance policies to highlight the advantages of one.

"WE'D LIKE TO TAKE YOU UPSTAIRS AND SHOW YOU THE REAL GRACIOUSNESS OF FRATERNITY LIFE, BUT IT'S SORT OF A RULE AROUND HERE TO WAIT UNTIL THE RUSHEE IS PLEDGED."

Reprinted by permission of Richard N. Bibler.

■ Selecting Items for Comparison

Any items you compare must share some common ground. For example, you could compare two golfers on driving ability, putting ability, and sand play, or two cars on appearance, gas mileage, and warranty; but you can't meaningfully compare a golfer with a car, any more than you could compare guacamole with Guadalajara or chicken with charcoal. There's simply no basis for comparison.

Any valid comparison, on the other hand, presents many possibilities. Suppose you head the music department of a large store and have two excellent salespeople working for you. The manager of the store asks you to prepare a one- or two-page report that compares their qualifications for managing the music department in a new branch store. Assessing their abilities becomes the guiding purpose that motivates and controls the writing. On the spot you can rule out points such as eye color, hair style, and religion, which have no bearing on job performance. Instead, you must decide what managerial traits the job will require and the extent to which each candidate possesses them. Your thinking might result in a list like this.

Points of Similarity or Difference	Pat	Mike
1. Ability to deal with customers, sales skills	Excellent	Excellent
2. Effort: regular attendance, hard work on the job	Excellent	Excellent
3. Leadership qualities	Excellent	Good
4. Knowledge of ordering and accounting procedures	Good	Fair
5. Musical knowledge	Excellent	Good

This list tells you which points to emphasize and suggests Pat as the candidate to recommend. You might briefly mention similarities (points 1 and 2) in an introductory paragraph, but the report would focus on differences (points 3, 4, and 5), since you're distinguishing between two employees.

EXERCISE   *Say you want to compare two good restaurants in order to recommend one of them. List the points of similarity and difference that you might discuss. Differences should predominate because you will base your decision on them.*

■ Developing a Comparison

Successful comparisons rest upon ample, well-chosen details that show just how the items under consideration are alike and different. Such support helps the reader grasp your meaning. Read the following two student paragraphs and note how the concrete details convey the striking differences between south and north 14th Street:

On 14th Street running south from P Street are opulent department stores, such as Woodward and Lothrop and Julius Garfinkle, and small but expensive clothing stores with richly dressed mannequins in the windows. Modern skyscraping office buildings harbor banks and travel bureaus on the ground floors and insurance companies and corporation headquarters in the upper stories. Dotting the concretescape are high-priced movie theaters, gourmet restaurants, multilevel parking garages, bookstores, and candy-novelty-gift shops, all catering to the prosperous population of the city. This section of 14th Street is relatively clean: The city maintenance crews must clean up after only a nine-to-five populace and the Saturday crowds of shoppers. The pervading mood of the area is one of bustling wealth during the day and, in the night, calm.

Crossing P Street toward the north, one notes a gradual but disturbing change in the scenery of 14th Street. Two architectural features assault the eyes and automatically register as tokens of trouble: the floodlights that leave no alley or doorway in shadows and the riot screens that cage in the store windows. The buildings are old, condemned, decaying monoliths, each occupying an entire city block. Liquor stores, drugstores, dusty television repair shops, seedy pornographic bookstores that display photographs of naked bodies with the genital areas blacked out by strips of tape, discount stores smelling perpetually of stale chocolate and cold popcorn, and cluttered pawnshops--businesses such as these occupy the street level. Each is separated from the adjoining stores by a littered entranceway that leads up a decaying wooden stairway to the next two floors. All the buildings are three stories tall; all have most of their windows broken and blocked with boards or newspapers; and all reek of liquor, urine, and unidentifiable rot. And so the general atmosphere of this end of 14th Street is one of poverty and decay.

Student Unknown

Vivid details depict with stark clarity the economic differences between the two cultures.

■ Organizing a Comparison

You can use either of two basic patterns to organize a comparison paper: block or alternating. The paper may deal with similarities, differences, or some combination of them.

The Block Pattern   The block pattern first presents all of the points of comparison for one item and then all of the points of comparison for the other. Here is the comparison of the two salespeople, Pat and Mike, outlined according to the block pattern:

    I. Introduction: mentions similarities in sales skills and effort but recommends Pat for promotion.
   II. Specific points about Mike
      A. Leadership qualities
      B. Knowledge of ordering and accounting procedures
      C. Musical knowledge

III. Specific points about Pat
    A. Leadership qualities
    B. Knowledge of ordering and accounting procedures
    C. Musical knowledge
IV. Conclusion: reasserts that Pat should be promoted.

The block pattern works best with short papers or ones that include only a few points of comparison. The reader can easily remember all the points in the first block while reading the second.

The Alternating Pattern   The alternating pattern presents a point about one item, then follows immediately with a corresponding point about the other. Organized in this way, the Pat-and-Mike paper would look like this:

I. Introduction: mentions similarities in sales skills and effort but recommends Pat for promotion.
II. Leadership qualities
    A. Mike's qualities
    B. Pat's qualities
III. Knowledge of ordering and accounting procedures
    A. Mike's knowledge
    B. Pat's knowledge
IV. Musical knowledge
    A. Mike's knowledge
    B. Pat's knowledge
V. Conclusion: reasserts that Pat should be promoted.

For longer papers that include many points of comparison, use the alternating method. Discussing each point in one place highlights similarities and differences; your reader doesn't have to pause and reread in order to grasp them. The alternating plan also works well for short papers.

Once you select your pattern, arrange your points of comparison in an appropriate order. Take up closely related points one after the other. Depending on your purpose, you might work from similarities to differences or the reverse. Often, a good writing strategy is to move from the least significant to the most significant point so that you conclude with punch.

EXERCISE   *Using the points of comparison you selected for the exercise on page 122, prepare outlines for a paper organized according to the block and then the alternating pattern.*

■ Using Analogy

An *analogy,* a special type of comparison, calls attention to one or more similarities underlying two different kinds of items that seem to have nothing in common. While some analogies stand alone, most clarify concepts in other kinds of writing. Whatever their role, they follow the same organizational pattern as ordinary comparisons.

An analogy often explains something unfamiliar by likening it to something familiar. Here is an example:

> The atmosphere of Earth acts like any window in serving two very important functions. It lets light in, and it permits us to look out. It also serves as a shield to keep out dangerous or uncomfortable things. A normal glazed window lets us keep our houses warm by keeping out cold air, and it prevents rain, dirt, and unwelcome insects and animals from coming in. . . . Earth's atmospheric window also helps to keep our planet at a comfortable temperature by holding back radiated heat and protecting us from dangerous levels of ultraviolet light.
>
> Lester del Ray, *The Mysterious Sky*

Conversely, an analogy sometimes highlights the unfamiliar in order to help illuminate the familiar. The following paragraph discusses the qualities and obligations of an unfamiliar person, the mountain guide, to shed light on a familiar practice—teaching:

> The mountain guide, like the true teacher, has a quiet authority. He or she engenders trust and confidence so that one is willing to join the endeavor. The guide accepts his leadership role, yet recognizes that success (measured by the heights that are scaled) depends upon the close cooperation and active participation of each member of the group. He has crossed the terrain before and is familiar with the landmarks, but each trip is new and generates its own anxiety and excitement. Essential skills must be mastered; if they are lacking, disaster looms. The situation demands keen focus and rapt attention: slackness, misjudgment, or laziness can abort the venture.
>
> Nancy K. Hill, "Scaling the Heights: The Teacher as Mountaineer"

When you develop an analogy, keep these points in mind:

1. Your readers must be well acquainted with the familiar item. If they aren't, the point is lost.
2. The items must indeed have significant similarities. You could develop a meaningful analogy between a kidney and a filter or between cancer and anarchy but not between a fiddle and a flapjack or a laser and limburger cheese.
3. The analogy must truly illuminate. Overly obvious analogies, such as one comparing a battle to an argument, offer few or no revealing insights.
4. Overextended analogies can tax the reader's endurance. A multipage analogy between a heart and a pump would likely overwhelm the reader with all its talk of valves, hoses, pressures, and pumping.

■ Ethical Issues

Although an old adage declares that "comparisons are odious," most people embrace comparisons except when they are unfair. Unfortunately, this situation occurs all too often. For example, advertisers commonly magnify trivial drawbacks in competitive products while exaggerating the benefits of their own merchandise. Politicians run attack ads that distort their opponents' views and demean the opponents' character. And when scientific theories clash, supporters of one view have been known to alter their findings in order to undermine the other position. Your readers expect any comparison to meet certain ethical standards. Ask and answer these questions to help ensure that those you write measure up.

- Have I avoided skewing one or both of my items in order to ensure a particular outcome?

- Are the items I'm comparing properly matched? It would be unethical to compare a student essay to a professional one in order to demonstrate the inadequacy of the former.

- If I'm using an analogy, is it appropriate? Comparing immigration officials to Nazi storm troopers is ethically odious: It trivializes the suffering and deaths of millions of Nazi victims and taints the officials with a terrible label.

■ Writing a Comparison

Planning and Drafting the Comparison

Don't write merely to fulfill an assignment; if you do, your paper will likely ramble aimlessly and fail to deliver a specific message. Instead, build your paper around a clear sense of purpose. Do you want to show the superiority of one product or method over another? Do you want to show how sitcoms today differ from those twenty years ago? Purpose governs the details you choose and the organization you follow.

Whether you select your own topic or write on an assigned one, answer these questions:

What purpose will my comparison serve?
Who will be my audience and why will they want to read the essay?
What points of similarity or difference will I discuss?

To develop the comparison, draw up a chart similar to this one.

Item A	**Item B**
First point of comparison	First point of comparison
Second point of comparison	Second point of comparison

Next, brainstorm each point in turn, recording appropriate supporting details. When you finish, stand back and ask these questions:

Do all the details relate to my purpose?
Do any new details come to mind?
In what order should I organize the details?

When you decide upon an order, copy the points of comparison and the details, arranged in the order you will follow, into a chart like the one below.

Item A	**Item B**
First point of comparison	First point of comparison
First detail	First detail
Second detail	Second detail
Second point of comparison	Second point of comparison

Use the introduction to identify your topic and arouse the reader's interest. If you intend to establish the superiority of one item over the other, you might call attention to your position. If you're comparing something unfamiliar with something familiar, you might explain the importance of understanding the unfamiliar item.

Organize the body of your paper according to whichever pattern—block or alternating—suits its length and the number of points you're planning to take up. If you explain something familiar by comparing it with something unfamiliar, start with the familiar item. If you try to show the superiority of one item over another, proceed from the less to the more desirable one. Note that both of the Pat-and-Mike outlines (pages 123, 124) put Mike ahead of Pat, the superior candidate.

Write whatever kind of conclusion will round off your discussion effectively. Many comparison papers end with a recommendation or a prediction. A paper comparing two brands of stereo receivers might recommend purchasing one of them. A paper comparing a familiar sport, such as football, with an unfamiliar one, such as rugby, might predict the future popularity of the latter. Unless you've written a lengthy paper, don't summarize the likenesses and differences you've presented. If you've done a proper writing job, your reader already has them clearly in mind.

Revising the Comparison

Revise your paper in light of the general guidelines in Chapter 3 and the questions that follow:

- Have I accomplished my purpose, whether to choose between alternatives or acquaint the reader with something unfamiliar?
- For something unfamiliar, have I shown clearly just how it is like and unlike the familiar item?
- Have I consistently written with my audience in mind?
- Have I considered all points of similarity and difference that relate to my purpose?
- Have I included appropriate supporting details?
- Are my comparisons arranged effectively?
- Have I considered appropriate ethical issues?

EXAMPLE STUDENT ESSAY OF COMPARISON

Different Shifts, Different Actions
Claire Mutter

1   The nursing team in a small hospital meets the routine and special daily needs of patients. A registered professional nurse usually leads the team, and members often include registered and practical nurses, nurse's aides, and attendants. Although all nurses care for patients, the duties and working conditions of team members on the first and second shifts differ considerably.

2   The first shift begins at 7:00 A.M., when nurses awaken patients and prepare them for laboratory tests, X-rays, or medications. Additional nursing duties include taking temperatures, pulses, and respirations and giving enemas or preoperative injections. Team members also serve breakfast and then administer medications such as pain pills.

3   By this time doctors have arrived to visit their patients. The nursing station swirls with activity. Doctors write new orders at desks cluttered with their patients' charts. Laboratory and X-ray technicians explain test results. The pharmacist brings medications and inquires about any new orders for drugs. Inhalation and physical therapists check charts for their new orders. The dietitian asks why Mr. Bowers is not eating his prescribed foods. Telephones ring and patients' signal lights flash continually. The members of the nursing team, all with their own duties, try desperately to keep up with these frenzied activities, which leaves little time to spend with their patients. This pace continues through most of the first shift.

4   Second shift team members, starting work at 3:00 P.M., usually can devote more attention to their patients' personal needs. To prepare for supper, nurses clear flowers and cards from tables, wash faces and hands where necessary, and position patients for eating comfort. After supper, when visitors have departed, team members inform patients about

their conditions and teach them how to care for themselves
after discharge. For example, they show diabetic patients
how to administer insulin injections and to care for their
skin, and tell them what foods to eat.

To prepare patients for the night, nurses straighten and   5
change beds and give last medications. By 10:00 most
patients are asleep. Calmness and quiet prevail at the nursing station, with only two or three nurses doing their
charting--recording how patients have tolerated treatment
and medication. Except for an occasional signal light from a
patient, activities cease for the night.

Although both shifts have the same responsibilities, the   6
care and welfare of the patient, the second shift usually
works in a much more relaxed atmosphere. Fewer staff people
and a slower pace result in more personalized treatment.

DISCUSSION QUESTIONS

1. Comment on the significance of the phrase "the duties and working conditions"
   in paragraph 1.
2. Point out effective supporting details in the essay. What do they accomplish?
3. What pattern of organization does the writer use?
4. Explain why the writer ends the third sentence of paragraph 5 as follows:
   "recording how patients have tolerated treatment and medication." What can
   you learn from this explanation?

SUGGESTIONS FOR WRITING

1. Write a properly focused comparison essay on one of the topics below or another
   that your instructor approves. Determine the points you will discuss and how you will
   develop and arrange them. Emphasize similarities, differences, or both.

   a. Two sportscasters (or news commentators or talk show hosts)

   b. The physical or mental demands of two jobs

   c. Male and female responses to stress

   d. Online and traditional shopping

   e. Something natural and something artificial

   f. The playing styles of two NBA or WNBA superstars

   g. Two computer languages

   h. A high-pressure and a no-pressure salesperson

   i. Online and traditional dating

   j. The business, residential, or slum districts of two cities or a wealthy and a work-
      ing-class residential district in the same city

   k. A favorite social spot during the day and during the evening

l. Conventional and digital photography

m. The effectiveness of two pieces of writing

n. Traditional and extreme sports

o. Two techniques for doing something in your field

p. Two musical groups

q. Two managers (or styles of managing)

r. Authoritarian vs. permissive parenting

s. Two products being considered for purchase

t. Two video games

2. **Develop an analogy based on one of the following sets of items or another set that your instructor approves. Proceed as you would for any other comparison.**

a. The offerings in a college catalog and a restaurant

b. A conquering army and a swarm of locusts

c. Driving on certain highways and gambling

d. A heart and a pump

e. Writing and gardening

f. A teacher and a merchant

g. Cancer and anarchy

h. A parent and a farmer

i. A brain and a computer

j. Developing an idea and building a house

k. Succeeding at school and winning a military campaign

l. A workaholic and an alcoholic

m. A mob and a storm

n. A kidney and a filter

o. A cluttered attic and a disorderly mind

p. Reading a book and exploring a new place

q. A rock concert and a circus

r. A party and a circus

s. Casinos and robbery

t. Contemporary America and an amusement park

The Critical Edge

Although you rely on your own knowledge or findings to develop many comparisons, in some cases you'll synthesize (see pages 72–73) material from other sources.

Let's say that your business management instructor has asked you to prepare a report on the management styles of two high-profile chief executive officers (CEOs) at Fortune 500 companies that manufacture the same kinds of products. You realize that you'll need to do some reading in business periodicals like *Forbes, Fortune,* and the *Wall Street Journal* in order to complete this assignment. Your sources reveal that the first CEO favors a highly centralized managerial structure with strict limits on what can be done by all employees except top executives. The company has pursued foreign markets by establishing factories overseas and has aggressively attempted to merge with or acquire its domestic competitors. The second CEO has established a decentralized managerial structure that allows managers at various levels of the company to make key decisions. The company has also established a strong foreign presence, but it has done so primarily by entering into joint ventures with foreign firms. Most of its domestic expansion has resulted from the construction of new plants rather than from mergers or takeovers. Both CEOs have borrowed heavily to finance their companies' expansion. These three differences and one similarity are your points of comparison, which you can organize using either the block or alternating pattern. You might conclude by indicating why you prefer one of the two management styles.

After you've read the views expressed by your sources, examine them critically. Does any of the information about the two CEOs seem slanted so that it appears to misrepresent their management styles? For example, do any of the writers seem to exaggerate the positive or negative features of centralized or decentralized management? Do appropriate examples support the writers' contentions? Does any relevant information appear to be missing? Does any source contain material that isn't related to your purpose? Judging the works of others in this fashion will help you write a better report.*

SUGGESTIONS FOR WRITING

1. Read "Sexual Harassment Is a Serious Problem at Universities" (pages 566–71) and "Sexual Harassment Is Overestimated" (pages 571–76) and then compare the views of these two writers.

2. Read several reviews of the same movie and then compare what the critics have written.

3. Write a criticism of a comparison you recently read that you thought was unreasonable.

---

*Because you'll rely on published sources, it is important to read the sections on card catalogs and periodical indexes in Chapter 20 and those on handling quotations and avoiding plagiarism in Chapter 21 before you start to write. As always, follow your instructor's guidelines for documenting sources.

c h a p t e r

10

....

Cause and Effect: Explaining Why

Cause and effect, like the two sides of a coin, are inseparably linked and together make up *causation*. Cause probes the reasons why actions, events, attitudes, and conditions exist. Effect examines their consequences. Causation is important to us because it can explain historical events, natural happenings, and the actions and attitudes of individuals and groups. It can help us anticipate the consequences of personal actions, natural phenomena, or government policies.

Everyone asks and answers questions of causation. Scott wonders why Sue *really* broke off their relationship, and Jennifer speculates on the consequences of changing her major. People wonder why child abuse and homelessness are on the rise, and millions worry about the effects of corporate cost cutting and violence in our schools.

Inevitably, therefore, you will need to write papers and reports that employ causation. Your instructors might ask you to write on topics such as the causes of the American Revolution, the consequences of white-collar crime, the reasons why so many couples are divorcing, or the effects of different fertilizers on plant growth. An employer may want a report on why a certain product malfunctions, what might happen if a community redesigns its traffic pattern, or how a school closing might affect business.

■ Patterns in Causal Analysis

Several organizational patterns are possible for a causal analysis. Sometimes, a single cause produces several effects. For instance, poor language skills prevent college students from keeping up with required reading, taking adequate notes, and writing competent papers and essay exams. To explore such a single cause–multiple effect relationship, construct outlines similar to the following two:

I. Introduction: identifies cause	I. Poor language skills
II. Body	II. Body
A. Effect number 1	A. Can't keep up with required reading
B. Effect number 2	B. Can't take adequate notes
C. Effect number 3	C. Can't write competent papers or exams
III. Conclusion	III. Conclusion

Alternatively, you might discuss the cause after the effects are presented.

On the other hand, several causes may join forces to produce one effect. Zinc production in the United States, for example, has decreased over the last few years because it can be produced more cheaply abroad than it can here, it is being replaced on cars by plastics and lighter metals, and it cannot be recycled. Here's how you might organize a typical multiple cause–single effect paper:

I. Introduction: identifies effect	I. Decrease in U.S. zinc production
II. Body	II. Body
A. Cause number 1	A. Produced more cheaply abroad
B. Cause number 2	B. Replaced on cars by plastics, lighter metals
C. Cause number 3	C. Cannot be recycled
III. Conclusion	III. Conclusion

Sometimes discussion of the effect follows the presentation of causes.

At times a set of events forms a causal chain, with each event the effect of the preceding one and the cause of the following one. For example, a student sleeps late and so misses breakfast and ends up hungry and distracted, which in turn results in a poor performance on an exam. Interrupting the chain at any point halts the sequence. Such chains can be likened to a row of upright dominoes that fall one after the other when the first one is pushed. Belief in a domino theory, which held that if one nation in Southeast Asia fell to the communists all would, one after the other, helped bring about U.S. entry into the Vietnam War. Causal chains can also help explain how devices function and some social changes proceed. The following outlines typify the arrangement of a paper explaining a causal chain:

I. Introduction	I. Introduction
II. Body	II. Body
A. Cause	A. Sleep late

B. Effect	B. Miss breakfast
C. Cause	C. Become hungry and distracted
D. Effect	D. Perform poorly on exam
III. Conclusion	III. Conclusion

Papers of this kind resemble process analyses, but process is concerned with *how* the events occur, cause and effect with *why*.

In many situations the sequence of causes and effects is too complex to fit the image of a chain. Suppose you are driving to a movie on a rainy night. You approach an intersection screened by bushes and, because you have the right-of-way, start across. Suddenly a car with unlit headlights looms directly in your path. You hit the brakes but skid on the slippery pavement and crash into the other car, crumpling its left fender and damaging your own bumper. Later, as you think about the episode, you begin to sense its complexities.

Obviously, the *immediate cause* of the accident was the other driver's failure to heed the stop sign. But other causes also played roles: the bushes and unlit headlights that kept you from seeing the other car sooner; the starts and stops, speedups and slowdowns that brought the two cars to the intersection at the same time; the wet pavement you skidded on; and the movie that brought you out in the first place.

You also realize that the effects of the accident go beyond the fender and bumper damage. After the accident, a police officer ticketed the other driver. As a result of the delay, you missed the movie. Further, the accident unnerved you so badly that you couldn't attend classes the next day and therefore missed an important writing assignment. Because of a bad driving record, the other driver lost his license for sixty days. Clearly, the effects of this accident rival the causes in complexity.

Here's how you might organize a multiple cause–multiple effect essay:

I. Introduction	I. The accident
II. Body	II. Body
A. Cause number 1	A. Driver ran stop sign
B. Cause number 2	B. Bushes and unlit headlights impaired vision
C. Cause number 3	C. Wet pavement caused skidding
D. Effect number 1	D. Missed the movie
E. Effect number 2	E. Unnerved so missed classes next day
F. Effect number 3	F. Other driver lost license
III. Conclusion	III. Conclusion

In some situations, however, you might first present the effects, then turn to the causes.

EXERCISE

1. Read the following selection and then arrange the events in a causal chain:

Although some folk societies still exist today, similar human groups began the slow process of evolving into more complex societies many millennia ago, through settlement in villages and through advances in technology and organizational structure. This gave rise to the second level of organization: civilized preindustrial, or "feudal," society. Here there is a surplus of food because of the selective cultivation of grains—and also because of the practice of animal husbandry. The food surplus permits both the specialization of labor and the kind of class structure that can, for instance, provide the leadership and command the manpower to develop and maintain extensive irrigation systems (which in turn makes possible further increases in the food supply). . . .

Gideon Sjöberg, "The Origin and Development of Cities"

2. **Trace the possible effects of the following occurrences:**

   a. You pick out a salad at the cafeteria and sit down to eat. Suddenly you notice a large green worm on one of the lettuce leaves.

   b. As you leave your composition classroom, you trip and break your arm.

   c. Your boss has warned you not to be late to work again. You are driving to work with ten minutes to spare when you get a flat tire.

■ Reasoning Errors in Causal Analysis

Ignoring Multiple Causes

An effect rarely stems from a single cause. The person who believes that permissive parents have caused the present upsurge of venereal disease or the one who blames television violence for the climbing numbers of emotionally disturbed children oversimplifies the situation. Permissiveness and violence perhaps did contribute to these conditions. Without much doubt, however, numerous other factors also played important parts.

Mistaking Chronology for Causation

Don't assume that just because one event followed another the first necessarily caused the second. This kind of faulty thinking feeds many popular superstitions. Horace walks under a ladder, later stubs his toe, and thinks that his path caused his pain. Sue breaks a mirror just before Al breaks their engagement; then she blames the cracked mirror. Many people once believed that the election of Herbert Hoover as President in 1928 brought on the Great Depression in 1929. Today some people believe that the testing of atomic weapons has altered our weather patterns. Don't misunderstand: One event *may* cause the next; but before you go on record with your conclusion, make sure that you're not dealing with mere chronology.

Confusing Causes with Effects

Young children sometimes declare that the moving trees make the wind blow. Similarly, some adults may think that Pam and Paul married because they fell in love, when in reality economic necessity mandated the vows, and love came later. Scan your evidence carefully in order to avoid such faulty assertions.

EXERCISE

1. **Which of the following statements point toward papers that will focus on causes? Which point toward papers focusing on effects? Explain your answers.**

   a. Most of the problems that plague newly married couples are the direct outgrowth of timidity and pride.

   b. The Marshall Plan was designed to aid the economic recovery of Europe after World War II.

   c. The smoke from burning poison ivy can bring on a skin rash and lung irritation.

   d. Popularity in high school stems largely from good looks, a pleasing personality, participation in school activities, the right friends, and frequent dates.

2. **Identify which of the following paragraphs deals with causes, which with effects. List the causes and effects.**

   a.   Color filters offer three advantages in black-and-white photography. First, a particular color will be lightened by a filter of the same color. For example, in a photograph of a red rose in a dark blue vase, both will appear almost the same shade of gray if no filter is used. However, when photographed through a red filter, the rose will appear much lighter than the vase; and through a blue filter the vase will appear much lighter than the rose. This effect can be useful in emphasizing or muting certain objects in a photograph. Second, a particular color filter will darken its complementary color in the scene. Consequently, any orange object will appear darker than normal if a blue filter is used. Finally, color filters can reduce or increase atmospheric haze. For example, in a distant aerial shot there will often be so much haze that distant detail is obscured. To eliminate haze almost entirely, the photographer can use a deep red filter. On the other hand, if more haze is desired in order to achieve an artistic effect, varying shades of blue filters can be used.

   Timothy Kelly

   b.   Overeating, which has become a national pastime for millions of Americans, has several roots. For example, parents who are concerned that their children get enough to eat during the growing years overfeed them and thereby establish a lifetime overeating habit. The child who is constantly praised for cleaning up his plate experiences a sort of gratification later on as he cleans up all too many plates. The easy availability of so much food is a constant temptation for many people, especial-

ly the types of food served at fast-food restaurants and mer-
chandised in the frozen food departments of supermarkets.
Equally tempting are all the snack foods constantly advertised
on TV. But many people don't need temptation from the outside;
their overeating arises from such psychological factors as ner-
vousness, boredom, loneliness, insecurity, an overall discontent with life, or an aversion to exercise. Thus, overeating can
actually be a symptom of psychological surrender to, or withdrawal from, the complexities and competition of modern life.

Kenneth Reichow

■ Ethical Issues

Causation is not immune from abuse, either accidental or deliberate. Imagine
the consequences of an article that touts a new herbal remedy but fails to mention several potentially serious side effects that could harm many users. Think
about the possible strain on your relationship with a friend if she unjustly suspected you of starting a vicious rumor about her. Writing cause-and-effect papers creates an ethical responsibility. Asking and answering these questions will
help you meet that obligation.

- Have I tried to uncover all of the causes that might result in a particular
  outcome? A report blaming poor instruction alone for a high student
  failure rate in a certain town's public schools almost certainly overlooks
  such factors as oversized classes, inadequate facilities, and poor home
  environments.

- Have I carefully weighed the importance of the causes I've uncovered?
  If a few, but not most, of the classes in the school system with problems
  are oversized, then the report should not stress their significance.

- Have I tried to uncover and discuss every important effect, even one
  that might damage a case I'm trying to make? A report emphasizing the
  beneficial effects of jogging would be dangerously negligent if it failed
  to note the potential for injury.

- What would be the consequences if people act on my analysis?

Careful evaluation of causes and effects not only fulfills your writing obligation
but also your ethical one.

■ Writing a Causal Analysis

Planning and Drafting the Causal Analysis

Because you have probably speculated about the causes and effects of several
campus, local, state, or national problems, writing this type of paper should pose
no great difficulty. If you choose your own topic, perhaps your personal experi-

ence will suggest something promising. Topics such as "Why I Dislike (or Like) Foreign Cars" and "How My Father's (or Someone Else's) Death Has Changed My Life" might work well. Nonpersonal topics also offer writing possibilities. For instance, "What's Behind Teenage Suicides?" and "The Impact of Global Markets on American Corporations" would allow you to draw on library resources.

The strategies on pages 14–20 can also help you find several topics. Answer these questions about each potential candidate:

> What purpose will guide this writing?
> Who is my audience? Will the topic interest them? Why or why not?
> Shall I focus on causes, effects, or both?

Brainstorming your topic for supporting details should be easy. If you're dealing with causes, pose these questions about each one:

> How significant is this cause?
> Could it have brought about the effect by itself?
> Does it form part of a chain?
> Precisely how does it contribute to the effect?

For papers dealing with effects, substitute the following questions for the ones above:

> How important is this effect?
> What evidence will establish its importance?

Charting your results can help you prepare for writing the paper. To tabulate causes, use an arrangement like this one:

Cause	Contribution to Effect
First cause	Specific contribution
Second cause	Specific contribution

For effects, use this chart:

Effect	Importance
First effect	Why important
Second effect	Why important

Once your items are tabulated, examine them carefully for completeness. Perhaps you've overlooked a cause or effect or have slighted the significance of one you've already mentioned. Think about the order in which you'd like to discuss your items and prepare a revised chart that reflects your decision.

Use the opening of your paper to identify your topic and indicate whether you plan to discuss causes, effects, or both. You can signal your intention in a number of ways. To prepare for a focus on causes, you might use the words *cause, reason,* or *stem from,* or you might ask why something has occurred. To signal a paper on effects, you might use *effect, fallout,* or *impact,* or you might ask what has happened since something took place. Read these examples:

Signals causes: Midville's recent decrease in street crime stems primarily from its expanded educational program, growing job opportunities for young people, and falling rate of drug addiction.

Signals effects: Since my marriage to Rita, how has my social life changed?

At times you may choose some dramatic attention-getter. For a paper on the effects of radon, a toxic radioactive gas present in many homes, you might note that "Although almost everyone now knows about the hazards associated with smoking, eating high-cholesterol foods, and drinking excessively, few people are aware that just going home could be hazardous to one's health." If you use an arresting statement, be sure the content of your paper warrants it.

How you organize the body of the paper depends on your topic. Close scrutiny may reveal that one cause was indispensable; the rest merely played supporting roles. If so, discuss the main cause first. In analyzing your automobile mishap, which fits this situation, start with the failure of the other driver to yield the right-of-way; then fan out to any other causes that merit mentioning. Sometimes you'll find that no single cause was essential but that all of them helped matters along. Combinations of this kind lie at the heart of many social and economic concerns: inflation, depression, and urban crime rates, to name just a few. Weigh each cause carefully and rank them in importance. If your topic and purpose will profit from building suspense, work from the least important cause to the most important. Otherwise, reverse the order. For analyzing causal chains, chronological order works effectively.

If space won't permit you to deal adequately with every cause, pick out the two or three you consider most important and limit your discussion to them. To avoid giving your reader an oversimplified impression, note that other causes exist. Even if length poses no problem, don't attempt to trace every cause to some more remote cause and then to a still more remote one. Instead, determine some sensible cutoff point that accords with your purpose, and don't go beyond it.

Treat effects as carefully as you do causes. Keep in mind that effects often travel in packs, and try to arrange them in some logical order. If they occur together, consider order of climax. If one follows the other in a chainlike sequence, present them in that fashion. If space considerations dictate, limit your discussion to the most interesting or significant effects. Whatever order you choose for your paper, don't jump helter-skelter from cause to effect to cause in a way that leaves your reader bewildered.

As you write, don't restrict yourself to a bare-bones discussion of causes and effects. If, for instance, you're exploring the student parking problem on your campus, you might describe the jammed lots or point out that students often miss class because they have to drive around and look for spots. Similarly, don't simply assert that the administration's insensitivity contributes to the problem.

Instead, cite examples of the college's refusal to answer letters about the situation or to discuss it. To provide statistical evidence of the problem's seriousness, you might note the small number of lots, the limited spaces in each, and the approximate number of student cars on campus.

It's important to remember, however, that you're not just listing causes and effects; you're showing the reader their connection. Let's see how one student handled this connection. After you've read "Why Students Drop Out of College," the student essay that follows in this chapter, carefully re-examine paragraph 3. Note how the sentence beginning "In many schools" and the two following it show precisely how poor study habits develop. Note further how the sentence beginning "This laxity produces" and the three following it show precisely how such poor habits result in "a flood of low grades and failure." Armed with this information, readers are better able to avoid poor study habits and their consequences.

Causal analyses can end in several ways. A paper discussing the effects of acid rain on America's lakes and streams might specify the grave consequences of failing to deal with the problem or express the hope that something will be done. Frequently, writers use their conclusions to evaluate the relative importance of their causes or effects.

Revising the Causal Analysis

Follow the guidelines in Chapter 3 and answer these questions as you revise your causal analysis:

Have I made the right decision in electing to focus on causes, effects, or both?

Have I ferreted out all important causes and effects? Mistakenly labeled something as an effect merely because it follows something else? Confused causes with effects?

Am I dealing with a causal chain? An immediate cause and several supporting causes? Multiple causes and effects?

Have I presented my causes and effects in an appropriate order?

Have I supported my discussion with sufficient details?

Have I considered appropriate ethical issues?

EXAMPLE STUDENT ESSAY OF CAUSE AND EFFECT

Why Students Drop Out of College

Diann Fisher

1   Each fall a new crop of first-year college students, wavering between high hopes for the future and intense anxiety about their new status, scan college maps searching for

their classrooms. They have been told repeatedly that college is the key to a well-paying job, and they certainly
don't want to support themselves by flipping hamburgers or
working at some other dead-end job. So, notebooks at the
ready, they await what college has in store. Unfortunately
many of them--indeed, over 30 percent--will not return after
the first year. Why do so many students leave? There are several reasons. Some find the academic program too hard, some
lack the proper study habits or motivation, others fall victim to the temptations of the college environment, and a
large group leave for personal reasons.

Not surprisingly, the academic shortcomings of college   2
students have strong links to high school. In the past, a
high school student who lacked the ability or desire to take
a college-preparatory course could settle for a diploma in
general studies and afterward find a job with decent pay.
Now that possibility scarcely exists, so many poorly prepared students feel compelled to try college. Getting
accepted by some schools isn't difficult. Once in, though,
the student who has taken nothing beyond general mathematics, English, and science faces serious trouble when confronted with college algebra, first-year composition, and
biological or physical science. Most colleges do offer remedial courses and other assistance that may help some weaker
students to survive. In spite of everything, however, many
others find themselves facing ever-worsening grade-point
averages and either fail or just give up.

Like academic shortcomings, poor study habits have   3
their roots in high school, where even average students can
often breeze through with a minimum of effort. In many
schools, outside assignments are rare and so easy that they
require little time or thought to complete. To accommodate
slower students, teachers frequently repeat material so
many times that slightly better students can grasp it without opening their books. And when papers are late, teachers
often don't mark them down. This laxity produces students
who can't or don't want to study, students totally unprepared for the rigorous demands of college. There, courses

may require several hours of study each week in order to be passed with even a C̲. In many programs, outside assignments are commonplace and demanding. Instructors expect students to grasp material after one explanation, and many won't accept late papers at all. Students who don't quickly develop disciplined study habits face a flood of low grades and failure.

4   Poor student motivation aggravates faulty study habits. Students who thought high school was boring find even less allure in the more challenging college offerings. Lacking any commitment to do well, they shrug off assigned papers, skip classes, and avoid doing required reading. Over time, classes gradually shrink as more and more students stay away. With final exams upon them, some return in a last-ditch effort to salvage a passing grade, but by then it is too late. Eventually, repetition of this scenario forces the students out.

5   The wide range of freedoms offered by the college environment can overwhelm even well-prepared newcomers. While students are in high school, parents are on hand to make them study, push them off to class, and send them to bed at a reasonable hour. Once away from home and parents, however, far too many students become caught up in a constant round of parties, dates, bull sessions, and other distractions that seem more fascinating than school work. Again, if such behavior persists poor grades and failure result.

6   Personal reasons also take a heavy toll on students who might otherwise complete their programs successfully. Often, money problems are at fault. For example, a student may lose a scholarship or grant, fail to obtain needed work, or find that the family can no longer afford to help out. Some students succumb to homesickness; some are forced out by an illness, injury, or death in the family; and yet others become ill or injure themselves and leave to recuperate. Finally, a considerable number become disillusioned with their programs or the size, location, or atmosphere of their schools and decide not to return.

What happens to the students who drop out? Some re-enroll   7
in college later, often in less demanding two- and four-year
schools that offer a better chance of academic success. Of
the remainder, the great bulk find civilian jobs or enlist
in the armed forces. Most, whatever their choice, go on to
lead productive, useful lives. In the meantime, campus newcomers need to know about the dangers that tripped up so many
of their predecessors and make every effort to avoid them.

DISCUSSION QUESTIONS

1. Identify the thesis statement in this essay.
2. Trace the causal chain that makes up paragraph 2.
3. What is the function of the first sentence in paragraph 3?
4. In which paragraphs does the writer discuss causes? Effects?

SUGGESTIONS FOR WRITING   *Use one of the topics below, or another that your instructor approves, to develop a causal analysis. Determine which causes and/or effects to consider. Scrutinize your analysis for errors in reasoning, settle on an organization, and write the essay.*

1. Reasons why relationships fail
2. The effect of some friend, acquaintance, public figure, or writer on your life
3. Causes, effects, or both of road rage
4. Effects of divorce on children
5. Why you are a _____ major
6. Causes, effects, or both of the popularity of the Internet
7. Causes of school violence
8. Effects of the popularity of casino gambling
9. Causes, effects, or both of the cell phone phenomenon
10. Reasons why you have a particular habit or participate in a particular sport
11. Causes or effects of sleep deprivation
12. Reasons why _____ is a popular celebrity
13. Effects of some recent Supreme Court decision or change in public policy
14. Causes, effects, or both of some family crisis in your life
15. Causes, effects, or both of our hunger for heroes
16. Reasons why herbal medicines enjoy widespread popularity
17. Effects of drinking on college students
18. Causes of procrastination
19. Reasons why the national crime rate has decreased
20. Causes and effects of violence at sporting events

The Critical Edge

Although nearly everyone recognizes the role of causation in human affairs, differences of opinion often surface about the causes and effects of important matters. What lies behind the widespread incivility in the United States today? Why are women more likely than men to leave management jobs? How do video games affect children? What impact does the high divorce rate have on American society? Obviously such questions lack simple answers; and as a result investigators, even when they agree on the causes and effects involved, often debate their relative importance.

Suppose your women's studies instructor has asked you to investigate the departure of women from managerial positions. A library search reveals several articles on this topic as well as a number of reasons for resigning. Some women leave because they find it harder to advance than men do, and as a result they seldom attain senior positions. Others leave because they receive lower salaries than their male counterparts. Still others leave because of the stifling effects of corporate rigidity, unrealistic expectations, the demands of raising a family, or possibly diminished chances of marriage. Although most articles cite these causes, their relative importance is debatable. One writer, for example, emphasizes family concerns by discussing them last and at greatest length. Another puts the chief blame on obstacles to upward mobility—the existence of a "glass ceiling" that blocks women from upper-level positions along with an "old-boy network" of entrenched executives that parcels out jobs among its members.

Once you've finished your research, you're ready to synthesize (see pages 72–73) the views of your sources as well as your own views. Before you start to write, though, take some time to consider carefully each cause and effect you've uncovered. Obviously you should ground your paper on well-supported and widely acknowledged causes and effects, but you might also include more speculative ones as long as you clearly indicate their secondary nature. To illustrate, one writer, while mentioning corporate rigidity as a reason that women leave management jobs, clearly labels this explanation as a theory and backs it with a single example. As you examine your material, ask yourself these critical questions as well as any others that occur to you: Does any writer exhibit obvious bias? Do the studies cited include a sufficient number of examples to be meaningful? Do the statistics appear reliable, or are some out of date, irrelevant, or skimpy? Have the writers avoided the reasoning errors discussed on page 135? Whenever you find a flaw, note where the problem lies so that you can discuss it in your writing if you choose. Such discussions often clear up common misconceptions. There are various possibilities for organizing your paper. If your sources substantially agree on the most important cause, you might begin with that one and then take up the others. A second possibility, the order-of-climax arrangement, reverses the procedure by starting with secondary causes and ending with the most significant one. You can use the same options for organizing effects. When no clear consensus exists about the relative importance of the different causes and effects, there is no best arrangement of the material.*

SUGGESTIONS FOR WRITING

1. Read three articles on the causes of a major social problem such as domestic violence and incorporate those causes and your own views in a paper.

2. Read two articles that disagree about the effects of a proposed government program such as oil and gas drilling on public land and write a paper that incorporates the writers' views and presents your own conclusions.

3. Write an essay that corrects a common misconception about the causes or effects of a matter about which you feel strongly. Possibilities might include the causes of homelessness or the impact of capital punishment on murder rates in different states.

*Because this type of paper draws upon published information, it is important to read the sections on card catalogs and periodical indexes in Chapter 20 and those on handling quotations and avoiding plagiarism in Chapter 21 before you start to write. As always, follow your instructor's guidelines for documenting sources.

chapter 11

Definition: Establishing Boundaries

That movie was egregious.

Once the bandage is off the wound, swab the proud flesh with the disinfectant.

Speaking on statewide television, Governor Blaine called his opponent a left-winger.

Do you have questions? You're not alone. Many people would question the sentences above: "What does *egregious* mean?" "How can flesh be *proud?*" "What does the governor mean by *left-winger?* What specific policies does the opponent support that warrant this label?" To avoid puzzling and provoking your own readers, you'll often need to explain the meaning of some term. The term may be unfamiliar *(egregious),* used in an unfamiliar sense *(proud flesh),* or mean different things to different people *(left-winger).* Whenever you clarify the meaning of some term, you are *defining.*

Humans are instinctively curious. We start asking about meanings as soon as we can talk, and we continue to seek, as well as supply, definitions all through life. In school, instructors expect us to explain all sorts of literary, historical, scientific, technical, and social terms. On the job, a member of a company's human resources department might prepare a brochure that explains the meaning of such terms as *corporate responsibility* and *product stewardship* for new employees. An accountant might define *statistical sampling inventory* in a report calling for a change in the inventory system. A special education teacher might write a memo explaining *learning disabled* to the rest of the staff.

When you define, you identify the features that distinguish a term, thereby putting a fence around it, establishing its boundaries, and separating it from all others. Knowing these features enables both you and your reader to use the term appropriately.

Sometimes a word, phrase, or sentence will settle a definition question. To clear up the mystery of "proud flesh," all you'd need to do is insert the parenthetical phrase "(excessively swollen and grainy)" after the word *proud*. But when you're dealing with new terms—*information superhighway* and *virtual reality* are examples—brief definitions won't provide the reader with enough information for proper understanding.

Abstract terms—those standing for things we can't see, touch, or otherwise detect with our five senses—often require extended definitions, too. It's impossible to capture the essence of *democracy* or *hatred* or *bravery* in a single sentence: The terms are too complex, and people have too many differing ideas about what they mean. The same holds true for some concrete terms—those standing for actions and things we can perceive with our five senses. Some people, for instance, limit the term *drug pusher* to full-time sellers of hard drugs like cocaine and heroin. Others, at the opposite extreme, extend the term to full- and part-time sellers of any illegal drug. Writing an argument recommending life sentences for convicted drug pushers would require you to tell just what you mean by the term so that the reader would have solid grounds for judging your position.

■ Types of Definitions

Three types of definitions—synonyms, essential definitions, and extended definitions—serve writers' needs. Although the first two seldom require more than a word or a sentence, an extended definition can run to several pages. The three types, however, are related. Synonyms and essential definitions share space between the covers of dictionaries, and both furnish starting points for extended definitions.

Synonyms

Synonyms are words with very nearly the same meanings. *Lissome* is synonymous with *lithe* or *nimble,* and *condign* is a synonym of *worthy* and *suitable.* Synonyms let writers clarify meanings of unfamiliar words without using cumbersome explanations. To clarify the term *expostulation* in a quoted passage, all you'd have to do is add the word *objection,* in brackets, after it. Because synonyms are not identical twins, using them puts a slightly different shade of meaning on a message. For example, to "protest" and to "object" are certainly similar in many ways. Yet the claim that we "object" to the establishment of a nuclear waste site in our area fails to capture the active and sustained commitment implied in our willingness to "protest" against such a site. Still, synonyms provide a convenient means of breaking communications logjams.

Essential Definitions

An essential definition does three things: (1) names the item being defined, (2) places it in a broad category, and (3) distinguishes it from other items in that category. Here are three examples:

Item Being Defined	Broad Category	Distinguishing Features
A howdah	is a covered seat	for riding on the back of an elephant or camel.
A voiceprint	is a graphical record	of a person's voice characteristics.
To parboil	is to boil meat, vegetables, or fruits	until they are partially cooked.

Writing a good essential definition requires careful thought. Suppose your instructor has asked you to write an essential definition of one of the terms listed in an exercise, and you choose *vacuum cleaner*. Coming up with a broad category presents no problem: A vacuum cleaner is a household appliance. The hard part is pinpointing the distinguishing features. The purpose of a vacuum cleaner is to clean floors, carpets, and upholstery. You soon realize, however, that these features alone do not separate vacuum cleaners from other appliances. After all, carpet sweepers also clean floors, and whisk brooms clean upholstery. What then does distinguish vacuum cleaners? After a little thought, you realize that, unlike the other items, a vacuum cleaner works by suction. You then write the following definition:

> A vacuum cleaner is a household appliance that uses suction to clean floors, carpets, and upholstery.

The same careful attention is necessary to establish the distinguishing features of any essential definition.

Limitations of Essential Definitions   Essential definitions have certain built-in limitations. Because of their brevity, they often can't do full justice to abstract terms such as *cowardice, love, jealousy, power*. Problems also arise with terms that have several settled meanings. To explain *jam* adequately, you'd need at least three essential definitions: (1) a closely packed crowd, (2) preserves, and (3) a difficult situation. But despite these limitations, an essential definition can be useful by itself or as part of a longer definition. Writers often build an extended definition around an essential definition.

Pitfalls in Preparing Essential Definitions   When you prepare an essential definition, guard against these flaws:

> *Circular definition.* Don't define a term by repeating it or changing its form slightly. Saying that a psychiatrist is "a physician who practices psychiatry" will only frustrate someone who's never heard of psychiatry. Repress circularity and provide the proper insight by choosing terms the reader can relate to, for example, "A psychiatrist is a physician who diagnoses and treats mental disorders."

Overly broad definition. Shy away from definitions that embrace too much territory. If you define a skunk as "an animal that has a bushy tail and black fur with white markings," your definition is not precise. Many cats and dogs also fit this description. But if you add "and that ejects a foul-smelling secretion when threatened," you will clear the air—of any misconceptions at least.

Overly narrow definition. Don't hem in your definition too closely, either. "A kitchen blender is a bladed electrical appliance used to chop foods" illustrates this error. Blenders perform other operations, too. To correct the error, add the missing information: "A kitchen blender is a bladed electrical appliance used to chop, mix, whip, liquefy, or otherwise process foods."

Omission of main category. Avoid using "is where" or "is when" instead of naming the main category. Here are examples of this error: "A bistro is where food and wine are served" and "An ordination is when a person is formally recognized as a minister, priest, or rabbi." The reader will not know exactly what sort of thing (a bar? a party?) a *bistro* is and may think that *ordination* means a time. Note the improvement when the broad categories are named: "A bistro is a small restaurant where both food and wine are served" and "An ordination is a ceremony at which a person is formally recognized as a minister, priest, or rabbi."

EXERCISE

1. **Identify the broad category and the distinguishing traits in each of these essential definitions:**

   a. Gangue is useless rock accompanying valuable minerals in a deposit.

   b. A catbird is a small American songbird with a slate-colored body, a black cap, and a catlike cry.

   c. A soldier is a man or woman serving in an army.

   d. Myelin is a white, fatty substance that forms a sheath around some nerve fibers.

   e. A gargoyle is a waterspout carved in the likeness of a grotesque animal or imaginary creature and projecting from the gutter of a building.

   f. A magnum is a wine bottle that holds about two-fifths of a gallon.

2. **Indicate which of the following statements are acceptable essential definitions. Explain what is wrong with those that are not. Correct them.**

   a. A scalpel is a small knife that has a sharp blade used for surgery and anatomical dissections.

   b. A puritan is a person with puritanical beliefs.

   c. A kraal is where South African tribes keep large domestic animals.

   d. A rifle is a firearm that has a grooved barrel and is used for hunting large game.

   e. A motorcycle is a two-wheeled vehicle used mainly for human transportation.

   f. Fainting is when a person loses consciousness owing to inadequate flow of blood to the brain.

3. **Write an essential definition for each of the following terms:**

   a. groupie   **c.** hit man   **e.** pushover

   b. happy hour   **d.** jock   **f.** hard grader

Extended Definitions

Sometimes it's necessary to go beyond an essential definition and write a paragraph or whole paper explaining a term. New technical, social, and economic terms often require extended definitions. To illustrate, a computer scientist might need to define *data integrity* so that computer operators understand the importance of maintaining it. Terms with differing meanings also frequently require extended definitions. To let voters know just what he means by *left-winger*, Governor Blaine might detail the kinds of legislation his opponent favors and opposes. Furthermore, extended definition is crucial to interpretation of the law, as we see when courts clarify the meaning of concepts such as obscenity.

Extended definitions are not merely academic exercises; they are fundamental to your career and your life. A police officer needs to have a clear understanding of what counts as *reasonable grounds for search and seizure;* an engineer must comprehend the meaning of *stress;* a nuclear medical technologist had better have a solid grasp of *radiation.* And all of us are concerned with the definition of our basic rights as citizens.

Extended definitions are montages of other methods of development—narration, description, process analysis, illustration, classification, comparison, and cause and effect. Often, they also define by negation: explaining what a term *does not* mean. The following paragraphs show how one writer handled an extended definition of *sudden infant death syndrome.* The student began by presenting a case history (illustration), which also incorporated an essential definition and two synonyms.

> Jane and Dick Smith were proud, new parents of an eight-pound, ten-ounce baby girl named Jenny. One summer night, Jane put Jenny to bed at 8:00. When she went to check on her at 3:00 A.M., Jane found Jenny dead. The baby had given no cry of pain, shown no sign of trouble. Even the doctor did not know why she had died, for she was healthy and strong. The autopsy report confirmed the doctor's suspicion--the infant was a victim of "sudden infant death syndrome," also known as SIDS or crib death. SIDS is the sudden and unexplainable death of an apparently healthy, sleeping infant. It is the number-one cause of death in infants after the first week of life and as a result has been the subject of numerous research studies.

DISCUSSION QUESTIONS

1. What synonyms does the writer use?
2. Which sentence presents an essential definition?

In the next paragraph, the writer turned to negation, pointing out some of the things that researchers have ruled out about SIDS.

Although researchers do not know what SIDS is, they do know what it is <u>not</u>. They know it cannot be predicted; it strikes like a thief in the night. Crib deaths occur in seconds, with no sound of pain, and they always happen when the child is sleeping. Suffocation is <u>not</u> the cause, nor is aspiration or regurgitation. Researchers have found no correlation between the incidence of SIDS and the mother's use of birth control pills or tobacco or the presence of fluoride in water. Since it is not hereditary or contagious, only a slim chance exists that SIDS will strike twice in the same family.

Finally, the student explored several proposed causes of SIDS as well as how parents may react to the loss of their child.

As might be expected, researchers have offered many theories concerning the cause of crib death. Dr. R. C. Reisinger, a National Cancer Institute scientist, has linked crib deaths to the growth of a common bacterium, <u>E. coli</u>, in the intestines of newborn babies. The organisms multiply in the intestines, manufacturing a toxin that is absorbed by the intestinal wall and passes into the bloodstream. Breast milk stops the growth of the organism, whereas cow's milk permits it. Therefore, Dr. Reisinger believes, bottle-fed babies run a higher risk of crib death than other babies. . . .

The loss of a child through crib death is an especially traumatic experience. Parents often develop feelings of guilt and depression, thinking they somehow caused the child's death. To alleviate such feelings, organizations have been established to help parents accept the fact that they did not cause the death.

Trudy Stelter

■ Ethical Issues

How we define can have devastating consequences. For centuries, the practice of defining Africans as "subhuman" helped justify the slave trade and slavery. During the 1930s and early 1940s, labeling Jews as "vermin" was used to fuel the attempt to exterminate them both in Nazi Germany and much of Western Europe. Even in the absence of malice, definition can have far-reaching effects, both good and bad. For instance, a change in the federal definition of "poverty" can increase or decrease by millions the number of individuals and households eligible for benefits such as Medicaid. Although the consequences of your writing won't approach those of the above examples, you'll nevertheless need to think about any possible ethical implications. Addressing the following questions will help you do this.

- Have I carefully evaluated all of the features of my definition? In clarifying what constitutes "excessive force" by the police, it would be unfair to include the reasonable means necessary to subdue a highly dangerous suspect.

- Have I slanted my definition to reflect some prejudice? Let's say a writer opposed to casino gambling is defining "gambling addicts." The paper should focus on those who spend an excessive amount of time in casinos, bet and often lose large sums of money, and in so doing neglect family, financial, and personal obligations. It would be unfair to include those who visit casinos occasionally and strictly limit their losses.

- Have I avoided unnecessary connotations that might be harmful? A definition of teenagers that overemphasized their swift changes in mood might be unfair, perhaps even harmful, since it may influence the reactions of readers.

■ Writing an Extended Definition

Planning and Drafting the Extended Definition

If you choose your own topic, pick an abstract term or one that is concrete but unfamiliar to your reader. Why, for instance, define *table* when the discussion would likely ease the reader into the Land of Nod? On the other hand, a paper explaining *computer virus* might well prove interesting and informative. Use one of the strategies on pages 14–20 to unearth promising topics. Then answer these questions about them:

Which topic holds the most promise? Why?

What purpose will guide my writing? To clarify a technical or specialized concept? To show what the term means to me? To persuade the reader to adopt my attitude toward it? To discuss some neglected facet of it?

For what audience should I write?

Here's a helpful process to follow as you think your definition through. First, select a clear example that illustrates what you wish to define: the United States could exemplify *democracy*. Then brainstorm to uncover major identifying characteristics. For democracy your list might include majority rule, free elections, a separately elected chief executive, and basic human rights. Next, test these characteristics against other legitimate examples and retain only the characteristics that apply. Britain is clearly a democracy but doesn't have a separately elected chief executive. Finally, test the unfolding definition against a clear counter-example, perhaps the People's Republic of China. If the definition fits the example, something is wrong.

Now evaluate what methods you might use to develop your definition. Each method has its own set of special strengths, as the following list shows:

Narration. Tracing the history of a new development or the changing meaning of a term

Description. Pointing out interesting or important features of a device, an event, or an individual

Process. Explaining what a device does or how it is used, how a procedure is carried out, or how a natural event takes place

Illustration. Tracing changes in meaning and defining abstract terms

Classification. Pointing out the different categories into which an item or an event can be grouped

Comparison. Distinguishing between an unfamiliar and a familiar item

Cause and effect. Explaining the origins and consequences of events, conditions, problems, and attitudes

Negation. Placing limitations on conditions and events and correcting popular misconceptions

Examine your topic in light of this listing and select the methods of development that seem most promising. Don't hesitate to use a method for some purpose not mentioned here. If you think that a comparison will help your reader understand some abstract term, use it.

Chart the methods of development you'll use, and then brainstorm each method in turn to gather the details that will inform the reader. When you've finished, look everything over, rearrange the details as necessary, add any new ones you think of, and prepare a revised chart. The example that follows is for a paper utilizing four methods of development.

Narration	**Classification**	**Process**	**Negation**
First supporting detail	First supporting detail	First supporting detail	First supporting detail
Second supporting detail	Second supporting detail	Second supporting detail	Second supporting detail

Definition papers can begin in various ways. If you're defining a term with no agreed-upon meaning (for example, *conservatism*), you might note some differing views of it and then state your own. If the term reflects some new social, political, economic, or technological development (such as the *wireless Internet*), you might mention the events that brought it into being. A colloquial or slang term often lends itself nicely to an attention-getting opener. A paper defining *chutzpah* might begin by illustrating the brash behavior of someone with this trait. Often an introduction includes a short definition, perhaps taken from a dictionary. If you do include a dictionary definition, use the full name of the dictionary (*Webster's New World Dictionary* says . . .). Several dictionary titles include the word *Webster,* and unless you use the full name your reader won't know which one you mean. Draw on a dictionary definition, however, only as a last resort.

In writing the body of the paper, present the methods of development in whatever order seems most appropriate. A paper defining *drag racing* might first describe the hectic scene as the cars line up for a race, then classify the different categories of vehicles, and finally explain the steps in a race. One defining *intellectual* might start by showing the differences between intellectuals and scholars, then name several prominent intellectuals and note how their insights have altered our thinking, and conclude by trying to explain why many Americans hold intellectuals in low regard.

Definition papers can end, as well as begin, in a number of ways. If you're defining some undesirable condition or event (such as *sudden infant death syndrome*), you might express hope for a speedy solution. If you're reporting on some new development (like *information superhighway*), you might predict its economic or social impact. Often, a summary of your main points is effective. Choose whichever type of ending best supports your main idea.

Revising the Extended Definition

Use the general guidelines in Chapter 3 and these specific questions as you revise your extended definition:

Are my purpose and audience clear and appropriate?
If I've used an essential definition, does it do what it should and avoid the common pitfalls?
Are the methods of development suitable for the topic?
Is the paper organized effectively?
Are there other factors or examples I need to consider?
Have I considered appropriate ethical issues?

EXAMPLE STUDENT ESSAY OF DEFINITION

The Food Chain

Michael Galayda

1   It is a truism that we must eat to stay alive and that all the plants and animals we dine on must do the same. How many of us, though, ever stop to consider whether or not any pattern underlies all the cross-dining that goes on? There is a pattern, and to understand it we must first familiarize our-

selves with the concept of a food chain. Such a chain can be defined as a hierarchy of organisms in a biological community, or ecosystem, with each member of the chain feeding on the one below it and in turn being fed upon by the one above it. To put the matter more simply, a food chain starts with a great quantity of plant stuffs which are eaten by a large number of very hungry diners. These diners are then eaten by a lesser number of other animals, which in turn fall prey to an even smaller number of creatures. With the passage of time, the uneaten organisms die and become part of the soil for the plant to grow in.

To illustrate, let's look for a moment at one particular   2
biological community, a marshy ecosystem, and a few events that might take place there. First, there are the marsh grasses, with millions of grasshoppers busily feeding upon them. When one grasshopper isn't looking, a shrew sneaks up and eats it. This process is repeated many times as the day wears on. Later, toward sunset, as the stuffed and inattentive shrew is crossing an open stretch of ground, a hawk swoops out of the sky and eats the rodent. The food chain is completed when the marsh hawk dies and its corpse fertilizes the marsh grasses.

This illustration is not meant to suggest that hawks eat   3
only shrews or shrews eat only grasshoppers; the cycle is much more complicated than that, involving what biologists call trophic levels--the different feeding groups in an ecosystem. For example, some creatures eat green plants and some eat meat. There are five major trophic levels. The beginning point for any food chain is green plants, known as producers, which absorb sunlight and through the process of photosynthesis turn carbon dioxide, water, and soil nutrients into food, especially carbohydrates, that animals can assimilate.

All of the other life forms subsist either directly or   4
indirectly on the producers. Animals that feed directly on green plants are the <u>herbivores</u>, called primary consumers. This group includes, among other creatures, most insects, most rodents, and hooved animals. The secondary consumers

are the carnivores and omnivores. The term <u>carnivore</u>, meaning an animal that eats only flesh, is more familiar than the term <u>omnivore</u>, which designates an animal that eats both green plants and flesh. Carnivores include such animals as lions, leopards, eagles, and hawks; whereas omnivores are represented by foxes, bears, humans, and so on.

5   The last feeding group in the food chain consists of the decomposers: bacteria and fungi. These microorganisms recycle the waste products of living animals and the remains of all dead things--plants, herbivores, omnivores, and carnivores alike--into fertilizers that plants, the producers, can use.

6   Obviously each trophic level must produce more energy than it transfers to the next higher level. With animals, a considerable part of this energy is lost through body heat. The muscles that pump the lungs, continually pushing air out of the body and sucking it back in, consume energy. The muscles in the limbs sweat out energy. All of the life-supporting systems of the organism use energy to keep it going. Everything from worms to people lives in accordance with this law of energy loss. As long as life's fires burn, energy is lost, never to be regained.

7   Throughout history we humans have tried to manipulate the food chain so as to provide ever-greater outputs of energy. On the one hand, we have tried, by whatever means we could employ, to rid our fields of harmful birds, insects, and rodents, and our animals of diseases and parasites. On the other, we have constantly striven to produce healthier and more productive strains of plants and animals. Often these attempts have been spectacularly successful. Sometimes, though, the results have proved disastrous, as with the insecticide DDT.

8   Farmers first began using DDT on a large scale in 1946, right after it had proved its effectiveness in tropical military operations in World War II. As expected, the product proved equally effective as an agricultural pesticide, but there were some unexpected and disastrous side effects. The

difficulties were caused by excessive DDT washing off crops, entering irrigation canals, and from there flowing to streams, rivers, and lakes. All living creatures in the path of the chemical were contaminated--worms, fish, ducks, indeed all forms of aquatic life. Contaminated worms poisoned songbirds, causing massive die-offs of birds, and many humans developed serious health problems from eating contaminated aquatic animals. Although Congress has severely restricted the use of DDT in this country, the whole episode stands as a warning of what can happen when humans manipulate the food chain.

As time continues and the population grows, efforts will   9
be made to further increase the food supply. Let us hope that in doing so we won't act in haste and create catastrophes of even greater magnitude.

DISCUSSION QUESTIONS

1. Identify the essay's essential definition and explain how it functions.
2. What is accomplished by the last three sentences in paragraph 1?
3. What method of development does the writer use in paragraph 2?
4. What methods of development are combined in paragraphs 3–5?
5. Cite three places in the essay where the writer uses brief definitions.

SUGGESTIONS FOR WRITING   *Write a properly focused extended definition using one of the following suggestions or one approved by your instructor. The term you define may be new, misused, or misunderstood or may have a disputed meaning. Develop the essay by any combination of writing strategies.*

1. Integrity
2. Campus gambling
3. Depression
4. School violence
5. Stress
6. Human genome
7. Extreme sports
8. Body piercing
9. Tae-Bo
10. Cybervandals
11. Campus security
12. Feminist
13. Hate crimes
14. Family values
15. Some term from your field
16. Senior citizen
17. Addiction
18. The Internet
19. The Christian Right
20. Rap music

The Critical Edge

Definitions are always social creations. The way various people and communities understand and use any word determines its definition. As a result, writers who use complex words such as *justice, love,* or *charisma* to convey a message may need to consult a number of sources to determine how others have used the words. With their findings of this research in mind, the writers can stake out their own meanings of those words.

If you were writing a paper defining *dance* for a humanities class, you would probably find several conflicting meanings of the term. Frank Thiess, writing in *The Dance as an Artwork,* defines dance as the use of the body for expressive gesture. But as you mull over that definition, you realize that it is both too broad and too narrow. While some forms of dance, such as ballet, feature expressive gesture, so does pantomime or even a shaken fist; and neither of these qualifies as dance. A square dance clearly qualifies, but does it represent expressive gesture? Susanne Langer, in *Philosophy in a New Key,* defines dance as "a play of Powers made visible," pointing to the way dancers seem to be moved by forces beyond themselves. You recognize that this definition may apply to religious dance forms, that dancers sometimes appear swept away by the music, and that you yourself have experienced a feeling of power when dancing. Nevertheless, upon reflection you decide that often it's the dancer's skill that attracts us, and rarely do we dance to reveal invisible powers. Finally, you discover that Francis Sparshott, in *The Theory of the Arts,* defines dance as a rhythmical, patterned motion that transforms people's sense of their own existence according to the dance they do. As you evaluate Sparshott's contention, you decide that it has considerable merit, although you aren't convinced that every dance transforms our sense of existence. When you think about the kinds of dance you know and the various definitions you have uncovered, you conclude that these writers, like the blind men who felt different parts of an elephant and tried to describe it, are each only partly correct. For your humanities paper, you decide to synthesize (see pages 72–73) the different definitions. You might explain that all dance involves a rhythmical, patterned movement of the body for its own sake. Sometimes such movement can transform our sense of existence, as in trance dances or even waltzes. Other dances, such as story ballets, use rhythmical movements as expressive gestures that tell stories or convey emotions. Still other dances may suggest the manifestation of powers beyond the dances themselves. You proceed to explain each of these features with details drawn both from your sources and from personal experience.

Carrying out this type of project requires you to look critically at the definitions of others. Do they accurately reflect the examples you know about? Do they describe examples that do not fit the definition? Are any parts of the definition questionable? Once you've answered these questions, you can then draw on the appropriate elements of the definitions to formulate your own. You might organize such a paper by developing each definition in a separate section, first presenting it in detail and then pointing out its strengths and weaknesses. In the final section, you could offer your own definition and support it with your reasoning and suitable examples.*

SUGGESTIONS FOR WRITING

1. Read the two essays on sexual harassment in the Reader (pages 566–71 and 571–76) as well as several others on this topic that you find in the library. Reflect on the different definitions of sexual harassment and then, drawing on your reading, offer your own definition.

2. Read "The Sweet Smell of Success . . ." (pages 540–42) and "I Have a Dream" (pages 576–79). Then write your own definition of success, taking into account the views expressed in these essays.

3. Do some reading about an abstract term like *bravery, democracy,* or *hatred* in at least three sources. Use the sources to develop your own definition of the term.

---

*Because you'll draw upon published sources, it is important to read the sections on card catalogs and periodical indexes in Chapter 20 and those on handling quotations and avoiding plagiarism in Chapter 21 before you start to write. As always, follow your instructor's guidelines for documenting sources.

chapter
12

Argument: Convincing Others

"What did you think of that movie?"

"Great!"

"What do you mean, *great*? I thought the acting was wooden and the story completely unbelievable."

"That's about what I'd expect from you. You wouldn't know a good movie if it walked up and bit you."

"Oh yeah? What makes you think you're such a great . . .?"

Argument or quarrel? Many people would ask, "What's the difference?" To them, the two terms convey the same meaning, both calling to mind two angry people, shouting, trading insults, and sometimes slugging it out. In writing, however, *argument* stands for something quite different: a paper, grounded on logical, structured evidence, that attempts to convince the reader to accept an opinion, take some action, or do both.

The ability to argue effectively will help you succeed both in class and on the job. A business instructor may ask students to defend a particular management style. A political science instructor may want you to support or oppose limiting the number of terms that members of a legislature can serve. A special education instructor may have students make a written case for increased funding for exceptional students. In the workplace, a computer programmer may argue that the company should change its account-keeping program, an automotive service manager call for new diagnostic equipment, and a union president make a case that a company's employees merit raises.

Arguments don't always involve conflicts. Some simply support a previously established decision or course of action, as when a department manager sends her boss a memo justifying some new procedure that she implemented. Others try to establish some common ground, just as you might do when you and your date weigh the pros and cons of two films and pick one to see.

When preparing to write an argument, you need to be aware that certain kinds of topics just aren't arguable. There's no point, for instance, in trying to tackle questions of personal preference or taste (Is red prettier than blue?). Such contests quickly turn into "it is," "it isn't" exchanges that establish nothing except the silliness of the contenders. Questions of simple fact (Was Eisenhower first elected President in 1952?) don't qualify either; one side has all the ammunition. Bickering will never settle these issues; reference books quickly will. We turn to argument when there is room for disagreement.

When you write an argument, you don't simply sit down and dash off your views as though they came prefabricated. Instead, argument represents an opportunity to think things through, to gradually, and often tentatively, come to some conclusions, and then, in stages, begin to draft your position with the support you have discovered. You should try to keep an open mind as you formulate and then express your views. And remember, you rarely start from scratch. Instead, you join a conversation where ideas and evidence have already been exchanged. As a result, you need to be thoughtful and informed.

The most successful arguments rest on a firm foundation of solid, logical support. In addition, many arguments include emotion because it can play an important part in swaying reader opinion. Furthermore, writers often make ethical appeals by projecting favorable images of themselves since readers form conclusions based on their judgments of the writer.

■ The Rational Appeal

In society, and certainly in professional circles, you are usually expected to reach your conclusions on the basis of good reasons and appropriate evidence. Reasons are the key points you'll use to defend your conclusions. If, for instance, you support the needle-exchange program for intravenous drug users, one reason might be the considerable reduction in AIDS-related deaths that could result. If you oppose the program, one reason may be the drug dependency that will continue.

To convince readers, your reasons must be substantiated by evidence. If you favor needle exchange, you could cite figures that project the number of deaths that will be prevented. If you're against the program, you might quote a respected authority who verifies that dependency will become entrenched.

When you appeal to reason in an argument, then, you present your reasons and evidence in such a way that if your readers are also reasonable they will likely agree with you, or at least see your position as plausible. That assumes, of course, that you and your readers start from some common ground about the principles you share and what you count as evidence. Evidence falls into several categories: established truths, opinions of authorities, primary source information, statistical findings, and personal experience. The strongest arguments usually combine several kinds of evidence.

Established Truths

These are facts that no one can seriously dispute. Here are some examples:

Historical fact: The First Amendment to the United States Constitution prohibits Congress from abridging freedom of the press.

Scientific fact: The layer of ozone in the earth's upper atmosphere protects us from the sun's harmful ultraviolet radiation.

Geographical fact: The western part of the United States has tremendous reserves of coal.

Established truths aren't arguable themselves but do provide strong backup for argumentative propositions. For example, citing the abundant coal supply in the western regions could support an argument that the United States should return to coal to supply its energy needs.

Some established truths, the result of careful observations and thinking over many years, basically amount to enlightened common sense. The notion that everyone possesses a unique combination of interests, abilities, and personality characteristics illustrates this kind of truth. Few people would seriously question it.

Opinions of Authorities

An authority is a recognized expert in some field. Authoritative opinions—the only kind to use—play a powerful role in winning readers over to your side. The views of metropolitan police chiefs and criminologists could support your position on ways to control urban crime. Researchers who have investigated the effects of air pollution could help you argue for stricter smog-control laws. Whatever your argument, don't settle for less than heavyweight authorities, and, when possible, indicate their credentials to your reader. This information makes their statements more persuasive. For example, "Ann Marie Forsythe, a certified public accountant and vice-president of North American operations for Touche Ross Accounting, believes that the President's tax cut proposal will actually result in a tax increase for most Americans." You should, of course, also cite the source of your information. Follow your instructor's guidelines.

The following paragraph, from an article arguing that extra-high-voltage electric transmission lines pose a health hazard, illustrates the use of authority:

> Robert Becker, a physician and director of the Orthopedic–Biophysics Laboratory at the Syracuse, New York, Veterans Administration Hospital–Upstate Medical Center, has been researching the effects of low-frequency electric fields (60 Hz) for fifteen years. Testifying at health and safety hearings for proposed lines in New York, he said that exposure to the fields can produce physiological and functional changes in humans—anything from increased irritability and fatigue to raised cholesterol levels, hypertension and ulcers. Studies of rats exposed to low-level electric fields showed tumor growths and abnormalities in development. Dr. Becker be-

lieves we are performing unauthorized medical experiments by exposing people to the electromagnetic fields surrounding the transmission lines.

Kelly Davis, "Health and High Voltage: 765 KV Lines"

Beware of biased opinions. The agribusiness executive who favors farm price supports or the labor leader who opposes any restrictions on picketing may be writing merely to guard old privileges or garner new ones. Unless the opinion can stand especially close scrutiny, don't put it in your paper; it will just weaken your case with perceptive readers.

Because authorities don't always see eye to eye, their views lack the finality of established truths. Furthermore, their opinions will convince only if the audience accepts the authority *as* authoritative. Although advertisers successfully present football stars as authorities on shaving cream and credit cards, most people would not accept their views on the safety of nuclear energy.

Primary Source Information

You'll need to support certain types of arguments with primary source information—documents or other materials produced by individuals directly involved with the issue or conclusions you reached by carrying out an investigation yourself. To argue whether the United States should have dropped the atom bomb on Japan to end World War II, for example, you would want to examine the autobiographies of those involved in making the decision and perhaps even the documents that prompted it. To take a position on the violence mentioned in some gangster rap, you would want to analyze the actual lyrics in a number of songs. To make a claim about the press coverage of the Persian Gulf War, you would want to read the newspaper and magazine accounts of correspondents who were on the scene. To convince readers to adopt your solution for the homeless problem, you might want to visit a homeless shelter or interview (in a safe place) some homeless people. This type of information can help you reach sound conclusions and build strong support for your position. Most college libraries contain a significant amount of primary source materials. Document the sources you use according to your instructor's guidelines.

Statistical Findings

Statistics—data showing how much, how many, or how often—can also buttress your argument. Most statistics come from books, magazines, newspapers, handbooks, encyclopedias, and reports, but you can use data from your own investigations as well. *Statistical Abstract of the United States* is a good source of authoritative statistics on many different topics.

Because statistics are often misused, many people distrust them, so any you offer must be reliable. First, make sure your sample isn't too small. Don't use a one-day traffic count to argue for a traffic light at a certain intersection. City Hall might counter by contending that the results are atypical. To make your case, you'd need to count traffic for perhaps two or three weeks. Take care not to push statistical claims too far. You may know that two-thirds of Tarrytown's factories pollute the air excessively, but don't argue that the same figures probably apply to your town. There's simply no carryover. Keep alert for biased statistics; they can cause as serious a credibility gap as biased opinions. Generally, recent data are better than old data, but either must come from a reliable source. Older information from the *New York Times* would probably be more accurate than current data from some publication that trades on sensationalism. Note how the following writer uses statistics in discussing America's aging population and its impact on the federal budget:

> . . . In 1955 defense spending and veterans benefits accounted for almost 70 percent of federal outlays. By 1995 their share was 19 percent. In the same period social security and Medicare (which didn't exist until 1965) went from 6 percent to 34 percent of the budget. Under present trends, their share would rise to 39 percent by 2005, projects the Congressional Budget Office. . . . Between 2010 and 2020, the older-than-65 population will rise by about a third; in the next decade, it will rise almost another third. Today, about one in eight Americans is older than 65; by 2030, the proportion is projected to be one in five. The older-than-85 population will rise even faster.
>
> Robert J. Samuelson, "Getting Serious"

Again, follow your instructor's guidelines when documenting your sources.

Personal Experience

Sometimes personal experience can deliver an argumentative message more forcefully than any other kind of evidence. Suppose that two years ago a speeder ran into your car and almost killed you. Today you're arguing for stiffer laws against speeding. Chances are you'll rely mainly on expert opinions and on statistics showing the number of people killed and injured each year in speeding accidents. However, describing the crash, the slow, pain-filled weeks in the hospital, and the months spent hobbling around on crutches may well provide the persuasive nudge that wins your reader over.

Often the experiences and observations of others, gathered from books, magazines, or interviews, can support your position. If you argue against chemical waste dumps, the personal stories of people who lived near them and suffered the consequences—filthy ooze in the basement, children with birth defects, family members who developed a rare form of cancer—can help sway your reader.

Despite its usefulness, personal experience generally reinforces but does not replace other kinds of evidence. Unless it has other support, readers may reject it as atypical or trivial.

Once you've selected the appropriate type(s) of evidence, certain standards govern the use of that evidence. Merely because a piece of information is in some way connected to your topic does not necessarily qualify it for inclusion in your paper. Readers won't be convinced that trains are dangerous merely because you were in a train wreck. In order to defend a position with suitable evidence, you need to understand and apply the following principles.

- The evidence must relate specifically to the position you are arguing. The fact that most Americans are immigrants or descendants of immigrants has no bearing on whether the country is admitting too many or too few immigrants. In order to make a case for or against some policy on immigration, the evidence would have to focus on its good or bad results.

- The evidence shouldn't lead you to reach an exaggerated conclusion. Studies showing that TV violence causes children to play more aggressively *do not* warrant the conclusion that it causes children to kill others.

Sometimes unwarranted conclusions result because a writer fails to take competing claims and evidence into consideration. To illustrate, evidence shows that children in Head Start programs do better than others during the first three years of school. Other evidence, however, shows that in later years these students do not do significantly better. Therefore, you shouldn't argue that Head Start ensures continuing success at all grade levels.

An argument, then, consists of a conclusion you want to support, your reasons for that conclusion, and the evidence that supports your reasons. But how are reasons and evidence fitted together? Rational appeals include three reasoning strategies: induction, deduction, and analogy.

Induction

Induction moves from separate bits of evidence to a general observation. Suppose that on a hot, humid summer day you go to the kitchen to eat some potato chips from a bag opened the day before. As you start to munch, you make these observations:

Chip 1: limp and stale
Chip 2: limp and stale
Chip 3: limp and stale
Chip 4: limp and stale
Chip 5: limp and stale

At this point, you decide that the rest of the chips are probably stale too, and you stop eating. Inductive reasoning has led you, stale chip by stale chip, to a conclusion about the whole bag.

But probability is not proof. To prove something by induction, we must check every bit of evidence, and often that's just not practical or possible. Nonetheless, induction has great value for the conduct of human affairs. Say a food company has test marketed a new spaghetti sauce and now wants to decide whether it should start selling the product nationwide. A poll of 1,200 users, representing a cross section of the market, indicates that 78 percent rate the sauce "excellent." As a result, the company decides to go ahead. Induction has led it to conclude that future customers will favor the sauce as much as past customers did. Polls that sample political preferences and other public attitudes also operate inductively.

You have several options for organizing an inductive argument. You might begin by posing some direct or indirect question in order to snare your reader's interest, or you might simply state the position you will argue. The body of the paper provides the supporting evidence. In the conclusion you could reaffirm your position or suggest the consequences of that position. The following short example illustrates inductive argument:

> Bologna is perhaps the most popular of all luncheon meats. Each day, thousands of individuals consume bologna sandwiches at noontime without ever considering the health consequences. Perhaps they should.
>
> The sodium content of bologna is excessively high. On the average, three ounces contain over 850 milligrams, three times as much as a person needs in a single day. In addition, bologna's characteristic flavor and reddish color are caused by sodium nitrite, which is used to prevent the growth of botulism-causing organisms. Unfortunately, sodium nitrite combines with amines, natural compounds already in most foods, to form nitrosamines, which have been proved to cause cancer in laboratory animals. Finally, from a nutrition standpoint, bologna is terrible. The fat content is around 28 percent, the water content ranges upward from 50 percent, and the meat includes very little protein.
>
> Health-conscious people, then, will choose better fare for lunch.
>
> Alison Russell

Deduction

Deduction is the reverse of induction. Instead of formulating a conclusion after considering pieces of evidence, you start with an observation that most people accept as true and then show how certain conclusions follow from that observation. For example, to convince a friend to study harder, you begin with the assumption that a profitable career requires a good education; proceed to argue that for a good education students must study diligently; and conclude that, as a result, your friend should spend more time with the books. Politicians who assert that we all want to act in ways beneficial to future generations, then point out how the policies they favor will ensure that outcome, argue deductively.

As with induction, you have several options when organizing a deductive argument. You might begin with the position you intend to prove, with a question that will be answered by the argument, or with a synopsis of the argument. The body of the paper works out the implications of your assumption. In the conclusion you could directly state (or restate, in different words) your position, suggest the consequences of adopting or not adopting that position, or pose a question that is easily answered after reading the argument. Here is a short example of deductive argument:

The recent spot-checks of our rooms by the dorm's head advisor are an unacceptable invasion of privacy. This practice should stop immediately.

The United States Constitution prohibits searches by police officers unless these officers have adequate reason. That is why the police need a search warrant before they can search any home. If they fail to obtain one, a case that ends up in court will likely be thrown out. Our right to privacy, then, can't be violated without due cause.

If the police can't search our homes without good reason, why should our head advisor spot-check our rooms for signs of wrongdoing?

Sammy Borchardt

A common and powerful form of deduction called *reductio ad absurdum* ("to reduce to absurdity") is used to attack an opponent's position by showing that its consequences are absurd if carried to their logical end. To counter the position that the government should impose no restrictions on the public's right to bear arms, you might point out that, carried to its logical extreme, such a policy would allow individuals to own bazookas, cannons, and nuclear bombs. This absurd result makes it clear that certain restrictions should apply to our right to bear arms. The question then becomes where we should draw the ownership line.

Often, a deductive argument is built around a categorical syllogism, a set of three statements that follow a fixed pattern to ensure sound reasoning. The first statement, called the *major premise,* names a category of things and says that all or none of them shares a certain characteristic. The *minor premise* notes that a thing or group of things belongs to that category. The *conclusion* states that the thing or group shares the characteristics of the category. Here are two examples:

Major premise:	All persons are mortal.
Minor premise:	Sue Davis is a person.
Conclusion:	Therefore, Sue Davis is mortal.

Major premise:	No dogs have feathers.
Minor premise:	Spot is a dog.
Conclusion:	Therefore, Spot does not have feathers.

Note that in each case both major and minor premises are true and the conclusion follows logically.

Syllogisms frequently appear in stripped-down form, with one of the premises or the conclusion omitted. The following example omits the major premise: "Because Wilma is a civil engineer, she has a strong background in mathematics." Obviously the missing major premise is as follows: "All civil engineers have strong backgrounds in mathematics."

Syllogistic Argument at Work　A syllogism can occur anywhere in an essay: in the introduction to set the stage for the evidence, at various places in the body, even in the conclusion in order to pull the argument together. Here is an example that uses a syllogism in the introduction:

> In 1966, when the Astrodome was completed in Houston, Texas, the managers concluded that it would be impossible to grow grass indoors. To solve their problem, they decided to install a rug-like synthetic playing surface that was fittingly called Astro-turf. In the ensuing years, many other sports facilities have installed synthetic turf. Unfortunately, this development has been accompanied by a sharp rise in the number and severity of injuries suffered by athletes--a rise clearly linked to the surface they play upon. <u>Obviously, anything that poses a threat to player safety is undesirable. Because synthetic turf does this, it is undesirable and should be replaced by grass</u>.
>
> Denny Witham

To support his position, the writer then notes that turf, unlike grass, often becomes excessively hot, tiring players and increasing their chances of injury; that seams can open up between sections of turf and lead to tripping and falling; that players can run faster on artificial turf and thus collide more violently; and that the extreme hardness of the turf leads to torn ligaments and tissues when players slam their toes into it.

Avoiding Misuse of Syllogisms　Two cautions are in order. *First,* make sure any syllogism you use follows the proper order. The writer of the following passage has ignored this caution:

> And that's not all. Newton has stated openly that he favors federally funded abortions for the poor. Just the other day, the American Socialist party took this same stand. In my book, Newton's position puts him squarely in the Socialist camp. I strongly urge anyone supporting this man's candidacy to reconsider. . . .

Restated in syllogistic form, the writer's argument goes like this:

> Socialists favor federally funded abortions for the poor.
> Newton favors federally funded abortions for the poor.
> Therefore, Newton is a Socialist.

The last two statements reverse the proper order, and as a result the syllogism proves nothing about Newton's politics: he may or may not be "in the Socialist camp."

Second, make sure the major premise of your syllogism is in fact true. Note this example:

> All conservatives are opposed to environmental protection.
> Mary is a conservative.
> Therefore, Mary is opposed to environmental protection.

But is every conservative an environmental Jack the Ripper? In some communities, political conservatives have led fights against air and water pollution, and most conservatives agree that at least some controls are worthwhile. Mary's sympathies, then, may well lie with those who want to heal, rather than hurt, the environment.

EXERCISE   *Which of these syllogisms is satisfactory, which have false major premises, and which is faulty because the last two statements reverse the proper order?*

1. All singers are happy people.
   Mary Harper is a singer.
   Therefore, Mary Harper is a happy person.

2. All cowards fear danger.
   "Chicken" Cacciatore is a coward.
   Therefore, "Chicken" Cacciatore fears danger.

3. All cats like meat.
   Towser likes meat.
   Therefore, Towser is a cat.

4. No salesperson would ever misrepresent a product to a customer.
   Sabrina is a salesperson.
   Therefore, Sabrina would never misrepresent a product to a customer.

Analogy in Argument

An analogy compares two unlike situations or things. Arguers often use analogies to contend that because two items share one or more likenesses, they are also alike in other ways. Familiar analogies assume that humans respond to chemicals as rats do and that success in school predicts success on the job. You have used analogy if you ever pressed your parents for more adult privileges, such as a later curfew, by arguing that you were like an adult in many ways.

Because its conclusions about one thing rest upon observations about some different thing, analogy is the weakest form of rational appeal. Analogies never prove anything. But they often help explain and show probability and therefore are quite persuasive.

For an analogy to be useful, it must feature significant similarities that bear directly on the issue. In addition, it must account for any significant differences between the two items. It is often helpful to test an analogy by listing the similarities and differences. Here's an effective analogy, used to back an argument that a liberal education is the best kind to help us cope successfully with life:

> Suppose it were perfectly certain that the life and fortune of every one of us would, one day or other, depend upon his winning or losing a game of chess. Don't you think that we should all consider it to be a primary duty to learn at least the names and the moves of the pieces; to have a notion of a gambit, and a keen eye for all the means of giving and getting out of check? Do you not think that we should look with a disapprobation amounting to scorn, upon the father who al-

lowed his son, or the state which allowed its members, to grow up without knowing a pawn from a knight?

Yet it is a very plain and elementary truth, that the life, the fortune, and the happiness of every one of us, and, more or less, of those who are connected with us, do depend upon our knowing something of the rules of a game infinitely more difficult and complicated than chess. It is a game which has been played for untold ages, every man and woman of us being one of the two players in a game of his or her own. The chessboard is the world, the pieces are the phenomena of the universe, the rules of the game are what we call the laws of Nature. The player on the other side is hidden from us. We know that his play is always fair, just, and patient. But also we know, to our cost, that he never overlooks a mistake, or makes the smallest allowance for ignorance. To the man who plays well, the highest stakes are paid, with that sort of overflowing generosity with which the strong shows delight in strength. And one who plays ill is checkmated—without haste, but without remorse. . . .

Well, what I mean by Education is learning the rules of this mighty game. In other words, education is the instruction of the intellect in the law of Nature, under which name I include not merely things and their forces, but men and their ways; and the fashioning of the affections and of the will into an earnest and loving desire to move in harmony with those laws. For me, education means neither more nor less than this. Anything which professes to call itself education must be tried by this standard, and if it fails to stand the test, I will not call it education, whatever may be the force of authority, or of numbers, upon the other side.

Thomas Henry Huxley, "A Liberal Education and Where to Find It"

To develop an argument by analogy, brainstorm the two items being compared for significant similarities and prepare a chart that matches them up. The greater the number and closeness of these similarities, the better the argument by analogy.

■ The Emotional Appeal

Although effective argument relies mainly on reason, an emotional appeal can lend powerful reinforcement. Indeed, emotion can win the hearts and the help of people who would otherwise passively accept a logical argument but take no action. Each Christmas, newspapers raise money for local charities by running stark case histories of destitute families. Organizations raise funds to fight famine by displaying brochures that feature skeletal, swollen-bellied children. Still other groups use emotion-charged stories and pictures to solicit support for environmental protection, to combat various diseases, and so on. Less benignly, advertisers use emotion to play upon our hopes, fears, and vanities in order to sell mouthwash, cars, clothes, and other products. Politicians paint themselves as God-fearing, honest toilers for the public good while lambasting their opponents as the uncaring tools of special interests. In evaluating or writing an argument, ask yourself whether the facts warrant the emotion. Is the condition of the destitute family truly cause for pity? Is any politician unwaveringly good, any other irredeemably bad?

The following passage, from a student argument favoring assisted suicide for the terminally ill, represents an appropriate use of emotion:

> When I visited Grandpa for the last time, he seemed imprint-
> ed on the hospital bed, a motionless, skeleton-like figure
> tethered by an array of tubes to the droning, beeping machine at
> his bedside. The eyes that had once sparkled with delight as he
> bounced grandchildren on his knee now stared blankly at the
> ceiling, seemingly ready to burst from their sockets. His
> mouth, frozen in an open grimace, emitted raspy, irregular
> noises as he fought to breathe. Spittle leaked from one corner
> of his mouth and dribbled onto the sheet. A ripe stench from the
> diaper around his middle hung about the bedside, masking the
> medicinal sickroom smells. As I stood by the bedside, my mind
> flashed back to the irrepressible man I once knew, and tears
> flooded my eyes. Bending forward, I planted a soft kiss on his
> forehead, whispered "I love you, Gramps," and walked slowly
> away.
>
> Dylan Brandt Chafin

To develop an effective emotional appeal, identify the stories, scenes, or events of the topic that arouse the strongest emotional response within you. Do some thinking about the types of words that will best convey the emotion you feel. Then write the section so that it builds to the kind of emotional conclusion that will help your argument.

■ The Ethical Appeal

Before logic can do its work, the audience must be willing to consider the argument. If a writer's tone offends the audience, perhaps by being arrogant or mean-spirited, the reasoning will fail to penetrate. But if the writer comes across as pleasant, fair-minded, and decent, gaining reader support is much easier. The image that the writer projects is called the *ethical appeal*.

If you write with a genuine concern for your topic, a commitment to the truth, and a sincere respect for others, you will probably come across reasonably well. When you finish writing, check to see that an occasional snide comment or bitter remark didn't slip unnoticed onto the page. In the following introductory paragraph, from an essay arguing that many universities violate the Constitution by imposing campus rules that restrict freedom of speech, the student establishes an appealing ethical image:

> Most of us would agree that educated people should not
> indulge in name-calling and stereotyping in their speaking and
> writing. To do so is an essential mark of irrational prejudice.

Nevertheless, such speaking and writing are protected by the
United States Constitution, which prohibits anyone from abridging freedom of expression. Today, many colleges and universities, in a well-meaning attempt to shield particular groups
from unwelcome or insensitive words, are subverting this prohibition. Former Supreme Court Justice William Brennan, noted for
his liberal views, has stated, "If there is a bedrock principle
underlying the First Amendment, it is that the government may
not prohibit the expression of an idea simply because society
finds the idea offensive or disagreeable."

Linda Kimrey

The writer opposes on constitutional grounds any attempts to ban the expression of two forms of "irrational prejudice." Nevertheless, she characterizes
these attempts as "well-meaning" and acknowledges that they are prompted by
worthy motives. As a result, she emerges as fair-minded, decent, sensitive, and
concerned, an image she maintains throughout the essay.

■ Ferreting Out Fallacies

Fallacies are lapses in logic that reflect upon your ability to think clearly, and
therefore they weaken your argument. The fallacies described below are among
the most common. Correct any you find in your own arguments, and call attention to those used by the opposition.

Hasty Generalization

Hasty generalization results when someone bases a conclusion on too little evidence. The student who tries to see an instructor during one of her office
hours, finds her out, and goes away muttering, "She's never there when she
should be" is guilty of hasty generalization. Perhaps the instructor was delayed
by another student, attended a special department meeting, or went home ill.
Even if she merely went shopping, that's not a good reason for saying she always
shirks her responsibility. Several more unsuccessful office visits would be
needed to make such a charge stick.

Non Sequitur

From the Latin "It does not follow," the *non sequitur* fallacy draws unwarranted
conclusions from seemingly ample evidence. Consider this example: "Bill's
been out almost every night for the last two weeks. Who is she?" These evening
excursions, however numerous, point to no particular conclusion. Bill may be
studying in the library, participating in campus organizations, taking night
classes, or walking. Of course, he *could* be charmed by a new date, but that conclusion requires other evidence.

Stereotyping

A person who commits this fallacy attaches one or more supposed characteristics to a group or one of its members. Typical stereotypes include "Latins make better lovers," "Blondes have more fun," and "Teenagers are lousy drivers." Stereotyping racial, religious, ethnic, or nationality groups can destroy an argument. The images are often malicious and always offensive to fair-minded readers.

Card Stacking

In card stacking, the writer presents only part of the available evidence on a topic, deliberately omitting essential information that would alter the picture considerably. For instance: "College students have a very easy life; they attend classes for only twelve to sixteen hours a week." This statement ignores the many hours that students must spend studying, doing homework and/or research, writing papers, and the like.

Either/Or Fallacy

The either/or fallacy asserts that only two choices exist when, in fact, several options are possible. A salesperson who wants you to buy snow tires may claim, "Either buy these tires or plan on getting stuck a lot this winter." But are you really that boxed in? You might drive only on main roads that are plowed immediately after every snowstorm. You could use public transportation when it snows. You could buy radial tires for year-round use. If very little snow falls, you might not need special tires at all.

Not all either/or statements are fallacies. The instructor who checks a student's record and then issues a warning, "Make at least a *C* on your final, or you'll fail the course," is not guilty of a reasoning error. No other alternatives exist. Most situations, however, offer more than two choices.

Begging the Question

A person who begs the question asserts the truth of some unproven statement. Here is an example: "Vitamin A is harmful to your health, and all bottles should carry a warning label. If enough of us write the Food and Drug Administration, we can get the labeling we need." But how do we know vitamin A does harm users? No evidence is offered. People lacking principles often use this fallacy to hit opponents below the belt: "We shouldn't allow a right-wing sympathizer like Mary Dailey to represent us in Congress." Despite a lack of suitable evidence, voters often accept such faulty logic and vote for the other candidate.

Circular Argument

Circular argument, a first cousin to begging the question, supports a position merely by restating it. "Pauline is a good manager because she runs the company effectively" says, in effect, that "something is because something is." Repetition replaces evidence.

Arguing off the Point

The writer who argues off the point, which is sometimes called "ignoring the question" or "a red herring," sidetracks an issue by introducing irrelevant information. To illustrate: "The Ford Thunderbolt is a much better value than the Honda Harmony. Anyway, far too many foreign cars are coming into the country. As a result, thousands of auto workers have lost their jobs and had to take lower-paying jobs. Many Americans strongly oppose this state of affairs." The writer sets out to convince us that the American car is superior in value but then abruptly shifts to the plight of downsized auto workers—a trend that has no bearing on the argument.

The Argument Ad Hominem

The Latin term "to the man" designates an argument that attacks an individual rather than that individual's opinions or qualifications. Note this example: "Sam Bernhard doesn't deserve promotion to personnel manager. His divorce was a disgrace, and he's always writing letters to the editor. The company should find someone more suitable." This attack completely skirts the real issue—whether Sam's job performance entitles him to the promotion. Unless his personal conduct has caused his work to suffer, it should not enter into the decision.

Appeal to the Crowd

An appeal of this sort arouses an emotional response by playing on the irrational fears and prejudices of the audience. Terms like *communists, fascists, bleeding hearts, right-winger, welfare chiselers,* and *law and order* are tossed about freely to sway the audience for or against something. Consider:

> The streets of our country are in turmoil. The universities are filled with students rebelling and rioting. Communists are seeking to destroy our country. Russia is threatening us with her might, and the public is in danger. Yes, danger from within and without. We need law and order. Yes, without law and order our nation cannot survive. Elect us, and we shall by law and order be respected among the nations of the world. Without law and order our republic shall fall.

Tapping the emotions of the crowd can sway large groups and win acceptance for positions that rational thinking would reject. Think what Adolf Hitler, the author of the foregoing excerpt, brought about in Germany.

Guilt by Association

This fallacy points out some similarity or connection between one person or group and another. It tags the first with the sins, real or imagined, of the second. The following excerpt from a letter protesting a speaker at a lecture series illustrates this technique:

> The next slated speaker, Dr. Sylvester Crampton, was for years a member of the Economic Information Committee. This foundation has very strong ties with other ultraright-wing groups, some of which have been labeled fascistic. When he speaks next Thursday, whose brand of Americanism will he be selling?

Post Hoc, ergo Propter Hoc

The Latin meaning, "after this, therefore because of this," refers to the fallacy of assuming that because one event follows another, the first caused the second. Such shoddy thinking underlies many popular superstitions ("If a black cat crosses your path, you'll have bad luck") and many connections that cannot be substantiated ("I always catch cold during spring break"). Sometimes one event does cause another: A sudden thunderclap might startle a person into dropping a dish. At other times, coincidence is the only connection. Careful thinking will usually lay far-fetched causal notions to rest.

Faulty Analogy

This is the error of assuming that two circumstances or things are similar in all important respects, when in fact they are not. Here's an example: Harvey Thompson, high school football coach, tells his players, "Vince Lombardi won two Super Bowls by insisting on perfect execution of plays and enforcing strict disciplinary measures. We're going to win the conference championship by following the same methods." Thompson assumes that because he and Lombardi are coaches, he can duplicate Lombardi's achievements by using Lombardi's methods. Several important differences, however, mark the two situations:

1. Lombardi had very talented players, obtained through the player draft or trades; Thompson can choose only from the students in his high school.

2. Lombardi's players were paid professionals who very likely were motivated, at least in part, by the financial rewards that came from winning the Super Bowl; Thompson's players are amateurs.

3. "Perfect execution of plays" is probably easier to attain on the professional level than in high school because of the players' experience.

4. Despite Lombardi's rigid disciplinary measures, very few of his players quit, perhaps because they were under contract. Could Thompson expect his players, essentially volunteers, to accept the kind of verbal and physical rigors Lombardi was famous for?

EXERCISE *Identify and explain the fallacies in the following examples. Remember that understanding the faulty reasoning is more important than merely naming the fallacy.*

1. After slicing a Golden Glow orange, Nancy discovers that it is rotten. "I'll never buy another Golden Glow product," she declares emphatically.

2. A campaigning politician states that unless the federal government appropriates funds to help people living in poverty, they will all starve.

3. A husband and wife see an X-rated movie called *Swinging Wives*. A week later the husband discovers that his wife, while supposedly attending an evening class, has been unfaithful to him. He blames the movie for her infidelity.

4. "Look at those two motorcycle riders trying to pick a fight. All those cycle bums are troublemakers."

5. "Bill really loves to eat. Some day he'll have a serious weight problem."

6. "Because no-fault divorce is responsible for today's skyrocketing divorce rate, it should be abolished."

7. "This is the best-looking picture in the exhibit; it's so much more attractive than the others."

8. "I do not support this school millage proposal. It's sponsored by James McAndrews, who's about the most ill-tempered, quarrelsome person I've ever met. I'd never favor anything he supports."

9. "My position on social and economic issues is easy to state. I am against wooly-brained do-gooders and big-spending, pie-in-the-sky social programs that have brought us to the brink of social disaster. I stand foursquare behind our free-enterprise system, which has given us a standard of living the whole world envies; and if elected, I will defend it with everything at my command."

10. "I am against the proposed ban on smoking in public places. As long as I don't inhale and I limit my habit to ten cigarettes a day, my health won't suffer."

11. "Life today has become far too frenzied and stressful. It was much better a century ago."

■ Ethical Issues

When writing an argument we attempt to alter attitudes or spark some action. These objectives create an ethical responsibility for both the quality and the possible consequences of our arguments. Suppose a doctor writing a nationally syndicated advice column recommends an over-the-counter herbal product but fails to disclose that it may cause a serious reaction in users who also take a certain prescription drug. Clearly this writer has acted irresponsibly and risks legal action if some readers suffer harm. Asking and answering the following questions will help you avoid any breach of ethics.

■ Have I carefully considered the issue I'm arguing and the stance I'm taking? Since you're trying to convince readers to adopt your views, you'll need either to make sure they are credible or make very clear that your position is tentative or dependent on certain conditions.

■ Am I fair to other positions on the issue? Careless or deliberate distortion of opposing views is ethically dishonest and could raise questions about your credibility.

■ Are my reasons and evidence legitimate? Presenting flawed reasons as if they were credible or falsifying evidence are attempts to deceive the reader.

■ Do I use fallacies or other types of faulty thinking to manipulate the reader unfairly?

■ What consequences could follow if readers adopt my position? Say a writer strongly opposes genetically modified foods and advocates disrupting installations that help develop them. If some who agree act on the recommendation, innocent people could be injured.

■ Writing an Argument

Planning and Drafting the Argument

Some instructors assign argumentative topics, and some leave the choice of topic to you. If you will be choosing, many options are available. Interesting issues—some local, some of broader importance—crowd our newspapers, magazines, and TV airways, vying for attention. Because several of them have probably piqued your interest, there's a good chance you won't have to rely on the strategies on pages 14–20 for help in choosing your topic.

Some students approach an argument with such strong attitudes that they ignore evidence that contradicts their thinking. Don't make this mistake. Instead, maintain an open mind as you research your issue, and then, after careful thought, choose the position you'll take. Often, several possible positions exist. On the question of whether handguns should be banned, the positions might include (1) banning the possession of handguns by anyone except law officers and military personnel, (2) eliminating all restrictions on handgun possession, (3) banning handguns for persons with criminal records or a history of mental problems, and (4) banning certain types of handguns, such as "Saturday night specials" and all-plastic handguns. Even if you don't shift your position, knowing the opposition's strengths allows you to counter or neutralize them, and thus enhance your argument. Suppose you favor the first position. You need to know that half of our state constitutions grant citizens the right to own guns. Unless you acknowledge and somehow counter this fact, your case will suffer and perhaps even founder.

As you investigate the various positions, ask and answer the following questions about each:

What kinds of evidence support it?
How substantial is the evidence?
If the evidence includes statistics and authoritative opinions, are they reliable?
    Flawed for some reason?
What are the objections to each position, and how can they be countered?
If the issue involves taking some action, what might be its consequences?

One effective technique for developing an argument is to write a dialogue between two or more people that explores the various sides of an issue without trying to arrive at any conclusion. The beginning of such a dialogue on a handgun ban might look like the following:

Doug: We need a ban on handguns. The United States has the highest
        murder rate in the industrialized world and the largest number
        of people owning guns. This is no coincidence. A handgun
        makes it easy to kill people.

Leslie: Are handguns really the cause of the high murder rate? Just
        owning a gun doesn't make someone kill. Most legitimate hand-
        gun owners will never use their guns on another human being.
        Many people kill with illegal weapons, including already banned
        semiautomatic weapons. So it isn't clear that a ban would actu-
        ally prevent murders.

> *Kyra:*   I don't think a ban on handguns would prevent a black market in guns. Drugs are illegal and seem to be readily available.
>
> *Doug:*   I didn't say a ban on handguns would prevent all murders.

Writing such a dialogue can help start your mental juices flowing, help you see the issue from many sides, and help you develop effective material for your paper.

As you contemplate your position and evidence, consider the purpose of your argument and how that might affect the strategies you choose to employ. Arguments are written for several purposes, each requiring a different approach. Some arguments *try to establish that something is a fact*—nursing is hard work, dormitories are poor study places, bologna is an unhealthy food. This type of paper usually relies on assorted evidence, perhaps some combination of statistics, authoritative opinion, and personal experience. To prove that nursing is quite demanding, you might narrate and describe some of the strenuous activities in a typical nursing day, cite hospital nursing supervisors who verify the rigors of the job, and perhaps give statistics on nurses who quit the profession because of stress.

Other arguments *defend or oppose some policy*—for example, whether first-year students should be allowed cars on campus or a company should begin drug-testing its employees—*or support or oppose some action or project,* such as the construction of a study lounge for students or the purchase of more microfilm readers for the library. In this type of paper, you usually discuss the need for the policy or action, how it can best be met, the cost or feasibility of your recommendation, and the benefits that will result. For instance, if you believe the library needs more microfilm readers, you might explain the problems that students currently experience (perhaps long lines, papers turned in late), cite the number of new microfilm readers you think necessary, indicate the cost of purchasing them, and then detail the improvements that will follow (perhaps shorter waiting time, fewer late papers).

Still other arguments *assert the greater value of someone or something,* as when a supervisor ranks one candidate for promotion ahead of another. To write this type of paper, generally you would indicate what you're trying to prove; identify the points on which the items will be evaluated; and then, using reasons along with details, examples, or statistics, demonstrate that one of the items has greater worth than the other. Often such an argument will be deductive as you show how your conclusions follow from agreed-upon values.

With an argument, as with any essay, purpose and audience are closely linked. For example, imagine that your audience is a group of readers who are neutral or opposed to your position; there's no point in preaching to the converted. Take a little time to analyze these readers so that you can tailor your arguments appropriately. Pose these questions as you proceed:

What are the readers' interests, expectations, and needs concerning this issue?
What evidence is most likely to convince them?
What objections and consequences would probably weigh most heavily with them?
How can I answer the objections?

To convince an audience of farmers that the federal school lunch program needs expanding, you might stress the added income they would gain. For nutritionists, you might note the health benefits that would result, and for school officials, the improved class performance of the students. Even though you are unlikely to convince everyone, it is best to adopt the attitude that most readers are willing to be convinced if your approach is appealing and your evidence is sound.

If you're arguing an emotionally charged issue such as gun control or federally funded abortions for the poor, you may want to use *Rogerian argument.* Named for psychologist Carl Rogers, this type of argument attempts to reduce the antagonism that people with opposing views might feel toward your position. To succeed, you must show that you understand and respect the opposing position as well as acknowledge its good points. You try to establish some common point of agreement, then show how the conclusion you want really follows from the reader's own values and assumptions without compromising your own. For example, if you want stricter gun-control laws, you might begin by acknowledging that the Constitution grants citizens the right to bear arms and that you believe anyone with legitimate uses for guns—hunters, target shooters, and the like—should have access to them. Moving on, you might point out that gun owners and those who agree with the Second Amendment support the proper, safe use of firearms and are concerned about firearm abuse. You might then possibly agree with the premise that people, rather than guns themselves, kill people, and for that reason, no one wants criminals to have guns. Finally, you might demonstrate that requiring computer background checks before issuing handgun permits would deprive criminals of such weapons while protecting the constitutional right to bear arms.

When you have a good grasp on your position, reasons, evidence, and the approach you want to take, you're ready to draft your paper. A typical introduction arouses the reader's interest and may also present the proposition—a special thesis statement that names the issue and indicates which position the writer will take. It can declare that something is a fact, support a policy, call for a certain action, or assert that something has greater value than something else. Here are examples:

1. Carron College does not provide adequate recreational facilities for its students. *(Declares something is fact.)*
2. Our company's policy of randomly testing employees for drug use has proved effective and should be continued. *(Supports policy.)*
3. Because the present building is overcrowded and unsafe, the people of Midville should vote funds for a new junior high school. *(Calls for action.)*
4. The new Ford Fire-Eater is superior to the Honda Harmony in performance and economy. *(Asserts value.)*

Any of the techniques on pages 211–13 can launch your paper. For example, in arguing for stepped-up AIDS education, you might jolt your reader by describing a dying victim. If your issue involves unfamiliar terms, you might define them up front; and if the essay will be long, you could preview its main points.

After the introduction comes the evidence, arranged in whatever order you think will work best. If one of your points is likely to arouse resistance, hold it back and begin by making points your reader can more easily accept. Argument always goes more smoothly if you first establish some common ground of agreement that recognizes the values of your reader. Where strong resistance is not a factor, you could begin or end with your most compelling piece of evidence.

The strategies discussed in earlier chapters can help you develop an argument. Some papers incorporate one strategy, while others rely on several. Let's see how you might combine several in an argument against legalized casino gambling. You might open with a brief *description* of the frantic way an all-too-typical gambling addict keeps pulling the lever of a slot machine, his eyes riveted on the spinning dials, his palms sweating, as flashing lights and wailing sirens announce winners at other machines. Next, you could offer a brief *definition* of gambling fever so that the writer and reader are on common ground, and, to show the dimensions of the problem, *classify* the groups of people who are especially addicted. Then, after detailing the negative *effects* of the addiction, you might end by *comparing* gambling addiction with drug addiction, noting that both provide a "high" and both kinds of addicts know their habits hurt them.

Whatever strategies you use, make sure that substantiating evidence is embedded within them. Strategies by themselves won't convince. To illustrate, in discussing the negative effects of gambling, you might cite statistics that show the extent and nature of the problem. An expert opinion might validate your classification of addicts. Or you might use personal experience to verify gambling's addictive effects.

Besides presenting evidence, use this part of your paper to refute, that is, to point out weaknesses or errors in the opposing position. You might try the following:

- *Point out any evidence that undermines that position.* If one viewpoint holds that drug testing violates cherished privacy rights, you might note that employers already monitor phone calls, check employees' desks, and violate privacy in other ways.

- *Identify faulty assumptions and indicate how they are faulty: they don't lead to the implied conclusion, they lack the effectiveness of an alternative, or they are false or unsupported.* If you oppose drug testing, you could point out problems in the assumption that such tests are necessary to protect the public. Closer supervision of work performance might be a better protection; after all, fatigue, stress, negligence, and alcohol abuse can all result in serious problems, and they are not detected by drug tests.

- *Identify problems in the logic of the argument.* Are there missing premises, faulty connections between reasons, or conclusions that don't follow from the premises? The argument against drug testing usually proceeds by asserting that privacy is a fundamental right, that drug testing violates privacy, and that therefore drug testing should not be allowed. There is a missing premise, however: that because privacy is a fundamental right it should never be violated. This premise is, in fact, at the heart of the dispute and therefore cannot be accepted as a reason to disallow drug testing.

You can place refutations throughout the body of the paper or group them together just ahead of the conclusion. Whatever you decide, don't adopt a gloating or sarcastic tone that will alienate a fair-minded reader. Resist the urge to engage in *straw man* tactics—calling attention to imaginary or trivial weaknesses of the opposing side so that you can demolish them. Shrewd readers easily spot such ploys. Finally, don't be afraid to concede secondary or insignificant points to the opposition. Arguments have two or more sides; you can't have all the ammunition on your side. (If you discover you must concede major points, however, consider switching sides.) Here is a sample refutation from a student paper:

> Not everyone agrees with workplace drug testing for employees in public transportation companies, electric utilities, nuclear power plants, and other industries involving public safety. Critics assert that such tests invade privacy and therefore violate one of our cherished freedoms. While the examination of one's urine does entail inspection of something private, such a test is a reasonable exception because it helps ensure public safety and calm public fears. Individuals have a right to be protected from the harm that could be caused by an employee who abuses drugs. An airline pilot's right to privacy should not supersede the security of hundreds of people who could be injured or killed in a drug-induced accident. Thus the individual's privacy should be tempered by concern for the community--a concern that benefits all of us.
>
> Annie Louise Griffith

Conclude in a manner that will sway the reader to your side. Depending on the argument, you might restate your position, summarize your main points, predict the consequences if your position does or doesn't prevail, or make an emotional appeal for support or action.

Revising the Argument

Review the guidelines in Chapter 3 and ponder these questions as you revise your argument paper:

- Is my topic controversial? Have I examined all of the main positions? Assessed the evidence supporting each one? Considered the objections to each position and how they can be countered? Weighed the consequences if a position involves taking some action?
- Is the paper aimed at the audience I want to reach? Have I tailored my argument to appeal to that audience?

Is my evidence sound, adequate, and appropriate to the argument? Are my authorities qualified? Have I established their expertise? Are they biased? Will my audience accept them as authorities? Do my statistics adequately support my position? Have I pushed my statistical claims too far?

If I've used analogy, are my points of comparison pertinent to the issue? Have I noted any significant differences between the items being compared?

If I've included an emotional appeal, does it center on those emotions most likely to sway the reader?

Have I made a conscious effort to present myself in a favorable light?

Is my proposition clearly evident and of the appropriate type—that is, one of fact, policy, action, or value? If the proposition takes the form of a syllogism, is it sound? If faulty, have I started with a faulty premise? Reversed the last two statements of the syllogism?

Is my evidence effectively structured? Have I adequately refuted opposing arguments? Developed my position with one or more writing strategies?

Is my argument free of fallacies?

Have I considered appropriate ethical issues?

EXAMPLE STUDENT ESSAY OF ARGUMENT

The Right to Bear Arms

Brenda Buehrle

1   The right of citizens to bear arms is often discussed in heated tones and emotional language. Political assassinations, for example, inevitably spark an outcry for control of firearms, as do workplace and school shootings. These appeals are frequently countered by jingles such as "When guns are outlawed, only outlaws will have guns." If we bypass such pleas and examine the issue from a constitutional perspective, we find that there is ample legal justification for the right to bear arms.

2   The first thing we should consider is the original intent of the Second Amendment to the United States Constitution, which states: "A well-regulated militia being necessary to the security of a free State, the right of the people to keep and bear arms shall not be infringed." When the purpose of any constitutional provision or law is in question, a good procedure is to return to the thoughts and words of those who originally framed it. For the Second Amendment, it is neces-

sary to examine the ideas of George Mason, the Virginia con-
stitutionalist. Mason wrote several specific safeguards of
individual rights into the Virginia constitution of 1776.
The Bill of Rights--that is, the first ten amendments added
to the United States Constitution in 1791--incorporates
many of Mason's safeguards. R. A. Rutland's edition of
Mason's papers reveals clearly that his conception of the
militia--that group empowered by law to bear arms--went far
beyond an organized group of men in uniform. During a debate
in Richmond on June 16, 1788, Mason rhetorically said, "I
ask, who are the militia?" and then answered his own question with these words: "They consist now of the whole people, except a few public officials." There can be little
doubt that George Mason, "father of the Bill of Rights,"
never intended to restrict the right to bear arms to a relatively few men in uniform. Therefore, the original concept
of the Second Amendment was that the militia consisted of
all people; and to ensure security of a free country, the
people had the right to keep and bear arms.

Early in this century Congress interpreted the militia   3
more narrowly than Mason did. On January 23, 1903, Congress
defined the militia as all able-bodied male citizens more
than eighteen and less than forty-five years of age. These
men were divided into two classes: the organized militia, to
be known as the National Guard of the State, Territory, or
District of Columbia, and the remainder, to be known as the
Reserve Militia. Thus, the Congress classified all males
within certain age limits, and not in the National Guard, as
members of the militia. These men would now seem to be the
"people to keep and bear arms" whose right to firearms
"shall not be infringed" under the Second Amendment. Furthermore, under the broad doctrine of equal rights, it would
appear that women should also be included, if they fall into
the proper age groups eligible for military service.

Since no provision of the United States Constitution   4
defines the rights of gun owners throughout the fifty
states, the state constitutions certainly would seem to be

the highest law in such cases, as provided in the Ninth and Tenth Amendments. These reserve to the states and the people all rights and powers not spelled out in the United States Constitution. Because the Second Amendment does not definitely state the rights of gun owners, the federal government cannot alter the rights that are defined in individual state constitutions. At least half of these state constitutions go beyond the Second Amendment by spelling out that the right to bear arms is an individual right for personal protection or defense of home and property and has nothing to do with a "well-regulated militia." Among these states are Arizona, Michigan, and Pennsylvania. For example, Arizona's constitution states, "The right of the individual citizen to bear arms in defense of himself or the State shall not be impaired. . . ." Michigan's says, "Every person has a right to keep and bear arms for the defense of himself and the State." Pennsylvania's constitution is emphatic: "The right of the citizens to bear arms in defense of themselves and the State shall not be questioned." Given such declarations, the states with these and similar provisions could not possibly prohibit ownership of handguns or any other arms.

5   It should be clear that the Second Amendment was not originally intended to apply only to militia but to the "whole people." In addition, Congress has indicated that the militia consists of all able-bodied young and middle-aged males (and now perhaps females also). Furthermore, 50 percent of the state constitutions define and protect the rights of individual gun owners. Is it not evident that the right to bear arms is rooted in solid legal precedent?

DISCUSSION QUESTIONS

1. Identify the writer's proposition. Is it one of fact, policy, action, or value?
2. What type of evidence does the writer use in her argument?
3. Reread the last two sentences in paragraph 3. Indicate why the phrasing "would now seem" and "it would appear" is appropriate here.
4. What type of conclusion does the writer use? Why is the question that ends it effective?

SUGGESTIONS FOR WRITING   *Write a properly focused argument on some topic you feel strongly about. Study all sides of the issue so you can argue effectively and appeal to a particular audience. Support your proposition with logical evidence. Here are some possibilities to consider if your instructor gives you a free choice:*

1. Compulsory composition classes in college
2. Requiring safety locks on firearm triggers
3. Prohibiting development of private property to save endangered species
4. Prayer in public schools
5. Some aspect of Native American or Hispanic affairs
6. Filters on Internet stations at public libraries
7. Legalizing marijuana for medical purposes
8. Gay rights
9. Coed military training
10. Bilingual instruction in schools
11. The effectiveness of some kind of alternative medicine (or some particular diet)
12. Coping with school violence
13. Taxpayer funding for professional athletic facilities
14. Use of animals for research
15. A campus, local, or state issue
16. A national missile defense system
17. Privatizing a small portion of social security payroll taxes
18. Publicly funded private school vouchers
19. U.S. participation in peace-keeping missions
20. Virtual universities where all classes are conducted on the Internet

A successful argument, by its very nature, requires critical thinking. This chapter has given you the tools you'll need to test the logic and evaluate the evidence offered in support of argumentative positions. After all, rarely will you generate an idea on your own and then argue for it. Instead, because most important issues have already been debated in print, you'll enter a discussion that's already underway. Sometimes it's on a topic of national interest, such as the desirability of politically correct speech and writing or the need to limit the number of terms elected officials can serve. At other times, the topic may be more localized: Should your state outlaw teacher strikes, your company install new equipment to control air pollution, or your college reduce its sports programs? On any of these issues you begin to form your own view as you read and assess the arguments of other writers.

A good way to take stock of conflicting opinions is to make a chart that summarizes key reasons and evidence on each side of the argument. Here is a segment of a chart that presents opposing viewpoints on whether industrial air pollution poses a significant threat of global warming:

Pro-threat side

Industrial emissions of carbon dioxide, methane, and chlorofluorocarbons let sun's rays in but keep heat from escaping.

                                    Andrew C. Revkin

Atmospheric levels of carbon dioxide are now 25 percent higher than in 1860. Computer models indicate a continuing rise will cause a temperature increase of 3–9°F.

                                    Revkin

No-threat side

Natural sources account for almost 50 percent of all carbon dioxide production.

                                    Dixy Lee Ray

The computer models are inaccurate, don't agree with each other, and fail to account for the warming effects of the oceans.

                                    H. E. Landsberg

Even though you investigate the reasons and evidence of others, deciding what position to take and how to support it—that is, establishing your place in the debate—is the real work of synthesis. (See pages 72–73.) Therefore, after evaluating your sources, outline the main points you want to make. You can then incorporate material that supports your argument. Let's say that you're considering the issue of global warming. After examining the differing viewpoints, you might conclude that although those who believe that global warming is occurring sometimes overstate their case, those who disagree tend to dismiss important scientific evidence. Because global warming is a serious possibility if not a certainty, you decide to argue for immediate environmental action. You might begin your paper by pointing out the dire consequences that will ensue if global warming becomes a reality, then offer evidence supporting this possibility, acknowledge and answer key opposing viewpoints, and finally offer your recommendations for averting a crisis.*

SUGGESTIONS FOR WRITING

1. Read several sources that explore the problem of spouse abuse and write an argument that incorporates the views expressed in the sources and suggests the extent of the problem.

2. Read several sources that take different positions on the question of whether the United States should be "the world's police officer" and write an argument that draws on those sources.

3. Read several sources that explore the issue of children suing parents or guardians for physical or sexual abuse and then write an argument that incorporates the views expressed in those sources.

*Before starting to write this type of paper, it is important to read the sections on card catalogs and periodical indexes in Chapter 20 and those on handling quotations and avoiding plagiarism in Chapter 21. As always, follow your instructor's guidelines for documenting sources.

chapter 13

Mixing
the Writing Strategies

■ Why and How to Mix Strategies

Writing strategies seldom occur in pure form. Writers nearly always mix them in assorted combinations for various purposes, not just in papers of definition and argument, as we've noted in Chapters 11 and 12, but also in papers of narration, description, process analysis, illustration, classification, comparison, and cause and effect. An essay that is primarily narration might contain descriptive passages or note an effect. A comparison might include illustrations or carry an implied argument. The purpose, audience, and occasion of the individual essay dictate the mixture, which can't be predetermined. Your best bet is to familiarize yourself with the individual strategies and use them as needed.

Assignments in other classes and on the job will also require you to mix the writing strategies. Your political science professor might ask for a paper that evaluates the advantages of a democratic state over a totalitarian one. You could open with contrasting *definitions* of the two forms of government and then, to make them more concrete, offer XYZ as an *illustration* of a typical democracy, ABC as a typical totalitarian state. After *describing* the key characteristics of each type, you might *compare* their social, economic, and religious effects on their citizens.

At work, a sales manager might have to write a year-end analysis that *compares* sales trends in the first and second quarters of the year, suggests the *causes* of any areas of weakness, and *classifies* the regions with superior potential in the upcoming year. And almost any employee could be asked to compose a report that *defines* and *illustrates* a problem, examines its *causes,* and *argues* for a particular solution.

When tackling a multistrategy writing assignment, break the project into separate stages. Determine first what you need to accomplish, then which strategies will serve your purpose, and finally how best to implement and organize them. It also helps to list all the strategies before you start reflecting on which ones to use. After a brief consideration of ethical issues, let's apply these guidelines to the writing of a problem/solution report and then to an evaluation report, two common projects that rely on a mix of writing strategies.

■ Ethical Issues

As you might guess, when your writing includes several strategies, the ethical issues pertinent to each apply. You may, however, need to consider additional issues with problem/solution and evaluation reports.

> *Problem/Solution* What consequences might follow if my recommendation is adopted? If a college with a grade inflation problem implements a policy that instructors grant no more than 10 percent A's and 20 percent B's, some students who do excellent work could be denied the grades they deserve.
>
> *Evaluation* Are my evaluation criteria fair? When evaluating the job performance of the clerks in a bookstore, it would seem unfair and discriminatory to include their ability to do heavy lifting if a number of them are older employees.

■ Problem/Solution Report

Suppose many students have experienced serious delays in getting to use the computers in your college library and you want to report the situation to the administration. Your goal is to eliminate the problem. After a little thought, you realize that you must first demonstrate that a problem exists and that it warrants action.

Before you can write such a report, you need to investigate the extent of the problem (does it really need solving?), look for its causes (possibly hidden causes), and determine the possible effects. Almost always these are your first steps before you decide on any solutions. Often you can find effective solutions by addressing the causes of the problem, but you might also explore new ways of improving the situation. You'll want to consider carefully whether your solution will work. After you review your options, you decide to use illustration and description to demonstrate the problem, and then to examine the effects and their causes.

Here's how you might proceed as you write the report. Your introduction states the problem. Then you portray a typical evening with long lines of students waiting to use the computers, while others mill around, grumble, and sometimes leave in disgust. Next, you take up effects, noting a number of occasions when both you and your friends have turned in late papers due to unavailable computers and received low grades. Turning to causes, you report your findings. Perhaps the library lacks funds to buy more computers. Perhaps it needs to expand its hours, or instructors need to schedule research projects at differing times.

The solution you recommend will, of course, depend on the cause(s). If extending the library hours would solve the problem, then purchasing more computers would just waste funds. The best solution may consist of several actions: buying a few computers, extending the library hours, and persuading instructors to stagger their research assignments. In some cases, you may have to explain the process of implementing your solution and/or defend (argue) its feasibility by showing that it will not have unacceptable consequences. For instance, in our computer example, you would need to consider the costs of keeping the library open and staffed for longer hours.

■ Evaluation Report

Imagine that your school has been experimenting with metal whiteboards that use markers instead of chalk. The administration has asked you to assess how effectively these boards serve student and instructor needs and to present your findings in an evaluation report.

As you think the project through, you realize that you first need to determine the key criteria for evaluation, which you decide are glare, the quality of the writing left by the markers, and the effectiveness of erasing. Because these boards compete with conventional blackboards, you decide that you need a comparison of the two that includes a description of the whiteboards and illustrations supporting your observations. You also decide that a discussion of the effects the boards have on students would be in order.

After drawing your conclusions, you begin your report by indicating why it's being written, providing a definition and description of the whiteboards, and noting the criteria you will use. Following this introduction, you discuss each criterion in turn, describing with illustrative examples how well the whiteboard measures up in comparison to conventional blackboards. You also note the effects of any shortcomings on students. In your conclusion, you argue that the irregular performance of the markers, the glare of the whiteboard surfaces, and the difficulty of erasing the marking frustrate students and make classes more difficult for instructors to conduct. You recommend that the college discontinue using whiteboards except in computer classrooms where chalk dust damages the units.

EXERCISE   *Suggest what combination of writing strategies you might use in each of the situations on page 190.*

1. The company you work for, school you attend, or club you belong to has a serious morale problem. You have been asked to evaluate its various dimensions, propose feasible solutions, and then make a recommendation to the appropriate person.

2. Your company, school, or club is about to purchase some specific type of new equipment. You have been asked to write a report examining the available brands and recommending one.

3. Your local newspaper has asked you to write about your college major or occupation and how you regard it. The article will help high school students decide whether this major or occupation would be appropriate for them.

4. Your general science instructor has asked you to study and report on some industrial chemical. The report must answer typical questions a layperson would likely ask about the chemical.

The margin notes on the following essay show the interplay of several writing strategies.

EXAMPLE ESSAY USING SEVERAL WRITING STRATEGIES

Bruce Jay Friedman

Eating Alone in Restaurants

Bruce Jay Friedman (born 1930) is a native of New York City and a 1951 graduate of the University of Missouri, where he majored in journalism. Between 1951 and 1953, he served in the U.S. Air Force and for the next decade was editorial director of a magazine management company. He now freelances. A versatile writer, Friedman has produced novels, plays, short stories, and nonfiction, earning critical acclaim as a humorist. In our selection, taken from The Lonely Guy's Book of Life *(1979), he offers the urban male who must dine out alone witty advice on coping with the situation.*

> Illustration in narrative form

1   Hunched over, trying to be as inconspicuous as possible, a solitary diner slips into a midtown Manhattan steakhouse. No sooner does he check his coat than the voice of the headwaiter comes booming across the restaurant.

2   "Alone again, eh?"

3   As all eyes are raised, the bartender, with enormous good cheer, chimes in: "That's because they all left him high and dry."

4   And then, just in case there is a customer in the restaurant who isn't yet aware of the situation, a waiter shouts out from the buffet table: "Well, we'll take care of him anyway, won't we fellas!"

Haw, haw, haw, and a lot of sly winks and pokes in the ribs.   5

Eating alone in a restaurant is one of the most terrifying experiences in America.   6

Sniffed at by headwaiters, an object of scorn and amusement to couples, the solitary diner is the unwanted and unloved child of Restaurant Row. No sooner does he make his appearance than he is whisked out of sight and seated at a thin sliver of a table with barely enough room on it for an hors d'oeuvre. Wedged between busboy stations, a hair's breadth from the men's room, there he sits, feet lodged in a railing as if he were in Pilgrim stocks, wondering where he went wrong in life.   7

| Definition |
| Description |
| Effect |

Rather than face this grim scenario, most Lonely Guys would prefer to nibble away at a tuna fish sandwich in the relative safety of their high-rise apartments.   8

What can be done to ease the pain of this not only starving but silent minority—to make dining alone in restaurants a rewarding experience? Absolutely nothing. But some small strategies *do* exist for making the experience bearable.   9

Before You Get There

Once the Lonely Guy has decided to dine alone at a restaurant, a sense of terror and foreboding will begin to build throughout the day. All the more reason for him to get there as quickly as possible so that the experience can soon be forgotten and he can resume his normal life. Clothing should be light and loose-fitting, especially around the neck—on the off chance of a fainting attack during the appetizer. It is best to dress modestly, avoiding both the funeral-director-style suit as well as the bold, eye-arresting costume of the gaucho. A single cocktail should suffice; little sympathy will be given to the Lonely Guy who tumbles in, stewed to the gills. (The fellow who stoops to putting morphine in his toes for courage does not belong in this discussion.) En route to the restaurant, it is best to play down dramatics, such as swinging the arms pluckily and humming the theme from *The Bridge on the River Kwai*.   10

| Step in process |

| Description |

Once You Arrive

The way your entrance comes off is of critical importance. Do not skulk in, slipping along the walls as if you are carrying some dirty little secret. There is no need, on the other hand, to fling your coat arrogantly at the hatcheck girl, slap the headwaiter across the cheeks with your gloves and demand to be seated immediately. Simply walk in with a brisk rubbing of the hands and approach the headwaiter. When asked how many are in your party, avoid cute responses such as "Jes lil ol' me." Tell him you are a party of one; the Lonely Guy who does not trust his voice can simply lift a finger. Do not launch into a story about how tired you are of taking out fashion models, night after night, and what a pleasure it is going to be to dine alone.   11

| Step in process |

| Comparison |

It is best to arrive with no reservation. Asked to set aside a table for one, the restaurant owner will suspect either a prank on the part of an ex-waiter, or a terrorist plot, in which case windows will be boarded up and the kitchen bomb-swept. An advantage of the "no reservation" approach is that you will appear to have just stepped off the plane from Des Moines, your first night in years away from Marge and the kids.   12

| Effect |

All eyes will be upon you when you make the promenade to your table. Stay as close as possible to the headwaiter, trying to match him step for step.   13

This will reduce your visibility and fool some diners into thinking you are a member of the staff. If you hear a generalized snickering throughout the restaurant, do not assume automatically that you are being laughed at. The other diners may all have just recalled an amusing moment in a Feydeau farce.

14   If your table is unsatisfactory, do not demand imperiously that one for eight people be cleared immediately so that you can dine in solitary grandeur. Glance around discreetly and see if there are other possibilities. The ideal table will allow you to keep your back to the wall so that you can see if anyone is laughing at you. Try to get one close to another couple so that if you lean over at a 45-degree angle it will appear that you are a swinging member of their group. Sitting opposite a mirror can be useful; after a drink or two, you will begin to feel that there are a few of you.

Definition

15   Once you have been seated, and it becomes clear to the staff that you are alone, there will follow The Single Most Heartbreaking Moment in Dining Out Alone—when the second setting is whisked away and yours is spread out a bit to make the table look busier. This will be done with great ceremony by the waiter—angered in advance at being tipped for only one dinner. At this point, you may be tempted to smack your forehead against the table and curse the fates that brought you to this desolate position in life. A wiser course is to grit your teeth, order a drink and use this opportunity to make contact with other Lonely Guys sprinkled around the room. A menu or a leafy stalk of celery can be used as a shield for peering out at them. Do not expect a hearty greeting or a cry of "huzzah" from these frightened and browbeaten people. Too much excitement may cause them to slump over, curtains. Smile gently and be content if you receive a pale wave of the hand in return. It is unfair to imply that you have come to help them throw off their chains.

Effect   16   When the headwaiter arrives to take your order, do not be bullied into ordering the last of the gazelle haunches unless you really want them. Thrilled to be offered anything at all, many Lonely Guys will say "Get them right out here" and wolf them down. Restaurants take unfair advantage of Lonely Guys, using them to get rid of anything from withered liver to old heels of roast beef. Order anything you like, although it is good to keep to the light and simple in case of a sudden attack of violent stomach cramps.

Some Proven Strategies

Step in process

17   Once the meal is under way, a certain pressure will begin to build as couples snuggle together, the women clucking sympathetically in your direction. Warmth and conviviality will pervade the room, none of it encompassing you. At this point, many Lonely Guys will keep their eyes riveted to the restaurant paintings of early Milan or bury themselves in a paperback anthology they have no wish to read.

Effect

18   Here are some ploys designed to confuse other diners and make them feel less sorry for you:

Classification

19   ■ After each bite of food, lift your head, smack your lips thoughtfully, swallow and make a notation in a pad. Diners will assume you are a restaurant critic.

20   ■ Between courses, pull out a walkie-talkie and whisper a message into it. This will lead everyone to believe you are part of a police stake-out team, about to bust the salad man as an international dope dealer.

21   ■ Pretend you are a foreigner. This is done by pointing to items on the menu with an alert smile and saying to the headwaiter: "Is good, no?"

22 ▪ When the main course arrives, brush the restaurant silverware off the table and pull some of your own out of a breastpocket. People will think you are a wealthy eccentric.

23 ▪ Keep glancing at the door, and make occasional trips to look out at the street, as if you are waiting for a beautiful woman. Half-way through the meal, shrug in a world-weary manner and begin to eat with gusto. The world is full of women! Why tolerate bad manners! Life is too short.

The Right Way

24   One other course is open to the Lonely Guy, an audacious one, full of perils, but all the more satisfying if you can bring it off. That is to take off your dark glasses, sit erectly, smile broadly at anyone who looks in your direction, wave off inferior wines, and begin to eat with heartiness and enormous confidence. As outrageous as the thought may be—enjoy your own company. Suddenly, titters and sly winks will tail off, the headwaiter's disdain will fade, and friction will build among couples who will turn out to be not as tightly cemented as they appear. The heads of other Lonely Guys will lift with hope as you become the attractive center of the room.

Step in process

Implied argument

25   If that doesn't work, you still have your fainting option.

The Critical Edge

Most writing, including writing that draws on outside sources, uses a mixture of several strategies. As you determine which strategies will help you present your ideas, you can draw upon the principles of critical thinking that you used with each individual strategy. You can, for example, evaluate the merits of different writers' opinions, look for evidence of bias, weigh the type and amount of support backing each assertion, and select the key points you'll include in your paper.

    Let's say that you're taking an elementary education class and are asked to write a paper evaluating the effectiveness of computers as an educational tool in elementary schools. Obviously, this assignment would require you to synthesize (see pages 72–73) the results of your outside reading and very likely the conclusions drawn from one or more observations of computer use in classrooms. It would, in short, require both secondary (that is, library) research and direct observations (see pages 417–23), a form of primary research.

    You might begin your paper by describing a typical morning's activities in a computer-equipped classroom, noting particularly the students' responses to computer instruction. Next, you might classify the different uses of computers in the classroom and provide a brief history of the movement toward this type of instruction. You could proceed by citing the positive effects of computers in the classroom, as noted by those who advocate their use, and then evaluate whether these claims are exaggerated or reflect any bias. For example, you might notice some kind of bias in a comparison of classrooms with and without computers and then suggest how to make such a comparison so as to eliminate the bias. Finally, you might also critically examine the objections of those who oppose computer instruction. After you've completed this research and analysis, you could argue for or against the use of computers as an educational tool. Even though this type of assignment may seem overwhelming, you can meet the challenge if you tackle the project one stage at a time.*

SUGGESTIONS FOR WRITING

1. Using a combination of strategies, write a paper that investigates and assesses the placement of students with mental and emotional handicaps in "mainstream" rather than special classes. You might visit classrooms with and without handicapped students.

2. Examine several sources that favor or oppose the use of community tax revenues to modernize an existing sports stadium or construct a new one. Then use a combination of strategies to write a paper that presents and assesses your findings.

3. Investigate in outside sources a current national phenomenon such as the upsurge in sensationalist television programming, the popularity of diet and exercising, or the increase in antismoking sentiment. Then use a combination of strategies to write a paper that presents and assesses these findings.

4. Identify what you consider a problem with some social policy of your college. Discuss this problem with several responsible students and also examine any available printed material that addresses this policy. Then use a combination of strategies to write a paper that identifies the problem and proposes a reasonable solution.

5. Identify what you consider a problem with some local, state, or national law. Perhaps you see it as unjust, unfairly applied, outdated, or the like. Examine several sources that discuss this law and then use a combination of strategies to write a paper that identifies the problem and proposes a reasonable solution.

*Because you'll need to consult library sources, it is important to read the sections on card catalogs and periodical indexes in Chapter 20 and those on handling quotations and avoiding plagiarism in Chapter 21 before you start to write. As always, follow your instructor's guidelines for documenting sources.

Paragraphs

Imagine the difficulty of reading a magazine article or book if you were faced with one solid block of text. How could you sort its ideas or know the best places to pause for thought? Paragraphs help guide readers through longer pieces of writing. Some break lengthy discussions of one idea into segments of different emphasis, thus providing rest stops for readers. Others consolidate several briefly developed ideas. Yet others begin or end pieces of writing or link major segments together. Most paragraphs, though, include a number of sentences that develop and clarify one idea. Throughout a piece of writing, paragraphs relate to one another and reflect a controlling purpose. To make paragraphs fit together smoothly, you can't just sit down and dash them off. Instead, you first need to reflect on the entire essay, then channel your thoughts toward its different segments. Often you'll have to revise your paragraphs after you've written a draft.

■ Characteristics of Effective Paragraphs

Unity

A paragraph with unity develops one, and only one, key controlling idea. To ensure unity, edit out any stray ideas that don't belong and fight the urge to take interesting but irrelevant side trips; they only create confusion about your destination.

The following paragraph *lacks unity:*

> The psychiatric nurse deals with dangerous mental patients, pathological personalities who may explode into violence at any moment. Sigmund Freud was one of the first doctors to study mental disorders. Today psychotherapy is a well-established medical discipline.

What exactly is this writer trying to say? We can't tell. Each sentence expresses a different, undeveloped idea:

1. Job of the psychiatric nurse
2. Freud's pioneering work in studying mental disorders
3. Present status of psychotherapy

In contrast, the following paragraph develops and clarifies only one central idea, the professional responsibilities of a psychiatric nurse:

> Psychiatric nurses deal with dangerous mental patients, pathological personalities who may explode into violence at any moment. For this reason, they must remain on guard at all times. When a patient displays anger or violence, they cannot respond in kind but must instead show tolerance and understanding. Furthermore, they must be able to recognize attempts at deception. Sometimes a mentally ill person, just prior to launching an attack, will act in a completely normal way in order to deceive the intended victim. The nurse must recognize this behavior and be alert for any possible assault.

> > Peggy Feltman

Because no unrelated ideas sidetrack the discussion of responsibilities, the paragraph has unity. To check your paragraphs for unity, ask yourself what each one aims to do and whether each sentence helps that aim.

EXERCISE   *After reading the next two paragraphs, answer the questions that follow.*

1.   The legend--in Africa--that all elephants over a large geographical area go to a common "graveyard" when they sense death is approaching led many hunters to treat them with special cruelty. Ivory hunters, believing the myth and trying to locate such graveyards, often intentionally wounded an elephant in the

hopes of following the suffering beast as it made its way to the place where it wanted to die. The idea was to wound the elephant seriously enough so that it thought it was going to die but not so seriously that it died in a very short time. All too often, the process resulted in a single elephant being shot or speared many times and relentlessly pursued until it either fell dead or was killed when it finally turned and charged its attackers. In any case, no wounded elephant ever led its pursuers to the mythical graveyard with its hoped-for booty of ivory tusks.

Kris Hurrell

2. When I was growing up, I spent many happy hours with my brothers and sisters playing jungle games in the woodlot behind our farm home. This lot, ten acres of dense-set poplars and birches standing amidst the blackened stumps of an old pine forest, provided a perfect setting for our jungle adventures. At times we acted out African versions of cowboys and Indians; at others we sought the long-lost treasures of fabled diamond mines. Often our adventures pitted Tarzan against tomb robbers and poachers. Besides serving as a playground, our woodlot furnished most of the fuel for the iron stoves in our kitchen and living room. I can still remember the backbreaking work of chopping up stumps and fallen trees and hauling them to the house. In the winter, the woodlot offered fine small-game hunting. In the summer, it provided a cool refuge from the heat that blistered the fields and farmhouse. Today, farm and woodlot are gone, swallowed up by a sprawling suburb. I wonder whether the children who live there ever want to play jungle games or regret that there's no place for them.

Student Unknown

1. Which of these paragraphs lacks unity? Refer to the paragraphs when answering.

2. How would you improve the paragraph that lacks unity?

The Topic Sentence

The topic sentence states the main idea of the paragraph. Think of the topic sentence as a rallying point, with all supporting sentences developing the idea it expresses. A good topic sentence helps you gauge what information belongs in a paragraph, thus ensuring unity. At the same time, it informs your reader about the point you're making.

Placement of the topic sentence varies from paragraph to paragraph, as the following examples show. As you read each, note how supporting information develops the topic sentence, which is italicized.

Topic Sentence Stated First   Many paragraphs open with the topic sentence. The writer reveals the central idea immediately and then builds from a solid base.

> *Starting about one million years ago, the fossil record shows an accelerating growth of the human brain.* It expanded at first at the rate of one cubic inch of additional gray matter every hundred thousand years; then the growth rate doubled; it doubled again; and finally it doubled once more. Five hundred thousand years ago the rate of growth hit its peak. At that time, the brain was expanding at the phenomenal rate of ten cubic inches every hundred thousand years. No other organ in the history of life is known to have grown as fast as this.
>
> Robert Jastrow, *Until the Sun Dies*

Topic Sentence Stated Last   In order to emphasize the support and build gradually to a conclusion, a topic sentence can end the paragraph. This position creates suspense as the reader anticipates the summarizing remark.

> An experience of my own comes handily to mind. Some years ago, when the Restaurant de la Pyramide in Vienne was without question one of the best half-dozen restaurants in the world, I visited it for the first time. After I had ordered my meal, the sommelier[wine steward] appeared to set before me a wine list of surpassing amplitude and excellence. But as I cast my eyes down this unbelievable offering of the world's most tantalizing wines, the sommelier bent over me and pointed out a wine of which I had never heard, ticketed at a price one-fifth that of its illustrious neighbors. "Monsieur," said the sommelier, "I would suggest this one. It is a local wine, a very good wine. It is not a great wine, but after all, monsieur, you are likely to pass this way only once. The great wines you will find everywhere; this wine you will find only in Vienne. I would like you to try it, while you have the opportunity." *This, to my mind, was true sophistication—on the part of M. Point for having the wine and on the part of the waiter for offering it.*
>
> Stephen White, "The New Sophistication: Defining the Terms"

Topic Sentence Stated First and Last   Some paragraphs lead with the main idea and then restate it, usually in different words, at the end. This technique allows the writer to repeat an especially important idea.

> *Everything is changing.* . . . This is a prediction I can make with absolute certainty. As human beings, we are constantly in a state of change. Our bodies change every day. Our attitudes are constantly evolving. Something that we swore by five years ago is now almost impossible for us to imagine ourselves believing. The clothes we wore a few years ago now look strange to us in old photographs. The things we take for granted as absolutes, impervious to change, are, in fact, constantly doing just that. Granite boulders become sand in time. Beaches erode and shape new shorelines. Our buildings become outdated and are replaced with mod-

ern structures that also will be torn down. Even those things which last thousands of years, such as the Pyramids and the Acropolis, also are changing. This simple insight is very important to grasp if you want to be a no-limit person, and are desirous of raising no-limit children. *Everything you feel, think, see, and touch is constantly changing.*

Wayne Dyer, *What Do You Really Want for Your Children?*

Topic Sentence Stated in the Middle   On occasion, the topic sentence falls between one set of sentences that provides background information and a follow-up set that develops the central idea. This arrangement allows the writer to shift the emphasis and at the same time preserve close ties between the two sets.

Over the centuries, China has often been the subject of Western fantasy. In their own way, a number of scholars, journalists, and other travelers have perpetuated this tradition in recent years, rushing to rediscover the country after its long period of isolation. Some of these visitors, justifiably impressed by the Communists' achievements in eliminating the exploitative aspects of pre-1949 mandarin society, propagated the view that the revolution, after its initial successes, had continued to "serve the people," and that China was "the wave of the future"—a compelling alternative to the disorder and materialism of contemporary Western society. Human rights were not at issue, they argued, because such Western concepts were inapplicable to China. *In the past year, however, the Chinese have begun to speak for themselves, and they are conveying quite a different picture.* In the view of many of its own people, China is a backward and repressive nation. "China is Asia's Gulag Archipelago," an elderly Chinese scholar said to me shortly after I had arrived in China last spring. "I was in Germany right after the Second World War, and I saw the horrors of Buchenwald and other concentration camps. In a way—in its destruction of the human spirit these past two decades—China has been even worse."

David Finkelstein, "When the Snow Thaws"

Topic Sentence Implied   Some paragraphs, particularly in narrative and descriptive writing, have no topic sentence. Rather, all sentences point toward a main idea that readers must grasp for themselves.

[Captain Robert Barclay] once went out at 5 in the morning to do a little grouse shooting. He walked at least 30 miles while he potted away, and then after dinner set out on a walk of 60 miles that he accomplished in 11 hours without a halt. Barclay did not sleep after this but went through the following day as if nothing had happened until the afternoon, when he walked 16 miles to a ball. He danced all night, and then in early morning walked home and spent a day partridge shooting. Finally he did get to bed—but only after a period of two nights and nearly three days had elapsed and he had walked 130 miles.

John Lovesey, "A Myth Is as Good as a Mile"

The details in this paragraph collectively suggest a clear central idea: that Barclay had incredible physical endurance. But writing effective paragraphs without topic sentences challenges even the best writers. Therefore, control most of your paragraphs with clearly expressed topic sentences.

EXERCISE   *Identify the topic sentences in each of the following paragraphs and explain how you arrived at your decisions. If the topic sentence is implied, state the central idea in your own words.*

1.   Last winter, while leafing through the Guinness Book of World Records, I came across an item stating that the tallest sunflower ever had been grown by G. E. Hocking, an Englishman. Fired by a competitive urge, I planted a half acre of sunflower seeds. That half acre is now a magnificent 22,000 square feet of green and gold flowers. From the elevated rear deck of my apartment, I can look out over the swaying mass of thick, hairy green stalks and see each stalk thrusting up through the darker heart-shaped leaves below and supporting an ever-bobbing imitation of the sun. In this dwarf forest, some of the flower heads measure almost a foot in diameter. Though almost all my plants are now blooming, none will top the sixteen feet, two inches reached by Hocking's plant. My tallest is just thirteen feet even, but I don't think that's too bad for the first attempt. Next year, however, will be another matter. I plan to have an automatic watering system to feed my babies.

                                                                Joseph Wheeler

2.   What my mother never told me was how fast time passes in adult life. I remember, when I was little, thinking I would live to be at least as old as my grandmother, who was dynamic even at ninety-two, the age at which she died. Now I see those ninety-two years hurtling by me. And my mother never told me how much fun sex could be, or what a discovery it is. Of course, I'm of an age when mothers really didn't tell you much about anything. My mother never told me the facts of life.

                                        Joyce Susskind, "Surprises in a Woman's Life"

3.   The UN's International Labor Organization estimates that as many as 200 million children go to work rather than to school. They are in developing nations throughout the world, making everything from clothing and shoes to handbags and carpets. These children are the dark side of the new global economy, an international underclass working 12 or more hours a day, six or seven days a week. In the carpet factories of India, they are often separated from their families for years at a time. In the leather-handbag plants of Thailand, children report being forced to ingest amphetamines just to keep up their strength. In the charcoal industry of Brazil, tens of thousands of children work in a soot-drenched hell producing ingredients for steel alloys used in the manufacture of American cars. Child laborers everywhere develop arthritis and carpal tunnel syndrome from the repetitive work; their respiratory systems are damaged by inhaling toxic chemicals in poorly ventilated workshops; their posture is permanently altered by the long hours in cramped conditions. And the products they make are in homes across America,

serving as a bitterly ironic commentary on what we consider a child's right to a carefree youth.

Mark Schapiro, "Children of a Lesser God"

4.   The first hostage to be brought off the plane was a dark little man with a bald head and a moustache so thick and black that it obliterated his mouth. Four of the masked terrorists were guarding him closely, each with a heavy rifle held ready for fire. When the group was about fifty feet from the plane, a second hostage, a young woman in flowered slacks and a red blouse, was brought out in clear view by a single terrorist, who held a pistol against the side of her head. Then the first four pushed the dark little man from them and instructed him to kneel on the pavement. They looked at him as they might an insect. But he sat there on his knees, seemingly as indifferent as if he had already taken leave of his body. The shots from the four rifles sounded faintly at the far end of the field where a group of horrified spectators watched the grisly proceedings.

Bradley Willis

EXERCISE   *Develop one of the ideas below into a topic sentence. Then write a unified paragraph that is built around it.*

1. The career (or job or profession) I want is _____.
2. The one quality most necessary in my chosen field is _____.
3. The most difficult aspect of my chosen field is _____.
4. One good example of the American tendency to waste is _____.
5. The best (or worst) thing about fast-food restaurants is _____.
6. The college course I find most useful (or interesting) is _____.
7. Concentration (or substitute your own term here) is an important part of a successful golf game (or substitute your own sport).
8. The one place where I feel most at home is _____.
9. More than anything else, owning a pet (or growing a garden) involves _____.

Write a topic sentence that would control a paragraph on each of the following:

1. Preparations for traveling away from home
2. Advantages of having your own room
3. Some landmark of the community in which you live
4. The price of long-distance telephone calls
5. Registering for college courses
6. A cherished memento or souvenir

7. High school graduation
8. New Year's resolutions

Adequate Development

Students often ask for guidelines on paragraph length: "Should I aim for fifty to sixty words? Seven to ten sentences? About one-fourth of a page?" The questions are natural, but the approach is wrong. Instead of targeting a particular length, ask yourself what the reader needs to know. Then supply enough information to make your point clearly. Developing a paragraph inadequately is like inviting guests to a party but failing to tell them when and where it will be held. Skimpy paragraphs force readers to fill in the gaps for themselves, a task that can both irritate and stump them. On the other hand, a paragraph stuffed with useless padding dilutes the main idea. In all cases, the reader, the information being presented, and the publication medium determine the proper amount of detail. A newspaper might feature short paragraphs including only key facts, whereas a scientific journal might have lengthy paragraphs that offer detailed development of facts.

The details you supply can include facts, figures, thoughts, observations, steps, lists, examples, and personal experiences. Individually, these bits of information may mean little, but added together they clearly illustrate your point. Keep in mind, however, that development isn't an end in itself but instead advances the purpose of the entire essay.

Here are two versions of a paragraph, the first inadequately developed:

Underdeveloped Paragraph

Most of the delegates to the Constitutional Convention of 1787 feared too much democracy. As a result, they drafted the Constitution as a document outlining a limited democracy. Indeed, some of the provisions were simply undemocratic. But despite reflecting the delegates' distrust of popular rule, the Constitution did provide a framework in which democracy could evolve.

Adequately Developed Paragraph

Most of the delegates to the Constitutional Convention of 1787 feared too much democracy. As a result, they drafted the Constitution as a document outlining a limited democracy. Indeed, some of the provisions were simply undemocratic: *universal suffrage was denied; voting qualifications were left to the states; and women, blacks, and persons without property were denied the federal franchise. Until the passage of the Seventeenth Amendment in 1913, senators were not popularly elected but were chosen by state legislators.* But despite reflecting the delegates' distrust of popular rule, the Constitution did provide a framework in which democracy could evolve.

The first paragraph lacks examples of undemocratic provisions, whereas the second one provides the needed information.

Readability also helps set paragraph length. Within a paper, paragraphs signal natural dividing places, allowing the reader to pause and absorb the material presented up to that point. Too little paragraphing overwhelms the reader with long blocks of material. Too much creates a choppy Dick-and-Jane effect that may seem simplistic, even irritating. To counter these problems, writers sometimes use several paragraphs for an idea that needs extended development, or they combine several short paragraphs into one.

EXERCISE

1. **Indicate where the ideas in this long block of material divide logically; explain your choices.**

> During the summer following graduation from high school, I could hardly wait to get to college and "be on my own." In my first weeks at State University, however, I found that independence can be tough and painful. I had expected raucous good times and a carefree collegiate life, the sort depicted in old beach movies and suggested by the selective memories of sentimental alumni. Instead, all I felt at first was the burden of increasing responsibilities and the loneliness of "a man without a country." I discovered that being independent of parents who kept at me to do my homework and expected me to accomplish certain household chores did not mean I was free to do as I pleased. On the contrary, living on my own meant that I had to perform for myself all the tasks that the family used to share. Studying became a full-time occupation rather than a nightly duty to be accomplished in an hour or two, and my college instructors made it clear that they would have little sympathy for negligence or even for my inability to do an assignment. But what was more troubling about my early college life than having to do laundry, prepare meals, and complete stacks of homework was the terrifying sense of being entirely alone. I was independent, no longer a part of the world that had seemed to confine me, but I soon realized that confinement had also meant security. I never liked the feeling that people were watching over me, but I knew that my family and friends were also watching out for me--and that's a good feeling to have. At the university no one seemed particularly to be watching, though professors constantly evaluated the quality of my work. I felt estranged from people in those first weeks of college life, desperately needing a confidant but fearful that the new and tenuous friendships I had made would be damaged if I were to confess my fears and problems. It was simply too early for me to feel a part of the uni-

versity. So there I was, independent in the fullest sense, and
thus "a man without a country."

2. **The following short, choppy units are inadequately developed. List some details you could use to expand one of them into a good paragraph.**

I like living in a small town because the people are so friendly. In addition, I can always get the latest gossip from the local busybody.

In a big city, people are afraid to get too friendly. Everything is very private, and nobody knows anything about anybody else.

3. **Scan the compositions you have written in other classes for paragraphs that are over- or underdeveloped. Revise any you find.**

Organization

An effective paragraph unfolds in a clear pattern of organization so that the reader can easily follow the flow of ideas. Usually when you write your first draft, your attempt to organize your thoughts will also organize your paragraphs. Writers do not ordinarily stop to decide on a strategy for each paragraph. But when you revise or are stuck, it's useful to understand the available choices. Here are some options:

1. The strategies discussed in Chapters 4–12
2. Order of climax

The choice you make depends upon your material and purpose in writing.

Writing Strategies   These include all of the following patterns:

Time sequence (narration)
Space sequence (description)
Process analysis
Illustration
Classification
Comparison
Cause and effect
Definition
Argument

Four example paragraphs follow. The first, organized by *time sequence,* traces the final years of the Model T Ford, concluding with a topic sentence that sums up its impact.

In 1917 the Model T lost much of its attraction when its exterior appearance was drastically altered. The famous flat-sided brass radiator disappeared and the new style featured (in the words of the catalogue) "The stream-lined hood, large radiator and enclosed fan, crown fenders, black finish and nickel trimmings" ("crown fenders" would be described in England as domed mudguards). Electric lighting and starting followed in 1919, and the model then continued with little alteration until 1927, when it was finally withdrawn. After a considerable pause it was replaced by the Model A, a very conventional machine with wire wheels, three-speed gearbox and four-wheel brakes (the "T" had never made this concession to progress and continued to the last with two minute brake drums on the back wheels only). While it was in preparation, others had taken the lead and the "A" never replaced the immortal "T" in the public fancy. Indeed, the "Tin Lizzy" or "Flivver" had become almost a national characteristic, and at the end of its eighteen years in production the total number sold was fifteen million.

Cecil Clutton and John Stanford, *The Vintage Motor-Car*

The next paragraph, organized by *space sequence,* describes a ceramic elf, starting from the bottom and working up to the top. Other common spatial arrangements include top to bottom, left to right, right to left, nearby to far away, far away to nearby, clockwise, and counterclockwise.

The ceramic elf in our family room is quite a character. His reddish-brown slippers, which hang over the mantel shelf, taper to a slender point. Pudgy, yellow-stockinged legs disappear into a wrinkled tunic-style, olive-green jacket, gathered at the waist with a thick, brown belt that fits snugly around his roly-poly belly. His short, meaty arms hang comfortably, one hand resting on the knapsack at his side and the other clutching the bowl of an old black pipe. An unkempt, snow-white beard, dotted by occasional snarls, trails patriarch-fashion from his lower lip to his belt line. A button nose capped with a smudge of gold dust, mischievous black eyes, and an unruly snatch of hair peeking out from under his burnt-orange stocking cap complete Bartholomew's appearance.

Maria Sanchez

Although descriptive paragraphs, like those developed by narration, often lack topic sentences, our example leads off with the central idea.

Here is a paragraph showing *process* development.

Making beer nuts is a quick, simple procedure that provides a delicious evening snack. You'll need six cups of raw peanuts, three cups of sugar, and one-and-one-half cups of water. To begin, combine the sugar and water in a two-quart saucepan and stir to dissolve the sugar. Next, add the peanuts and stir again until all of the peanuts are covered by the sugar-water solution. Leave the pan, uncovered, on a burner set at medium-high heat for ten to twelve minutes, until the sugar crystallizes and coats the peanuts thoroughly. Stay at the stove during the heat-

```
ing process and stir the mixture every two or three minutes to
ensure even coating of the nuts. When the peanuts are thoroughly
coated, pour them onto an ungreased cookie sheet and bake at 350
degrees for about thirty minutes, stirring and lightly salting
at ten-minute intervals. Serve your beer nuts fresh out of the
oven or eat them at room temperature.
```
Kimberlee Walters

Again, the topic sentence comes first.

The final example illustrates development by *comparison* and also proceeds from an opening topic sentence.

> There is an essential difference between a news story, as understood by a newspaperman or a wire-service writer, and the newsmagazine story. The chief purpose of the conventional news story is to tell what happened. It starts with the most important information and continues into increasingly inconsequential details, not only because the reader may not read beyond the first paragraph but because an editor working on galley proofs a few minutes before press time likes to be able to cut freely from the end of the story. A newsmagazine is very different. It is written to be read consecutively from beginning to end, and each of its stories is designed, following the critical theories of Edgar Allan Poe, to create one emotional effect. The news, what happened that week, may be told in the beginning, the middle, or the end; for the purpose is not to throw information at the reader but to seduce him into reading the whole story, and into accepting the dramatic (and often political) point being made.

Otto Friedrich, "There Are 00 Trees in Russia"

Order of Climax   Climactic order creates a crescendo pattern, starting with the least emphatic detail and progressing to the most emphatic. The topic sentence can begin or end the paragraph, or it can remain implied. This pattern holds the reader's interest by building suspense. On occasion, writers reverse the order, landing the heaviest punch first; but such paragraphs can trail off, leaving the reader dissatisfied.

Here is a paragraph illustrating climactic order:

```
The speaking errors I hear affect me to different degrees.
I'm so conditioned to hearing "It don't make any difference" and
"There's three ways to solve the problem" that I've almost
accepted such usage. However, errors such as "Just between you
and I, Arnold loves Edna" and "I'm going back to my room to lay
down" still offend my sensibility. When hearing them, I usually
just chuckle to myself and walk away. The "Twin I's"--irreve-
lant and irregardless--are another matter. More than any other
errors, they really grate on my ear. Whenever I hear "that may
be true, but it's irrevelant" or "Irregardless of how much I
study, I still get C's," I have the urge to correct the speaker.
```

It's really surprising that more people don't clean up their
language act.

Valerie Sonntag

> **EXERCISE** *From a magazine or newspaper article, select four paragraphs that illus-*
> *trate different patterns of organization. Identify the topic sentence in*
> *each case; or if it is implied, state it in your own words. Point out the*
> *organization of each paragraph.*

Coherence

Coherent writing flows smoothly and easily from one sentence and paragraph
to another, clarifying the relationships among ideas and thus allowing the
reader to grasp connections. Because incoherent writing fails to do this, it confuses, and sometimes even irritates, the reader.

Here is a paragraph that lacks coherence:

> I woke up late. I had been so tired the night before that I had forgotten to set
> the alarm. All I could think of was the report I had stayed up until 3 A.M. typing,
> and how I could possibly get twenty copies ready for next morning's 9 o'clock sales
> meeting. I panicked and ran out the door. My bus was so crowded I had to stand.
> Jumping off the bus, I raced back up the street. The meeting was already under
> way. Mr. Jackson gestured for me to come into the conference room. Inserting the
> first page of the report into the copier, I set the dial for twenty copies and pressed
> the print button. The sign started flashing CALL KEY OPERATOR. The machine
> was out of order. Mr. Jackson asked whether the report was ready. I pointed to the
> flashing red words. Mr. Jackson nodded grimly without saying anything. He left me
> alone with the broken machine.

This paragraph has some degree of unity: most of its sentences relate to the
writer's disastrous experience with the sales report. Unfortunately, though, its
many gaps in logic create rather than answer questions, and in very bumpy
prose, at that. Note the gap between the third and fourth sentences. Did the
writer jump out of bed and rush right out the door? Of course not, but the
reader has no real clue to the actual sequence of events. Another gap occurs between the next two sentences, leaving the reader to wonder why the writer had
to race up the street upon leaving the bus. And who is Mr. Jackson? The paragraph never tells, but the reader will want to know.

Now read this rewritten version, additions italicized:

> I woke up late *because* I had been so tired the night before that I had forgot-
> ten to set the alarm. All I could think of was the report I had stayed up until 3 A.M.
> typing, and how I could possibly get twenty copies ready for next morning's
> 9 o'clock sales meeting. *When I realized it was 8:30,* I panicked. *Jumping out of bed, I*
> *threw on some clothes, grabbed the report,* and ran out the door. My bus was so crowded
> I had to stand *and could not see out the window. Two blocks beyond my stop, I realized I*
> *should have gotten off. "Stop!" I cried and,* jumping off the bus, raced back up the
> street. *When I reached the office, it was 9:15, and* the meeting was already underway.
> Mr. Jackson, *the sales manager,* saw me and gestured for me to come into the confer-

ence room. *"One moment,"* *I said as calmly as I could and hurried to the copier.* Inserting the first page of the report into it, I set the dial for twenty copies and pressed the print button. *Immediately,* the sign started flashing CALL KEY OPERATOR. The machine was out of order. *The next thing I knew,* Mr. Jackson *was at my side* asking whether the report was ready. I pointed to the flashing red words, *and* Mr. Jackson nodded grimly without saying anything. *Turning on his heel,* he *walked away and* left me alone with the broken machine.

As this example shows, correcting an incoherent paragraph may call for anything from a single word to a whole sentence or more.

Coherence derives from a sufficient supply of supporting details and your firm sense of the way your ideas go together. If you brainstorm your topic thoroughly and think carefully about the relationships between sentences, incoherence isn't likely to haunt your paragraphs.

As you write, and especially when you revise, signal connections to the reader by using *transitions*—devices that link sentences to one another. These are the most common transitional devices:

1. Connecting words and phrases
2. Repeated key words
3. Pronouns and demonstrative adjectives
4. Parallelism

You can use them to furnish links both within and between paragraphs.

Connecting Words and Phrases   These connectors clarify relationships between sentences. The following list groups them according to function:

Showing similarity: in like manner, likewise, moreover, similarly

Showing contrast: at the same time, but, even so, however, in contrast, instead, nevertheless, still, on the contrary, on the other hand, otherwise, yet

Showing results or effects: accordingly, as a result, because, consequently, hence, since, therefore, thus

Adding ideas together: also, besides, first (second, third . . .), furthermore, in addition, in the first place, likewise, moreover, similarly, too

Drawing conclusions: as a result, finally, in brief, in conclusion, in short, to summarize

Pointing out examples: for example, for instance, to illustrate

Showing emphasis and clarity: above all, after all, again, as a matter of fact, besides, in fact, in other words, indeed, nonetheless, that is

Indicating time: at times, after, afterward, from then on, immediately, later, meanwhile, next, now, once, previously, subsequently, then, until, while

Conceding a point: granted that, of course, to be sure, admittedly

Don't overload your paper with connectors. In well-planned prose, your message flows clearly with only an occasional assist from them.

In the following excerpt, which clarifies the difference between workers and workaholics, the connectors are italicized:

My efforts to define workaholism and to distinguish workaholics from other hard workers proved difficult. *While* workaholics do work hard, not all hard workers are workaholics. Moonlighters, *for example,* may work 16 hours a day to make ends meet, but most of them will stop working when their financial circumstances permit. Accountants, *too,* seem to work non-stop, but many slow down after the April 15 tax deadline. Workaholics, *on the other hand,* always devote more time and thought to their work than their situation demands. Even in the absence of deadlines to meet, mortgages to pay, promotions to earn, or bosses to please, workaholics still work hard. What sets them apart is their attitude toward work, not the number of hours they work.

Marilyn Machlowitz, "Workaholism: What's Wrong with
Being Married to Your Work?"

DISCUSSION QUESTIONS

1. What ideas do each of the italicized words and phrases connect?
2. What relationship does each show?

Repeated Key Words   Repeating key words, especially those that help convey a paragraph's central idea, can smooth the reader's path. The words may appear in different forms, but their presence keeps the main issues before the reader. In the following paragraph, the repetition of *majority, minority,* and *will* aids coherence, as does the more limited repetition of *government* and *interests.*

Whatever fine-spun theories we may devise to resolve or obscure the difficulty, there is no use blinking the fact that the *will* of the *majority* is not the same thing as the *will* of all. *Majority* rule works well only so long as the *minority* is *willing* to accept the *will* of the *majority* as the *will* of the *nation* and let it go at that. Generally speaking, the *minority* will be *willing* to let it go at that so long as it feels that its essential *interests* and rights are not fundamentally different from those of the current *majority,* and so long as it can, in any case, look forward with confidence to mustering enough votes within four or six years to become itself the *majority* and so redress the balance. But if it comes to pass that a large *minority* feels that it has no such chance, that it is a fixed and permanent *minority* and that another group or class with rights and *interests* fundamentally hostile to its own is in permanent control, then *government* by *majority* vote ceases in any sense to be *government* by the *will* of the people for the good of all, and becomes *government* by the *will* of some of the people for their own *interests* at the expense of the others.

Carl Becker, *Freedom and Responsibility in the American Way of Life*

EXERCISE   *Write a paragraph using one of the following sentences as your topic sentence. Insert the missing key word and then repeat it in your paragraph to help link your sentences together.*

1. _____ is my favorite relative.
2. I wish I had (a, an, some, more) _____.
3. _____ changed my life.
4. _____ is more trouble that it's worth.
5. A visit to _____ always depresses me.
6. Eating _____ is a challenge.
7. I admire _____.

Pronouns and Demonstrative Adjectives   Pronouns stand in for nouns that appear earlier in the sentence or in previous sentences. Mixing pronouns and their nouns throughout the paragraph prevents monotony and promotes clarity. We have italicized the pronouns in the following excerpt from an article about the writer's first visit to a gambling casino.

> There are three of *us* on this trip, two veterans of Atlantic City and *I*, a neophyte, all celebrating the fact that *we* have recently become grandmothers. One of *my* companions is the canny shopper in *our* crowd; as a bargain-hunter *she* knows the ways of the world. *I* have followed *her* through discount shops and outlet stores from Manhattan's Lower East Side to the Secaucus, New Jersey, malls. . . . Without saying a word, *she* hands *me* a plastic container of the kind that might hold two pounds of potato salad, and takes one *herself*. *She* drags *me* off to the change booth, where *she* exchanges bills for tubes of silver, careful not to let *me* see just how much. *I* do the same. Then *she* leads *me* to a clattering corner, where a neon sign winks on and off, *Quartermania*. "Let's try to find a couple of machines that only have handles," *she* says. . . .
>
> Eileen Herbert Jordan, "My Affair with the One-Armed Bandit"

All the pronouns in the excerpt refer to the writer, her bargain-hunting friend, or the whole group.

Four demonstrative adjectives—*this, that, these,* and *those*—also help hook ideas together. Demonstratives are special adjectives that identify or point out nouns rather than describe them. Here is an example from the Declaration of Independence:

> We hold *these* truths to be self-evident, that all men are created equal, that they are endowed by their Creator with certain unalienable Rights, that among *these* are Life, Liberty, and the pursuit of Happiness. That to secure *these* rights, Governments are instituted among Men, deriving their just powers from the consent of the governed. That whenever any Form of Government becomes destructive of *these* ends, it is the Right of the People to alter or to abolish it, and to institute new Government, laying its foundation on such principles and organizing its power in such form, as to them shall seem most likely to effect their Safety and Happiness.

EXERCISE   *In a magazine, newspaper, textbook, or some other written source, find two paragraphs that use pronouns and demonstrative adjectives to increase coherence. Copy the paragraphs, underline the pronouns and demonstrative adjectives, and explain what each refers to.*

Parallelism   Parallelism uses repetition of grammatical form to express a series of equivalent ideas. Besides giving continuity, the repetition adds rhythm and balance to the writing. Note how the following italicized constructions tie together the unfolding definition of poverty:

> *Poverty is staying* up all night on cold nights to watch the fire, knowing one spark on the newspaper covering the walls means your sleeping children die in flames. In summer *poverty is watching* gnats and flies devour your baby's tears when he cries. The screens are torn and you pay so little rent you know they will never be fixed. *Poverty means* insects in your food, in your nose, in your eyes, and crawl-

ing over you when you sleep. *Poverty is hoping* it never rains because diapers won't dry when it rains and soon you are using newspapers. *Poverty is seeing* your children forever with runny noses. Paper handkerchiefs cost money and all your rags you need for other things. Even more costly are antihistamines. *Poverty is cooking* without food and cleaning without soap.

Jo Goodwin Parker, "What Is Poverty?"

■ Paragraphs with Special Functions

Special-function paragraphs include introductions, transitional paragraphs, and conclusions. One-paragraph introductions and conclusions appear in short, multiparagraph essays. Transitional paragraphs occur primarily in long compositions.

Introductions

A good introduction acquaints and coaxes. It announces the essay's topic and may directly state the thesis. In addition, it sets the tone—somber, lighthearted, angry—of what will follow. An amusing anecdote would not be an appropriate opening for a paper about political torture.

With essays, as with people, first impressions are important. If your opening rouses interest, it will draw the reader into the essay and pave the way for your ideas. If, instead, you'd like to try your hand at turning the reader away, search for a beginning that is mechanical, plodding, and dull. Your success will astonish you. Here are some bad openings:

In this paper I intend to . . .
Wars have always afflicted humankind.
As you may know, having too little time is a problem for many of us.
In the modern world of today . . .

How would you respond to these openings? Ask yourself that same question about every opening you write.

Gear the length of the introduction to that of the essay. Although longer papers sometimes begin with two or more introductory paragraphs, generally the lead-in for a short essay is a single paragraph. Here are some possibilities for starting an essay. The type you select depends on your purpose, subject, audience, and personality.

A Directly Stated Thesis This is a common type of opening, orienting the reader to what will follow. After providing some general background, the writer of our example narrows her scope to a thesis that previews the upcoming sections of her essay.

An increasing number of midlife women are reentering the workforce, pursuing college degrees, and getting more involved in the public arena. Several labels besides "midlife" have been attached to this type of person: the mature woman, the older

```
woman, and, more recently, the re-entry woman. By definition,
she is between thirty-five and fifty-five years old and has been
away from the business or academic scene anywhere from fifteen
to thirty years. The academic community, the media, marketing
people, and employers are giving her close scrutiny, and it is
apparent that she is having a greater impact on our society than
she realizes.
```
                                                          Jo Ann Harris

A Definition   This kind of introduction works particularly well in a paper that acquaints the reader with an unfamiliar topic.

> You are completely alone in a large open space and are struck by a terrifying, unreasoning fear. You sweat, your heart beats, you cannot breathe. You fear you may die of a heart attack, although you do not have heart disease. Suppose you decide you will never get yourself in this helpless situation again. You go home and refuse to leave its secure confines. Your family has to support you. You have agoraphobia—a disabling terror of open spaces.
>   "Controlling Phobias Through Behavior Modification"

A Quotation   A beginning quotation, particularly from an authority in the field, can be an effective springboard for the ideas that follow. Make sure any quote you use relates clearly to your topic.

> The director of the census made a dramatic announcement in 1890. The Nation's unsettled area, he revealed, "has been so broken into by isolated bodies of settlement that there can hardly be said to be a frontier line." These words sounded the close of one period of America's history. For three centuries before, men had marched westward, seeking in the forests and plains that lay beyond the settled areas a chance to begin anew. For three centuries they had driven back the wilderness as their conquest of the continent went on. Now, in 1890, they were told that a frontier line separating the settled and unsettled portions of the United States no longer existed. The west was won, and the expansion that had been the most distinctive feature of the country's past was at an end.
>   Ray Allen Billington, "The Frontier Disappears"

An Anecdote or Personal Experience   A well-told personal anecdote or experience can lure readers into the rest of the paper. Like other introductions, this kind should bear on what comes afterward. Engle's anecdote, like the stories she reviews, demonstrates that "women also have dark hearts."

> My mother used to have a little china cream and sugar set that was given to her by a woman who later killed her children with an axe. It sat cheerfully in the china cabinet, as inadequate a symbol as I have ever seen of the dark mysteries within us. Yet at least it was there to remind us that no matter how much Jesus wanted us for a sunbeam, we would still have some day to cope with a deeper reality than common sense could explain. It stood for strange cars not to get into, running shoes to wear when you were out alone at night and the backs of Chinese restaurants you were not supposed to go into.
>   Marian Engle, review of *The Goddess and Other Women* by Joyce Carol Oates

An Arresting Statement   Sometimes you can jolt the reader into attention, using content, language, or both, particularly if your essay develops an unusual or extreme position.

> It's like Pearl Harbor. The Japanese have invaded, and the U.S. has been caught short. Not on guns and tanks and battleships—those are yesterday's weapons—but on mental might. In a high-tech age where nations increasingly compete on brainpower, American schools are producing an army of illiterates. Companies that cannot hire enough skilled workers now realize they must do something to save the public schools. Not to be charitable, not to promote good public relations, but to survive.
>
> Nancy Perry, "Saving the Schools: How Business Can Help"

Interesting Details   These details pique curiosity and draw the reader into the paper.

> It is Friday night at any of the ten thousand watering holes of the small towns and crossroads hamlets of the South. The room is a cacophony of the ping-pong-ding-ding ding of the pinball machine, the pop-fizz of another round of Pabst, the refrain of "Red Necks, White Socks and Blue Ribbon Beer" on the juke box, the insolent roar of a souped-up engine outside and, above it all, the sound of easy laughter. The good ole boys have gathered for their fraternal ritual—the aimless diversion that they have elevated into a life-style.
>
> Bonnie Angelo, "Those Good Ole Boys"

A Question   A provocative question can entice the reader into the essay to find the answer.

> When you leave your apartment or house, do you begin to feel better? If you leave for a week-long trip, do you find your head clears, your migraine disappears, dizziness stops, your aches and pains subside, depression fades away, and your entire attitude is better? If so, chemical pollution of the atmosphere in your home may be making you ill.
>
> Marshall Mandell, "Are You Allergic to Your House?"

EXERCISE

1. Explain why each of the preceding introductions interests or does not interest you. Does your response stem from the topic or the way the author introduces it?

2. Find magazine articles with effective introductory paragraphs illustrating at least three different techniques. Write a paragraph explaining why each impresses you.

Transitional Paragraphs

In the midst of a lengthy essay, you may need a short paragraph that announces a shift from one group of ideas to another. Transitional paragraphs summarize previously explained ideas, repeat the thesis, or point to ideas that follow. In our example, Bruno Bettelheim has been discussing a young boy named Joey who has turned into a kind of human machine. After describing Joey's assorted delusions, Bettelheim signals his switch from the delusions to the fears that caused them.

> What deep-seated fears and needs underlay Joey's delusional system? We were long in finding out, for Joey's preventions effectively concealed the secret of his autistic behavior. In the meantime we dealt with his peripheral problems one by one.
>
> Bruno Bettelheim, "Joey: 'A Mechanical Boy'"

The following transitional paragraph looks back as well as ahead:

> Certainly these three factors--exercise, economy, conven-
> ience of shortcuts--help explain the popularity of bicycling
> today. But a fourth attraction sometimes overrides the others:
> the lure of the open road.
>
> Mike Bernstein

Conclusions

A conclusion rounds out a paper and signals that the discussion has been completed. Not all papers require a separate conclusion; narratives and descriptions, for example, generally end when the writer finishes the story or concludes the impression. But many essays benefit from a conclusion that drives the point home a final time. To be effective, a conclusion must mesh logically and stylistically with what comes earlier. A long, complex paper often ends with a summary of the main points, but any of several other options may be used for shorter papers with easy-to-grasp ideas. Most short essays have single-paragraph conclusions; longer papers may require two or three paragraphs.

Here are some cautions about writing your conclusion:

1. Don't introduce new material. Draw together, round out, but don't take off in a new direction.
2. Don't tack on an ending in desperation when the hour is late and the paper is due tomorrow—the so-called midnight special. Your reader deserves better than "All in all, skiing is a great sport" or "Thus we can see that motorcycle racing isn't for everyone."
3. Don't apologize. Saying that you could have done a better job makes a reader wonder why you didn't.
4. Don't moralize. A preachy conclusion can undermine the position you have established in the rest of your composition.

The following examples illustrate several common types of conclusions.

Restatement of the Thesis   The following conclusion reasserts Jordan's thesis that "a mood of antisocial negativism is creeping through the structure of American life, corroding our ideals, and suffocating the hopes of poor people and minorities."

> There is room for honest differences about each of these key issues, but the new negativism's overt greed and the implicit racism of its loud "No" to minority

aspirations indicate that this is a poisonous movement that denies the moral ideals and human values that characterize the best in America's heritage.

Vernon E. Jordan, Jr., "The New Negativism"

A Summary   A summary draws together and reinforces the main points of a paper.

> There are, of course, many other arguments against capital punishment, including its high cost and its failure to deter crime. But I believe the most important points against the death penalty are the possibility of executing an innocent man, the discriminatory manner in which it is applied, and the barbaric methods of carrying it out. In my opinion, capital punishment is, in effect, premeditated murder by society as a whole. As the old saying goes, two wrongs don't make a right.
>
> Diane Trathen

A Question   The paragraph below concludes an argument that running should not be elevated to a religion, that its other benefits are sufficient. A final question often prompts the reader to think further on the topic. If your essay is meant to be persuasive, be sure to phrase a concluding question so that the way a reasonable person would answer emphasizes your point of view.

> Aren't those gifts enough? Why ask running for benefits that are plainly beyond its capacity to bestow?
>
> James Fixx, "What Running Can't Do for You"

A Quotation   A quotation can capture the essence of your thought and end the essay with authority.

> "We had no idea of the emotional involvement and the commitment of these women," Richard says. "Suddenly a constituency arose. Suddenly there are thousands and thousands of women who don't care about your moral position or mine—they want a baby."
>
> David Zimmerman, "Are Test-Tube Babies the Answer for the Childless?"

Ironic Twist or Surprising Observation   These approaches prompt the reader to think further about a paper's topic. The following paragraph points out the ironic refusal of the government to confront poverty that exists a mere ten blocks away from its offices:

> Thus, a stark contrast exists between the two cultures of 14th Street, which appears to be like an earthworm with half of its body crushed by poverty but the other half still alive, wriggling in wealth. The two are alike only in that each communicates little with the other because of the wide disparity between the lives of the people and the conditions of the envi-

```
ronments. The devastating irony of the situation on 14th Street
lies in the fact that only ten blocks away sit the very govern-
ment institutions that could alleviate the poverty--the Senate,
the House of Representatives, and the White House.
```

Student Unknown

Clever or Lighthearted Ending   In our example, the writer, capitalizing on the essay's topic, ends by exaggerating the fault being criticized.

```
Because using clichés is as easy as falling off a log, it
goes without saying that it would be duck soup to continue in
this vein till hell freezes over. However, since that would be
carrying coals to Newcastle, let's ring down the curtain and bid
adieu to the fair topic of the cliché. (No use beating a dead
horse.)
```

Student Unknown

Personal Challenge   A challenge often prompts the reader to take some action.

```
And therein lies the challenge. You can't merely puff hard
for a few days and then revert to the La-Z-Boy recliner, smugly
thinking that you're "in shape." You must sweat and strain and
puff regularly, week in and week out. They're your muscles, your
lungs, your heart. The only caretaker they have is you.
```

Monica Duvall

Hope or Recommendation   Both a hope and a recommendation may restate points already made in the essay or suggest actions to take in order to arrive at a solution.

Periodically my pilot and I climb into our aircraft and head out over the Minnesota wilderness, following a succession of electronic beeps that lead to some of the last remaining wolves in the lower 48 states. We hope that the data we collect will provide a better understanding of the wolf. We especially hope that our work will help guide authorities into a management program that will insure the perpetuation of the species in the last vestiges of its former range.

L. David Mech, "Where Can the Wolves Survive?"

I who am blind can give one hint to those who can see—one admonition to those who would make full use of the gift of sight: Use your eyes as if tomorrow you would be stricken blind. And the same method can be applied to the other senses. Hear the music of voices, the song of the bird, the mighty strains of an orchestra, as if you would be stricken deaf tomorrow. Touch each object you want to touch as if tomorrow your tactile sense would fail. Smell the perfume of flowers, taste with relish each morsel, as if tomorrow you could never smell and taste again. Make the most of every sense; glory in all the facets of pleasure and beauty which the world reveals to you through the several means of contact which Nature provides. But of all the senses, I am sure that sight must be the most delightful.

Helen Keller, "Three Days to See"

EXERCISE

1. Explain why each of the foregoing conclusions does or does not interest you. Does your response stem from the topic or from the author's handling of it?

2. Copy effective concluding paragraphs, illustrating at least three different techniques, from magazine articles. Then write a paragraph explaining why each impresses you.

• •

chapter 15

Effective Sentences

A sentence is a group of words that begins with a capital letter; ends with a period, question mark, or exclamation point; and makes sense by itself. The elements that comprise sentences include subjects, predicates, direct objects, indirect objects, subject complements, object complements, phrases, and clauses.

Sentences take many forms, some straightforward and unadorned, others intricate and ornate, each with its own stylistic strengths. Becoming familiar with these forms and their uses gives you the option to

- emphasize or de-emphasize an idea
- combine ideas into one sentence or keep them separate in more than one sentence
- make sentences sound formal or informal
- emphasize the actor or the action
- achieve rhythm, variety, and contrast.

Effective sentences bring both exactness and flair to your writing.

■ Sentence Strategies

Effective sentences stem, at least in part, from selecting the right word order for independent clauses, coordinating and subordinating effectively, correctly positioning movable modifiers, using parallel structures, choosing the right verb voice, and avoiding fragments except for particular effects. Usually it's best to work on these different strategies as you revise rather than pausing to refine each sentence after you write it.

Word Order in Independent Clauses

Most independent clauses follow a similar arrangement. First comes the subject, then the verb, and finally any other element needed to convey the main message.

> Barney blushed. *(subject, verb)*

> They built the dog a kennel. *(subject, verb, indirect object, direct object)*

> Samantha is an architect. *(subject, verb, subject complement)*

This arrangement puts the emphasis on the subject, right where it's usually wanted.

But the pattern doesn't work in every situation. Occasionally, a writer wants to emphasize some element that follows the verb, create an artistic effect, or give the subject unusual emphasis. Enter inverted order and the expletive construction.

Inverted Order   To invert a sentence, move to the front the element you want to emphasize. Sometimes the rest of the sentence follows in regular subject-then-verb order; sometimes the verb precedes the subject.

> Lovable he isn't. *(subject complement, subject, verb)*

> This I just don't understand. *(direct object, subject, verb)*

> Tall grow the pines in the mountains. *(subject complement, verb, subject)*

Sentences that ask questions typically follow an inverted pattern.

> Is this your coat? *(verb, subject, subject complement)*

> Will you let the cat out? *(verb, subject, verb, direct object)*

Most of your sentences should follow normal order: Readers expect it and read most easily through it. Furthermore, don't invert a sentence if the result would sound strained and unnatural. A sentence like "Fools were Brett and Amanda for quitting college" will only hinder communication.

Expletives   An expletive fills a vacancy in a sentence without contributing to the meaning. English has two common expletives, *there* and *it*. Ordinarily, *there* functions as an adverb, *it* as a pronoun, and either can appear anywhere in a sentence. As expletives, however, they alter normal sentence order by beginning sentences and anticipating the real subjects or objects.

Expletives are often used unnecessarily, as in the following example:

There were twenty persons attending the sales meeting.

This sentence errs on two counts: Its subject needs no extra emphasis, and it is very clumsy. Notice the improvement without the expletive and the unneeded words:

Twenty persons attended the sales meeting.

When the subject or object needs highlighting, leading off with an expletive will, by altering normal order, call it more forcefully to the reader's attention.

> *Normal order:* A fly is in my soup.
> He seeks her happiness.

> *Expletive construction:* There is a fly in my soup. *(expletive anticipating subject)*
> It is her happiness he seeks. *(expletive anticipating object)*

Once in a while you'll find that something just can't be said unless you use an expletive.

There is no reason for such foolishness.

No other construction can express exactly the same thought.

EXERCISE   *Indicate which of these sentences follow normal order, which are inverted, and which have expletive constructions. Rewrite so that all will be in normal order.*

1. Dick Lewis is a true friend.
2. It was her car in the ditch.
3. An intelligent person is she.
4. May I go to the movie with you?
5. A sadder but wiser man he became.
6. There are many dead fish on the beach.
7. The instructor gave the class a long reading assignment.
8. The Willetts have bought a new house.
9. It is Marianne's aim to become a lawyer.
10. Harry works at a supermarket.

Coordination and Subordination

Coordination and subordination are ways to rank ideas in sentences. Coordination makes ideas equal; subordination makes them unequal. To understand coordination and subordination, you need to know about four kinds of sentences: simple, compound, complex, and compound–complex.

Simple Sentences A simple sentence has one subject and one predicate. Some simple sentences consist merely of a single noun and a single verb.

> Millicent shouted.

Others can include elements such as compound subjects, compound verbs, direct objects, indirect objects, and subject complements.

> Jim and Sue have bought a car. *(compound subject, direct object)*

> Lucretia Borgia smiled and mixed her guests a cocktail. *(compound verb, indirect object, direct object)*

> Autumn is a sad season. *(subject complement)*

Most simple sentences are rather short and easy to understand. This trimness can add punch to your writing, but it can also make your writing sound childish and may waste words.

> The audience was young and friendly. It was responsive. It cheered for each speaker.

Combined into a single simple sentence, the information is easier to follow and more interesting to read:

> The young, friendly, responsive audience cheered for each speaker.

Compound Sentences A compound sentence contains two or more independent clauses, each holding the same (coordinate) rank. As a result, the idea in the first clause receives the same emphasis as the idea in the second.
    In some cases, a comma and a coordinating conjunction *(and, but, or, nor, for, yet, so)* link successive clauses.

> Name the baby Huey, *or* I'll cut you out of my will.

> The audience was young, friendly, and responsive, *so* it cheered for each speaker.

In others, a semicolon and a conjunctive adverb *(for example, however, in fact, likewise, meanwhile, instead,* and the like) furnish the connection.

> Tod wants to see the play; *in fact,* he's talked about it for weeks.

> Today, many young women do not rush into marriage and motherhood; *instead,* they spend several years establishing careers.

Finally, a writer may omit any connecting word and separate the clauses with a semicolon.

> The sky grew pitch black; the wind died; an ominous quiet hung over the whole city.

Be sure to read this Hemingway novel; it suggests how to cope gracefully with pressure.

As the preceding sentences show, compound sentences allow writers to express simple relationships among simple ideas. However, such sentences have one important limitation: It is impossible to highlight one particular idea. To do this, we need to use complex sentences.

Complex Sentences   A complex sentence has one independent clause and one or more dependent clauses. Relegating an idea to a dependent clause shows that the writer wishes it to receive less emphasis than the idea in the main clause. In the following examples the dependent clauses are italicized.

Because the young, friendly audience was responsive, it cheered for each speaker.

After the dance was over, Arthur collapsed on the sofa.

Once they had reached the lakeshore, the campers found a level spot *where they could pitch their tent.*

Unlike compound sentences, complex ones allow writers to vary the emphasis of ideas.

While I watered the grass, I discussed stock options with Liz.

I watered the grass *while I discussed stock options with Liz.*

The first sentence emphasizes the talk with Liz, the second watering the lawn.
Often, shifting emphasis allows a writer to change the meaning of a sentence.

While his bicycle was damaged, Pat walked to work.

While Pat walked to work, his bicycle was damaged.

Furthermore, complex sentences signal *how* ideas relate. Note the various relationships in the following sentences:

Because she was swimming well, Millicent did 200 laps today. *(reason)*

The Sears Tower is taller *than the Empire State Building. (extent)*

Ms. Yoshira is the executive *for whom I am working. (relationship between persons)*

Compound–Complex Sentences   This type of sentence features two or more independent clauses and one or more dependent clauses. Here are two examples with the dependent clauses italicized:

Ms. Harris works as an investment manager, and Mr. Williams, *who lives next door to her,* owns a jewelry store.

If you are to communicate properly, your thoughts must be clear and correct; thoughts are wasted *when language is muddled.*

Compound–complex sentences allow writers to present more intricate relationships than do other kinds of sentences. In the following example, three sentences—one compound and two simple—have been rewritten as a compound–complex sentence. Notice how subordination improves the compactness and smoothness of the final version.

> Mary hated to be seen in ugly clothing, but she wore an ugly dress with red polka dots. She had received the dress as a Christmas present. Her Aunt Ida had given it to her.

> Mary hated to be seen in ugly clothing; nevertheless, she wore an ugly red-polka-dot dress that *her Aunt Ida had given her for Christmas.*

The second version condenses thirty-five words to twenty-six.

EXERCISE

A. Label the independent and dependent clauses in the sentences below. Then identify each sentence as simple, compound, complex, or compound–complex.

1. A career in broadcasting requires good verbal skills, an extensive wardrobe, and a pleasant smile.

2. Because its bag was too full, the vacuum cleaner backfired, leaving the room dirtier than it had been before.

3. Leave your boots in the back hall, please.

4. When Tom arrived home, his roommate asked him where he had really gone; six hours seemed too long a time to spend in the library.

5. My orange tree blossomed last week; however, the grapefruit trees have withered, probably because of the freeze last month.

6. Kites make good gifts for children; even if a child already has a kite, a second one will come in handy if the first one becomes tangled in a tree.

7. It's risky to confide in a co-worker because one can never be sure that the confidence will be kept.

8. I know why he moved here: He likes having the only dental practice in this part of the state.

9. The pencil and the stapler are on the table next to the window in Mr. Brigg's office.

10. Don't add bleach to your load of colored shirts; the colors will fade and the fibers weaken.

B. Using coordination and subordination, rewrite the following passages to reduce words and/or improve smoothness.

1. He played the piano. He played the organ. He played the French horn. He did not play the viola.

2. The weather was icy cold and windy. Lee was wearing only a T-shirt and athletic shorts.

3. Life on Venus may be possible. It will not be the kind of life we know on Earth. Life on Mars may be possible. It will not be the kind of life we know on Earth.

4. He felt his classmates were laughing at his error. He ran out of the room. He vowed never to return to that class.

5. Albert lay in bed. He stared at the ceiling. Albert thought about the previous afternoon. He had asked Kathy to go to dinner with him. She is a pretty, blonde-haired woman. She sits at the desk next to his. They work at Hemphill's. She had refused.

6. I went to the store to buy a box of detergent. I saw Bill there, and we talked about last night's game.

7. Tim went to the newsstand. He bought a magazine there. While he was on the way home, he lost it. He had nothing to read.

Positioning of Movable Modifiers

Movable modifiers can appear on either side of the main statement or within it.

Modifiers After Main Statement Sentences that follow this arrangement, frequently called *loose sentences,* occur more commonly than either of the others. They mirror conversation, in which a speaker first makes a statement and then adds on further thoughts. Often, the main statement has just one modifier.

> Our company will have to file for bankruptcy *because of this year's huge losses. (phrase as modifier)*

Or it can head up a whole train of modifiers.

> He burst suddenly into the party, *loud, angry, obscene. (words as modifiers)*

> The family used to gather around the hearth, *doing such chores as polishing shoes, mending ripped clothing, reading, chatting, always warmed by one another's presence as much as by the flames. (words and phrases as modifiers)*

> Sally stared in disbelief, and then she smiled, *slowly, tremulously, as if she couldn't believe her good fortune. (words and clause as modifiers)*

> There are three essential qualities for buzzard country: *a rich supply of unburied corpses, high mountains, a strong sun. (noun-base groups as modifiers)*
> John D. Stewart, "Vulture Country"

A sentence may contain several layers of modifiers. In the following example, we've indented and numbered to show the different layers.

1. The men struggled to the top of the hill,
   2. thirsty,
   2. drenched in sweat,
   2. and cursing in pain
      3. as their knapsack straps cut into their raw, chafed shoulders
         4. with every step.

In this sentence, the terms numbered 2 refer to *men* in the item numbered 1. Item 3 is linked to *cursing* in the preceding item 2, and item 4 is linked to *cut* in item 3.

The modifiers-last arrangement works well for injecting descriptive details into narratives and also for qualifying, explaining, and presenting lists in other kinds of writing.

Modifiers Before Main Statement   Sentences that delay the main point until the end are called *periodic*. In contrast to loose sentences, they lend a formal note to what is said, slowing its pace, adding cadence, and making it more serious.

> *If you can keep your head when everyone around you is panicking,* you probably don't understand the situation. *(clauses as modifiers)*

> *From the onset of his journey to the heart of darkness,* Marlow witnesses many incidents that reveal the human capacity for evil. *(phrases as modifiers)*

> *The danger of sideswiping another vehicle, the knowledge that a hidden bump or hole could throw me from the dune buggy,* both of these things added to the thrill of the race. *(noun plus phrase and noun plus clause as modifiers)*

> *When so large a percentage of our college students admits to cheating, when so many professors practice grade inflation, when administrators fail to face up to these problems,* our colleges are in serious trouble. *(clauses as modifiers)*

> 1. *When the public protests,*
>   2. *confronted with some obvious evidence of the damaging results of pesticide applications,* it is fed little tranquilizing pills of half truth. *(clause and phrase as modifiers)*
>
> Rachel Carson, *Silent Spring*

As shown in the Carson example, periodic sentences can also have layers of modifiers.

Positioning the modifiers before the main point throws the emphasis upon the end of the sentence, adding force to the main point. The delay also lets the writer create sentences that, like the first example, carry stings, ironic or humorous, in their tails.

Modifiers Within Main Statement   Inserting one or more modifiers into a main statement creates a sentence with *interrupted order*. The material may come between the subject and the verb or between the verb and the rest of the predicate.

> The young girl, *wearing a tattered dress and looking anything but well-off herself,* gave the beggar a ten-dollar bill. *(phrases between subject and verb)*

> Dewey declared, *in a loud, happy voice,* that the concert was the best he'd ever heard. *(phrase between verb and rest of predicate)*

> The bedsprings, *bent and rusted, festooned with spider webs,* lay on top of the heap. *(words and phrase between subject and verb)*

> The evolutionists, *piercing beneath the show of momentary stability,* discovered, *hidden in rudimentary organs,* the discarded rubbish of the past. *(one phrase between subject and verb, another between verb and rest of predicate)*

By stretching out the main idea, inserted modifiers slow the forward pace of the sentence, giving it some of the formality and force of a periodic sentence.

EXERCISE *Identify each sentence as loose, periodic, or interrupted. Rewrite each as one of the other kinds.*

1. Victoria, rejected by family and friends, uncertain where to turn next, finally decided to start a new life in Chicago.
2. When told that she had to have her spleen removed, the woman gasped.
3. Tom missed the bus because his wife had forgotten to reset the alarm after she got up and he had cut himself several times while shaving.
4. Good health, warm friends, a beautiful summer evening—the best things cannot be purchased.
5. A customer, angry and perspiring, stormed up to the claims desk.
6. Stopping just short of the tunnel entrance, the freight train avoided a collision with the crowded commuter train stalled inside.
7. The new kid hammered away at the fading champ, determination in his eyes and glory in his fists.
8. The new tract house sparkled in the sunlight, pink and trim, its lawn immaculate, its two bushes and newly planted crab apple tree, by their very tininess, making the yard look vaster than its actual size.
9. Bright red and skin stinging after a day at the beach, Steve will remember the sunscreen next time.
10. Saloons, gaudily painted and beckoning with promises of extraordinary pleasures, lined the town's main street.
11. In being whisked from Lyons, France, to Tel Aviv to Sri Lanka for location shots, the Hollywood star gave new force to the phrase *international celebrity.*
12. The first graders stood in line, talking and giggling, pushing at one another's caps and pencil boxes and kicking one another's shins, unmindful of the drudgery that awaited them within the old schoolhouse.

Using Parallelism

Parallelism presents equivalent ideas in grammatically equivalent form. Dressing them in the same grammatical garb calls attention to their kinship and adds smoothness and polish. The following sentence pairs demonstrate the improvement that parallelism brings:

Nonparallel: James's outfit was *wrinkled, mismatched,* and *he needed to wash it. (words and independent clause)*

Parallel: James's outfit was *wrinkled, mismatched,* and *dirty. (words)*

Nonparallel: Oscar likes *reading books, attending plays,* and *to search for antiques. (different kinds of phrases)*

Parallel: Oscar likes *reading books, attending plays,* and *searching for antiques. (same kind of phrases)*

Nonparallel: Beth performs her tasks *quickly, willingly,* and *with accuracy.* *(words and phrase)*

    Parallel: Beth performs her tasks *quickly, willingly,* and *accurately.* *(words)*

Nonparallel: The instructor complimented me *for taking part in class discussions and because I had written a superb theme. (phrase and clause)*

    Parallel: The instructor complimented me *for taking part in class discussions and for writing a superb theme. (phrases)*

As the examples show, revising nonparallel sentences smooths out bumpiness, binds the ideas together more closely, and lends them a more finished look.

Parallelism doesn't always stop with a single sentence. Writers sometimes use it in a series of sentences:

> He had never lost his childlike innocence. He had never lost his sense of wonder. He had never lost his sense of joy in nature's simplest gifts.

For an example of parallelism that extends over much of a paragraph, see pages 210–11.

Repeating a structure through several sentences of a paragraph beats a tattoo that drums the points home more forcefully and adds rhythm to the prose. But don't overuse the technique, or it will lose its impact and seem irritating and artificial.

Balance, a special form of parallelism, positions two grammatically equivalent ideas on opposite sides of some pivot point, such as a word or punctuation mark.

Hope for the best, and prepare for the worst.

Many are called, but few are chosen.

When I'm right, nobody ever notices; when I'm wrong, nobody ever forgets.

The sheep are in the meadow, and the cows are in the corn.

Like regular parallel sentences, balanced sentences sometimes come in series:

> The tension in this city is not between white people and Negro people. The tension is, at bottom, between justice and injustice, between the forces of light and the forces of darkness. And if there is a victory, it will be a victory not merely for fifty thousand Negroes, but a victory for justice and the forces of light.
>
> Martin Luther King, Jr., "Pilgrimage to Nonviolence"

Balance works especially well for pitting contrasting or clashing ideas against each other. It sharpens the difference between them while achieving compactness and lending an air of insight to what is said.

EXERCISE   *Identify each sentence as nonparallel, parallel, or balanced; then rewrite each nonparallel sentence to make it parallel.*

1. Professor Bartlett enjoys helping students, counseling advisees, and participation in faculty meetings.

2. I can still see Aunt Alva striding into the corral, cornering a cow against a fencepost, try to balance herself on a one-legged milking stool, and butt her head into the cow's belly.

3. The city plans on building a new fishing pier and on dredging the channel of the river.

4. Elton plans on vacationing in New York, but Noreen wants to raft down the Colorado River.

5. Being half drunk and because he was already late for work, Tom called his boss and said he was too ill to come in that day.

6. The novel's chief character peers through a tangle of long hair, slouches along in a shambling gait, and gets into trouble constantly.

7. You can take the boy out of the country, but you can't take the country out of the boy.

8. Joe's problem is not that he earns too little money but spending it foolishly.

9. The room was dark, gloomy, and everything was dusty.

10. The apparition glided through the wall, across the room, and up the fireplace chimney.

Choosing the Right Verb Voice

A sentence's verb voice derives from the relationship between the subject and the action. A sentence in the *active voice* has a subject that does something plus a verb that shows action.

The boy hit the target.

The girl painted the garage.

This pattern keeps the key information in the key part of the sentence, making it strong and vigorous and giving the reader a close-up look at the action.

The *passive voice* reverses the subject–action relationship by having the subject receive, rather than perform, the action. It is built around a form of the verb *to be,* for example, *is, are, was, were.* Some sentences identify the actor by using a prepositional phrase; others don't mention the actor at all.

The target was hit by the boy. *(actor identified)*

The federal debt limit is to be increased. *(actor unidentified)*

Demoting or banishing the actor dilutes the force of the sentence, puts greater distance between the action and the reader, and almost always adds extra words to the message.

Most writers who overuse the passive voice simply don't realize its effects on their writing. Read the following paragraph, written mainly in the passive voice:

Graft becomes possible when gifts are given to police officers or favors are done for them by persons who expect preferential treatment in return. Gifts of many kinds may be received by officers. Often free meals are given to them by the owners of restaurants on their beats. During the Christmas season, they may be given liquor, food, or theater tickets by merchants. If favored treatment is not received by the donors, no great harm is done. But if traffic offenses, safety code violations, and other infractions are overlooked by the officers, corruption results. When such corruption is exposed by the newspapers, faith is lost in law enforcement agencies.

This impersonal, wordy passage plods across the page and therefore lacks any real, persuasive impact. Now note the livelier, more forceful tone of this rewritten version.

> Graft becomes possible when police officers accept gifts or favors from persons who expect preferential treatment in return. Officers may receive gifts of many kinds. Restaurant owners often provide free meals for officers on the beat. During the Christmas season, merchants may give them liquor, food, or theater tickets. If donors do not receive favored treatment, no great harm is done. But if officers overlook traffic offenses, safety code violations, and other infractions, corruption results. When the newspapers expose such corruption, citizens lose faith in law enforcement agencies.

Don't misunderstand: The passive voice does have its uses. It can mask identities—or at least try to. A child may try to dodge responsibility by saying, "Mother, while you were out, the living room lamp got broken." Less manipulatively, reporters may use it to conceal the identity of a source.

Technical and scientific writing customarily uses the passive voice to explain processes.

> In the production of steel, iron ore is first converted into pig iron by combining it with limestone and coke and then heating the mixture in a blast furnace. Pig iron, however, contains too many impurities to be useful to industry, and as a result must be refined and converted to steel. In the refining process, manganese, silicon, and aluminum are heated with the pig iron in order to degas it, that is, to remove excess oxygen and impurities from it. The manganese, silicon, and aluminum are vaporized while the iron remains in the liquid state and the impurities are carried away by the vapors. Once this step has been completed, the molten steel is poured into ingots and allowed to cool. The steel is now ready for further processing.

Putting such writing in the passive voice provides a desirable objective tone and puts the emphasis where it's most important: on the action, not the actor. On occasion, everyday writing also uses the passive voice.

The garbage is collected once a week, on Monday.

These caves were formed about 10 million years ago.

In the first case, there's no need to tell who collects the garbage; obviously, garbage collectors do. In the second, the writer may not know what caused the formation, and saying "Something formed these caves about 10 million years ago" would sound ridiculous. In both situations, the action, not the actor, is paramount.

Unless special circumstances call for the passive voice, however, use the active voice.

EXERCISE *After determining whether each sentence below is in active or passive voice, rewrite the passive sentences as active ones.*

1. Mary's parents gave her a sports car for her sixteenth birthday.
2. Fires were left burning by negligent campers.
3. The new ice arena will be opened by the city in about two weeks.
4. Harry left the open toolbox out in the rain.
5. Corn was introduced to the Pilgrims by friendly American Indians.
6. Maude took a trip to Sante Fe, New Mexico.
7. We have just installed a new computer in our main office.
8. The club president awarded Tompkins the Order of the Golden Mace.
9. The sound of war drums was heard by the missionaries as they floated down the river.
10. Objections were raised by some members of the legislature to the ratification of the proposed amendment.

Using Fragments

A fragment is a part of a sentence that is capitalized and punctuated as if it were a complete sentence.

Although fragments are seldom used in formal prose, they form the backbone of most conversations. Here's how a typical bit of dialogue might go:

"Where are you going tonight?" *(sentence)*
"To Woodland Mall." *(fragment)*
"What for?" *(fragment)*
"To buy some shoes." *(fragment)*
"Alone?" *(fragment)*
"No, with Maisie Perkins." *(fragment)*
"Can I come too?" *(sentence)*
"Sure." *(fragment)*

As with most conversations, the sprinkling of complete sentences makes the fragments clear.

Writers of nonfiction use fragments to create special effects. In the following passage, the fragment emphasizes the importance of the question it asks and varies the pace of the writing:

> Before kidney transplants, people had an ethical unease about renal dialysis—the artificial kidney machine. Unquestionably it was a great technical advance making it possible to treat kidney dysfunctions from which thousands die. But the machine was, and is, expensive and involves intensive care of the patient by doctors and nurses. For whom the machine? In the United States the dilemma was evaded but not solved by having lay panels, like juries, making life-or-death choices. In Britain, where the National Health Service entitles everyone, rich or poor, to have access to any necessary treatment, the responsibility rests on the medical staff. It was (and still is) a difficult decision.
>
> Lord Ritchie-Calder, "The Doctor's Dilemma"

Once in a while, as in the following examples, a writer will use a whole series of fragments. In the Ciardi selection, the fragments heighten the ironic effect. In the following one, they create a kaleidoscopic effect that mirrors the
kaleidoscopic impressions offered by the Jazz Age itself.

> Or look at any of the women's magazines. There, as Bernard DeVoto once
> pointed out, advertising begins as poetry in the front pages and ends as pharma-
> copoeia and therapy in the back pages. The poetry of the front matter is the
> dream of perfect beauty that must be hers. These, the flawless teeth. This, the
> baby skin that must be hers. This, the perfumed breath she must exhale. This, the
> sixteen-year-old figure she must display at forty, at fifty, at sixty, and forever.
>
> John Ciardi, "What Is Happiness?"

> The Jazz Age offers a kaleidoscope of shifting impressions. Of novelties
> quickly embraced and quickly discarded. Of flappers flaunting bobbed hair and
> short skirts. Of hip flasks and bootleg whisky, fast cars and coonskin coats, jazz and
> dancing till dawn. And overall a sense of futility, an uneasy conviction that all the
> gods were dead.
>
> Elliott L. Smith and Andrew W. Hart,
> *The Short Story: A Contemporary Looking Glass*

Before using any fragment in your own writing, think carefully about your
intended effect and explore other ways of achieving it. Unless only a fragment
will serve your needs, don't use one; fragments are likely to be viewed as unin-
tentional—and thus errors—in the work of inexperienced writers.

EXERCISE   *Each of the following passages includes one or more fragments. Identify
each and explain its function.*

1.   Anthropologists came to Indian country only after the tribes had agreed to
live on reservations and had given up their warlike ways. Had the tribes been given
a choice of fighting the cavalry or the anthropologists, there is little doubt as to
whom they would have chosen. In a crisis situation, men always attack the biggest
threat to their existence. A warrior killed in battle could always go to the happy
hunting grounds. But where does an Indian laid low by an anthro go? To the library?

> Vine Deloria, Jr., "Custer Died for Your Sins"

2.   He [Richard Wagner] wrote operas; and no sooner did he have the synopsis
of a story, but he would invite—or rather summon—a crowd of his friends to his
house and read it aloud to them. Not for criticism. For applause. When the complete poem was written, the friends had to come again, and hear *that* read aloud.
Then he would publish the poem, sometimes years before the music that went
with it was written. He played the piano like a composer, in the worst sense of what
that implies, and he would sit down at the piano before parties that included some
of the finest pianists of his time, and play for them, by the hour, his own music,
needless to say. He had a composer's voice. And he would invite eminent vocalists
to his house, and sing them his operas, taking all the parts.

> Deems Taylor, "The Monster"

■ Beyond the Single Sentence

What makes a team successful? Skilled players, to be sure, but teamwork as well. Most sentences are part of a team; and unless they work in harmony, the composition will suffer, however good each of them may be.

Harmony—the rhythmic interplay of sentences—demands, first of all, sentences of different lengths. If all your sentences drag on and on, your reader may get bogged down and lose the train of thought. If all are clipped, the ideas may seem simplistic, and the sentences will jerk along like a car with a misfiring engine. And if all of them are middling long, their plodding, monotonous pace may bring boredom and inattention.

Content sets the pattern of sentence lengths, and often your ideas will lead naturally to the proper mix of long and short sentences. But don't count on it. Chances are you will need to make adjustments. Once you have finished a draft of your paper, read it over, see how its rhythms strike your inner ear, and put check marks by stretches that "sound" wrong. For instance, you might need to condense a set of jolting primer-book sentences into one or two sentences that present their ideas in a series:

Original Version

Members of the Unification Church actively recruit converts. They do it in shopping malls. College campuses are also recruiting sites. They talk about the benefits of world unity and sell books as well as records. Donations are also solicited. Listeners receive invitations to a dinner. There the guests learn more about the sect.

Revised Version

Members of the Unification Church recruit converts in such places as shopping malls and college campuses. They talk about the benefits of world unity, sell books and tapes, ask for donations, and invite listeners to a dinner to learn more about the sect.

If a key point is submerged in a long sentence, highlight it as a separate thought, thereby giving it the recognition it deserves. Here is an example:

Original Version

Employers find mature women to be valuable members of their organizations. They are conscientious, have excellent attendance records, and stay calm when things go awry, *but unfortunately many employers exploit them.* Despite their desirable qualities, most remain mired in clerical, sales, and elementary teaching positions. On the average they earn two-thirds as much as men.

Revised Version

Employers find mature women to be valuable members of their organizations. They are conscientious, have excellent attendance records, and stay calm when things go awry. *Unfortunately, though, many employers exploit them.* Despite their desirable qualities, most remain mired in clerical, sales, and elementary teaching positions. On the average they earn two-thirds as much as men.

In the following paragraph, the sentences differ considerably in length.

> To protest that some fairly improbable people, some people who could not possibly respect themselves, seem to sleep easily enough is to miss the point entirely, as surely as those people miss it who think that self-respect has necessarily to do with not having safety pins in one's underwear. There is a common superstition that "self-respect" is a kind of charm against snakes, something that keeps those who have it locked in some unblighted Eden, out of strange beds, ambivalent conversations, and trouble in general. It does not at all. It has nothing to do with the face of things, but concerns instead a separate peace, a private reconciliation.
>
> Joan Didion, "On Self-Respect"

Much of the appealing rhythm of this passage stems from varied sentence length. The first two rather long sentences (forty-nine and thirty-six words) are followed by the very brief "It does not at all," which gains emphasis by its position. The last sentence adds variety by means of its moderate length (nineteen words), quite apart from its interesting observation on the real nature of self-respect.

Look to the structures of your sentences as well as their length. Do they resemble a streetful of row houses built from the same blueprint? If they are all simple, with few modifiers, your readers may underrate the importance of your message. To correct row-house sentences, draw upon the patterns you learned about earlier in this chapter. Try inverting sentence order or positioning modifiers at different points. Combine sentences. Turn a statement into a question. Build from several blueprints. Try anything as long as the structures go together and you don't warp meanings.

The following example illustrates how sentence combining adds smoothness and interest to a piece of writing.

Original Version

Before deaf children can speak, they must learn the speech sounds of the English language. This is a process that requires them to practice breath control, to mouth vowels, and to study the speech positions of the mouth and tongue for many hours. A speech specialist helped my brother do these things. The specialist started with him before he was two years old. She built up his vocabulary by teaching him a series of related words. Each of these words identified something in his environment. My brother proved to be an apt student. He soon learned to talk.

Revised Version

Before deaf children can speak, they must learn the speech sounds of the English language, a process that requires them to practice breath control, mouth vowels, and study the speech positions of the mouth and tongue for many hours. A speech specialist helped my brother do these things. Starting before he was two years old, she built up his vocabulary by teaching him a series of related words, each identified with something in his environment. My brother proved to be an apt student and soon learned to talk.

EXERCISE   *Revise the following passages to improve their style.*

1.   Andrew Carnegie came to America from Scotland. He worked as a factory hand, a telegrapher, and a railway clerk to support himself. His savings from these jobs were invested in oil and later in the largest steel works in the country. Historians do not agree in their assessments of Carnegie. Some have considered him as a cruel taskmaster and others as a benevolent benefactor. His contributions to American society, however, cannot be denied. He established public libraries all across the country and spent much time in promoting peace. Good or bad, he ranks as one of our most noteworthy nineteenth-century immigrants.

2.   She went to the seashore. She found some seashells. She picked up the seashells. She put the seashells into a basket. She had a whole basketful of seashells. She went home with the basket. She took the shells out of the basket. She put the shells on a dinette table. She brought jeweler's tools to the table. She pierced holes in the shells. She strung the shells on small chains. The chains were gold and silver. She made twenty necklaces. The selling price of the necklaces was $10 apiece. She earned $175 profit. She used her profits to go to the shore again. She could afford to stay for a week this time.

chapter 16

Diction, Tone, Style

Your decisions about words and sentences set the tone and style of your writing. Not only do you choose sentence strategies for correctness and effectiveness, but you also choose words for accuracy and effect. Sentences must be clear and effective; so must words. Diction deals broadly with words, not in isolation but as parts of sentences, paragraphs, and essays. Every time you write and revise, diction comes into play.

■ Toward Clear Diction

Clear diction stems from choosing words with the right meanings, using abstract and concrete words appropriately, and picking terms that are neither too specific nor too general. Dictionaries and thesauruses can help guide your choices.

Word Meanings

Make sure the words you use mean what you think they do, so that inaccurate words will not distort your message. Sound-alike word pairs often trip up unwary writers. Take *accept* and *except* for example. *Accept* means "to approve." *Ex-*

cept, when used as a verb, means "to exclude or omit." If you want to indicate approval but you say, "The following new courses were *excepted* by the committee," think of the obvious consequences. Likewise, consider the distinction between *continual* (frequently or regularly repeated) and *continuous* (uninterrupted). If you illustrate your popularity by saying "My phone rings *continuously*," your reader will wonder why you never answer it and how you ever sleep.

Concrete and Abstract Words

A concrete word names or describes something that we can perceive with one or more of our five senses. A thing is concrete if we can weigh it, measure it, hold it in our hands, photograph it, taste it, sniff it, add salt to it, drop it, smash into it, or borrow it from a neighbor. If it's abstract, we can't do any of these things. *Eric Clapton* is a concrete term, as are *Swiss cheese, petroleum, maple syrup,* and *Dallas*. On the other hand, *jealousy, power, conservatism, size,* and *sadness* are abstract terms.

Concrete words evoke precise, vivid mental images and thus help convey a message. The images that abstract terms create differ from person to person. Try this test: Ask several of your friends to describe what comes to mind when they think of *joy, hatred, fear,* or some other abstract term. To illustrate, the word *hatred* might call up images of a person with cold, slitted eyes, a grimly set jaw, and tightly clenched fists. As you can see, concrete terms help us specify what we mean and thus enhance communication.

In the following passage, the concrete diction is italicized:

> To do without self-respect . . . is to be an unwilling *audience of one* to an interminable *documentary* that details one's failings, both real and imagined, with *fresh footage spliced* in for every *screening*. There's *the glass you broke* in anger, there's *the hurt on X's face; watch now, this next scene, the night Y came back from Houston,* see how you muff this one. To live without self-respect is to *lie awake some night,* beyond the reach of *warm milk, phenobarbital,* and *the sleeping hand on the coverlet,* counting up the sins of commission and omission, the trusts betrayed, the promises subtly broken, the gifts irrevocably wasted through sloth or cowardice or carelessness. However long we postpone it, we eventually lie down alone in that notoriously *uncomfortable bed,* the one we make ourselves. Whether or not we sleep in it depends, of course, on whether or not we respect ourselves.
>
> Joan Didion, "On Self-Respect"

Now note how vague and colorless the passage becomes without the concrete diction:

> To do without self-respect is to be continuously aware of your failings, both real and imagined. Incidents stay in your mind long after they are over. To live without self-respect means being bothered by intentional or unintentional failings, trusts betrayed, promises subtly broken, and gifts irrevocably wasted through sloth or cowardice or carelessness. However long we postpone it, we eventually must come to terms with who we are. How we respond to this situation depends, of course, on whether or not we respect ourselves.

EXERCISE   *Underline the concrete terms in the following passage:*

> The fog which rises from the river has no color, no texture, no taste, smell, or sound. It is sheer vision, a vision of purity, a slow, mesmeric, inexorable erasure of the slate. You see fog mushrooming along the river's course. Gently, it obliterates the alders tangled on the banks, wipes out the road. Buildings without foundations, trees without trunks, hang in the air like mirages. Sun may be shining brightly on them, or rain drenching them, or stars twinkling above or among them. Slowly the fog reaches higher and spreads. Ridgepoles, small topmost branches, and your own dooryard vanish. There is nothing left now but shining mist. It is all, and you float on it, utterly alone, as one imagines he might in empty space if flung off by earth; as the mind does, drifting into sleep; as the spirit does, having escaped its mortal frame.
>
> Gladys Hasty Carroll, *Sing Out the Glory*

Specific and General Terms

One concrete term can be more specific or more general than another. As we move from *Lassie* to *collie* to *dog* to *mammal* and finally to *animal*, we become less and less specific, ending with a term that encompasses every animal on earth. With each step we retain only those features that fit the more general term. Thus, when we move from *collie* to *dog*, we leave out everything that makes collies different from terriers, greyhounds, and other breeds.

The more specific the term, the less difference among the images it calls to mind. If you say *animal* to a group of friends, one may think of a dog, another of a horse, and a third of a gorilla. *Collie,* on the other hand, triggers images of a large, long-haired, brown and white dog with a pointed muzzle.

Ask yourself how specific you need to be and then act accordingly. Often, the more specific term will be the better choice. If, for instance, you're describing a wealthy jet-setter, noting that he drives a Ferrari, not just a car, helps establish his character. But if you're writing a narrative about your flight to New Orleans and your experience at Mardi Gras, nothing is gained by naming the make of car you rented and used uneventfully during your stay.

EXERCISE

1. **Arrange each set of words from less specific to more specific.**

   a. man, ex-President, human being, Bill Clinton, American

   b. Forest Hills Apartments, building, structure, condominium, dwelling

2. **Expand each of the following words into a series of four or more that become progressively more specific. Use 1a or 1b as a pattern.**

   a. activity   **c.** political party   **e.** device

   b. event   **d.** institution   **f.** reading matter

Dictionaries and Thesauruses

Get the dictionary habit and learn to use a thesaurus. These will increase your vocabulary as well as your skill at using words you already know.

Dictionaries   Dictionaries are storehouses of word meanings. In general, dictionary makers do not try to dictate how words should be used. Instead, they note current and past meanings. When a word gains or loses a meaning or a newly minted word enjoys wide circulation, dictionary makers observe and record. Most users, however, regard dictionaries as authorities on correctness.

Dictionaries supply much more than word meanings. Figure 16.1, an annotated entry from a college-level dictionary, shows what they can provide. Some dictionary entries include idioms, irregular forms of words, usage labels, and supplementary information, as well.

Idioms   Idioms express meanings that differ from those of the words that make them up. Here are two examples.

I won't *put up with* any foolishness.

The dowager *gave me the cold shoulder.*

Put up with means "tolerate"; *gave me the cold shoulder* means "snubbed me." Looking up the most prominent word of an unfamiliar idiom may lead you to a listing and a definition.

Irregular Forms   Any irregular forms are indicated. In *Webster's New World Dictionary,* the entry for the verb *spring* notes that the other forms are *sprang, sprung,* and *springing.* This information helps you use correct forms in your writing.

Usage Labels   Usage labels help you determine whether a word suits the circumstances of your writing. Here are the most common labels:

Label	Meaning
Colloquial	Characteristic of informal writing and speaking; should not be considered nonstandard.
Slang	Informal, newly coined words and expressions or old expressions with new meanings.
Obsolete	No longer in use but found in past writing.
Archaic	Still finds restricted use, for example, in legal documents; otherwise not appropriate.
Poetic	Used only in poetry and in prose with a poetic tone.
Dialect	Used regularly only in a particular geographical location such as the southeastern United States or the Scottish Lowlands.

Supplementary Information   While focusing primarily on individual words, college-level dictionaries often provide several other kinds of information. These may include a history of the language, lists of standard abbreviations and

Spelling, Syllabication. When a word has variant spellings, some dictionaries indicate a preferred version. Alphabetically close variants appear in the same entry. Dots or hyphens separate syllables and tell where to divide a word written on two lines.

Parts of Speech. Each word is classified by grammatical function. Usually, abbreviations such as *n* (noun), *adj.* (adjective), and *vt.* (transitive verb) identify the part of speech.

Pronunciation. Dictionaries indicate preferred as well as secondary pronunciations. Accent marks (') show which syllable gets the primary stress and which the secondary stress, if any. To determine the pronunciation, follow the key at the bottom of the page.

Etymology. This term means the origin and development of words. Most college dictionaries limit the entry to the root (original) word and an abbreviation for the original language. The abbreviation key near the front of the dictionary identifies the language.

man-i-fold (man´ ə fōld´) *adj.* [ME. see MANY & -FOLD] 1. having many and various forms, features, parts, etc. *[manifold wisdom]* 2. of many sorts; many and varied; multifarious: used with a plural noun *[manifold duties.]* 3. being such in many and various ways or for many reasons *[a manifold villain]* 4. comprising, consisting of, or operating several units or parts of one kind: said of certain devices —*n.* 1. something that is manifold 2. a pipe with one inlet and several outlets or with one outlet and several inlets, for connecting with other pipes, as, in an automobile, for conducting exhausts from each cylinder into a single exhaust pipe —*vt.* 1. to make manifold; multiply 2. to make more than one copy of *[to manifold a letter with carbon paper]* —*SYN.* see MANY — **man´i-fold´er** *n.* —**man´i-fold´ly** *adv.* —**man´i-fold´ness** *n.*

< OE. *manigfeald:*

MANIFOLD
(A. manifold; B. cylinders)

Additional Word Formations. These are words derived from the one being defined. Their parts of speech are also indicated. Because they have the same basic meaning as the parent word, definitions are omitted.

Meanings. Meanings are grouped by parts of speech. Sometimes usage is briefly illustrated (*manifold* duties). Some dictionaries list meanings in historical order, others according to frequency of use. The front part of the dictionary specifies the arrangement.

Synonyms. These are words close in meaning to the one being defined. Although no synonym carries exactly the same meaning as the original, the two may be interchangeable in some situations.

Figure 16.1 From *Webster's New World Dictionary of the American Language,* Third College Edition.

of colleges and universities, biographical notes on distinguished individuals, and geographical notes on important locations.

While any dictionary is better than none, some clearly outrank others in usefulness. A pocket dictionary is handy but not as comprehensive as a desk dictionary. Excellent desk-sized dictionaries include the following:

The American Heritage Dictionary
Funk and Wagnall's Standard College Dictionary
The Random House Dictionary of the English Language
Webster's Tenth New Collegiate Dictionary
Webster's New World Dictionary of the American Language

Unabridged (complete) dictionaries such as *Webster's Third New International Dictionary* and the *Oxford English Dictionary* can be found in college and public libraries. There you'll also find a variety of specialized dictionaries. Your librarian can direct you to dictionaries that list terms in particular fields.

EXERCISE   *Use a good desk dictionary to look up the specified information for each of the following lists of words:*

1. Variant spellings:

airplane	aesthete	gray	tornadoes
color	gaily	theater	usable

2. Syllabication and the syllable that receives the main stress:

anacrusis	cadenza	harbinger	misanthrope
baccalaureate	exclamation	ionize	sequester

3. Parts of speech:

before	fair	separate	to
deep	here	then	where

4. Etymology:

carnival	Icarian	phenomenon	supercilious
fiduciary	lethargy	sabotage	tawdry

5. Idiomatic phrases:

beat	get	jump	put
eat	high	make	set

6. Synonyms:

attack	ghastly	mercy	plot
distress	keep	object	range

Thesauruses   Thesauruses list synonyms for words but omit the other elements in dictionary entries. Figure 16.2 shows a typical entry. Note that the items are grouped according to parts of speech, and some are cross-indexed.

A thesaurus will help you find a word with just the right shade of meaning or a synonym when you want to avoid repetition. But synonyms are never exactly equal, nor are they always interchangeable. To illustrate, *old* means "in existence or use for a long time"; *antiquated* conveys the notion that something is old-fashioned or outdated. Therefore, use the thesaurus along with the dictionary. Only then can you tell which synonym fits a specific sentence.

247. FORMLESSNESS

.1 NOUNS **formlessness, shapelessness;** amorphousness, amorphism, amorphia; **chaos,** confusion, messiness, orderlessness; disorder 62; entropy; anarchy 740.2; **indeterminateness, indefiniteness,** indecisiveness, vagueness, mistiness, haziness, fuzziness, blurriness, unclearness, obscurity.

.2 unlicked cub, diamond in the rough.

.3 VERBS **deform, distort** 249.5; unform, unshape; disorder, jumble, mess up, muddle, confuse; obfuscate, obscure, fog up, blur.

.4 ADJS **formless, shapeless,** featureless, characterless, nondescript, inchoate, lumpen, blobby *or* baggy [both informal], inform: amorphous, amorphic, amorph(o)-: **chaotic, orderless,** disorderly 62.13, unordered, unorganized, confused, anarchic 740.6; kaleidoscopic; **indeterminate, indefinite,** undefined, indecisive, vague, misty, hazy, fuzzy, blurred *or* blurry, unclear, obscure.

.5 **unformed, unshaped,** unshapen, unfashioned, unlicked; uncut, unhewn.

Figure 16.2   From *Roget's International Thesaurus*, 5th edition, Peter Mark Roget. Copyright © 1992 by HarperCollins Publishers, Inc. Reprinted by permission of Harper-Collins Publishers, Inc.

Excellent guides to synonyms include the following:

Roget's International Thesaurus
Webster's New Dictionary of Synonyms
Modern Guide to Synonyms and Related Words

■ Toward Rhetorical Effect

Rhetorical effect refers to the response that the manner of writing, not the message, generates in the reader. Successful writers create a desired response through the level of their diction and the tone of their writing.

Level of Diction

What level of diction is best? The answer depends upon the writer's audience and purpose. Think about a safety engineer who investigates a serious industrial accident on which she must write two reports, one for the safety director of the company, who represents a technical audience, and another for the local newspaper, read by a general audience. Although the two accounts would deal with the same matter, clearly they would use very different language: specialized and formal in the first case, everyday and more relaxed in the second. In each case, the language would reflect the background of the audience. As you write, always choose language suited to your audience and purpose.

Edited American English follows the familiar grammatical rules maintained in most formal and academic writing. Generally, everything you write for college courses or on the job should be in edited American English. *Nonstandard English* refers to any version of the language that deviates from these rules. Here is an example from Mark Twain's famous novel *The Adventures of Huckleberry Finn:*

> You don't know about me without you have read a book by the name of *The Adventures of Tom Sawyer,* but that ain't no matter. That book was made by Mr. Mark Twain, and he told the truth, mainly. There was things which he stretched, but mainly he told the truth. That is nothing. I never seen anybody but lied one time or another, without it was Aunt Polly, or the widow, or maybe Mary. Aunt Polly— Tom's Aunt Polly, she is—and Mary, and the Widow Douglas is all told about in that book, which is mostly a true book, with some stretchers, as I said before.

Nonstandard English does have a place in writing. Fiction writers use it to narrate the talk of characters who, if real, would speak that way. Journalists use it to report eyewitness reactions to accidents and crimes, and people who compile oral histories use it to record the recollections of people they interview.

Edited American English includes four levels of usage: formal, informal, formal–informal and technical. Another commonly recognized category is colloquial language and slang.

Formal Level   The formal level, dignified and serious, is suitable for important political, business, and academic occasions. Its vocabulary is marked by many abstract and multisyllabic words but no slang or contractions. Long sentences and deliberately varied sentence patterns help give it a strong, rhythmic flow. Sentences are often periodic, and many have parallel or balanced structures. (See pages 226–27.) Overall, formal prose impresses the reader as authoritative, stately, and graceful.

The following excerpts from John F. Kennedy's inaugural address illustrate the formal level:

> Now the trumpet summons us again—not as a call to bear arms, though arms we need; not as a call to battle, though embattled we are; but a call to bear the burden of a long twilight struggle, year in and year out, "rejoicing in hope, patient in tribulation," a struggle against the common enemies of man: tyranny, poverty, disease, and war itself. . . .
>
> In the long history of the world, only a few generations have been granted the role of defending freedom in its hour of maximum danger. I do not shrink from this responsibility; I welcome it. I do not believe that any of us would exchange places with any other people or any other generation. The energy, the faith, the devotion which we bring to this endeavor will light our country and all who serve it, and the glow from that fire can truly light the world.
>
> And so, my fellow Americans, ask not what your country can do for you; ask what you can do for your country.

The first sentence opens with parallelism to show contrast: "not as a call to bear arms, though arms we need" and "not as a call to battle, though embattled we are." In the second paragraph, parallelism in the second sentence shows contrast; in the last sentence it does not. Except for the second sentence in paragraph 2, all of the sentences are periodic rather than loose. Thus, not until the end of the opening sentence do we learn the nature of the "long twilight struggle" to which "the trumpet summons us." Time and again Kennedy uses elevated diction—polysyllabic words like *embattled, rejoicing, tribulation, tyranny, poverty, generations, devotion,* and *endeavor,* along with shorter abstract words like *hope, freedom,* and *faith.* These carefully controlled sentence patterns, along with this wording, lend rhythmical dignity to the whole passage.

Informal Level   Informal writing resembles orderly, intelligent conversation. Earmarked by relatively ordinary words, loose sentences, and numerous shorter, less varied sentence structures than formal prose, informal writing may include contractions or even slang, and it is more likely than formal writing to use the pronouns *I, me, my, you,* and *yours.* Casual and familiar rather than dignified and rhythmic, informal writing does not usually call attention to itself. Nevertheless, the language is precise and effective. Here is an example:

> There was a distressing story in the paper a few months ago. I wish I'd clipped it out and saved it. As it is, I can only hope I remember it fairly accurately. There was a group of people who wanted a particular dictionary removed from the shelves of the local library because it contained a lot of obscenity. I think they said there were sixty-five or so dirty words in it. Some poor woman who was acting as a spokesman for the group had a list of offending words, which she started to read aloud at a hearing. She managed to read about twenty of them before she started sobbing uncontrollably and couldn't continue.
>
> Thomas H. Middleton, "The Magic Power of Words"

Unlike the Kennedy excerpt, this one has relatively uncomplicated sentences. Three of them—the fourth, sixth, and seventh—are loose rather than periodic. The passage includes two contractions, *I'd* and *couldn't,* one casual expression, *a lot of,* and the pronoun *I.* Most of the words are very short, and none would be out of place in an ordinary conversation.

Formal–Informal Level   As life has become less formal, informal diction has become increasingly widespread. Today many articles and books, even ones on relatively serious topics, mix informal and formal elements. Here is an example:

> . . . faith in sports has been vigorously promoted by industry, the military, government, the media. The value of the arena and the locker room has been imposed on our national life. Coaches and sportswriters are speaking for generals and businessmen, too, when they tell us that a man must be physically and psychologically "tough" to succeed, that he must be clean and punctual and honest, that he must bear pain, bad luck, and defeat without whimpering or making excuses. A man must prove his faith in sports and the American Way by whipping himself into shape, playing by the rules, being part of the team, and putting out all the way. If his faith is strong, he will triumph. It's his own fault if he loses, fails, remains poor.
>
> Robert Lipsyte, *Sports World*

All these sentences except the next to last are loose. Two are quite long, four quite short, and only two have parallel phrases or clauses. Although a few expressions—"bear," "the American Way," "triumph"—echo formal diction, most of the words have an informal ring, and two expressions, "whipping himself into shape" and "putting out all the way," skirt the edges of slang.

Technical Level   A specialist writing for others in the same field or for sophisticated nonspecialists writes on the technical level, a cousin to the formal level. Technical language uses specialized words that may be unfamiliar to a general audience. Its sentences tend to be long and complex, but unlike formal diction it doesn't lean toward periodic sentences, parallelism, and balance. Read this example from the field of entomology, the study of insects:

> The light organs of fireflies are complex structures, and recent studies using the electron microscope show them to be even more complex than once supposed. Each is composed of three layers: an outer "window," simply a transparent portion of the body wall; the light organ proper; and an inner layer of opaque, whitish cells filled with granules of uric acid, the so-called "reflector." The light organ proper contains large, slablike light cells, each of them filled with large granules and much smaller, dark granules, the latter tending to be concentrated around the numerous air tubes and nerves penetrating the light organ. These smaller granules were once assumed by some persons to be luminous bacteria, but we now know that they are mitochondria, the source of ATP [adenosine triphosphate] and therefore of the energy of light production. The much larger granules that fill most of the light cells are still of unknown function; perhaps they serve as the source of luciferin.
>
> Howard Ensign Evans, *Life on a Little-Known Planet*

Note the specialized vocabulary—*granules, uric acid, mitochondria,* and *luciferin*—as well as the length and complexity of the sentences. Five sentences make up the passage, the shortest having twenty-four words. None is periodic, and none has a parallel or balanced structure.

Every field has *jargon*, specialized terms or inside talk that provides a convenient shorthand for communication among its members. For an audience of biologists, you may write that two organisms have a *symbiotic relationship*, meaning "mutually beneficial"; for psychology majors, you might use *catalepsy* instead of "a temporary loss of consciousness and feeling, often accompanied by muscular rigidity." As a general rule, use technical terms only if your audience will know their meanings. If you must use unfamiliar words when writing for a general audience, define them the first time they appear.

Colloquial Language and Slang   *Colloquial* originally meant "the language of ordinary conversation between people of a particular region." *Slang*, according to *Webster's Tenth New Collegiate Dictionary*, is "an informal nonstandard vocabulary composed typically of coinages, arbitrarily changed words, and extravagant, forced, or facetious figures of speech." These two categories shade into each other, and even authorities sometimes disagree on whether to label a term *colloquial* or *slang*. The word *bender*, meaning "a drinking spree," seems firmly in the colloquial camp, and *bummer*, a term recently used by young people to mean "a bad time," is just as clearly slang. *Break a leg* is theater slang used to wish a performer success. But what about *guy* and *kid*? Once they were slang, but so many people have used them for so long that they have now become colloquial.

Regardless of their labels, colloquial and slang terms are almost never appropriate in formal writing. They sometimes serve a useful purpose in informal writing by creating a special effect or increasing audience appeal. Even so, careful writers use them sparingly. Some readers may not understand some colloquial language, and slang usually becomes dated quickly. The following paragraph uses colloquial and slang expressions successfully:

> . . . When I was just a kid on Eighth Avenue in knee pants . . . [Big Bill] was trying to get himself killed. He was always in some fight with a knife. He was always cutting or trying to cut somebody's throat. He was always getting cut or getting shot. Every Saturday night that he was out there, something happened. If you heard on Sunday morning that somebody had gotten shot or stabbed, you didn't usually ask who did it. You'd ask if Big Bill did it. If he did it, no one paid much attention to it, because he was always doing something like that. They'd say, "Yeah, man. That cat is crazy."
>
> Claude Brown, *Manchild in the Promised Land*

Kid, yeah, and *cat* reflect the speech of Brown's characters and thus add authenticity to his account. Despite the informal diction, Brown uses parallelism in the second, third, and fourth sentences; repetition of "he was always" emphasizes the single-minded self-destructiveness of Big Bill's behavior.

EXERCISE   *Identify the level of diction in each of the following passages. Support your answers with examples from the passages. Point out slang or colloquial expressions.*

1.   We may now recapitulate the reasons which have made it necessary to substitute "space-time" for space and time. The old separation of space and time rested upon the belief that there was no ambiguity in saying that two events in distant places happened at the same time; consequently it was thought that we could describe the topography of the universe at a given instant in purely spatial terms. But now that simultaneity has become relative to a particular observer, this is no longer possible. What is, for one observer, a description of the state of the world at a given instant, is, for another observer, a series of events at various different times, whose relations are not merely spatial but also temporal.

Bertrand Russell, *The ABC of Relativity*

2.   In some ways I am an exceptionally privileged woman of thirty-seven. I am in the room of a private, legal abortion hospital, where a surgeon, a friend of many years, is waiting for me in the operating room. I am only five weeks pregnant. Last week I walked out of another hospital, unaborted, because I had suddenly changed my mind. I have a husband who cares for me. He yells because my indecisiveness makes him anxious, but basically he has permitted the final choice to rest in my hands: "It would be very tough, especially for you, and it is absolutely insane, but yes, we could have another baby." I have a mother who cares. I have two young sons, whose small faces are the most moving arguments I have against going through with this abortion. I have a doctorate in psychology, which among other

advantages, assures me of the professional courtesy of special passes in hospitals, passes that at this moment enable my husband and my mother to stand in my room at a nonvisiting hour and yell at each other over my head while I sob.
    Magda Denes, *In Necessity and Sorrow: Life and Death in an Abortion Hospital*

3.   I have just spent two days with Edward T. Hall, an anthropologist, watching thousands of my fellow New Yorkers short-circuiting themselves into hot little twitching death balls with jolts of their own adrenalin. Dr. Hall says it is overcrowding that does it. Overcrowding gets the adrenalin going, and the adrenalin gets them queer, autistic, sadistic, barren, batty, sloppy, hot-in-the-pants, charred-in-the-flankers, leering, puling, numb—the usual in New York, in other words, and God knows where else. Dr. Hall has the theory that overcrowding has already thrown New York into a state of behavioral sink. Behavioral sink is a term from ethology, which is the study of how animals relate to their environment. Among animals, the sink winds up with a "population collapse" or "massive die-off." O rotten Gotham.
    Tom Wolfe, *The Pump House Gang*

Tone

Tone reveals the author's attitude toward the topic and the reader. Every piece of writing has a tone, intended or otherwise, that stems from the meanings and connotations of words, the sentence patterns, and the rhythm of the prose.

Denotation and Connotation   The denotation of a word is its direct, essential meaning: what the word always stands for. The word *book,* for example, denotes "a set of printed or blank sheets bound together along one edge to form a volume." This definition is objective and neutral: It does not assign any special value or convey any particular attitude toward the word or what the word stands for. Connotations are the values and emotional associations that accompany a word. When the self-made man snorts "book learnin'" at his better-educated junior partner, he assigns a value and an attitude—that he ranks experience higher than the knowledge gained from books.

Some words—*death,* for instance—almost always carry strong connotations or emotional associations. *Webster's Tenth New Collegiate Dictionary* defines it as "a permanent cessation of all vital functions" or "the end of life," but it means much more. All of us have hopes, fears, and memories about death, feelings that color our responses whenever we hear or read the word. Likewise, we have personal responses to words like *sexy, cheap, radical, politician,* and *mother.* Experience, to a considerable extent, conditions how we think and feel about a word. To an Olympic swimmer who has won a gold medal, *swimming* may stir pleasant memories of the victory and the plaudits that went with it. The victim of a near-drowning, however, might react to the same word with something approaching horror.

Nonetheless, cultural connotations are more important than personal ones. Cultural connotations develop the way individual ones do, but on a much larger scale, growing out of the common experiences of many speakers and writers and changing with usage and circumstances.

Context, the parts of a passage that precede and follow a word, also affects connotation. Note, for instance, the different associations of *dog* in these sentences:

That movie is a real dog.

I sure am putting on the dog!

It's a dog-eat-dog world.

Your dog-in-the-manger attitude makes you very unpopular.

Denotation is sometimes called the language of science and technology, connotation, the language of art. But we need both to communicate effectively. Denotation allows us to convey precise, essential meanings. Connotation adds richness, warmth, and bite. Without these qualities our language would be bland and sterile, our lives bleak and mechanical.

Objective Tone   An objective tone keeps the writer's personality and opinions out of the message. Here is an example:

> Myopia is a condition of the eye that makes distant vision blurry. In brief, the myopic individual is nearsighted. When the eye is normal, rays of light pass through it and come to focus on the retina, located at the back of the eye. In the myopic eye, however, the rays of light come together a little in front of the retina. As a result, the distant image is not seen clearly. Myopia may result from the eye itself being too long or the lens of the eye being too flat. In either case, the rays converge in front of the retina, and the nearsighted individual is likely to have difficulty making out distant objects.
>
> Janine Neumann

This tone suits a popular explanation of a medical condition. The prose is businesslike and authoritative, the sentence patterns uncomplicated, and nothing reveals the person behind the words.

Other Attitudes   Sometimes you write merely to inform, sometimes to persuade. In persuasive writing, let your attitude toward your topic set the tone. Decide how subtle, flamboyant, or formal your writing should be and what special tone—satiric, cynical, serious, mock pompous, bawdy, playful—will win your reader over.

Every essay has combined characteristics that give it a special tone. The following excerpts illustrate some of tone's many dimensions:

> Unless you have led an abnormally isolated adulthood, the chances are excellent that you know many people who have at one time or another committed an act, or consorted with someone who was committing an act, for which they might

have been sent to prison. We do not consider most of these people, or ourselves, criminals; the act is one thing, the criminality of it quite something else. Homicide, for example, is in our law not a crime; murder only is proscribed. The difference between the two is the intention, or to be more accurate, society's decision about the nature of that intention.

> Bruce Jackson, "Who Goes to Prison: Caste and Careerism in Crime"

Here we have a sophisticated and rather formal tone. Terms like *consorted* and *proscribed,* while exactly suited to Jackson's meaning, do not form part of most people's word kits. The complexity of the first sentence and the varied patterns of the others add to the air of sophistication. The emphatic *quite,* meaning "entirely," is cultivated usage; and along with *society's decision,* it lends the tone a wry touch.

> Cans. Beer cans. Glinting on the verges of a million miles of roadways, lying in scrub, grass, dirt, leaves, sand, mud, but never hidden. Piels, Rheingold, Ballantine, Schaeffer, Schlitz, shining in the sun or picked by moon or the beams of headlights at night; washed by rain or flattened by wheels, but never dulled, never buried, never destroyed. Here is the mark of savages, the testament of wasters, the stain of prosperity.
>
> Who are these men who defile the grassy borders of our roads and lanes, who pollute our ponds, who spoil the purity of our ocean beaches with the empty vessels of their thirst? Who are the men who make these vessels in millions and then say, "Drink and discard"? What society is this that can afford to cast away a million tons of metal and to make a wild and fruitful land a garbage heap?
>
> Marya Mannes, "Wasteland"

Rhythm and word choice contribute equally to the tone of this passage. The excerpt opens with imagistic sentence fragments that create a panoramic word picture of our littered roadways. Then complete sentences and somber commentary follow. Words and patterns are repeated, mixing the dignified language of epic and religion with common derogatory terms—*testament, purity, vessels,* and *fruitful* set against *savages, wasters, defile,* and *garbage heap*—to convey the contradictions Mannes deplores. The rhetorical questions, used instead of accusations, add a sense of loftiness to her outrage, helping create a tone both majestic and disdainful.

> *Erethizon dorsatus,* an antisocial character of the Northern U.S. and Canadian forest, commonly called a porcupine, looks like an uncombed head, has a grumpy personality, fights with his tail, hides his head when he's in trouble, attacks backing up, retreats going ahead, and eats toilet seats as if they were Post Toasties. It's a sad commentary on his personality that people are always trying to do him in.
>
> R. T. Allen, "The Porcupine"

The tone of this passage is affectionately humorous. Allen sets this tone by noting the porcupine's tousled appearance, testy personality, and peculiar habits, such as eating outdoor toilet seats (for their salt content, as Allen later explains). The net effect is to personify porcupines, making them seem like the eccentric reprobate human that others regard with amused toleration.

The final passage begins by referring to a "promissory note": the Constitution and the promise of life, liberty, and the pursuit of happiness spelled out in the Declaration of Independence.

It is obvious today that America has defaulted on this promissory note in so far as her citizens of color are concerned. Instead of honoring this sacred obligation, America has given the Negro people a bad check; a check which has come back marked "insufficient funds." But we refuse to believe that the bank of justice is bankrupt. We refuse to believe that there are insufficient funds in the great vaults of opportunity of this nation. And so we've come to cash this check, a check that will give us upon demand the riches of freedom and the security of justice.

We have also come to this hallowed spot to remind America of the fierce urgency of now. This is no time to engage in the luxury of cooling off or to take the tranquilizing drug of gradualism. Now is the time to make real the promises of democracy; now is the time to rise from the dark and desolate valley of segregation to the sunlit path of racial justice; now is the time to lift our nation from the quicksands of racial injustice to the solid rock of brotherhood; now is the time to make justice a reality for all of God's children.

Martin Luther King, Jr., "I Have a Dream"

This writing speaks passionately for freedom and justice. Its most obvious rhetorical strategy is metaphor, first the extended one of the promissory note, then brief separate metaphors that make the same point. The repetition of *now* sharpens the insistent tone. Eloquence comes through parallelism, repetition, and words like *sacred* and *hallowed,* vividness through figures of speech like "vaults of opportunity" and "sunlit path of racial justice." Like George Orwell, Mark Twain, Joseph Conrad, and other masters of tonal effects whose work appears in this book, King uses both rhythm and diction to create a tone that infuses and invigorates his message.

EXERCISE   *Characterize the tone of each of the following paragraphs. Point out how word choice, sentence structure, rhythm, and other elements contribute to it.*

1.   When I awoke, dimly aware of some commotion and outcry in the clearing, the light was slanting down through the pines in such a way that the glade was lit like some vast cathedral. I could see the dust motes of wood pollen in the long shaft of light, and there on the extended branch sat an enormous raven with a red and squirming nestling in its beak.

The sound that awoke me was the outraged cries of the nestling's parents, who flew helplessly in circles around the clearing. . . . And he, the murderer, the black bird at the heart of life, sat there, glistening in the common light, formidable, unperturbed, untouchable. The sighing died. It was then I saw the judgment. It was the judgment of life against death. I will never see it again so forcefully presented. I will never hear it again in notes so tragically prolonged. For in the midst of protest, they forgot the violence. There, in that clearing, the crystal note of a song sparrow lifted hesitantly in the hush. And, finally, after painful fluttering, another took the song, and then another, the song passing from one bird to another, doubtfully at first, as though some evil thing was being slowly forgotten. Till suddenly they took heart and sang from many throats joyously together as birds are known to sing. They sang under the brooding shadow of the raven. In simple truth they had forgotten the raven, for they were the singers of life, and not of death.

Loren Eiseley, "The Judgment of the Birds"

2.   America, which leads the world in almost every economic category, leads it above all in the production of schlock. Christmas toys broken before New Year's, wash-n-wear suits that neither wash well nor wear well, appliances that expire a month after the guarantee, Barbie dolls, frozen pizza—these are but a few of the shoddy goods whose main contribution to our civilization, apart from a momentary satisfaction to the purchaser, is to swell the sanitary-fill schlock heaps that are the feces of our Gross (and how!) National Product.

Robert Claiborne, "Future Schlock"

3.   Babe Ruth was *** The Sultan of Swat ***
Babe Ruth was *** THE BAMBINO ***
Babe Ruth was what you came to see!!!!
It was like going to a carnival, with Babe as both the star performer and the side-show attraction. Hell, that's what we called him: "You big ape." He was what a home-run hitter was supposed to look like. Wide, flat nose. Big feet. Little ankles. Belly hanging over his belt. All he had to do was walk on to the field and everybody would applaud. The air became charged with electricity. You just felt that something great was going to happen.

He'd twirl that big 48-ounce bat around in little circles up at the plate as if he were cranking it up for the Biggest Home Run Ever Hit—*you felt that*—and when he'd hit one he would hit it like nobody has hit it before or since. A mile high and a mile out. I can see him now, as I did so many times, just look up, drop the bat and start to trot, the little pitter-patter pigeon-toed, high-bellied trot that seemed to say, I've done it before and I'll do it again, but this one was for you.

Leo Durocher, *Nice Guys Finish Last*

■ Special Stylistic Techniques

The style of a piece of writing is its character or personality. Like people, writing can be many things: dull, stuffy, discordant, sedate, lively, flamboyant, eccentric, and so on. Figurative language and irony can contribute to your own distinctive writing style.

Figurative Language

Figurative language uses concrete words in a nonliteral way to create sharply etched sensory images that catch and hold the reader's attention. Besides energizing the writing, figurative language helps to strengthen the reader's grip on its ideas. Five figurative devices are especially important: simile, metaphor, personification, overstatement, and understatement.

Simile and Metaphor   A *simile* directly compares two unlike things by the use of *like* or *as*. "Todd is as restless as an aspen leaf in a breeze" and "Her smile flicked on and off like a sunbeam flashing momentarily through a cloud bank" are similes. A *metaphor* also compares unlike things, but without using *like* or *as*. Some metaphors include a linking verb (*is, are, were,* and so on); others do not. "The moon was a wind-tossed bark" and "The curtain of darkness fell over the land" are both metaphors. Here is an excerpt that contains similes and metaphors:

> The field is a sea of deep, dark green, a sea made up of mil-
> lions of small blades of grass blended together as one. Each
> blade is a dark green spear, broad at the bottom and narrowing
> to a needle point at the tip. Its full length is arched so that,
> viewed from one end, it looks like a shallow trough with paper-
> thin sides. On the inner side of this trough, small ridges and
> shallow valleys run from base to tip. To a finger rubbed across
> them, they feel like short, bristly hairs.
>
> Daniel Kinney

DISCUSSION QUESTIONS

1. Locate the similes in this passage and explain how they help the reader.
2. Locate the metaphors and point out how each heightens the sensory impact of the writing.

Writers too often snatch hastily at the first similes and metaphors that come to mind and end up strewing their pages with overused and enfeebled specimens. Johnny is "as blind as a bat," Mary runs around "like a chicken with its head cut off"—and the writing slips into trite gear. Other comparisons link items that are too dissimilar. For example, "The wind whistled through the trees like a herd of galloping horses" would only puzzle a reader.

Personification   This is a special sort of metaphor that assigns human qualities or traits to something nonhuman: a plant, an abstraction, a nonliving thing. Here are some examples:

The vine clung stubbornly to the trunk of the tree.

May fortune smile upon you.

The waves lapped sullenly against the base of the cliff.

Each of these sentences assigns its subject a different emotional quality—stubbornness, friendliness, gloom—each figurative rather than literal: Vines aren't stubborn, fortune doesn't smile, and waves aren't sullen.

Personification sometimes extends beyond a single sentence. To illustrate, the following passage carries a single image through two paragraphs:

> "I figured when my legislative program passed the Congress," [Lyndon] John-
> son said in 1971, "that the Great Society had a real chance to grow into a beautiful
> woman. And I figured her growth and development would be as natural and in-
> evitable as any small child's. In the first year, as we got the laws on the books, she'd
> begin to crawl. Then in the second year, as we got more laws on the books, she'd
> begin to walk, and the year after that, she'd be off and running, all the time grow-

ing bigger and healthier and fatter. And when she grew up, I figured she'd be so big and beautiful that the American people couldn't help but fall in love with her, and once they did, they'd want to keep her around forever, making her a permanent part of American life, more permanent than the New Deal.

"But now Nixon has come along and everything I've worked for is ruined. There's a story in the paper every day about him slashing another one of my Great Society programs. I can just see him waking up in the morning, making that victory sign of his and deciding which program to kill. It's a terrible thing for me to sit by and watch someone else starve my Great Society to death. She's getting thinner and thinner and uglier and uglier all the time; now her bones are beginning to stick out and her wrinkles are beginning to show. Soon she'll be so ugly that the American people will refuse to look at her; they'll stick her in a closet to hide her away and there she'll die. And when she dies, I too will die."

Doris Kearns, "Who *Was* Lyndon Baines Johnson?"

Through personification, Johnson expresses affection for his social program, disapproval of Nixon's policies, and sorrow over the coming demise of the "child" he has so carefully nurtured.

Personification works best when it is used in moderation and doesn't make outrageous comparisons. Dishes don't run away with spoons except in nursery rhymes.

Overstatement   Overstatement, sometimes called hyperbole, deliberately and drastically exaggerates in order to make a point. An example is "Wilfred is the world's biggest fool."

One of the best examples of sustained overstatement is Mark Twain's essay "Fenimore Cooper's Literary Offences." In it, Twain claims, "In one place in *Deerslayer,* and in the restricted space of two-thirds of a page, Cooper has scored 114 offences against literary art out of a possible 115." Twain also asserts, "There have been daring people in the world who claimed that Cooper could write English, but they are all dead now. . . ." Through such exaggerations, Twain mocks the shortcomings of Cooper's novels.

Used sparingly, overstatement is emphatic, adding real force to an event or situation. Writers who consistently exaggerate, however, risk losing their credibility.

Understatement   Understatement makes an assertion in a humble manner without giving something its due, as when a sportscaster calls a team's 23–2 record "pretty fair." By drawing attention to the thing it appears to slight, this soft-spoken approach offers writers an effective strategy. Here is an example:

> To assume that Heidi Mansfield lacks the qualifications for this position is not unwarranted.

Without ever actually calling Mansfield unqualified, the statement suggests that she is. Similarly, when a meat company executive says, "It is not unlikely that beef prices will jump ten cents a pound in the next two months," we might as well count on spending another dime. As these statements show, understatement not infrequently has an ulterior motive.

EXERCISE   *Identify the similes, metaphors, personifications, overstatements, or understatements in these sentences.*

1. The old table greedily sucked up the linseed oil.
2. Russia's social and economic system is a giant staircase that leads nowhere.
3. Stanley has the bile of human meanness by the quart in every vein.
4. Their music sounds like the drumming of an infant's fists against the sides of a crib.
5. The foundations of our divorce are as strong as ever.
6. It is not unlike Muriel to be late.
7. You're the world's biggest liar!
8. "Fashion, though folly's child, and guide of fools, Rules e'en the wisest, and in learning rules."
9. Einstein's theories have had some impact on modern science.
10. I'm as tired as a farm horse at sunset.

Irony

Irony occurs when a writer intentionally states one thing but actually means something different or even opposite. A certain point is thus highlighted. The sportswriter who refers to the "ideal conditions" for a tennis tournament when rain has drenched the courts and forced cancellation of matches speaks ironically. Here is a longer example of the same sort of irony:

> The baron, though a small man, had a large soul, and it swelled with satisfaction at the consciousness of being the greatest man in the little world about him. He loved to tell long stories about the dark old warriors whose portraits looked grimly down from the walls around, and he found no listeners equal to those that fed at his expense. He was much given to the marvellous, and a firm believer in all those supernatural tales with which every mountain and valley in Germany abounds. The faith of his guests exceeded even his own; they listened to every tale of wonder with open eyes and mouths, and never failed to be astonished, even though repeated for the hundredth time. Thus lived the Baron Von Landshort, the oracle of his table, the absolute monarch of his little territory, and happy, above all things, in the persuasion that he was the wisest man of the age.
>
> Washington Irving, "The Spectre Bridegroom"

Irving never directly states the baron's shortcomings. Rather, suggestive details such as the swelling of the baron's soul, his belief in the supernatural, and his deception by the sponging guests portray one who, far from being "the wisest man of the age," is pompous, superstitious, and gullible.

■ Eliminating Flawed Diction

Diction flaws include wordiness, euphemisms, clichés, mixed metaphors, and sexist language. As you revise, stay alert for these culprits and eliminate any that you find.

Wordiness

Wordiness is verbal obesity, and like physical obesity it has more than one cause. Some writers overnourish their prose to make it sound more impressive, some to pad an assignment, and some simply because they don't realize they're doing it. Whatever the reason, the results are the same: ponderous, slow-moving papers that lack punch. To inject vigor, strip your prose down to fighting weight by cutting out every word that doesn't serve a purpose. If five words are doing the work of one, drop four.

The two major forms of wordiness, deadwood and gobbledygook, often occur together. *Deadwood*, which does nothing but take up space and clutter the writing, is bracketed in the following sentence:

> Responsible parents [of today] neither allow their children[to have] absolute freedom [to do as they please] nor severely restrict their children's activities.

Now read the sentence without the deadwood:

> Responsible parents neither allow their children absolute freedom nor severely restrict their children's activities.

Careful revision has increased the clarity and reduced the words from twenty-three to fourteen.

Gobbledygook consists of long, abstract, or technical words that help create unnecessarily long and complex sentences. Some people who write it mistakenly believe it "dignifies" their thoughts. Others want to conceal their meanings by clouding their statements. And some naively think that long words are better than short ones. All of these writers use gobbledygook, but none of their readers appreciates it. Here are some samples of gobbledygook followed by revised versions in plain English:

Original Version	**Revised Version**
The fish exhibited a 100 percent mortality response.	All the fish died.
We have been made cognizant of the fact that the experiment will be terminated in the near future.	We have learned that the experiment will end soon.

Euphemisms

Euphemisms take the sting out of something unpleasant or add stature to something humble. Familiar expressions include *pass away* for *die, preowned* for *used,* and *sanitation engineer* for *garbage collector.*

In most cases, the writer simply intends to cushion reality. But euphemisms also have grisly uses. Mobsters don't *beat up* merchants who refuse *protection* (itself a euphemism); they *lean on* them. Hitler didn't talk about *exterminating the Jews* but about *the final solution to the Jewish problem.* These euphemisms don't just blur reality; they blot out images of horror. Of merchants with broken limbs and bloodied faces. Of cattle cars crammed with men, women, and children en route to death camps. Of barbed wire and gas ovens and starved corpses in the millions.

Any euphemism, however well-intentioned, probably obscures an issue. On occasion you may need one in order to protect the sensitive reader, but usually you will serve readers best by using direct expressions that present reality, not a tidied-up version.

Clichés and Mixed Metaphors

Clichés   Clichés are expressions that have become flat and stale from overuse. Rather than responding to experience with their own perceptions, writers sometimes resort to oft-repeated words or phrases that stem from patterned thinking. Dullness follows. Daily conversation abounds with stale, trite expressions because talk is unplanned, but writing allows you time to find invigorating and effective language. Your individual response is what draws the reader's interest, and only fresh thinking will produce that response. The following list of clichés barely "scratches the surface":

acid test	burn the midnight oil	green with envy
almighty dollar	chip off the old block	last but not least
beat a hasty retreat	clear as a bell	nipped in the bud
better late than never	cool as a cucumber	rears its ugly head
black sheep	easier said than done	set the world on fire
blind as a bat	goes without saying	sick as a dog

Mixed Metaphors   Clichéd writing often suffers as well from mixed metaphors—inappropriate combinations that startle or amuse the reader. How would you respond if you came across this example?

When he opened that can of worms, he bit off more than he could chew.

Can you visualize someone chewing a mouthful of worms? The point is obvious.

Sexist Language

Sexist language can assume several guises. Sometimes it appears as unneeded information that dilutes or even demeans someone's accomplishments. It can occur when the writer uses gender-exclusive pronouns like *he* and *she* inappropriately. And it may attach arbitrary gender labels to persons and groups. All U.S. government agencies, most businesses, and most academic publications prohibit sexist language. Deliberate or accidental, such language has no place in your writing. These guidelines will help you avoid it.

1. Don't unnecessarily mention a person's appearance, spouse, or family.

> *Sexist:*   The cute new loan officer at the Godfather Finance Company is a real hit with customers.
>
> *Sexist:*   Craig Helmond, husband of nationally known cardiologist Dr. Jennifer Helmond, won election to the Beal City Board of Education.

> *Sexist:*   After eight years of attending college part time, Angelica Denham, a three-time grandmother, was awarded a bachelor of science degree.

> *Nonsexist:*   The efficient new loan officer at the Godfather Finance Company is a real hit with customers.

> *Nonsexist:*   Craig Helmond, an accountant at Oakwood Growth Enterprise, won election to the Beal City Board of Education.

> *Nonsexist:*   After eight years of attending college part time, Angelica Denham was awarded a bachelor of science degree.

Note how, in each case, the sentence has been rewritten to include only relevant information.

2. Use the pronouns *he, him, his,* and *himself* only when referring to antecedents that are clearly masculine and *she, her, hers,* or *herself* only when their antecedents are clearly feminine.

> *Sexist:*   Each tourist must carry *his* passport with *him* at all times.

> *Sexist:*   If a collector wishes to find an out-of-print book, she should try http://www.bibliofind.com on the Web.

Correct this type of error by substituting plural antecedents and pronouns for the singular ones or by rewriting the sentence to eliminate the pronouns.

> *Nonsexist:*   Tourists must carry *their* passports with *them* at all times.

> *Nonsexist:*   Any collector wishing to find an out-of-print book should try http://www.bibliofind.com on the Web.

3. Don't use occupational labels that imply the positions are held only by one sex.

Sexist	Nonsexist
chairwoman	chair
draftsman	drafter
fireman	fire fighter
policeman	police officer
postman	letter carrier
weatherman	weather reporter

A word of caution here. To avoid sexism, some writers substitute the suffix *-person* for *-man* in many job titles (such as *handyperson* for someone who does odd jobs). Such attempts, however, often create awkward expressions that you should avoid.

EXERCISE   *The following sentences are flawed by wordiness, euphemisms, clichés,*
mixed metaphors, and sexist language. When you have identified the
faults, revise the sentences.

1. The American eagle will never, in the face of foreign threats, pull in its horns
   or draw back into its shell.

2. Last summer, I was engaged in the repair of automobiles.

3. You're looking as bright as a button this morning.

4. My mother was called to her heavenly reward last winter.

5. Any student wishing to attend summer school at Burns State College must pay
   his tuition one week before registration day.

6. My brother is in the process of pursuing a curriculum of industrial chemistry.

7. The ball's in your court, and if you strike out, don't expect me to pick up the
   pieces.

8. The beautiful, sultry-voiced clerk quickly filled the order.

9. Winning first prize for her essay was a real feather in Peggy's cap.

10. Our company plans to confer retirement on 200 employees by year's end.

chapter 17

The Essay Examination

Instructors use essay examinations to gauge your grasp of ideas, noting how well you apply, analyze, challenge, compare, or otherwise handle them. Facts and figures, on the other hand, are more often tested by objective examinations. Writing essay answers under pressure and with minimal time to rethink and revise differs from writing at home. Instructors expect reasonably complete and coherent answers but not models of style or neatness. They do expect legibility. An effective presentation increases your chances for success; the skills learned in composition class can help you achieve it. A plan, a thesis, specific support, staying on track, and the pointers presented in this chapter—all are grade boosters.

■ Studying for the Examination

Here are some pointers for studying:

1. Allow adequate preparation time. For a comprehensive test, start reviewing several days in advance. For one that covers a small segment of the course, a day or two should be enough.
2. Reread the key points you've marked in your class notes and textbook. Use them to develop a set of basic concepts.

3. Make up a set of sample questions related to these concepts and do some freewriting to answer them. Even if none of the questions appears on the test, your efforts will ease pretest jitters and supply insights that apply to other questions.

4. Answer your questions by drawing upon your concepts and supplying details from your notes and textbook.

■ Types of Test Questions

Some instructors favor narrow, highly focused test questions with detailed answering instructions. Others like broad items, perhaps with simple directions such as "Write for twenty minutes." The sample questions below range from very broad to very narrow. Note how when answering them you can often use the writing strategies discussed in Chapters 4–12.

1. Analyze the *influences* of the industrial revolution on European society.

2. Discuss the most important *causes* of the Spanish–American War.

3. *Compare and contrast* the David statues of Michelangelo and Bernini.

4. Select three different camera shots used in the movie *Titanic*. Identify at least one scene that *illustrates* each shot; then explain how each shot functions by *describing* the relationship between the shot and the action or dialogue.

5. Discuss the stock market plunge of October 27, 1997. Consider the major *factors* involved, such as the liberal lending practices of international banks, the growth in global manufacturing capacity, the severe recessions and monetary turmoil in Pacific Rim countries like Thailand and Malaysia, the concerns of Wall Street, and how these *factors* interacted. Use a thesis statement that signals the points you will discuss.

A highly focused question such as item 5 suggests how to organize and develop the essay. If you know the answer, you can begin writing quickly. In contrast, item 1 forces you to focus and narrow the subject before you respond. Answering this type of item requires careful planning.

■ Preparing to Write

You can't get from Pocatello to Poughkeepsie without knowing and following an appropriate route. The same principle applies to exam writing. Often students fail to read general directions or to answer what is asked. Low grades follow. To avoid penalizing yourself, scan the test items, noting how many must be answered and which ones, if any, are optional. When you have a choice, select the questions you can answer most thoroughly. Pay attention to any suggestions or requirements concerning length (one paragraph, two pages) or relative weight (25 points, 30 minutes, 40 percent), and budget your time accordingly.

The first requirement for most essay tests is to read the question for *key words*. Does the instructor want you to analyze, compare, criticize, defend, describe, discuss, evaluate, illustrate, explain, justify, trace, or summarize? If you are asked to explain how Darwin's theory of evolution affected nineteenth-century thinking, do just that; you won't like your grade if, instead, you summarize the theory. Merely putting ideas on paper, even perceptive ideas, does not substitute for addressing the question.

> **EXERCISE**   *Indicate what each of the following questions calls for. What is required? By what methods—arguing, describing, or the like—would you develop the answer?*
>
> 1. Distinguish between mild depression and severe depression. You might focus on the nature, the symptoms, or the potential treatments of each condition.
> 2. Support or refute the following statement: Because waste incineration generates stack gases and ash that contain high levels of toxic substances, it is not an acceptable solution to waste-disposal problems.
> 3. Explain how to clean an automobile carburetor.
> 4. Briefly relate the events in the Book of Job and then explain the significance of the tale. Could the tale be called symbolic? Why or why not?

When you have the essay question clearly in mind, don't immediately start writing. A jackrabbit start spells trouble. Instead, take a few moments to plan your answer. Following these steps will help you do this:

1. Jot down specific supporting information from your reading and lecture notes.
2. Make a rough outline that sketches the main points you'll cover and an effective order for presenting them.
3. Prepare a thesis statement that responds to the question and will control your answer.

Writing an essay exam, like writing an essay, is a front-end-loaded process. Much of the brain work occurs before you put your answer on paper. You won't get to Poughkeepsie just by starting to drive.

■ Writing the Examination Answer

Here are some guidelines that will help you write a successful exam:

1. Position your thesis statement at the beginning of your answer. Make sure each paragraph is controlled by a topic sentence tied to the thesis statement.
2. Don't become excessively concerned about your wording. Focus on content and, if time permits, make stylistic changes later.
3. Fight the impulse to jot down everything you know about the general subject. The grader doesn't want to plow through verbiage to arrive at your answer.

The following essay illustrates these guidelines:

Question:	Discuss the various appeals described by classical rhetoric that an orator can use. Give a brief example of each kind of appeal.
Answer: *Thesis statement previews* *focus and order of answer*	Classical rhetoric defines three major appeals—logical, emotional, and ethical—that orators may use to win support from their audience.
Topic sentence: *Example 1:* *Example 2:*	Most rhetoricians agree that any argument must be based on logic; that is, it must appeal to the intellect of the listeners. Unless it does, the orator will fail to convince them. For example, a speaker who is urging the election of a candidate and presents the candidate's voting record is appealing to logic, asking the audience to understand that the voting record predicts how the candidate will continue to vote if elected. Likewise, a candidate for public office who describes how a tax cut will stimulate the economy and create new jobs is using a logical appeal.
Topic sentence: *Example 1:* *Example 2:*	In addition to logic, emotional appeals are a powerful means of swaying people, especially groups. Though emotional appeals work along with logical appeals, they are quite different because they are directed at the listener's hopes, fears, and sympathies. The presidential candidate who indicates that a vote for an opponent is a vote to increase government spending and risk a financial crisis is making an emotional appeal. So, too, is the gubernatorial candidate who asserts that her state's industry can be revitalized and serve as a model for all other states.
Topic sentence: *Example 1:* *Example 2:*	The ethical appeal is more subtle than either of the other two but probably just as important. The orator must strike the audience as a sensible, good person if they are to believe the message. Sometimes the speaker's logic and also the tone—moderate, sensible, or wise—will convey sufficient ethical appeal. At other times, a speaker will use statements that are deliberately intended to create ethical appeal. "In developing this program, I will work closely with both houses of the legislature, including the members of both political parties" and "De-

spite our differences, I believe my opponent to be a decent, honest person" are examples of such statements.

Restatement of thesis: In any speech, all these appeals—logical, emotional, and ethical—work together to convince an audience.

Student Unknown

In contrast, the next two responses to the same question illustrate common faults of examination essays.

Answer A

1   There are three basic appeals that a speaker can make to captivate an audience. These are the ethical appeal, the logical appeal, and the emotional appeal.

2   The first of these—the ethical appeal—includes all the speaker's efforts to be viewed as rational, wise, good, and generous. Needless to say, the ethical appeal is very important. Without it, no one would pay attention to the speaker's argument.

3   The second appeal—logical—is also extremely important. It carries the burden of the argument from speaker to listener and appeals to the intellect of the audience.

4   Emotional appeal—the third and final one—is made to the passions and feelings of the listeners. The significance of such an appeal is obvious.

5   A speaker often uses all three appeals to win an audience over.

Answer *A* starts with a thesis statement and includes brief definitions of the three appeals; however, it omits any concrete examples and includes no specific details. As a result, the significance of the emotional appeal is not "obvious," as paragraph 4 claims, nor does the answer offer any hints as to why the other appeals are important. This response resembles an outline more than an answer and suggests the student lacked the knowledge to do a good job.

Answer B

1   Orators may make three different kinds of appeals to win favor from an audience: emotional appeal, logical appeal, and ethical appeal.

2   Let's start with emotional appeal because this is the one that is not essential to a speech. Logical and ethical appeals are always included; emotional appeal may be used to help sway an audience, but without logical and ethical appeals no argument is accepted. This simply makes sense: If there is no logic, there is no argument; and if the speaker doesn't come across as an ethical person—someone to be relied upon—then no one will accept the message. But emotional appeal is different. Unemotional arguments may be accepted.

3   Nevertheless, emotional appeal is important. It includes whatever a speaker does to move the feelings of the audience. The speaker asks, "Don't you want to protect your families?" Such an appeal is emotional. A speaker may appeal to the prejudices or biases of listeners. Someone at a Ku Klux Klan rally does that. So does a minister who exhorts people to be "saved." Both speakers address the emotions of the groups they talk to.

4   There is a very fine use of emotional appeal in the "Letter from Birmingham Jail" by Martin Luther King, Jr. At one point King asks his audience of white clergy how they would feel if, like blacks, they had to deny their children treats such as amusement parks and had to fear for the lives of their families, and so on. He also describes the bombings and burnings that blacks are subjected to. All the details move readers emotionally, so that they come to sympathize with blacks who live in fear.

5   Logical appeal, as noted earlier, is crucial. The speaker must seem to have an intelligent plan. The listeners want the plan to meet their needs.

6   The other appeal is the ethical one. It is made when speakers make themselves seem generous, good, and wise.

7   All three appeals can be used in one speech, although the logical and ethical appeals are essential to it.

Although the writer opens with an acceptable thesis statement, this answer shows little evidence of advance planning. Does it make sense to begin in paragraph 2 with an appeal tagged "not essential"? And note how the paragraph drifts from the emotional appeal to the other two types, despite its topic sentence. Paragraphs 3 and 4 do focus on the emotional appeal and ironically, through specific examples, make a good case for its importance. Paragraphs 5 and 6 shortchange logical and ethical appeals by saying next to nothing about them. The essay contradicts itself: If logical and ethical appeals are the essential ones and emotional appeals "not essential," why is more than half of the essay about emotional appeal?

EXERCISE   *Read the examination questions and answers below. Then respond to the questions that follow the answers.*

A. Question

Living organisms are composed of cells. On the basis of structure, biologists categorize cells into two groups: the prokaryotic cells and the eukaryotic cells. What are the major differences between prokaryotic cells and eukaryotic cells, and in which living organisms are these cells found?

Answer

1   Eukaryotic cells have a true nucleus and their genetic material, the DNA-containing chromosomes, is located within this nucleus, which is surrounded by a nuclear membrane. Prokaryotic cells lack a true nucleus, and their genetic material lies free in the cytoplasm of the cell.

2   Eukaryotic cells are also much more complex than prokaryotic cells. Eukaryotic cells commonly contain organelles such as mitochondria, a Golgi complex, lysosomes, an endoplasmic reticulum, and in photosynthetic cells, chloroplasts. These organelles are typically lacking in the simpler prokaryotic cells.

3   Prokaryotic cells make up the structure of all bacteria and the blue-green algae. These are the simplest of all known cellular organisms. All other cellular organisms, including humans, are composed of eukaryotic cells.

Scott Wybolt

a. Does the response answer the question that was asked? Discuss.

B. Question

Analyze the significant relationships between imagination and reality in Coleridge's "This Lime-Tree Bower My Prison." In your answer, you might consider some of the following questions: What is the importance of setting in the poem? Is the speaker's mind a form of setting? How is reality implicitly defined in the poem? How, and through what agencies, can reality be transmitted? What relationship is finally perceived between the spiritual and the concrete? How does friendship or fellow feeling trigger the essential insights revealed in the poem?

Answer

1   Coleridge's "This Lime-Tree Bower My Prison" shows imagination to be a powerful force that can control one's perception of reality and that is, in itself, a kind of reality—perhaps the most important reality. Thus, imagination and reality are more intimately linked and more similar in Coleridge's poem than they are ordinarily thought to be.

2   The relationship between imagination and reality is revealed by the speaker of "Lime-Tree Bower," although he doesn't openly state it. The technique for revelation is dramatic monologue, with the speaker seemingly talking spontaneously as his situation gives rise to a series of thoughts.

3   As the poem begins, the speaker finds himself "trapped" at home in his lime-tree bower, while his friends go on a walk he had hoped to take with them. This situation at first bothers the speaker, causing him to feel imprisoned. As the poem progresses, however, the speaker begins to imagine all the places his friends are visiting on their walk. Though he laments not being with them, he shows excitement as he describes the scenes his friends are viewing: the "roaring dell," the sea, and so on. Thus the speaker recognizes that he is able to participate imaginatively in the walk and, in doing so, to escape his "prison" reality and enter the reality of his friends.

4   The moment of recognition occurs at the beginning of stanza three: "A delight / Comes sudden on my heart, and I am glad / As I myself was there!" Interestingly, however, this point marks a turn in the speaker's thoughts. Once again he realizes where he actually is—the lime-tree bower. But now he appreciates its beauties. The natural beauties he imagined have taught him to appreciate the beauties of nature right before him. He has learned that there is "No plot so narrow, be but Nature there." The lime-tree bower is no longer a prison but a rich and beautiful, if somewhat small, world.

5   Imagination has again shaped the speaker's perceptions of reality. It controls the perception of circumstances—whether one views a place as a prison or a microcosm of a larger world, with beauties and possibilities in its own right. The use of imagination can teach one about reality, as it has Coleridge's speaker. And, if one surrenders to it completely—as the speaker does when he envisions the world of the walkers—imagination is a delightful reality, as valid as the reality of the place in which one sits.

6   Imagination and reality are merged in "This Lime-Tree Bower My Prison," and though this identification is apparently temporary, one may learn through imagination how to cope with and enjoy reality. Thus, imagination is intimately involved in shaping the perception of reality.

Lori McCue

a. Which of the possible approaches suggested in the question does the student select?

b. Which of the other questions does she indirectly answer? Which ones are not addressed?

c. Identify the thesis statement and explain how it controls the answer.

d. Show how the answer demonstrates careful planning.

e. Point out some effective supporting details.

chapter

18

Writing About Literature

Teachers of literature generally expect you to write about what you've read. Typically they might ask you to

- show how an author handled one element of a short story, play, or poem
- compare how two different works treat a particular element
- weigh several elements and then determine the writer's intention
- air your reactions to some work.

Writing about literature offers several benefits. Weighing and recording your thoughts on the different elements sharpen your critical thinking ability. Literary papers also pay artistic dividends, as careful reading and subsequent writing deepen your appreciation of the writer's craft. Furthermore, you'll feel a sense of accomplishment as you coherently express your perceptions. Finally, writing a literature paper offers yet another opportunity to apply the writing guidelines discussed in Chapters 1–3. Focusing, gathering information, organizing, writing, revising, and editing—the old familiar trail leads to success here too.

■ The Elements of Literature

Most writing assignments on literature will probably feature one or more of the following elements:

Plot	Symbols
Point of view	Irony
Character	Theme
Setting	

Depending on the work, some of these will be more important than others. Read the following story by Stephen Crane, "The Bride Comes to Yellow Sky." The discussions that follow it point out the basic features of each element and offer useful writing suggestions.

The Bride Comes to Yellow Sky

Stephen Crane

I

The great Pullman was whirling onward with such dignity of motion that a glance from the window seemed simply to prove that the plains of Texas were pouring eastward. Vast flats of green grass, dull-hued spaces of mesquit and cactus, little groups of frame houses, woods of light and tender trees, all were sweeping into the east, sweeping over the horizon, a precipice.

A newly married pair had boarded this coach at San Antonio. The man's face was reddened from many days in the wind and sun, and a direct result of his new black clothes was that his brick-colored hands were constantly performing in a most conscious fashion. From time to time he looked down respectfully at his attire. He sat with a hand on each knee, like a man waiting in a barber's shop. The glances he devoted to other passengers were furtive and shy.

The bride was not pretty, nor was she very young. She wore a dress of blue cashmere, with small reservations of velvet here and there, and with steel buttons abounding. She continually twisted her head to regard her puff sleeves, very stiff, straight, and high. They embarrassed her. It was quite apparent that she had cooked, and that she expected to cook, dutifully. The blushes caused by the careless scrutiny of some passengers as she had entered the car were strange to see upon this plain, under-class countenance, which was drawn in placid, almost emotionless lines.

They were evidently very happy. "Ever been in a parlor-car before?" he asked, smiling with delight.

"No," she answered; "I never was. It's fine, ain't it?"

"Great! And then after a while we'll go forward to the diner, and get a big lay-out. Finest meal in the world. Charge a dollar."

"Oh, do they?" cried the bride. "Charge a dollar? Why, that's too much—for us—ain't it, Jack?"

"Not this trip, anyhow," he answered bravely. "We're going to go the whole thing."

Later he explained to her about the trains. "You see, it's a thousand miles from one end of Texas to the other; and this train runs right across it and never stops but four times." He had the pride of an owner. He pointed out to her the dazzling fittings of the coach; and in truth her eyes opened wider as she contemplated the sea-green figured velvet, the shining brass, silver, and glass, the wood that gleamed as darkly brilliant as the surface of a pool of oil. At one end a bronze figure sturdily held a support for a separated chamber, and at convenient places on the ceiling were frescos in olive and silver.

To the minds of the pair, their surroundings reflected the glory of their marriage that morning in San Antonio; this was the environment of their new estate; and the man's face in particular beamed with an elation that made him appear ridiculous to the negro porter. This individual at times surveyed them from afar with an amused and superior grin. On other occasions he bullied them with skill in ways that did not make it exactly plain to them that they were being bullied. He subtly used all the manners of the most unconquerable kind of snobbery. He oppressed them; but of this oppression they had small knowledge, and they speedily forgot that infrequently a number of travelers covered them with stares of derisive enjoyment. Historically there was supposed to be something infinitely humorous in their situation.

"We are due in Yellow Sky at 3:42," he said, looking tenderly into her eyes.

"Oh, are we?" she said, as if she had not been aware of it. To evince surprise at her husband's statement was part of her wifely amiability. She took from a pocket a little silver watch; and as she held it before her, and stared at it with a frown of attention, the new husband's face shone.

"I bought it in San Anton' from a friend of mine," he told her gleefully.

"It's seventeen minutes past twelve," she said, looking up at him with a kind of shy and clumsy coquetry. A passenger, noting this play, grew excessively sardonic, and winked at himself in one of the numerous mirrors.

At last they went to the dining car. Two rows of negro waiters, in glowing white suits, surveyed their entrance with the interest, and also the equanimity, of men who had been forewarned. The pair fell to the lot of a waiter who happened to feel pleasure in steering them through their meal. He viewed them with the manner of a fatherly pilot, his countenance radiant with benevolence. The patronage, entwined with the ordinary deference, was not plain to them. And yet, as they returned to their coach, they showed in their faces a sense of escape.

To the left, miles down a long purple slope, was a little ribbon of mist where moved the keening Rio Grande. The train was approaching it at an angle, and the apex was Yellow Sky. Presently it was apparent that, as the distance from Yellow Sky grew shorter, the husband became commensurately restless. His brick-red hands were more insistent in their prominence. Occasionally he was even rather absent-minded and far-away when the bride leaned forward and addressed him.

As a matter of truth, Jack Potter was beginning to find the shadow of a deed weigh upon him like a leaden slab. He, the town marshal of Yellow Sky, a man known, liked, and feared in his corner, a prominent person, had gone to San Antonio to meet a girl he believed he loved, and there, after the usual prayers, had actually induced her to marry him, without consulting Yellow Sky for any part of the transaction. He was now bringing his bride before an innocent and unsuspecting community.

Of course people in Yellow Sky married as it pleased them, in accordance with a general custom; but such was Potter's thought of his duty to his friends, or of their idea of his duty, or of an unspoken form which does not control men in these matters, that he felt he was heinous. He had committed an extraordinary crime. Face to face with this girl in San Antonio, and spurred by his sharp impulse, he had gone headlong over all the social hedges. At San Antonio he was like a man hidden in the dark. A knife to sever any friendly duty, any form, was easy to his hand in that remote city. But the hour of Yellow Sky—the hour of daylight—was approaching.

He knew full well that his marriage was an important thing to his town. It could only be exceeded by the burning of the new hotel. His friends could not forgive him. Frequently he had reflected on the advisability of telling them by telegraph, but a new cowardice had been upon him. He feared to do it. And now the train was hurrying him toward a scene of amazement, glee, and reproach. He glanced out of the window at the line of haze swinging slowly in toward the train.

Yellow Sky had a kind of brass band, which played painfully, to the delight of the populace. He laughed without heart as he thought of it. If the citizens could dream of his prospective arrival with his bride, they would parade the band at the station and escort them, amid cheers and laughing congratulations, to his adobe home.

He resolved that he would use all the devices of speed and plainscraft in making the journey from the station to his house. Once within that safe citadel, he could issue some sort of vocal bulletin, and then not go among the citizens until they had time to wear off a little of their enthusiasm.

The bride looked anxiously at him. "What's worrying you, Jack?"

He laughed again. "I'm not worrying, girl; I'm only thinking of Yellow Sky."

She flushed in comprehension.

A sense of mutual guilt invaded their minds and developed a finer tenderness. They looked at each other, with eyes softly aglow. But Potter often laughed the same nervous laugh; the flush upon the bride's face seemed quite permanent.

The traitor to the feelings of Yellow Sky narrowly watched the speeding landscape. "We're nearly there," he said.

Presently the porter came and announced the proximity of Potter's home. He held a brush in his hand, and, with all his airy superiority gone, he brushed Potter's new clothes as the latter slowly turned this way and that way. Potter tumbled out a coin and gave it to the porter, as he had seen others do. It was a heavy and muscle-bound business, as that of a man shoeing his first horse.

The porter took their bag, and as the train began to slow they moved forward to the hooded platform of the car. Presently the two engines and their long string of coaches rushed into the station of Yellow Sky.

"They have to take water here," said Potter, from a constricted throat and in mournful cadence, as one announcing death. Before the train stopped his eye had swept the length of the platform, and he was glad and astonished to see there was none upon it but the station-agent, who, with a slightly hurried and anxious air, was walking toward the water-tanks. When the train had halted, the porter alighted first, and placed in position a little temporary step.

"Come on, girl," said Potter, hoarsely. As he helped her down they each laughed on a false note. He took the bag from the negro, and bade his wife cling to his arm. As they slunk rapidly away, his hang-dog glance perceived that they were unloading the two trunks, and also that the station-agent, far ahead near the baggage-car, had turned and was running toward him, making gestures. He laughed, and groaned as he laughed, when he noted the first effect of his marital bliss upon Yellow Sky. He gripped his wife's arm firmly to his side, and they fled. Behind them the porter stood, chuckling fatuously.

II

The California express on the Southern Railway was due at Yellow Sky in twenty-one minutes. There were six men at the bar of the Weary Gentleman saloon. One was a drummer[1] who talked a great deal and rapidly; three were Texans who did not care to talk at that time; and two were Mexican sheepherders, who did not talk as a general practice in the Weary Gentleman saloon. The barkeeper's dog lay on the boardwalk that crossed in front of the door. His head was on his paws, and he glanced drowsily here and there with the constant vigilance of a dog that is kicked on occasion. Across the sandy street were some vivid green grass-plots, so wonderful in appearance, amid the sands that burned near them in a blazing sun, that they caused a doubt in the mind. They exactly resembled the grass mats used to represent lawns on the stage. At the cooler end of the railway station, a man without a coat sat in a tilted chair and smoked his pipe. The fresh-cut bank of the Rio Grande circled near the town, and there could be seen beyond it a great plum-colored plain of mesquit.

Save for the busy drummer and his companions in the saloon, Yellow Sky was dozing. The new-comer leaned gracefully upon the bar, and recited many tales with the confidence of a bard who has come upon a new field.

"—and at the moment that the old man fell downstairs with the bureau in his arms, the old woman was coming up with two scuttles of coal, and of course—"

The drummer's tale was interrupted by a young man who suddenly appeared in the open door. He cried: "Scratchy Wilson's drunk, and has turned loose with both hands." The two Mexicans at once set down their glasses and faded out of the rear entrance of the saloon.

The drummer, innocent and jocular, answered: "All right, old man. S'pose he has? Come in and have a drink, anyhow."

But the information had made such an obvious cleft in every skull in the room that the drummer was obliged to see its importance. All had become instantly solemn. "Say," said he, mystified, "what is this?" His three companions made the introductory gesture of eloquent speech; but the young man at the door forestalled them.

"It means, my friend," he answered, as he came into the saloon, "that for the next two hours this town won't be a health resort."

The barkeeper went to the door, and locked and barred it; reaching out of the window, he pulled in heavy wooden shutters, and barred them. Immediately a solemn, chapel-like gloom was upon the place. The drummer was looking from one to another.

"But say," he cried, "what is this, anyhow? You don't mean there is going to be a gun-fight?"

"Don't know whether there'll be a fight or not," answered one man, grimly; "but there'll be some shootin'—some good shootin'."

The young man who had warned them waved his hand. "Oh, there'll be a fight fast enough, if any one wants it. Anybody can get a fight out there in the street. There's a fight just waiting."

The drummer seemed to be swayed between the interest of a foreigner and a perception of personal danger.

"What did you say his name was?" he asked.

"Scratchy Wilson," they answered in chorus.

"And will he kill anybody? What are you going to do? Does this happen often? Does he rampage around like this once a week or so? Can he break in that door?"

"No; he can't break down that door," replied the barkeeper. "He's tried it three times. But when he comes you'd better lay down on the floor, stranger. He's dead sure to shoot at it, and a bullet may come through."

---

[1]Traveling salesman

Thereafter the drummer kept a strict eye upon the door. The time had not yet been called for him to hug the floor, but, as a minor precaution, he sidled near to the wall. "Will he kill anybody?" he said again.

The men laughed low and scornfully at the question.

"He's out to shoot, and he's out for trouble. Don't see any good in experimentin' with him."

"But what do you do in a case like this? What do you do?"

A man responded: "Why, he and Jack Potter—"

"But," in chorus the other men interrupted, "Jack Potter's in San Anton'."

"Well, who is he? What's he got to do with it?"

"Oh, he's the town marshal. He goes out and fights Scratchy when he gets on one of these tears."

"Wow!" said the drummer, mopping his brow. "Nice job he's got."

The voices had toned away to mere whisperings. The drummer wished to ask further questions, which were born of an increasing anxiety and bewilderment; but when he attempted them, the men merely looked at him in irritation and motioned him to remain silent. A tense waiting hush was upon them. In the deep shadows of the room their eyes shone as they listened for sounds from the street. One man made three gestures at the barkeeper; and the latter, moving like a ghost, handed him a glass and a bottle. The man poured a full glass of whisky, and set down the bottle noiselessly. He gulped the whisky in a swallow, and turned again toward the door in immovable silence. The drummer saw that the barkeeper, without a sound, had taken a Winchester from beneath the bar. Later he saw this individual beckoning to him, so he tiptoed across the room.

"You better come with me back of the bar."

"No, thanks," said the drummer, perspiring: "I'd rather be where I can make a break for the back door."

Whereupon the man of bottles made a kindly but peremptory gesture. The drummer obeyed it, and, finding himself seated on a box with his head below the level of the bar, balm was laid upon his soul at sight of various zinc and copper fittings that bore a resemblance to armorplate. The barkeeper took a seat comfortably upon an adjacent box.

"You see," he whispered, "this here Scratchy Wilson is a wonder with a gun—a perfect wonder; and when he goes on the wartrail, we hunt our holes—naturally. He's about the last one of the old gang that used to hang out along the river here. He's a terror when he's drunk. When he's sober he's all right—kind of simple—wouldn't hurt a fly—nicest fellow in town. But when he's drunk—whoo!"

There were periods of stillness. "I wish Jack Potter was back from San Anton'," said the barkeeper. "He shot Wilson up once—in the leg—and he would sail in and pull out the kinks in this thing."

Presently they heard from a distance the sound of a shot, followed by three wild yowls. It instantly removed a bond from the men in the darkened saloon. There was a shuffling of feet. They looked at each other. "Here he comes," they said.

III

A man in a maroon-colored flannel shirt, which had been purchased for purposes of decoration, and made principally by some Jewish women on the East Side of New York, rounded a corner and walked into the middle of the main street of Yellow Sky. In either hand the man held a long, heavy, blue-black revolver. Often he yelled, and these cries rang through a semblance of a deserted village, shrilly flying over the roofs in a volume that seemed to have no relation to the ordinary vocal strength of a man. It was as if the surrounding stillness formed the arch of a tomb over him. These cries of ferocious challenge rang against walls of silence. And his boots had red tops with gilded imprints, of the kind beloved in winter by little sledding boys on the hillsides of New England.

The man's face flamed in a rage begot of whisky. His eyes, rolling, and yet keen for ambush, hunted the still doorways and windows. He walked with the creeping movement of the midnight cat. As it occurred to him, he roared menacing information. The long revolvers in his hands were as easy as straws; they were moved with an electric swiftness. The little fingers of each hand played sometimes in a musician's way. Plain from the low collar of the shirt, the cords of his neck straightened and sank, straightened and sank, as passion moved him. The only sounds were his terrible invitations. The calm adobes preserved their demeanor at the passing of this small thing in the middle of the street.

There was no offer of fight—no offer of fight. The man called to the sky. There were no attractions. He bellowed and fumed and swayed his revolvers here and everywhere.

The dog of the barkeeper of the Weary Gentleman saloon had not appreciated the advance of events. He yet lay dozing in front of his master's door. At sight of the dog, the man paused and raised his revolver humorously. At sight of the man, the dog sprang up and walked diagonally away, with a sullen head, and growling. The man yelled, and the dog broke into a gallop. As it was about to enter an alley, there was a loud noise, a whistling, and something spat the ground directly before it. The dog screamed, and, wheeling in terror, galloped headlong in a new direction. Again there was a noise, a whistling, and sand was kicked viciously before it. Fear-stricken, the dog turned and flurried like an animal in a pen. The man stood laughing, his weapons at his hips.

Ultimately the man was attracted by the closed door of the Weary Gentleman saloon. He went to it and, hammering with a revolver, demanded drink.

The door remaining imperturbable, he picked a bit of paper from the walk, and nailed it to the framework with a knife. He then turned his back contemptuously upon this popular resort and, walking to the opposite side of the street and spinning there on his heel quickly and lithely, fired at the bit of paper. He missed it by a half-inch. He swore at himself, and went away. Later he comfortably fusilladed the windows of his most intimate friend. The man was playing with this town: it was a toy for him.

But still there was no offer of fight. The name of Jack Potter, his ancient antagonist, entered his mind, and he concluded that it would be a glad thing if he should go to Potter's house, and by bombardment induce him to come out and fight. He moved in the direction of his desire, chanting Apache scalp-music.

When he arrived at it, Potter's house presented the same still front as had the other adobes. Taking up a strategic position, the man howled a challenge. But this house regarded him as might a great stone god. It gave no sign. After a decent wait, the man howled further challenges, mingling with them wonderful epithets.

Presently there came the spectacle of a man churning himself into deepest rage over the immobility of a house. He fumed at it as the winter wind attacks a prairie cabin in the North. To the distance there should have gone the sound of a tumult like the fighting of two hundred Mexicans. As necessity bade him, he paused for breath or to reload his revolvers.

IV

Potter and his bride walked sheepishly and with speed. Sometimes they laughed together shamefacedly and low.

"Next corner, dear," he said finally.

They put forth the efforts of a pair walking bowed against a strong wind. Potter was about to raise a finger to point the first appearance of the new home when, as they circled the corner, they came face to face with a man in a maroon-colored shirt, who was feverishly pushing cartridges into a large revolver. Upon the instant the man dropped his revolver to the ground and, like lightning, whipped another from its holster. The second weapon was aimed at the bridegroom's chest.

There was a silence. Potter's mouth seemed to be merely a grave for his tongue. He exhibited an instinct to at once loosen his arm from the woman's grip, and he dropped the bag to the sand. As for the bride, her face had gone as yellow as old cloth. She was a slave to hideous rites, gazing at the apparitional snake.

The two men faced each other at a distance of three paces. He of the revolver smiled with a new and quiet ferocity.

"Tried to sneak up on me," he said. "Tried to sneak up on me!" His eyes grew more baleful. As Potter made a slight movement, the man thrust his revolver venomously forward. "No; don't you do it, Jack Potter. Don't you move a finger toward a gun just yet. Don't you move an eyelash. The time has come for me to settle with you, and I'm goin' to do it my own way, and loaf along with no interferin'. So if you don't want a gun bent on you, just mind what I tell you."

Potter looked at his enemy. "I ain't got a gun on me, Scratchy," he said. "Honest, I ain't." He was stiffening and steadying, but yet somewhere at the back of his mind a vision of the Pullman floated: the sea-green figured velvet, the shining brass, silver, and glass, the wood that gleamed as darkly brilliant as the surface of a pool of oil—all the glory of the marriage, the environment of the new estate. "You know I fight when it comes to fighting, Scratchy Wilson; but I ain't got a gun on me. You'll have to do all the shootin' yourself."

His enemy's face went livid. He stepped forward, and lashed his weapon to and fro before Potter's chest. "Don't tell me you ain't got no gun on you, you whelp. Don't tell me no lie like that. There ain't a man in Texas ever seen you without no gun. Don't take me for no kid." His eyes blazed with light, and his throat worked like a pump.

"I ain't takin' you for no kid," answered Potter. His heels had not moved an inch backward. "I'm takin' you for a damn fool. I tell you I ain't got a gun, and I ain't. If you're goin' to shoot me up, you better begin now; you'll never get a chance like this again."

So much enforced reasoning had told on Wilson's rage; he was calmer. "If you ain't got a gun, why ain't you got a gun?" he sneered. "Been to Sunday-school?"

"I ain't got a gun because I've just come from San Anton' with my wife. I'm married," said Potter. "And if I'd thought there was going to be any galoots like you prowling around when I brought my wife home, I'd had a gun, and don't you forget it."

"Married!" said Scratchy, not at all comprehending.

"Yes, married. I'm married." said Potter, distinctly.

"Married?" said Scratchy. Seemingly for the first time, he saw the drooping, drowning woman at the other man's side. "No!" he said. He was like a creature allowed a glimpse of another world. He moved a pace backward, and his arm, with the revolver, dropped to his side. "Is this the lady?" he asked.

"Yes; this is the lady," answered Potter.

There was another period of silence.

"Well," said Wilson at last, slowly, "I s'pose it's all off now."

"It's all off if you say so, Scratchy. You know I didn't make the trouble." Potter lifted his valise.

"Well, I 'low it's off, Jack," said Wilson. He was looking at the ground. "Married!" He was not a student of chivalry; it was merely that in the presence of this foreign condition he was a simple child of the earlier plains. He picked up his starboard revolver, and, placing both weapons in their holsters, he went away. His feet made funnel-shaped tracks in the heavy sand.

Plot

Plot Factors   Plot is the series of events that moves a narrative along. The opening of a story with a conventional plot introduces important characters and sets the stage for what happens. Then one or more conflicts develop, some pitting person against person, others setting characters against society, nature, fate, or themselves. Action gradually builds to a climax, where events take a decisive turn. The ending can do a number of things—clear up unanswered questions, hint at the future, state a theme, or reestablish some sort of relationship between two foes. In "The Bride," Potter experiences two conflicts: one with Scratchy Wilson and the other within himself over his marriage. The climax comes when Potter and Scratchy meet face to face, and Scratchy learns about his old adversary's marriage. As Scratchy walks away, we sense that the two old foes have had their last confrontation, that Potter's marriage has altered forever the relationship between them.

To organize plots, writers use a number of techniques. In foreshadowing, for example, the writer hints at later developments, thus creating interest and building suspense. In H. H. Munro's short story "The Open Window," a visitor to a country house observes that "An undefinable something about the room seemed to suggest masculine habitation." Yet he accepts the story of a young girl that her uncle, the man of the house, had lost his life in a bog three years before. Because he ignores his observation and accepts the girl's story at face value, the visitor is terrified by the sudden appearance of the uncle, who seems to be a ghost. The careful reader, however, senses what's coming and enjoys the trick more for having been in on it.

When using a flashback, another organizational technique, the writer interrupts the flow of events to relate one or more happenings that occurred before the point at which the story opened, then resumes the narrative at or near the point of interruption. Ernest Hemingway's short story "The Short Happy Life of Francis Macomber" provides an illustration. As the story opens, we meet characters who hint that Macomber displayed cowardice by running from, rather than shooting, a charging, wounded lion. A bit later the story flashes back to detail the actual incident. Flashbacks supply essential information and either create or resolve suspense.

Not every plot unfolds in clear stages. Many modern stories lack distinct plot divisions and focus on psychological, not physical, conflicts. In extreme cases, writers may abandon the traditional plot structure and present events in a disorganized sequence that helps accomplish some literary purpose, such as reflecting a character's disturbed state of mind. Joyce Carol Oates's short story "How I Contemplated the World from the Detroit House of Correction and Began My Life Over Again" fits this mold. To dramatize her chief character's mental turmoil, Oates presents the story as a series of notes for an English composition. These notes, labeled "Events," "Characters," "Sioux Drive," "Detroit," and "That Night," are internally disorganized and arranged in a jumbled sequence.

A poem sometimes includes a series of actions and events, as Edwin Arlington Robinson's "The Miller's Wife" illustrates:

> The miller's wife had waited long,
>   The tea was cold, the fire was dead;
> And there might yet be nothing wrong
>   In how he went and what he said:
> "There are no millers any more,"
>   Was all that she had heard him say:
> And he had lingered at the door
>   So long that it seemed yesterday.
>
> Sick with a fear that had no form
>   She knew that she was there at last;
> And in the mill there was a warm
>   And mealy fragrance of the past.
> What else there was would only seem
>   To say again what he had meant;
> And what was hanging from a beam
>   Would not have heeded where she went.
>
> And if she thought it followed her,
>   She may have reasoned in the dark
> That one way of the few there were
>   Would hide her and would leave no mark;
> Black water, smooth above the weir
>   Like starry velvet in the night,
> Though ruffled once, would soon appear
>   The same as ever to the sight.

Most poems, however, present a series of images, building statements that make a philosophical point rather than tell a conventionally plotted story.

Writing About Plot   Unless your instructor asks for a plot summary, don't merely repeat what happens in the story. Instead, help your reader understand what's special about the plot and how it functions. Does it build suspense, mirror a character's confusion, shape a conflict, show how different lives can intersect, or help reveal a theme?

Before starting to write, answer the following questions:

What are the key events of the story? Do they unfold in conventional fashion or deviate from it in some way?

Does the writer use foreshadowing or flashback? If so, for what purpose?

Is the plot believable and effective, or does it display weakness of some sort?

Does it include any unique features?

Is it similar to the plot of another story or some type of story?

What plot features could I write about? What examples from the story would support my contentions?

As you prepare your analysis, determine the important events and how they relate to your topic. If the story is disjointed or incoherent, arrange the events so that they make sense and ask yourself why the writer chose that sequence. To mirror the main character's disordered state of mind? To show that life is chaotic and difficult to understand? Similarly, assess the reason for any use of foreshadowing or flashback. Does it build, create, or resolve suspense?

Not all plots are successful. A character's actions may not fit his or her personality or the situation. The plot might be too hard to follow or fail to produce the desired effect, as in a mystery where the clues are too obvious to create suspense. Or a writer might rely on chance or coincidence to resolve a conflict or problem: It's unacceptable to have the cavalry charge in gallantly out of nowhere and rescue the hero.

If there's something unique about the plot—perhaps a surprise event that works well—describe it and tell how it functions in the story, or perhaps you can compare the plot with one in another story in order to show how both develop some key insight.

The organization of a paper on plot is simple: You'll either present a thesis and then support it with examples taken from the text, or you'll write a comparison. Writing about "The Bride Comes to Yellow Sky," you could show how foreshadowing moves the story toward an inevitable showdown. As support, you could cite the deliberate, forward motion of the train, the repeated emphasis on clocks and time, the repeated suggestions of Potter's anxiousness, and Scratchy's ongoing conflict with Potter. As a more ambitious project, you might compare the plot of "The Bride" to that of a conventional western showdown, noting any important differences and what they accomplish. A more critical approach would be to argue that the plot is implausible, citing Potter's unplanned marriage and the coincidence of his return to Yellow Sky precisely when Scratchy Wilson was drunk and shooting up the town.

EXERCISE   *In a short story with a strong plot line, identify conflicts and climax and tell what the ending accomplishes. Point out any use of foreshadowing or flashback.*

Point of View

Point-of-View Factors   The point of view is the vantage point from which the writer of a literary work views its events. A writer may adopt either a first-person or a third-person point of view. In *first-person* narration, someone in the work tells what happens and is identified by words like *I, me, mine,* and *my.* A *third-*

person narrator stays completely out of the story and is never mentioned in any way. "The Bride Comes to Yellow Sky" illustrates third-person narration.

The most common form of first-person narration features a narrator who takes part in the action. This technique puts the readers directly on the scene and is excellent for tracing the growth or deterioration of a character. Instead of participating in the action, the narrator may view it from the sideline, an approach that preserves on-the-scene directness and allows the narrator to comment on the characters and issues. The narrator, however, cannot enter the mind and reveal the unspoken thoughts of anyone else.

Third-person narrators don't participate in the action but can survey the whole literary landscape and directly report events that first-person narrators would know only by hearsay. Most third-person narrators reveal the thoughts of just one character. Others, with *limited omniscience,* can enter the heads of several characters, while still others display *full omniscience* and know everything in the literary work, including all thoughts and feelings of all characters. Omniscience allows the narrator to contrast two or more sets of thoughts and feelings and draw general conclusions from them. The narrator of Stephen Crane's "The Open Boat" is fully omniscient. The story is about four shipwrecked sailors adrift in a lifeboat, and the narrator, knowing what they all think, traces their developing awareness that nature is completely indifferent to their plight.

Yet another type of third-person narration, *dramatic,* has emerged in contemporary fiction. A dramatic narrator, like a motion-picture camera, moves about recording the characters' actions and words but without revealing anyone's thoughts. Stories with surprise endings often use this technique.

Writing About Point of View   For a paper about point of view, ask and answer these questions:

What point of view is used? Why is it used?

Is it suitable for the situation? Why or why not?

If the story uses first-person narration, is the narrator reliable? What textual evidence supports my answer?

What focus would produce an effective paper? What textual evidence could support its discussion?

Various reasons might prompt the choice of a particular point of view. For example, an author might use the first person to show a character's mental deterioration. A third-person narrator might enter two minds to contrast opposing attitudes toward some incident or enter no minds at all, in order to heighten the emotional impact of a story's climax.

If a point of view seems unsuitable, say so and suggest why. Suppose a man is planning an elopement that will create a surprising ending. A point of view that revealed the man's thoughts would give away that ending.

First-person narrators are sometimes unreliable; that is, they offer the reader a warped view of things. To gauge reliability, compare the narrator's version of the facts with what the work otherwise reveals. The narrator may come off as stupid, psychologically warped, or too biased to view events fairly. If so, speculate on the reasons. A mentally unreliable narrator may be meant, for example, to heighten the horror of events.

Although organization can vary, papers on point of view basically follow a cause-and-effect format, first identifying the point of view used and then demonstrating, with examples, its effect on the story and reader. In "The Bride," the third-person point of view allows Crane to shift from Potter and his new wife to the men in the saloon to the rampaging Scratchy and then to Potter and Scratchy as they confront each other. Shifting scenes in this way builds a sense of impending conflict, which would be difficult to produce with a first-person narrator, who could not move about in this fashion.

EXERCISE   *Read the following two excerpts and answer the questions that follow them:*

Max shook his head no at the mugger, his mouth in a regretful pout.

The teenager lunged at Max's chest with the blade. Instinctively, Max moved one step to his right. He didn't shift far enough. The knife sank into him. Max lowered his head and watched as the metal disappeared into his arm and chest. He felt nothing. With the blade all the way in, the teenager's face was only inches from Max's; he stared at the point of entry, stunned, his mouth sagging open. The mugger's eyes were small and frightened. Max didn't like him. He put his hand on the kid's chest and pushed him away. He didn't want to die looking into scared eyes.

The mugger stumbled back, tripped over his feet and fell. . . . Max felt the point of the blade in his armpit. He realized he wasn't cut. The stupid kid had stuck the knife in the space below Max's armpit, the gap between his arm and chest. He had torn Max's polo shirt, but missed everything else. For a moment the knife hung there, caught by the fabric. Max raised his arm and the switchblade fell to the ground.

The teenager jumped to his feet and ran away, heading uptown.

Rafael Yglesias, *Fearless*

"Now!" I cry, aloud or to myself I don't know. Everything has boiled down to this instant. There's nothing in the world except the hand of the gate judge, lowering in slow motion to the catch that contains us. I see each of his fingers clearly, separately, as they fold around the lever, I see the muscles in his forearm harden as he begins to push down.

Wheeling and spinning, tilting and beating, my breath the song, the horse the dance. Time is gone. All the ordinary ways of things, the gettings from here to there, the one and twos, forgot. The crowd is color, the whirl of a spun top. The noises blend into a waving band that flies around us like a ribbon on a string. Beneath me four feet dance, pounding and leaping and turning and stomping. My legs flap like wings. I sail above, first to one side, then the other, remembering more than feeling the slaps of our bodies together. Things happen faster than understanding, faster than ideas. I'm a bird coasting, shot free into the music, spiraling into a place without bones or weight.

Michael Dorris, *A Yellow Boat in Blue Water*

1. In this third-person excerpt, Yglesias depicts the climax of an unsuccessful mugging, entering one character's mind but not the other's. Whose mind does he enter, and how does he convey the other person's mental state?

2. What does Dorris accomplish by using the first-person point of view?

Character

Character Factors   The characters in a literary work function in various ways. Some are centers of physical and mental action. Others furnish humor, act as narrators, provide needed information, act as *foils* who highlight more important characters by contrast, serve as symbols, or simply populate the landscape. In "The Bride," the drummer helps funnel information to the reader. He asks questions, the bartender answers them, and the reader learns all about Scratchy.

Writers present characters in several ways. Some tell the reader point-blank that a person is brave, stupid, self-serving, or the like. But most authors take an indirect approach by indicating how their characters look and act, what they think and say, how they live, and how other characters regard them.

Beware of uncritically accepting Character X's assessment of Character Y. X may be prejudiced, simpleminded, a deliberate liar, or too emotionally involved or disturbed to be objective. To illustrate, Scratchy Wilson, despite the bartender's fearful comments, proves to be something less than a real terror. He makes no real attempt to break down any doors and toys with, rather than shoots, the dog and Potter.

In picturing Potter, Crane first notes his appearance and self-conscious behavior, then delves into his mind to show the turmoil his marriage has stirred. Somewhat later, the bartender adds his brush strokes to Potter's portrait. At the confrontation, we again observe Potter's thoughts and behavior, as well as what he says to Scratchy. From all this, Potter emerges not as a mere one-dimensional lawman but as someone with a recognizably lifelike personality.

Some characters remain static; others mature, gain insight, or deteriorate in some telling way. Potter changes. As the story unfolds he abandons his doubts about the course he's charted and ends up fully committed to "the environment of the new estate." Scratchy, on the other hand, ends just as he started, "a simple child of the earlier plains."

Writing About Character   Start the process by asking yourself these questions:

What characters offer the potential for a paper?
What are their most important features, and where in the story are these features revealed?
Do the characters undergo any changes? If so, how and why do the changes occur?
Are the characters believable, true to life? If not, why?
What focus would produce an effective paper?
What textual evidence could support the discussion?

Usually, you'll write about the main character, but at times you might choose the chief adversary or some minor character. For a lesser character, point out how that person interacts with the main one.

Most main characters change; most lesser ones do not. But sometimes a main character remains frozen, allowing the writer to make an important point. To show that a certain social group suffers from paralysis of the will, an author might create a main character who begins and ends weak and ineffectual. Whatever the situation, when you determine what purpose your character serves, tell the reader.

Think hard about your character's credibility. Ask yourself if he or she is true to life. Cruel stepmothers, brilliant but eccentric detectives, mad scientists, masked seekers after justice—these and other stereotyped figures don't square with real-life people, who are complex mixtures of many traits. Inconsistent acts or unexplained and unmotivated personality changes don't ring true: Most people behave the same in similar situations and change only when properly motivated. Not every character needs to be a full-dress creation, but all require enough development to justify their roles.

Start your paper by identifying your character's role or personality; then back your contention with illustrations that support it, possibly following the sequence in which the writer presents them. If a character changes, say so, tell why, and indicate the results of the change, again using supporting examples. Such a paper is usually a cause-and-effect analysis. Papers that evaluate two characters are essentially comparisons.

For an example of a paper analyzing a character, see pages 291–93.

EXERCISE   *Write a paragraph describing the personality of the character in the following passage:*

The thousand injuries of Fortunato I had borne as I best could, but when he ventured upon insult, I vowed revenge. You, who so well know the nature of my soul, will not suppose, however, that I gave utterance to a threat. *At length* I would be avenged; this was a point definitely settled—but the very definiteness with which it was resolved precluded the idea of risk. I must not only punish, but punish with impunity. A wrong is unredressed when retribution overtakes its redresser. It is equally unredressed when the avenger fails to make himself felt as such to the one who has done the wrong.

Edgar Allan Poe, "The Cask of Amontillado"

Setting

Setting Factors   Setting locates characters in a time, place, and culture so they can think, feel, and act against this background. Writers can generate feelings and moods by describing settings. Sunny spring landscapes signal hope or happiness, dark alleys are foreboding, and thunderstorms suggest violent possibilities. Poetry, especially, uses setting to create mood. In "Cannery Town in August," Lorna Dee Cervantes combines images of tired, work-stained employees, a noisy workplace, and dismal streets to evoke an unpleasant setting.

All night it humps the air.
Speechless, the steam rises
from the cannery columns. I hear
the night bird rave about work
or lunch, or sing the swing shift
home. I listen, while bodyless
uniforms and spinach specked shoes

drift in monochrome down the dark
moon-possessed streets. Women
who smell of whiskey and tomatoes,
peach fuzz reddening their lips and eyes—
I imagine them not speaking, dumbed
by the can's clamor and drop
to the trucks that wait, grunting
in their headlights below.
They spotlight those who walk
like a dream, with no one
waiting in the shadows
to palm them back to living.

Setting can also help reveal a character's personality. In this excerpt from Amy Tan's novel *The Joy Luck Club,* the size and contents of the wealthy merchant Wu Tsing's house reflect the owner's love of wealthy display:

As soon as we walked into that big house, I became lost with too many things to see; a curved staircase that wound up and up, a ceiling with faces in every corner, then hallways twisting and turning into one room then another. To my right was a large room, larger than I had ever seen, and it was filled with stiff teakwood furniture: sofas and tables and chairs. And at the other end of this long, long room, I could see doors leading into more rooms, more furniture, then more doors. To my left was a darker room, another sitting room, this one filled with foreign furniture: dark green leather sofas, paintings with hunting dogs, armchairs, and mahogany desks. And as I glanced in these rooms I would see different people. . . .

Settings sometimes function as symbols, reinforcing the workings of the other elements. A broad, slowly flowing river may stand for time or fate, a craggy cliff for strength of character, a blizzard-swept plain for the overwhelming power of nature. The following section, a discussion of symbols, points out some symbolic settings in "The Bride."

At times, setting provides a clue to some observation about life. At one point in Stephen Crane's story "The Open Boat," the men spot a nearby flock of seagulls sitting comfortably on the turbulent waves. Juxtaposing the complacent gulls and the imperiled men suggests the philosophical point of the story: that the universe is indifferent to human aspirations and struggles.

Shifts in setting often trigger shifts in a character's emotional or psychological state. Jack Potter, typically calm and assured in Yellow Sky, displays great awkwardness and embarrassment in the unfamiliar environment of the Pullman car.

Writing About Setting Begin your search for a topic by identifying the settings in the story and then asking these questions about each one:

What are its key features?
What does it accomplish? Does it create a mood? Reveal a character? Serve as a symbol? Reinforce the story's point? How does it accomplish these things?
In what ways does it support or interfere with the story?
Does the setting seem realistic? If not, why not?
What focus would produce an effective paper? What textual evidence would support it?

Check the impact of setting on mood by seeing how well the two match up for each setting. Sometimes, as in "The Bride," the two bear little or no relationship to each other. In other cases, the two intertwine throughout the work.

Try to establish connections between settings and characters. If an emotionally barren individual always appears against backdrops of gloomy furnished rooms, cheerless restaurants, and decaying slums, you can assume that the writer is using setting to convey character. Look for links between changes in characters and changes in settings. If the setting remains the same, point out any shifts in the way the character views it.

Occasionally, a writer drums home settings so insistently that they overpower the characters and story line. A novel about the super rich may linger so lovingly over their extravagant surroundings that the plot lacks force and the characters seem mere puppets. If the setting hobbles the other elements, identify this flaw in your analysis.

When you write about setting, describe it and discuss its impact on the story's other elements, supporting your claims with specific examples. In writing about "The Bride," you might argue that Crane used as his chief setting a pulp fiction cliché of a western town in order to heighten the atypical nature of the showdown. As support, you could cite such stock features as the train station, saloon, dog, and dusty streets, all of which point toward an actual shootout rather than Scratchy Wilson's backdown.

EXERCISE   *What mood does the following description of a room generate? What does it suggest about the situation of the room's inhabitants, two women in an Old Ladies' Home?*

Marian stood enclosed by a bed, a washstand, and a chair; the tiny room had altogether too much furniture. Everything smelled wet—even the bare floor. She held onto the back of the chair, which was wicker and felt soft and damp. . . . How dark it was! The window shade was down, and the only door was shut. Marian looked at the ceiling. . . . It was like being caught in a robbers' cave. . . .

Eudora Welty, "A Visit of Charity"

Symbols

Symbol Factors   To strengthen and deepen their messages, writers use symbols: names, persons, objects, places, colors, or actions that have a significance beyond their surface meaning. A symbol may be very obvious—as a name like Mr. Grimm, suggesting the person's character—or quite subtle, as an object representing a universal human emotion.

Some symbols are private and others conventional. A private symbol has special significance within a literary work but not outside it. Conventional symbols are deeply rooted in our culture, and almost everyone knows what they represent. We associate crosses with Christianity and limousines with wealth and power. In "The Bride," the plains pouring eastward past the Pullman windows, Scratchy's eastern clothing, and the mirage-like grass plots in front of the saloon are all private symbols that stand for the passing of the Old West. Because people of Crane's time associated Pullman cars with an urbane, eastern lifestyle, the Pullman is a conventional symbol that represents the new order of things. Like the Pullman, a symbol may appear more than once in a literary work.

Whether or not a recurring item is a symbol depends upon its associations. In Ernest Hemingway's novel *A Farewell to Arms,* rain may fairly be said to symbolize doom because it consistently accompanies disasters, and one of the main characters says that she has visions of herself lying dead in the rain. But if rain is randomly associated with a rundown lakeside resort, a spirited business meeting, a cozy weekend, and the twentieth-anniversary celebration of a happy marriage, the writer probably intends no symbolism.

Writing About Symbols   When you examine the symbols in a literary work, think about these questions:

What symbols are used and where do they appear?
Are they private or conventional?
What do they appear to mean?
Do any of them undergo a change in meaning? If so, how and why?
Which symbol(s) could I discuss effectively?
What textual evidence would support my interpretation?

To locate symbols, read the literary work carefully, looking for items that seem to have an extended meaning. You might, for example, discover that the cracked walls of a crumbling mansion symbolize some character's disordered mental state or that a voyage symbolizes the human journey from birth to death. Several symbols often mean the same thing; writers frequently use them in sets. In "Bartleby the Scrivener," for instance, Herman Melville uses windows that look upon walls, a folding screen, and a prison to symbolize Bartleby's alienated condition, that is, his mental separation from those around him. Determining whether each symbol is private or conventional can provide clues to its meaning.

Sometimes a symbol changes meaning during the course of a work. A woman who regards her lover's large, strong hands as symbols of passion may, following an illness that leaves him a dangerous madman, view them as symbols of danger and brute strength. Note any changes you discover, and suggest what they signify.

A word of caution: Don't let symbol hunting become an obsession. Before you assert that something has a different and deeper meaning than its surface application, make sure the evidence in the work backs your claim.

For each symbol you discuss, state what you think it means and then support your position with appropriate textual evidence. You could argue, for example, that the Pullman car in "The Bride" symbolizes the Eastern civilization that is encroaching on the West, offering as evidence the car's "figured velvet . . . shining brass, silver, and glass" and darkly gleaming wood appointments.

EXERCISE   *Read the following poem and answer the questions that follow:*

Heritage

Margaret Abbott

We were building there together,
Two children playing blocks,
And I debated whether
To copy your cautious scheme
That would withstand the knocks
Of a careless hand or try
My own impracticable plan
Of block on block until a high
Column, random and unsure, would stand
Memento to my dream.
I looked at you and planned
My tower. Each block fanned
My zeal. The shaft rose higher
And higher, like a spire
To my joy. I knew it could not last at all,
And yet—yet, when I saw it fall,
Some nameless hope came tumbling, too.
I crept, forlornly, close to you
And laid a finger on your solid square
And wished my heart would learn to care
For safety. Then, within that selfsame hour,
My traitor hands began another tower.

1. What does the "high / Column, random and unsure" symbolize? The "solid square"?

2. What is the significance of the final statement?

Irony

Irony Factors   Irony features some discrepancy, some difference between appearance and reality, expectation and outcome. Sometimes a character says one thing but means something else. The critic who, tongue in cheek, says that a clumsy dancer is "poetry in motion" speaks ironically.

Irony also results when the reader or a character recognizes something as important, but another character does not. In "The Bride" this situation occurs when Potter, not knowing that Scratchy is on a rampage, flees the station agent, who tries to let him know. A character's behavior sometimes offers ironic contrasts, too. There's high irony in the contrast between Potter's unflinching face-off with Scratchy and his fear of telling the townsfolk about his marriage.

At times the ending of a work doesn't square with what the reader expects: the confrontation between Potter and Scratchy ends not in a fusillade of bullets but a flurry of words. To add to the irony, Potter wins because he is armed with a new and unfamiliar weapon—his wife. The emotional impact of an ironic ending depends upon the circumstances of plot and character. As Scratchy walks off, we're likely to view matters with amusement. In other cases, we might register joy, horror, gloom, or almost anything else.

Writing About Irony   Start by answering these questions:

> Where does irony occur?
> What does it accomplish?
> What could my thesis be, and how could I support it?

In probing for irony, check for statements that say one thing and mean something else, situations in which one character knows something that another doesn't, and contrasts between the ways characters should and do behave. Review the plot to see whether the outcome matches the expectations.

To prove that irony is intended, examine the context in which the words are spoken or the events occur. Also, tell the reader what the irony accomplishes. In "The Bride," it is ironic that someone as wild as Scratchy Wilson would be awed by, and retreat from, Potter's wife; yet this irony is central to the idea that the Old West, despite its violence, was no match for the civilizing forces of the East.

EXERCISE   *Discuss the irony in this poem:*

Yet Do I Marvel

Countee Cullen

I doubt not God is good, well-meaning, kind,
And did He stoop to quibble could tell why
The little buried mole continues blind,
Why flesh that mirrors Him must some day die,
Make plain the reason tortured Tantalus[1]
Is baited by the fickle fruit, declare
If merely brute caprice dooms Sisyphus[2]
To struggle up a never-ending stair.
Inscrutable His ways are, and immune
To catechism by a mind too strewn
With petty cares to slightly understand
What awful brain compels His awful hand.
Yet do I marvel at this curious thing:
To make a poet black, and bid him sing!

Theme

Theme Factors   The theme of a literary work is its controlling idea, some observation or insight about life or the conditions and terms of living, such as the prevalence of evil, the foolishness of pride, or the healing power of love. Many

---

[1] In Greek mythology, a king confined to hell who is teased by water and fruit trees forever beyond his reach.

[2] In Greek mythology, a king confined to hell who must continually roll a heavy rock up a hill and then see it roll back down.

literary works suggest several themes: sometimes one primary motif and several related ones, sometimes a number of unrelated motifs. Theme is central to a work of literature; frequently all of the other elements help develop and support it.

On occasion, the writer or a character states the theme directly. Mrs. Alving, the main character in Henrik Ibsen's play *Ghosts*, notes that the dead past plays a powerful and evil role in shaping human lives:

> . . . I am half inclined to think that we are all ghosts, Mr. Manders. It is not only what we have inherited from our fathers and mothers that exists again in us, but all sorts of old dead ideas and all kinds of old dead beliefs and things of that kind. They are not actually alive in us; but there they are dormant, all the same, and we can never be rid of them.

Ordinarily, though, the theme remains unstated and must be deduced by examining the other elements of the literary work.

Writing About Theme   Before you begin writing, ask and answer these questions:

> What are the themes of this work? Which of these should I write about? Are they stated or unstated?
> If stated, what elements support them?
> If unstated, what elements create them?
> What, if any, thematic weaknesses are present?

Check the comments of the characters and the narrator to see whether they state the themes directly. If they don't, assess the interaction of characters, events, settings, symbols, and other elements to determine them.

Let's see how the elements of Nathaniel Hawthorne's short story "Young Goodman Brown" work together to yield the primary theme. The story has four characters—Goodman Brown; his wife, Faith; Deacon Gookin; and Goody Cloyse—whose names symbolically suggest that they are completely good. Another symbol, Faith's pink hair ribbon, at first suggests innocence and later its loss. The story relates Brown's nighttime journey into a forest at the edge of a Puritan village and subsequent attendance at a baptismal ceremony for new converts to the Devil. He proceeds into the forest, suggestive of mystery and lawlessness, during a dark night, suggestive of evil, where he meets his guide, the Devil in the guise of his grandfather. As he proceeds, Brown vacillates between reluctance to join the Devil's party and fascination with it. Innocent and ignorant, he is horrified when he finds that the deacon and Goody Cloyse seem to be in league with the Devil. Brown tries to preserve his pure image of his wife, Faith, but her pink ribbon falls out of a tumultuous sky seemingly filled with demons, and Brown sees her at the baptismal ceremony. He shrieks out to her to "resist the wicked one" and is suddenly alone in the woods, not knowing whether she obeyed. The end of the story finds Brown back in his village, unable to view his wife and neighbors as anything but totally evil.

In light of these happenings, it's probably safe to say that the primary theme of the story is somewhat as follows:

Human beings are a mixture of good and evil, but some individuals can't accept this fact. Once they realize that "good" people are susceptible to sin, they decide that everyone is evil, and they become embittered for life.

Point out any thematic weakness that you find. Including a completely innocent major character in a story written to show that people are mixtures of good and evil would contradict the writer's intention.

A paper on theme is basically an argument, first presenting your interpretation and then supporting it with textual evidence. You might argue that the primary theme of "The Bride" is the demise of the Old West under the civilizing influence of the East. You could cite the luxurious Pullman car in contrast to the drab town, Potter's uncomfortable submission to the waiter and porter, and Scratchy Wilson's retreat at the story's end. In addition, you could suggest a related theme: People out of their element often founder—sometimes even appear ridiculous. As support, you might point to Potter's behavior on the train, the drummer's subdued attitude when Scratchy's arrival is imminent, and Scratchy's reaction when told about Potter's wife.

EXERCISE   *State the controlling idea of this poem by Emily Dickinson:*

'Twas like a Maelstrom, with a notch,
That nearer, every Day,
Kept narrowing its boiling Wheel
Until the Agony

Toyed coolly with the final inch
Of your delirious Hem—
And you dropt, lost,
When something broke—
And let you from a Dream—

As if a Goblin with a Gauge—
Kept measuring the Hours—
Until you felt your Second
Weigh, helpless, in his Paws—

And not a Sinew—stirred—could help,
And sense was setting numb—
When God—remembered—and the Fiend
Let go, then, Overcome—

As if your Sentence stood—pronounced—
And you were frozen led
From Dungeon's luxury of Doubt
To Gibbets, and the Dead—

And when the Film had stitched your eyes
A Creature gasped "Reprieve"!
Which Anguish was the utterest—then—
To perish, or to live?

■ Ethical Issues

When you write about literature, you'll need to be aware of certain ethical considerations. Imagine someone reading only part of a short story and then writing a scathing analysis that suggests he has read the entire work. Imagine a thematic analysis of a novel that deliberately ignores large sections of the text in order to develop a twisted interpretation about the evils of capitalism. Imagine citing atypical quotations from the heroine of a play that deliberately create a distorted impression of her character. To help fulfill your ethical responsibility, ask and answer the following questions.

- Have I read the entire work carefully?

- Is my interpretation supported by the preponderance of textual evidence? Does it avoid deliberate distortion? A student who emphasizes a story's passing description of the pleasant feelings that accompany cocaine use while downplaying the drug's progressive effects that destroy a character could send a dangerous message.

- Have I avoided using quotations that are atypical or taken out of context?

- Is my interpretation fair to the text and the author rather than distorting events to promote an agenda?

■ Writing a Paper on Literature

The Writing Procedure

Focusing, gathering information, organizing, writing, revising, and editing—the same procedure leads to success in a literature paper as in any other type.

First, make sure you *understand the assignment*. Let's assume you have been asked to do the following:

> Write a 750-word essay that analyzes one of the elements in Stephen Crane's "The Bride Comes to Yellow Sky." Take into account all the pertinent factors of whatever element you choose.

For this assignment you could focus on plot, point of view, character, setting, symbols, irony, or theme.

Next, *decide upon a suitable topic*. For papers on literature, your best approach is to reread the work carefully and then reflect on it. As you do this for the assignment on "The Bride," you rule out a paper centering on plot, setting, irony, point of view, or theme. Because your class has discussed the first three so thoroughly, you doubt you can offer anything more. The matter of the narrator stumps you; you can understand why Crane uses a third-person narrator who airs Potter's thoughts, but you can't see what's accomplished by the brief looks into other characters' minds. Regarding theme, you doubt you can do justice to the topic in 750 words. As you mentally mine character and symbolism for possible topics, your thoughts turn to the many gunfighters you've watched in the movies and read about in western fiction. Because gunfighters have always fascinated you and Scratchy Wilson seems an intriguing example of the breed, you decide to analyze his character.

To complete the next stage, *gathering information,* reread the story again and as you do, list all pertinent information about Scratchy that might help develop a character analysis. Your efforts might yield these results:

1. Scratchy "a wonder with a gun."
2. "about the last one of the old gang that used to hang out along the river here."
3. "He's a terror when he's drunk," the opposite otherwise.
4. Potter "goes out and fights Scratchy when he gets on one of these tears."
5. Has shot Scratchy once, in the leg.
6. Does nothing to stop "tears" from happening.
7. On street, Scratchy "in a rage begot of whisky." Neck works angrily.
8. Utters "Cries of ferocious challenge."
9. Moves with "the creeping movement of the midnight cat."
10. Guns move "with an electric swiftness."
11. Clothes—maroon shirt, gilded red-topped boots—not adult western garb.
12. Doesn't shoot dog.
13. Doesn't try breaking down doors.
14. Warns Potter not to go for gun rather than shooting him.
15. Says he'll hit Potter with gun, not shoot him, if Potter doesn't "mind what I tell you."
16. Only sneers when Potter calls him "damn fool," and when Potter says, "If you're goin' to shoot me up, you better begin now; you'll never get a chance like this again."
17. Backs down and walks away when confronted with Potter's marriage.

List in hand, you are now ready to *organize your information.* As you examine your items and answer the questions about character on page 279, you start to realize that Scratchy is not merely a one-dimensional gunslinging menace. To reflect your discovery, you prepare a formal topic outline.

   I. Bartender's assessment
      A. Evidence that Scratchy is a menace
         1. A wonder with a gun
         2. Former outlaw gang member
         3. A terror when drunk
      B. Contradictory evidence
         1. Mild when sober
         2. Only one actual shootout with Potter

II. Scratchy's behavior
   A. Evidence that Scratchy is a menace
      1. Rage
      2. Wary movements
      3. Skillful handling of guns
   B. Contradictory evidence
      1. Mode of dress
      2. Failure to shoot dog
      3. Failure to try breaking down doors
      4. Behavior during confrontation
      5. Final retreat

The next stage, *developing a thesis statement*, presents few difficulties. After examining the outline and thinking about its contents, you draft the following sentence:

```
A close look at Scratchy Wilson shows that he has much more
depth than his pulp fiction counterparts.
```

Drawing on your notes and following your outline, you now *write a first draft* of your essay, and then follow up with the necessary revising and editing. In addition, you review the story and verify your interpretation.

As you *prepare your final draft*, follow these guidelines.

Handling Quotations   Like aspirin, quotations should be used when necessary, but not to excess. Cite brief, relevant passages to support key ideas, but fight the urge to quote huge blocks of material. Place short quotations, less than five lines long, within quotation marks and run them into the text. For longer passages, omit the quotation marks and indent the material ten spaces from the left-hand margin. When quoting poetry, use a slash mark (/) to show the shift from one line to the other in the original: "A honey tongue, a heart of gall, / Is fancy's spring, but sorrow's fall." Pages 397–400 provide added information on handling quotations.

Documentation   Document ideas and quotations from outside sources by following the guidelines on pages 391–97.

If your instructor wants you to document quotations from the work you're writing about, include the information within parentheses following the quotations. For fiction, cite the page number on which the quotation appeared: (83). For poetry, cite the word "line" or "lines" and the appropriate numbers: (lines 23–24). For plays, cite act, scene, and line numbers, separated by periods: (1.3.18–19). When discussing a work of fiction not in your textbook, identify the book you used as your source. Your instructor can then easily check your information. In short papers like the one below, internal documentation is often omitted.

Tense   Write your essay in the present rather than the past tense. Say "In *The Sound and the Fury,* William Faulkner uses four narrators, each of whom provides a different perspective on the events that take place," not ". . . William Faulkner used four narrators, each of whom provided a different perspective on the events that took place."

EXAMPLE STUDENT ESSAY ON LITERATURE

Scratchy Wilson: No Cardboard Character

Wendell Stone

Stephen Crane's "The Bride Comes to Yellow Sky" is artful on several counts. For one thing, the story is rich in irony. It makes use of an elaborate set of symbols to get its point across. It is filled with vivid language, and in Jack Potter and Scratchy Wilson it offers its readers two very unusual characters. Potter's actions and thoughts clearly show that he is a complex person. In fact, his complexity is so conspicuous that it becomes easy to regard Scratchy as nothing more than a one-dimensional badman. But this judgment is mistaken. A close look at Scratchy shows that he, like Potter, has much more depth than his pulp fiction counterparts.

Nothing in what the bartender says about Scratchy hints that there is anything unusual about the old outlaw. We learn that Scratchy is "a wonder with a gun," that he is "about the last one of the old gang that used to hang out along the river here," and that "He's a terror when he's drunk" but mild-mannered and pleasant at other times. One thing may strike the careful reader as a little odd, though. Although Potter "goes out and fights Scratchy when he gets on one of these tears," he has wounded Scratchy just once, and then only in the leg. Apparently, Potter has been able to talk the supposed terror out of a shootout each of the other times. Nor has Potter apparently tried doing anything to stop Scratchy's "tears."

As he steps onto the main street of Yellow Sky, Scratchy seems every bit as menacing as the bartender has described him. His face flames "in a rage begot of whisky," the cords in his neck throb and bulge with anger, and he hurls "cries

of ferocious challenge" at the barricaded buildings.
Scratchy is clearly no stranger to either weapons or
shootouts. He walks with "the creeping movement of the midnight cat," moves his revolvers with "an electric swiftness," and keeps constantly on the alert for an ambush.

Nevertheless, Scratchy comes across as less than totally
menacing. For one thing, his maroon shirt and gilded, red-
topped boots make him look not like a westerner but like some
child's notion of one. When he sees the dog, he deliberately
shoots to frighten rather than to kill it. And in spite of
all his bluster, he makes no real attempt to break down any
doors and get at the people hiding behind them. Scratchy's
clothing shows that eastern ways have touched even this
"child of the earlier plains." But one could easily argue
that eastern gentleness has had some slight softening influence on him, too. Be that as it may, it seems evident that
Scratchy, perhaps without quite realizing it himself, is
mainly play-acting when he goes on his rampages and that
Potter knows this.

During the whole final confrontation, Scratchy seems
more of an actor than a gunman wanting revenge against his
"ancient antagonist." Instead of shooting when Potter makes
a slight movement, Scratchy warns him not to go for a gun and
says that he intends to take his time settling accounts, to
"loaf along with no interferin.'" Significantly, he threatens to hit Potter with a gun, not shoot him, if the marshal
does not "mind what I tell you." Even when Potter, recovered
from his brief fright, calls Scratchy a "damn fool" and says
"If you're goin' to shoot me up, you better begin now: you'll
never get a chance like this again," Scratchy does nothing
except sneer. This confrontation, like all but one of the
others, ends with no shots fired. But one thing is different. Potter's marriage has forced Scratchy to realize that
something unstoppable is changing the Old West forever. When
he drops his revolver to his side, stands silent for a while,
and then says, "I s'pose it's all off now," we sense that he
means not just this episode but any future clashes as well.

```
     Scratchy is not a cardboard creation. His behavior is by
no means as easily explainable as it at first seems, and he
is capable of some degree of insight. Nonetheless, Scratchy
remains very much a creature of the past, something that
time has passed by. As he leaves, his feet make "funnel-
shaped tracks," reminiscent of hourglasses, in the sand.
Soon these tracks, along with Scratchy and his way of life,
will disappear.
```

Including the Views of Others

Obviously you are not the first one to write about an established piece of literature. To help deepen your understanding, your instructor may ask you to draw upon various sources that analyze the work you are discussing.

As you read these secondary sources, jot down any insights you find helpful. Be sure to record the name of the author and the source so that you can document appropriately and therefore avoid plagiarism. (For an explanation of plagiarism and when you need to document a source, see "Avoiding Plagiarism" in Chapter 21.) Keep track of where you disagree or have a different insight. Some students keep a reading journal in which they record useful quotes or information about both the piece of literature and the secondary source.

When you write the paper, you can synthesize (see pages 72–73) the views of the critics you've read and offer them as additional support for your view. Alternatively, you might summarize the conclusions, or perhaps the conflicting views, of critics and then offer your own observations along with appropriate support. Think of writing in response to others' views as entering a conversation with friends about a good book; they have their opinions, but your insights will add something to the discussion.

EXERCISE   *Using the guidelines offered in this chapter, write a short essay comparing and contrasting the two writers' assessments of the women in the following poems. (You might find it helpful to review pages 120–27 on comparison.) Limit your focus and back any general statements you make with appropriate support from the poems.*

There Is a Garden in Her Face

Thomas Campion (1617)

There is a garden in her face,
Where roses and white lilies grow;
A heavenly paradise is that place,
Wherein all pleasant fruits do flow.
There cherries grow which none may buy
Till "Cherry ripe" themselves do cry.

Those cherries fairly do inclose
Of orient pearl a double row,

Which when her lovely laughter shows,
They look like rosebuds filled with snow;
Yet them nor peer nor prince can buy,
Till "Cherry ripe" themselves do cry.

Her eyes like angels watch them still;
Her brows like bended bows do stand.
Threat'ning with piercing frowns to kill
All that attempt with eye or hand
Those sacred cherries to come nigh,
Till "Cherry ripe" themselves do cry.

Sonnet 130

William Shakespeare (1609)

My mistress' eyes are nothing like the sun;
Coral is far more red than her lips red;
If snow be white, why then her breasts are dun;
If hairs be wires, black wires grow on her head.
I have seen roses damask'd, red and white,
But no such roses see I in her cheeks;
And in some perfumes there is more delight
Than in the breath that from my mistress reeks.
I love to hear her speak, yet well I know
That music hath a far more pleasing sound;
I grant I never saw a goddess go;
My mistress, when she walks, treads on the ground.
And yet, by heaven, I think my love as rare
As any she belied with false compare.

chapter 19

Business Letters and Résumés

Businesspeople aren't the only ones who write business letters. You write quite a few yourself, or soon will, especially to request information, place orders, register complaints, and apply for jobs. There's nothing mysterious or difficult about business correspondence. True, it follows its own special format, but otherwise it breaks no new writing ground. As always, deciding what to say and how to say it is vital to your success.

As you turn to business writing, pay particular attention to audience. Ask yourself these questions: To whom should I write? Why that person? What is his or her position in the organization? How will this person likely receive the communication? What action can he or she take? After all, you wouldn't write the president of a large company to inquire about a recent order you haven't received.

■ Letter Language

Effective letter language weaves conciseness, informality, and courtesy into a three-strand finished fabric.

Conciseness Concise writing avoids word clutter and gets directly to the point, saving the reader time and enlivening the message. As you write and revise, guard against two kinds of wordiness: deadwood and gobbledygook. *Dead-*

wood repeats the same thing or uses excess words to deliver its message. Here are some examples of deadwood and ways of correcting them:

Deadwood	Correction
in view of the fact that, due to the fact that	because
had the effect of causing	caused
would you be kind enough to	would you please
I want to take this opportunity to thank you	thank you
in the event that	if
personally, I believe	I believe
I want to make it clear that	[simply state what you want known]

Gobbledygook uses inflated, elaborately polite expressions that make writing stiff, stuffy, and distant. Note how the corrections soften the standoffish tone:

Gobbledygook	Correction
enclosed please find	I am enclosing
subsequent to the purchase of your	after buying your
in accordance with the terms of your warranty	your warranty provides
reference is made herewith	I am referring to
the said lawnmower	this lawnmower

Informality   Informal language is everyday language. Friendly and relaxed, it has the air of face-to-face conversation between writer and reader. To achieve it, use simple words and sentence structures; personal pronouns like *I, me, you,* and *your* are appropriate. At the same time, though, don't go overboard and resort to slang or overly casual expressions. Saying "When you guys packed my radio, you must have goofed; when I got it, it was busted" raises questions about your seriousness.

Courtesy   In your business letters, as in your direct dealings with others, courtesy plays a key role in helping you accomplish your objective. Here are some guidelines to keep in mind.

First, try to adopt what is sometimes called the "you" approach. That is, focus on the reader's concerns and values while avoiding expressions of sarcasm, anger, or disappointment. Assume, for example, that a well-established landscaping company has done a poor job of seeding your lawn, and the work has to be repeated. Nothing would be gained by attacking the company's integrity and declaring "I am not going to pay you until you redo your shoddy work." Indeed, the letter could spark an angry refusal or result in an unwarranted delay. If, however, you stress how the job reflects poorly on the company's excellent reputation and note that "You will receive the final $500 payment when the lawn is reseeded consistent with your high-quality work," you are much more likely to achieve your goal.

Sarcasm and anger aren't the only forms of discourtesy. Curt demands and writing with negative implications can also be offensive to readers. Consider these examples:

| *Curt*: | I want you to send me . . . I need a copy of . . . |
| *Negative*: | I take the position that . . . |

Note how rewriting has eliminated the discourtesy.

| *Courteous*: | Would you please send me . . . |
| *Courteous*: | I think you'll find that . . . |

As you prepare your letter, try changing places with your reader. How would you react to the message? If you're pleased with what you see, courtesy should be no problem.

■ Parts of the Business Letter

The letter in Figure 19.1, labeled to show the parts of a business letter, is set up in the modified block format, a very common one for business correspondence.

Heading   Spell out every word except for the two-letter state abbreviation used by the postal service. Begin the heading at the center of the sheet.

Inside Address   *Ms.* is an acceptable personal title for both married and single women. If you don't know the name of the person you want to reach, begin the inside address with the job title or name of the department, for example, *Vice-President for Research* or *Sales Department.* If you don't know the job title or department, start with the company name. Use abbreviations only if they are part of the company name. Begin the inside address two spaces below the heading in long letters and three to eight spaces in shorter letters. The shorter the letter, the more space should be left.

Salutation   Standard practice calls for addressing individuals by both personal title and last name: *Dear Ms. Barnes.* If the inside address begins with a job title or the name of a department, use that title or department name for the salutation, for instance, *Vice-President for Research* or *Sales Department.* If the inside address begins with the name of the company, try to determine which department would answer it and use the department name as a salutation. The letters throughout the chapter illustrate these conventions. The salutation comes two spaces below the inside address.

Recently, a more informal salutation for individuals has been gaining popularity. This salutation uses the recipient's full name without a personal title, and the letter also omits the title from the inside address. Here is an example.

Leslie Avery
Calmath Chemical Company
239 Dorman Drive
Birmingham AL 35207

Dear Leslie Avery:

Before using this new form of salutation, check with your instructor.

Heading

Inside
address

Salutation

Body

Complimentary
close

Signature

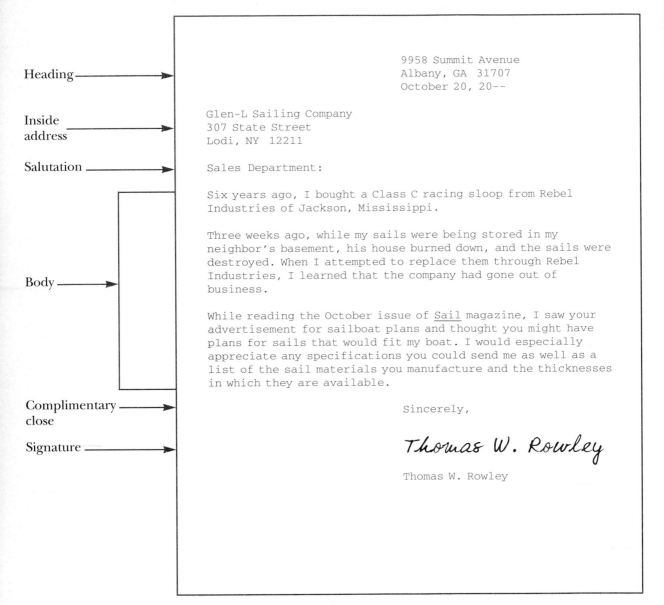

9958 Summit Avenue
Albany, GA 31707
October 20, 20--

Glen-L Sailing Company
307 State Street
Lodi, NY 12211

Sales Department:

Six years ago, I bought a Class C racing sloop from Rebel
Industries of Jackson, Mississippi.

Three weeks ago, while my sails were being stored in my
neighbor's basement, his house burned down, and the sails were
destroyed. When I attempted to replace them through Rebel
Industries, I learned that the company had gone out of
business.

While reading the October issue of <u>Sail</u> magazine, I saw your
advertisement for sailboat plans and thought you might have
plans for sails that would fit my boat. I would especially
appreciate any specifications you could send me as well as a
list of the sail materials you manufacture and the thicknesses
in which they are available.

Sincerely,

Thomas W. Rowley

Thomas W. Rowley

Figure 19.1   Modified Block Form

Body   Most letters are one page or less. Try to keep your paragraphs short—about seven lines at most. Begin the body two spaces below the salutation. If the letter contains only one brief paragraph, double-space the typing. Otherwise use single spacing with double spacing between paragraphs.

Complimentary Close   Acceptable closings are *Sincerely, Sincerely yours,* and *Yours truly.* Type the complimentary close two spaces below the last line of the body and line it up with the center of the sheet.

Signature Both typewritten and handwritten signatures are necessary. Leave four spaces between the complimentary close and the typed signature. Line the typed signature up with the center of the sheet.

Enclosure Notation The abbreviation *Enc.,* used in several of our sample letters, indicates that a brochure, drawing, check, money order, or other document accompanies the letter. It starts at the left-hand margin. If more than one item accompanies a letter, the notation should indicate how many there are. Important documents are often named:

Enc. 3
Enc. Money Order

Type business letters on 8½ × 11-inch unlined white paper and center them on the page. For full-page letters, make the side margins one inch wide; for shorter letters, make wider margins. In all cases, establish top and bottom margins of roughly equal width.

■ Preparation for Mailing

To ensure that the Post Office's optical scanners can read your envelope, type the address entirely in capital letters and without punctuation. Position the address between one-half and three inches from the bottom of the envelope and at least one inch from the right-hand edge. Figure 19.2 shows a properly typed address. Use the standard state abbreviations, which are readily available.

Proofread your letter carefully, sign it, and then fold it neatly in thirds (Figure 19.3) so that it will fit into a number 10 size business envelope.

```
DJ ASSOCIATES
230 PARK AVE S
NEW YORK NY 10003-1502


                      MS SHARON CUSTOMER
                      806 S ARLINGTON MILL DRIVE APT 1A
                      ARLINGTON VA 22204-2921
```

Figure 19.2

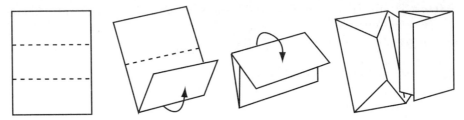

Figure 19.3

■ E-Mail Correspondence

E-mail is quick, can carry a number of attachments, allows for prompt responses, and saves paper. As a result, many students now use e-mail to communicate with friends and faculty as well as for business purposes, including job applications.

E-mail is usually more informal than conventional business correspondence but should follow good business writing practices. Because it is so easy to send and the receiver can promptly ask follow-up questions, writers may be tempted to dash off incomplete, error-riddled messages. Remember that both you and your reader are busy; try to write clearly so that follow-up exchanges are unnecessary. Remember also that your e-mail can be forwarded to other people, so make sure your messages reflect well on you.

■ Types of Letters

Of the many kinds of business letters, the ones you'll most likely write are inquiries, orders, complaints, and job applications. Here are guidelines and models.

Letters of Inquiry

Your letters of inquiry may be written to request information about a vacation spot, a hobby, or a project that you are working on; or you may write for data to be used in a research paper (see Figure 19.4). Here's how to proceed:

1. Identify yourself, indicate the kind of information you're after, and explain why you need it.
2. To avoid inconveniencing your reader, keep your questions to a minimum, make them clear, and word them so they can be answered briefly.
3. If you have three or more questions, set them up in a numbered list so the reader is less likely to miss answering one.
4. If you're using the information for a research paper and it's appropriate to do so, offer to supply a copy of your paper. Acknowledge the source of information when you write the paper.
5. Close by expressing appreciation for any help the reader can give.

```
                                    325 Darrin Hall
                                    Prentice College
                                    Barstow, ME 04611
                                    January 3, 20--

Mr. John Antwerp
Antrim Industries, Inc.
6431 Honeysuckle Avenue
Modesto, CA 95355

Dear Mr. Antwerp:

Your article in the December issue of Modern Health, in which
you describe the features of your company's new comprehensive
medical program, greatly interested me.

I am an environmental health student investigating the benefits
that small companies have realized by instituting such
programs. Can you help me by answering the following questions?

    1. To what extent has the number of employees calling in
       sick increased or decreased since your program began?

    2. To what extent has the program affected worker
       productivity and efficiency?

    3. How do the costs of the program compare with those of the
       medical insurance you used to provide through a private
       insurance company?

Thank you for any information you can supply. If you wish, I
will be happy to send you a copy of my finished report.

                                    Sincerely,

                                    René M. Hewitt

                                    René M. Hewitt
```

Figure 19.4   The Pointers Applied: Sample Inquiry Letter

EXERCISE   *Write a letter of inquiry that requests one of the following kinds of information:*

1. More details about a project reported in a magazine or newspaper article
2. Performance data for something you might buy

3. Detailed information about the credit policies of a company

4. Information for a research paper

5. Your congressional reprensentative's, mayor's or other public officials's position on an issue you're concerned about

6. Membership information for a club or professional organization

Order Letters

Order letters, used to order sports equipment, hobby supplies, appliances, furniture, clothing, and the like, must be brief and to the point (see Figure 19.5). Write the letter as follows:

1. Identify the merchandise by name, model or catalog number, size, weight, color, finish, or whatever else is needed.

2. To order a single item, write the letter in paragraph form. Otherwise set up a numbered list.

3. Specify how many items of each sort you want, the cost of a single item, and the total cost of the order.

4. Indicate when you wish to pay and how: by check, money order, or credit card. If you are enclosing payment, say so.

5. If you're ordering a gift to be shipped to someone at another address, be sure to include that address in the body of your letter.

EXERCISE   *Write one of the following letters:*

1. Order one or more pieces of furniture, household appliances, garden implements, or automobile accessories.

2. Order a gift to be shipped to a friend or relative.

Claim Letters

Writing a claim (complaint) letter is unpleasant but sometimes necessary. An improperly filled order, damaged or shoddy merchandise, a misunderstanding about prices—these and many other situations can result in claims. The letter points out the problem and asks that it be corrected.

When writing your letter, don't let anger make you discourteous. Remember, you're trying to settle a problem, not antagonize your reader. These guidelines will help you get a quick, favorable response:

1. If you are writing to a large company and don't know the name of the department that handles claims, address your letter to "Customer Adjustments Department" or "Claims Department." For small companies, write to the sales department. Your letter should then quickly reach someone who can help you.

2. Begin the body of the letter by identifying the problem precisely. Tell what happened and when, giving size, colors, model numbers, order number, prices—whatever the reader needs to investigate and make an adjustment.

3. If you've suffered serious inconvenience, mentioning it may speed the settlement.

4. Clearly state the adjustment you want.

5. Back your position with supporting evidence or arguments, positioned at whatever point in the letter seems most appropriate.

6. End courteously by expressing hope for a speedy settlement or offering any further information needed to reach that settlement.

Figure 19.6 shows a typical claim letter.

```
                                    420 Bayshore Drive
                                    Durham, NC 27701
                                    October 30, 20--

Order Department
Fitzpatrick Manufacturing Company
123 Getty Street
Philadelphia, PA 19141

Order Department:

Please ship the following merchandise as advertised in the
October 20-- issue of Better Homes and Gardens:

   1   Model 979-14/ES Luxury Kitchen
       Center.  Unit price: $141.77        $141.77

   1   Model 5109/WN Whippet five-quart
       Automatic Oriental Wok.
       Unit price:  $35.67.                  35.67
       TOTAL                               $177.44

Please send the order at your earliest convenience to the above
address.  I have enclosed a check for the total amount.

                        Sincerely yours,

                        Cheryl A. Forrest

                        Cheryl A. Forrest

Enc. Check
```

Figure 19.5   The Pointers Applied: Sample Order Letter

815 Buckaroo Lane
Dallas, TX 75226
July 10, 20--

Customer Relations Department
Carlson Craft
P.O. Box 87
Mankato, MN 56001

Customer Relations Department:

On June 12, I sent a check for $15.19 and an order for 150 imprinted white luncheon napkins, style 7219. These napkins were intended for my wedding reception.

The napkins came today, but instead of saying "Kathleen and Ward" they have the wrong imprint--"Kathleen and Lard." I am enclosing one of them to show you the mistake.

My wedding is less than five weeks off, and I'd like to settle the details of the reception well before then. Therefore, I'd appreciate a replacement order as soon as possible.

My fiancé and I both hope you'll take care of this matter promptly.

Yours truly,

Kathleen M. Van Meer

Kathleen M. Van Meer

Enc.

Figure 19.6   The Pointers Applied: Sample Claim Letter

EXERCISE   *Write a claim letter calling attention to one of the following:*

1. An improperly or incompletely filled order
2. An order that was delivered late
3. Merchandise damaged in transit because of improper packing
4. Improper billing by a credit card company or utility

Memos

Although memorandums, or memos, are rarely written by students, they will almost certainly be an important part of your on-the-job writing. The most common kind of business correspondence, memos are used to present data, announce meetings or their results, announce or suggest policy changes, request action, ask for recommendations, explain procedures, and perform many other functions.

Because memos are so common, most medium-sized and large companies provide printed memo forms. A memo consists of two parts: the heading and the body. A basic heading includes spaces for the names of the receiver and sender, the date, and the subject.

```
To: _____

From: _____

Date: _____

Subject: _____
```

To ensure that you write effective memos, follow these guidelines.

1. Make sure that your subject line states precisely what you're writing about. For example, if you're announcing a meeting, be sure to indicate its exact purpose. If you merely say "special meeting," you lessen the chance that your message will be read.

2. Consider how much background information you'll need to supply for the reader. Perhaps the subject line will provide all the background that's necessary. If this is not the case, however, include whatever is required in an introduction.

3. When you write the body of the memo, ask yourself what kinds of information the reader will need and how detailed it should be. Here are several kinds of memos and the basic information you might provide.

   Announcement of a Meeting: Date, time, and place; details concerning matters to be discussed; indication of any materials participants need to bring.

   Announcement of an Appointment: Name of appointee and position; appointee's background and qualifications; duties of job if unfamiliar to readers.

   Report of Safety Violations: Location and nature of violations; unless the information is obvious, why violations are dangerous and how to correct them.

   Report of Minor Mishap: When, where, and why mishap occurred; results of mishap; how to prevent recurrence.

4. Determine the need for a conclusion. Among the most common endings are those that offer to provide more information, make recommendations, and set starting dates for procedures and policies. Don't provide a conclusion unless one is clearly needed.

Figure 19.7 illustrates a typical memo.

To: All Department Supervisors
From: Gregory Conti, Production Planner
Date: July 5, 20--
Subject: Special meeting to draft flow chart
         for production of Data Star unit

Engineering has recently introduced a number of changes in the
design of the Data Star unit. As all of you know by now, these
changes have made it necessary for us to rework all of the
I/O and CPU boards in stock as well as the sensor packages and
purge systems of the last eight units. Consequently, we
have fallen behind our schedule for completing the twenty
units needed for the Russian shipment this October.

In an effort to correct this situation, I am calling a special meeting for the purpose of drawing up a new production
flow chart. This chart will be my primary tool for producing
a new, and speedier, production schedule. The meeting will be
held in the main conference room on July 9. It will begin at
1:30 p.m. and end when the objective has been met. All department supervisors are required to attend as the outcome
will affect all departments. At the meeting, you will be
asked to submit a status report on all jobs currently listed
in your work areas.

If you need further information about this meeting, call me
at extension 356.

Figure 19.7   The Pointers Applied: Sample Memorandum

EXERCISE   *Write a memorandum that does the following:*

1. Announces an appointment
2. Reports a safety violation
3. Reports a minor mishap

Job Application Letters

Once you've finished your academic preparation and started looking for a permanent job, you'll have to write one or more job application letters. In the meantime, you may need to write one to apply for a summer job (see Figures 19.8 and 19.9).

Take great care to do a first-rate job. Companies scan applications carefully and immediately discard those that fail to measure up. Grammatical or punctuation errors, misspellings, strikeovers, obvious erasures, smudge marks, beverage stains—all can earn your letter a quick trip to the reject pile. Be sure to in-

1407 East Elm Street
Big Rapids, MI 49307
February 24, 20--

Ms. Helen Thompson
Medical Records Administrator
St. Luke's Hospital
411 West Cooper Street
Saginaw, MI 48602

Dear Ms. Thompson:

Ms. Leslie Goldstein, director of your nursing department, has
informed me that you intend to hire an assistant administrator. I
believe that my formal training in medical records administration and
my hospital experience qualify me for this position. Please regard
this letter as my formal application.   ── Attracts interest

On May 24, 20--, I will receive a bachelor of science degree in medical
records administration from Ferris State University. This program
offers a thorough background in medical terminology, health science,
technical skills, and personnel management, and emphasizes health
administration.

As an intern, I served three months in the medical records department
of a large hospital, learning the day-to-day operations of such a
department and the managerial skills necessary to hold a supervisory
position. To help pay for my education, I have worked three summers as   Establishes
a server. This job has provided experience in meeting and dealing with   superiority
people on a one-to-one basis.

While in college, I have been social chairman of the Ferris Medical
Records Association and a member of the American Medical Records
Association. The enclosed résumé provides further information about
my experience and background.

May I arrange an interview to discuss my qualifications in greater
detail? You can reach me by writing to the above address or by   ── Requests
calling (231) 796-7791 Monday through Friday from 2 to 5 P.M.   interview

                    Sincerely,

                    Karen K. Auernhamer

                    Karen K. Auernhamer

Enc.

Figure 19.8 The Pointers Applied: Sample Job Application Letter [Permanent Job]

2439 South Lake Road
Fenton, MI 48438
March 27, 20--

Mr. Roger Updike
General Manager
Martin Buick-Olds, Inc.
Fenton, MI 48439

Dear Mr. Updike:

According to the weekly bulletin of the Drake College Placement
Bureau, you have several summer openings for automotive
technicians. I believe my academic training and practical
experience have provided me with the qualifications needed to
fill one of these positions.

I am a second-year student in the automotive service program at
Drake College and expect to receive my bachelor of science
degree in May 20--. My overall academic average is 3.08 on a
4.0 scale.

I have worked nine months as a co-op auto mechanic, and I owned
a lawn-care service for one year. The co-op position has given
me hands-on experience working with automobiles, and both positions have taught me the value of teamwork. I am hardworking,
responsible, and quick to learn, and I will do an effective job
for you.

If you desire further information concerning my background and
qualifications, the Drake Placement Bureau can supply you with
my college transcripts. Just call (231) 892-2319, extension
2607, and request them.

I will be happy to come in for an interview at some mutually
convenient time. My number is (231) 892-9531, or you can reach
me at the above address.

Sincerely yours,

Philip Thomas Dieck

Philip Thomas Dieck

Figure 19.9   The Pointers Applied: Sample Job Application Letter [Summer Job]

clude enough information for the employer to evaluate your qualifications. Here are some guidelines:

1. If you know an opening exists, begin by naming the position and how you heard of it—through an advertisement or from an instructor, for example. Using a name implies a recommendation by that person. If you're writing to ask whether an opening exists, specify exactly what position you're after. In either case, proceed by naming one or two of your qualifications or mentioning some service you can provide.

2. Establish your superiority over other candidates. Elaborate on the qualities mentioned at the start and present others that suit you for the position. If you have earned the money for some or all of your college expenses or had on-the-job supervisory experience, note these facts; employers like candidates who are ambitious and possess leadership potential.

3. Don't take a "hard-sell" approach. Assertions such as "I'm just the person you're looking for" or "You'll be making a mistake if you bypass me" will likely backfire. On the other hand, don't sell yourself short with statements such as "Although I have little on-the-job experience, I think I can probably handle your job." Instead, say something like "I'm confident my academic training has prepared me to handle this job successfully." In short, don't cast yourself in a negative light; accentuate the positive without bragging.

4. Keep your letter short by referring the reader to your résumé for further information. (Summer jobs often don't require résumés.)

5. End by requesting an interview. Provide a phone number so the employer can contact you quickly. If you can be reached only at certain times, specify them.

■ Résumés

The résumé, sent with the application letter, elaborates on the qualifications mentioned in that letter and presents others that the employer is likely to find useful (see Figure 19.10). Since it, like the letter, helps to sell you as a candidate, spare no effort to ensure that it's attractive, well-organized, and easy to read. Here are some tips:

1. Capitalize the main headings to make them stand out on the page.

2. To condense information, use phrases and clauses rather than complete sentences.

3. List your most recent education and employment experience first and then work backward so the employer can quickly gauge what you've done recently.

4. Don't try to cram too much material onto a page. Ample white space is important.

5. Center the heading at the top of the page.

Karen K. Auernhamer

1407 East Elm Street   Home Phone:(231) 796-7791
Big Rapids, MI 49307   E-mail:Auernh@aol.com

Employment Objective
   To work in a technical or an assistant managerial position in a medical records
   department, gain experience, and eventually assume an administrative position

Education
   Bachelor of science in Medical Records Administration. Ferris State University,
   Big Rapids, MI. May 2001

   Academic Honors
   Grade Point Average 3.85 (of 4.0) in Medical Records Courses

   Selected Course Work
   Legal Aspects of Health Care   Health Data and Analysis
   Quality Assurance   Principles of Information Systems

   Familiar with the Following Computer Programs
   Office 97(all features)   3M Coding Software
   Visio   E and M Calculator

Employment Experience
   Technical Trainee (Internship Program). Entered new patient information into
   computer systems, processed insurance claims, assisted in managing patient charts,
   and assisted in other technical duties in the medical records department. Saginaw
   Osteopathic Hospital, Saginaw, MI 48602. June 2000 to August 2000

   Server at Zehnder's of Frankenmuth. 215 South Main Street, Frankenmuth, MI
   48734. Summers of 1997, 1998, 1999

Professional Interests
   Member, American Medical Records Association, Ferris Medical Records
   Association (Social Chair)

References will be furnished upon request

Figure 19.10   The Pointers Applied: Sample Résumé

Typically, information is grouped under the six headings below. If you are a recent graduate with little or no full-time work experience, list education before work experience. If you've worked for a number of years, however, reverse the order.

1. *Heading.* Include your name, address, phone number, and e-mail address if you have one. Don't date the résumé; it will then become obsolete more quickly than it otherwise would.

2. *Employment Objective.* State your immediate work goal and the direction you hope your career will take. Avoid any impression that you will soon

move on to another organization or try for the boss's job. If you can't specify your objective in a believable manner, leave it out.

3. *Education.* List pertinent facts of your college education. Note any academic honors, such as a good (above 3.0) grade-point average, a scholarship, or a certificate of commendation. If you've taken elective courses in your major or have a minor in a closely related field, so indicate.

4. *Employment Experience.* Highlight your full-time, part-time, volunteer, and summer work experience. If a job was seasonal, note this fact to avoid the impression that you were fired. Mention any promotions or raises you've received and any supervisory experience you've had. Don't mention any job duties unless they are similar to those of the job you're after.

5. *Professional Interests.* Cite membership in professional organizations. In addition, note any special skills such as training in lifesaving, fluency in a foreign language, or familiarity with some specialized form of communication.

6. *References.* List references only if you are answering an advertisement that asks for them. Otherwise, indicate that they will be furnished on request. Typical references include instructors, supervisors, and prominent community leaders who know you. Never use names of relatives or name anyone as a reference without first obtaining permission. For each reference, give the person's name, including a personal title, position, business address, and telephone number. An example follows:

> Ms. Brenda Pretzer
> Director, Medical Records Department
> Saginaw Osteopathic Hospital
> 515 North Michigan Avenue
> Saginaw, MI 48602
> Telephone: (517) 776-2682

EXERCISE

1. Write a letter applying for an advertised job or one that someone has told you about.

2. Write a letter applying for a position for which there may or may not be a vacancy.

3. Prepare a résumé to accompany your letter.

Research Guide

Much of your college and workplace writing will require some type of research—obtaining information from one or more sources to help achieve your writing purpose. The nature of your writing task and the demands of the situation determine the format you use and the way you document your sources.

This section of the text explores in detail the research tools and procedures you will use to develop various types of papers and reports. Sometimes you'll draw upon books, magazines, newspapers, and other printed sources, as well as electronic sources, in order to prepare a longer library research paper; at other times you'll do the same for shorter papers. Still other situations call for using primary research—the type in which you develop the information you use—to accomplish your purpose. The three chapters in this section will help you to meet these writing demands.

Chapter 20 explains how to choose a suitable library research topic and then focuses on carrying out the necessary steps to write a research paper. The chapter includes a continuing case history that leads to a finished paper complete with margin notes that will provide guidance as you prepare your own paper.

Chapter 21 shows how to prepare correct references for your paper's bibliography. It also shows the correct formats for references within the body of the paper, explains how to handle quotations, and offers guidelines for avoiding plagiarism.

Chapter 22 explains and illustrates the most common types of primary research strategies—interviews, questionnaires, and direct observations. In each case, student models, annotated with margin notes, embody the key features of that strategy.

Together, the material in these three chapters should provide all the information you'll need to complete your writing assignments that require research.

chapter 20

The Library Research Paper

Scene: A dark, sinister-looking laboratory. In the center of the stage stands a large laboratory bench crowded with an array of mysterious chemistry apparatus. Tall, cadaverous, and foreboding, Dr. Frankenslime leers as he pours the contents of a tube through a funnel and into a bubbling flask. A short, hunched-over figure looks on with interest. Suddenly the doctor spreads his arms wide and flashes a sardonic smile.

Frankenslime: Igor! At last! At last I've got it! With this fluid, I can control . . .

Research yes. But not all researchers are mad scientists, or scientists, or even mad. You might not be any of these things, but no doubt you'll be asked to prepare a *library research paper* for your composition class. This assignment calls for you to gather information from a variety of sources and then to focus, organize, and present it in a formal paper that documents your sources. The procedure will familiarize you with the mechanics of documentation, and when you finish you'll have a solid grasp of your topic and pride in your accomplishment. In addition, the experience will help you learn how to meet the research demands of other courses and your job.

For many students, the thought of writing a research paper triggers feelings of anxiety and fears of drudgery. Some feel overwhelmed by the amount of material in a college library and the need to make a lengthy search for useful information. Others doubt that they could have anything more to say about any topic they might choose: What's the point of simply rehashing what experts have already said much better? Still others are daunted by how much there might actually be to say about their topic.

But writing a research paper really isn't so formidable. You can acquaint yourself with the various library resources that will provide easy access to the information you need. Reading what others have written on a topic will give you a chance to draw your own conclusions. And as a writer you can limit your topic so that it doesn't balloon out of control.

Research writing is common both in the classroom and on the job. A history professor might require a long report on the causes of the Vietnam War. A business instructor might ask you to trace the history of a company, evaluate an advertising campaign, or review the latest styles of management. A building trades instructor might call for a short report that compares the effectiveness of several new insulating materials. At work, a marketing analyst might report on the development costs, sales potential, and competition for a product the company is considering introducing. An engineer might write a journal article that summarizes recent developments in plastic fabrication. A physical therapist might prepare a seminar paper that evaluates different exercise programs to follow arthroscopic surgery.

Whatever the writing project, let your purpose guide your research and determine the information you elect to use. When you write, the conclusions you have reached from thinking about what you have read and your purpose in communicating, not your notes, should dictate what you say.

■ Learning About Your Library

Before starting a library research paper, take time to familiarize yourself with your library. Many college libraries offer guided tours, and almost all of them display floor plans that show where and how the books are grouped. If your library doesn't have tours, browse through it on your own and scan its contents. As you do, note the following features:

Card Catalog: The card catalog indexes the library's books and often most of its other holdings as well. Although most colleges now have computerized card catalogs, a few use conventional catalogs, which consist of files of 3 x 5-inch cards. Pages 323–29 discuss computerized catalogs and pages 330–31 the conventional type.

Computerized Databases: These databases, like printed periodical indexes, provide listings of articles in magazines and newspapers, and some even provide the full text of the article. Information may be on compact discs or transmitted to the library by wire from another location. Pages 331–36 discuss databases.

Computers with Internet Access: These computers connect users to a worldwide network of organizations and individuals, providing access to an almost endless variety of information. Pages 336–43 discuss the Internet.

Stacks: These are the bookshelves that hold books and bound periodicals (magazines and newspapers). Stacks are either open or closed. Open stacks allow you to go directly to the books you want, take them off the shelf, and check them out. Closed stacks do not allow you direct access to shelved material. Instead, a staff member brings you what you want.

Periodical Area: Here you'll find current and recent issues of magazines and newspapers. If your topic calls for articles that have appeared within the last few months, you're likely to find them in this area.

Microfilm and Microfiche Files: Microfilm is a filmstrip bearing a series of photographically reduced printed pages. Microfiche is a small card with a set of photographically reduced pages mounted on it. Often, most of a library's magazine and newspaper collection is on film. Ask a librarian how to work the viewing machines. Once you can run them, you'll have access to many library resources.

Circulation Desk: Here's where you check materials in and out, renew books you want to keep longer, and pay overdue fines. If you can't find something you want, the desk clerk will tell you whether it's missing, on reserve, or checked out. If it's out, fill out a hold card, and the library will notify you when it is available.

Reserve Area: This area contains books that instructors have had removed from general circulation so students can use them for particular courses. Ordinarily, you can keep these books for only a few hours or overnight.

Reference Area: This area houses the library's collection of encyclopedias, periodical indexes, almanacs, handbooks, dictionaries, and other research tools that you'll use as you investigate your topic. You'll also find one or more reference guides—Eugene P. Sheehy's *Guide to Reference Books* (1996), for example—that direct you to useful reference tools. To ensure that these books are always available, they must be used in the library. Someone is usually on duty to answer questions.

■ Choosing a Topic

Instructors take different approaches in assigning library research papers. Some want explanatory papers, other want papers that address a two-sided question, and still others allow students a free choice. An explanatory paper takes no position but provides information that gives the reader a better grasp of the topic. For example, it may explain the key advantages of solar heating, thereby clearing up popular misconceptions. An argument paper, on the other hand, attempts to sway the reader toward one point of view—for instance, that solar heat is commercially feasible. Some instructors specify not only the type of paper but also the topic. Others restrict students to a general subject area, ask them to pick topics from lists, or give them free choice. If you have little to say in the selection, take a positive view: At least you won't have to wrestle with finding a topic.

Whatever the circumstances, it's a good idea to follow a pacing schedule that establishes completion dates for the various stages of your paper. Such a timetable encourages you to plan your work, clarifies both your progress and the work remaining, and provides an overview of the entire project. You can use the following sample schedule as a guide, modifying the stages or adding other ones as necessary.

Sample schedule for a library research paper

Activity	Targeted Completion Date
Topic Selection	_____
Working Bibliography	_____
Research Question and Tentative Thesis	_____

Note Taking   ———————

Working Outline   ———————

First Draft   ———————

Revised Drafts   ——————— ——————— ———————

    Date Due: ———————

Topics to Avoid

If you have free rein to pick your topic, how should you proceed? To begin, rule out certain types of topics.

- Those based entirely on personal experience or opinion such as "The Thrills I Have Enjoyed Waterskiing" or "Colorado Has More [or Less] Scenic Beauty than New Mexico." Such topics can't be supported by library research. Don't hesitate, however, to include personal judgments and conclusions that emerge from your reading.

- Those fully explained in a single source. An explanation of a process, such as cardiopulmonary resuscitation, or the description of a place, such as the Gobi Desert, does not require coordination of materials from various sources. Although you may find several articles on such topics, basically they will repeat the same information.

- Those that are brand new. Often it's impossible to find sufficient source material about such topics.

- Those that are overly broad. Don't try to tackle such elephant-sized topics as "The Causes of World War II" or "Recent Medical Advances." Instead, slim them down to something like "The Advent of Jet Fighters" or "Eye Surgery with Laser Beams."

- Those that have been worked over and over, such as abortion and the legal drinking age. Why bore your reader with information and arguments that are all too familiar already?

EXERCISE   *Using the advice on topics to avoid, explain why each of the following would or would not be suitable for a library research topic:*

1. Genetic counseling
2. Neoconservatism
3. The fiber optics revolution
4. How last night's riot got started
5. Building a rock garden
6. A Third World hot spot as described on the evening news
7. Reforming the financing of presidential election campaigns

Drawing on Your Interests

Let your interests guide your choice. A long-standing interest in basketball might suggest a paper on the pros and cons of expanding the number of teams in the National Basketball Association. An instructor's lecture might spark your interest in a historical event or person, an economic crisis, a scientific development, a sociological trend, a medical milestone, a political scandal, or the influences on an author. An argument with a friend might spur you to investigate latch-key children. A television documentary might arouse your curiosity about a group of primitive people. A recent article or novel might inspire you to explore the occult or some taboo.

Be practical in selecting a topic. Why not get a head start on a particular aspect of your major field by researching it now? Some management, marketing, or advertising strategy; the beginnings of current contract law; medical ethics—all of these topics, and many others, qualify. Think about your audience, the availability of information, and whether you can fit it into the guidelines for your paper.

To develop a focus for your paper, it's often helpful to brainstorm, skim encyclopedia articles and other materials, and utilize the branching or clustering technique. If you're exploring the topic of child abuse, preparing a clustering diagram like the one in Figure 20.1 can help you decide how to narrow your topic as well as provide a rough map of areas to research. The more you brainstorm, the richer your map will be. Brainstorming often results in a series of questions, perhaps based on the writing strategies discussed in Chapters 4–12, that will help guide your research. Often it is helpful to state your main research question, followed by a series of related questions that elaborate on it. From our cluster example, a student wishing to explore the topic of psychological abuse might develop the following set of questions:

What can be done to help victims of psychological abuse?
    What is psychological abuse?
    What long-term and short-term effects does it have on a child?
    How can a child living at home be helped?
        Are there services to help limit the abuse?
        Is family therapy an option?
            What is family therapy, and what does it do?
    What psychological help is available for an adult who experienced
        childhood abuse?
        What therapies work best?
        What do they do?
        How effective are they?

These questions make research easier. After all, the purpose of research is to answer questions. Later, as you examine source material, you will be seeking specific answers, not just randomly searching for information.

Encyclopedias are usually neither current enough nor sufficiently detailed to be major sources for a paper. They can, however, provide an overview of a topic's essential points and alert you to areas of controversy that you'll need to

Figure 20.1   Clustering Diagram on Child Abuse

investigate in order to produce a thoughtful paper. You can consult both general and specialized encyclopedias, and other specialized publications are also available. If, for instance, you need material on a historical figure, you can check the *Dictionary of American Biography* for deceased American figures, the *Dictionary of National Biography* for deceased British figures, and the *McGraw-Hill Encyclopedia of World Biography.* Your librarian can suggest other useful resources. Once you've found your focus, the branching technique will allow you to expand the list of items obtained by brainstorming.

More often than not, things won't fall neatly into place as you probe for a topic and then a focus. Don't be discouraged by false starts and blind alleys. Think of yourself as an explorer who will gradually become well-versed in your chosen topic.

CASE HISTORY

Keith Jacque was a first-year composition student majoring in criminal justice when he wrote the library research paper at the end of this chapter. The assignment was to write about a recent technological development or an innovative solution to a social problem. Intrigued by the possible solutions to the problem of prison overcrowding, Keith decided to explore several options: building more prisons, developing early release programs for the least dangerous criminals, setting up house-arrest programs verified by electronic monitoring systems, utilizing halfway houses, converting empty military bases into prisons, and re-evaluating legal codes to determine which offenses should require incarceration. After a little thought, Keith realized that in order to develop his paper properly he would need to concentrate on only one option. Because he had recently watched a televised report on electronic monitoring and found it interesting, he decided to investigate this alternative.

To establish a focus for his paper, Keith drafted a series of questions suggested by the writing strategies discussed in Chapters 4–12. Here are the questions he developed:

> Could I *narrate* a brief history of electronic monitoring?
> Could I *describe* how a monitoring system works?
> Could I *classify* monitoring systems?
> Could I *compare* monitoring systems to anything?
> Could I explain the *process* involved in monitoring?
> What *causes* led to the development of monitoring?
> What *effects* is monitoring likely to have?
> What systems best *illustrate* the essence of monitoring?
> Is there a widely accepted *definition* of electronic monitoring?
> Could I *argue* for or against the expanded use of monitoring?

These writing strategies can often help you narrow a subject down to a manageable topic.

For background reading, Keith consulted two general encyclopedias: the *Encyclopedia Americana* and the *Encyclopaedia Britannica*. After preparing a list of possible entries that included "electronic monitoring," "electronic surveillance," "electronic incarceration," "home incarceration," and "house arrest," he began searching for those entries but found none of them. Next, he decided to look in more specialized publications. Not knowing how to proceed, he asked a reference librarian, who directed him to the latest editions of the *Encyclopedia of Crime and Justice* and the *McGraw-Hill Encyclopedia of Science and Technology*. These sources also contained no useful information.

At this point, drawing on what he had learned from his criminal justice instructor and the television report, Keith brainstormed in order to determine a possible focus for his paper. He came up with the following list:

1. Brief history of electronic monitoring
2. Technical problems in developing systems
3. Types of monitoring systems
4. Benefits of monitoring
5. Problems associated with monitoring

Upon reflection, Keith eliminated the second item because it would require reading highly technical material, which he might not understand. The other items were interesting to him, and he believed that they would also interest his audience—fellow students at the vocationally oriented school he attended.

Next, Keith used branching to expand his list and guide his library search, concentrating on what he knew at this stage.

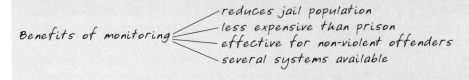

Benefits of monitoring
- reduces jail population
- less expensive than prison
- effective for non-violent offenders
- several systems available

Problems associated with monitoring
- signal interference problems
- legal concerns

This case history continues on page 344.

■ Assembling a Working Bibliography

Once you have a topic, you're ready to see whether the library has the resources you'll need to complete the project. This step requires you to check additional reference tools and compile a working bibliography—a set of cards that list promising sources of information. This section discusses these reference tools and how to use them.

Encyclopedias

What They Are   Encyclopedias fall into two categories, general and specialized. General encyclopedias, the *Encyclopedia Americana* and the *Encyclopaedia Britannica,* for instance, offer articles on a wide range of subjects. Specialized encyclopedias cover one particular field, such as advertising or human behavior. Here's a sampling of specialized encyclopedias:

> *Encyclopedia of Advertising*
> *Encyclopedia of Education*
> *Encyclopedia of Environmental Science*
> *Encyclopedia of Human Behavior: Psychology, Psychiatry, and Mental Health*
> *Encyclopedia of Social Work*
> *Encyclopedia of World Art*
> *Harper's Encyclopedia of Science*
> *International Encyclopedia of the Social Sciences*
> *McGraw-Hill Encyclopedia of Science and Technology*

How to Use Them Encyclopedias are sometimes a convenient launching pad for your investigation because they provide an overview of the broad field your topic fits into. For a nonspecialized topic, like the impact of commercial television during the 1950s, check the articles on television in one or more general encyclopedias. For a specialized aspect of television, say the development of the picture tube, consult one or more specialized encyclopedias, such as *Harper's Encyclopedia of Science* and the *McGraw-Hill Encyclopedia of Science and Technology,* along with the general encyclopedias. During this search you'll re-encounter material you scanned while trying to focus on a topic.

Some instructors allow you to acknowledge encyclopedias as a source; others prohibit their use; and still others allow material from specialized, but not general, encyclopedias. As always, follow your instructor's wishes.

If you will be using encyclopedia sources, jot down the following information for each note you take:

> Title of article
> Author(s) of article (Not always available. Sometimes only initials at the end of an article identify an author. In that case, check the list of contributors at the front of the first volume for the full name.)
> Name of encyclopedia
> Year of publication
> For specialized encyclopedias, also include the number of volumes in the set, the encyclopedia editor, and the place of publication.

Most importantly, check for bibliographies at the ends of articles and copy down any reference that looks promising.

Computer-Based Encyclopedias Today, a number of encyclopedias, both general and specialized, are available on computer compact discs or over the Internet. They are easy to search and often allow you to search for a key phrase such as "Greek architecture." The results will guide you not only to articles devoted to your topic but also to others that refer to it, even if only in a paragraph. If you use an electronic encyclopedia, write down, in addition to the other source information, the publication medium, the name of the vendor (Microsoft, for example, for a Microsoft product), and the name and date of the electronic publication.

When you've finished your exploratory reading in encyclopedias, turn to the card catalog and periodical indexes—the prime sources of information for library research papers.

Computerized Card Catalog

What It Is A computerized card catalog lists all the books in the library, usually along with other holdings like magazines, newspapers, government documents, and electronic recordings. It may also provide additional information, such as whether a book has been checked out and, if so, the return date. Some catalogs even include the holdings of nearby libraries. Books are usually cataloged using Library of Congress call numbers, although some libraries use the Dewey decimal system.

Several catalog systems are available, all having similar terminals that consist essentially of a viewing screen and a keyboard on which to enter requests for information. Some terminals also have printers for copying material shown on the screen. To use the unit properly, read the instructions at the terminal or ask a librarian. Remember, a computer can't think. It can only match the string of letters you type to similar strings of letters in its database. If you misspell a word, you will not find any matches.

Most systems let you conduct searches by author, title, subject, and key terms—those appearing in book titles and descriptions. Typically, you'll begin by typing in a code—say A for "author," T for "title," S for "subject," and KT for "key term"—then an equal sign and your specific search request. Searching may require you to view a series of screens having increasingly specific information, with the final screen providing information about a single book. Figure 20.2 illustrates a two-screen subject search. Figures 20.3, 20.4, and 20.5 show the screens obtained in author, title, and key term searches. Note that all four screens provide identical information about the book. Most libraries have handouts and training programs that explain the different symbols and options of their specific system.

Often, a key term search (see Figure 20.5) can be the most helpful way to approach a topic. In this type of search, the computer checks the titles and descriptions of books for the key terms you enter and lists any that it finds. Different key terms will produce varying strings of articles, so it is a good idea to try different words or phrases for the same topic. For example, if you're searching for material on "electric cars," you might also try "electronic cars," "alternative fuels," and so on. Because such searches are very rapid, you can experiment with different combinations of terms to focus your search. If, for instance, you're asked to write a paper on some aspect of Japanese culture, you might investigate such combinations as "Japanese business," "Japan and education," and "Japanese feminists." Because key term searches allow you to use logical terms like *and, or, but,* and *not,* they are especially useful for narrowing a broad focus.

Obtaining the Books   Start your search for useful books by looking up any promising titles found in encyclopedia bibliographies or other sources. Use the appropriate code and enter the title into the computer exactly. Once you've found the screen for a book that appears useful, write down any subject headings for it that appear on the screen. You can use these headings for a subject search.

Next, draw up a list of promising subject headings and check them in the computer. If you're investigating satanic cults, your headings might include "devil worship," "satanism," "diabolism," and "cult."

Successful subject and key term searches often turn up more book titles than a single screen can accommodate, a situation illustrated by the top screen in Figure 20.2. In this case, using a key designated at the bottom of the screen will let you review the rest of the list. With especially long lists, you may need to

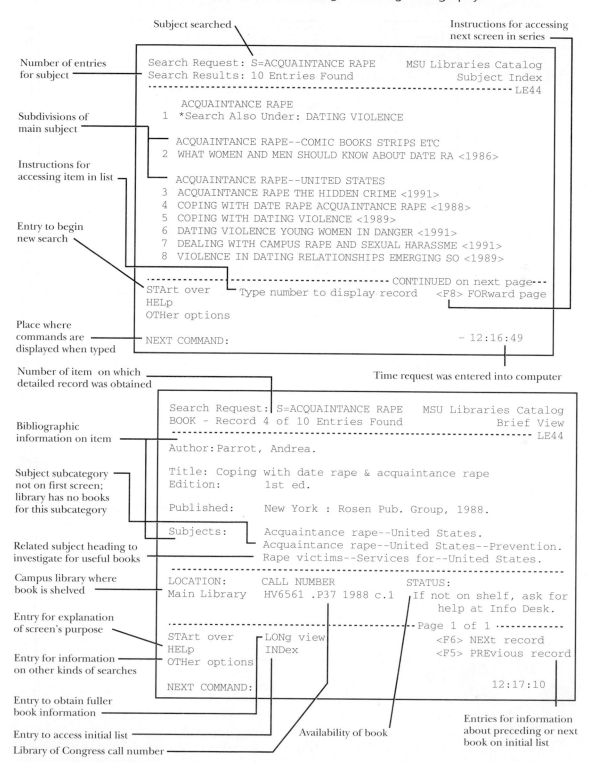

Subject searched

Instructions for accessing next screen in series

Number of entries for subject

Subdivisions of main subject

Instructions for accessing item in list

Entry to begin new search

Place where commands are displayed when typed

```
Search Request: S=ACQUAINTANCE RAPE    MSU Libraries Catalog
Search Results: 10 Entries Found              Subject Index
------------------------------------------------------------LE44
      ACQUAINTANCE RAPE
  1  *Search Also Under: DATING VIOLENCE

      ACQUAINTANCE RAPE--COMIC BOOKS STRIPS ETC
  2  WHAT WOMEN AND MEN SHOULD KNOW ABOUT DATE RA <1986>

      ACQUAINTANCE RAPE--UNITED STATES
  3  ACQUAINTANCE RAPE THE HIDDEN CRIME <1991>
  4  COPING WITH DATE RAPE ACQUAINTANCE RAPE <1988>
  5  COPING WITH DATING VIOLENCE <1989>
  6  DATING VIOLENCE YOUNG WOMEN IN DANGER <1991>
  7  DEALING WITH CAMPUS RAPE AND SEXUAL HARASSME <1991>
  8  VIOLENCE IN DATING RELATIONSHIPS EMERGING SO <1989>
------------------------------------------- CONTINUED on next page---
STArt over         Type number to display record   <F8> FORward page
HELp
OTHer options

NEXT COMMAND:                                     - 12:16:49
```

Number of item on which detailed record was obtained

Time request was entered into computer

Bibliographic information on item

Subject subcategory not on first screen; library has no books for this subcategory

Related subject heading to investigate for useful books

Campus library where book is shelved

Entry for explanation of screen's purpose

Entry for information on other kinds of searches

Entry to obtain fuller book information

Entry to access initial list

Library of Congress call number

Availability of book

Entries for information about preceding or next book on initial list

```
Search Request: S=ACQUAINTANCE RAPE    MSU Libraries Catalog
BOOK - Record 4 of 10 Entries Found            Brief View
------------------------------------------------------------ LE44
Author:Parrot, Andrea.

Title: Coping with date rape & acquaintance rape
Edition:      1st ed.

Published:    New York : Rosen Pub. Group, 1988.

Subjects:     Acquaintance rape--United States.
              Acquaintance rape--United States--Prevention.
              Rape victims--Services for--United States.
---------------------------------------------
LOCATION:     CALL NUMBER          STATUS:
Main Library  HV6561 .P37 1988 c.1 If not on shelf, ask for
                                    help at Info Desk.
------------------------------------- Page 1 of 1 ------------
STArt over    LONg view            <F6> NEXt record
HELp          INDex                <F5> PREvious record
OTHer options

NEXT COMMAND:                         12:17:10
```

Figure 20.2   Subject Search
Screens courtesy of Michigan State University libraries' online "Magic" system.

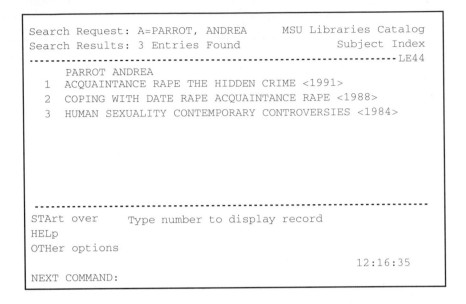

```
Search Request: A=PARROT, ANDREA      MSU Libraries Catalog
Search Results: 3 Entries Found                Subject Index
----------------------------------------------------------LE44
       PARROT ANDREA
  1    ACQUAINTANCE RAPE THE HIDDEN CRIME <1991>
  2    COPING WITH DATE RAPE ACQUAINTANCE RAPE <1988>
  3    HUMAN SEXUALITY CONTEMPORARY CONTROVERSIES <1984>




    ----------------------------------------------------------
STArt over     Type number to display record
HELp
OTHer options
                                            12:16:35

NEXT COMMAND:
```

```
Search Request: A=PARROT, ANDREA      MSU Libraries Catalog
BOOK - Record 2 of 3 Entries Found               Brief View
---------------------------------------------------------- D3BB
Author:Parrot, Andrea.

Title: Coping with date rape & acquaintance rape
Edition:      1st ed.

Published:    New York : Rosen Pub. Group, 1988.

Subjects:     Acquaintance rape--United States.
              Acquaintance rape--United States--Prevention.
              Rape victims--Services for--United States.
    ----------------------------------------------------------
LOCATION:     CALL NUMBER         STATUS:
Main Library  HV6561 .P37 1988 c.1 If not on shelf, ask for
                                    help at Info Desk.
    ----------------------------------------- Page 1 of 1 -----------
STArt over    LONg view              <F6> NEXt record
HELp          INDex                  <F5> PREvious record
OTHer options
                                            14:02:20

NEXT COMMAND:
```

Figure 20.3   Author Search

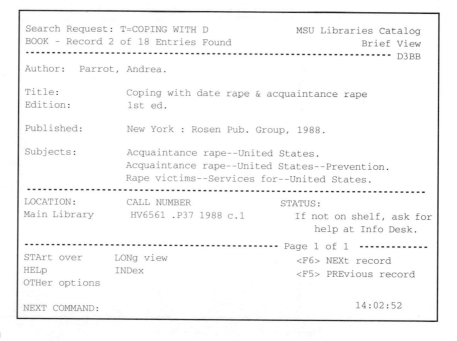

Repetition indicates that original title uses *&* instead of *and*

```
Search Request: T=COPING WITH D            MSU Libraries Catalog
Search Results: 18 Entries Found                       Title Index
-------------------------------------------------------- LE44
  1 COPING WITH DATE RAPE & ACQUAINTANCE RAPE. PARROT ANDREA <1988>
  2 COPING WITH DATE RAPE AND ACQUAINTANCE RAPE. PARROT ANDREA <1988>
  3 COPING WITH DATING VIOLENCE. RUE NANCY N <1989>
  4 COPING WITH DEATH. RAAB ROBERT A <1978>
  5 COPING WITH DEATH AND DYING AN INTERDISCIPLINARY APPROACH <1985>
  6 COPING WITH DEATH IN THE FAMILY. SCHNEIDERMAN GERALD <1979>
  7 COPING WITH DEATH ON CAMPUS <1985>
  8 COPING WITH DESTITUTION POVERTY AND RELIEF IN WESTERN EUROPE.
    MITCHISON ROSALIND <1991>
  9 COPING WITH DIFFICULT PEOPLE. BRAMSON ROBERT M <1981>
 10 COPING WITH DIFFICULT TEACHERS. BERGREEN GARY <1988>
    COPING WITH DISABILITY INVENTORY A STUDY OF THE RELIABILITY AND
    VALIDITY OF AN INSTRUMENT DESIGNED TO MEASURE COPING B
 11 KULKARNI MADHAV R <1985>

------------------------------------------ CONTINUED on next page --
STArt over     Type number to display record      <F8> FORward page
HELp
OTHer options

NEXT COMMAND:                                          12:15:07
```

```
Search Request: T=COPING WITH D            MSU Libraries Catalog
BOOK - Record 2 of 18 Entries Found                     Brief View
-------------------------------------------------------- D3BB
Author:  Parrot, Andrea.

Title:            Coping with date rape & acquaintance rape
Edition:          1st ed.

Published:        New York : Rosen Pub. Group, 1988.

Subjects:         Acquaintance rape--United States.
                  Acquaintance rape--United States--Prevention.
                  Rape victims--Services for--United States.
------------------------------------------------------------------
LOCATION:         CALL NUMBER              STATUS:
Main Library      HV6561 .P37 1988 c.1     If not on shelf, ask for
                                           help at Info Desk.
------------------------------------------- Page 1 of 1 ------------
STArt over     LONg view                  <F6> NEXt record
HELp           INDex                       <F5> PREvious record
OTHer options

NEXT COMMAND:                                          14:02:52
```

Figure 20.4   Title Search

```
Search Request: K=ACQUAINTANCE AND RAPE        MSU Libraries Catalog
Search Results: 29 Entries Found                     Key Term Index
------------------------------------------------------------- D3BB
     DATE  TITLE:                                  AUTHOR:
15  1993  Beyond the legal definition: u <microfilm> Campbell, Rebecca M
16  1993  Beyond the legal definition: understanding Campbell, Rebecca M
17  1993  Coping with date rape & acquaintance rape  Parrot, Andrea
18  1993  Date rape : the secret epidemic : what it  Boumil, Marcia M
19  1993  When "I love you" turns violent : abuse in Johnson, Scott A
20  1991  Acquaintance gang rape on campus           O'Sullivan, Chris S
21  1991  Acquaintance rape : the hidden crime
22  1991  Dating violence : young women in danger
23  1991  Dealing with campus rape and sexual harass
24  1990  The date rape epidemic : profitable myth   Anderson, James D
25  1989  Coping with dating violence                Rue, Nancy N
26  1989  Violence in dating relationships : emergin
27  1988  Coping with date rape & acquaintance rape  Parrot, Andrea
28  1988  I never called it rape : the Ms. report on Warshaw, Robin
------------------------------------------- CONTINUED on next page----

STArt over       Type number to display record      <F8> FORward page
HELp                                                 <F7> BACk page
OTHer options
                                                          11:14:18

NEXT COMMAND:
```

```
Search Request: K=ACQUAINTANCE AND RAPE        MSU Libraries Catalog
BOOK - Record 17 of 29 entries found                     Brief View
------------------------------------------------------------- D3BB
Author:  Parrot, Andrea.

Title:           Coping with date rape & acquaintance rape
Edition:         1st ed.

Published:       New York : Rosen Pub. Group, 1988.

Subjects:        Acquaintance rape--United States.
                 Acquaintance rape--United States--Prevention.
                 Rape victims--Services for--United States.
-------------------------------------------------------------
LOCATION:        CALL NUMBER            STATUS:
Main Library     HV6561 .P37 1988 c.1      If not on shelf, ask for
                                              help at Info Desk.

------------------------------------------- Page 1 of 1 ------------
STArt over     LONg view                   <F6> NEXt record
HELp           INDex                        <F5> PREvious record
OTHer options
                                                          11:49:21

NEXT COMMAND:
```

Figure 20.5   Key Term Search

narrow your focus and start searching anew. For example, "Japan and education" might be narrowed to "Japan and primary education."

When a check of your subject headings yields nothing, don't give up. Perhaps your list doesn't include any headings that are actually used. To find the right headings, turn to the *Library of Congress Subject Headings,* if your library catalogs books according to the Library of Congress system. If it uses the Dewey decimal system, then consult the *Sears List of Subject Headings.* If, for example, you're researching the subject of multiculturalism and your library uses the Library of Congress system, don't expect to find anything cataloged under that heading. Instead, as the *Subject Headings* guide shows, books on multiculturalism are cataloged under "Pluralism (social studies)."

When you have found a promising title, entering its number, or a command and the number, will call up a screen with relevant information. This is illustrated by the bottom screen in Figure 20.2. With some systems, this screen indicates whether the book is in the library or checked out and tells you how to proceed if you can't find it on the shelf. With other systems, you can get the information by entering a command. Some systems will even allow you to reserve a book by entering the request into the computer.

If your terminal has a printer, use it to make a copy of each promising reference. Otherwise, record the following information on a 3 × 5-inch note card:

Author(s)
Title
Editor(s) and translator(s), as well as author(s) of any supplementary material
Total number of volumes (if more than one) and the number of the specific volume that you want to use
City of publication
Name of publisher
Date of publication

Also, copy the book's call number in the upper left-hand corner of the card.

Next, scan the books themselves. If your library stacks are closed, give the librarian a list of your call numbers and ask to see the books. If you can enter the stacks, locate the general areas where your books are shelved. Once you find a number range that includes one of your call numbers, follow the trail of guides on the book spines until you find your book. Spend a few extra minutes browsing in the general area of each book; you may discover useful sources that you overlooked in the card catalog.

Skim each book's table of contents and any introductory material, such as a preface or introduction, to determine its scope and approach. Also check the index and note the pages with discussions that relate to your topic. Finally, thumb through any portions that look promising. If the book won't help you, throw away the note card.

If a book is missing from the shelf and the computer hasn't indicated that someone has checked it out, then it's probably on reserve. Check at the circulation desk; if the book is on reserve, go to that section and examine it there. If someone has checked the book out and the due date is some time away, perhaps a library nearby will have a copy.

Conventional Card Catalog

If your college, like many, has converted to a computerized card catalog, you can skip to the section on periodical indexes, pages 331–36. Some schools, however, continue to use a conventional card catalog, either as their principal reference tool or as an important backup to the often overburdened computer system.

What It Is   A conventional card catalog is a file of 3 × 5-inch cards that indexes all the books in the library and sometimes other holdings, such as magazines and newspapers, as well. Some libraries have their catalogs on microfiche cards or microfilms, which are read with a special viewing device.

The card catalog contains three kinds of cards—author, title, and subject—for each nonfiction item cataloged. Fiction has author and title cards only. Except for the top line, which differs for the different types of cards, all cards for the same book are identical. Figure 20.6 shows a typical author card. The cards are filed alphabetically, and the three kinds may be filed together, separately, or in some other manner, for example, title and author cards together, subject cards elsewhere. In alphabetizing the cards, librarians follow certain standard practices.

1. Title and subject cards are filed alphabetically according to the first word that is *not* an article (*a, an, the*).
2. Cards are filed word by word rather than strictly letter by letter. Thus, *Chicken and Turkey Tapeworms* precedes *Chicken Beacon*, and *Chicken Raising Made Easy* precedes *The Chicken-bone Special*.
3. "Mc" names are filed under "Mac."
4. Numbers and abbreviations are filed alphabetically as if they were spelled out. For example, the title card for the novel *Mr. Bridge* is filed under "Mister."

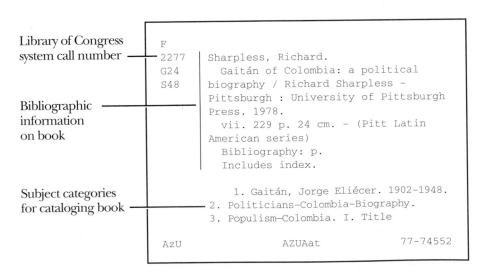

Library of Congress
system call number

F
2277
G24
S48

Sharpless, Richard.
   Gaitán of Colombia: a political
biography / Richard Sharpless -
Pittsburgh : University of Pittsburgh
Press. 1978.
   vii. 229 p. 24 cm. - (Pitt Latin
American series)
   Bibliography: p.
   Includes index.

Bibliographic
information
on book

Subject categories
for cataloging book

   1. Gaitán, Jorge Eliécer. 1902-1948.
2. Politicians-Colombia-Biography.
3. Populism—Colombia. I. Title

AzU   AZUAat   77-74552

Figure 20.6   Author Card

5. Names of people precede identical names of places and things. Thus, "Snow, C. P., *The Masters*" comes before *"Snow at Evening."*

Knowing these conventions will lessen tedious thumbing through the cards.

How to Use It   Follow the procedure given on pages 324 and 329 for computerized card catalogs, making any needed modifications.

Exercise

1. **Select five of the following subjects. Go to the card catalog and find one book about or by each. List each book's call number, author, title, publisher, and date of publication. Because subject headings may vary, investigate related categories, if necessary, to find an entry. To illustrate, if you find nothing under "mountaineering," check "mountain climbing" or "backpacking."**

1. AIDS research	16. Home schooling
2. The American family	17. The Internet and business
3. The American workplace	18. The Internet and games
4. Campaign reform	19. Stephen King
5. Cancer research	20. Bobby Knight
6. Charter schools	21. Barbara Mandrell
7. Children and divorce	22. Mountaineering
8. Hillary Clinton	23. Colin Powell
9. Diets	24. Robots
10. Electric cars	25. Laura Schlessinger
11. Gloria Estefan	26. School vouchers
12. Bill Gates	27. Tupac Shakur
13. Genetic research	28. Telecommunication
14. Global warming	29. Andrew Weil
15. HMOs	30. Oprah Winfrey

2. **Provide your instructor with a list of the books you found that appear useful for developing your paper's topic. For each book, furnish the information specified in Exercise 1 above, along with a brief note indicating why you think the book will be useful.**

Periodical Indexes

What They Are   Periodical indexes catalog articles in magazines and newspapers. Indexes may be in book form, on microfilm or microfiche, or computerized. Some are offered in two or more forms. Computerized indexes, called *databases,* are available to libraries through subscription. Depending upon the particular database, information may be furnished on compact discs or transmitted via wire from a mainframe computer to the library. The term *CD-ROM* (compact disc, read-only memory) designates the first type of system, and *online* designates the second type. Databases are accessed through terminals equipped with a keyboard and a viewing screen. Some have printers that can supply lists of references and even copies of articles.

In some cases, terminals are intended for student operation; others are operated by library personnel. If you use a database, you may have to pay a service fee, but it's likely to be small.

Updated frequently, sometimes every week, periodical indexes provide access to information that hasn't yet found its way into books and perhaps never will. Their listings allow you to examine new topics, follow developments in older ones, and explore your topic in greater depth than you could by using books alone. In short, indexes help you avoid doing a superficial paper.

The *Readers' Guide to Periodical Literature,* available since 1900 in printed form, is now available online and on compact discs. The *Guide* indexes the material in over 200 widely circulated magazines—*Harper's, Newsweek, Scientific American,* and the like. Articles are indexed by subject and author, and other categories are indexed by title and author. The *Guide* is especially useful for finding material on historical events (say the Persian Gulf War or the Iran-Contra hearings) and on social, political, and economic developments (for instance, the assisted-suicide movement and the drive to limit the terms of officeholders). The *Guide* also includes scientific, technical, and even literary articles intended for a general audience rather than specialists, but such articles do not include all the available research.

The first pages in the printed version of the *Guide* identify the abbreviations used for the magazines indexed. Figure 20.7 shows the arrangement of

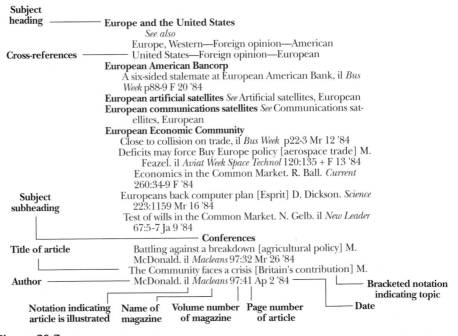

Figure 20.7

From *Readers' Guide to Periodical Literature,* May, 1984. Copyright © 1984 by the H. W. Wilson Company. Reproduced by permission.

the index and the "see also" cross-references that direct you to related subject headings.

The *Magazine Index,* available on microfilm or online, indexes some four hundred popular publications by author, title, and subject. Updated monthly, it covers a five-year period and includes references to articles no more than two weeks old. The viewing machines for units using microfilm resemble small television sets and have motorized controls that allow swift movement through the filmstrip. Accompanying the viewer are coded reels of microfilm containing the indexed articles, together with a reader/printer that allows you to read articles and obtain printed copies. Your librarian will demonstrate how these machines work. The producers of the index also publish a listing of recent articles on twenty to thirty current topics.

The *National Newspaper Index* covers five national newspapers: the *Christian Science Monitor,* the *Los Angeles Times,* the *New York Times,* the *Wall Street Journal,* and the *Washington Post.* It is available on microfilm, on compact discs, and on-line. Each monthly issue covers two-and-one-half years of references, and back issues can be obtained on microfiche cards. Microfilm units have the same kind of viewer as the microfilm version of the *Magazine Index.*

The *New York Times Index* comes in printed and online form. It indexes, by subject, all news articles, book reviews, commentaries, and features that have appeared in the paper and briefly summarizes each listing. The index entries refer to the "late city edition" of the paper, the one most libraries have on microfilm. If your library subscribes to a regional edition, an article may appear on another page or not at all.

NewsBank may be your best bet for a topic of regional interest. This CD-ROM database covers more than five hundred newspapers in all fifty states and Canada, indexing articles on politics, economics, business, the environment, and the entertainment world. It also offers the full text of many articles. A loose-leaf notebook version of *NewsBank,* accompanied by the articles on microfiche cards, is also available.

Periodical databases allow you to search quickly and effectively for articles in journals, magazines, and newspapers. Some databases such as *ERIC* (Educational Resources Information Center) or *Medline* (National Library of Medicine) give you access to citations of articles appearing in professional journals in a specific area. These articles, however, are usually aimed at a specialized audience and may be difficult to comprehend. Perhaps the best place to start a search is with a general periodical database such as *First Search* or *InfoTrac.* These databases provide access to listings of articles, arranged and subdivided by subject, that have appeared in over a thousand magazines and newspapers, including the entries in various other indexes. Articles are sometimes accompanied by abstracts—brief summaries of the articles' main points—and in some cases the full articles may be available on screen. *A word of caution: Don't mistake an abstract for the full article; an abstract is a 200–300 word summary of a journal article and should not be used as a source. Always take notes on the full article.* These databases are easy to operate. Your library probably has handouts that explain how to use your school's system and probably offers training sessions as well.

Because most periodical indexes, like *InfoTrac*, are organized around subject headings, it's a good idea to try a variety of subject terms since each will yield different articles. If your entry matches a subject heading or you are referred to a cross-reference, the computer will use a series of screens to direct you to a list of articles.

Along the way, one of the screens may list subdivisions of the request being searched, as in the following example:

Acquaintance Rape, subdivisions of

—analysis
—cases
—investigation
—laws, regulations, etc.
—media coverage
—moral and ethical aspects
—personal narratives
—prevention
—psychological aspects
—research
—social aspects
—statistics
—studying and teaching
—usage

Such a listing can uncover facets of your topic that you hadn't considered and that might enrich your final paper. For example, the subdivision "personal narratives" might contain an experience that would provide a powerful opening for the paper. Similarly, articles cataloged under "statistics" could provide information on the scope of the acquaintance rape problem.

If your entries don't match a subject heading, the computer may automatically switch to a key term search (see page 324) and display a list of articles. If your subject yields only a few articles, you can initiate a key term search that may uncover more. Just follow the instructions for beginning the search and then enter your key term. If, for example, your topic is "teenage suicide," type "teenagers and suicide" onto the screen that's already showing and press the search or enter key. The computer will check titles and abstracts for the key terms and provide a list of the corresponding articles. Allow ample time to explore a number of possibilities. If you try several terms related to your topic, you will find a wider variety of articles that serve your purpose.

The final result of any search is a listing of articles like the following one, obtained through *InfoTrac*, for the "psychological aspects" subdivision of the subject heading "acquaintance rape":

```
An open letter to a rape victim. Gail Elizabeth Wyatt. Essence,
April 1992 v22 n12 p80(3). Mag. Coll.: 64B0749.
--Abstract Available--
Holdings: AS Magazine Collection
```

```
Between seduction and rape. (date rape) Kathy Dobie. Vogue, Dec
1991 v181 n12 p154(4). Mag. Coll.: 62G6035.
--Abstract Available--
Holdings: AS Magazine Collection

Rape on campus: is your daughter in danger? Kate Fillion.
Chatelaine, August 1991 v64 n8 p33(5). Mag. Coll.: 61A5794.
Holdings: AS Magazine Collection
```

This listing shows that all three magazines are available in the library and that two articles are abstracted in the computer. (If the database provides the full text of an article, the notation "full text available" will appear after the citation.) The coded notation "Mag. Coll." indicates that the magazine is available on microfilm. The first two numbers and the letter in the code identify the number of the microfilm cassette. The remaining numbers indicate the microfilm page on which the article starts. The exact listings of your system may be somewhat different from what's shown here; the same kind of information, however, should be available.

Besides the previously mentioned specialized indexes, many others are available that you could use to supplement your search of general indexes. Here is a brief sampling of some of them:

Applied Science and Technology Index, 1958–date (indexed by subject)

Education Index, 1929–date (indexed by subject and author)

Humanities Index, 1974–date (indexed by subject and author)

International Index to Periodicals, 1907–1964 (indexed by subject and author; titled *Social Sciences and Humanities Index,* 1965–1974, and then separated into the *Humanities Index* and the *Social Sciences Index*)

Social Sciences and Humanities Index, 1965–1974 (indexed by subject and author)

Social Sciences Index, 1975–date (indexed by subject and author)

All come in printed form, and most are also available on compact discs and online.

With periodical indexes, as with the card catalog, don't give up if a subject heading you're exploring yields few or no entries. Instead, explore related headings. For example, if your topic is teenage marriages, look also under "adolescence," "divorce," "teen pregnancies," and the like. Browse through the system and try a variety of options. Use this as an opportunity to gain different perspectives on your research project.

Obtaining the Articles   If the index is computerized and provides printouts, print a copy of each promising reference you find. Otherwise, copy the following information on a 3 × 5-inch note card.

Author(s), if identified

Title of article

Name of periodical

Volume or issue number (for professional and scholarly journals only)

Date of periodical

For newspapers, the edition name (city, metro) if more than one published, and section letter

The page range of the entire article

Obtain printout copies of whatever articles you can and check the topic sentences of paragraphs for essential points. Also, scan any accompanying abstracts or summaries. If an article appears useful, check to see whether it has a bibliography, which might include additional useful sources. Keep the note cards for articles that seem promising—and any useful articles—and throw away the others.

Check the remaining references, including the ones from encyclopedia bibliographies, against the library's periodical catalog to see which periodicals are available and where they are located. Libraries frequently keep current issues in a periodical room or some other special section. Back issues of magazines are often kept on microfilm or bound into hardcover volumes and shelved. Most newspapers are on microfilm. Check the articles for which you don't have printouts in the same manner that you checked the others.

EXERCISE   *Select five of the following subjects and find one magazine article about each. Use at least three different periodical indexes to locate the articles. List the author, if given; the title of the article; the name of the magazine; its date; the page range; and the name of the index used. Because subject categories may vary, investigate related categories, if necessary, to find an entry. To illustrate, if you find nothing under "bioengineered foods," check "genetically modified foods" or "bioaltered foods."*

1. Animal rights
2. Bandwidth technology
3. Bioengineered foods
4. Black holes
5. Tony Blair
6. Campaign funds
7. Campus drinking
8. Cellular phones
9. Corporate mergers
10. DNA testing
11. Fiber optics
12. Alan Greenspan
13. Hedge funds
14. Laser surgery
15. NASDAQ stock exchange
16. National missile defense system
17. Rosie O'Donnell
18. Shaquille O'Neal
19. Oral history
20. Racial profiling
21. John Rocker
22. Sport utility vehicles
23. Telemarketing
24. Televangelism
25. Unemployment
26. Vegetarianism
27. Venus or Serena Williams
28. Wiretapping
29. X-ray astronomy
30. Yale University

The Internet

What It Is   The Internet is a worldwide network that links the computer systems of educational institutions, government agencies, businesses, professional organizations, and individuals. The Internet offers a number of services, including the World Wide Web, electronic mail (e-mail), newsgroups, and list-servs. It allows you to check the holdings of college libraries; obtain information from online books, magazines, and newspapers; access research and government documents; gather viewpoints and information from numerous organizations and individuals; and communicate with people around the world or at the next computer station. This abundance of information and perspectives, sometimes not more than a day old, can greatly enhance your research. But remember that you'll still need to consult traditional sources in addition to using the Internet.

You can easily learn how to access the Internet and World Wide Web if you don't already know how. Your school may offer training sessions that you can attend. In addition, a number of excellent, easy-to-follow books are available. Whether enrolled in a training session or learning on your own, you'll need to obtain a log-on name, your own password, and an e-mail address if you plan to use your school's computers. If you encounter problems, personnel in the computer labs can probably answer many of your questions.

World Wide Web   During the 1990s the World Wide Web exploded into national prominence. The Web gained quick popularity because it is easy to use and offers visuals, including many sites dedicated to art, and hypertext, that is, text with color-coded words that can link you to other related sites. Web pages can include text, graphics, sound, video clips, entire computer programs, files that can be downloaded, and even animated images.

To use the World Wide Web, you need access to a computer with a Web browser such as *Netscape Navigator* or *Microsoft Internet Explorer,* and an Internet service provider such as *America Online, CompuServe,* or another provider to connect you to the Web. The format of these services is user-friendly and, in addition, most colleges have training programs. The top of the screen on any browser features a tool bar that you can click on to save locations for future reference, stop the transfer of data, or initiate a search.

Each Web page has an address called a URL (uniform resource locator), which allows the browser to locate that page. Here is a sample address:

http://www.whitehouse.gov

How to Use It   The Internet includes millions of computers and offers a stupendous amount of information. As a result, finding just the material you want can be quite difficult. To solve this problem, several indexes, or *search engines,* have been developed that can connect any search term or terms with potentially millions of sites that include the key words. The easiest way to connect with these search engines is to simply select the search command or its nearest equivalent on your browser or Internet service. This will connect you with a specific search engine but also give you a choice of several others. You can also enter the direct address (URL) in the address window. Figure 20.8 provides the addresses of several popular search engines. Because the various search engines often select differently and produce different results, it's a good idea to use several engines while conducting your search.

Search Engine	Address
Alta Vista	http://www.altavista.com
Google	http://www.google.com
Go	http://www.go.com
Lycos	http://www.lycos.com
Excite	http://www.excite.com
WebCrawler	http://webcrawler.com
Yahoo	http://www.yahoo.com

Figure 20.8   Popular Search Engines

While each search engine works in a slightly different manner, they all provide similar sorts of information. When prompted by the key words you enter, the engine searches and returns lists of links to information containing these words. Such engines simplify the job of finding what you want on the Internet. Still, expect the job to require patience since search engines often provide information that isn't useful. For that reason, you'll often want to narrow your search when you begin. Single terms such as "health," "cancer," or "crime" could give you a million possible sites; instead, you may want to search for "ovarian cancer" or even "ovarian cancer cures." Most search engines also let you add more key words that will further narrow what has already been found. Different words or phrases can produce different results, so you'll want to try a variety of words for the same topic.

You can scroll through the list of sites the engine has found. The sites are usually accompanied by a short description that may help you decide whether they are useful. If you select any highlighted words, the search engine will transfer the data from that site and will connect you to a Web page.

Figures 20.9, 20.10, and 20.11 show the results of searching the subject "robotics advances." Figure 20.9 shows a search engine screen with the search subject entered, Figure 20.10 shows some of the Web sites found during the search, and Figure 20.11 shows a Web page with potentially useful information.

When viewing a Web page, you may notice menus, highlighted words, or specially marked graphics. These features, called *hyperlinks,* will usually take you to a different location: another section within the original page, a different page within the same domain, or even a new page on a computer in a different country. Following these hyperlinks allows you to explore related information from a variety of sources. As you move from Web page to Web page, browsers provide an easy way to navigate. *Netscape,* for example, has "back" and "forward" buttons that allow you to move to other sites. If you move back far enough, you will eventually get back to your main search site or even your home page. When you find an interesting site, you can print it out, or you can "bookmark" the site, allowing you easy future reference to the page. You'll need to keep track of any site addresses that you use since you'll include them in your bibliography.

Figure 20.9   Screen Showing Search Entry

Evaluating Internet Material   Because anyone can post virtually anything on the Internet, it is crucial that you check the accuracy and validity of any information you obtain from it. A source that sounds like a research center, for example, the Institute for Social Justice, could be a political or even a cult organization giving out one-sided or false information for its own purposes. While articles for professional journals are reviewed by experts to ensure that the information is reliable, no such safeguard exists on the Internet. Carelessly researched or ethically questionable material can and does appear. Here are some guidelines for checking the validity of an Internet source:

1. Is the source identified as a reputable professional organization, such as the American Cancer Society, a university like MIT, or a government agency like the Department of Justice? Keep in mind that anyone can use a professional-sounding name, so be alert.

Figure 20.10   Screen Showing Sites Found During Search

2. Is there an identified author whose credentials you can check and who speaks with some authority? If there is no e-mail contact listed or you can't find another way to verify the contents of the Web site, don't use it.

3. Is the tone of the site professional? Does it maintain an objectice stance and support its position with credible evidence?

4. Is the information consistent with the other material you have found? If the site disagrees with the standard information, does it offer adequate support for its claims?

5. Does the site explain how the data were obtained?

6. Does the site appear to misuse any data? For instance, is the sample too small? Are the claims pushed too far? Are the statistics biased?

1997 FLORIDA CONFERENCE ON RECENT ADVANCES IN ROBOTICS

Florida International University
Miami, Florida
April 10-11, 1997

http://www1.eng.fiu.edu/me/robotics/flconf.htm

REGISTRATION FORM

The 1997 Florida Conference on Recent Advances in Robotics was organized by Florida International University (FIU) in Miami on April 10-11, 1997. The annually-held conference was started nine years ago and has been organized in various cities in Florida. It was held in Miami for the first time.

TECHNICAL PROGRAM

Thursday – April 10, 1997

Session: Design I

Chair: R. Schoepherster, Florida International University
Co-Chair: H. Zhuang, Florida Atlantic University

- Design and Construction of a Prototype Force-Reflecting Manual Controller, P. Batsomboon, S. Tosunoglu, Florida International University, Miami, and D. W. Repperger, Wright Patterson Air Force Base, Dayton, Ohio.

- Design and Realization of an Automated Log Strip Separator (LSS), I. N. Tansel, T. T. Arkan, W. Y. Bao, J. Shaw, C. A. Velez, T. C. Yih, S. Tosunoglu, I. Fernandez, and B. Tansel, Florida International University, Miami.

- Contactless Gripper for Silicon Wafers, J. Jin, and T. C. Yih, Florida International University.

Figure 20.11   Screen Showing Potentially Useful Source

Take a look at this sample Web site.

School Vouchers: Clearly a Moral Wrong!

Rev. James W. Watkins

Would it seem a wise use of taxes to neglect needed improvements in your public water system, while using available public monies to buy a limited few citizens Perrier? School vouchers are similarly flawed in both concept and design.

First, what limited experiments with school vouchers have shown is that these newly proposed multimillion dollar tax expenditures could more than bankrupt public education budgets nationwide—while also raising taxes. School voucher proposals are totally out of sync with current efforts toward leaner, less costly government.

Second, school voucher plans are simply not fair. Vouchers are designed to transfer tax dollars to private schools. If parents want to send a child to private school, that is their right. But exactly why should the average taxpayer be asked to pay for it?

Third, many school voucher plans include parochial school tuition. Americans have never thought it proper to use generally collected tax revenues to teach specific sectarian religious doctrine. School voucher plans that entangle religion and government in an unhealthy way should be rejected on that ground alone.

Not one argument favoring school vouchers really bears up under scrutiny. When we hear "paying twice for my child's education is not fair," it sounds as if the only reason a citizen pays school taxes is as a payment for their [sic] child's education. What's being asked for is a voucher acting as a refund on their taxes, should they choose private school for their children. Historically, it has been a civil duty obligatory for all our citizens, parents or not, to support public education through taxation.

Parents who have chosen private schools or home schooling have every right to do so. But this does not relieve them of their community responsibility to support public education any more than not owning a car relieves one from that portion of their [sic] taxes slated for highway construction. . . .

The address of this Web site is <http://www.mainstreamop.org/vouch1.htm>. Its home page reveals that "mainstreamop" is an organization established to fight the Religious Right. Thus the site may present a clear bias. The excerpt's author is a minister, and it's unclear what authority he brings to a discussion of school vouchers. Certainly the excerpt offers no evidence to back its claims and as a result does not represent an objective, expert opinion. It does, however, suggest that at least some Christian ministers oppose vouchers.

Sometimes, of course, you may want to check out pages that present the views of individuals or organizations with strong but slanted positions to gain a better understanding of their thinking, but don't consider such pages to be reliable sources. When using the Internet, "Reader beware" is a prudent attitude.

E-Mail   Once you get an e-mail address, you can communicate over the Internet with anyone else who has an address. It's a good idea to jot down the e-mail addresses of other students in your class so that you can exchange ideas. With some systems you can even exchange full drafts of your papers. Your instructor may create a distribution list that allows you to forward ideas and responses to the entire class by sending them to a single address.

You can also use e-mail to ask knowledgeable people about your research topic and get swift answers to your questions. Use this approach, however, as a last resort since busy people have limited time. If you must contact experts, don't bother them with questions that you could easily answer by reading background material. Reserve e-mail for specific queries that defy answer after extensive research. Most search engines have clearly identified directories that allow you to look up an e-mail address if you know a person's name. Sometimes you can find the name of an expert through the Web pages of major universities. If you do get a response to your query, evaluate it carefully; an overburdened expert may dash off a quick response while doing something else.

Newsgroups   A newsgroup is a group of people who discuss a common interest by posting their responses to a common address for everyone to read. These discussions can be informal and often are not monitored; as a result, they leave something to be desired as a source for research. Still, your university system will likely give you access to newsgroups, so ask your computer center for an instruction sheet. A word of caution: Many newsgroups are intolerant of uninformed people intruding upon their conversation. Common netiquette (the etiquette of the Internet) calls for you to read what has already been written and to think before you write.

Listservs   A listserv consists of numerous e-mail addresses that make up a mailing list of people interested in a particular topic. Once you sign up, everything posted to that listserv will be sent to your e-mail address. People who subscribe to three or four listservs may receive thirty or forty e-mail messages every day. If you post a question on a listserv, you may get dozens of responses from professionals interested in the topic, and sorting out the validity of the different responses can be difficult. As with newsgroups, netiquette calls for you to acquire an understanding of your subject and follow the discussions on the listserv for some time before you post a question or a response. Your university computer professionals can probably supply you with instructions on how to find and sign up for a listserv. You can access a subject index of listservs at http://www.liszt.com.

FAQs   Whenever you find a promising Web site, newsgroup, or listserv, you will often see a line for FAQs (frequently asked questions). It's a good idea to read the FAQs first since they may well answer your questions.

EXERCISE

1. **Using an appropriate search engine, find information on each of the following topics:**

   a. the Vietnam War

   b. current crime statistics

   c. sexual harassment

   d. current government immigration policy

2. **Enter the name of a major university into a search engine and then search. You should find that university's home page. Try to access the university's library to find what books are available on a topic of your choice. You might try schools like Harvard, Duke, or Notre Dame.**

Primary Research Findings

Besides relying on library materials, you may wish to use information obtained by conducting primary research. Chapter 22 provides detailed instructions for interviewing specialists, sending out questionnaires, and making direct observations. Before doing any type of primary research, always get your instructor's permission.

Adjusting Your Topic

After finishing your search for sources, you may need to adjust the scope and emphasis of your topic. If you start with "America's First Nuclear-Powered Submarine" but fail to turn up enough sources, you might expand your emphasis to "America's First Nuclear-Powered Warships." On the other hand, if you're working with "America's First Nuclear-Powered Warships" and find yourself floundering in an ocean of sources, you might zero in on one type of vessel. Gathering evidence helps to develop your judgment about how many sources you need to do the job.

CASE HISTORY (Continued from page 322)

Once Keith Jacque had selected a focus for his paper on electronic monitoring, he began compiling his working bibliography. First he turned to the computerized card catalog and began his search for books and government documents by typing in the subject entry "house arrest," but he found nothing. Next he tried "electronic monitoring of prisoners." This entry yielded a cross-reference directing him to the entries "punishment—United States" and "criminal statistics—analysis." These two entries yielded a list of seven books and eleven government documents. Further examination revealed that three of the books and four of the documents appeared promising.

Keith's search for periodical articles took him to the college's *InfoTrac* database. Using this system, he found three useful subject headings: "home detention," "electronic monitoring of prisoners," and "criminal statistics—analysis." A search of these subjects turned up twenty-four journal articles, all of which were available in the library. Eight looked as if they would be useful. Three newspaper articles seemed suitable, and a search of *NewsBank* revealed another promising newspaper article.

Since his library offered access to the Internet, Keith also searched the World Wide Web. He used the Lycos and Yahoo search engines and entered complete phrases such as "electronic incarceration," "home detention," "electronic monitoring," and "incarceration, electronic." Many of the Web sites he found were not relevant to his topic, but he persisted and finally found two that seemed promising. One, from an organization concerned with public policy, discussed the indirect costs of incarceration. The other, from the Probation Division of Georgia's Department of Corrections, discussed alternatives to jail sentences.

After completing his search for library and Internet sources, Keith sought and obtained his instructor's permission to conduct primary research on his topic. Unsure of how to proceed, he talked to his advisor in the criminal justice department. She suggested that he ask the director of Michigan's electronic surveillance program for a personal interview. (See pages 406–08). He was able to obtain the interview, which provided information on the scope, operation, and success rate of the program as well as the savings it has achieved.

Satisfied that ample information was available, Keith carefully evaluated the content of the articles and of pertinent sections of the books and government documents he had located. His instructor had suggested that one good way to approach a topic is to pose a question about it and then draft a *tentative* answer, if possible. Here's how Keith proceeded:

> Q.   What benefits does electronic monitoring offer jurisdictions that adopt it?
>
> A.   Electronic monitoring is less expensive than incarceration, presents no serious problems, and offers a choice among several systems.

This answer provided a *tentative thesis,* an informed opinion that guided Keith's later note taking, giving him a sense of direction and indicating what information would probably prove useful and what was likely to be useless. Tentative theses can be altered slightly or changed completely if necessary. If later reading indicated that electronic monitoring can sometimes be more expensive than incarceration, Keith could alter his thesis accordingly.

This case history continues on page 351.

■ Taking Notes

To take notes, read your references carefully and record significant information. You might review or even expand your original research questions (page 321) so that you can read with a better sense of purpose. Notes are the raw materials for your finished product, so develop them accurately.

Evaluating Your Sources

Evaluate your sources by considering these factors.

The Expertise of the Author   Judge an author's expertise by examining his or her professional status. Say you're searching for information on some new cancer-treating drug. An article by the director of a national cancer research center would be a better bet than one by a staff writer for a magazine. Similarly, a historian's account of a national figure will probably have more balance and depth than a novelist's popularized account of that person's life. Gauging a writer's credentials is not difficult. Articles in periodicals often note authors' job titles along with their names. Some even supply thumbnail biographies. For a book, check its title page, preface, or introduction, and—if it's been left on— the dust jacket. Finally, notice whether the writer has other publications on this general subject. If your sources include two or more items by one person or if that person's name keeps cropping up as you take notes, you're probably dealing with an expert.

The Credibility of the Publication   A book's credibility hinges on its approach and its reception by reviewers. Cast a cautious eye on books that take a popular rather than a scholarly approach. For research papers, scholarly treatments provide more solid fare. Weigh what reviewers said when a book first appeared. Two publications excerpt selected reviews and provide references to others. The *Book Review Digest* (1905–date) deals mainly with nontechnical works, while the *Technical Book Review Index* (1935–date) covers technical and scientific books. Turn first to the volume for the year the book came out. If you don't find any reviews, scan the next year's index. Often books published in the fall are not reviewed until the following year.

Periodical articles can also take a scholarly or popular tack. Editors of specialized journals and of some wide-circulation magazines—for example, *Scientific American* and *The Atlantic Montly*—publish only in-depth, accurate articles. Most newsstand publications, however, popularize to some extent, and some deliberately strive for sensationalism. Popularizing may result in broad, general statements, skimpy details, and a sensational tone.

Don't automatically reject a source because the writer lacks expertise or offers a popularized treatment. Often, especially when writing about a current topic, you'll need to use material that falls short in some way. Remember, though, that you undertake research to become more knowledgeable than general readers are about a topic. When information in popular periodicals provides less than adequate coverage, candidly acknowledge the shortcomings.

Mechanics of Note Taking

Generally your most effective approach to note taking is to use note cards. Copy each note on a 4 × 6-inch card to avoid confusion with the smaller bibliography cards. Record only one note per card, even when you take several notes from a single page; you may use the notes at different points. If you can't fit a note on a single card, continue the note on a second card and paper-clip or staple the two together. Cards allow you to test different arrangements of notes and use the best one to write the paper.

Before you take a note, indicate its source at the bottom of the card. You will then have all the details necessary for documenting the information if you use it in your paper. Usually, the author's last name and the page number suffice, since your bibliography card contains all other details. To distinguish between two authors with the same last name or between two works by the same author, add initials or partial titles. *Don't forget to include the page number or numbers for each note.* Otherwise, you'll have to waste time looking them up when you cite your sources in the paper.

Summarize briefly the contents of the note at the top of the card. Later, when you construct an outline, these notations will help you sort your cards into categories and subcategories.

Responding to Notes

As you take notes, reflect on your topic and try to come up with new ideas, see connections to other notes, and anticipate future research. Think of yourself as having a conversation with your sources, and jot down your responses on the backs of your note cards. Ask yourself these questions: Does this information agree with what I have learned so far? Does it suggest any new avenues to explore? Does it leave me with questions about what's been said? Although it may take a few minutes to record your responses to a note, this type of analysis will help you write a paper that reflects *your* opinions, decisions, and evaluations, not one that smacks of notes merely patched together from different sources.

Types of Notes

A note can be a summary, paraphrase, or quotation. *Whenever you use any kind of note in your paper, give proper credit to your source. Failure to do so results in plagiarism—that is, literary theft—a serious offense even when committed unintentionally.* Pages 400–02 discuss plagiarism, and pages 376–97 explain proper documentation of sources.

Summary A summary condenses original material, presenting its core ideas *in your own words*. In order to write an effective summary, you must have a good grasp of the information, and this comprehension ensures that you are ready to use the material in your paper. You may include brief quotations if you enclose them in quotation marks. A properly written summary presents the main points in their original order without distorting their emphasis or meaning, and it omits supporting details and repetition. Summaries, then, serve up the heart of the matter.

Begin the summarizing process by asking yourself, "What points does the author make that have an important bearing on my topic and purpose?" To answer, note especially the topic sentences in the original, which often provide essential information. Copy the points in order; then condense and rewrite them in your own words. Figure 20.12 summarizes the Bertrand Russell passage that follows. We have underscored key points in the original.

Necessity for law

About a century and a half ago, there began a still-existing preference for impulsive actions over deliberate ones. Those responsible for this development believed that people are naturally good but institutions have perverted them. Actually, unfettered human nature breeds violence and brutality, and law is our only protection against anarchy. The law assumes the responsibility for revenge and settles disputes equitably. It frees people from the fear of being victimized by criminals and provides a means of catching them. Without it, civilization could not endure.

Russell, pp. 63-65

Figure 20.12 Summary

Under the influence of the romantic movement, a process began about a hundred and fifty years ago, which has continued ever since—a process of revaluing the traditional virtues, placing some higher on the scale than before, and others lower. The tendency has been to exalt impulse at the expense of deliberation. The virtues that spring from the heart have come to be thought superior to those that are based upon reflection: a generous man is preferred to a man who is punctual in paying his debts. *Per contra*, deliberate sins are thought worse than impulsive sins: a hypocrite is more harshly condemned than a murderer. The upshot is that we tend to estimate virtues, not by their capacity for providing human happiness, but by their power of inspiring a personal liking for the possessors, and we are not apt to include among the qualities for which we like people, a habit of reflecting before making an important decision.

The men who started this movement were, in the main, gentle sentimentalists who imagined that, when the fetters of custom and law were removed, the heart would be free to display its natural goodness. Human nature, they thought, is good, but institutions have corrupted it; remove the institutions and we shall all become angels. Unfortunately, the matter is not so simple as they thought. Men who follow their impulses establish governments based on pogroms, clamour for war with foreign countries, and murder pacifists and Negroes. Human nature unrestrained by law is violent and cruel. In the London Zoo, the male baboons fought over the females until all the females were torn to pieces; human beings, left to the ungoverned impulse, would be no better. In ages that have had recent experience of anarchy, this has been obvious. All the great writers of the middle ages were passionate in their admiration of the law; it was the Thirty Years' War that led Grotius to become the first advocate of international law. Law, respected and enforced, is in the long run the only alternative to violent and predatory anarchy; and it is just as necessary to realize this now as it was in the time of Dante and Grotius.

What is the essence of law? On the one hand, it takes away from private citizens the right of revenge, which it confers upon the government. If a man steals your money, you must not steal it back, or thrash him, or shoot him; you must establish the facts before a neutral tribunal, which inflicts upon him such punishment as has seemed just to the disinterested legislators. On the other hand, when two men have a dispute, the law provides a machinery for settling it, again on principles laid down in advance by neutrals. The advantages of law are many. It diminishes the amount of private violence, and settles disagreements in a manner more nearly just than that which would result if the disputants fought it out by private war. It makes it possible for men to work without being perpetually on the watch against bandits. When a crime has been committed it provides a skilled machine for discovering the criminal.

Without law, the existence of civilized communities is impossible. In international law, there is as yet no effective law, for lack of an international police force capable of overpowering national armies, and it is daily becoming more evident that this defect must be remedied if civilization is to survive. Within single nations there is a dangerous tendency to think that moral indignation excuses the extralegal punishment of criminals. In Germany an era of private murder (on the loftiest grounds) preceded and followed the victory of the Nazis. In fact, nine-tenths of what appeared as just indignation was sheer lust for cruelty; and this is equally true in other countries where mobs rob the law of its functions. In any civilized community, toleration of mob rule is the first step towards barbarism.

Bertrand Russell, "Respect for Law," *San Francisco Review,* Winter 1958, 63–65.

EXERCISE

A. Select two passages that your instructor approves from an essay in the Reader and prepare summary note cards for them.

B. Submit summaries of three pieces of information that you plan to use in writing your paper; also submit complete versions of the original.

Paraphrase   To paraphrase is to restate material *in your own words* without attempting to condense it. Unlike a summary, a paraphrase allows you to present an essentially complete version of the original material. A note of caution, however: Don't copy the original source nearly verbatim, changing only a word here and there. To do so is to plagiarize. To avoid this offense, follow a read, think, and write-without-looking-at-the-original strategy when you take notes so that you concentrate on recording the information in your own words. Then verify the accuracy of your notes by checking them against the original source. Here is a sample passage; Figure 20.13 is its paraphrase.

> Over time, more and more of life has become subject to the controls of knowledge. However, this is never a one-way process. Scientific investigation is continually increasing our knowledge. But if we are to make good use of this knowledge, we must not only rid our minds of old, superseded beliefs and fragments of magic, but also recognize new superstitions for what they are. Both are generated by our wishes, our fears, and our feelings of helplessness in difficult situations.
>
> Margaret Mead, "New Superstitions for Old," *A Way of Seeing*, New York: McCall, 1970. 266.

> ### Combatting Superstitions
>
> As time has passed, knowledge has asserted its sway over larger and larger segments of human life. But the process cuts two ways. Science is forever adding to the storehouse of human knowledge. Before we can take proper advantage of its gifts, however, we must purge our minds of old and outmoded convictions, while recognizing the true nature of modern superstitions. Both stem from our desires, our apprehensions, and our sense of impotence under difficult circumstances.
>
> Mead, p. 266

Figure 20.13   Paraphrase

EXERCISE   *Paraphrase a short passage from one of your textbooks. Submit a complete version of the passage with the assignment.*

Quotation   A quotation is a copy of original material. Since your paper should demonstrate that you've mastered your sources, don't rely extensively on quotations. You need practice in expressing yourself. As a general rule, avoid quotations except when

- the original displays special elegance or force

- you really need support from an authority

- you need to back up your interpretation of a passage from a literary work.

Paraphrasing a passage as well-written as the one below would rob it of much of its force.

> Man is himself, like the universe he inhabits, like the demoniacal stirring of the ooze from which he sprang, a tale of desolation. He walks in his mind from birth to death the long resounding shores of endless disillusionment. Finally, the commitment to life departs or turns to bitterness. But out of such desolation emerges the awful freedom to choose beyond the narrowly circumscribed circle that delimits the rational being.
>
> Loren Eiseley, *The Unexpected Universe*

Special rules govern the use of quotations. If, for clarity, you need to add an explanation or substitute a proper name for a personal pronoun, enclose the addition in *brackets*.

> The Declaration of Independence asserts that "the history of the present King of Great Britain [George III] is a history of repeated injuries and unsurpations. . . ."

If your keyboard doesn't have brackets, insert them neatly with a dark pen.

Reproduce any grammatical or spelling errors in a source exactly as they appear in the original. To let your reader know that the original author, not you, made the mistake, insert the Latin word *sic* (meaning "thus") within brackets immediately after the error.

> As Wabash notes, "The threat to our enviroment [sic] comes from many directions."

If you're using the MLA documentation system and exclude an unneeded part of a quotation, show the omission with an ellipsis—three spaced periods— within square brackets. Indicate omissions *within sentences* as follows:

> Writing in *The Age of Extremes*, Eric Hobsbawm observed, "What struck both the opponents of revolution and the revolutionists was that, after 1945, the primary form of revolutionary struggle [. . .] seemed to be guerilla warfare."

When an omission comes *at the end of a sentence* and what is actually quoted can also stand as a complete sentence, use an unspaced period followed by an ellipsis within square brackets.

> In his second inaugural address, Lincoln voiced his hopes for the nation: "With malice toward none, with charity for all, with firmness in the right as God gives us to see the right, let us strive on to finish the work we are in. [. . .]"

Do the same when you drop *a whole sentence* within a quoted passage.

> According to newspaper columnist Grace Dunn, "Williamson's campaign will undoubtedly focus primarily on the legalized gambling issue because he hopes to capitalize on the strong opposition to it in his district. [. . .] Nonetheless, commentators all agree he faces an uphill fight in his attempt to unseat the incumbent."

Don't change or distort when you delete. Tampering like the following violates ethical standards:

Original passage:	This film is poorly directed, and the acting uninspired; only the cameo appearance by Laurence Olivier makes it truly worth seeing.
Distorted version:	This film is [. . .] truly worth seeing.

When an ellipsis is already present in material you quote, *do not* set it off with brackets.

If you're using the APA documentation system, never enclose ellipsis within brackets.

You can summarize or paraphrase original material but retain a few words or phrases to add vividness or keep a precise shade of meaning. Simply use quotation marks but no ellipsis.

> Presidential spokesperson Paula Plimption notes that because of the "passionate advocacy" of its supporters, the push to roll back property taxes has been gaining momentum across the country.

When you copy a quotation onto a note card, put quotation marks at the beginning and the end so you won't mistake it for a paraphrase or a summary when you write the paper. If the quoted material starts on one page and ends on the next, use a slash mark (/) to show exactly where the shift comes. Then if you use only part of the quotation in your paper, you'll know whether to use one page number or two.

Don't expect to find a bonanza on every page you read. Sometimes one page will yield several notes, another page nothing. If you can't immediately gauge the value of some material, take it down. Useless information can be discarded later. Place a rubber band around your growing stack of note cards. Store them in a large envelope closed with a snap or string and labeled with your name and address. Submit them with your completed paper if your instructor requests.

CASE HISTORY (Continued from page 345)

Working bibliography in hand, Keith Jacque prepared note cards. Most of his notes were summaries of the source material, but in a few cases he chose quotations because of the importance of the source or the significance of the material. For example, one quotation cited a former U.S. Attorney General who pointed out the disproportionate number of crimes committed by habitual violent offenders. Another quotation cited a key reason for the growing use of electronic monitoring: the high cost of prisons. Still another detailed various difficulties encountered in transmitting signals.

As Keith took notes, a plan for his paper began to emerge. The introduction would explain the reasons behind the growing use of electronic monitoring. The body would present a brief history of monitoring and then detail the different kinds of available systems, examine the problems encountered when using them, and point out their effectiveness.

This case history continues on page 354.

■ Organizing and Outlining

Next comes your formal outline, the blueprint that shows the divisions and subdivisions of your paper, the order of your ideas, and the relationships between ideas and supporting details. An outline is a tool that benefits both writer and reader.

A formal outline follows the pattern shown below:

I.
   A.
   B.
      1.
      2.
         a.
         b.
II.

You can see the significance of an item by its numeral, letter, or number designation and by its distance from the left-hand margin; the farther it's indented, the less important it is. All items with the same designation have roughly the same importance.

Developing Your Outline

Developing an outline is no easy job. It involves arranging material from various sources in an appropriate manner. Sorting and re-sorting your note cards is a good way to proceed. First, determine the main divisions of your paper by checking the summarized notations at the tops of your cards, and then make one stack of cards for each division. Next, review each stack carefully to determine further subdivisions and sort it into smaller stacks. Finally, use the stacks to prepare your outline.

There are two types of formal outlines: *topic* and *sentence.* A topic outline presents all entries as words, short phrases, or short clauses. A sentence outline presents them as complete sentences. To emphasize the relationships among elements, items of equal importance have parallel phrasing. Although neither is *the* preferred form, a sentence outline includes more details and also your attitude toward each idea. Many students first develop a topic outline, do additional research, and then polish and expand this version into a sentence outline. While it's easy to be sloppy in a topic outline, forming a sentence outline requires you to reach the kinds of conclusions that will be the backbone of your paper. The following segments of a topic and a sentence outline for a paper on tranquilizer dependence illustrate the difference between the two:

Topic Outline

II. The tranquilizer abuse problem
    A. Reasons for the problem
        1. Overpromotion
        2. Overprescription
        3. Patient's misuse
            a. Dosage
            b. Length of usage
    B. Growth of the problem

Sentence Outline

II. Tranquilizers are widely abused.
    A. Several factors account for the abuse of tranquilizers.
        1. Drug companies overpromote their product.
        2. Doctors often unnecessarily prescribe tranquilizers.
        3. Patients often do not follow their doctors' instructions.
            a. Some patients take more than prescribed doses.
            b. Some continue to use tranquilizers beyond the prescribed time.
    B. The problem of tranquilizer abuse appears to be growing.

Note that the items in the sentence outline are followed by periods, but those in the topic outline are not.

Keying Your Note Cards to Your Outline

When your outline is finished, key your note cards to it by writing at the top of each card the letters and numbers—such as IIA or IIIB2—for the appropriate outline category. Now arrange the cards into one stack, following the order shown in the outline. Finally, start with the top card in the stack and number all of them consecutively. If they later fall off the table or slide out of place, you can easily put them in order again. You might have a few stragglers left over when you complete this keying. Some of these may be worked into your paper as you write or revise it.

CASE HISTORY (Continued from page 352)

Sorting and re-sorting was challenging and at times frustrating for Keith. Since some of his material could be arranged in different ways, he found himself experimenting, evaluating, and rearranging as he tried various options. After much thought and some trial and error, the following *initial draft* of his outline emerged:

I. Reasons why monitoring used
  A. Serious crime problem and number of people in prisons
  B. High cost of prisons
II. Brief history of electronic monitoring
III. Types of monitoring systems
  A. Programmed-contact systems
  B. Continuous-contact systems
  C. Hybrid systems
IV. Problems with these systems
  A. Practical problems
    1. Offenders' problems
    2. Transmission difficulties
  B. Legal problems
    1. Do the systems violate constitutional rights?
    2. "Net-widening" effect
V. Effectiveness of electronic monitoring
  A. Effectiveness with low-risk offenders
  B. Cost effectiveness
VI. Expanded use of monitoring likely

This version is marked by nonparallel structure and inadequate attention to some points. Despite these weaknesses, it provided an adequate blueprint for the first draft of Keith's paper.

This case history concludes on page 358.

■ Ethical Issues

When you present the information you've gathered from a variety of sources, you'll want to proceed in an ethically responsible way. Asking and answering the following questions will help you do just that.

- Have I carefully researched my topic so that my conclusions are well-founded? Imagine the consequences if slipshod testing by an auto company led to the erroneous conclusion that the steering mechanism on one of its models met current safety standards.

- Have I adequately acknowledged any evidence that runs counter to the conclusions I draw? A paper that stresses the advantages of charter schools but deliberately avoids mentioning their disadvantages could be a form of deception.

- Have I properly documented my sources? Using someone else's words or ideas without giving proper credit is a form of academic dishonesty (see pages 400–02).

- Have I honestly represented the authority of my sources? If you read an article touting almond extract as a cure for cancer that was written by a practicing foot doctor, it would be dishonest to suggest that the article was written by a "prominent research scientist." Refer to someone as an "expert" only when that person's credentials warrant the label.

- Could my information have an undersirable effect on readers? If so, how can I address their concerns? A report describing a new antibiotic-resistant strain of tuberculosis might alarm some readers, and therefore the writer could provide appropriate reassurances of the limited risk to most people.

■ Writing Your Research Paper

Some students think of a library research paper as a series of quotations, para-phrases, and summaries, one following the other throughout the paper. Not so. Without question, you use the material of others, but *you* select and organize it according to *your purpose. You* develop insights, and *you* draw conclusions about what you've read. You can best express your conclusions by setting your notes aside, stepping back to gain some perspective, and then expressing your sense of what you've learned. Many students find it helpful to write two or three pages on which they summarize what they want to say as well as whom they want to reach with their message and why. Like all forms of writing, research papers are written for some purpose and aimed at some audience.

Writing the First Draft

Your final research results will be expressed in a thesis. You've already drafted a tentative thesis (see page 345), and now you'll probably refine or revise it to ac-commodate any changes in your perspective on the topic. Position the thesis in the introductory part of your paper unless you're analyzing a problem or rec-ommending a solution; then you might hold back the thesis until later in the essay. If you do hold it back, state the problem clearly at the outset. Because of the paper's length, it's a good idea to reveal your organizational plan in your in-troductory section.

Write the paper section by section, following the divisions of your outline. But keep in mind that you're not locked into its pattern. If you see an oppor-tunity to develop an important idea that you omitted from your outline, try it. If you discover that it might be better to introduce an item earlier than you in-tended, go ahead. Just be sure to check your organization later. As you write, think of yourself as supporting the conclusions you have reached with the appropriate material on your note cards, not just as stringing these cards together. You will then incorporate the material on your note cards with your own assessments and with transitional elements that clarify your information and orient the reader. As you proceed, here again you'll use the writing strategies presented earlier in the book.

Because of this paper's length, you will probably need to connect its major sections with transitional paragraphs that pull together the material already covered and prepare the reader for what follows. Don't fret if the style bumps along or connections aren't always clear. These problems can be smoothed out when you revise. You will, of course, need to know how to document your sources properly, handle quotations, and avoid plagiarism. Chapter 21 presents guidelines on these important subjects.

On occasion you may want to include supplementary information that would interrupt the flow of thought if you placed it in the paper. When this happens, use an *explanatory note.*[1] A typical explanatory note might clarify or elaborate on a point, discuss some side issue, or define a term used in a specialized way.

When you finish writing, let this version sit for a day or two. Then revise it, just as you would with a shorter essay. Keep track of all sources so that preparing the bibliography will go smoothly.

Preparing Your Finished Copy

Follow the revision guidelines in Chapter 3. In addition, verify that you have

- included all key information
- clearly organized your material
- not overloaded your paper with quotations
- worked in your own observations
- put in-text documentation and source information in proper form.

Prepare your final draft with a typewriter or word-processor. If using a word-processor, be sure you have access to a laser or inkjet printer that produces dark, readable copy. Don't use a dot-matrix printer. Double-space throughout, including indented block quotations and the list of works you used to prepare the paper.

Two systems for formatting and documenting library research papers are in common use: the Modern Language Association (MLA) system, favored by many English and humanities instructors, and the American Psychological Association (APA) system, used by many social science and psychology instructors.

---

[1]This is an explanatory note. Position it at the bottom of the page, spaced four lines away from the main text. If more than one note occurs on a page, double-space between them. If the note carries over to the next page, separate it from your text with a solid, full-length line. Put two spaces above the line and two spaces below it.

MLA System for Preparing Papers

- Number each page in the upper right-hand corner, one-half inch from the top. Precede each page number with your last name.

- Starting one inch from the top of the first page, type your full name, the instructor's name, the course designation, and the date, all flush with the left-hand margin.

- Double-space below the date, and center the title; then double-space before starting the first paragraph.

- Leave one-inch margins on all four sides except at the top of the first page. Indent the first line of each paragraph five spaces or one-half inch.

- The MLA system does not require a title page. If your instructor wants one, however, center (1) the title of the paper about two inches below the top of the sheet, (2) your name in the middle of the sheet, and (3) the instructor's name, course designation, and date about two inches from the bottom. Use capital and lowercase letters for everything. Repeat the title, again in capital and lowercase letters, on the first text page, centered about two inches from the top.

- Begin the bibliography on a new page that follows the text of the paper, and give it the heading "Works Cited," without quotation marks. Center the heading on the page.

- List each bibliography entry alphabetically according to the author's last name or, if no author is given, by the first significant word in the title. For a work with more than one author, alphabetize by the name that comes first. If there's more than one entry for an author, substitute three unspaced hyphens, followed by a period and a double space, for the author's name in the second and subsequent entries.

- Begin the first line of each entry at the left-hand margin and indent any subsequent lines five spaces.

APA System for Preparing Papers

- The APA system requires a title page. Center (1) the title of the paper about four inches from the top and (2) your name, two spaces below the title. About three-fourths of the way from the top, provide the course designation, the name of your instructor, and the date, typed double-spaced and flush with the right-hand margin. Two inches from the top of the page, type the words "Running Head" without quotation marks, flush with the left-hand margin; then type a colon and a word or phrase that identifies the paper's topic. Type the running head in capital letters; type everything else in capital and lowercase letters.

- Repeat the title of the paper on the first text page, centered about one-and-a-half inches from the top and typed in capital and lowercase letters.

- Number every page of the text in the upper right-hand corner, starting with the title page. Position the first two or three words of the title five spaces to the left of the page number.

- Leave one-inch margins at the bottom and at both sides of each page. Indent the first line of each paragraph five spaces.

- Begin the bibliography on a new page that follows the text of the paper, and give it the heading "References," without quotation marks. Center this heading on the page. Follow the alphabetizing and positioning guidelines for the MLA system except that if the listing includes more than one entry for an author, repeat the author's name.

- Indent the first line of each entry five spaces and begin any subsequent lines at the left-hand margin.

EXAMPLE STUDENT RESEARCH PAPER

CASE HISTORY (Concluded)

Using his outline and thesis statement as a guide, Keith prepared a first draft of his paper, following the MLA format required by his instructor. It didn't all come easily. In order to ensure an effective presentation, he checked his note cards carefully to determine which material would provide the strongest support for his conclusions. He was careful to use his own words except when he was quoting. To achieve smoothness, he tried to connect his major sections with transitions, aware that he could polish these connections when he revised the paper.

When he had completed the first draft, Keith set it aside for two days in order to distance himself from his writing. Then he returned to it and revised it carefully. Reading the paper from the perspective of a slightly skeptical critic, he looked for unsupported claims, questions that readers might have, sections that might be confusing or poorly organized, and weak transitions. Like most writers, Keith found sections that could be improved. Next, he revised his initial topic outline and followed it when drafting the sentence outline that appears on pages 359–60. Keith then prepared the final draft of the paper itself, which is on pages 361–73. Direct your attention to its noteworthy features, which include italicized notations indicating where Keith used the writing strategies discussed earlier in the text.

Sentence Outline

Thesis statement: House arrest offers a choice of several monitoring systems, presents no insurmountable problems, proves effective in controlling low-risk offenders, and costs less than incarceration.

I. The use of house arrest stems from the country's serious crime problem.

   A. Violent crimes are committed by a small number of repeat offenders.

   B. These crimes have led to tougher crime-control legislation.

   C. This legislation has increased the country's prison population and the cost of incarceration.

   D. As a result, many jurisdictions have adopted house-arrest programs for low-risk offenders.

II. Electronic monitoring has a short history.

   A. The idea first appeared in the comic Spiderman.

   B. A New Mexico judge asked computer companies to develop an electronic bracelet.

   C. Monitoring was first used in 1984 to control offenders, and the concept quickly spread across the country.

III. Electronic monitoring devices fall into three categories.

   A. A programmed-contact system calls the offender's home during curfew periods and reports absences.

      1. A computer may simply record the offender's voice.

      2. A computer may compare the voice heard over the phone to a recording of the offender's voice.

      3. The offender may wear an encoded bracelet and insert it into a special telephone transmitter.

      4. A camera may transmit photos of the offender over telephone lines.

Sentence outline: note use of complete sentences throughout, use of periods following section and subsection markers, and the indentation arrangement

     B. A continuous-signal system requires the offender to wear a transmitter that sends uninterrupted electronic signals.

     C. A hybrid system combines programmed-contact and continuous-signal techniques.

        1. The programmed-contact component usually includes voice- and photo-transmission units.

        2. Jurisdictions can tailor systems to their needs.

IV. Electronic systems have created practical and legal problems.

     A. Practical problems include both difficulties experienced by offenders and transmission difficulties.

        1. Encoded bracelets can cause offenders discomfort and embarrassment.

        2. Telephone lines and objects in the offender's home can interfere with signal pickup.

     B. Legal problems include possible constitutional infringements and the net-widening effect.

        1. Charging surveillance fees and limiting surveillance to the least dangerous persons may infringe on offenders' equal-protection rights.

        2. Monitoring may violate the right to privacy of others in offenders' homes.

        3. Net-widening can result in an excessive number of individuals under house arrest.

 V. Electronic monitoring has proved effective with low-risk offenders.

     A. The great majority of offenders successfully complete monitoring programs.

     B. Monitoring costs less than incarceration.

VI. The advantages of house arrest should increase its use.

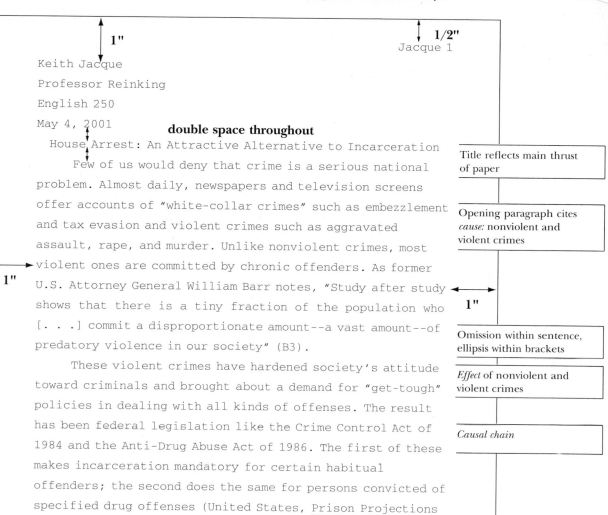

1"   **1/2"**

Jacque 1

Keith Jacque

Professor Reinking

English 250

May 4, 2001   **double space throughout**

House Arrest: An Attractive Alternative to Incarceration

Few of us would deny that crime is a serious national problem. Almost daily, newspapers and television screens offer accounts of "white-collar crimes" such as embezzlement and tax evasion and violent crimes such as aggravated assault, rape, and murder. Unlike nonviolent crimes, most violent ones are committed by chronic offenders. As former U.S. Attorney General William Barr notes, "Study after study shows that there is a tiny fraction of the population who [. . . .] commit a disproportionate amount--a vast amount---of predatory violence in our society" (B3).

These violent crimes have hardened society's attitude toward criminals and brought about a demand for "get-tough" policies in dealing with all kinds of offenses. The result has been federal legislation like the Crime Control Act of 1984 and the Anti-Drug Abuse Act of 1986. The first of these makes incarceration mandatory for certain habitual offenders; the second does the same for persons convicted of specified drug offenses (United States, Prison Projections 12). The introduction of mandatory sentencing guidelines, now common on the state as well as the federal level, provides consistent punishment for similar crimes. It has led, however, to an explosion in the number of prison inmates, which by mid-1999 totaled over 1.8 million, including a 4.4 percent increase between mid-1997 and mid-1998 (Gearan A1). Between 1980 and 1995, the nation's prison population grew 242 percent ("Inmate Populations" 10). Many of these inmates are guilty of nonviolent offenses. In 1997,

1"

1"

Title reflects main thrust of paper

Opening paragraph cites *cause:* nonviolent and violent crimes

Omission within sentence, ellipsis within brackets

Effect of nonviolent and violent crimes

Causal chain

1"

three-fourths of all prisoners fell into the nonviolent
category (Richey 3).

It is likely that the prison population will continue
to grow. The National Council on Crime and Delinquency has
estimated that the total number of prisoners might reach 1.4
million by the year 2000, a jump of 24 percent over the 1995
level ("Inmate Populations" 10). The Bureau of Prisons has
projected construction costs of some four billion dollars
for new federal prisons scheduled to open in the 1996-2006
decade and between ten billion and fourteen billion dollars
for the new state prisons required to house the anticipated
increase in prisoners ("Inmate Populations" 10).

Even these figures don't tell the whole story. Director
of the Federal Bureau of Prisons J. Michael Quinlan comments
that over the lifetime of a prison, "construction costs are
only 5-7 percent of the total expense. This means that from
15-20 times the construction costs will have to be budgeted
over the life of each prison now being built" (114).
Underestimating operating costs can result in unused
facilities as in Florida where, in 1992, two newly
constructed 900-person prisons and a 336-person death-row
facility remained empty because the state lacked the money
to operate them (Katel 63).

Overcrowding and the high costs of prisons have
seriously undermined state spending on public services and
created a number of hidden expenses. In Michigan, for
example, corrections spending increased over 300 percent
between 1979 and 1989, as compared to a 98 percent increase
in social services spending and a 40 percent increase in
education spending (Baird 122). And these figures do not
include hidden costs such as welfare payments to the
families of imprisoned offenders and the loss of tax
revenues from prisoners removed from the job market (Lynch).

Faced with the social and educational consequences of
current policy, many state legislators have recommended

Statistics, forecasts of prisoner increases, costs provide interest, depth

Author's name introduces short run-in quote within quotation marks; page number follows quote

Effect of underestimating costs

Comparison of spending figures

Jacque 3

using prison space only for violent offenders and
developing, for nonviolent ones, low-cost alternatives that
provide adequate public protection. At times, results have
been mixed. In the early 1980s, for example, the state of
Georgia attempted to relieve severe prison overcrowding by
greatly expanding the use of closely supervised probation.
While significant cost savings were realized, tremendous
work overloads on the probation staff resulted, according to
the Georgia Probation Division.

House arrest--a strategy that confines nonviolent
offenders to their homes and monitors their compliance with
electronic devices--avoids the drawbacks of other approaches.
It offers a choice of several monitoring systems, presents no
insurmountable problems, is effective in controlling low-
risk offenders, and costs less than incarceration.

Electronic monitoring[1] has curious roots--the comic
Spiderman. The idea first occurred in 1979 to New Mexico
Judge Jack Love, who observed that Kingpin, Spiderman's
nemesis, used an electronic bracelet to control his crime-
fighter enemy. Love asked computer companies to develop a
similar device (Scaglione, "Jails" 32; Sullivan 51). The
first house-arrest program using electronic monitoring was
implemented in 1984, and five years later programs had been
established in over a hundred jurisdictions across more than
thirty states (Peck 26; Scaglione, "Under Arrest" 26). By
1993, the number of offenders being electronically
monitored totaled 65,650 nationwide (Carey and McLean 1).

[1] This alternative is sometimes called electronic
tethering, electronic surveillance, electronic house
arrest, or electronic incarceration.

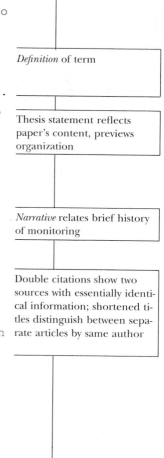

Definition of term

Thesis statement reflects
paper's content, previews
organization

Narrative relates brief history
of monitoring

Double citations show two
sources with essentially identical information; shortened titles distinguish between separate articles by same author

Explanatory note

Jacque 4

Classification of monitoring systems

The U.S. Department of Justice classifies electronic monitoring systems according to their signaling characteristics (United States, <u>Electronic Monitoring</u> 1). Types include programmed contact, continuous signal, and hybrid systems--a combination of the first two.

Definition of system

With a programmed-contact system, a computer calls an offender's residence on a random basis during established curfew periods and reports any unauthorized absence to correctional authorities. Various levels of sophistication are possible depending upon how much certainty is desired. In the simplest system, the computer merely records the offender's voice. Correctional authorities then review the taped responses the next day to determine any curfew violations. A variant approach uses a prerecording of the offender's voice, which the computer compares to the voice heard during random calls. If the two do not match, the computer can immediately notify authorities of a violation. Voice systems are comparatively inexpensive as no special equipment needs to be installed in the offender's home or worn by the individual (Hofer and Meierhoefer 36-37).

Comparison of systems

A more sophisticated means of checking on offenders makes use of an encoded bracelet worn by the offender. Again, a computer calls randomly during curfew. Instead of answering in the usual manner, however, the offender responds by inserting the bracelet into a special transmitter attached to the telephone. The bracelets can be made in such a way that unauthorized attempts to remove them will damage their transmitting ability (Hofer and Meierhoefer 36-37).

Process explained

Visual verification probably offers the best assurance against curfew violation. A special camera that can transmit photographs over telephone lines is installed in the offender's home. During calls, the computer can request the

Jacque 5

monitored individual to provide a variety of poses to the camera. These photographs can then be stored in the computer for later review or compared immediately to a reference key for the individual (Hofer and Meierhoefer 37).

Continuous-signal systems, unlike programmed-contact systems, require the offender to wear a transmitter that sends a continuous sequence of electronic signals, often several times a minute, to his or her home telephone. If a break in transmission occurs during a detention period, the monitoring computer notifies authorities. The transmitters are relatively small and generally worn on a tamper-resistant strap around the ankle. Attempts to remove the strap could cause the unit to stop sending signals or could be detected during periodic inspections. These systems provide a greater degree of supervision than programmed-contact systems, which check on offenders only intermittently (Hofer and Meierhoefer 38-39).

Comparison of systems; *definition* of system

Comparison of systems

Hybrid systems combine programmed-contact and continuous-signal techniques in order to realize the advantages of each (United States, Electronic Monitoring 1). Typically, the programmed-contact component includes both voice and video units. This component can function as a backup for continuous-signal monitoring or as a supplement to it. In the first case, the computer is programmed to call for voice-video identification whenever the offender's transmitter fails to send a continuous signal. In the second case, the computer randomly calls for voice-video verification as well as receives transmitter signals (Scaglione, "Jails" 36).

Jurisdictions can develop hybrid systems tailored to their individual needs. For example, a house-arrest program for drunk drivers could employ a continuous-signal transmitter supplemented by random telephone verification.

Jacque 6

Home monitoring equipment could even include a Breathalyzer to determine and transmit to the computer the offender's blood-alcohol level during telephone verification calls (Scaglione, "Jails" 36). A variation of this type of system is used in Annapolis, Maryland, where video cameras have been installed in the homes of some convicted drunk drivers. The offenders are called periodically and required to give themselves a blood-alcohol test in front of the camera (Peck 28).

Not surprisingly, electronic monitoring has resulted in some practical problems and legal concerns. Most problems arise with those who wear encoded verification bracelets or transmitters. These offenders complain that the devices cause physical discomfort or embarrassment. Correction officials can adjust the fit of the device or suggest that offenders wear a cut-off tube sock, tennis-type wrist band, or other type of padding under the strap. Wearers, however, must find their own ways of coping with embarrassment. In studying the electronic monitoring of federal parolees, Beck, Klein-Saffran, and Wooten found that offenders could be quite innovative in explaining why they were wearing units. When questioned by strangers, "the majority told the truth, while other parolees stated that [the unit] was a heart monitor, pager, battery charger for a video camera, or a fish caller" (29).

Transmitting difficulties have created other practical problems. In some areas, existing telephone lines may be inadequate or incompatible with the transmitting characteristics of certain monitoring systems. In other cases, the offender's home may cause difficulties. Ford and Schmidt, who conducted research for the National Institute of Justice, point out that

> The typical room has dead space in which the
> receiver cannot pick up the transmitter's

Cites article with three authors; page number follows quotation

Brackets enclose explanatory words inserted into quotation

Extended quotation indented ten spaces, without quotation marks, double spaced

Jacque 7

signal. In particular, metal tends to limit the range of the transmitter; kitchens are therefore an especially difficult environment. Transmission breaks have also been attributed to metal furniture, faulty wiring, other electronic devices, bathroom fixtures, waterbeds, and even certain sleeping positions. Mobile homes constitute a problem for offenders trying to do yard chores: The range outside the building is as little as ten feet, as compared to as much as 200 feet from a mainframe building. (3)

Other researchers have noted similar interference problems. In one situation, authorities suspected noncompliance when they discovered breaks in an offender's continuous signal transmissions. These breaks always occurred during the same time period and only on Sundays. Investigation revealed that a large rock and metal coffee table was blocking the signal from the transmitter on the offender's ankle while he was watching football on television (Beck, Klein-Saffran, and Wooten 27).

Most practical problems associated with electronic monitoring pose no serious challenge. Troublesome bracelets and transmitters can be adjusted or padded. Offenders often develop ingenious explanations for the units they wear. Difficulties in signal transmission can often be overcome by having trained technicians install equipment or by having offenders slightly modify their routine. Legal problems, on the other hand, pose a greater challenge.

Electronic surveillance programs necessarily involve some type of entry into offenders' homes. Therefore, they need careful examination to ensure that they don't violate the equal protection and right to privacy provisions of the Constitution. The American Civil Liberties Union is

Period precedes citation

Transition paragraph summarizes solutions to practical problems, looks ahead to legal problems

concerned that two common practices--charging a fee to cover surveillance costs and restricting surveillance to classes of offenders least likely to violate house arrest--may infringe on the equal protection clause of the Constitution. The first practice, the ACLU notes, can discriminate against young and indigent offenders by imprisoning them because they cannot pay their fees. The second, by singling out persons guilty only of property crimes and without serious criminal records or histories of drug abuse, may target disproportionately high numbers of white-collar offenders (Petersilia 3).

These concerns can be answered. Because electronic monitoring programs are always voluntary, participants essentially waive their right to privacy. By agreeing to a program in lieu of prison, they have indicated their willingness to undergo surveillance. Still, as the Bureau of Justice Assistance notes, court rulings may uphold a convicted person's right to privacy if electronic surveillance "cannot be justified in terms of an articulated security interest, ability to deter future criminal conduct or ability to reduce the risk of flight" (United States, Electronic Monitoring 5). Furthermore, electronic monitoring can invade the privacy of others in the offender's home. Family members who have not committed an offense and have not waived their right to privacy can accidentally be photographed or recorded. To prevent such intrusions, Kentucky, Nevada, and West Virginia have banned the use of equipment that might accidentally record extraneous sights and sounds. And because North Carolina prohibits photographing juveniles, visual verification cannot be used in that state (Scaglione, "Jails" 34).

Besides protecting an offender's constitutional rights, correction officials must try to avoid a "net-

Quotation indicates precise conditions that justify monitoring

Jacque 9

widening" effect when electronic monitoring is used. This
effect occurs when a judge approves surveillance for
offenders who would formerly have received probation but
denies it to anyone who would formerly have gone to prison.
The result is a "widening of the net of social control" to
encompass more individuals. When such abuses take place, the
system does not provide an option for those who would
otherwise have gone to prison, and it serves as a new form of
punishment for those who would otherwise have been placed on
probation. Prison overcrowding is not reduced, and the costs
of punishment actually rise because of the excess number of
individuals under surveillance (Morris and Tonry 225). The
net-widening effect has been avoided in some jurisdictions
by establishing strict rules for the selection of
participants. New Jersey, for instance, restricts
alternative punishment programs to offenders who have
already been sentenced to prison (Hofer and Meierhoefer 22).

Definition of term

A personal interview with Richard N. Irrer, who
supervises the Michigan Department of Corrections
electronic monitoring program, has provided convincing
evidence that monitoring works well in supervising low-risk
prisoners. Monitoring began experimentally in 1986, and the
following year the program was expanded to include the
entire state. Offenders monitored by the department include
circuit-court probationers, prison parolees, and prisoners
released from halfway houses. By mid-2000, some twenty-nine
hundred offenders were being monitored.

Interview supplements library research

Classification of offenders

The department uses the continuous-signal monitoring
system exclusively. Before being fitted with bracelets,
offenders are fully briefed on the operation of the system
and must read and sign a set of rules and regulations that
includes a list of possible penalties for violations. These
preliminaries and the fact that the program includes only

Jacque 10

carefully screened offenders with minimum-security status
have undoubtedly helped the program achieve its high success
rate. For 2000, according to Irrer, only 2.2 percent of the
offenders were arrested for new felonies, and just 6.7
percent disappeared. The penalty for program violators
depends on the status of the violator and the nature of the
crime. For example, parolees and probationers who commit
serious violations may go to prison, while prisoners on
furlough from halfway houses may be returned there. Minor
violations could result in extended curfew hours.

Classification of punishments

    The Michigan program has also been a financial success.
Imprisoning offenders costs the state an average of $65 a
day. In contrast, Irrer notes, electronic monitoring costs
just $7.30 a day, and financially able offenders must
reimburse the state. Those who can't pay must perform
community service. Earlier findings reported by Hofer and
Meierhoefer also reveal wide spreads between the costs of
imprisoning and monitoring offenders (54-55). Clearly,
electronic monitoring can significantly reduce the
country's enormous prison costs.

Arguments in favor
of monitoring

Comparison of costs

Independent conclusion
concerning savings in
prison costs

    Electronic monitoring is not a cure-all for prison
overcrowding. But it does offer a number of advantages that
deserve serious consideration: Several systems are
available; no insurmountable problems are evident; low-risk
offenders are effectively controlled; and the costs are less
than those for incarceration. As we move on into the twenty-
first century, authorities in increasing numbers can be
expected to establish house-arrest programs that monitor
compliance with electronic devices.

Independent conclusion
draws together and reinforces
main points of paper;
predicts future of house-
arrest programs

Jacque 11

Works Cited

Baird, Christopher. "Building More Prisons Will Not Solve
    Prison Overcrowding." <u>America's Prisons: Opposing
    Viewpoints</u>. Ed. David Bender, Bruno Leone, and
    Stacey Tipp. San Diego: Greenhaven, 1991. 118-24.

Barr, William. "Corraling the Hard-Core Criminal."
    <u>Detroit News and Free Press</u> 18 Oct. 1992, state
    ed.: B3.

Beck, James L., Jody Klein-Saffran, and Harold B. Wooten.
    "Home Confinement and the Use of Electronic
    Monitoring with Federal Parolees." <u>Federal Probation</u>
    Dec. 1990: 22-31.

Carey, Anne R., and Elys A. McLean. "Electronic Prison
    Bars." <u>USA Today</u> 30 Sept. 1993: A1.

Ford, Daniel, and Annesley K. Schmidt. <u>Electronically
    Monitored Home Confinement</u>. United States. National
    Institute of Justice, Department of Justice.
    Washington: GPO, 1989.

Gearan, Anne. "1.8M in U.S. Prisons, the Most Ever." <u>USA
    Today</u> 15 March 1999: A1.

Georgia State. Probation Division of the Georgia Department
    of Corrections. <u>Alternatives to Incarceration</u>. 1 July
    1997. 3 Feb. 1998 <http://www.harvard.edu/~innovat/
    aiga87. html>.

Hofer, Paul J., and Barbara S. Meierhoefer. <u>Home
    Confinement: An Evolving Sanction in the Federal
    Criminal Justice System</u>. Washington: Federal
    Judicial Center, 1987.

Entry for collection containing several authors' contributions compiled by three editors

Entry for newspaper article

Entry for occupational journal article with three authors

Entry for newspaper item with two authors

Entry for government document, two authors given

Entry for Internet report, no author given

Entry for book with two authors

Jacque 12

"Inmate Populations, Costs and Projection Models."
   Corrections Compendium Jan. 1997: 10-11.

Entry for interview

Irrer, Richard N. Personal interview. 20 Feb. 2001.

Entry for popular magazine
article with one author

Katel, Peter. "New Walls, No Inmates." Newsweek 18 May
   1992: 63.

Entry for Internet report,
one author given

Lynch, Allen. Cost Effectiveness of Incarceration. Leroy
   Collins Institute for Public Policy. 1 July 1997
   <http://www.dos.state.fl.us/fgils/agencies/fcc/
   reports/crime.html>.

Morris, Norval, and Michael Tonry. Between Prison and
   Probation: Intermediate Punishments in a Rational
   Sentencing System. New York: Oxford UP, 1990.

Peck, Keenan. "High-Tech House Arrest." Progressive July
   1988: 26-28.

Entry for government
document, one author given

Petersilia, Joan. House Arrest. United States. National
   Institute of Justice, Department of Justice.
   Washington: GPO, 1988.

Quinlan, J. Michael. "Building More Prisons Will Solve
   Prison Overcrowding." America's Prisons: Opposing
   Viewpoints. Ed. David Bender, Bruno Leone, and
   Stacey Tipp. San Diego: Greenhaven, 1991. 112-16.

Richey, Warren. "Bulging Cells Renew Debate Over Prisons
   As Tools to Fight Crime." Christian Science Monitor
   22 Jan. 1997: 3.

Entry for occupational
journal article with
one author

Scaglione, Fred. "Jails Without Walls." American City &
   County Jan. 1989: 32-40.

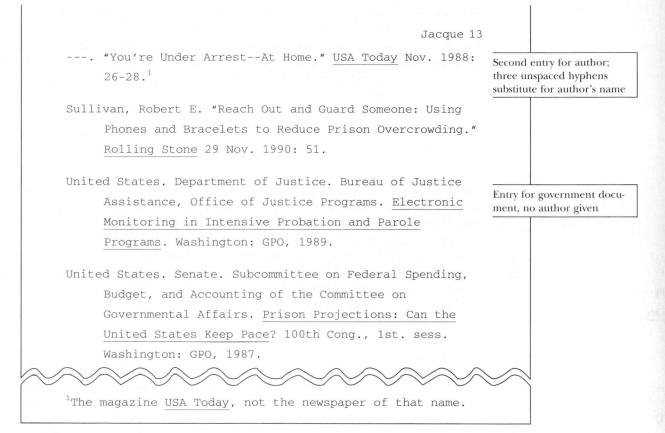

Jacque 13

---. "You're Under Arrest--At Home." <u>USA Today</u> Nov. 1988: 26-28.[1]

> Second entry for author; three unspaced hyphens substitute for author's name

Sullivan, Robert E. "Reach Out and Guard Someone: Using Phones and Bracelets to Reduce Prison Overcrowding." <u>Rolling Stone</u> 29 Nov. 1990: 51.

United States. Department of Justice. Bureau of Justice Assistance, Office of Justice Programs. <u>Electronic Monitoring in Intensive Probation and Parole Programs</u>. Washington: GPO, 1989.

> Entry for government document, no author given

United States. Senate. Subcommittee on Federal Spending, Budget, and Accounting of the Committee on Governmental Affairs. <u>Prison Projections: Can the United States Keep Pace</u>? 100th Cong., 1st. sess. Washington: GPO, 1987.

[1]The magazine <u>USA Today</u>, not the newspaper of that name.

■ Using a Word Processor

A word processor can help you with the various stages of library research. Several guidelines will enhance your efficiency as you proceed.

Taking Notes

Students with portable units sometimes take them into the library and enter notes as they read their sources, despite the inconvenience that often results. In most cases, though, you will find it works best to take notes on cards, then afterward enter them and your bibliographical references into your word processor. You can type notes into one central file and distribute them later to separate files by topic or distribute them as you go along.

As you proceed, take great care to distinguish between your notes and your thoughts about them. One good way to do this is to establish some system, such as typing notes in boldface and putting brackets around your thoughts. To avoid inadvertently using the exact words of others without giving proper credit, always put quotation marks around directly quoted material. As an added safeguard you might also use different spacing for quotations. To identify the sources of your notes, you could number them to match the number of the source or end each note with the author's name. For an anonymous source use a shortened title. Finally, don't neglect to keep printout copies of your notes and bibliography to guard against accidental erasure or a power surge.

Outlining

Many word-processing programs provide options that facilitate outlining. With some programs you can compare two arrangements side by side; others enable you to call up your stored and organized notes on one side of the screen and create your outline on the other side.

Don't let any limitations in your program cramp your explorations of possibilities. If your program lets you compare two outlines but you'd like to check more, make a second and if necessary a third printout; then examine them side by side. Similarly, if an outline includes more items than a single screen will accommodate, continue on a second screen and use printouts to check the complete product.

Drafting

Students follow different approaches when drafting on a word processor. Some follow the outline section by section, entering their notes and any thoughts that previously occurred to them, then go through everything again and add more material. Others finish off one section before moving on to the next, some by focusing on their notes and then developing thoughts that elaborate on them, others by developing their thoughts and working in their notes afterward. Follow the procedure that works best for you.

When you write the paper, fight the urge simply to string your notes together. Such an approach results in a draft that lurches from one bit of information to another without any consistent style or proper attention to the underlying thesis. If you find yourself merely typing in notes, stop, open a separate file, read each note carefully, and then enter your thoughts concerning it. When you've examined all the notes, begin the drafting process over again, integrating your notes and your thoughts in the new file.

As you compose, don't overfill any of your files; too many words leave little room for revision. You can avoid this problem by establishing a separate file for each section of your paper.

Revising and Formatting

Students often hesitate to revise research papers because of their length. A word processor gives you an edge. You can isolate different sections and experiment with them; move large sections of the text around; or, if you used separate files for different sections, change transitions to reflect different orders. When you make such changes, check to see that you maintain the flow of the paper. An adjustment in one section must mesh logically and stylistically with what precedes and follows. Reviewing a printout offers the best opportunity to check your paper's continuity. As you revise, always keep copies of earlier versions. Some part that seemed ineffective may fill a gap or take on a new look in view of your changes.

Finally, the formatting capabilities of word processors can be a powerful asset. Most programs will position page numbers, set margins properly, and add your name at the top of each page. Some programs will also indent bibliographic entries properly. Don't, however, neglect your instructor's specifications with regard to spacing, print style, and the like.

Documenting Sources

In order to acknowledge and handle sources, you must know how to (1) prepare proper bibliographical references, (2) document sources within your text, (3) handle quotations, and (4) avoid plagiarism.

The kind of information included in bibliographical references depends on the type of source and the documentation system. Two systems are in common use: the Modern Language Association (MLA) system and the American Psychological Association (APA) system. The entries that follow illustrate basic MLA and APA conventions. For more information, consult the *MLA Handbook for Writers of Research Papers,* 5th ed., 1999, and the *Publication Manual of the American Psychological Association,* 5th ed., 2001. When documenting online sources, consult the Web site noted on page 385 to supplement the information in the *Manual.*

■ Preparing Proper MLA and APA Bibliographic References

Books

The basic bibliographic reference for a book includes the name of the author, the title of the book, the place of publication, the name of the publisher, and the date of publication. Other information is added as necessary. The order of presentation depends upon which system of listing sources, the MLA or APA, is used. Note that the APA system uses initials rather than first and middle names for authors, editors, and translators.

■ *A Book with One Author*

Wilk, Max. <u>Every Day's a Matinee</u>. New York: Norton, 1975.

MLA

Wilk, M. (1975). *Every day's a matinee*. New York: W. W. Norton.

APA

■ *A Book with Two Authors*

Duncan, Dayton, and Ken Burns. <u>Lewis & Clark</u>. New York: Knopf, 1997.

MLA

Duncan, D., & Burns, K. (1997). *Lewis & Clark*. New York: Alfred Knopf.

APA

Note that the APA system reverses the name of the second author and uses "&" instead of "and" between the names. In titles and subtitles, only the first word and proper nouns and adjectives are capitalized. Both the MLA and APA systems use the hanging indent for entries in the reference list. Start the first line of each entry flush to the left margin and indent all subsequent lines five spaces.

■ *A Book with More Than Three Authors*

Alder, Roger William, et al. <u>Mechanisms in Organic Chemistry</u>. New York: Wiley, 1971.

MLA

Alder, R. W., Finn, T., Bradley, M. A., & Li, A. W. (1971). *Mechanisms in organic chemistry*. New York: John Wiley.

APA

The MLA system permits the use of "et al." for four or more authors or editors (listing all authors is also permitted); the APA system gives up to and including six author or editor names in the reference list. Substitute "et al." for the seventh or more.

■ *A Book with a Title That Includes Another Title*

The MLA offers two options: You may omit underlining the embedded title, or you may set it off with quotation marks.

Tanner, John. <u>Anxiety in Eden: A Kierkegaardian Reading of Paradise Lost</u>. Oxford: Oxford UP, 1992.

MLA

MLA   Tanner, John. <u>Anxiety in Eden: A Kierkegaardian Reading of</u>
<u>"Paradise Lost."</u> Oxford: Oxford UP, 1992.

The APA offers no guidelines for this specific situation. However the general guidelines for italics apply if you use the first option.

APA   Tanner, J. (1992). *Anxiety in Eden: A Kierkegaardian reading of*
Paradise Lost. Oxford: Oxford University Press.

■ A Book with Corporate or Association Authorship

MLA   United Nations, Public Administration Division. <u>Local Government</u>
<u>Training</u>. New York: UN, 1968.

APA   United Nations, Public Administration Division. (1968). *Local*
government training. New York: Author.

When the author of the work is also the publisher, the APA system uses the word "Author" following the place of publication. If the work is published by another organization, its name replaces "Author."

■ An Edition Other Than the First

MLA   Turabian, Kate L. <u>A Manual for Writers of Term Papers, Theses,</u>
<u>and Dissertations</u>. 6th ed. Chicago: U of Chicago P, 1996.

APA   Turabian, K. L. (1996). *A manual for writers of term papers,*
theses, and dissertations (6th ed.). Chicago: University of
Chicago Press.

■ A Book in Two or More Volumes

MLA   Bartram, Henry C. <u>The Cavalcade of America</u>. 2 vols. New York:
Knopf, 1959.

APA   Bartram, H. C. (1959). *The cavalcade of America* (Vols. 1–2). New
York: Alfred Knopf.

■ A Reprint of an Older Work

MLA   Matthiessen, F. O. <u>American Renaissance: Art and Expression in</u>
<u>the Age of Emerson and Whitman</u>. 1941. New York: Oxford UP,
1970.

APA   Matthiessen, F. O. (1970). *American renaissance: Art and*
expression in the age of Emerson and Whitman. New York:
Oxford University Press. (Original work published 1941)

■ *A Book with an Editor Rather Than an Author*

Deetz, James, ed. <u>Man's Imprint from the Past: Readings in the</u>   `MLA`
<u>Methods of Archaeology</u>. Boston: Little, 1971.

Deetz, J. (Ed.). (1971). *Man's imprint from the past: Readings*   `APA`
in the methods of archaeology. Boston: Little, Brown.

■ *A Book with Both an Author and an Editor*

Melville, Herman. <u>The Confidence Man</u>. Ed. Hershel Parker. New   `MLA`
York: Norton, 1971.

Melville, H. (1971). *The confidence man* (H. Parker, Ed.). New   `APA`
York: W. W. Norton. (Original work published 1857)

■ *A Translation*

Beauvoir, Simone de. <u>All Said and Done</u>. Trans. Patrick O'Brian.   `MLA`
New York: Putnam, 1974.

Beauvoir, S. de. (1974). *All said and done* (P. O'Brian, Trans.).   `APA`
New York: G. P. Putnam. (Original work published 1972)

■ *An Essay or Chapter in a Collection of Works by One Author*

Woolf, Virginia. "The Lives of the Obscure." <u>The Common Reader,</u>   `MLA`
<u>First Series</u>. New York: Harcourt, 1925. 111–18.

Woolf, V. (1925). The lives of the obscure. In V. Woolf, *The*   `APA`
common reader, first series (pp. 111–118). New York:
Harcourt Brace.

■ *An Essay or Chapter in an Anthology*

Angell, Roger. "On the Ball." <u>Subject and Strategy</u>. Ed. Paul   `MLA`
Eschholz and Alfred Rosa. New York: St. Martin's, 1981.
34-41.

Angell, R. (1981). On the ball. In P. Eschholz & A. Rosa (Eds.),   `APA`
Subject and strategy (pp. 34–41). New York: St. Martin's
Press.

Periodicals

Periodicals include newspapers, popular magazines, and specialized occupational and scholarly journals. The basic information for a periodical article includes the name of the article's author, the name of the periodical, the title of the article, the date of publication, the page range of the entire article, and, for scholarly journals, the volume number of the periodical. Again, the order of presentation depends on the documentation system used. The MLA and APA systems capitalize periodical titles identically; however, the MLA style omits an introductory *the* from these titles. As illustrated by our example for a signed article in a daily newspaper, the two systems follow a different format for showing when an article does not appear on consecutive pages. Note also that the systems capitalize the titles of articles differently and that the APA system precedes page numbers for newspaper articles with "p." or "pp."

■ *An Article in a Scholarly Journal Consecutively Paged Through the Entire Volume*

MLA Pfennig, David. "Kinship and Cannibalism." <u>Bioscience</u> 47 (1997):
       667-75.

APA Pfennig, D. (1997). Kinship and cannibalism. *Bioscience, 47,*
       667-675.

■ *An Article in a Scholarly Journal That Pages Each Issue Separately*

MLA Block, Joel W. "Sodom and Gomorrah: A Volcanic Disaster."
       <u>Journal of Geological Education</u> 23.5 (1976): 74-77.

APA Block, J. W. (1976). Sodom and Gomorrah: A volcanic disaster.
       Journal of Geological Education, 23(5), 74-77.

■ *An Unsigned Article in a Scholarly Journal*

MLA "Baby, It's Cold Inside." <u>Science</u> 276 (1997): 537-38.

APA Baby, it's cold inside. (1997). *Science, 276,* 537-538.

■ *A Signed Article in an Occupational or a Popular Magazine*

MLA Gopnik, Adam. "The Good Soldier." <u>New Yorker</u> 24 Nov. 1997:
       106-14.

APA Gopnik, A. (1997, November 24). The good soldier. *The New
       Yorker, 73,* 106-114.

■ *An Unsigned Article in an Occupational or a Popular Magazine*

```
"Robot Productivity." Production Engineering May 1982: 52-55.
```
MLA

```
Robot productivity. (1982, May). Production Engineering, 29,
    52-55.
```
APA

■ *A Signed Article in a Daily Newspaper*

```
Wade, Nicholas. "Germ Weapons: Deadly but Hard to Use." New York
    Times 26 Nov. 1997, national ed.: A13+.
```
MLA

```
Wade, N. (1997, November 26). Germ weapons: Deadly but hard to
    use. The New York Times, pp. A13, A15.
```
APA

■ *An Unsigned Article in a Daily Newspaper*

```
"The Arithmetic of Terrorism." Washington Post 14 Nov. 1997:
    A26.
```
MLA

```
The arithmetic of terrorism. (1997, November 14). The Washington
    Post, p. A26.
```
APA

Encyclopedia Articles

When documenting familiar works, such as the *Encyclopedia Americana,* the basic information for the MLA system includes the name of the article's author, if known, the title of the article, the name of the encyclopedia, and the date of the edition.

```
Sobieszek, Robert A. "Photography." World Book Encyclopedia.
    1991 ed.
```
MLA

The APA system requires additional information for all encyclopedia citations, as does the MLA system when less familiar publications are documented. Again, the order of presentation differs for the two systems.

```
Fears, J. Rufus. "Emperor's Cult." Encyclopedia of Religion. Ed.
    Mircea Eliade. 16 vols. New York: Macmillan, 1987.
```
MLA

```
Fears, J. R. (1987). Emperor's cult. In The encyclopedia of
    religion (Vol. 5, pp. 101-102). New York: Macmillan.
```
APA

For an anonymous article, references for both the MLA and APA systems begin with the article's title. With the APA system, position the publication date, within parentheses, after this title. The remaining format is identical to the citations with an author.

Government Documents

The basic information for a federal, state, or foreign government publication that is documented using the MLA system includes the name of the author, the title of the publication, the name of the government and the agency issuing the publication, the place of publication, the name of the printing group, if known, and the date. If no author is named, begin by identifying the government and then cite the government agency as the author. The APA system presents similar information but omits the government name, adds a cataloging code where one exists, and follows a different order of presentation.

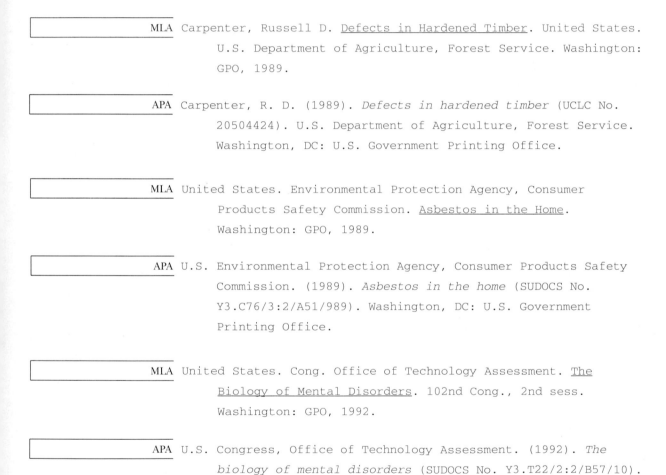

MLA Carpenter, Russell D. <u>Defects in Hardened Timber</u>. United States.
    U.S. Department of Agriculture, Forest Service. Washington:
    GPO, 1989.

APA Carpenter, R. D. (1989). *Defects in hardened timber* (UCLC No.
    20504424). U.S. Department of Agriculture, Forest Service.
    Washington, DC: U.S. Government Printing Office.

MLA United States. Environmental Protection Agency, Consumer
    Products Safety Commission. <u>Asbestos in the Home</u>.
    Washington: GPO, 1989.

APA U.S. Environmental Protection Agency, Consumer Products Safety
    Commission. (1989). *Asbestos in the home* (SUDOCS No.
    Y3.C76/3:2/A51/989). Washington, DC: U.S. Government
    Printing Office.

MLA United States. Cong. Office of Technology Assessment. <u>The
    Biology of Mental Disorders</u>. 102nd Cong., 2nd sess.
    Washington: GPO, 1992.

APA U.S. Congress, Office of Technology Assessment. (1992). *The
    biology of mental disorders* (SUDOCS No. Y3.T22/2:2/B57/10).
    Washington, DC: U.S. Government Printing Office.

Other Sources

The information presented and the order of presentation depend on the type of source and the documentation system.

■ Book Reviews

Koenig, Rhoda. "Billy the Kid." Rev. of <u>Billy Bathgate</u>, by E. L.   MLA
    Doctorow. <u>New York</u> 20 Feb. 1989: 20-21.

Koenig, R. (1989, February 20). Billy the Kid [Review of the   APA
    book *Billy Bathgate*]. *New York, 21,* 20-21.

If the review is untitled, follow the above formats but omit the missing element.

■ Published Interviews

Noriega, Manuel. "A Talk with Manuel Noriega." By Felipe   MLA
    Hernandez. <u>News Report</u> 20 March 1997: 28-30.

The APA system does not include a documentation format for published interviews. If you are using the APA format and your paper includes material from a published interview, we suggest that you document as follows:

Hernandez, F. (1997, March 20). A talk with Manuel Noriega.   APA
    [Interview with Manuel Noriega]. *News Report, 15,* 28-30.

If the interview is untitled, in place of a title, use the word "Interview," without quotation marks or underlining, for the MLA system. For the APA system, follow the example above, omitting any mention of a title.

■ Personal Interviews

If you conducted the interview yourself and are using the MLA system, start with the name of the person interviewed and follow it with the kind of interview and the date conducted.

Newman, Paul. Personal interview. 18 May 2001.   MLA

For the APA system, a personal interview is considered personal correspondence and is not included in the References list. Instead, use an in-text parenthetical citation. Include the name of the person interviewed, the notation "personal communication," and the date: (P. Newman, personal communication, May 18, 2001).

■ Audiovisual Media

<u>Frankenstein</u>. Dir. James Whale. Perf. Boris Karloff, John Boles,   MLA
    Colin Clive, and Mae Clarke. Universal, 1931.

If you are interested in the contribution of a particular person, start with that person's name. Use the term *film* in MLA format, and use the same model for vidoecassette and DVD recordings.

Whale, James, dir. <u>Frankenstein</u>. Perf. Boris Karloff, John   MLA
    Boles, Colin Clive, and Mae Clarke. Universal, 1931.

In APA format, the citation begins with an individual's name and his or her contribution to the *motion picture* (use this term, not *film*). The country of origin (where it was made and released) is now required.

APA   Whale, J. (Director). (1931). *Frankenstein* [Motion Picture].
        United States: Universal.

■ *Television and Radio Programs*

Basic citations follow the formats below:

MLA   Washington Week in Review. Prod. S. Ducat. PBS. WKAR, East
        Lansing. 6 Jan. 1995.

APA   Ducat, S. (Producer). (1995, January 6). *Washington week in review*
        [Television Broadcast]. Washington, DC: Public Broadcasting Service.

Use these formats when additional information is pertinent:

MLA   Peril at End House. By Agatha Christie. Dir. Renny Rye. Prod.
        Brian Eastman. Perf. David Suchet and Hugh Fraser. Mystery.
        Introd. Diana Rigg. PBS. WKAR, East Lansing. 12 Aug. 1993.

APA   Exton, C. (Script Writer). (1993). *Peril at end house* [Television
        Series Episode] (R. Rye, Director). In B. Eastman (Producer),
        Mystery. Washington, DC: Public Broadcasting Service.

With the APA system, the name of the script writer appears in the author's position. Any in-text references begin with the first name in the bibliographical reference (for example, Exton, 1993).

■ *Music and Sound Recordings*

MLA   Smith, Bessie. The World's Greatest Blues Singer. LP. Columbia, 1948.

In MLA style, list the medium (Audiocassette, LP, etc.) only when the recording is not a CD. If you mention the name of a particular item on the recording, set it off with quotation marks, as shown below. If the recording date is important, place it before the medium.

MLA   Smith, Bessie. "Down Hearted Blues." The World's Greatest Blues
        Singer. LP. Columbia, 1948.

The APA format requires indetification of all formats, including a CD:

APA   Smith, B. (1997). *The Essential Bessie Smith* [CD]. New York:
        Columbia Records.

APA   Smith, B. (1948). Down hearted blues. On *The world's greatest
        blues singer* [CD]. New York: Columbia Records. (Original
        recording February 17, 1923)

Recording dates, if different than the copyright year, follow the entry, enclosed in parentheses, with no final period.

■ Computer Software

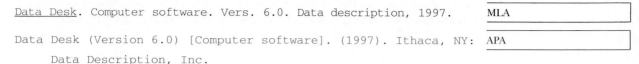

Data Desk. Computer software. Vers. 6.0. Data description, 1997.   MLA

Data Desk (Version 6.0) [Computer software]. (1997). Ithaca, NY: APA
     Data Description, Inc.

In the APA system, only specialized software or computer programs are listed in the References. Standard commercial software and languages should be cited by their proper name and version in the text itself.

■ CD-ROMs and Other Databases

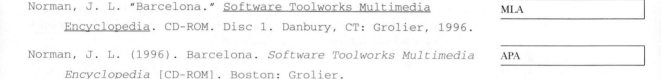

Norman, J. L. "Barcelona." Software Toolworks Multimedia   MLA
     Encyclopedia. CD-ROM. Disc 1. Danbury, CT: Grolier, 1996.

Norman, J. L. (1996). Barcelona. *Software Toolworks Multimedia*   APA
     Encyclopedia [CD-ROM]. Boston: Grolier.

The APA *Manual* (5th ed.) takes the view that all aggregated databases are the same type of source, regardless of the format or manner of access (CD-ROM, library or university server, or on-line Web supplier). Follow the model above when you need to cite an entire CD-ROM (not a document from it). In a reference to information taken from a database (even a CD-ROM), give a "retreival statement" containing the date you retrieved the document, article, piece of data, etc. as well as the full, correct name of the database. When you retrieve information from an online database, end the entry with a correct and complete URL for the specific document or version. In this case, the name of the database is omitted, unless this information will help in retrieval from a large or complex site. (See online models in the next section.)

Online Sources

The most recent edition of the *Publication Manual of the American Psychological Association* provides the APA's newest guidelines for documenting online sources. You can also consult the association's Web site for its most up-to-date information about citing electronic sources:

     http://www.apastyle.org/elecref.html

The examples here follow the published guidelines for the MLA (1999) and the APA (2001). Be sure to ask your instructor which format to follow and then use that format consistently. Often, data from the Internet are incomplete, perhaps lacking an author, a title, or any recognizable page or paragraph number. Include all the available information. The recommendation from APA is that you cite document locations rather than home pages and that the referenced address actually works for that file. Remember: your goal is to allow your reader to find the source.

■ Books

The basic information for a book documented by the MLA system includes the name(s) of the author(s), if known; the title of the book; the place and date of original publication, if applicable; the electronic site, if named; the date of electronic publication if the online version has never been published in print, or if it is part of a scholarly project; the sponsor of the site; the date the material was retrieved; and the online address.

MLA Locke, John. <u>An Essay Concerning Human Understanding.</u>. London,
       1690. Institute of Learning Technologies. 1995. Columbia
       U. 24 June 2000 <http://www.ilt.columbia.edu/projects/
       digitexts/locke/understanding/title.html>.

The APA *Publication Manual* does not show a model for documenting online books, however, the *Manual* treats all nonperiodical internet documents in one category, including multipage or multipart documents such as books or reports. Follow the general guidelines for a printed book and conclude with appropriate electronic source information, as modeled here.

APA Locke, J. (1995). *An essay concerning human understanding.* New
       York: Columbia University. (Original work published 1690)
       Retrieved June 24, 2000, from http://www.ilt.columbia.edu/
       projects/digitexts/locke/understanding/title.html

When some of the basic information is not provided, use whatever is available.

MLA Chaney, Walter J., William J. Diehm, and Frank Seeley. <u>The</u>
       <u>Second 50 Years: A Reference Manual for Senior Citizens.</u>
       Weed, CA: London Circle, 1999. 8 August 2000
       <http://londoncircle.com/2d50html>.

APA Chaney, W. J., Diehm, W. J., & Seeley, F. (1999). *The second 50*
       years: A reference manual for senior citizens. Weed, CA:
       London Circle. Retrieved August 8, 2000, from
       http://www.londoncircle.com/2d50.html

To cite part of an electronic book, place the part's title after the name(s) of the author(s) or, in APA format, after the date of publication. APA also cites a chapter or section identifier following the title of the complete document.

MLA Dawson, Marie. Introduction. <u>Methods of Sociological</u>
       <u>Investigation</u>. New York: Harmon, 1997. 6 Sept. 2000
       <http://www.harmon.edu/edu-books.html>.

APA Trochim, W. M. K. Language of research. In *The research methods knowledge base*
       (Foundations sec.). Cincinnatti, OH: Atomic Dog. Retrieved September 6,
       2001, from http://www.trochim.human.cornell.edu/kb/language.htm

- *Periodicals on the World Wide Web*

Periodicals online include specialized occupational and scholarly journals, popular magazines, newspapers, and newsletters. The basic information for a periodical includes the author's name, if known; the title of the article; the title of the periodical; the volume number; the date the article was published; the number of paragraphs in the article or its page numbers; the date the material was retrieved; and the online address.

The APA recommends using the models for print periodicals when documenting online articles that do not vary from their printed versions. In such cases, add [Electronic version] after the title and before the period to complete the citation. When the electronic format alters the printed version (e.g., no pagination, added data or links), then cite as an online document, using a retrieval statement and the name of the database and/or the URL. APA guidelines ask for the identification of the server or the Web site in a retrieval statement only when it would be helpful in finding the source; for example, it is not necessary to state "Retrieved from the World Wide Web" since it is the most common access point to the Internet.

Cervetti, Nancy. "In the Breeches, Petticoats, and Pleasures of
    Orlando." <u>Journal of Modern Literature</u> 20.2 (1996): 32
    pars. 8 Jan. 1998 <http://www.indiana.edu/~iupress/
    journals/mod-art2.html>.

> MLA

Cervetti, N. (1996). In the breeches, petticoats, and pleasures of
    Orlando. *Journal of Modern Literature, 20*(2). Retrieved January 8,
    1998, from http://www.indiana.edu/~iupress/journals/mod-art2.html

> APA

Navarro, Mireya. "Women in Sports Cultivating New Playing
    Fields." <u>New York Times on the Web</u> 13 Feb. 2001. 22 Feb.
    2001 <http://www.nytimes.com>.

> MLA

Navarro, M. (2001, February 13). Women in sports cultivating new
    playing fields. *The New York Times on the Web.* Retrieved
    February 22, 2001, from http://www.nytimes.com

> APA

"No Link Found in Violence, Videos." <u>Boston Globe Online</u> 8 Aug.
    2000. 27 Aug. 2000 <http://www.boston.com/dailyglobe2/
    ...nk_found_in_violence_videos+.shtml>.

> MLA

No link found in violence, videos. (2000, August 8). *Boston Globe
    Online*, p. A14. Retrieved August 27, 2000, from http://www.
    boston.com/dailyglobe2/...nk_found_in_violence_videos+.shtml

> APA

MLA Oakes, Jeannie. "Promotion or Retention: Which One Is Social?"
     <u>Harvard Education Letter</u>. Jan.–Feb. 1999. 7 pars. 8 Aug.
     2000 <http://www.edletter.org/past/issues/1999-jf/
     promotion.shtml>.

APA Oakes, J. (1999, January–February). Promotion or retention:
     Which one is social? *Harvard Education Letter*. Retrieved
     August 8, 2000, from http://www.edletter.org/past/
     issues/1999-jf/promotion.shtml

■ *Periodicals Accessed Through an Online Library Service or Large Network Provider*

Increasingly, full-text articles are available online at libraries or at home through services such as Lexis-Nexis, ProQuest Direct, and America Online. These services may or may not provide an online address for accessed material. If you know the service's home page, and you're documenting by the MLA system, cite the author's name, if known; the title of the article; the title of the periodical; the date the article was published; the page numbers for the article; the name of the database; the name of the library service; the name of the library; the date the material was accessed; and the online address of the service's home page.

MLA Clemetson, Lynette. "A Ticket to Private School." <u>Newsweek</u> 27
     Mar. 2000. <u>Lexis-Nexis</u>. Ferris State University Library Web
     Database Access. 5 May 2000 <http://library.ferris.edu/
     databaseframes.html>.

The APA documentation system provides the same information but omits any online addresses except World Wide Web addresses.

APA Clemetson, L. (2000, March 27). A ticket to private school.
     Newsweek. Retrieved May 5, 2000, from Ferris State
     University Library Web Database Access (Lexis-Nexis).

For MLA style, when no online address is provided, it is necessary to identify the keyword or keywords (the path) you used to find the material.

MLA Mayo Clinic Health Information: Lung Cancer. 21 Feb. 2000.
     America Online. 10 June 2000. Keywords: Cancer; Lung
     Cancer.

APA Mayo Clinic health information: Lung cancer. (2000, February
     21). Retrieved June 10, 2000, from America Online.
     Keywords: Cancer; Lung Cancer.

If you had accessed this source through a library, you would name the library after you named the service. APA style prefers that the URL that leads directly to the document file be provided, following the word *from.*

■ *Encyclopedia Articles*

The basic information for an encyclopedia article accessed through the World Wide Web includes the author's name, if known; the title of the article; the name of the encyclopedia; the date of the edition; and the online address. MLA style also names the vendor. For encyclopedia articles accessed through a CD-ROM, name this media after the title of the database for MLA format. The format is not required information in APA style, unless this information is needed for retrieval.

Daniel, Ralph Thomas. "The History of Western Music." <u>Britannica</u>
    <u>Online: Macropaedia</u>. 1995. Encyclopaedia Britannica. 14 June
    1995 <http://www.eb.com:180/cgi-bin/g:DocF=macro/
    5004/45/0.html>.

> MLA

Daniel, R. T. (1995). The history of western music. In *Britannica*
    Online: Macropaedia. Retrieved June 14, 1995, from
    http://www.eb.com:180/cgi-bin/g:DocF=macro/5004/45/0.html

> APA

■ *Government Documents*

The basic information for a government document includes the name of the author, if known; the title; the name of the government and agency issuing the document; the place of publication and printing group, if known; the date of publication; the date the material was retrieved; and the online address. If no author is given, begin by identifying the government and then give the government agency as the author. For the APA system, omit the government name, and add a cataloging code, if one is available.

Georgia State. Probation Division of the Georgia Department of
    Corrections. <u>Alternatives to Incarceration</u>. 1 July 1997.
    3 Feb. 1998 <http://www.harvard.edu/~innovat/aiga87.html>.

> MLA

Probation Division of the Georgia Department of Corrections. (1997, July
    1). *Alternatives to Incarceration*. (CSP No. 239875). Retrieved
    February 3, 1998, from http://www.harvard.edu/~innovat/aiga87.html

> APA

■ *Personal Home Page*

The basic information for a personal home page documented according to the MLA system includes the name of its originator, if known; the title of the site, if any (use *Home page* or other such description if no title is given); the date the material was retrieved from the site; and the online address.

Lanthrop, Olin. Home page. 24 June 2000 <http://
    www.cognivis.com/olin/photos.htm>.

> MLA

The APA *Manual* offers no specific guidelines for personal home pages. We suggest that you follow the pattern below, which conforms to general APA practice. Note that the APA system, unlike the MLA, includes the date of the latest Web page revision, if known, in parentheses.

APA   Lanthrop, O. (2000, May 28). Home page. Retrieved June 24, 2000,
        from http://www.cognivis.com/olin/photos.htm

■ *Newsgroups, Electronic Mailing Lists, and E-mail*

MLA gives guidelines for including newsgroups, electronic mailing lists (some-times called listservs), and e-mail within the Works Cited list. APA format treats e-mail as personal communications, which are cited in parentheses in the text only. Newsgroups, online forums, discussion groups, and electronic mailing lists that maintain archives can be cited in the References, but the APA cautions that there must be a scholarly purpose. When in doubt, treat as a personal communication.

MLA   Corelli, Aldo. "Colleges and Diversity." Online posting. 20 Apr.
        1993. 25 Apr. 1993 <learninghouse.michigan.edu>.

MLA   Nicholson, Brad. "Casino Gambling." E-mail to author. 2 Feb. 2001.

        . . . as reported in his study (B. Nicholson, personal
        communication, February 2, 2001).

APA   Trehub, A. (2002, January 28). The conscious access hypothesis [Msg.
        18]. Message posted to University of Houston Psyche Discussion
        Forum: http://listserv.uh.edu/cgi-bin/wa?A2=ind0201&L=psyche-
        b&F=&S=&P=2334

EXERCISE

A. Using the MLA system, write a proper reference for each of the unstyled information sets that follow:

1. A book titled Gas Conditioning Fact Book. The book was published in 1962 by Dow Chemical Company in Midland, Michigan. No author is named.

2. An unsigned article titled Booze Plays a Big Role in Car Crashes. The article was published in the November 28, 1997, state edition of the Detroit News. It appears on page 2 of section C.

3. An essay written by C. Wright Mills and titled The Competitive Personality. The essay appeared in a collection of Mills's writings entitled Power, Politics, and People. The collection was published in 1963 by Ballantine Books in New York. The book is edited and introduced by Irving Louis Horowitz. The essay appears on pages 263 through 273.

4. An unsigned article titled Global Warming Fears on Rise. The article was published in the October 25, 1997, issue of Newswatch magazine. It appears on pages 29 to 31.

5. A book written by Paul Theroux and titled The Kingdom by the Sea. The book was published in 1983 by the Houghton Mifflin Company in Boston.

6. A book written by Kate Chopin and titled The Awakening. The book, edited by Margaret Culley, was published in 1976 by W. W. Norton and Company in New York.

7. An article written by James E. Cooke and titled Alexander Hamilton. The article appears on pages 31 and 32 of the World Book Encyclopedia, Volume 9, published in 1996.

8. An article written by Sarah McBride and titled Young Deadbeats Pose Problems for Credit-Card Issuers. The article was published in the November 28, 1997, Midwest edition of the Wall Street Journal. It appears on pages 1 and 6 of section B.

9. A book written by Magdalena Dabrowski and Rudolph Leopold and titled Egon Schiele. The book was published in 1997 by the Yale University Press in New Haven, Connecticut.

10. A book written by Jean Descola and titled A History of Spain. The book, translated by Elaine P. Halperin, was published in 1962 by Alfred A. Knopf in New York.

11. An article written by John T. Flanagan and Raymond L. Grimer and titled Mexico in American Fiction to 1850. The article was published in 1940 in a journal called Hispania. It appears on pages 307 through 318. The volume number is 23.

12. A United States government document titled Marine Fisheries Review. It was published by the National Marine Fisheries Service of the U.S. Department of Commerce in 1993. No author is given.

13. A book written by David Kahn and titled The Codebreakers. The second edition of the book was published in 1996 by Scribner's in New York.

14. A book written by Joseph Blotner and titled Faulkner: A Biography. The book was published in two volumes in 1974 by Random House in New York.

15. An article written by Calvin Tompkins and titled The Importance of Being Elitist. The article was published in the November 24, 1997, issue of the New Yorker. It appears on pages 58 through 69.

16. A book written by Thomas Beer and titled Stephen Crane: A Study in American Letters. The book was published in 1923 and reprinted in 1972 by Octagon Books in New York.

17. A review of a book written by Jacques Barzun and titled The Culture We Deserve. The review, by Beth Winona, appeared in the March 1989 issue of American Issues magazine and was titled Barzun and Culture. It appeared on pages 46 through 50.

18. An interview of playwright Neil Simon. The interview was titled Neil Simon on the New York Theater and appeared in the September 3, 1997, issue of the Long Island News, on pages C4–5. The interviewer was Pearl Barnes.

19. A film titled Casablanca. The film was directed by Michael Curtiz and starred Humphrey Bogart, Ingrid Bergman, Claude Rains, and Paul Henreid. It was released in 1942 by Warner Brothers.

20. A television program titled Grizzly. It appeared on WNTR, New York, on February 3, 1997. The station is part of the CBS network.

B. **Prepare a proper MLA entry for each of the works you plan to use in writing your paper.**

■ Handling In-Text Citations

Both the MLA and APA systems use notations that appear within the text and are set off by parentheses. The systems are illustrated by the following examples.

Basic Citation Form

For the MLA system, the parenthetical citation consists of the last name of the author and the page number(s) of the material from the publication you are citing. The APA system adds the year to the citation. At the writer's option, the items may be grouped together within parentheses or separated when the author is named in the text, as shown in the following examples. The bibliographic references preceding the passages follow the MLA format.

■ *Bibliographic Reference*

Rothenberg, Randall. "Life in Cyburbia." Esquire Feb. 1996: 56-63.

■ *Passage and Citation*

> MLA

A mania for the Internet has invaded many important aspects of our culture. Newspapers run stories on it, businesses have rushed to set up Web sites, and the Speaker of the House of Representatives has stated that even our poorest children have a stake in the Internet (Rothenberg 59).

> MLA

Rothenberg states that a mania for the Internet has invaded many important aspects of our culture. Newspapers run stories on it, businesses have rushed to set up Web sites, and the Speaker of the House of Representatives has stated that even our poorest children have a stake in the Internet (59).

> APA

. . . our poorest children have a stake in the Internet (Rothenberg, 1996, p. 59).

> APA

Rothenberg (1996) states . . . have a stake in the Internet (p. 59).

■ *Bibliographic Reference*

Weider, Benjamin, and David Hapgood. The Murder of Napoleon. New York: Congdon, 1982.

■ *Passage and Citation*

> MLA

Four different autopsy reports were filed. All the reports agreed that there was a cancerous ulcer in Napoleon's stomach, but none of them declared that the cancer was the cause of death. Nevertheless, cancer has become accepted as the cause (Weider and Hapgood 72).

. . . Nevertheless, cancer has become accepted as the cause (Weider & Hapgood, 1982, p. 72).

APA

If a source has more than three authors (or more than six in the APA system), use "et al.," meaning "and others," for all but the first-named one.

■ *Bibliographic Reference*

Baugh, Albert C., et al. <u>A Literary History of England</u>. New York: Appleton, 1948.

■ *Passage and Citation*

Although no one knows for certain just when Francis Beaumont and John Fletcher started collaborating, by 1610 they were writing plays together (Baugh et al. 573).

MLA

. . . writing plays together (Baugh et al., 1948, p. 573).

APA

Authors with the Same Last Name

If your in-text citations include authors with the same last name, use the initials of their first names to distinguish them in all citations.

■ *Bibliographic References*

Adler, Jerry. "Search for an Orange Thread." <u>Newsweek</u> 16 June 1980: 32–34.

Adler, William L. "The Agent Orange Controversy." <u>Detroit Free Press</u> 18 Dec. 1979, state ed.: B2.

■ *Passage and Citation*

As early as 1966, government studies showed that dioxin-contaminated 2,4,5-T caused birth defects in laboratory animals. Later studies also found that this herbicide was to blame for miscarriages, liver abscesses, and nerve damage (J. Adler 32).

MLA

. . . miscarriages, liver abscesses, and nerve damage (J. Adler, 1980, p. 32).

APA

Separate Works by the Same Author

If your references include two or more works by the same author, add shortened titles to your in-text citation when following the MLA system. Underline shortened book titles and enclose article and essay titles in quotation marks. For APA format, use the author, name, publication year, and page reference entry in all cases.

■ *Bibliographic References*

Mullin, Dennis. "After U.S. Troops Pull Out of Grenada." U.S.
        News & World Report 14 Nov. 1983: 22-25.

---. "Why the Surprise Move in Grenada--and What Next." U.S.
        News & World Report 7 Nov. 1983: 31-34.

■ *Passage and Citation*

MLA

As the rangers evacuated students, the marines launched
another offensive at Grand Mal Bay, then moved south to
seize the capital and free the governor (Mullin, "Why the
Surprise" 33).

APA

. . . and free the governor (Mullin, 1983b, p. 33).

As the APA example illustrates, if two works by the same author appeared in the same year, order hem alphabetically by title and then place an "a" or a "b," without quotes, after the date. This permits accurate reference to each title.

Two Separate Sources for the Same Citation

If two or more sources provide essentially the same or related information and you wish to cite them in one parenthetical citation, alphabetize them according to the first author's last name. Separate each source with a semicolon and position the grouped citations within the same parentheses.

■ *Bibliographic References*

Bryce, Bonnie. "The Controversy over Funding Community
        Colleges." Detroit Free Press 13 Nov. 1988, state ed.: A4.

Warshow, Harry. "Community College Funding Hits a Snag." Grand
        Rapids Press 15 Nov. 1988, city ed.: A2.

■ *Passage and Citation*

MLA

In contending that a 3 percent reduction in state funding
for community colleges would not significantly hamper their
operations, the governor overlooked the fact that community

```
college enrollment was expected to jump by 15 percent during
the next year (Bryce A4; Warshow A2).
```

```
. . . enrollment was expected to jump by 15 percent
during the next year (Bryce, 1988, p. A4; Warshow, 1988,
p. A2).
```
| APA |

Unsigned References

When you use a source for which no author is given, the in-text citation consists of all or part of the title, the appropriate page numbers, and, for the APA system, the date.

■ *Bibliographic Reference*

```
"Money and Classes." Progressive Oct. 1997: 10.
```

■ *Passage and Citation*

```
According to the General Accounting Office, repairing the
country's dilapidated school buildings would carry a
price tag of over 110 billion dollars. Furthermore,
constructing the 6,000 buildings needed to end classroom
overcrowding would cost many billions more ("Money and
Classes" 10).
```
| MLA |

```
. . . many billions more ("Money and classes," 1997,
p. 10).
```
| APA |

Citing Quotations

When the quotation is run into the text, position the citation as shown below.

■ *Bibliographic Reference*

```
Schapiro, Mark. "Children of a Lesser God." Harper's Bazaar Apr.
     1996: 205—06+.
```

■ *Passage and Citation*

```
U.N. investigators who have studied the extent of child
labor in third-world countries estimate that "as many as
200 million children go to work rather than to school
[. . .] making everything from clothing and shoes to
handbags and carpets" (Schapiro 205).
```
| MLA |

```
". . . handbags and carpets" (Schapiro, 1996, p. 205).
```
| APA |

With longer, indented (displayed) quotations, leave two character(letter) spaces after the end punctuation and type the citation in parentheses.

■ *Bibliographic Reference*

```
Newhouse, John. "The Diplomatic Round: A Freemasonry of
     Terrorism." New Yorker 8 July 1985: 46-63.
```

■ *Passage and Citation*

MLA

```
One commentator offers this assessment of why foreign
terrorist groups don't operate in this country:
          The reason that America has been spared so far,
          apparently, is that it is less vulnerable than
          Europe, especially to Middle Eastern extremists.
          Moving in and out of most European countries
          isn't difficult for non-Europeans; border
          controls are negligible. But American customs
          and immigration authorities, being hyper-alert
          to drug traffic, tend to pay attention to even
          marginally doubtful people, and a would-be
          terrorist [. . .] could come under surveillance
          for the wrong reason. (Newhouse 63)
```

APA

```
. . . could come under surveillance for the wrong
reason. (Newhouse, 1985, p. 63)
```

Indirect Citations

If you use a quotation from person A that you obtained from a book or article written by person B, or you paraphrase such a quotation, put "qtd. in" (for quoted in) before author B's name in an MLA parenthetical citation. In and APA format, use "as cited in."

■ *Bibliographic Reference*

```
Klein, Joe. "Ready for Rudy." New York 6 Mar. 1989: 30-37.
```

■ *Passage and Citation*

MLA

```
Rudolph Giuliani favors the death penalty for "the murder
of a law-enforcement officer, mass murder, a particularly
heinous killing" but would impose it only "when there is
```

certainty of guilt well beyond a reasonable doubt" (qtd.
in Klein 37).

". . . there is certainty of guilt well beyond a
reasonable doubt" (as cited in Klein, 1989, p. 37).

APA

Authors Identified in Text

Sometimes you'll want to introduce a paraphrase, summary, or quotation with
the name of its author. In this case the page number may be positioned immediately after the name or follow the material cited.

■ Bibliographic Reference

Jacoby, Susan. "Waiting for the End: On Nursing Homes." New York
   Times Magazine 31 Mar. 1974, city ed., sec. 6: 80.

■ Passage and Citation

Susan Jacoby (80) sums up the grim outlook of patients in
bad nursing homes by noting that they are merely waiting to
die.

MLA

Susan Jacoby sums up the grim outlook of patients in bad
nursing homes by noting that they are merely waiting to die
(80).

MLA

Susan Jacoby (1974, p. 80) sums up . . .

APA

Susan Jacoby (1974) sums up . . . waiting to die (p. 80).

APA

EXERCISE   *Using the MLA system, write a proper in-text citation for each of the
bibliographic references you prepared for part B on page 391. Assume
that you have not used the author's name to introduce the material
you cite.*

■ Handling Quotations

Set off quotations fewer than five lines long (fewer than forty words long for the
APA system) with quotation marks and run them into the text of the paper. For
longer quotes, omit the quotation marks and indent the material ten spaces
from the left-hand margin (five spaces for the APA system). Double-space the
typing. If you quote part or all of one paragraph, don't further indent the first
line. If you quote two or more consecutive paragraphs, indent each one's first
line three additional spaces (five for the APA system). Use single quotation

marks for a quotation within a shorter quotation and double marks for a quotation within a longer, indented quotation. The following examples illustrate the handling of quotations. The documentation and indentation follow the MLA guidelines.

■ *Short Quotation*

Ellen Goodman offers this further observation about writers who peddle formulas for achieving success through selfishness: "They are all Doctor Feelgoods, offering placebo prescriptions instead of strong medicine. They give us a way to live with ourselves, perhaps, but not a way to live with each other" (16).

■ *Quotation Within Short Quotation*

The report further stated, "All great writing styles have their wellsprings in the personality of the writer. As Buffon said, 'The style is the man'" (Duncan 49).

■ *Quotation Within Longer, Indented Quotation*

Barbara Tuchman's The Proud Tower presents a somewhat different view of the new conservative leaders:

> Besides riches, rank, broad acres, and ancient lineage, the new government also possessed, to the regret of the liberal opposition, and in the words of one of them, "an almost embarrassing wealth of talent and capacity." Secure in authority, resting comfortably on their electoral majority in the House of Commons and on a permanent majority in the House of Lords, of whom four-fifths were conservatives, they were in a position, admitted the same opponent, "of unassailable strength." (4)

Always provide some context for material that you quote. Various options exist. When you quote from a source for the first time, you might provide the author's full name and the source of the quotation, perhaps indicating the author's expertise as well. The passage just above omits the author's expertise; the passage below includes it.

Writing in Newsweek magazine, Riena Gross, chief psychiatric social worker at Illinois Medical Center in

```
Chicago, said, "Kids have no real sense that they belong
anywhere or to anyone as they did ten or fifteen years
ago. Parents have loosened the reins, and kids are kind
of floundering" (74).
```

Or you might note the event prompting the quotation and then the author's name.

```
Addressing a seminar at the University of Toronto, Dr.
Joseph Pomeranz speculated that "acupuncture may work by
activating a neural pain suppression mechanism in the brain"
(324).
```

On other occasions you might note only the author's full name and expertise.

```
Economist Richard M. Cybert, president of Carnegie-Mellon
University, offers the following sad prediction about the
steel industry's future: "It will never be as large an
industry as it has been. There are a lot of plants that
will never come back and many laborers that will never be
rehired" (43).
```

When quoting from a source with no author given, introduce the quotation with the name of the source.

```
Commenting upon the problems that law enforcement
personnel have in coping with computer crime, Credit and
Financial Management magazine pointed out, "A computer
crime can be committed in three hundredths of a second,
and the criminal can be thousands of miles from the
'scene,' using a telephone" ("Computer Crime" 43).
```

After first citing an author's full name, use only the last name for subsequent references.

```
In answering the objections of government agencies to
the Freedom of Information Act, Wellford commented,
"Increased citizen access should help citizens learn of
governmental activities that weaken our First Amendment
freedoms. Some administrative inconvenience isn't too
large a price to pay for that" (137).
```

Page numbers are not helpful when you cite passages from plays and poems since these literary forms are available in many editions. When you quote from a play, identify the act, scene, and line numbers. Use Arabic numbers separated by periods. Here's how to cite Act 2, Scene 1, lines 295–300 of Shakespeare's *Othello:*

```
        That Cassio loves her, I do well believe it;
        That she loves him, 'tis apt, and of great credit:
        The Moor, how be it that I endure him not,
        Is of a constant, loving, noble nature;
        And I dare think he'll prove to Desdemona
        A most dear husband. (Othello 2.1. 295-300)
```

When quoting from a short poem, use "line" or "lines" and the line number(s).

```
In "Dover Beach," Matthew Arnold offers this melancholy
assessment of the state of religion:
        The Sea of Faith
        Was once, too, at the full, and round earth's shore
        Lay like the folds of a bright girdle furl'd.
        But now I only hear
        Its melancholy, long, withdrawing roar. (lines
        21-25)
```

In quoting poetry that has been run into the text, use a slash mark (/) to indicate the shift from one line to the next in the original:

```
In his ode "To Autumn," Keats says that Autumn is the "Season
of mists and mellow fruitfulness, / Close bosom-friend of
the maturing sun" (lines 1-2).
```

■ Avoiding Plagiarism

Plagiarism occurs when a writer uses another person's material without properly acknowledging the debt. Sometimes plagiarism is deliberate, but often it happens because students simply don't understand what must be acknowledged and documented. Deliberate or not, plagiarism is absolutely unacceptable. *Any summary, paraphrase, or quotation you include in your paper must be documented as must statistics and graphics.* The only types of information escaping this requirement are those listed below:

1. Common knowledge. Common knowledge is information that most educated people would know. For instance, there's no need to document a statement that the Disney theme parks in California and Florida attract thousands of visitors each year. However, if you include precise daily, monthly, or yearly figures, then documentation is necessary.

2. Your own conclusions. As you write your paper, you'll incorporate your own conclusions at various points. (See the margin notes accompanying Keith Jacque's library research paper, page 370, for examples.) Such

comments require no documentation. The same holds true for your own research. If you polled students on a campus issue, simply present the findings as your own.

3. **Facts found in many sources.** Facts such as the year of Shakespeare's death, the size of the 2001 national budget surplus, and the location of the Taj Mahal need not be documented.

4. **Standard terms.** Terms widely used in a particular field require no documentation. Examples include such computer terms as *mouse, floppy disk,* and *download.*

Any piece of information not set off with quotation marks must be in your own words. Otherwise, even though you name your source, you plagiarize by stealing the original phrasing.

The following passages illustrate the improper and proper use of source material.

Original Passage

One might contend, of course, that our country's biological diversity is so great and the land is so developed—so criss-crossed with the works of man—that it will soon be hard to build a dam anywhere without endangering some species. But as we develop a national inventory of endangered species, we certainly can plan our *necessary* development so as to exterminate the smallest number possible. [. . .]

James L. Buckley, "Three Cheers for the Snail Darter,"
National Review, September 14, 1979: 1144–45.

■ *Plagiarism*

Our country's biological diversity is so great and the land is so developed that it will soon be hard to build a dam anywhere without endangering some species. But as we develop a national inventory of endangered species, we certainly can plan our necessary development so as to exterminate the smallest number possible.

This writer clearly plagiarizes. The absence of Buckley's name and the failure to enclose his words in quotation marks create the impression that this passage is the student's own work.

■ *Plagiarism*

Our country's biological diversity is so great and the land so developed that in the near future we may pose a threat to some creature whenever we construct a dam. By developing a national inventory of endangered species, however, we can plan necessary development so as to preserve as many species as possible (Buckley 1144).

This version credits the ideas to Buckley, but the student has plagiarized by failing to put quotation marks around the phrasing (underlined above) that was copied from the original. As a result, readers will think that the passage represents the student's own wording.

■ *Proper Use of Original*

```
America has so many kinds of plants and animals, and it
is so built up, that in the near future we may pose a
threat to some living thing just by damming some
waterway. If, however, we knew which of our nation's
plants and animals were threatened, we could use this
information to preserve as many species as we can
(Buckley 1144).
```

This student has identified the author and used her own words. As a result, no plagiarism occurs.

Plagiarism is a serious offense because it robs the original writer of recognition. Students caught plagiarizing risk failure in the course or perhaps suspension from school. Whenever you are unsure whether material requires documentation, supply a reference. And always handle direct quotations by following the guidelines beginning on page 397.

22

. . . .

Additional Research Strategies: Interviews, Questionnaires, Direct Observations

The library isn't the only source of information for research writing. Investigators also gather information through *primary research*, which includes such activities as consulting public records in local, state, and federal archives, performing experiments, conducting interviews, sending out questionnaires, and making direct observations of various kinds.

This chapter focuses on the latter three types, the most common primary research strategies.

■ The Value of Primary Research

What makes primary research so valuable? First, it allows individuals and organizations to collect recent information, often unavailable elsewhere, that precisely suits their needs. A company that has developed a new product can't turn to published data to estimate its sales prospects; such information simply doesn't exist. But polling test users with a well-crafted questionnaire could suggest some answers and perhaps also some tips for improving the product. Similarly, someone wanting to gauge the success of an ongoing clothing drive by a local charitable organization might interview its director.

Even when published material exists, it may not contain desired information. Although numerous articles discuss student attitudes about required courses, you probably wouldn't find a report that explores student reaction to a new general-education requirement at your school. You could, however, assemble this information by distributing a questionnaire. The findings might even contradict, and therefore cause you to question, the conclusions of others.

Primary research can also yield unexpected and significant material. Suppose you're investigating adult illiteracy, and you interview a professor with a specialty in this area of study. She explains the reasons why people who can't read resist help and supplies several relevant examples. Such information might not appear anywhere in print. Certainly the resulting report would carry more weight and elicit more interest than one without such insights.

You can integrate primary research into a report that consists largely of *secondary research,* the kind that depends on library materials. The student who wrote the research paper on electronic monitoring (see pages 361–73) incorporated the results of a personal interview with the director of Michigan's electronic monitoring program. This interview provided information on the scope, operation, success rate, and cost advantage of the program. Often, however, writers detail the findings of primary research in separate reports. This would be the case if, for example, your employer asked you to interview users of a new computer system in order to determine their degree of satisfaction with it.

■ General Principles for Primary Research

Primary research, like all research, requires well-formulated questions. Such questions must be specifically focused, contain clearly defined terms, and be answerable by the actual research. A vague, general question such as "What attitudes do Americans have about their government?" lacks the necessary precision and therefore can't be resolved. What kind(s) of attitudes? What level or branch of government? Which Americans? How would you gather their opinions? A more realistic question might be "According to the Mason College faculty, how adequate is the new congressional proposal for funding academic research in this country?" You could easily develop and distribute to faculty members a questionnaire addressing the different provisions of the proposal. In addition, you can't resolve ethical or philosophical questions through primary research. While you could use a questionnaire to determine student attitudes about the police using sobriety check lanes, such information won't decide the ethical issue of whether the police should use such check lanes.

For valid results, conduct your primary research in an impartial manner. Always aim to determine facts rather than to justify some belief you hold. This means, first of all, that you must develop questions that have no built-in bias. If you poll other students and ask them to tell you "how core-course teachers on this campus marked their papers unreasonably hard," those responding might falsify their answers to give you what you want. Instead, use neutral phrasing such as "Do you believe core-course teachers on this campus mark your papers fairly or unfairly? Explain." Second, don't rely on atypical sources and situations for your data. If you investigate the adequacy of parking space on campus, don't deliberately observe the parking lots on a day when some special event has flooded the campus with visitors. Careful readers will see what you have done and reject your findings.

Just as you avoid bias when gathering information, so also do you report your results fairly. For one thing, don't use inaccurate interpretations of your findings to make them agree with the conclusions you're after. If you believe peer editing produces questionable results, don't claim that the students in a class you observed spent their time sneering at one another's work when in fact they offered constructive criticism. While such criticism can sometimes be straightforward, certainly most people wouldn't consider it sneering. Similarly, don't report conclusions that are unsupported by your actual research. If you observe a large number of violent acts while watching Saturday cartoons, don't leap to the conclusion that the violence in the cartoons causes violent behavior in children. You simply don't have the evidence needed to support that assertion. Finally, don't cover up results that you don't like. If your survey of teachers' marking practices shows that most of your respondents believe core-course instructors mark fairly, don't hide the fact because it doesn't match what you expected to discover. Instead, report your findings accurately and rethink your original position. The following section further explores ethical matters.

■ Ethical Issues

Today most people chuckle at an advertising ploy for a product recommended by "nine out of ten doctors." We recognize that the doctors were hand picked and don't represent an objective sample of adequate size. As a result, little harm occurs. With primary research, however, distorted investigating and reporting are sometimes hard to detect and can have significant consequences.

Say the officials of Anytown, USA, alarmed at a sharp rise in auto accidents caused by distracted drivers, schedule a special meeting attempting to ban cell phone calls by those driving within city limits. It would be unethical for a reporter opposed to the ban to write a supposedly objective feature article on the issue but include interviews only with people who share his views. Now suppose a presumably neutral group in the city of Lost Wages distributes a questionnaire to residents to gauge their reaction to a proposed gambling casino. It would be unethical to include a biased question such as "Should the city deprive its citizens of the revenue that a casino can provide?" Finally, imagine that a city manager, concerned by reports of motorists running the red light at a major intersection, gets the Department of Public Safety to investigate. A department employee conducts a twenty-minute observation, then writes a report concluding that surveillance cameras are not needed there. Clearly, the employee has acted unethically in drawing a conclusion after such a limited observation. To help ensure that your primary research reports are ethically responsible, ask and answer the following questions.

- Have I attempted to avoid bias in gathering and evaluating information?
- Are my data based on an adequate sample size? If not, have the limitations of the sample been clearly indicated?
- Is my information presented objectively and completely without any intentional effort to omit findings that run counter to my position?
- Are the people involved, whether I'm preparing an interview, questionnaire, or direct observation report, aware that they are part of a study and how the information will be used? Are they protected from harm that might result from their inclusion?
- Do I have permission to name in my report persons interviewed or observed?
- In an interview report, would the interviewee recognize and accept statements attributed to him or her?
- Have I noted any apparent bias in the interviewee?
- In a questionnaire report, have I avoided any biased questions?

■ Interviews

During an interview, questions are asked and answered. Some interviews amount to little more than brief, informal chats. Others, like those discussed here, may feature extended conversations, involve a series of questions, and require careful preparation. Interviewing an informed person provides you with firsthand answers to your queries, lets you ask follow-up questions, and gives you access to the most up-to-date thinking.

If you major in a business program, an instructor may require you to question a personnel manager about the company's employee relations program. If your field is social work, you might have to interview a case worker as part of your study of some kind of family problem. On the job, you might have to talk with prospective employees and then assess their suitability for a position in the company. Police officers routinely interview witnesses to accidents and crimes, and journalists do the same in pursuit of stories.

Choosing the Interviewee

Professional and technical personnel are a rich source of interview candidates. The faculty of any university can provide insights into a wide range of subjects. Doctors, pharmacists, and other health professionals can draw upon their expertise to help you, as can lawyers, engineers, researchers, corporation managers, and employees at every level of government—federal, state, and local.

Whom you interview depends, of course, on what you wish to know. For information on the safe disposal of high-level nuclear waste, you might consult a physics professor. If you want an expert view on the causes of homelessness, contact an authority such as a sociologist, who could provide objective information.

If, however, you want to gain a sense of what it's like to be homeless, you might interview the manager of a shelter or (in a safe place) one or more homeless people.

Preparing for the Interview

If you don't relish the thought of phoning to request an interview, keep in mind that most interviewees are eager to discuss their areas of expertise and are often flattered by the opportunity. The worst that can happen is a turndown, and in that event you can always find someone else in the same field.

Before you phone, review your own upcoming commitments and try to determine which ones you could reschedule if necessary. You may need to make an adjustment to accommodate the schedule of a busy person. When you call, indicate who you are, that you are requesting an interview, the subject of the interview, and how much time you'd like.

If the person agrees to meet with you, then ask when it would be convenient. Carefully record the time, day, and place of the interview, and if for any reason you need to cancel be sure to call well in advance.

Before the interview, do as much background reading as possible. This reading will help you develop a list of key questions and avoid those with obvious and readily available answers. Write out your questions to help ensure that the interview will proceed smoothly.

Good questions permit elaboration and don't call for simple "yes" or "no" answers. To illustrate:

Poor: Is it difficult to work with adult illiterates?
          (The obvious answer is "yes.")

Better: What have you found most challenging about working with adult illiterates?

On the other hand, don't ask overly broad questions that can't be answered in a relatively brief interview.

Poor: What's wrong with primary-school education?

Better: Why do you think so many children have trouble learning to read?

Avoid questions that are biased and may insult the interviewee.

Poor: Why do you bother to work with adult illiterates?

Better: Why did you decide to work with adult illiterates?

Likewise, avoid questions that restrict the interviewee's options for answering.

Poor: What do you think accounts for the poor academic performance of so many American secondary-school students—too much TV watching or overly large classes?

Better: People often blame the poor academic performance of so many American students on too much TV watching or overly large classes. What importance do you attach to these factors? Do you think other factors contribute to the problem?

The number of questions you prepare depends on the length of the interview. It's a good idea to draft more questions than you think you'll have time to ask, then arrange them from most to least important. If the interviewee keeps to the schedule, you'll obtain your desired information. If the interviewee grants you extra time, your written follow-up will have even more substance.

Conducting the Interview

Naturally you'll want to arrive on time and to bring a notepad and a pen. Sometimes you can tape-record an interview but only if you ask permission first. Because most people warm up slowly, you might start with one or two brief, general questions that provide you with useful background. Possibilities include "What is the nature of your specialty?" and "How long have you been employed in this field?"

Proceed by asking your most important questions first. If you believe that a question hasn't been answered or that an answer is incomplete, don't hesitate to ask follow-up questions.

As the interview unfolds, take notes but don't attempt to copy everything that's said. Instead, jot down key phrases and ideas that will serve as memory prompts. If you want to capture an essential explanation or some other important material in the interviewee's own words, ask the person to go slowly while you copy them down. When the interview is over, thank the person for talking to you. You may also offer to supply a copy of the finished report. With the answers to your questions fresh in your mind, expand on your notes by filling in details, supplying necessary connections between points that were made, and noting your reactions.

Writing About the Interview

The project you're working on determines how to handle your interview information. If you're preparing a library research paper, include the material, suitably presented, at the appropriate spot and document it according to whatever system, MLA or APA, you're using (see page 383).

Often, however, you'll be asked to prepare a separate report of the interview. Then, as with any other report, you'll need to organize and present the material in an effective order. Your topic, purpose, and audience will determine the arrangement you select. In any event, remember to establish the context for the report, identify the interviewee and his or her position, and present the information accurately.

EXAMPLE STUDENT INTERVIEW REPORT

Budget Cuts Affect State Police:
An Interview Report with Officer Robert Timmons
Holly Swain

Confronted with a billion-dollar budget deficit, the state legislature and the governor have been forced to make sharp budget cuts. One of these cuts is the allocation to the state police. This decision has threatened the loss of some police jobs and aroused considerable controversy. How, many ask, will the police, who were already on a tight budget, be able to provide the public with adequate protection when they have even less money and fewer personnel?

When Trooper Robert Timmons, a state police officer based in Marywood County, first heard that the governor might call for police cutbacks, he didn't believe they would become a reality. Timmons thought the governor was just making "political noise." Actually, the state police head did at first propose cutting 350 jobs, Timmons's among them, to help meet a $19 million cutback. This proposal was rejected in favor of one that combined demotions, pay cuts, and the elimination of special programs. In addition, the amounts allotted for other purposes were also cut.

All of these actions, Timmons says, have had an unfortunate effect on the operations of the state police. As an example, he mentions a sergeant who was demoted to "accident reconstructionist," a job requiring him to review severe accidents and reconstruct what happened for the court. This demotion, Timmons says, has taken an excellent police officer out of the field, where he's most needed, and put him behind a desk.

Timmons notes several bad effects of cuts in the allocation for gasoline. Because of these cuts, troopers are expected to drive just ninety miles a night. Timmons thinks this limitation has a "direct effect on the public." A motorist stranded on a freeway might not be

| Paragraph 1: establishes context for interview |
| Sentence 1, paragraph 2: identifies interviewee and his position |
| Remainder of report: presents information provided by interviewee |

spotted and aided by a trooper who is unable to make another run through that territory. Late-night accidents might go undiscovered, with serious or fatal consequences for those involved. Many more speeders and drunk drivers will escape being caught.

As of now, Timmons says, there are only 3,000 state police, about 400 fewer than needed. Each year, 100 to 200 officers retire. These vacancies need to be filled, but according to Timmons the state academy has been closed for over a year. The personnel shortages that already exist and the cutbacks resulting from the state's budget troubles are making it harder and harder for the state police to do an adequate job of protecting the public.

Officer Timmons understands that the state government needs to control its spending. However, he believes that the present budget cutbacks for a department that is already understaffed are very unwise. "I feel the governor should have given the matter more thought," he says.

■ Questionnaires

A questionnaire consists essentially of a series of statements or questions to which recipients are asked to respond. Questionnaires help individuals and organizations determine what select groups of people think about particular products, services, issues, and personal matters. You yourself have probably completed a variety of questionnaires, including teacher evaluations and market surveys.

Questionnaires are used extensively both on campus and in the workplace. A social science instructor might ask you to prepare a survey that explores community reaction to a recently implemented curfew for teenagers. A business instructor might want you to survey a test-market group to determine its response to some new product. In fact, some marketing classes focus on survey techniques. But even if marketing isn't your specialty, learning how to construct questionnaires can serve you well in your career. If you work in the hotel, restaurant, or health service field, you could use a questionnaire to gauge customer satisfaction. The same holds true if you manage or own a small repair service. As a landscape specialist, you might survey the people in your community to learn what planting and maintenance services they desire.

Developing the Questionnaire

When you develop a questionnaire, you need to target precisely what you want to know and what group you intend to survey. You could survey restaurant customers to determine their attitudes about the service and the quality of the food or to assess the types of food they prefer. Zero in on only one area of interest and then explore it with appropriate questions.

Begin the questionnaire with a clear explanation of what you intend to accomplish, and supply brief but clear instructions on how to respond to each part. Keep the questionnaire as short as possible, preferably no longer than a page or two. The longer the survey, the less likely that people will answer all the questions.

As you draw up your questions, take care to avoid these common errors:

1. Don't ask two questions in the same sentence. Their answers may be different.

Unacceptable: Do you find that this year's Ford Taurus has better acceleration and fuel economy than last year's model?

To correct this fault, use separate sentences.

Better: Do you find that this year's Ford Taurus has better acceleration than last year's model?

Better: Do you find that this year's Ford Taurus has better fuel economy than last year's model?

2. Don't include vague or ambiguous questions. Since people won't understand your intent, their answers may not reflect their beliefs.

Unacceptable: Is assisted suicide a good idea?

Better: Should assisted suicide be permitted for terminally ill patients?

3. Avoid biased questions. They might antagonize those who don't share your views and cause them not to complete the questionnaire.

Unacceptable: Should Century City taxpayers continue to waste money on renovating the North Park Bridge?

Better: Should Century City taxpayers spend an additional $100,000 to complete the North Park Bridge renovation?

Most questionnaire items fall into the categories that follow. The information you want determines which you choose. Often you'll need to include several or all of the categories in your questionnaire.

Two-Choice Items   Some items have two possible responses: yes/no, true/false, male/female.

Example: Do you plan to repaint your house during the summer months?

☐ yes
☐ no

Multiple-Choice Items   Often there are several possible responses to a questionnaire item. When you prepare this type of item, make sure that you include all significant choices and that the choices share some common ground. Don't ask if someone's primary vehicle is a subcompact, compact, full-size, or foreign car as size and place of manufacture are unrelated. To determine whether the vehicle is domestic or foreign, use a separate item.

Example: Check the income group that describes your combined family income.
  ☐ less than $10,000 a year
  ☐ $10,000–$20,000 a year
  ☐ $20,000–$30,000 a year
  ☐ $30,000–$40,000 a year
  ☐ $40,000–$50,000 a year
  ☐ over $50,000 a year

Checklists   Checklists allow respondents to mark more than one option. They can help you determine the range of factors that led to a decision.

Example: Please check any of the following factors that help explain why you decided not to re-enroll your child in Good Growth Private School:
  ☐ can no longer afford tuition
  ☐ moved
  ☐ dissatisfaction with child's progress
  ☐ disagree with school's educational approach
  ☐ conflict with teacher
  ☐ conflict with other staff
  ☐ child unhappy with school
  ☐ child had conflict with other children

Ranking Lists   Sometimes you may need to ask people to rank their preferences. This information will help you select the most suitable option from among several possibilities.

Example: Designating your first choice as "1," please rank your preferences in music from 1 through 5.
  ☐ classical
  ☐ country and western
  ☐ jazz
  ☐ rock and roll
  ☐ heavy metal
  ☐ rap

Using the responses to this item, the manager of a local radio station could broadcast the type of music that listeners clearly prefer.

Scale Items   When you are trying to determine the extent to which members of a group support or oppose some issue, using a scale can be helpful. Be sure to have people respond to a statement, *not* a question.

Example: Please circle the response that best reflects your feelings about the statement below.
SA = strongly agree, A = agree, N = no opinion,
D = disagree, SD = strongly disagree
Women should be allowed to fly combat aircraft in time of war.   SA   A   N   D   SD

Open-Ended Items   When you want to gather ideas from other people, you might turn to open-ended items—those that don't limit the reader's response. If you do, keep such items narrow enough to be manageable. You should know, however, that readers are less likely to complete open-ended items and that they are difficult to sort and tally.

Example: Please list the three improvements that you would most like to see in Lowden's high school curriculum.

_____

_____

_____

_____

_____

_____

_____

EXAMPLE STUDENT QUESTIONNAIRE

Survey on Public Smoking

Kelly Reetz

Please take a few minutes to fill out this questionnaire. My purpose is to determine the smoking habits and attitudes toward public smoking of Bartram College male smokers.

1. Do you smoke cigarettes? (check one)

    _____ yes

    _____ no

> Two-choice item

2. If you smoke, indicate how many cigarettes each day. (check one)

    _____ less than half a pack

    _____ between a half and a whole pack

    _____ between one and two packs

    _____ more than two packs

> Multiple-choice item

3. If you smoke, what are you likely to do upon entering a public place with no posted smoking restrictions? (check one)

_____ smoke freely

_____ check to see whether your smoking is bothering others

_____ ask others whether they would be bothered if you smoke

_____ not smoke

4. Check the statements you believe are true.

_____ My health is at risk only if I am a smoker.

_____ Secondhand smoke contains the same ingredients as directly inhaled smoke.

_____ Secondhand smoke poses no health risk to nonsmokers.

_____ Secondhand smoke poses a health risk to nonsmokers.

_____ Secondhand smoke poses less of a health risk than directly inhaled smoke.

5. Please rate each of the statements below, using the following scale: SA = strongly agree, A = agree, N = no opinion, D = disagree, SD = strongly disagree

_____ There should be no restrictions on public smoking.

_____ Smoking should be prohibited in stores, banks, offices, and workshops.

_____ Smoking and nonsmoking sections in restaurants should be separated by a barrier that smoke cannot penetrate.

_____ Smokers and nonsmokers should have separate workplace lounges.

_____ All public smoking should be prohibited.

6. Please add one or two comments you might have regarding public smoking.

_____

_____

_____

Testing and Administering the Questionnaire

When you have finished making out the questionnaire, ask several people to respond to the items and gauge their effectiveness. Are any items vague, ambiguous, biased, or otherwise faulty? If so, rewrite and retest them.

To ensure that you obtain an accurate assessment, make certain that you select an appropriate cross-section of recipients. To illustrate, assume that you and many of your campus friends dislike early morning classes. You decide to draw up a questionnaire to sample the attitudes of other students. You suspect that many students share your dislike, and you plan to submit your findings to the college president for possible action. To obtain meaningful results, you'll have to sample a sizable group of students. Furthermore, this group will need to include representative numbers of first-year students, sophomores, juniors, and seniors, as these classes may not share a uniform view. Failure to sample properly can call your results into question and cause the administration to disregard them. Proper sampling, on the other hand, pinpoints where dissatisfaction is greatest and suggests a possible response. Thus if first-year students and sophomores register the most objections, the administration might decide to reduce the number of 100- and 200-level classes meeting at 8 A.M.

Totaling the Responses

When the recipients have finished marking the questionnaire, you will need to total the responses. Even without computer scoring, this job is easier than you might think. Simply prepare a table that lists the questionnaire items and the possible responses to each; then go through the questionnaire and add up the number of times each response is marked.

When you finish, turn your numbers into percentages, which provide an easier-to-understand comparison of the responses. Simply divide the number of times each possible response is checked by the total number of questionnaires and then multiply the result by 100.

Writing the Questionnaire Report

When you write your report, don't merely fill it with numbers and responses to the questionnaire items. Instead, look for patterns in the responses and try to draw conclusions from them. Follow the order of the questionnaire items in presenting your findings.

Typically, a report consists of two or three sections. The first, "Purpose and Scope," explains why the survey was performed, how many questionnaires were distributed and returned, and how the recipients were contacted. The second section, "Results," reports the conclusions that were drawn. Finally, if appropriate, a "Recommendations" section offers responses that seem warranted based on the survey findings.

EXAMPLE STUDENT QUESTIONNAIRE REPORT

Findings from Smoking Questionnaire

Distributed to Bartram College Students

Kelly Reetz

Purpose and Scope of Survey

This survey was carried out to determine the smoking habits and attitudes toward public smoking of Bartram College's male students. The assignment was one of my requirements for completing Public Health 201. Each of the 240 male students in Crandall Hall received a copy of the questionnaire in his mailbox, and 72 completed questionnaires were returned. This latter number equals 10 percent of the college's male student population and therefore can be considered a representative sample. Of those responding, 37, or 51 percent, were cigarette smokers. Thirty-five, or 49 percent, were nonsmokers. Of the smokers, all but 11 percent smoked over a pack of cigarettes a day.

| Provides background details on project, profile of respondents |

Results of Survey

Smokers seemed fairly considerate of nonsmokers in public places. Only 16 percent said they would smoke freely. In fact, 51 percent said they wouldn't smoke at all. The remaining 33 percent indicated they would either look around to see whether they were bothering others or ask others whether they objected to cigarette smoke.

| Discusses responses to questionnaire item 3 |

In general, respondents seemed aware that secondhand smoke poses a health risk. Seventy-six percent believe that such smoke contains the same ingredients as directly inhaled smoke, and an amazing 96 percent believe that anyone exposed to secondhand smoke may be at risk. Only 3 percent think no health risk is involved.

| Discusses responses to questionnaire item 4 |

Opinions were strongly divided on the matter of banning all public smoking, with 79 percent strongly opposed and 21 percent strongly in favor. As might be expected, all of the

| Discusses responses to questionnaire item 5 |

smokers fell in the first group, but a surprising 51 percent of the nonsmokers did too. A sharp division was equally apparent between supporters and opponents of restaurant barriers, with 81 percent for or strongly for them and 19 percent against or strongly against them. In contrast to the findings on a smoking ban, all of the smokers favored barriers. Respondents overwhelmingly endorsed, 90 percent to 10 percent, prohibiting smoking in stores and banks and providing separate workplace lounges. Nobody registered a "no opinion" vote on any of the statements under item 5.

Responses to items 3-5 reveal an awareness among smokers of the dangers posed by secondhand cigarette smoke, a concern for the well-being of nonsmokers, and a willingness to accept restrictions, though not an outright ban, on public smoking. This attitude was consistent for both light and heavy smokers. For their part, about half the nonsmokers showed a tolerant attitude by supporting smoking restrictions but rejecting an outright ban.

| | Discusses patterns in responses to items 3-5 |

No smokers, but 71 percent of the nonsmokers, responded to the request to provide one or two additional comments. All of these comments dealt with how the respondents would act if bothered by someone else's smoke. Two-thirds said they would move to another spot, half of the remainder said they would ask the smoker to stop, and the other half said they would remain silent rather than risk an argument.

| | Discusses responses to item 6 |

Recommendations

As noted previously, this survey included only male students. To determine how its results compare with those for females, the same questionnaire should be administered to a similar group of female students.

■ Direct Observations

Often direct observation is the most effective means of answering research questions. If you want to know the extent and nature of violence in children's TV cartoons, watching a number of shows will tell you. Similarly, a researcher who seeks information about living conditions in an inner-city area of some metropolis can obtain it by visiting that locale. Such observations furnish firsthand answers to our questions.

In college and on the job, you may need to report your own observations. If you're majoring in business, an instructor might require a report on the work habits of employees at a small local company. If your field is biology, you might need to assess and report on the environmental health of a marsh, riverbank, or other ecological area. On the job, a factory superintendent might observe and then discuss in writing the particulars of some problem-plagued operation. Police officers routinely investigate and report on accidents, and waste-management specialists inspect and report on potential disposal sites.

The following suggestions will help you make your observations, record them, and then write your report.

Preparing to Make the Observations

First, determine the purpose of your observations and keep the purpose firmly in mind as you proceed. Otherwise, you'll overlook important details and record less-than-helpful information. Obviously, observing a classroom to assess the interaction of students calls for a different set of notes than if you were observing the teacher's instructional style or the students' note-taking habits.

Next, establish the site or sites that will best supply you with the information you need. If you're trying to determine how college students interact in the classroom, then the time of day, kind of class, and types of students will all make a difference. You might have to visit more than one class in order to observe the different types of behavior.

If your observations will take place on private property or will involve an organized group such as a class or a legislative body, you'll need to obtain permission and to make an appointment. Also, you might want to supplement your observations with an interview. Ordinarily, the interview will take place after you make your observations so that you can ask about what you've seen. However, if technical information is needed in advance, the interview should precede the observations.

Because you'll probably be making a great many individual observations, try to develop a chart and a code for recording them. Suppose you're comparing the extent to which students interact with one another and with the instructor in remedial and nonremedial composition courses. After much thought, you might develop a chart like the one following:

Class Designation: Composition 100				
Minutes into observation when interaction occurred	Classroom location of interacting students	Number and sex of students	Subject of interaction	Length of interaction

With certain kinds of observations, using a chart will not be possible.

In developing your code, you would undoubtedly use M = male and F = female to distinguish the sexes. To show the location of the interacting students, FC = front of class, MC = middle of class, and BC = back of class would probably work quite well. Coding the kinds of interactions presents a more difficult task. Here, after considering several possibilities, you might decide upon these symbols: CR = class related, SR = school related, SP = sports, D = dating, O = other matters. To save writing time, you'd probably want to use "min." for "minutes" and "sec." for "seconds" when recording the lengths of the interactions.

Making the Observations

If your visit involves a scheduled appointment, be sure to arrive on time and be ready to take notes. Select a location where you can observe without interfering. If you are observing people or animals, remember that they need to adjust to you before they will behave naturally.

Before you begin taking notes, record any pertinent general information. If you're observing a class, you might note the time it is meeting, its size, the name of the instructor, and whether he or she is present when you arrive. If you're observing an apartment, pertinent information would include the location and condition of the building, the time of the visit, and the general nature of the environment. Note also whether the landlord as well as the tenant knew you were coming: It is amazing how much cleanup landlords can carry out when they know an observer will soon arrive.

Don't feel as though you must take extensive notes. Do, however, record enough details to ensure that you won't forget any events, activities, or features that are important. If you have a chart and coding system, rely on it as much as possible when recording information. Refer to the chart at the top of page 420 for how the coded notes for part of a classroom visit might look.

If you haven't developed a chart, take enough notes so that you can produce a thorough report. Try to follow some note-taking pattern. When observing the condition of an apartment, you could proceed from room to room, jotting down observations such as "Front hallway, entranceway: paint peeling in large strips from wall, paint chips on floor. Hallway dark, bulb burned out. Linoleum curling up along sides. Cockroaches running along lower molding." Remain as objective as possible as you take notes. Record what you see, hear, and smell, and avoid loaded language. If you must record a subjective impression, identify it as such.

Ask questions if necessary, but rely primarily on what you observe, not what you're told. If the landlord of a run-down apartment you're visiting tells you that he's repainting the building but you see no signs that this is happening, ignore what he says or report it along with an appropriate cautionary comment. When you finish, thank the person(s) who made your observations possible or helped you in other ways.

When you leave the observation site, expand your notes by adding more details. Supply any needed connections and record your overall impressions. To illustrate, suppose you are expanding your notes on student interactions in a composition class. You might note that the greatest number of interactions occurred before and immediately after the instructor arrived, that all student-

Class Designation: Composition 100				
Minutes into observation when interaction occurred	Classroom location of interacting students	Number and sex of students	Subject of interaction	Length of interaction
0	FC	M-M	SP	1 min. 30 sec.
3	MC	F-F	D	
Instructor arrived				
5	FC, MC, BC	M-M-M-F-F	CR	3 min. 45 sec.
20	FC, MC	M-F-M	CR	1 min.

student interactions involved individuals seated together, that student-instructor interactions included students in all parts of the room, and that all the latter interactions were about subject-related matters. This information might stimulate interesting speculation concerning the student-student and student-teacher relationships in the class, causing you to conclude that the students were hesitant about having exchanges with the instructor. As you proceed, record only what you actually observed, not what you wanted or expected to observe.

If upon reviewing your notes you find that you require more information, you may need to arrange a second or even a third visit to the observation site.

Writing the Report

Once your notes are in final form, you can start writing your report. On the job your employer may specify a certain form to follow. As a general rule, all such reports reflect their purposes, focus on relevant information, and remain objective.

Usually you begin by explaining the reason for the investigation, noting any preliminary arrangements that were made, and if appropriate, providing an overview of the observation site. Depending upon the nature of the report, the primary means of organization may be as follows:

1. *Narration.* A report on the changing conduct of a child over a three-hour period in a day-care center would probably be organized by narration.
2. *Description.* A report assessing the tornado damage in a large urban area could present its details in spatial order.
3. *Classification.* A visit to a toxic-waste dump suspected of violating state regulations might produce a report classifying the types of wastes improperly stored there.

4. *Point-by-point comparison.* If you're comparing two possible sites for a baseball stadium, shopping mall, or other structure, a point-by-point comparison will probably best suit your purpose.

5. *Cause and effect.* This pattern works well for reporting events whose effects are of special concern, such as the testing of a new siren intended to scare birds from an airport runway.

6. *Process.* This arrangement is indicated when readers will want to know step-by-step how some process—for example, a new test for determining the mineral content of water—is carried out.

Conclude the report by discussing the significance of the findings and making any other comments that seem justified.

EXAMPLE STUDENT OBSERVATION REPORT

Observations of an Inner-City Apartment Building

Caleb Thomas

To fulfill part of the requirements for Social Service 321, I observed the housing conditions in an inner-city residential area. The building I selected is located in the city of Grand Mound, at the corner of Division Avenue and Hall Street, an area where most of the residents hold minimum-wage jobs or receive some form of public assistance.

> Gives reason for visit, location of site

I met the building supervisor, who had agreed to this visit, at 9:30 A.M. on Friday, April 13, 2001. The brick sides of the three-story apartment building appeared to be in good repair, but one second-story window was broken out and boarded up. Most windows had standard window shades, but a few were blocked with sheets or black plastic bags. Two had no coverings of any kind. Overall, the building's appearance was similar to that of several nearby apartment buildings.

> Notes preliminary arrangements, provides overview of site location

Heavy traffic clogged Division Avenue at the time of my visit. Next to the apartment building stood three single-story wooden buildings housing an adult video store, a bar, and a novelty shop, all with boarded windows and peeling paint. Across the street, a single-

> Continues overview of site location

story Goodwill Store occupied the entire block. In front of it, three women in short skirts walked slowly back and forth, eyeing the cars that passed. Two men sat on crates, their backs to the building, drinking something out of paper bags.

Describes building's hallway

The supervisor opened the unlocked metal door of the apartment building, and we went in. The hallway was lighted by a single dim bulb located on the wall toward the rear. Other bulbs along the wall and in two light fixtures hanging from the ceiling appeared burned out. Scraps of newspaper and chips of paint that had peeled from the ceiling and walls littered the floor. A strong urine-like smell pervaded the air.

Describes apartment hallway

Stating that he couldn't show me an occupied apartment because he "respected the privacy of the tenants," the supervisor took me to an unoccupied apartment on the first floor. He had trouble unlocking the wooden door; the key appeared to stick in the lock. The inside of the door had two bolt locks, one a few inches above the door handle and the other one near the floor. The door opened into a short hall with rooms off either side. Here, as in the building entrance, paint chips from the peeling walls and ceiling littered the floor. A battered socket on the wall held a single bulb, but when I flicked its switch, the bulb did not light. On the hall floor, linoleum curled at the edges. When I bent down to examine it more closely, several cockroaches scurried under the curl.

Describes apartment living room

The first door on the right-hand side of the hall led into a 10-by-12-foot room that the supervisor identified as the living room. Here the walls had been recently painted-- by a former tenant, the supervisor said--and a strong paint smell was still apparent. However, nothing else had been done to the rest of the room. The radiator was unshielded, several nail heads protruded from the stained and uncovered wooden floor, and the sagging ceiling had several long cracks. Plaster chips dotted the floor.

Describes apartment kitchen

A small kitchen was situated behind the living room. Again, linoleum floor covering curled from the baseboard, and cockroaches scurried for cover. The kitchen was furnished with a battered-looking gas stove, but there was no refrigerator (the supervisor said one was on order). The surface of the sink was chipped and had many brownish stains. When I turned on the faucet, a rusty brown stream of water spurted out. I asked for a sample to be tested for lead content, but the supervisor refused.

The bathroom, located at the end of the hall, had no radiator. Its floor tiles, broken in a number of places, exposed a foot-long section of rotted wood. The toilet, with seat missing, would not flush when I tried it but simply made a hissing noise. A brown stain spread over the bottom of the bathtub and a large portion of its sides. The wall tiles around the tub bulged outward and appeared ready to collapse into the tub. The supervisor offered the observation that there had been "some trouble with the plumbing."

> Describes apartment bathroom

Two small bedrooms opened off the left side of the hall. Like the living room both had unprotected radiators, uncovered wooden floors, and cracked ceilings. Walls were papered rather than painted, but long strips of the wallpaper were missing. In one bedroom a piece of plasterboard hung on the wall as if covering a hole. The windows in both bedrooms were covered with sheets tacked to the wall.

> Describes apartment bedrooms

When I had finished looking at the bedrooms, the supervisor quickly escorted me from the apartment and the building, declaring that he was too busy to show me any other vacant apartments. He also said he had no time to answer any questions.

Clearly the building I visited fails to meet city housing code: The living conditions are not what most people would consider acceptable. A careful investigation, including a test of the water and of the paint for lead content, seems called for to determine whether this apartment constitutes a health risk.

> Discusses significance of findings

Reader

Strategies for Successful Reading

Effective reading is not the passive process that many people imagine. On the contrary, it requires the ongoing interaction of your mind and the printed page. Bringing your own knowledge and experience to bear on a piece of writing can help you assess its events, ideas, and conclusions. For example, an understanding of marriage, love, and conflict, as well as experience with divorce, can help readers comprehend an essay that explores divorce. As you read, you must also understand each point that's made, consider how the various parts fit together, and try to anticipate the direction the writing will take. Successful reading, then, requires work. Fortunately, you can follow specific strategies to help yourself read better.

■ Following an Effective Reading Strategy

Different purposes require different approaches to reading. When reading for pleasure, you can relax and proceed at your own pace, slowing down to savor a section you especially enjoy, speeding up when you encounter less interesting material, and breaking off when you wish. Even so, you will get more satisfaction out of the material if you can relate it to your own knowledge and experience.

Reading for information/evaluation and to critique the writing call for a more methodical approach. Most of your college reading will require this kind of attention.

Strategies When Reading for Information/Evaluation

Because of the challenging nature of most college-level reading assignments, you should plan on more than one reading. A good first reading should orient you to the material. Before you begin, scan any accompanying biographical sketch and try to determine the writer's expertise and views on the topic. To illustrate, Alexander Petrunkevitch's background as a college professor and an author of internationally acclaimed books on spiders lends authority to his discussion of the survival process of the pepsis wasp in the essay "The Spider and the Wasp" (pages 465–67).

Next, see what the title tells you. Most titles identify the topic and often the viewpoint as well. Thus "The Sweet Smell of Success Isn't All That Sweet" (pages 540–41) suggests that the author isn't overly impressed with conventional attitudes toward success. Some titles signal the writer's primary strategy: "Close the Borders to All Newcomers" (pages 586–89) indicates development by argument and "Why Marriages Fail" (pages 533–36) development by causes. After evaluating the title, read the introductory paragraph(s) to see if you can determine the writer's main thesis.

Read the body of the essay quickly, noting any likely topic sentences that stand out (often the first or last sentence in a paragraph). Try to gain an idea of the essay's main thrust, the key ideas that support it, and the ways that they are organized. In your first reading, you can skim over the more difficult sections without trying to understand them fully. When you've finished, and before you reread the essay, think about what you've learned and then, either by saying it to yourself or jotting it down, express it *in your own words. For effective reading to take place, this activity is crucial.* You can hardly be said to understand what you've read, and you will be less likely to remember it, until you can state its essence in your own words. Next, go back and underline the thesis statement or, if one is not included, try to formulate one in your own words. Also look for any writing strategies the author has used. Finally, jot down questions that the first reading has raised in your mind.

On the second reading, which will take more time, you carefully absorb the writer's ideas. Read at a pace suitable to the material. Underline significant topic sentences as well as other key sentences, but keep in mind that underlining in itself doesn't ensure comprehension. Restating the ideas in your own words is more effective in this regard. As you proceed, carefully examine the supporting sentences to see how well they back up the main ideas. In addition, underline or note in the margin any ideas or facts you feel are important.

Consider reading as a kind of conversation with the text. Develop the habit of asking questions about facts, reasons, ideas—practically anything in the essay. Jot your queries and their answers in the margins. (On page 430 you can see how a student interacted with the first page of Amy Gross's essay "The Appeal of the Androgynous Man.") Good writers anticipate your questions and answer them; and because you have posed the questions yourself, you are more likely to see the connections in the text. If the author hasn't answered your questions, there may be problems with the work.

At times, unfamiliar words can hinder your grasp of the material. Whenever you encounter a new word, circle it, use context to help gauge its meaning, check the dictionary for the exact meaning, and then record it in the margin or some other convenient place. If the writing is peppered with words you don't know, you may have to read the whole piece just to figure out its general drift, then look up key words, and finally reread the material.

When the ideas of a single section prove difficult, restate the points of those sections you do understand. Then experiment by stating in your own words different interpretations of the problem section and see which one best fits the writing as a whole. When an entire essay is troublesome, state the ideas that are easier for you to understand and use them as keys to help unlock meanings that are difficult but not unintelligible. Save the most difficult sections until last. You might also want to discuss a difficult essay with others who are reading it.

Whenever you finish a major section of a lengthy essay, express your sense of what it means. If you have trouble seeing the connections between ideas, try outlining them, using as a starting point the topic sentences you've noted. When you finish an essay, do an overall summary.

To strengthen your grasp of material you'll need to remember for some time, try restating its main points a couple of days after the second reading. If anything has become hazy or slipped your mind, reread the appropriate section(s).

Strategies When Reading to Critique

In college you usually read not only to understand but also to judge. Your instructors will want to know what you think about what you've read.

Much of what written work conveys isn't always immediately apparent. Every writer makes assumptions, implies attitudes and values not directly stated, and has biases. For each major point that you encounter, ask yourself, "Why does the writer think this?" Then examine the supporting material for an answer.

Often, you'll be asked whether you agree or disagree with a piece of writing. Merely because information and ideas are in print does not mean that they are true or acceptable. An essay, for example, might include faulty logic, unreasonable ideas, suspect facts, or unreliable authorities. Don't hesitate to dispute the writer's information. Does it match your experience? Do the pieces of evidence support the claims? Do the ideas appear reasonable? Note any objections that you have. When you agree, try to suggest why, perhaps by citing additional support. A knowledge of the various reasoning fallacies can also help you critique a piece of writing. These fallacies are discussed on pages 172–75.

Does she favor androgynous men? What kind of appeal?

Amy Gross

both male and female in one

The Appeal of the Androgynous Man

Amy Gross, a native of Brooklyn, New York, earned a sociology degree at Connecticut College. Upon graduation, she entered the world of fashion publishing and has held writing or editorial positions at various magazines, including Talk, Mademoiselle, Good Housekeeping, Elle, *and* Mirabella. *She is the newly appointed editor-in-chief of* O, the Oprah Magazine. *In our selection, which first appeared in* Mademoiselle, *Gross compares androgynous men favorably to macho "all-men."*

She will give a woman's perspective. She writes for and edits women's magazines.

1   James Dean was my first androgynous man.[1] I figured I could talk to him. He was anguished and I was 12, so we had a lot in common. With only a few exceptions, all the men I have liked or loved have been a certain kind of man: a kind who doesn't play football or watch the games on Sunday, who doesn't tell dirty jokes featuring broads or chicks, who is not contemptuous of conversations that are philosophically speculative, introspective, or otherwise foolish according to the other kind of man. He is more self-amused, less inflated, more quirky, vulnerable and responsive than the other sort (the other sort, I'm visualizing as the guys on TV who advertise deodorant in the locker room). He is more like me than the other sort. He is what social scientists and feminists would call androgynous: having the characteristics of both male and female.

Seems like she is going to talk about the advantages of androgynous men as compared to other men. Sees them as better.

2   Now the first thing I want you to know about the androgynous man is that he is neither effeminate nor hermaphroditic. All his primary and secondary sexual characteristics are in order and I would say he's all-man, but that is just what he is not. He is more than all-man. *both male and female sex organs*

Attempt to counter stereotype? Can't androgynous men also be effeminate?

3   The merely all-man man, for one thing, never walks to the grocery store unless the little woman is away visiting her mother with the kids, or is in the hospital having a kid, or there is no little woman. All-men men don't know how to shop in a grocery store unless it is to buy a 6-pack and some pretzels. Their ideas of nutrition expand beyond a 6-pack and pretzels only to take in steak, potatoes, scotch or rye whiskey, and maybe a wad of cake or apple pie. All-men men have absolutely no taste in food, art, books, movies, theatre, dance, how to live, what are good questions, what is funny, or anything else I care about. It's not exactly that the all-man's man is an uncouth illiterate. He may be educated, well-mannered, and on a first-name basis with fine wines. One all-man man I knew was a handsome individual who gave the impression of being gentle, affectionate, and sensitive. He sat and ate dinner one night while I was doing something endearingly feminine at the sink. At one point, he mutely held up his glass to indicate in a primitive, even ape-like, way his need for a refill. This was in 1967, before Women's Liberation. Even so, I was disturbed. Not enough to break the glass over his handsome head, not even enough to mutely indicate the whereabouts of the refrigerator, but enough to remember that moment in all its revelatory clarity. No androgynous man

Suggests "All-men" men reject behaviors and interests they consider feminine, but isn't she stereotyping? Are all these men like this? She seems to be exaggerating.

---

[1]James Dean (1931–1955) was a 1950s film star who gained fame for his portrayals of restless, defiant young men.

would ever brutishly expect to be waited on without even a "please." (With a "please," maybe.)

The brute happened to be a doctor—not a hard hat—and, to all appearances, couth. But he had bought the whole superman package, complete with that fragile beast, the male ego. The androgynous man arrives with a male ego too, but his is not as imperialistic. It doesn't invade every area of his life and person. Most activities and thoughts have nothing to do with masculinity or femininity. The androgynous man knows this. The all-man man doesn't. He must keep a constant guard against anything even vaguely feminine (i.e., "sissy") rising up in him. It must be a terrible strain.   4

Male chauvinism is an irritation, but the real problem I have with the all-man man is that it's hard for me to talk to him. He's alien to me, and for this I'm at least half to blame. As his interests have not carried him into the sissy, mine have never taken me very far into the typically masculine terrains of sports, business and finance, politics, cars, boats and machines. But blame or no blame, the reality is that it is almost as difficult for me to connect with him as it would be to link up with an Arab shepherd or Bolivian sandalmaker. There's a similar culture gap.   5

It seems to me that the most masculine men usually end up with the most feminine women. Maybe they like extreme polarity. I like polarity myself, but the poles have to be within earshot. As I've implied, I'm very big on talking. I fall in love for at least three hours with anyone who engages me in a real conversation. I'd rather a man point out a paragraph in a book—wanting to share it with me—than bring me flowers. I'd rather a man ask what I think than tell me I look pretty. (Women who are very pretty and accustomed to hearing that they are pretty may feel differently.) My experience is that all-men men read books I don't want to see paragraphs of, and don't really give a damn what I or any woman would think about most issues so long as she looks pretty. They have a very limited use for women. I suspect they don't really like us. The androgynous man likes women as much or as little as he likes anyone.   6

Another difference between the all-man man and the androgynous man is that the first is not a star in the creativity department. If your image of the creative male accessorizes him with a beret, smock and artist's palette, you will not believe the all-man man has been seriously short-changed. But if you allow as how creativity is a talent for freedom, associated with imagination, wit, empathy, unpredictability, and receptivity to new impressions and connections, then you will certainly pity the dull, thick-skinned, rigid fellow in whom creativity sets no fires.   7

Nor is the all-man man so hot when it comes to sensitivity. He may be true-blue in the trenches, but if you are troubled, you'd be wasting your time trying to milk comfort from the all-man man.   8

This is not blind prejudice. It is enlightened prejudice. My biases were confirmed recently by a psychologist named Sandra Lipsetz Bem, a professor at Stanford University. She brought to attention the fact that high masculinity in males (and high femininity in females) has been "consistently correlated with lower overall intelligence and lower creativity." Another psychologist, Donald W. MacKinnon, director of the Institute of Personality Assessment and Research at the University of California in Berkeley, found that "creative males give more expression to the feminine side of their nature than do less creative men. . . . [They] score relatively high on femininity, and this despite the fact that, as a group, they do not present an effeminate appearance or give evidence of increased homosexual interests or experiences. Their elevated scores on femininity indicate rather an openness to their feelings and emotions, a   9 sensitive intellect and understanding self-awareness and wide-ranging interests including many which in the American culture are thought of as more feminine. . . ."

10   Dr. Bem ran a series of experiments on college students who had been categorized as masculine, feminine, or androgynous. In three tests of the degree of nurturance—warmth and caring—the masculine men scored painfully low (painfully for anyone stuck with a masculine man, that is). In one of those experiments, all the students were asked to listen to a "troubled talker"—a person who was not neurotic but simply lonely, supposedly new in town and feeling like an outsider. The masculine men were the least supportive, responsive or humane. "They lacked the ability to express warmth, playfulness and concern," Bem concluded. (She's giving them the benefit of the doubt. It's possible the masculine men didn't express those qualities because they didn't possess them.)

11   The androgynous man, on the other hand, having been run through the same carnival of tests, "performs spectacularly. He shuns no behavior just because our culture happens to label it as female and his competence crosses both the instrumental [getting the job done, the problem solved] and the expressive [showing a concern for the welfare of others, the harmony of the group] domains. Thus, he stands firm in his opinion, he cuddles kittens and bounces babies and he has a sympathetic ear for someone in distress."

12   Well, a great mind, a sensitive and warm personality are fine in their place, but you are perhaps skeptical of the gut appeal of the androgynous man. As a friend, maybe, you'd like an androgynous man. For a sexual partner, though, you'd prefer a jock. There's no arguing chemistry, but consider the jock for a moment. He competes on the field, whatever his field is, and bed is just one more field to him: another opportunity to perform, another fray. Sensuality is for him candy to be doled out as lure. It is a ration whose flow is cut off at the exact point when it has served its purpose—namely, to elicit your willingness to work out on the field with him.

13   Highly masculine men need to believe their sexual appetite is far greater than a woman's (than a nice woman's). To them, females must be seduced: Seduction is a euphemism for a power play, a con job. It pits man against woman (or woman against man). The jock believes he must win you over, incite your body to rebel against your better judgment: in other words—conquer you.

14   The androgynous man is not your opponent but your teammate. He does not seduce: he invites. Sensuality is a pleasure for him. He's not quite so goal-oriented. And to conclude, I think I need only remind you here of his greater imagination, his wit and empathy, his unpredictability, and his receptivity to new impressions and connections.

■ Reading as a Writer

All of us who write can use reading as a springboard for improving our writing. You can do several things to make your reading especially useful.

As you read, the views of others, the experiences they relate, and the information they present often deepen your understanding of yourself, your relationships, and your surroundings. In turn, this broadened perspective can supply you with writing ideas. When possibilities surface, be sure to record them. Some writers keep a reading journal in which they summarize what they've read and jot down writing ideas that come to mind. In addition, you can take down specific ideas, facts, and perhaps even a few particularly telling quotations that you discover. You may want to incorporate this material into your own writing at a later time. Carefully record the source so that you can document it properly in order to avoid plagiarism (see pages 400–02).

When you read various sources that explore the same topic or related topics, you may notice connections among their ideas. Since these connections can be fertile ground for a paper of your own, don't neglect to record them. Once you have jotted down these ideas, circle and label related thoughts. You can also draw a line linking the different thoughts to one another and to the main point that relates them. Express as a thesis statement your view of how these ideas fit together. Interacting with various sources and using their ideas to advance the purpose of your writing is a form of synthesis (see pages 72–73). When you proceed in this fashion, as in writing any paper, review your information, determine the points you want to make, and experiment until you find the order that works best. As you write, use the material from your sources as you would any support; be careful, however, to credit the authors properly in order to avoid plagiarism.

Let's see how you might use synthesis in writing an actual essay. Suppose, for example, you've read Amy Gross's "The Appeal of the Androgynous Man" (pages 430–32), Martin Gottfried's "Rambos of the Road" (pages 478–80), and Ellen Goodman's "The Company Man" (pages 486–87). You've noticed several connections among these essays. Gross describes "all-man" men who are insensitive in their treatment of women; Gottfried shows how some men need to assert their masculinity by driving aggressively; and Goodman characterizes a man who works himself to death. You might start your essay with Gross's definition of the "all-man" male and then cite some of her examples along with some of your own that identify how such a man would act. Next, you could stress that this particular concept of masculinity includes aggressiveness, then develop this point by using some illustrations from Gottfried's essay and from your own experience. Finally, you might conclude that being enslaved by such a narrow masculine role can have serious consequences and then support your view with material from Goodman's essay and from your own observations. All of these ideas and examples could help you build an essay that points out how men can sometimes become desensitized or trapped, even victimized, by living according to stereotypes of masculinity. If you will be writing a paper that synthesizes material from various sources, review pages 376–90 and 391–97 on how to document your sources properly.

Because writers solve problems, you'll want to pay attention to the techniques and strategies that other writers use. If you find an introduction, an organizational pattern, a transition, a certain description or comparison unusually engaging, study the writer's technique. Perhaps you can use it yourself. Similarly, observe when a piece of writing fails and try to determine why.

Narration

James Alexander Thom

The Perfect Picture[1]

James Alexander Thom (born 1933) is a native of Gosport, Indiana, where his parents were physicians, and a graduate of Butler University. Before becoming a free-lance writer in 1973, he worked as an editor for the Indianapolis Star *and the* Saturday Evening Post *and as a lecturer at Indiana University. He has authored one volume of essays and several historical novels, one of which,* Panther in the Sky, *earned the Best Novel Award from the Western Writers of America. His latest novel,* The Red Heart, *appeared in 1998. He is a contributor to many magazines. "The Perfect Picture" depicts an incident and an ethical dilemma that Thom experienced as a cub reporter.*

| Introduction: notes time, locale, and cause of action; first-person point of view | 1 | It was early in the spring about 15 years ago—a day of pale sunlight and trees just beginning to bud. I was a young police reporter, driving to a scene I didn't want to see. A man, the police-dispatcher's broadcast said, had accidentally backed his pickup truck over his baby granddaughter in the driveway of the family home. It was a fatality. |

Body: paragraphs 2–12; action begins

2 As I parked among police cars and TV-news cruisers, I saw a stocky white-haired man in cotton work clothes standing near a pickup. Cameras were trained on him, and reporters were sticking microphones in his face. Looking totally bewildered, he was trying to answer their questions. Mostly he was only moving his lips, blinking and choking up.

Time signal
Key event

3 After a while the reporters gave up on him and followed the police into the small white house. I can still see in my mind's eye that devastated old man looking down at the place in the driveway where the child had been. Beside the house was a freshly spaded flower bed, and nearby a pile of dark, rich earth.

Dialogue

4 "I was just backing up there to spread that good dirt," he said to me, though I had not asked him anything. "I didn't even know she was outdoors."

---

[1]Reprinted with permission from the August 1976 *Reader's Digest.* Copyright © 1976 by The Reader's Digest Assn., Inc.

He stretched his hand toward the flower bed, then let it flop to his side. He lapsed back into his thoughts, and I, like a good reporter, went into the house to find someone who could provide a recent photo of the toddler.

A few minutes later, with all the details in my notebook and a three-by-five studio portrait of the cherubic child tucked in my jacket pocket, I went toward the kitchen where the police had said the body was.

5   Time signal
      Secondary event

I had brought a camera in with me—the big, bulky Speed Graphic which used to be the newspaper reporter's trademark. Everybody had drifted back out of the house together—family, police, reporters and photographers. Entering the kitchen, I came upon this scene:

6

On a Formica-topped table, backlighted by a frilly curtained window, lay the tiny body, wrapped in a clean white sheet. Somehow the grandfather had managed to stay away from the crowd. He was sitting on a chair beside the table, in profile to me and unaware of my presence, looking uncomprehendingly at the swaddled corpse.

7   Key event

The house was very quiet. A clock ticked. As I watched, the grandfather slowly leaned forward, curved his arms like parentheses around the head and feet of the little form, then pressed his face to the shroud and remained motionless.

8   Time signal

In that hushed moment I recognized the makings of a prize-winning news photograph. I appraised the light, adjusted the lens setting and distance, locked a bulb in the flashgun, raised the camera and composed the scene in the viewfinder.

9

Every element of the picture was perfect: the grandfather in his plain work clothes, his white hair backlighted by sunshine, the child's form wrapped in the sheet, the atmosphere of the simple home suggested by black iron trivets and World's Fair souvenir plates on the walls flanking the window. Outside, the police could be seen inspecting the fatal rear wheel of the pickup while the child's mother and father leaned in each other's arms.

10

I don't know how many seconds I stood there, unable to snap that shutter. I was keenly aware of the powerful story-telling value that photo would have, and my professional conscience told me to take it. Yet I couldn't make my hand fire that flashbulb and intrude on the poor man's island of grief.

11   Conflict

At length I lowered the camera and crept away, shaken with doubt about my suitability for the journalistic profession. Of course I never told the city editor or any fellow reporters about that missed opportunity for a perfect news picture.

12   Time signal
      Action ends

Every day on the newscasts and in the papers, we see pictures of people in extreme conditions of grief and despair. Human suffering has become a spectator sport. And sometimes, as I'm watching news film, I remember that day.

13

Conclusion: paragraphs 13 and 14; indirectly states point; notes writer's reaction

I still feel right about what I did.

14

DISCUSSION QUESTIONS

1. Thom notes in his opening paragraph that he is "driving to a scene I didn't want to see." How does this statement help explain what happens later?
2. Paragraph 10 contains numerous descriptive details. What bearing do these details have on Thom's decision?
3. Do you think that Thom made the right decision? Why or why not?

TOWARD KEY INSIGHTS

How have the media affected our sense of privacy?

Is their influence good or bad?

To answer these questions, consider the role of the newspaper photographer in "The Perfect Picture," TV crews at disasters, and talk shows built around very personal revelations.

SUGGESTION FOR WRITING	*Write a personal narrative that features a conflict over a choice between an advantageous and a morally satisfying decision. State your point directly or indirectly, and use time signals and dialogue as necessary.*

Dan Greenburg

Sound and Fury

Dan Greenburg is a native of Chicago who holds a bachelor of fine arts from the University of Illinois and a master of fine arts from UCLA. A prolific writer, he has authored over forty books, including such best sellers as How to Be a Jewish Mother, How to Make Yourself Miserable, How to Avoid Love and Marriage, *and a series of more than twenty-four children's books,* The Zack Files. *His articles have appeared in a wide and diverse range of popular magazines and been reprinted in many anthologies of humor and satire. He has been a guest on* The Today Show, Larry King Live, Late Night with David Letterman, *and other major TV talk shows. In this selection, Greenburg relates a situation in which soft words defused a potentially explosive situation.*

1   We carry around a lot of free-floating anger. What we do with it is what fascinates me.

2   My friend Lee Frank is a stand-up comedian who works regularly in New York comedy clubs. Not long ago I accompanied him to one of these places, where he was to be the late-night emcee and where I myself had once done a stand-up act in a gentler era.

3   The crowd that night was a typical weekend bunch—enthusiastic, hostile and drunk. A large contingent of inebriated young men from Long Island had decided that a comedian named Rusty who was currently on stage was the greatest thing since pop-top cans and began chanting his name after almost everything he said: "Rus-TEE! Rus-TEE!"

4   My friend Lee knew he had a tough act to follow.

5   Indeed, the moment Lee walked on stage, the inebriated young men from Long Island began chanting "Rus-TEE! Rus-TEE!" and didn't give him a chance. Poor Lee, the flop sweat running into his eyes, tried every trick he knew to win them over, and finally gave up.

6   When he left the stage I joined him at the bar in the back of the club to commiserate.

"You did the best you could," I told him.   7

"I don't know," he said, "I could have handled it better."   8

"How?"   9

"I don't know," he said.   10

As we spoke, the young men who'd given him such a tough time trickled   11
into the bar area. One of them spotted Lee and observed to a companion that
Lee might want to do something about their heckling.

Lee thought he heard the companion reply, "I'm down," a casual acknowl-   12
edgment that he was willing to have a fistfight. Lee repeated their remarks to
me and indicated that he, too, was "down."

Though slight of frame, Lee is a black belt in Tae Kwon Do, has had skir-   13
mishes with three-card monte con men in Times Square, and once even cap-
tured a robber-rapist. I am also slight of frame but have had no training in martial arts. I did have one fistfight in my adult life (with a movie producer), but as
Lee's best friend, I assumed that I was "down" as well.

Considering that there were more than a dozen of them and only two of us,   14
the period of time that might elapse between our being "down" and our being
down seemed exceedingly brief.

The young man who'd made the remark drifted toward Lee.   15

The eyes of everyone in the bar shifted slightly and locked onto the two   16
men like heat-seeking missiles. Fight-or-flight adrenaline and testosterone
spurted into dozens of male cardiovascular systems. Safeties snapped off figurative weapons. Red warning lights lit up dozens of DEFCON systems; warheads
were armed and aimed. In a moment this bar area might very well resemble a
saloon in a B grade western.

"How ya doing?" said Lee, his voice flat as unleavened bread, trying to   17
make up his mind whether to be friendly or hostile.

"Okay," said the guy, a pleasant-looking, clean-cut kid in his mid-20s.   18

I was fascinated by what was going on between the two of them, each feel-   19
ing the other out in a neutral, unemotional, slightly bemused manner. I saw no
hostility here, no xenophobic loathing, just two young males jockeying for position, going through the motions, doing the dance, willing to engage at the
slightest provocation. I had seen my cat do this many times when a stranger
strayed onto his turf.

And then I had a sudden flash of clarity: These guys could either rip each   20
other's heads off now or they could share a beer, and both options would be
equally acceptable to them.

I'd felt close to critical mass on many occasions myself. But here, feeling   21
outside the action, I could see clearly that it had to do with the enormous reservoir of rage that we men carry around with us, rage that seethes just under the
surface and is ready to be tapped in an instant, with or without just provocation.

"What're you in town for?" asked Lee casually.   22

The guy was watching Lee carefully, making minuscule adjustments on his   23
sensing and triggering equipment.

"It's my birthday," said the guy.   24

Lee mulled over this information for a moment, still considering all his op-   25
tions. Then he made his decision.

"Happy birthday," said Lee finally, sticking out his hand.   26

The guy studied Lee's hand a moment. Then, deciding the gesture was sin-   27
cere, he took the hand and shook it.

"Thanks," he said, and walked back to his buddies.   28

29   All over the room you could hear safeties snapping on, warheads being un-armed. The incident was over, and in a moment it was as if it had never happened.

30   I felt I had just witnessed in microcosm the mechanism that triggers most acts of aggression, from gang fights to international conflagrations. It was so simple: a minor act of provocation. A decision on how to interpret it. Whether or not to escalate. And, in this particular case, a peaceful outcome. What struck me was how absolutely arbitrarily it had all been decided.

DISCUSSION QUESTIONS

1. Discuss the appropriateness of Greenburg's title.
2. Does this essay have a stated or an unstated point? If it is stated, indicate where. If it is unstated, express it in your own words.
3. The expression "our being down" occurs twice in paragraph 14. Explain what it means in each instance.
4. Discuss the effectiveness of the figurative language in paragraph 16.
5. In paragraph 21 Greenburg credits "feeling outside the action" for helping him understand the rage involved in this situation as well as in others. Explain what he means.
6. How often do you think that the "equally acceptable" options mentioned in paragraph 20 occur in confrontations?

TOWARD KEY INSIGHTS

What reasons can you give for the "free-floating anger" that Greenburg mentions at the outset of the essay?

How frequently and in what ways is this anger manifested?

What are some effective strategies for coping with this anger?

SUGGESTION FOR WRITING

Write a narrative about a small incident that turned into a serious confrontation. Possible incidents might include an improper or reckless action of another driver, a minor disagreement with a friend or spouse, or a retaliation for an action at a sporting event. The outcome can be peaceful or otherwise.

Maya Angelou

Momma's Encounter[1]

Maya Angelou has earned a reputation as one of this country's foremost black writers. Born (1928) Marguerite Johnson in St. Louis, Missouri, she spent much of her childhood in Stamps, Arkansas, the locale of our selection, where her grandmother ran a general store. Angelou has written plays, poems, and a six-part autobiography that includes I Know Why the Caged Bird Sings *(1970), from which our selection is taken. She has acted in numerous plays and has served as a television narrator, interviewer, and poet. At the January 1993 inauguration of President William Clinton, she recited a poem, "On the Pulse of Morning," that she had written especially for the occasion. In our selection, Angelou tells about an encounter in which her grandmother, whom she calls Momma, triumphs over a pack of taunting neighborhood children.*

1 "Thou shall not be dirty" and "Thou shall not be impudent" were the two commandments of Grandmother Henderson upon which hung our total salvation.

2 Each night in the bitterest winter we were forced to wash faces, arms, necks, legs and feet before going to bed. She used to add, with a smirk that unprofane people can't control when venturing into profanity, "and wash as far as possible, then wash possible."

3 We would go to the well and wash in the ice-cold, clear water, grease our legs with the equally cold stiff Vaseline, then tiptoe into the house. We wiped the dust from our toes and settled down for schoolwork, cornbread, clabbered milk, prayers and bed, always in that order. Momma was famous for pulling the quilts off after we had fallen asleep to examine our feet. If they weren't clean enough for her, she took the switch (she kept one behind the bedroom door for emergencies) and woke up the offender with a few aptly placed burning reminders.

4 The area around the well at night was dark and slick, and boys told about how snakes love water, so that anyone who had to draw water at night and then stand there alone and wash knew that moccasins and rattlers, puff adders and boa constrictors were winding their way to the well and would arrive just as the person washing got soap in her eyes. But Momma convinced us that not only was cleanliness next to Godliness, dirtiness was the inventor of misery.

5 The impudent child was detested by God and a shame to its parents and could bring destruction to its house and line. All adults had to be addressed as Mister, Missus, Miss, Auntie, Cousin, Unk, Uncle, Buhbah, Sister, Brother and a thousand other appellations indicating familial relationship and the lowliness of the addressor.

6 Everyone I knew respected these customary laws, except for the powhite-trash children.

[1]Editors' title.

7   Some families of powhitetrash lived on Momma's farm land behind the school. Sometimes a gaggle of them came to the Store, filling the whole room, chasing out the air and even changing the well-known scents. The children crawled over the shelves and into the potato and onion bins, twanging all the time in their sharp voices like cigarbox guitars. They took liberties in my Store that I would never dare. Since Momma told us that the less you say to whitefolks (or even powhitetrash) the better, Bailey and I would stand, solemn, quiet, in the displaced air. But if one of the playful apparitions got close to us, I pinched it. Partly out of angry frustration and partly because I didn't believe in its flesh reality.

8   They called my uncle by his first name and ordered him around the Store. He, to my crying shame, obeyed them in his limping dip-straight-dip fashion.

9   My grandmother, too followed their orders, except that she didn't seem to be servile because she anticipated their needs.

10   "Here's sugar, Miz Potter, and here's baking powder. You didn't buy soda last month, you'll probably be needing some."

11   Momma always directed her statements to the adults, but sometimes, Oh painful sometimes, the grimy, snotty-nosed girls would answer her.

12   "Naw, Annie . . ."—to Momma? Who owned the land they lived on? Who forgot more than they would ever learn? If there was any justice in the world, God should strike them dumb at once!—"Just give us some extry sody crackers, and some more mackerel."

13   At least they never looked in her face, or I never caught them doing so. Nobody with a smidgen of training, not even the worst roustabout, would look right in a grown person's face. It meant the person was trying to take the words out before they were formed. The dirty little children didn't do that, but they threw their orders around the Store like lashes from a cat-o'-nine tails.

14   When I was around ten years old, those scruffy children caused me the most painful and confusing experience I had ever had with my grandmother.

15   One summer morning, after I had swept the dirt yard of leaves, spearmint-gum wrappers and Vienna-sausage labels, I raked the yellow-red dirt, and made half-moons carefully, so that the design stood out clearly and mask-like. I put the rake behind the Store and came through the back of the house to find Grandmother on the front porch in her big, wide white apron. The apron was so stiff by virtue of the starch that it could have stood alone. Momma was admiring the yard, so I joined her. It truly looked like a flat redhead that had been raked with a big-toothed comb. Momma didn't say anything but I knew she liked it. She looked over toward the school principal's house and to the right at Mr. McElroy's. She was hoping one of those community pillars would see the design before the day's business wiped it out. Then she looked upward to the school. My head had swung with hers, so at just about the same time we saw a troop of the powhitetrash kids marching over the hill and down by the side of the school.

16   I looked to Momma for direction. She did an excellent job of sagging from her waist down, but from the waist up she seemed to be pulling for the top of the oak tree across the road. Then she began to moan a hymn. Maybe not to moan, but the tune was so slow and the meter so strange that she could have been moaning. She didn't look at me again. When the children reached halfway down the hill, halfway to the Store, she said without turning, "Sister, go on inside."

17   I wanted to beg her, "Momma, don't wait for them. Come on inside with me. If they come in the Store, you go to the bedroom and let me wait on them. They only frighten me if you're around. Alone I know how to handle them." But of course I couldn't say anything, so I went in and stood behind the screen door.

Before the girls got to the porch I heard their laughter crackling and pop- 18
ping like pine logs in a cooking stove. I suppose my lifelong paranoia was born
in those cold, molasses-slow minutes. They came finally to stand on the ground
in front of Momma. At first they pretended seriousness. Then one of them
wrapped her right arm in the crook of her left, pushed out her mouth and
started to hum. I realized that she was aping my grandmother. Another said,
"Naw, Helen, you ain't standing like her. This here's it." Then she lifted her
chest, folded her arms and mocked that strange carriage that was Annie Henderson. Another laughed, "Naw, you can't do it. You mouth ain't pooched out
enough. It's like this."

I thought about the rifle behind the door, but I knew I'd never be able to 19
hold it straight, and the .410, our sawed-off shotgun, which stayed loaded and
was fired every New Year's night, was locked in the trunk and Uncle Willie had
the key on his chain. Through the fly-specked screen-door, I could see that the
arms of Momma's apron jiggled from the vibrations of her humming. But her
knees seemed to have locked as if they would never bend again.

She sang on. No louder than before, but no softer either. No slower or 20
faster.

The dirt of the girls' cotton dresses continued on their legs, feet, arms and 21
faces to make them all of a piece. Their greasy uncolored hair hung down, uncombed, with a grim finality. I knelt to see them better, to remember them for
all time. The tears that had slipped down my dress left unsurprising dark spots,
and made the front yard blurry and even more unreal. The world had taken a
deep breath and was having doubts about continuing to revolve.

The girls had tired of mocking Momma and turned to other means of agi- 22
tation. One crossed her eyes, stuck her thumbs in both sides of her mouth and
said, "Look here, Annie." Grandmother hummed on and the apron strings
trembled. I wanted to throw a handful of black pepper in their faces, to throw
lye on them, to scream that they were dirty, scummy peckerwoods, but I knew I
was as clearly imprisoned behind the scene as the actors outside were confined
to their roles.

One of the smaller girls did a kind of puppet dance while her fellow clowns 23
laughed at her. But the tall one, who was almost a woman, said something very
quietly, which I couldn't hear. They all moved backward from the porch, still
watching Momma. For an awful second I thought they were going to throw a
rock at Momma, who seemed (except for the apron strings) to have turned into
stone herself. But the big girl turned her back, bent down and put her hands
flat on the ground—she didn't pick up anything. She simply shifted her weight
and did a hand stand.

Her dirty bare feet and long legs went straight for the sky. Her dress fell 24
down around her shoulders, and she had on no drawers. The slick pubic hair
made a brown triangle where her legs came together. She hung in the vacuum
of that lifeless morning for only a few seconds, then wavered and tumbled. The
other girls clapped her on the back and slapped their hands.

Momma changed her song to "Bread of Heaven, bread of Heaven, feed me 25
till I want no more."

I found that I was praying too. How long could Momma hold out? What 26
new indignity would they think of to subject her to? Would I be able to stay out
of it? What would Momma really like me to do?

Then they were moving out of the yard, on their way to town. They bobbed 27
their heads and shook their slack behinds and turned, one at a time:

"'Bye, Annie." 28

29   "'Bye, Annie."

30   "'Bye, Annie."

31   Momma never turned her head or unfolded her arms, but she stopped singing and said, "'Bye, Miz Helen, 'bye, Miz Ruth, 'bye, Miz Eloise."

32   I burst. A firecracker July-the-Fourth burst. How could Momma call them Miz? The mean nasty things. Why couldn't she have come inside the sweet, cool store when we saw them breasting the hill? What did she prove? And then if they were dirty, mean and impudent, why did Momma have to call them Miz?

33   She stood another whole song through and then opened the screen door to look down on me crying in rage. She looked until I looked up. Her face was a brown moon that shone on me. She was beautiful. Something had happened out there, which I couldn't completely understand, but I could see that she was happy. Then she bent down and touched me as mothers of the church "lay hands on the sick and afflicted" and I quieted.

34   "Go wash your face, Sister." And she went behind the candy counter and hummed, "Glory, glory, hallelujah, when I lay my burden down."

35   I threw the well water on my face and used the weekday handkerchief to blow my nose. Whatever the contest had been out front, I knew Momma had won.

36   I took the rake back to the front yard. The smudged footprints were easy to erase. I worked for a long time on my new design and laid the rake behind the wash pot. When I came back in the Store, I took Momma's hand and we both walked outside to look at the pattern.

37   It was a large heart with lots of hearts growing smaller inside, and piercing from the outside rim to the smallest heart was an arrow. Momma said, "Sister, that's right pretty." Then she turned back to the Store and resumed, "Glory, glory, hallelujah, when I lay my burden down."

DISCUSSION QUESTIONS

1. Does this narrative have a stated or an unstated point? If it is stated, indicate where. If it is unstated, express it in your own words.

2. Point out the contrast between Angelou's upbringing and that of the "powhite-trash" children. How does this contrast prepare the reader for the events that follow?

3. Explain what Angelou means in paragraph 22 when she says ". . . but I knew I was as clearly imprisoned behind the scene as the actors outside were confined to their roles."

4. Discuss the significance of the dialogue in paragraphs 28–31.

5. Suggest the significance of the pattern of hearts that Angelou draws in the front yard. Of Momma singing "Glory, glory, hallelujah, when I lay my burden down."

6. Angelou recalls that she was "around ten years old" when the encounter took place. Explain why her age was significant. How would her perception have differed had she been, say, eighteen?

7. Angelou uses the first-person point of view. Explain why third-person narration would have been inappropriate for this narrative.

TOWARD KEY INSIGHTS

Was Momma's strategy for enduring the children's taunts the most effective approach? Why or why not?

What else could she have done?

Has she really won?

Some argue that racism should always be actively confronted since passive endurance only perpetuates it. Do you agree? If not, when and how should racism be confronted and when should it be endured?

SUGGESTION FOR WRITING   *Write a narrative that illustrates how a friend, an acquaintance, or a family member achieved a personal triumph through turning the other cheek.*

Lewis Sawaquat

For My Indian Daughter

Lewis Sawaquat (born 1935), a Native American who numbers an Indian chief among his ancestors, is an active participant in the affairs of his tribe and in securing scholarships for Native American students. While serving in the U.S. Army, he completed a program in surveying and then spent the remainder of his enlistment in Korea. Later, he attended the Art Institute of Chicago. He is now a retired U.S. government surveyor. In "For My Indian Daughter," Sawaquat addresses anti-Indian prejudice and the development of his sense of "what it means to be Indian."

My little girl is singing herself to sleep upstairs, her voice mingling with the sounds of the birds outside in the old maple trees. She is two and I am nearly 50, and I am very taken with her. She came along late in my life, unexpected and unbidden, a startling gift.   1

Today at the beach my chubby-legged, brown-skinned daughter ran laughing into the water as fast as she could. My wife and I laughed watching her, until we heard behind us a low guttural curse and then an unpleasant voice raised in an imitation war whoop.   2

I turned to see a fat man in a bathing suit, white and soft as a grub, as he covered his mouth and prepared to make the Indian war cry again. He was middle-aged, younger than I, and had three little children lined up next to him, grinning foolishly. My wife suggested we leave the beach, and I agreed.   3

I knew the man was not unusual in his feelings against Indians. His beach behavior might have been socially unacceptable to more civilized whites, but his basic view of Indians is expressed daily in our small town, frequently on the editorial pages of the county newspaper, as white people speak out against Indian fishing rights and land rights, saying in essence, "Those Indians are taking our fish, our land." It doesn't matter to them that we were here first, that the U.S. Supreme Court has ruled in our favor. It matters to them that we have something they want, and they hate us for it. Backlash is the common explanation of   4 the attacks on Indians, the bumper stickers that say, "Spear an Indian, Save a Fish," but I know better. The hatred of Indians goes back to the beginning when white people came to this country. For me it goes back to my childhood in Harbor Springs, Mich.

5   **Theft:** Harbor Springs is now a summer resort for the very affluent, but a hundred years ago it was the Indian village of my Ottawa ancestors. My grandmother, Anna Showanessy, and other Indians like her, had their land there taken by treaty, by fraud, by violence, by theft. They remembered how whites had burned down the village at Burt Lake in 1900 and pushed the Indians out. These were the stories in my family.

6   When I was a boy my mother told me to walk down the alleys in Harbor Springs and not to wear my orange football sweater out of the house. This way I would not stand out, not be noticed, and not be a target.

7   I wore my orange sweater anyway and deliberately avoided the alleys. I was the biggest person I knew and wasn't really afraid. But I met my comeuppance when I enlisted in the U.S. Army. One night all the men in my barracks gathered together and, gang-fashion, pulled me into the shower and scrubbed me down with rough brushes used for floors, saying, "We won't have any dirty Indians in our outfit." It is a point of irony that I was cleaner than any of them. Later in Korea I learned how to kill, how to bully, how to hate Koreans. I came out of the war tougher than ever and, strangely, white.

8   I went to college, got married, lived in La Porte, Ind., worked as a surveyor and raised three boys. I headed Boy Scout groups, never thinking it odd when the Scouts did imitation Indian dances, imitation Indian lore.

9   One day when I was 35 or thereabouts I heard about an Indian powwow. My father used to attend them and so with great curiosity and a strange joy at discovering a part of my heritage, I decided the thing to do to get ready for this big event was to have my friend make me a spear in his forge. The steel was fine and blue and iridescent. The feathers on the shaft were bright and proud.

10   In a dusty state fairground in southern Indiana, I found white people dressed as Indians. I learned they were "hobbyists," that is, it was their hobby and leisure pastime to masquerade as Indians on weekends. I felt ridiculous with my spear, and I left.

11   It was years before I could tell anyone of the embarrassment of this weekend and see any humor in it. But in a way it was that weekend, for all its silliness, that was my awakening. I realized I didn't know who I was. I didn't have an Indian name. I didn't speak the Indian language. I didn't know the Indian customs. Dimly I remembered the Ottawa word for dog, but it was a baby word, *kahgee*, not the full word, *muhkahgee*, which I was later to learn. Even more hazily I remembered a naming ceremony (my own). I remembered legs dancing around me, dust. Where had that been? Who had I been? "Suwaukquat," my mother told me when I asked, "where the tree begins to grow."

12   That was 1968, and I was not the only Indian in the country who was feeling the need to remember who he or she was. There were others. They had powwows, real ones, and eventually I found them. Together we researched our past, a search that for me culminated in the Longest Walk, a march on Washington in 1978. Maybe because I now know what it means to be Indian, it surprises me that others don't. Of course there aren't very many of us left. The chances of an average person knowing an average Indian in an average lifetime are pretty slim.

Circle: Still, I was amused one day when my small, four-year-old neighbor 13 looked at me as I was hoeing in my garden and said, "You aren't a real Indian, are you?" Scotty is little, talkative, likable. Finally I said, "I'm a real Indian." He looked at me for a moment and then said, squinting into the sun, "Then where's your horse and feathers?" The child was simply a smaller, whiter version of my own ignorant self years before. We'd both seen too much TV, that's all. He was not to be blamed. And so, in a way, the moronic man on the beach today is blameless. We come full circle to realize other people are like ourselves, as discomfiting as that may be sometimes.

As I sit in my old chair on my porch, in a light that is fading so the leaves 14 are barely distinguishable against the sky, I can picture my girl asleep upstairs. I would like to prepare her for what's to come, take her each step of the way saying, there's a place to avoid, here's what I know about this, but much of what's before her she must go through alone. She must pass through pain and joy and solitude and community to discover her own inner self that is unlike any other and come through that passage to the place where she sees all people are one, and in so seeing may live her life in a brighter future.

DISCUSSION QUESTIONS

1. After reflecting on the entire essay, try to account for Sawaquat's choice of title.
2. Why, according to Sawaquat, are so many whites prejudiced against Indians?
3. The man who ridicules Sawaquat's daughter is described in paragraph 3 as being "white and soft as a grub." What does this description reveal about Sawaquat's attitude toward him?
4. Why was the "powwow" that Sawaquat discusses in paragraphs 9–10 an important event in his life?
5. What is accomplished by the repetition of "I didn't" in four consecutive sentences of paragraph 11?
6. Discuss the significance of the dialogue in paragraph 13.
7. Reflecting on his daughter's future, Sawaquat says in paragraph 14 that "much of what's before her she must go through alone." Explain what he means.

TOWARD KEY INSIGHTS

Many Native Americans say that they maintain their Indian identity only in their community—for example, by belonging to a tribe. With that in mind, is Sawaquat correct when he asserts that solving the Indian identity problem lies in discovering an "inner self that is unlike any other" and in seeing that "all people are one"? Why or why not?

SUGGESTION FOR WRITING

Write a narrative that relates an instance when you experienced some form of prejudice and how you coped with it. Your thesis may be stated or unstated.

Description

John V. Young

When the Full Moon Shines Its Magic over Monument Valley

John V. Young (1909–1999) was born in Oakland, California. After attending San Jose State Teachers College, he spent twelve years as a reporter and editor for several rural California newspapers, then held a series of personnel and public relations positions. In 1966, he became a full-time freelance writer, specializing in western travel pieces. His books include The Grand Canyon *(1969),* Ghost Towns of the Santa Cruz Mountains *(1979, 1984),* Hot Type and Pony Wire *(1980),* State Parks of New Mexico *(1984),* State Parks of Arizona *(1986), and* State Parks of Utah *(1989). His articles have appeared in the* New York Times *as well as in numerous travel publications. In the article that follows, he focuses on the sensations generated first by his surroundings and then by the moonrise.*

Title identifies dominant impression: magic

Introduction: paragraphs 1 and 2; identifies when, where, who, why. Touch impression

---

Sight impression
Comparisons

Body: paragraphs 3–8
Fixed vantage point
Sight impressions

Time signal

Sight impressions

Sound impressions

1   We were camped here in early spring, by one of those open-faced shelters that the Navajos have provided for tourists in this part of their vast tribal park on the Arizona–Utah border, 25 miles north of Kayenta. It was cool but pleasant, and we were alone, three men in a truck.

2   We were here for a purpose; to see the full moon rise over this most mysterious and lonely of scenic wonders, where fantastically eroded red and yellow sandstone shapes soar to the sky like a giant's chess pieces and where people—especially white strangers—come quickly to feel like pretty small change indeed.

3   Because all Navajo dwellings face east, our camp faced east—toward the rising sun and the rising moon and across a limitless expanse of tawny desert, that ancient sea, framed by the towering nearby twin pinnacles called The Mittens. We began to feel the magic even before the sun was fully down. It occurred when a diminutive wraith of a Navajo girl wearing a long, dark, velvet dress gleaming with silver ornaments drifted silently by, herding a flock of ghostly sheep to a waterhole somewhere. A bell on one of the rams tinkled faintly, and then its music was lost in the soft rustle of the night wind, leaving us with an impression that perhaps we had really seen nothing at all.

Just then, a large woolly dog appeared out of the gloom, seeming to materialize on the spot. It sat quietly on the edge of the glow from our campfire, its eyes shining like mirrors. It made no sound but when we offered food, it accepted the gift gravely and with much dignity. The dog then vanished again, probably to join the girl and her flock. We were not certain it was not part of the illusion.

4	Time signal Sight impression Comparison

As the sun disappeared entirely, the evening afterglow brush tipped all the spires and cliffs with magenta, deepening to purple, and the sand ripples stood out like miniature ocean waves in darkening shades of orange. Off to the east on the edge of the desert, a pale saffron glow told us the moon was about to rise behind a thin layer of clouds, slashed by the white contrail of an invisible jet airplane miles away.

5	Time signal Sight impressions Comparison Sight impressions

We had our cameras on tripods and were fussing with light meters, making casual bets as to the exact place where the moon would first appear, when it happened—instant enchantment. Precisely between the twin spires of The Mittens, the enormous globe loomed suddenly, seeming as big as the sun itself, behind a coppery curtain on the rim of creation.

6	Sight impressions Comparison Vivid language

We were as totally unprepared for the great size of the moon as we were for its flaming color, nor could we have prepared ourselves for the improbable setting. We felt like the wizards of Stonehenge, commanding the planets to send their light through the magic orifices in line at the equinox. Had the Navajo medicine men contrived this for our benefit?

7	Sight impressions
	Comparison

The massive disk of the moon seemed to rise very fast at first, an optical effect magnified by the crystalline air and the flatness of the landscape between us and the distant, ragged skyline. Then it seemed to pause for a moment, as if it were pinioned on one of the pinnacles or impaled on a sharply upthrusting rocky point. Its blazing light made inky shadows all around us, split by the brilliant wedge of the moon's path between the spires. The wind had stopped. There was not a sound anywhere, nor even a whisper. If a drum had sounded just then, it would not have been out of place, I suppose, but it would have frightened us half to death.

8	Sight impressions
	Vivid language
	Absent sound Impression

Before the moon had cleared the tops of The Mittens, the show was over and the magic was gone. A thin veil of clouds spread over the sky, ending the spell as suddenly as it had come upon us. It was as if the gods had decided that we had seen enough for mere mortals on one spring night, and I must confess it was something of a relief to find ourselves back on mundane earth again, with sand in our shoes and a chill in the air.

9	Conclusion: time signal; renames dominant impression
	Notes writer's reaction
	Touch impression

Discussion Questions

1. How does the last sentence in paragraph 7 ("Had the Navajo medicine men contrived this for our benefit?") relate to the purpose of the essay?
2. This description takes the form of a narrative. Where does the climax occur, and how does it affect the viewers?

Toward Key Insights

What makes certain experiences seem magical?
How important are such magical experiences, and how might they shape our perceptions of the everyday world?

| **SUGGESTION FOR WRITING** | *Select a place you know well and describe it by conveying some dominant impression that emerges during daylight hours. Settle on an appropriate vantage point and either identify the impression or allow readers to determine it for themselves.* |

Annie Dillard

In the Jungle

Annie Dillard was born in Pittsburgh (1945) and received her education at Hollins College in Virginia. For twelve years she lived in the Roanoke Valley of Virginia, where she investigated and wrote about the world of nature. Dillard's first prose book, Pilgrim at Tinker Creek *(1974), was compared favorably with Thoreau's* Walden *and won her the 1975 Pulitzer Prize. She has also written many other fiction and nonfiction books, including* Teaching a Stone to Talk, *from which our selection is taken. Her latest work,* A Short Guide to a Happy Life, *appeared in 1999. Her shorter pieces have appeared in upscale magazines such as* Harper's, The Yale Review, *and many anthologies. She has received numerous fellowship grants and awards. In our selection, Dillard shares her feelings about one of nature's most unspoiled places, the Ecuadorian jungle.*

1   Like any out-of-the-way place, the Napo River in the Ecuadorian jungle seems real enough when you are there, even central. Out of the way of *what?* I was sitting on a stump at the edge of a bankside palm-thatch village, in the middle of the night, on the headwaters of the Amazon. Out of the way of human life, tenderness, or the glance of heaven?

2   A nightjar in deep-leaved shadow called three long notes, and hushed. The men with me talked softly in clumps: three North Americans, four Ecuadorians who were showing us the jungle. We were holding cool drinks and idly watching a hand-sized tarantula seize moths that came to the lone bulb on the generator shed beside us.

3   It was February, the middle of summer. Green fireflies spattered lights across the air and illumined for seconds, now here, now there, the pale trunks of enormous, solitary trees. Beneath us the brown Napo River was rising, in all silence; it coiled up the sandy bank and tangled its foam in vines that trailed from the forest and roots that looped the shore.

4   Each breath of night smelled sweet, more moistened and sweet than any kitchen, or garden, or cradle. Each star in Orion seemed to tremble and stir with my breath. All at once, in the thatch house across the clearing behind us, one of the village's Jesuit priests began playing an alto recorder, playing a wordless song, lyric, in a minor key, that twined over the village clearing, that caught in the big trees' canopies, muted our talk on the bankside, and wandered over the river, dissolving downstream.

This will do, I thought. This will do, for a weekend, or a season, or a home.   5

Later that night I loosed my hair from its braids and combed it smooth—   6
not for myself, but so the village girls could play with it in the morning.

We had disembarked at the village that afternoon, and I had slumped on   7
some shaded steps, wishing I knew some Spanish or some Quechua so I could
speak with the ring of little girls who were alternately staring at me and smiling
at their toes. I spoke anyway, and fooled with my hair, which they were obviously
dying to get their hands on, and laughed, and soon they were all braiding my
hair, all five of them, all fifty fingers, all my hair, even my bangs. And then they
took it apart and did it again, laughing, and teaching me Spanish nouns, and
meeting my eyes and each other's with open delight, while their small brothers
in blue jeans climbed down from the trees and began kicking a volleyball
around with one of the North American men.

Now, as I combed my hair in the little tent, another of the men, a free-lance   8
writer from Manhattan, was talking quietly. He was telling us the tale of his life,
describing his work in Hollywood, his apartment in Manhattan, his house in
Paris. . . . "It makes me wonder," he said, "what I'm doing in a tent under a
tree in the village of Pompeya, on the Napo River, in the jungle of Ecuador."
After a pause he added, "It makes me wonder why I'm going *back*."

The point of going somewhere like the Napo River in Ecuador is not to see   9
the most spectacular anything. It is simply to see what is there. We are here on
the planet only once, and might as well get a feel for the place. We might as well
get a feel for the fringes and hollows in which life is lived, for the Amazon basin,
which covers half a continent, and for the life that—there, like anywhere else—
is always and necessarily lived in detail: on the tributaries, in the riverside villages, sucking this particular white-fleshed guava in this particular pattern of
shade.

What is there is interesting. The Napo River itself is wide (I mean wider   10
than the Mississippi at Davenport) and brown, opaque, and smeared with floating foam and logs and branches from the jungle. White egrets hunch on shoreline deadfalls and parrots in flocks dart in and out of the light. Under the water
in the river, unseen, are anacondas—which are reputed to take a few village toddlers every year—and water boas, stingrays, crocodiles, manatees, and sweet-
meated fish.

Low water bares gray strips of sandbar on which the natives build tiny palm-   11
thatch shelters, arched, the size of pup tents, for overnight fishing trips. You see
these extraordinarily clean people (who bathe twice a day in the river, and
whose straight black hair is always freshly washed) paddling down the river in
dugout canoes, hugging the banks.

Some of the Indians of this region, earlier in the century, used to sleep   12
naked in hammocks. The nights are cold. Gordon MacCreach, an American explorer in these Amazon tributaries, reported that he was startled to hear the Indians get up at three in the morning. He was even more startled, night after
night, to hear them walk down to the river slowly, half asleep, and bathe in the
water. Only later did he learn what they were doing: they were getting warm.
The cold woke them; they warmed their skins in the river, which was always
ninety degrees; then they returned to their hammocks and slept through the
rest of the night.

13   The riverbanks are low, and from the river you see an unbroken wall of dark forest in every direction, from the Andes to the Atlantic. You get a taste for looking at trees: trees hung with the swinging nests of yellow troupials, trees from which ant nests the size of grain sacks hang like black goiters, trees from which seven-colored tanagers flutter, coral trees, teak, balsa and breadfruit, enormous emergent silk-cotton trees, and the pale-barked *samona* palms.

14   When you are inside the jungle, away from the river, the trees vault out of sight. It is hard to remember to look up the long trunks and see the fans, strips, fronds, and sprays of glossy leaves. Inside the jungle you are more likely to notice the snarl of climbers and creepers round the trees' boles, the flowering bromeliads and epiphytes in every bough's crook, and the fantastic silk-cotton tree trunks thirty or forty feet across, trunks buttressed in flanges of wood whose curves can make three high walls of a room—a shady, loamy-aired room where you would gladly live, or die. Butterflies, iridescent blue, striped, or clear-winged, thread the jungle paths at eye level. And at your feet is a swath of ants bearing triangular bits of green leaf. The ants with their leaves look like a wide fleet of sailing dinghies—but they don't quit. In either direction they wobble over the jungle floor as far as the eye can see. I followed them off the path as far as I dared, and never saw an end to ants or to those luffing chips of green they bore.

15   Unseen in the jungle, but present, are tapirs, jaguars, many species of snake and lizard, ocelots, armadillos, marmosets, howler monkeys, toucans and macaws and a hundred other birds, deer, bats, peccaries, capybaras, agoutis, and sloths. Also present in this jungle, but variously distant, are Texaco derricks and pipelines, and some of the wildest Indians in the world, blowgun-using Indians, who killed missionaries in 1956 and ate them.

16   Long lakes shine in the jungle. We traveled one of these in dugout canoes, canoes with two inches of freeboard, canoes paddled with machete-hewn oars chopped from buttresses of silk-cotton trees, or poled in the shallows with peeled cane or bamboo. Our part-Indian guide had cleared the path to the lake the day before; when we walked the path we saw where he had impaled the lopped head of a boa, open-mouthed, on a pointed stick by the canoes, for decoration.

17   This lake was wonderful. Herons, egrets, and ibises plodded the sawgrass shores, kingfishers and cuckoos clattered from sunlight to shade, great turkeylike birds fussed in dead branches, and hawks lolled overhead. There was all the time in the world. A turtle slid into the water. The boy in the bow of my canoe slapped stones at birds with a simple sling, a rubber thong and leather pad. He aimed brilliantly at moving targets, always, and always missed; the birds were out of range. He stuffed his sling back in his shirt. I looked around.

18   The lake and river waters are as opaque as rain-forest leaves; they are veils, blinds, painted screens. You see things only by their effects. I saw the shoreline water roil and the sawgrass heave above a thrashing *paichi*, an enormous black fish of these waters; one had been caught the previous week weighing 430 pounds. Piranha fish live in the lakes, and electric eels. I dangled my fingers in the water, figuring it would be worth it.

19   We would eat chicken that night in the village, and rice, yucca, onions, beets, and heaps of fruit. The sun would ring down, pulling darkness after it

like a curtain. Twilight is short, and the unseen birds of twilight wistful, uncanny, catching the heart. The two nuns in their dazzling white habits—the beautiful-boned young nun and the warm-faced old—would glide to the open cane-and-thatch schoolroom in darkness, and start the children singing. The children would sing in piping Spanish, high-pitched and pure; they would sing "Nearer My God to Thee" in Quechua, very fast. (To reciprocate, we sang for them "Old MacDonald Had a Farm"; I thought they might recognize the animal sounds. Of course they thought we were out of our minds.) As the children became excited by their own singing, they left their log benches and swarmed around the nuns, hopping, smiling at us, everyone smiling, the nuns' faces bursting in their cowls, and the clear-voiced children still singing, and the palm-leafed roofing stirred.

The Napo River: it is not out of the way. It is *in* the way, catching sunlight 20 the way a cup catches poured water; it is a bowl of sweet air, a basin of greenness, and of grace, and, it would seem, of peace.

DISCUSSION QUESTIONS

1. Other than starting the essay, what does Dillard accomplish in paragraph 1?
2. Dillard uses a number of comparisons, such as "hand-sized tarantula" in paragraph 2, to clarify and enhance her description. Point out other comparisons and comment on their effectiveness.
3. Explain why you think Dillard includes paragraph 5 in the essay.
4. Point out the linking devices that Dillard uses to provide coherence in paragraphs 6–10.
5. Does Dillard use a fixed or moving vantage point? How do you account for her choice?
6. Explain why you think Dillard ends the final sentence of paragraph 18 with "figuring it would be worth it."
7. What types of sensory impressions are found in this essay?
8. What does Dillard accomplish in the final paragraph of her essay?

TOWARD KEY INSIGHTS

What are some key distinguishing features of a primitive locale such as a jungle, desert, or remote mountainous area?

Why would such a locale appeal to many people today?

What characteristics might distinguish those who are attracted to such locales?

SUGGESTION FOR WRITING

Write an essay describing noteworthy features of a densely populated metropolitan area. Select an appropriate vantage point and incorporate as many of the five kinds of sensory impressions as you can.

Lesley Hazleton

Assembly Line Adventure[1]

Lesley Hazleton (born 1945) is a native of England who earned a B.A. degree from Manchester University and an M.A. degree from the Hebrew University of Jerusalem before emigrating to the United States in 1979. Hazleton is a nationally known automotive journalist with wide-ranging interests that include baseball, psychology, and politics. She has authored six nonfiction books, and her numerous shorter pieces have appeared in a variety of major newspapers and popular magazines. Our essay is excerpted from her latest book, Driving to Detroit *(1998). In it she describes her brief introduction to auto assembly-line work and the lessons she learned from the experience.*

1   I'd toured many auto plants before, and physically this was not much different. That is, it was an assault on the senses: an enclosed, windowless world of harsh artificial light and hard concrete floors ringing with the discordant cacophony of industrial production. Metal rang on metal. Stamping presses clanked, power tools whined, pulleys groaned, hoists clanged, welding robots whooshed, sparks crackled, lasers beeped, compressed air hissed, bolts banged into place, trolleys rumbled down the aisles, and all the while, conveyor belts carrying cars in one stage or another of production, from bare metal frames to fully painted bodies, clattered and clanketed beside us and behind us and even over our heads.

2   At five in the afternoon, I started work, joining three other workers stationed around a huge rotating machine. Our job was to feed a robot.

3   Officially, we were preparing dashboard molds for foam injection. In fact, we were simply loading and unloading the machine for the robot, which injected the foam and then wiped its own nozzle as though it were wiping its nose—one of those infuriatingly human gestures that make you think, "Cute," and then hate yourself for having thought it.

4   This was one of the simplest tasks on the whole assembly line. Squirt some filler release into a hole. Lift a light plastic mold and place it on a protruding lip of the machine. Bang a board with your knee to drop three locks to hold the mold in place. Check the locks. Push a black button to bring the lip down into the right position for the next guy. Wait for the machine to rotate and present you with a new lip. And that was it. A ten-second job to be repeated ad infinitum.

5   Two hours later, I moved from one of the simplest jobs on the line to one of the most complicated: assembling the whole instrument panel. Steering wheel, indicator and wiper wands, gauges, dashboard line, the lot.

6   Audrey, the woman whose task it was to teach me this job, had a tough challenge ahead of her.

7   I guessed she was in her mid-thirties. Despite a mass of long brown curly hair, she had a boyish way to her, maybe because of the leather builder's apron she was wearing, its pockets so full of connectors and screws and bolts that it took me a while to realize she was six months pregnant.

8   "Is this your first?" I asked.

[1]Editors' title.

She burst out laughing. "Honey, I'm forty-three years old. And a grand- 9
mother. I married again not long ago, and"—she spread her arms wide and stared
at her belly—"just look what happened. This sure is the last thing I ever expected."

"How long will you go on working?" 10

She laughed again. "Do you know how much kids cost? I'm staying right 11
here till the day I pop."

She hadn't stopped working for a moment as we talked. She couldn't. The 12
line was rolling, and it was either keep up or bring everything to a halt. We were
standing *on* the line, a wide conveyor belt rumbling past an array of shelves
piled high with parts, and beneath an overhead rack dangling power tools and
bins of screws. On the line with us, every six feet or so, was a workstand holding
an empty dashboard shell, placed upside down on the stand so that it was easy
to work on. Audrey's job was to make it into a complete instrument panel.

For the first few moments, standing on the moving belt was almost child- 13
ishly fun. The world was reversed: you stood still and it went past you. Your
mind knew it was you moving, not the world, but your senses told you otherwise. And all the time, the belt vibrated gently underfoot; if it weren't for the
noise, it might even have been pleasantly sexy.

"Watch your head," Audrey said, and I ducked as a power wrench came 14
dangling past my right ear. Followed by another. And yet another. Even though
I reminded myself that it was me moving, not them, every time I looked up they
seemed to be aiming for my brains with a certain inexorable malevolence.

I spent the first half-hour watching Audrey and figuring out how to stay out 15
of the way. So far as I could make out, she had a total of some fifty separate procedures to complete in a logic-defying sequence of about three minutes. Each
step had to be performed in perfect timing, so that the right parts and tools
were at hand exactly when she needed them. And to add to the pressure, this
job was what they called a "show-stopper."

Farther on down the line, the completed instrument panel would be low- 16
ered into the "smile joint"—a large lazy U going from side to side of the car's
frame. If it didn't fit, the line would stop, and the whole plant would start running behind. "You can't go back and do it again," Audrey said. "You got to do it
perfect the first time."

I knew I'd never be able to do this job. Yet Audrey seemed convinced that 17
I was educable. She talked each movement out loud as she worked, with me following her around like a pet dog. Somehow, she convinced me to do a bit here
and a bit there, until within an hour, I had the beginning of it down pat:

Walk six stands down the line, past other team members at different stages 18
of the job, and read the manifest hanging on the dashboard shell. Pick up different parts from the shelves alongside the line, depending on whether this is to
be a sedan or a wagon, an automatic or a manual shift. Jam a leather sheath over
the sharp metal edge to the side of the module. Ease the parts into place. Snap-
connect electrical wires: gray to the right, blue to the middle, white to the left.

So far so good. I was feeling quite proud of myself. Trouble was, this was 19
only the beginning of the beginning.

The rest began to blur: Snap-connect a black fastener, then a yellow one. 20
Don't delay. If you go too slow, the line will take you past the parts you need,
and you'll have to start running back and forth for them. Pick up the steering
shaft from a shelf and ease its thirty-pound weight down through the center of
the module. Arrange the wires to run over the top of the shaft. Slip on and snap
a green fastener . . .

21   Or were those last two steps the other way round? "Here," said Audrey, re-doing my work.

22   Okay, now pick up two bronze-colored bolts and screws, two black bolts, a circular piece, and two silver bolts from those big bins alongside the line. Insert the silver bolts. Fine. Place the bronze-colored ones in one place, the black ones in another. Great. Pull down a power wrench from the overhead line . . .

23   I grabbed for it and missed. It began to recede from me. I stretched and yanked it down just in time to tighten the bolts. I had no idea of what I was bolting to what, or why. Neither, it turned out, did Audrey.

24   Right, you've got those bolts nice and tight. Now pick different bronze-colored bolts from another bin. No, not alongside the line—right here, hanging overhead. Fine. Insert them and tighten them by hand for now. What about the wrench? Not there yet, that comes soon. First, thread the electrical wires through the back of the module and out through this flap, then loop them over and under the shaft like so, and then . . .

25   Then what? I couldn't remember. And I was only a third of the way through the job.

26   "Don't worry," said Audrey. "It takes most people four days to learn this job. You're doing real good."

27   That was sweet of her, but it didn't feel real good to me. My attention strayed for a moment, I lost a beat, and suddenly the power tools and screw bins were bearing down on me way before I was ready for them. I worked as fast as I could, one eye on my hands, the other on the dangling wrench going past. I swore, lunged for it, and yanked at the cord as though if I pulled hard enough I could pull back the whole line and slow things down to my pace. I remembered Charlie Chaplin's desperation in *Modern Times,* and suddenly there was nothing remotely funny about it. I dropped a bolt, reached for the wrong wrench, and watched pathetically as Audrey stepped in and put everything to rights. I hadn't felt quite this incompetent since I was a kid trying to thread a sewing machine at school. I never did master that.

28   Every time I thought I had the hang of it all, another two steps somehow reversed themselves in my mind, or one slipped out of existence altogether. My ears were ringing, my mind was reeling, and my hands had never felt clumsier. I began to fumble the screws, inserting them at an angle so that they wouldn't tighten properly and had to be taken out and inserted anew. Audrey was working as hard as I was by now; we stood shoulder to shoulder, me fouling things up, her fixing them.

29   And suddenly it was ten o'clock, and there was a half-hour break for lunch. Ten at night, that is. By now, I was squinting to stop from seeing double. I was convinced that if I could just work through to the end of the shift, I'd get this job down pat. But as the line came to a halt and everything stopped moving, some remote part of my brain managed to signal a weak but just decipherable message that the pressure was getting to me. It was time to call it quits before I damaged a car, or myself, or worse still, somebody else.

30   "Don't you want some lunch before you go?" said Audrey. But I was too exhausted to even look at food. I needed fresh air. And solitude. And silence. I made my excuses, stuffed my yellow Kevlar gloves into my pocket as a memento, got lost twice trying to find the way out, and finally emerged into the parking lot.

31   Never had a parking lot seemed so beautiful: so quiet, so peaceful, so serene. Even the buzzing yellow of the sodium vapor lights seemed soothing. Behind me, the plant hummed gently, its skylights glowing into the night. Mid-

shift, I was the only person out here, and I had a flash of guilt mixed with giddy freedom, the kind that comes from playing hooky.

I found the truck, climbed in, made to start it up. Then stopped, hand in 32 midair, and sat staring at the instrument panel. Something was wrong. I took a moment to figure it out: I'd spent the past few hours working on upside-down instrument panels, and now I was seeing this one the right way up.

I reached out and examined it for its component parts, thinking of the 33 man or the woman who'd put it together, and appreciating the way it had been done. This thing I usually took so for granted that I'd never before paid a moment's attention to it, was now an astounding piece of mad-made—woman-made—complexity.

I started the truck and drove slowly out of the lot, wondering how long I'd 34 keep this awareness that cars are not merely machines, but things put together by human beings, products of real men and real women doing the kind of work that would drive most people crazy. Not long enough, for sure.

DISCUSSION QUESTIONS

1. Comment on the effectiveness of the essay's title.

2. Which of the five sensory impressions does Hazleton include? Refer to specific paragraphs when answering.

3. What is the dominant impression of this essay?

4. What time signals does Hazleton use? Refer to specific paragraphs when answering.

5. This description takes the form of a narrative with the action moving forward until a turning point is reached. Where does this turning point occur?

6. Identify the conclusion of the essay and what it accomplishes.

7. After reading Hazleton's description, how do you think you would tolerate working on an assembly line as a summer job? Discuss.

TOWARD KEY INSIGHTS

What jobs have you done or heard about that you would consider unbearable? What characteristics make them unbearable?

What jobs have you done or heard about that you would find enjoyable? What characteristics make them enjoyable?

SUGGESTION FOR WRITING

Write an essay describing your introduction to some new job. Use an appropriate number of sensory details that create a dominant impression and indicate your reaction to what you learned.

E. B. White

Once More to the Lake

E. B. White (1899–1985) was born in Mount Vernon, New York, and was a graduate of Cornell University. In 1927, he joined the staff of The New Yorker, *launched just two years before, and for several decades produced a steady flow of short pieces for it. Between 1937 and 1943, he also wrote a column, "One Man's Meat," for* Harper's. *He is the author of three critically acclaimed children's books,* Stuart Little *(1945),* Charlotte's Web *(1952), and* The Trumpet of the Swan *(1970) as well as numerous adult works, including several collections of his essays and poems. In "Once More to the Lake," White creates a vivid and memorable word picture of a summer vacation that had great meaning for him and that brought him a sobering insight.*

1   One summer, along about 1904, my father rented a camp on a lake in Maine and took us all there for the month of August. We all got ringworm from some kittens and had to rub Pond's Extract on our arms and legs night and morning, and my father rolled over in a canoe with all his clothes on; but outside of that the vacation was a success and from then on none of us ever thought there was any place in the world like that lake in Maine. We returned summer after summer—always on August 1st for one month. I have since become a salt-water man, but sometimes in summer there are days when the restlessness of the tides and the fearful cold of the sea water and the incessant wind which blows across the afternoon and into the evening make me wish for the placidity of a lake in the woods. A few weeks ago this feeling got so strong I bought myself a couple of bass hooks and a spinner and returned to the lake where we used to go, for a week's fishing and to revisit old haunts.

2   I took along my son, who had never had any fresh water up his nose and who had seen lily pads only from train windows. On the journey over to the lake I began to wonder what it would be like. I wondered how time would have marred this unique, this holy spot—the coves and streams, the hills that the sun set behind, the camps and the paths behind the camps. I was sure the tarred road would have found it out and I wondered in what other ways it would be desolated. It is strange how much you can remember about places like that once you allow your mind to return into the grooves which lead back. You remember one thing, and that suddenly reminds you of another thing. I guess I remembered clearest of all the early mornings, when the lake was cool and motionless, remembered how the bedroom smelled of the lumber it was made of and the wet woods whose scent entered through the screen. The partitions in the camp were thin and did not extend clear to the top of the rooms, and as I was always the first up I would dress softly so as not to wake the others, and sneak out into the sweet outdoors and start out in the canoe, keeping close along the shore in the long shadows of the pines. I remembered being very careful never to rub my paddle against the gunwale for fear of disturbing the stillness of the cathedral.

The lake had never been what you would call a wild lake. There were cottages sprinkled around the shores, and it was in farming country although the shores of the lake were quite heavily wooded. Some of the cottages were owned by nearby farmers, and you would live at the shore and eat your meals at the farmhouse. That's what our family did. But although it wasn't wild, it was a fairly large and undisturbed lake and there were places in it which, to a child at least, seemed infinitely remote and primeval.

I was right about the tar: it led to within half a mile of the shore. But when I got back there, with my boy, and we settled into a camp near a farmhouse and into the kind of summertime I had known, I could tell that it was going to be pretty much the same as it had been before—I knew it, lying in bed the first morning, smelling the bedroom, and hearing the boy sneak quietly out and go off along the shore in a boat. I began to sustain the illusion that he was I, and therefore by simple transposition, that I was my father. This sensation persisted, kept cropping up all the time we were there. It was not an entirely new feeling, but in this setting it grew much stronger. I seemed to be living a dual existence. I would be in the middle of some simple act, I would be picking up a bait box or laying down a table fork, or I would be saying something, and suddenly it would be not I but my father who was saying the words or making the gesture. It gave me a creepy sensation.

We went fishing the first morning. I felt the same damp moss covering the worms in the bait can, and saw the dragonfly alight on the tip of my rod as it hovered a few inches from the surface of the water. It was the arrival of this fly that convinced me beyond any doubt that everything was as it always had been, that the years were a mirage and there had been no years. The small waves were the same, chucking the rowboat under the chin as we fished at anchor, and the boat was the same boat, the same color green and the ribs broken in the same places, and under the floor-boards the same fresh-water leavings and debris— the dead hellgramite,[1] the wisps of moss, the rusty discarded fishhook, the dried blood from yesterday's catch. We stared silently at the tips of our rods, at the dragonflies that came and went. I lowered the tip of mine into the water, tentatively, pensively dislodging the fly, which darted two feet away, poised, darted two feet back, and came to rest again a little farther up the rod. There had been no years between the ducking of this dragonfly and the other one—the one that was part of memory. I looked at the boy, who was silently watching his fly, and it was my hands that held his rod, my eyes watching. I felt dizzy and didn't know which rod I was at the end of.

We caught two bass, hauling them in briskly as though they were mackerel, putting them over the side of the boat in a businesslike manner without any landing net, and stunning them with a blow on the back of the head. When we got back for a swim before lunch, the lake was exactly where we had left it, the same number of inches from the dock, and there was only the merest suggestion of a breeze. This seemed an utterly enchanted sea, this lake you could leave to its own devices for a few hours and come back to, and find that it had not stirred, this constant and trustworthy body of water. In the shallows, the dark, water-soaked sticks and twigs, smooth and old, were undulating in clusters on the bottom against the clean ribbed sand, and the track of the mussel was plain. A school of minnows swam by, each minnow with its small individual shadow,

3

4

5

6

---

[1]Insect used as bait.

doubling the attendance, so clear and sharp in the sunlight. Some of the other campers were in swimming, along the shore, one of them with a cake of soap, and the water felt thin and clear and unsubstantial. Over the years there had been this person with the cake of soap, this cultist, and here he was. There had been no years.

7   Up to the farmhouse to dinner through the teeming, dusty field, the road under our sneakers was only a two-track road. The middle track was missing, the one with the marks of the hooves and the splotches of dried, flaky manure. There had always been three tracks to choose from in choosing which track to walk in; now the choice was narrowed down to two. For a moment I missed terribly the middle alternative. But the way led past the tennis court, and something about the way it lay there in the sun reassured me; the tape had loosened along the backline, the alleys were green with plantains and other weeds, and the net (installed in June and removed in September) sagged in the dry noon, and the whole place steamed with midday heat and hunger and emptiness. There was a choice of pie for dessert, and one was blueberry and one was apple, and the waitresses were the same country girls, there having been no passage of time, only the illusion of it as in a dropped curtain—the waitresses were still fifteen; their hair had been washed, that was the only difference—they had been to the movies and seen the pretty girls with the clean hair.

8   Summertime, oh summertime, pattern of life indelible, the fade-proof lake, the woods unshatterable, the pasture with the sweetfern and the juniper forever and ever, summer without end; this was the background, and the life along the shore was the design, the cottages with their innocent and tranquil design, their tiny docks with the flagpole and the American flag floating against the white clouds in the blue sky, the little paths over the roots of the trees leading from camp to camp and the paths leading back to the outhouses and the can of lime for sprinkling, and at the souvenir counters at the store the miniature birch-bark canoes and the post cards that showed things looking a little better than they looked. This was the American family at play, escaping the city heat, wondering whether the newcomers in the camp at the head of the cove were "common" or "nice," wondering whether it was true that the people who drove up for Sunday dinner at the farmhouse were turned away because there wasn't enough chicken.

9   It seemed to me, as I kept remembering all this, that those times and those summers had been infinitely precious and worth saving. There had been jollity and peace and goodness. The arriving (at the beginning of August) had been so big a business in itself, at the railway station the farm wagon drawn up, the first smell of the pine-laden air, the first glimpse of the smiling farmer, and the great importance of the trunks and your father's enormous authority in such matters, and the feel of the wagon under you for the long ten-mile haul, and at the top of the last long hill catching the first view of the lake after eleven months of not seeing this cherished body of water. The shouts and cries of the other campers when they saw you, and the trunks to be unpacked, to give up their rich burden. (Arriving was less exciting nowadays, when you sneaked up in your car and parked it under a tree near the camp and took out the bags and in five minutes it was all over, no fuss, no loud wonderful fuss about trunks.)

10   Peace and goodness and jollity. The only thing that was wrong now, really, was the sound of the place, an unfamiliar nervous sound of the outboard motors. This was the note that jarred, the one thing that would sometimes break the illusion and set the years moving. In those other summertimes all motors were inboard; and when they were at a little distance, the noise they made was a sedative,

an ingredient of summer sleep. They were one-cylinder and two-cylinder engines, and some were make-and-break and some were jump-spark, but they all made a sleepy sound across the lake. The one-lungers throbbed and fluttered, and the twin-cylinder ones purred and purred, and that was a quiet sound too. But now the campers all had outboards. In the daytime, in the hot mornings, these motors made a petulant, irritable sound; at night, in the still evening when the afterglow lit the water, they whined about one's ears like mosquitoes. My boy loved our rented outboard, and his great desire was to achieve singlehanded mastery over it, and authority, and he soon learned the trick of choking it a little (but not too much), and the adjustment of the needle valve. Watching him I would remember the things you could do with the old one-cylinder engine with the heavy flywheel, how you could have it eating out of your hand if you got really close to it spiritually. Motor boats in those days didn't have clutches, and you would make a landing by shutting off the motor at the proper time and coasting in with a dead rudder. But there was a way of reversing them, if you learned the trick, by cutting the switch and putting it on again exactly on the final dying revolution of the flywheel, so that it would kick back against compression and begin reversing. Approaching a dock in a strong following breeze, it was difficult to slow up sufficiently by the ordinary coasting method, and if a boy felt he had complete mastery over his motor, he was tempted to keep it running beyond its time and then reverse it a few feet from the dock. It took a cool nerve, because if you threw the switch a twentieth of a second too soon you would catch the flywheel when it still had speed enough to go up past center, and the boat would leap ahead, charging bull-fashion at the dock.

We had a good week at the camp. The bass were biting well and the sun shone endlessly, day after day. We would be tired at night and lie down in the accumulated heat of the little bedrooms after the long hot day and the breeze would stir almost imperceptibly outside and the smell of the swamp drift in through the rusty screens. Sleep would come easily and in the morning the red squirrel would be on the roof, tapping out his gay routine. I kept remembering everything, lying in bed in the mornings—the small steamboat that had a long rounded stern like the lip of a Ubangi, and how quietly she ran on the moonlight sails, when the older boys played their mandolins and the girls sang and we ate doughnuts dipped in sugar, and how sweet the music was on the water in the shining night, and what it had felt like to think about girls then. After breakfast we would go up to the store and the things were in the same place—the minnows in a bottle, the plugs and spinners disarranged and pawed over by the youngsters from the boys' camp, the fig newtons and the Beeman's gum. Outside, the road was tarred and cars stood in front of the store. Inside, all was just as it had always been, except there was more Coca-Cola and not so much Moxie and root beer and birch beer and sarsaparilla. We would walk out with a bottle of pop apiece and sometimes the pop would backfire up our noses and hurt. We explored the streams, quietly, where the turtles slid off the sunny logs and dug their way into the soft bottom; and we lay on the town wharf and fed worms to the tame bass. Everywhere we went I had trouble making out which was I, the one walking at my side, the one walking in my pants.

One afternoon while we were there at the lake a thunderstorm came up. It was like the revival of an old melodrama that I had seen long ago with childish awe. The second-act climax of the drama of the electrical disturbance over a lake in America had not changed in any important respect. This was the big

11

12

scene, still the big scene. The whole thing was so familiar, the first feeling of op-pression and heat and a general air around camp of not wanting to go very far away. In mid-afternoon (it was all the same) a curious darkening of the sky, and a lull in everything that had made life tick; and then the way the boats suddenly swung the other way at their moorings with the coming of a breeze out of the new quarter, and the premonitory rumble. Then the kettle drum, then the snare, then the bass drum and cymbals, then crackling light against the dark, and the gods grinning and licking their chops in the hills. Afterward the calm, the rain steadily rustling in the calm lake, the return of light and hope and spirits, and the campers running out in joy and relief to go swimming in the rain, their bright cries per-petuating the deathless joke about how they were getting simply drenched, and the children screaming with delight at the new sensation of bathing in the rain, and the joke about getting drenched linking the generations in a strong inde-structible chain. And the comedian who waded in carrying an umbrella.

13   When the others went swimming my son said he was going in too. He pulled his dripping trunks from the line where they had hung all through the shower, and wrung them out. Languidly, and with no thought of going in, I watched him, his hard little body, skinny and bare, saw him wince slightly as he pulled up around his vitals the small, soggy, icy garment. As he buckled the swollen belt suddenly my groin felt the chill of death.

DISCUSSION QUESTIONS

1. In paragraph 4 White says that while doing or saying things "suddenly it would be not I but my father who was saying the words or making the gesture." Ex-plain what he means.
2. White supplies relatively little information about his son except to mention that his actions resemble White's own as a child. How do you account for this brief treatment?
3. What is the significance of the missing middle track of the road (paragraph 7) and the "nervous sound of the outboard motors" (paragraph 10)?
4. Throughout the essay White spices his descriptions with precise sensory impres-sions of sight, hearing, touch, taste, and smell. How do these sensory details en-hance his writing?
5. On what audience would this essay likely have the largest impact?
6. White's final sentence provides an indirect statement of his main point. What is the point?

TOWARD KEY INSIGHTS

In what ways is the lake part of E. B. White's sense of personal identity?

How and to what extent can places become part of our lives?

What kinds of circumstances or events are likely to become part of our identity?

SUGGESTION FOR WRITING

Write an essay describing a place you have re-visited after being absent for a number of years. Indicate what was similar and what was differ-ent and describe your reactions to the changes. Appeal to at least three of the five senses.

Process Analysis

Ian Dunbar

Fast Track to Perfection

Ian Dunbar is a veterinarian and behaviorist who has an international reputation for his "lure and reward" method of training animals. Born in England, he holds degrees from the Royal Veterinarian College of London University and in psychology from the University of California. He now heads the Center for Applied Animal Behavior at his California alma mater. Dunbar has written extensively about his speciality, most recently (1999) coauthoring a series of volumes on different breeds of dogs. In this selection, he shows readers how to apply his methods to training puppies.

Puppies mature at an astounding rate. Don't let yours fall behind on the developmental curve. Nearly everything a puppy needs to learn must be taught in 12 weeks—between the ages of 2 and 5 months. You can buy yourself time by knowing what and how to teach the puppy before you bring it home. Go to puppy classes, read behavior and training books, watch instructional videos and consult your veterinarian. Then raise your puppy perfectly by meeting these six training deadlines.

> Introduction
>
> 1 Warning
>
> Notes requirements, rewards of training a perfect dog

Deadline 1: Before You Bring Home a Puppy

Your puppy should be accustomed to a domestic environment before you bring it home—at around 8 weeks of age. Make sure it has been raised indoors and in close contact with people. It should be prepared for the clamor of everyday life—the noise of the vacuum cleaner, the hoopla surrounding sports programs on the television, children crying, adults arguing. Early exposure—before the pup's eyes and ears have fully opened—allows the puppy to gradually assimilate sights and sounds that otherwise might frighten.

> 2 Body: paragraphs 2–19
>
> First step and its actions
>
> Reason for action

The window for socializing begins to close by the time the pup turns 3 months of age, and its most impressionable learning period starts to fade by its fifth month.

> 3

Deadline 2: Puppy's First Day at Home

Misbehavior is the most common reason dogs end up in shelters. This is especially sad because owners can prevent most behavior problems. For instance, if you avoid leaving the pup unsupervised, it won't chew furniture and

> Second step and its actions
>
> 4

belongings or soil your house; while teeny accidents do little damage in themselves, they may set a precedent for habits in months to come.

5   When you cannot watch your pup, confine it to a crate or a puppy-proofed room, which should contain:

- a comfortable bed.

- a bowl of fresh water.

- a doggie toilet placed away from the bed and which simulates the outdoors. Lay down a sheet of linoleum and cover it with a disposable plastic sheet. Next lay newspaper or something absorbent. Top the three layers with dirt or sod to teach the pup to relieve itself on grass (or concrete slabs for city pups that relieve themselves curbside).

- Hollow chew toys with kibble inside to reward your puppy for chewing toys rather than furniture. During its first few weeks at home, a marvelous training ploy is to serve your puppy's food only in chew toys. After it's a chew toy-aholic—and has not had a chewing mishap for at least three months—begin to serve its dinner in a bowl.

6   At least every hour, release your puppy from its crate, quickly leash it and hurry it to its outdoor toilet area. Stand still and give the pup three minutes to produce. When it does, lavishly praise and offer *three* extra special treats. Freeze-dried liver treats work well because dogs love their strong smell.

7   If your puppy eliminates, it may be allowed supervised exploration of the house. If it does not eliminate, lead it back to its crate or puppy-proof room and try again in half an hour.

8   Keep up the once an hour schedule until your pup is at least 3 months old to make certain it never eliminates indoors. After 3 months of age pups start to develop the bladder control necessary for longer waits between potty breaks, but you must still be vigilant. One mistake can set a bad precedent.

9   Always reward your puppy for using its outdoors toilet area, but wait until it has completed its shots before taking it to public property; otherwise it can pick up other dogs' diseases. A pup must not walk or sniff where other dogs have been until it has developed sufficient immunity (between 3 and 4 months old).

Deadline 3: Puppy at 3 Months

10   By 3 months your pup must master socialization and basic manners. Pups that do not will have a hard time picking up these skills later in life. Unfortunately, the risk of disease means dog-to-dog socialization must wait. Meanwhile, teach your pup to be people-friendly.

11   As a general rule, your pup should socialize with at least 100 people before it is 3 months old. This is easier than it sounds. Invite eight friends over each Sunday to watch sports on the television. Each Monday invite eight different friends to watch *Ally McBeal* and *Dateline*. Catch up on outstanding social obligations by inviting family, friends and neighbors to weekly puppy parties. On another night, invite some neighborhood children. Socializing a puppy is great because it does wonders for *your* social life.

Show your guests how to hand feed the puppy's kibble to encourage and reward it for coming, sitting and lying down. Ask your puppy to come. Praise profusely as it approaches and offer a piece of kibble when it arrives. Back up, then do it again—and again and again. Then say "Puppy, Sit" and slowly move a piece of kibble from in front of the puppy's nose to between its eyes. As the puppy raises its nose to sniff, it will lower its rear and sit. If the puppy jumps up, you're holding the food too high. When your puppy sits, say "Good dog" and offer the kibble. Now say "Puppy, Down" and lower a piece of kibble from in front of the puppy's nose to between its forepaws. As the puppy lowers its head to follow the food, it will usually lie down. If your puppy stands, hide the kibble in your palm until it lies down. Then say "Good dog" and offer the food. Coach your guests until each can get the puppy to come, sit and lie down three times for a piece of kibble.

> 12 | Reason for action
>
> Feedback tells reader what to expect, how to react

When a puppy approaches promptly and happily, it is a sign the dog is people-friendly. Sitting and lying down on request indicates respect for the person issuing instructions. If your puppy is regularly hand-fed by guests, it will learn to enjoy people's company.

> 13 | Feedback explains significance of behavior

Deadline 4: Puppy at 4½ Months

Seemingly overnight, puppies become adolescents. Enroll in a training class before yours is 14 weeks old—that is, before it starts to test your limits. A professional will teach it to stop nipping and other behavior no-no's, as well as temper its hyper-turbo energy.

> Fourth step and its actions
>
> 14
>
> Reason for action

Most puppies can start classes at 3 months. Classrooms are generally safe places; the puppies are vaccinated, the floors regularly sterilized. I advise delaying walks in public places until your puppy is 4 months old because of the risk of disease.

> 15
>
> Reason for action

Puppy classes develop canine social savvy through play with other puppies in a controlled setting. Most classes are family-oriented, offering pups opportunities to socialize with all sorts of people—men, women and children. The number of behaviors your pup learns in its first training lesson will amaze you. Shy and fearful pups gain confidence. Bullies tone it down and become gentle. All dogs learn to come, sit and lie down when requested and listen to their owners and ignore distractions.

> 16

Deadline 5: Puppy at 5 Months

Take your dog everywhere—errands around town, car trips to visit friends, picnics in the park and especially to explore the neighborhood. And bring a little bag of kibble. Give a couple of pieces to each stranger who wants to meet your dog. Ask each person to offer the kibble only after your pup sits to say hello.

> Fifth step and its
>
> 17 | actions

At this point, you may come to believe the canine weight-pulling record exceeds 10,000 pounds. Your dog also may begin to ignore you. A few tips:

> 18

- **Make your dog walk for its dinner.** With kibble in hand, stand still and wait for the dog to sit. Ignore everything else your dog does; it will sit eventually. When it does, say "Good dog," offer the kibble, take one giant step forward, stand still and wait for your dog to sit again. Repeat this until your dog sits each time you stop. Now take two giant steps before your stop. Then three steps, five, eight, 10, 20 and so on. *Voilá*, your dog walks calmly and attentively by your side and sits each time you stop.

> Feedback tells reader what to expect

■ **Take a few time-outs on each walk.** Sit down, relax and allow the dog to settle down and watch the world go by. If your pup is not the sit-still type, take along a treat-stuffed chew toy as an incentive.

Warning

■ **Never take your dog's sound temperament for granted.** Outdoors can be scary and offer the occasional surprise. Give your dog a piece of kibble every time a big truck, noisy motorcycle or child on a skateboard whizzes by and your dog doesn't overreact.

Warning

■ **Don't make a habit of letting your dog off-leash to run and play with other dogs;** your dog may eventually refuse to come when called. Instead, take your dog's dinner to the park and, throughout its play session, call your dog every minute or so and have it sit for a couple of pieces of kibble. It will soon get the idea and its enthusiastic response will be the talk of the park.

Feedback tells reader what to expect

Deadline 6: Now and Forever

Sixth step and its actions

19   Continue walking your dog at least once a day and take it to a dog park several times a week. Find different walks and dog parks to meet a variety of dogs and people. If your dog always sees the same people and dogs, it may regress socially and become intolerant of strangers.

Reason for actions

20   Now enjoy life with your good-natured, well-mannered companion. Give your dog a special bone—Good dog!—and yourself a pat on the back—Good owner!

Conclusion; indicates results to expect

DISCUSSION QUESTIONS

1. Point out why Dunbar's title is appropriate. Refer to the essay when answering.
2. In paragraph 18 Dunbar states that the owner might "believe the canine weight-pulling record exceeds 10,000 pounds." Explain what he means.

TOWARD KEY INSIGHTS

Given the choice, what animal would you prefer to train? Why?
What animal would you least like to train? Why?

SUGGESTION FOR WRITING

Write an essay that provides directions for training a riding horse, hunting dog, or guard dog. Be sure to include the reason for any action whose purpose is not obvious and provide cautionary warnings whenever necessary.

Alexander Petrunkevitch

From The Spider and the Wasp[1]

Alexander Petrunkevitch (1875–1964) was a professor of zo-ology at Yale University for over a third of a century. He was born in Russia and emigrated to the United States in 1903, holding teaching positions at several universities before going to Yale. He gained international recognition for his investi-gations of spiders and his writings on them, in particular his Index Catalogue of Spiders of North, Central, and South America *(1911) and* An Inquiry into the Natural Classification of Spiders *(1933). A man of wide-reaching in-terests, Petrunkevitch also produced historical and philosophical works as well as transla-tions of Russian poetry. The following selection, excerpted from a 1952* Scientific Ameri-can *article, describes a natural process and analyzes the behavior of its two participants.*

1   In the adult stage the [pepsis] wasp lives only a few months. The female produces but a few eggs, one at a time at intervals of two or three days. For each egg the mother must provide one adult tarantula, alive but paralyzed. The mother wasp attaches the egg to the paralyzed spider's abdomen. Upon hatch-ing from the egg, the larva is many hundreds of times smaller than its living but helpless victim. It eats no other food and drinks no water. By the time it has finished its single Gargantuan meal and become ready for wasphood, nothing remains of the tarantula but its indigestible chitinous skeleton.

2   The mother wasp goes tarantula-hunting when the egg in her ovary is al-most ready to be laid. Flying low over the ground late on a sunny afternoon, the wasp looks for its victim or for the mouth of a tarantula burrow, a round hole edged by a bit of silk. The sex of the spider makes no difference, but the mother is highly discriminating as to species. Each species of pepsis requires a certain species of tarantula, and the wasp will not attack the wrong species. In a cage with a tarantula which is not its normal prey, the wasp avoids the spider and is usually killed by it in the night.

3   Yet when a wasp finds the correct species, it is the other way about. To iden-tify the species the wasp apparently must explore the spider with her antennae. The tarantula shows an amazing tolerance to this exploration. The wasp crawls under it and walks over it without evoking any hostile response. The molesta-tion is so great and so persistent that the tarantula often rises on all eight legs, as if it were on stilts. It may stand this way for several minutes. Meanwhile the wasp, having satisfied itself that the victim is of the right species, moves off a few inches to dig the spider's grave. Working vigorously with legs and jaws, it exca-vates—like a machine—a hole 8 to 10 inches deep with a diameter slightly larger than the spider's girth. Now and again the wasp pops out of the hole to make sure that the spider is still there.

4   When the grave is finished, the wasp returns to the tarantula to complete her ghastly enterprise. First she feels it all over once more with her antennae. Then her behavior becomes more aggressive. She bends her abdomen,

protruding her sting, and searches for the soft membrane at the point where the spider's legs join its body—the only spot where she can penetrate the horny skeleton. From time to time, as the exasperated spider slowly shifts ground, the wasp turns on her back and slides along with the aid of her wings, trying to get under the tarantula for a shot at the vital spot. During all this maneuvering, which can last for several minutes, the tarantula makes no move to save itself. Finally the wasp corners it against some obstruction and grasps one of its legs in her powerful jaws. Now at last the harassed spider tries a desperate but vain defense. The two contestants roll over and over on the ground. It is a terrifying sight and the outcome is always the same. The wasp finally manages to thrust her sting into the soft spot and holds it there for a few seconds while she pumps in the poison. Almost immediately the tarantula falls paralyzed on its back. Its legs stop twitching; its heart stops beating. Yet it is not dead, as is shown by the fact that if taken from the wasp it can be restored to some sensitivity by being kept in a moist chamber for several months.

5   After paralyzing the tarantula, the wasp cleans herself by dragging her body around the ground and rubbing her feet, sucks the drop of blood oozing from the wound in the spider's abdomen, then grabs a leg of the flabby, helpless animal in her jaws and drags it down to the bottom of the grave. She stays there for many minutes, sometimes for several hours, and what she does all that time in the dark we do not know. Eventually she lays her egg and attaches it to the side of the spider's abdomen with a sticky secretion. Then she emerges, fills the grave with soil carried bit by bit in her jaws, and finally tramples the ground all around to hide any trace of the grave from prowlers. Then she flies away, leaving her descendant safely started in life.

6   In all this the behavior of the wasp evidently is qualitatively different from that of the spider. The wasp acts like an intelligent animal. This is not to say that instinct plays no part or that she reasons as man does. But her actions are to the point; they are not automatic and can be modified to fit the situation. We do not know for certain how she identifies the tarantula—probably it is by some olfactory or chemo-tactile sense—but she does it purposefully and does not blindly tackle a wrong species.

7   On the other hand, the tarantula's behavior shows only confusion. Evidently the wasp's pawing gives it no pleasure, for it tries to move away. That the wasp is not simulating sexual stimulation is certain because male and female tarantulas react in the same way to its advances. That the spider is not anesthetized by some odorless secretion is easily shown by blowing lightly at the tarantula and making it jump suddenly. What, then, makes the tarantula behave as stupidly as it does?

8   No clear, simple answer is available. Possibly the stimulation by the wasp's antennae is masked by a heavier pressure on the spider's body so that it reacts as when prodded by a pencil. But the explanation may be much more complex. Initiative in attack is not the nature of tarantulas; most species fight only when cornered so that escape is impossible. Their inherited patterns of behavior apparently prompt them to avoid problems rather than attack them. For example, spiders always weave their webs in three dimensions, and when a spider finds that there is insufficient space to attach certain threads in the third dimension, it leaves the place and seeks another, instead of finishing the web in a single plane. This urge to escape seems to arise under all circumstances, in all phases of life, and to take the place of reasoning. For a spider to change the pattern of its web is as impossible as for an inexperienced man to build a bridge across a chasm obstructing his way.

In a way the instinctive urge to escape is not only easier but often more   9
efficient than reasoning. The tarantula does exactly what is most efficient in
all cases except in an encounter with a ruthless and determined attacker dependent for the existence of her own species on killing as many tarantulas as
she can lay eggs. Perhaps in this case the spider follows its usual pattern of trying to escape, instead of seizing and killing the wasp, because it is not aware
of its danger. In any case, the survival of the tarantula species as a whole is
protected by the fact that the spider is much more fertile than the wasp.

DISCUSSION QUESTIONS

1. Into how many steps is this natural process divided? In which paragraph or
   paragraphs is each discussed?
2. Characterize Petrunkevitch's attitude toward his topic. Is it completely objective,
   or does Petrunkevitch sometimes reveal his personal feelings? If he does, indicate where.
3. Petrunkevitch uses a number of transitional words and phrases to ensure a
   smooth flow of ideas. Indicate those transitional devices and the paragraphs in
   which they are found.
4. Where does the conclusion begin and what is its purpose?

TOWARD KEY INSIGHTS

When you read this essay, did you sympathize with the spider, the wasp, or neither?
How do you account for your feelings?

Critics of overly violent TV and movie dramas charge that such spectacles deaden
our capacity for human sympathy. Might televised nature programs depicting
the struggle for existence have a similar effect? Why or why not?

SUGGESTION FOR WRITING

*Write an essay explaining some process you per-
form frequently. Possibilities include flossing
your teeth, brewing a pot of coffee, or preparing
for a date.*

Beth Wald

Let's Get Vertical!

*Beth Wald (born 1960) first felt the attraction of the moun-
tains when, at age sixteen, she took a backpacking trip to
Canada. A native of Minnesota, she studied botany and
Russian at the University of Minnesota and then, in the
mid-1980s, began a dual career as a freelance writer and
photographer. Her career and her love of climbing have
taken her around the world. Her articles have appeared in a variety of climbing and outdoor magazines, as have her photographs, which include environmental and cultural*

subjects as well as sports and travel. From 1988 to 1992, she was a contributing editor for Climbing Magazine. *In our selection, Wald acquaints potential recruits with the sport of rock climbing.*

1   Here I am, 400 feet up on the steep west face of Devil's Tower,[1] a tiny figure in a sea of petrified rock. I can't find enough footholds and handholds to keep climbing. My climbing partner anxiously looks up at me from his narrow ledge. I can see the silver sparkle of the climbing devices I've jammed into the crack every eight feet or so.

2   I study the last device I've placed, a half-inch aluminum wedge 12 feet below me. If I slip, it'll catch me, but only after a 24-foot fall, a real "screamer." It's too difficult to go back; I have to find a way up before my fingers get too tired. I must act quickly.

3   Finding a tiny opening in the crack, I jam two fingertips in, crimp them, pull hard, and kick my right foot onto a sloping knob, hoping it won't skid off. At the same time, I slap my right hand up to what looks like a good hold. To my horror, it's round and slippery.

4   My fingers start to slide. Panic rivets me for a second, but then a surge of adrenalin snaps me back into action. I scramble my feet higher, lunge with my left hand, and catch a wider crack. I manage to get a better grip just as my right hand pops off its slick hold. My feet find edges, and I regain my balance. Whipping a chock (wedge) off my harness, I slip it into the crack and clip my rope through a carabiner (oblong metal snaplink). After catching my breath, I start moving again, and the rest of the climb flows upward like a vertical dance.

5   ***The Challenges and Rewards***   I've tried many sports, but I haven't found any to match the excitement of rock climbing. It's a unique world, with its own language, communities, controversies, heroes, villains, and devoted followers. I've lived in vans, tepees, tents, and caves; worked three jobs to save money for expenses; driven 24 hours to spend a weekend at a good rock; and lived on beans and rice for months at a time—all of this to be able to climb. What is it about scrambling up rocks that inspires such a passion? The answer is, no other sport offers so many challenges and so many rewards.

6   The physical challenges are obvious. You need flexibility, balance, and strength. But climbing is also a psychological game of defeating your fear, and it demands creative thinking. It's a bit like improvising a gymnastic routine 200 feet in the air while playing a game of chess.

7   Climbers visit some of the most spectacular places on earth and see them from a unique perspective—the top! Because the sport is so intense, friendships between climbers tend to be strong and enduring.

8   ***Anyone Can Climb***   Kids playing in trees or on monkey bars know that climbing is a natural activity, but older people often have to relearn to trust their instincts. This isn't too hard, though. The ability to maintain self-control in difficult situations is the most important trait for a beginning climber to have. Panic is almost automatic when you run out of handholds 100 feet off the ground. The typical reaction is to freeze solid until you fall off. But with a little discipline, rational thinking, and/or distraction tactics such as babbling to yourself, humming, or even screaming, fear can change to elation as you climb out of a tough spot.

---

[1]A large, flat-topped rock formation, 876 feet high, in northeastern Wyoming.

Contrary to popular belief, you don't have to be superhumanly strong to   9
climb. Self-confidence, agility, a good sense of balance, and determination will
get you farther up the rock than bulging biceps. Once you've learned the basics, climbing itself will gradually make you stronger, though many dedicated
climbers speed up the process by training at home or in the gym.

Nonclimbers often ask, "How do the ropes get up there?" It's quite simple;   10
the climbers bring them up as they climb. Most rock climbers today are "free
climbers." In free climbing, the rope is used only for safety in case of a fall, *not* to
help pull you up. (Climbing without a rope, called "free soloing," is a *very* dangerous activity practiced only by extremely experienced—and crazy—climbers.)

First, two climbers tie into opposite ends of a 150-foot-long nylon rope.   11
Then one of them, the belayer, anchors himself or herself to a rock or tree. The
other, the leader, starts to climb, occasionally stopping to jam a variety of aluminum wedges or other special gadgets, generically referred to as protection,
into cracks in the rock. To each of these, he or she attaches a snaplink, called a
carabiner, and clips the rope through. As the leader climbs, the belayer feeds
out the rope, and it runs through the carabiners. If the leader falls, the belayer
holds the rope, and the highest piece of protection catches the leader. The belayer uses special techniques and equipment to make it easy to stop falls.

When the leader reaches the end of a section of rock—called the pitch—and   12
sets an anchor, he or she becomes the belayer. This person pulls up the slack of
the rope as the other partner climbs and removes the protection. Once together
again, they can either continue in the same manner or switch leaders. These
worldwide techniques work on rock formations, cliffs, peaks, even buildings.

Rocks, Rocks Everywhere   Some of the best climbing cliffs in the country are in   13
the Shawangunk Mountains, only two hours from New York City. Seneca Rocks
in West Virginia draws climbers from Washington, D.C., and Pittsburgh, Pennsylvania. Chattanooga, Tennessee, has a fine cliff within the city limits. Most
states in the U.S. and provinces in Canada offer at least one or two good climbing opportunities.

Even if there are no large cliffs or rock formations nearby, you can climb   14
smaller rocks to practice techniques and get stronger. This is called bouldering.
Many climbers who live in cities and towns have created climbing areas out of
old stone walls and buildings. Ask someone at your local outdoor shop where
you can go to start climbing.

Get a Helping Hand   There's no substitute for an expert teacher when it comes   15
to learning basic techniques and safety procedures. One of the best (and least
expensive) ways to learn climbing is to convince a veteran climber in your area to
teach you. You can usually meet these types at the local crag or climbing shop.

As another option, many universities and colleges, some high schools, and   16
some YMCAs have climbing clubs. Their main purpose is to introduce people to
climbing and to teach the basics. Other clubs, such as the Appalachian Mountain Club in the eastern U.S. and the Mountaineers on the West Coast, also provide instruction. Ask at your outdoor shop for the names of clubs in your area.

If you live in a place completely lacking rocks and climbers, you can attend   17
one of the fine climbing schools at the major climbing area closest to you. Magazines like *Climbing, Rock & Ice,* and *Outside* publish lists of these schools. Once
you learn the basics, you're ready to get vertical.

In rock climbing, you can both lose yourself and find yourself. Life and all   18
its troubles are reduced to figuring out the puzzle of the next section of cliff or

forgotten in the challenge and delight of moving through vertical space. And learning how to control anxiety, how to piece together a difficult sequence of moves, and how to communicate with a partner are all skills that prove incredibly useful back on the ground!

DISCUSSION QUESTIONS

1. Discuss the effectiveness of Wald's title.
2. At the beginning of the essay, Wald notes that she is 400 feet up one side of Devil's Tower and positioned above her climbing partner. What do you think these statements accomplish?
3. In which paragraphs does Wald detail the actual process of climbing? What do the remaining paragraphs in the body of the essay accomplish?
4. Point out two places in the first four paragraphs where Wald cites reasons for her actions.
5. What attributes does Wald believe a rock climber must have? Refer to the essay when answering.
6. After reading this essay, are you ready to begin rock climbing? Does your answer stem from Wald's content, the manner of presentation, or both? Discuss.

TOWARD KEY INSIGHTS

What challenging activities appeal to you?
What level of risk are you willing to accept in an activity?
How do you account for your attitude about taking risks?

SUGGESTION FOR WRITING

Write a process paper in which you explain the attributes required and the steps involved in one of your recreational activities.

Richard Selzer

The Knife

Richard Selzer (born 1928) grew up in Troy, New York, where his father was a family doctor. He attended Union College and Albany Medical College. After service in the United States Army, he completed three years of postdoctoral training at Yale University and joined its medical faculty. Selzer's shorter writings, which include stories and essays, focus on medical topics and have appeared in a number of popular magazines. He has also written several books on medical topics, the latest of which, The Exact Location of the Soul *(2001), is the author's selection of his own classic essays, taken from three decades of writing. In "The Knife," Selzer traces the course of an operation while meditating on the nature of his calling.*

One holds the knife as one holds the bow of a cello or a tulip—by the stem. 1
Not palmed nor gripped nor grasped, but lightly, with the tips of the fingers. The
knife is not for pressing. It is for drawing across the field of skin. Like a slender
fish, it waits, at the ready, then, go! It darts, followed by a fine wake of red. The
flesh parts, falling away to yellow globules of fat. Even now, after so many times, I
still marvel at its power—cold, gleaming, silent. More, I am still struck with a kind
of dread that it is I in whose hand the blade travels, that my hand is its vehicle,
that yet again this terrible steel-bellied thing and I have conspired for a most unnatural purpose, the laying open of the body of a human being.

A stillness settles in my heart and is carried to my hand. It is the quietude 2
of resolve layered over fear. And it is this resolve that lowers us, my knife and
me, deeper and deeper into the person beneath. It is an entry into the body
that is nothing like a caress; still, it is among the gentlest of acts. Then stroke
and stroke again, and we are joined by other instruments, hemostats and forceps, until the wound blooms with strange flowers whose looped handles fall to
the sides in steely array.

There is sound, the tight click of clamps fixing teeth into severed blood ves- 3
sels, the snuffle and gargle of the suction machine clearing the field of blood
for the next stroke, the litany of monosyllables with which one prays his way
down and in: *clamp, sponge, suture, tie, cut.* And there is color. The green of the
cloth, the white of the sponges, the red and yellow of the body. Beneath the fat
lies the fascia, the tough fibrous sheet encasing the muscles. It must be sliced
and the red beef of the muscles separated. Now there are retractors to hold
apart the wound. Hands move together, part, weave. We are fully engaged, like
children absorbed in a game or the craftsmen of some place like Damascus.

Deeper still. The peritoneum, pink and gleaming and membranous, bulges 4
into the wound. It is grasped with forceps, and opened. For the first time we can
see into the cavity of the abdomen. Such a primitive place. One expects to find
drawings of buffalo on the walls. The sense of trespassing is keener now, heightened by the world's light illuminating the organs, their secret colors revealed—
maroon and salmon and yellow. The vista is sweetly vulnerable at this moment,
a kind of welcoming. An arc of the liver shines high and on the right, like a
dark sun. It laps over the pink sweep of the stomach, from whose lower border
the gauzy omentum is draped, and through which veil one sees, sinuous, slow
as just-fed snakes, the indolent coils of the intestine.

You turn aside to wash your gloves. It is a ritual cleansing. One enters this 5
temple doubly washed. Here is man as microcosm, representing in all his parts
the earth, perhaps the universe.

I must confess that the priestliness of my profession has ever been im- 6
pressed on me. In the beginning there are vows, taken with all solemnity. Then
there is the endless harsh novitiate of training, much fatigue, much sacrifice. At
last one emerges as celebrant, standing close to the truth lying curtained in the
Ark of the body. Not surplice and cassock but mask and gown are your regalia.
You hold no chalice, but a knife. There is no wine, no water. There are only the
facts of blood and flesh.

And if the surgeon is like a poet, then the scars you have made on count- 7
less bodies are like verses into the fashioning of which you have poured your
soul. I think that if years later I were to see the trace from an old incision of
mine, I should know it at once, as one recognizes his pet expressions.

But mostly you are a traveler in a dangerous country, advancing into the moist 8
and jungly cleft your hands have made. Eyes and ears are shuttered from the land

you left behind; mind empties itself of all other thought. You are the root of groping fingers. It is a fine hour for the fingers, their sense of touch so enhanced. The
blind must know this feeling. Oh, there is risk everywhere. One goes lightly. The
spleen. No! No! Do not touch the spleen that lurks below the left leaf of the
diaphragm, a manta ray in a coral cave, its bloody tongue protruding. One poke
and it might rupture, exploding with sudden hemorrhage. The filmy omentum
must not be torn, the intestine scraped or denuded. The hand finds the liver,
palms it, fingers running along its sharp lower edge, admiring. Here are the
twin mounds of the kidneys, the apron of the omentum hanging in front of the
intestinal coils. One lifts it aside and the fingers dip among the loops, searching, mapping territory, establishing boundaries. Deeper still, and the womb is
touched, then held like a small muscular bottle—the womb and its earlike ap-
pendages, the ovaries. How they do nestle in the cup of a man's hand, their
power all dormant. They are frailty itself.

9   There is a hush in the room. Speech stops. The hands of the others, assistants and nurses, are still. Only the voice of the patient's respiration remains. It
is the rhythm of a quiet sea, the sound of waiting. Then you speak, slowly, the
terse entries of a Himalayan climber reporting back.

10   "The stomach is okay. Greater curvature clean. No sign of ulcer. Pylorus,
duodenum fine. Now comes the gallbladder. No stones. Right kidney, left, all
right. Liver . . . uh-oh."

11   Your speech lowers to a whisper, falters, stops for a long, long moment,
then picks up again at the end of a sigh that comes through your mask like a
last exhalation.

12   "Three big hard ones in the left lobe, one on the right. Metastatic deposits.
Bad, bad. Where's the primary? Got to be coming from somewhere."

13   The arm shifts direction and the fingers drop lower and lower into the
pelvis—the body impaled now upon the arm of the surgeon to the hilt of the
elbow.

14   "Here it is."

15   The voice goes flat, all business now.

16   "Tumor in the sigmoid colon, wrapped all around it, pretty tight. We'll take
out a sleeve of the bowel. No colostomy. Not that, anyway. But, God, there's a
lot of it down there. Here, you take a feel."

17   You step back from the table, and lean into a sterile basin of water, resting
on stiff arms, while the others locate the cancer. . . .

18   What is it, then, this thing, the knife, whose shape is virtually the same as it
was three thousand years ago, but now with its head grown detachable? Before
steel, it was bronze. Before bronze, stone—then back into unremembered time.
Did man invent it or did the knife precede him here, hidden under ages of veg-
etation and hoofprints, lying in wait to be discovered, picked up, used?

19   The scalpel is in two parts, the handle and the blade. Joined, it is six inches
from tip to tip. At one end of the handle is a narrow notched prong upon
which the blade is slid, then snapped into place. Without the blade, the handle
has a blind, decapitated look. It is helpless as a trussed maniac. But slide on the
blade, click it home, and the knife springs instantly to life. It is headed now,
edgy, leaping to mount the fingers for the gallop to its feast.

20   Now is the moment from which you have turned aside, from which you
have averted your gaze, yet toward which you have been hastened. Now the
scalpel sings along the flesh again, its brute run unimpeded by germs or other
frictions. It is a slick slide home, a barracuda spurt, a rip of embedded talon.

One listens, and almost hears the whine—nasal, high, delivered through that gleaming metallic snout. The flesh splits with its own kind of moan. It is like the penetration of rape.

The breasts of women are cut off, arms and legs sliced to the bone to make   21
ready for the saw, eyes freed from sockets, intestines lopped. The hand of the surgeon rebels. Tension boils through his pores, like sweat. The flesh of the patient retaliates with hemorrhage, and the blood chases the knife wherever it is withdrawn.

Within the belly a tumor squats, toadish, fungoid. A gray mother and her   22
brood. The only thing it does not do is croak. It too is hacked from its bed as the carnivore knife lips the blood, turning in it in a kind of ecstasy of plenty, a gluttony after the long fast. It is just for this that the knife was created, tempered, heated, its violence beaten into paper-thin force.

At last a little thread is passed into the wound and tied. The monstrous   23
booming fury is stilled by a tiny thread. The tempest is silenced. The operation is over. On the table, the knife lies spent, on it side, the bloody meal smeardried upon its flanks. The knife rests.

And waits.   24

DISCUSSION QUESTIONS

1. Cite several parts of the essay to show that despite Selzer's use of medical terms he is writing for a lay audience.

2. Point out examples of effective description in paragraph 3 and explain what they contribute to the process.

3. Identify the signals that Selzer uses to help the reader follow the course of the operation.

4. Selzer includes numerous comparisons in his essay. Identify them and discuss their purpose.

5. Even though Selzer is not providing directions for someone to follow, he includes three warnings to himself in paragraph 8. What are they? What purpose do they serve?

6. In paragraph 9, Selzer notes that a hush occurs, speech and movement cease, and quiet prevails. Explain why.

7. Discuss the meaning and effectiveness of the sentence fragment that ends the essay.

TOWARD KEY INSIGHTS

What are the advantages of presenting an emotional, poetic account of a surgical procedure rather than treating it in an objective and clinical manner? Are there any disadvantages or dangers?

What other kinds of processes can be usefully described in an emotional fashion? What common characteristics, if any, do these processes share?

SUGGESTION FOR WRITING

Select some activity you're familiar with—perhaps planning a party, programming a computer, or dieting successfully—and describe the steps involved, using appropriate comparisons and figurative language.

Illustration

Sabrina Rubin Erdely

Binge Drinking, A Campus Killer

Sabrina Rubin Erdely is an award-winning investigative journalist based in Philadelphia. She is a Senior Writer at Philadelphia *magazine, where she has been on staff since 1995, and has contributed to a wide array of other magazines. Erdely's feature writing has earned her a number of awards, including a prestigious National Magazine Award nomination. Our selection focuses on a serious and growing problem at American colleges and universities.*

Introduction: identifies serious problem, point to be illustrated	1 Pregame tailgating parties, post-exam celebrations and Friday happy hours—not to mention fraternity and sorority mixers—have long been a cornerstone of the collegiate experience. But on campuses across America, these indulgences have a more alarming side. For some of today's college students, binge drinking has become the norm.
Body: paragraphs 2–39	2 This past February I headed to the University of Wisconsin-Madison, rated the No. 2 party school in the nation by the college guide *Princeton Review*, to see the party scene for myself. On Thursday night the weekend was already getting started. At a raucous off-campus gathering, 20-year-old Tracey Middler struggled to down her beer as fist-pumping onlookers yelled, "Chug! Chug! Chug!"
End of paragraph 2, paragraphs 3 and 5: first examples support main point, as do all examples	3 In the kitchen, sophomore Jeremy Budda drained his tenth beer. "I get real wasted on weekends," he explained. Nearby, a 19-year-old estimated, "I'll end up having 17, 18 beers."

4   Swept up in the revelry, these partiers aren't thinking about the alcohol-related tragedies that have been in the news. All they're thinking about now is the next party. The keg is just about empty.

5   As the 19-year-old announces loudly, these college students have just one objective: "to get drunk!"

6   The challenge to drink to the very limits of one's endurance has become a celebrated staple of college life. In one of the most extensive reports on college drinking thus far, a 1997 Harvard School of Public Health study found that 43 percent of college students admitted binge drinking in the preceding two weeks. (Defined as four drinks in a sitting for a woman and five for a man, a drinking binge is when one drinks enough to risk health and well-being.)

Illustration **475**

"That's about five million students," says Henry Wechsler, who co-authored 7
the study. "And it's certainly a cause for concern. Most of these students don't
realize they're engaging in risky behavior." University of Kansas Chancellor
Robert Hemenway adds, "Every year we see students harmed because of their
involvement with alcohol."

Indeed, when binge drinking came to the forefront last year with a rash 8
of alcohol-related college deaths, the nation was stunned by the loss. There
was Scott Krueger, the 18-year-old fraternity pledge at the Massachusetts Institute of Technology, who died of alcohol poisoning after downing the equivalent of 15 shots in an hour. There was Leslie Baltz, a University of Virginia
senior, who died after she drank too much and fell down a flight of stairs. Lor-
raine Hanna, a freshman at Indiana University of Pennsylvania, was left alone
to sleep off her night of New Year's Eve partying. Later that day her twin sister found her dead—with a blood-alcohol content (BAC) of 0.429 percent.
(Driving with a BAC of 0.1 percent and above is illegal in all states.)

> Brief examples feature different students, as do all examples, providing more evidence supporting paper's point

Experts estimate that excessive drinking is involved in thousands of student 9
deaths a year. And the Harvard researchers found that there has been a dramatic change in why students drink: 39 percent drank "to get drunk" in 1993,
but 52 percent had the same objective in 1997.

"What has changed is the across-the-board *acceptability* of intoxication," says 10
Felix Savino, a psychologist at UW-Madison. "Many college students today see
not just drinking but being *drunk* as their primary way of socializing."

The reasons for the shift are complex and not fully understood. But re- 11
searchers surmise that it may have something to do with today's instant-gratifi-
cation life-style—and young people tend to take it to the extreme.

In total, it is estimated that America's 12 million undergraduates drink the 12
equivalent of six million gallons of beer a week. When that's combined with
teenagers' need to drink secretly, it's no wonder many have a dangerous relationship with alcohol.

The biggest predictor of bingeing is fraternity or sorority membership. 13
Sixty-five percent of members qualified as binge-drinkers, according to the Harvard study.

August 25, 1997, was meant to be a night the new Sigma Alpha Epsilon 14
pledges at Louisiana State University in Baton Rouge would never forget, and
by 8 P.M it was certainly shaping up that way. The revelry had begun earlier with
a keg party. Then they went to a bar near campus, where pledges consumed
massive quantities of alcohol.

> Extended example: paragraphs 14–21

Among the pledges were Donald Hunt, Jr., a 21-year-old freshman and 15
Army veteran, and his roommate, Benjamin Wynne, a 20-year-old sophomore.
Friends since high school, the two gamely drank the alcoholic concoctions of-
fered to them and everyone else.

Before long, many in the group began vomiting into trash cans. (Donald 16
Hunt would later allege in a lawsuit that these "vomiting stations" were set up
for that very purpose, something the defendants adamantly deny.) About 9:30,
incapacitated pledges were taken back to sleep it off at the frat house.

The 911 call came around midnight. Paramedics were stunned at what they 17
found: more than a dozen young men sprawled on the floor, on chairs, on
couches, reeking of alcohol. The paramedics burst into action, shaking the
pledges and shouting, "Hey! Can you hear me?" Four couldn't be roused, and
of those, one had no vital signs: Benjamin Wynne was in cardiac arrest.

18   Checking to see that nothing was blocking Wynne's airway, the paramedics began CPR. Within minutes they'd inserted an oxygen tube into his lungs, hooked up an I.V., attached a cardiac monitor and begun shocking him with defibrillation paddles, trying to restart his heart.

19   Still not responding, Wynne was rushed by ambulance to Baton Rouge General Hospital. Lab work revealed that his blood-alcohol content was an astonishing 0.588 percent, nearly six times the legal driving limit for adults—the equivalent of taking about 21 shots in an hour.

20   Meanwhile, three other fraternity pledges were undergoing similar revival efforts. One was Donald Hunt. He would suffer severe alcohol poisoning and nearly die.

21   After working furiously on Wynne, the hospital team admitted defeat. He was pronounced dead of acute alcohol poisoning.

22   One simple fact people tend to lose sight of is that alcohol is a poison—often pleasurable, but a toxin nonetheless. And for a person with little experience processing this toxin, it can come as something of a physical shock.

23   In general, a bottle of beer has about the same alcohol content as a glass of wine or shot of liquor. And the body can remove only the equivalent of less than one drink hourly from the bloodstream.

24   Many students are not just experimenting once or twice. In the Harvard study, half of binge drinkers were "frequent binge drinkers," meaning they had binged three or more times in the previous two weeks.

25   It also is assumed by some that bingeing is a "guy thing," an activity that, like cigar smoking and watching televised sports, belongs in the realm of male bonding. Statistics, however, show that the number of heavy-drinking young women is significant. Henry Wechsler's Harvard study found that a hefty 48 percent of college men were binge drinkers, and women were right behind them at 39 percent.

Extended example:
paragraphs 26–32

26   Howard Somers had always been afraid of heights. Perhaps his fear was some sort of an omen. On an August day in 1997 he helped his 18-year-old daughter, Mindy, move into her dorm at Virginia Tech. As they unloaded her things in the eighth-floor room, Somers noted with unease the position of the window. It opened inward like an oven door, its lip about level with her bed. He mentioned it, but Mindy dismissed his concern with a smile.

27   "I have gone through more guilt than you can imagine," Somers says now quietly. "Things I wish I had said or done. But I never thought this would happen. Who would?"

28   Mindy Somers knew the dangers of alcohol and tried to stay aware of her limits. She'd planned not to overdo it that Friday night, since her mother was coming in that weekend to celebrate Mindy's 19th birthday on Sunday. But it was Halloween, the campus was alive with activity, and Mindy decided to stop in at several off-campus parties.

29   When she returned to her room at 3 A.M., she was wiped out enough to fall into bed fully clothed. Mindy's bed was pushed lengthwise against the long, low window. Her roommate and two other girls, who were on the floor, all slept too soundly to notice that sometime after 4 A.M. Mindy's bed was empty.

30   When the paperboy found her facedown on the grass at 6:45 A.M., he at first thought it was a Halloween prank. Police and EMTs swarmed to the scene in minutes. Somers was pronounced dead of massive chest and abdominal in-

Illustration   **477**

juries. She had a blood-alcohol content of 0.21 percent, equal to her having drunk about five beers in one hour.

Police surmised that Mindy had tried to get out of bed during the night but, disoriented, had slipped out the window, falling 75 feet to her death. "It was a strange, tragic accident," Virginia Tech Police Chief Michael Jones says. 31

A terrible irony was that the week prior to Mindy's death had been Virginia Tech's annual Alcohol Awareness Week. 32

While binge drinking isn't always lethal, it does have other, wide-ranging effects. Academics is one realm where it takes a heavy toll. 33

During my trip to Wisconsin most students told me they didn't plan on attending classes the following day. "Nah, I almost never go to class on Friday. It's no big deal," answered Greg, a sophomore. According to a survey of university administrators, 38 percent of academic problems are alcohol-related, as are 29 percent of dropouts. 34

Perhaps because alcohol increases aggression and impairs judgment, it is also related to 25 percent of violent crimes and roughly 60 percent of vandalism on campus. According to one survey, 79 percent of students who had experienced unwanted sexual intercourse in the previous year said that they were under the influence of alcohol or other drugs at the time. "Some people believe that alcohol can provide an excuse for inappropriate behavior, including sexual aggression," says Jeanette Norris, a University of Washington researcher. Later on, those people can claim, "It wasn't me—it was the booze." 35

Faced with the many potential dangers, college campuses are scrambling for ways to reduce binge drinking. Many offer seminars on alcohol during freshman orientation. Over 50 schools provide alcohol-free living environments. At the University of Michigan's main campus in Ann Arbor, for instance, nearly 30 percent of undergrads living in university housing now choose to live in alcohol-free rooms. Nationwide several fraternities have announced that by the year 2000 their chapter houses will be alcohol-free. 36

After the University of Rhode Island topped the *Princeton Review* party list two yeas in a row, administrators banned alcohol at all student events on campus; this year URI didn't even crack the top ten. Some campuses respond even more severely, unleashing campus raids and encouraging police busts. 37

Researchers debate, however, if such "zero-tolerance" policies are helpful or if they might actually result in more secret, off-campus drinking. Other academics wonder if dropping the drinking age to 18 would take away the illicit thrill of alcohol and lower the number of kids drinking wildly. Others feel this would just create more drinking-related fatalities. 38

Whatever it takes, changing student behavior won't be easy. "What you've got here are people who think they are having fun," Harvard's Henry Wechsler explains. "You can't change their behavior by preaching at them or by telling them they'll get hurt." 39

Around 2 A.M. at UW-Madison a hundred kids congregate at a downtown intersection in a nightly ritual. One girl is trying to pull her roommate up off the ground. "I'm not that drunk," the one on the ground insists. "I just can't stand up." 40

Conclusion: paragraphs 40–41; returns to opening example

Two fights break out. A police car cruises by and the crowd thins, some heading to after-hours parties. Then maybe at 3 or 4 A.M. they'll go home to get some sleep, so they will be rested for when they start to drink again. Tomorrow night. 41

DISCUSSION QUESTIONS

1. Discuss the effectiveness of Rubin Erdely's title.
2. What does Rubin Erdely accomplish in paragraphs 6–7 and in paragraphs 9–13, 22–25, and 33–38?
3. How do you account for the slang expressions found in this essay: "Chug! Chug! Chug!" in paragraph 2 and "wasted" in paragraph 3?
4. Comment on the effectiveness of the two-word sentence fragment that ends the essay.

TOWARD KEY INSIGHTS

Why would "many college students today see not just drinking but being *drunk* as their primary way of socializing"?
What can be done to counter this mind-set?

SUGGESTION FOR WRITING

Write an essay illustrating some type of benefit available on campus—perhaps academic counseling, the campus ministry, or some ethnic or racial organization. Develop your essay with several short examples or one extended one.

Martin Gottfried

Rambos of the Road

Martin Gottfried is a native of New York City and a writer on theatrical matters. Born in 1933, he earned an A.B. degree at Columbia University and then, after attending law school, served two years in the military intelligence branch of the U.S. Army. Following his discharge in 1959, he spent four years as a music and movie critic and since 1963 has worked as a drama critic. He has authored several books on the theater as well as magazine articles on a variety of topics. In our selection, Gottfried examines the driving behavior of all too many motorists.

1   The car pulled up and its driver glared at us with such sullen intensity, such hatred, that I was truly afraid for our lives. Except for the Mohawk haircut he didn't have, he looked like Robert De Niro in "Taxi Driver," the sort of young man who, delirious for notoriety, might kill a president.

2   He was glaring because we had passed him and for that affront he pursued us to the next stoplight so as to express his indignation and affirm his masculinity. I was with two women and, believe it, was afraid for all three of us. It was nearly midnight and we were in a small, sleeping town with no other cars on the road.

3   When the light turned green, I raced ahead, knowing it was foolish and that I was not in a movie. He didn't merely follow, he chased, and with his headlights turned off. No matter what sudden turn I took, he followed. My passengers were silent. I knew they were alarmed, and I prayed that I wouldn't be

Illustration **479**

called upon to protect them. In that cheerful frame of mind, I turned off my own lights so I couldn't be followed. It was lunacy. I was responding to a crazy *as* a crazy.

"I'll just drive to the police station," I finally said, and as if those were the magic words, he disappeared. 4

Elbowing Fenders: It seems to me that there has recently been an epidemic of auto macho—a competition perceived and expressed in driving. People fight it out over parking spaces. They bully into line at the gas pump. A toll booth becomes a signal for elbowing fenders. And beetle-eyed drivers hunch over their steering wheels, squeezing the rims, glowering, preparing the excuse of not having seen you as they muscle you off the road. Approaching a highway on an entrance ramp recently, I was strong-armed by a trailer truck so immense that its driver all but blew me away by blasting his horn. The behemoth was just inches from my hopelessly mismatched coupe when I fled for the safety of the shoulder. 5

And this is happening on city streets, too. A New York taxi driver told me that "intimidation is the name of the game. Drive as if you're deaf and blind. You don't hear the other guy's horn and you sure as hell don't see him." 6

The odd thing is that long before I was even able to drive, it seemed to me that people were at their finest and most civilized when in their cars. They seemed so orderly and considerate, so reasonable, staying in the right-hand lane unless passing, signaling all intentions. In those days you really eased into highway traffic, and the long, neat rows of cars seemed mobile testimony to the sanity of most people. Perhaps memory fails, perhaps there were always testy drivers, perhaps—but everyone didn't give you the finger. 7

A most amazing example of driver rage occurred recently at the Manhattan end of the Lincoln Tunnel. We were four cars abreast, stopped at a traffic light. And there was no moving even when the light had changed. A bus had stopped in the cross traffic, blocking our paths: it was normal-for-New-York-City gridlock. Perhaps impatient, perhaps late for important appointments, three of us nonetheless accepted what, after all, we could not alter. One, however, would not. He would not be helpless. He would go where he was going even if he couldn't get there. A Wall Street type in suit and tie, he got out of his car and strode toward the bus, rapping smartly on its doors. When they opened, he exchanged words with the driver. The doors folded shut. He then stepped in front of the bus, took hold of one of its large windshield wipers and broke it. 8

The bus doors reopened and the driver appeared, apparently giving the fellow a good piece of his mind. If so, the lecture was wasted, for the man started his car and proceeded to drive directly *into the bus*. He rammed it. Even though the point at which he struck the bus, the folding doors, was its most vulnerable point, ramming the side of a bus with your car has to rank very high on a futility index. My first thought was that it had to be a rental car. 9

Lane Merger: To tell the truth, I could not believe my eyes. The bus driver opened his doors as much as they could be opened and he stepped directly onto the hood of the attacking car, jumping up and down with both his feet. He then retreated into the bus, closing the doors behind him. Obviously a man of action, the car driver backed up and rammed the bus again. How this exercise in absurdity would have been resolved none of us will ever know for at that point the traffic unclogged and the bus moved on. And the rest of us, we passives of the world, proceeded, our cars crossing a field of battle as if nothing untoward had happened. 10

11   It is tempting to blame such belligerent, uncivil and even neurotic behavior on the nuts of the world, but in our cars we all become a little crazy. How many of us speed up when a driver signals his intention of pulling in front of us? Are we resentful and anxious to pass him? How many of us try to squeeze in, or race along the shoulder at a lane merger? We may not jump on hoods, but driving the gantlet, we seethe, cursing not so silently in the safety of our steel bodies on wheels—fortresses for cowards.

12   What is it within us that gives birth to such antisocial behavior and why, all of a sudden, have so many drivers gone around the bend? My friend Joel Katz, a Manhattan psychiatrist, calls it, "a Rambo pattern. People are running around thinking the American way is to take the law into your own hands when anyone does anything wrong. And what constitutes 'wrong'? Anything that cramps your style."

13   It seems to me that it is a new America we see on the road now. It has the mentality of a hoodlum and the backbone of a coward. The car is its weapon and hiding place, and it is still a symbol even in this. Road Rambos no longer bespeak a self-reliant, civil people tooling around in family cruisers. In fact, there aren't families in these machines that charge headlong with their brights on in broad daylight, demanding we get out of their way. Bullies are loners, and they have perverted our liberty of the open road into drivers' license. They represent an America that derides the values of decency and good manners, then roam the highways riding shotgun and shrieking freedom. By allowing this to happen, the rest of us approve.

DISCUSSION QUESTIONS

1. Identify the thesis statement of this essay.
2. What paragraphs make up the introduction? Besides starting the essay, what function do they perform?
3. Why are several examples a better choice for this essay than one extended example?
4. In what order does Gottfried arrange his examples?
5. What does Gottfried accomplish in paragraphs 11–12?
6. What function, other than ending the essay, is served by the final paragraph?

TOWARD KEY INSIGHTS

Do you agree with Gottfried's claim that the "new America we see on the road now . . . has the mentality of a hoodlum and the backbone of a coward"? Why or why not?

Where else have you encountered macho behavior? At athletic events? At activities that generate long lines? At political demonstrations?

What conclusions can you draw about those who engage in such behavior?

SUGGESTION FOR WRITING

Write an illustration essay exploring the behavior, good or bad, that you have experienced on campus, in the workplace, or while engaged in some activity such as shopping. Use several examples, arrange them in an appropriate order, and try to account for the behavior.

Illustration   **481**

Matea Gold and David Ferrell

Going for Broke

Matea Gold, a native of Northampton, Massachusetts, earned a B. A. degree from UCLA and then joined David Ferrell as a staff writer for the Los Angeles Times. *Gold earned Sacramento Press Club awards in 1994 and 1995, while Ferrell was a 1996 finalist for the Investigative Reporters and Editors Award, which recognizes outstanding investigative work. The information in this article is drawn from a seven-month nationwide investigation of legalized gambling. Its case studies offer a sobering view of the consequences of gambling addiction.*

1   Rex Coile's life is a narrow box, so dark and confining he wonders how he got trapped inside, whether he'll ever get out.

2   He never goes to the movies, never sees concerts, never lies on a sunny beach, never travels on vacation, never spends Christmas with his family. Instead, Rex shares floor space in cheap motels with other compulsive gamblers, comforting himself with delusional dreams of jackpots that will magically wipe away three decades of wreckage. He has lost his marriage, his home, his Cadillac, his clothes, his diamond ring. Not least of all, in the card clubs of Southern California, he has lost his pride.

3   Rex no longer feels sorry for himself, not after a 29-year losing streak that has left him scrounging for table scraps to feed his habit. Still, he agonizes over what he has become at 54 and what he might have been.

4   Articulate, intellectual, he talks about existential philosophy, the writings of Camus and Sartre. He was once an editor at Random House. His mind is so jampacked with tidbits about movies, television, baseball and history that card room regulars call him "Rex Trivia," a name he cherishes for the remnant of self-respect it gives him. "There's a lot of Rexes around these card rooms," he says in a whisper of resignation and sadness.

5   And their numbers are soaring as gambling explodes across America, from the mega-resorts of Las Vegas to the gaming parlors of Indian reservations, from the riverboats along the Mississippi to the corner mini-marts selling lottery tickets. With nearly every state in the union now sanctioning some form of legalized gambling to raise revenues, evidence is mounting that society is paying a steep price, one that some researchers say must be confronted, if not reversed.

6   Never before have bettors blown so much money—a whopping $50.9 billion last year—five times the amount lost in 1980. That's more than the public spent on movies, theme parks, recorded music and sporting events combined. A substantial share of those gambling losses—an estimated 30% to 40%—pours from the pockets and purses of chronic losers hooked on the adrenaline rush of risking their money, intoxicated by the fast action of gambling's incandescent world.

7   Studies place the total number of compulsive gamblers at about 4.4 million, about equal to the nation's ranks of hard-core drug addicts. Another 11 million,

known as problem gamblers, teeter on the verge. Since 1990, the number of Gamblers Anonymous groups nationwide has doubled from about 600 to more than 1,200.

8   Compulsive gambling has been linked to child abuse, domestic violence, embezzlement, bogus insurance claims, bankruptcies, welfare fraud and a host of other social and criminal ills. The advent of Internet gambling could lure new legions into wagering beyond their means.

9   Every once in a while, a case is so egregious it makes headlines: A 10-day-old baby girl in South Carolina dies after being left for nearly seven hours in a hot car while her mother plays video poker. A suburban Chicago woman is so desperate for a bankroll to gamble that she allegedly suffocates her 7-week-old daughter 11 days after obtaining a $200,000 life-insurance policy on the baby.

10   But these tragedies that flash before the public eye are just lightning strokes of a roiling night storm. Far more often, compulsive gambling bends lives more subtly, less sensationally, over the course of years.

11   Gwen, one of the unseen masses trying to keep her head above water, sits on an easy chair in the living room of her worn Jefferson Park bungalow, watching the movie "Titanic" on an old TV. Her hair is uncombed and there are bags under her eyes. She puffs on a cigarette and shakes her foot nervously. On the screen, the great ship begins to founder.

12   "That's me," she says, tears rolling down her checks. "I'm sinking."

13   Gwen has just come off a three-day bender at the Hollywood Park Casino in Inglewood. She blew a paycheck, emptied out her new checking account, gambled right through her work shift. Driving home from the casino, she contemplated veering off the road, ending it all. "I just don't want to be here," she mumbles, watching Titanic's Rose and Jack struggling to hold on to a piece of driftwood in the freezing sea. "I just feel like I'm living a hopeless life. So hopeless."

14   She's written bad checks and maxed out her credit cards. One bank closed her checking account after she put too many fake deposit slips in the ATM to withdraw cash. She lies. She tells her boss she needs a salary advance because her son is in the hospital. Late on the rent, she parks a block from the house to duck the landlord. For the last eight years, this has been her life, one so empty of joy and options that the card clubs have become her only hope of filling the hole.

15   She thinks back to that night a few years ago when, desperate to recoup her gambling losses, she pilfered several thousand dollars from the safe of a restaurant where she was working. She just needed something to get herself started, she told herself. She'd pay it back with the winnings. She blew it all in one weekend.

16   Overwhelmed by guilt, she came clean with her manager. She was booked, fingerprinted and briefly thrown behind bars. "It was the worst experience of my life," she says.

17   Gwen now makes monthly $75 restitution payments to the restaurant as part of her court-ordered probation.

18   "I have hurt so many people with my gambling," says Gwen. "I have lost best friends. After all the pain I've caused everybody, the pain I caused myself, I still have the urge to gamble. I never know what I'm going to do. I'm so afraid. I'm really afraid."

19   Science has begun to uncover clues to compulsive gambling—genetic predispositions that involve chemical receptors in the brain, the same pleasure pathways implicated in drug and alcohol addiction. But no amount of knowledge, no amount of enlightenment, makes the illness any less confounding, any less destructive. What the gamblers cannot understand about themselves is also

Illustration **483**

well beyond the comprehension of family members, who struggle for normality in a world of deceit and madness.

Money starts vanishing: $500 here, $200 there, $800 a couple of weeks later. 20 Where is it? The answers come back vague, nonsensical. It's in the desk at work. A friend borrowed it. It got spent on family dinners, car repairs, loans to in-laws. Exasperated spouses play the sleuth, combing through pockets, wallets, purses, searching the car. Sometimes the incriminating evidence turns up—a racing form, lottery scratchers, a map to an Indian casino. Once the secret is uncovered, spouses usually fight the problem alone, bleeding inside, because the stories are too humiliating to share.

"Anybody who is living with a compulsive gambler is totally overwhelmed," 21 says Tom Tucker, president of the California Council on Problem Gambling. "They're steeped in anger, resentment, depression, confusion. None of their personal efforts will ever stop a person from their [sic] addiction. And they don't really see any hope because compulsive gambling in general is such an under-recognized illness."

One Los Angeles woman, whose husband's gambling was tearing at her san- 22 ity, says she slept with her fists so tightly clenched that her nails sliced into her palms. She had fantasies of death—first her own, thinking he'd feel sorry for her and stop gambling. Later, she harbored thoughts of turning her rage on her husband. She imagined getting a gun, hiding in the closet and blasting him out of her life.

"The hurt was so bad I think I would have pulled the trigger," she says. 23 "There were times the pain was so much I thought being in jail, or being in the electric chair, would be less than this."

Five years in Gam-Anon, the 12-step support group for family and friends 24 of compulsive gamblers, has only begun to heal her. "I don't think I'm even halfway there," she says.

Too often, families of gambling addicts endure more than warped finances 25 and wrecked psyches. They have come to fear for their physical safety.

Trena, a 42-year-old Whittier homemaker, is among them. Several months 26 ago, after years of agony, she filed for divorce. Her husband, a manager in an industrial plant, was making decent money and took pride in his job. He had two good children and a nice home, an airy bungalow with hardwood floors and a white-brick fireplace. Inside him, though, was a fearsome need to fulfill some glossy vision.

Lottery keno became the rhythmic pulse of his life. For five years, Trena 27 says, she awoke in an empty bed every weekend. Her husband would be gone by 5:30 or 6, joining other keno regulars at the neighborhood doughnut shop, watching the numbers flash on an overhead monitor. He'd shuffle home hours later, refusing to divulge his losses.

Trena did what tens of thousands of spouses do: She struggled desperately 28 to pay the bills. She hid money in Cheerios boxes, books, couch cushions, under the doormat. She drew up household budgets—hundreds of them. They became her obsession. She drafted a new one almost every day, never able to get one to work.

Absurd dramas were played out. On paydays, when her husband's check 29 was directly deposited into their account, they would race each other to the bank. Trena would go to one branch, he'd head to another. She would sit at the drive-up window, jamming her withdrawal slip in the pneumatic tube the moment the bank opened. If she got the money, they could pay the utilities and keep the phone connected. If not, he'd be off to the races, the casinos or the doughnut shop.

30   Like a caged animal, she threw things—smashed a clock against the wall, broke the portable TV in the bedroom. She yelled, clawed and sometimes just sank down and cried. Trena had no money for herself, for the important personal things. She got nothing for her mom on Mother's Day.

31   Increasingly reclusive, she stopped returning calls. Chit-chatting with friends seemed a frivolous distraction when dealing with foreclosure notices, filing for bankruptcy or, worse, fending off her husband's angry demands for cash.

32   He would burst into the house shouting, "Give me my money!" Pacing, following her, tipping over plants, rifling through drawers, dumping them out to try to find it. "Don't you touch my money!"

33   Joining Gam-Anon, where Trena receives emotional support from the spouses of other gamblers, has helped her deal with her decade-long ordeal. She says she is not bitter and understands that compulsive gambling is an illness.

34   While her husband now lives with his parents, she remains in their home of 19 years, a place filled with memories as wistful as they are painful.

35   With drug or alcohol abusers, there is the hope of sobering up, an accomplishment in itself, no matter what problems may have accompanied their addictions. Compulsive gamblers often see no way to purge their urges when suffocating debts suggest only one answer: a hot streak. "They have nowhere to turn—they feel cornered," says Dr. Richard J. Rosenthal, a Beverly Hills psychiatrist who founded the California Council on Problem Gambling. "Very often they are motivated by their shame into more and more desperate attempts to avoid being found out."

36   David Phillips, a UC San Diego sociology professor, studied death records from 1982 to 1988—before legalized gambling exploded across America—and found that people in Las Vegas, Atlantic City and other gambling meccas showed significantly higher suicide rates than people in non-gambling cities.

37   Rex Trivia is not about to kill himself, but like most compulsive gamblers, he occasionally thinks about it. Looking at him, it's hard to imagine he once had a promising future as a smart young New York book editor. His pale eyes are expressionless, his hair yellowish and brittle. In his fifties, his health is failing: emphysema, three lung collapses, a bad aorta, rotting teeth.

38   His plunge has been so dizzying that at one point he agreed to aid another desperate gambler in a run of bank robberies—nine in all, throughout Los Angeles and Orange counties. When the FBI busted him in 1980, he had $50,000 in cash in a dresser drawer and $100,000 in traveler's checks in his refrigerator's vegetable crisper. Rex, who ended up doing a short stint in prison, hasn't seen that kind of money since.

39   At 11 P.M. on a Tuesday night, with a bankroll of $55—all he has—he is at a poker table in Gardena. With quick, nervous hands he stacks and unstacks his $1 chips. The stack dwindles. Down $30, he talks about leaving, getting some sleep. Midnight comes and goes. Rex starts winning. Three aces. Four threes. Chips pile up—$60, $70. "A shame to go when the cards are falling my way." He checks the time: "I'll go at 2. Win, lose or draw."

40   Fate, kismet, luck—the cards keep falling. At 2 A.M., Rex is up $97. He stands, leaves his chips on the table and goes out for a smoke. In the darkness at the edge of the parking lot, he loiters with other regulars, debating with himself whether to grab a bus and quit.

"I should go back in there and cash in and get out of here," he says. "That's 41 what I should do."

A long pause. Crushing out his cigarette, Rex turns and heads back inside. 42 He has made his decision.

"A few more hands." 43

DISCUSSION QUESTIONS

1. Discuss the irony of the essay's title.

2. Why do you think Gold and Ferrell repeat "never" five times in paragraph 2?

3. Identify the essay's thesis statement.

4. By referring to specific paragraphs, point out the various illustrations that the writers use in this essay.

5. Why do you think that Gold and Ferrell cite quotations at various points?

6. What do the writers accomplish by ending the selection with a continuation of the first example?

TOWARD KEY INSIGHTS

What factors account for the explosive growth of legalized gambling?
What benefits, if any, have resulted from this growth?
How should we address the problem of compulsive gambling?

SUGGESTION FOR WRITING

Write an essay illustrating addiction to television viewing or smoking. Choose an appropriate number of examples and develop them with specific details.

Ellen Goodman

The Company Man

Ellen Goodman (born 1941) is a native of Massachusetts and a 1963 graduate of Radcliffe College. A journalist since graduation, she has worked as a researcher and reporter for Newsweek *magazine as well as a writer for several major newspapers and a commentator for national radio and TV shows. She has also written articles for* MS., McCall's, *and the* Village Voice. *Book-length publications include* Turning Points *(1979),* Value Judgments *(1993), and several collections of newspaper columns. Her latest book, which she co-authored with Patricia O'Brien, is entitled* I Know Just What You Mean: The Power of Friendship in Women's Lives *(2000). She has received numerous writing awards including a 1980 Pulitzer Prize for distinguished commentary. Our selection, originally a newspaper article, depicts a workaholic whose total dedication to his job killed him.*

1   He worked himself to death, finally and precisely, at 3:00 A.M. Sunday morning.

2   The obituary didn't say that, of course. It said that he died of a coronary thrombosis—I think that was it—but everyone among his friends and acquaintances knew it instantly. He was a perfect Type A, a workaholic, a classic, they said to each other and shook their heads—and thought for five or ten minutes about the way they lived.

3   This man who worked himself to death finally and precisely at 3:00 A.M. Sunday morning—on his day off—was fifty-one years old and a vice-president. He was, however, one of six vice-presidents, and one of three who might conceivably—if the president died or retired soon enough—have moved to the top spot. Phil knew that.

4   He worked six days a week, five of them until eight or nine at night, during a time when his own company had begun the four-day week for everyone but the executives. He worked like the Important People. He had no outside "extracurricular interests," unless, of course, you think about a monthly golf game that way. To Phil, it was work. He always ate egg salad sandwiches at his desk. He was, of course, overweight, by 20 to 25 pounds. He thought it was okay, though, because he didn't smoke.

5   On Saturdays, Phil wore a sports jacket to the office instead of a suit, because it was the weekend.

6   He had a lot of people working for him, maybe sixty, and most of them liked him most of the time. Three of them will be seriously considered for his job. The obituary didn't mention that.

7   But it did list his "survivors" quite accurately. He is survived by his wife, Helen, forty-eight years old, a good woman of no particular marketable skills, who worked in an office before marrying and mothering. She had, according to her daughter, given up trying to compete with his work years ago, when the children were small. A company friend said, "I know how much you will miss him." And she answered, "I already have."

8   "Missing him all these years," she must have given up part of herself which had cared too much for the man. She would be "well taken care of."

9   His "dearly beloved" eldest of the "dearly beloved" children is a hardworking executive in a manufacturing firm down South. In the day and a half before the funeral, he went around the neighborhood researching his father, asking the neighbors what he was like. They were embarrassed.

10   His second child is a girl, who is twenty-four and newly married. She lives near her mother and they are close, but whenever she was alone with her father, in a car driving somewhere, they had nothing to say to each other.

11   The youngest is twenty, a boy, a high-school graduate who has spent the last couple of years, like a lot of his friends, doing enough odd jobs to stay in grass and food. He was the one who tried to grab at his father, and tried to mean enough to him to keep the man at home. He was his father's favorite. Over the last two years, Phil stayed up nights worrying about the boy.

12   The boy once said, "My father and I only board here."

13   At the funeral, the sixty-year-old company president told the forty-eight-year-old widow that the fifty-one-year-old deceased had meant much to the company and would be missed and would be hard to replace. The widow didn't look him in the eye. She was afraid he would read her bitterness and, after all, she would need him to straighten out the finances—the stock options and all that.

Illustration   487

Phil was overweight and nervous and worked too hard. If he wasn't at   14
the office, he was worried about it. Phil was a Type A, a heart-attack natural. You
could have picked him out in a minute from a lineup.

So when he finally worked himself to death, at precisely 3:00 A.M. Sun-   15
day morning, no one was really surprised.

By 5:00 P.M. the afternoon of the funeral, the company president had   16
begun, discreetly of course, with care and taste, to make inquiries about his replacement. One of three men. He asked around: "Who's been working the
hardest?"

DISCUSSION QUESTIONS

1. Goodman says that Phil was "a perfect Type A" (paragraph 2). After reflecting
   on her essay, explain the characteristics of this type.
2. Why do you think Goodman doesn't supply Phil's last name or the name of the
   company he works for?
3. What idea is Goodman trying to present?
4. Unlike the essay by Rubin Erdely, Goodman's uses one longer illustration
   rather than several shorter ones. Why?
5. What is the significance of Phil's oldest son going "around the neighborhood
   researching his father, asking the neighbors what he was like" (paragraph 9)?
   Why were they embarrassed?
6. How do you account for Goodman's relatively short paragraphs?

TOWARD KEY INSIGHTS

What social values would cause individuals to work themselves to death?

In that regard, what is the significance of the company president asking "Who's
   been working the hardest?"

Are these values basically good, or should we make some changes in our attitudes
   toward work and success? If so, what kinds of changes?

SUGGESTION FOR WRITING   *Using one extended example, write an essay
that illustrates the lifestyle of a laid-back em-
ployee or friend. Your paper need not, of course,
feature a death.*

Classification

Marion Winik

What Are Friends For?

Marion Winik (born 1958) is a graduate of Brown University and of Brooklyn College, where she earned a master of fine arts degree in creative writing. Since graduation, she has pursued a career in education, writing, and marketing. Her writings include poems, short stories, essays, and books, and the shorter pieces have appeared in a variety of major newspapers and popular magazines. Her most recent book, The Lunch-Box Chronicles: Notes from the Parenting Underground *(1998), discusses her experiences in raising her sons after her husband's death. In this selection, Winik takes a humorous look at the different categories of friends and the benefits derived from each one.*

Introduction: indicates value of friends	1

I was thinking about how everybody can't be everything to each other, but some people can be something to each other, thank God, from the ones whose shoulder you cry on to the ones whose half-slips you borrow to the nameless ones you chat with in the grocery line.

Body: paragraphs 2–14	2
First category	

Buddies, for example, are the workhorses of the friendship world, the people out there on the front lines, defending you from loneliness and boredom. They call you up, they listen to your complaints, they celebrate your successes and curse your misfortunes, and you do the same for them in return. They hold out through innumerable crises before concluding that the person you're dating is no good, and even then understand if you ignore their good counsel. They accompany you to a movie with subtitles or to see the diving pig at Aquarena Springs. They feed your cat when you are out of town and pick you up from the airport when you get back. They come over to help you decide what to wear on a date. Even if it is with that creep.

Second category: paragraphs 3–4	3

What about family members? Most of them are people you just got stuck with, and though you love them, you may not have very much in common. But there is that rare exception, the Relative Friend. It is your cousin, your brother, maybe even your aunt. The two of you share the same views of the other family members. Meg never should have divorced Martin. He was the best thing that ever happened to her. You can confirm each other's memories of things that happened a long time ago. Don't you remember when Uncle Hank and

488

Daddy had that awful fight in the middle of Thanksgiving dinner? Grandma always hated Grandpa's stamp collection; she probably left the window open during the hurricane on purpose.

While so many family relationships are tinged with guilt and obligation, a relationship with a Relative Friend is relatively worry-free. You don't even have to hide your vices from this delightful person. When you slip out Aunt Joan's back door for a cigarette, she is already there.   4

Then there is that special guy at work. Like all the other people at the job site, at first he's just part of the scenery. But gradually he starts to stand out from the crowd. Your friendship is cemented by jokes about co-workers and thoughtful favors around the office. Did you see Ryan's hair? Want half my bagel? Soon you know the names of his turtles, what he did last Friday night, exactly which model CD player he wants for his birthday. His handwriting is as familiar to you as your own.   5 Third category: paragraphs 5–6

Though you invite each other to parties, you somehow don't quite fit into each other's outside lives. For this reason, the friendship may not survive a job change. Company gossip, once an infallible source of entertainment, soon awkwardly accentuates the distance between you. But wait. Like School Friends, Work Friends share certain memories which acquire a nostalgic glow after about a decade.   6

A Faraway Friend is someone you grew up with or went to school with or lived in the same town as until one of you moved away. Without a Faraway Friend, you would never get any mail addressed in handwriting. A Faraway Friend calls late at night, invites you to her wedding, always says she is coming to visit but rarely shows up. An actual visit from a Faraway Friend is a cause for celebration and binges of all kinds. Cigarettes, Chips Ahoy, bottles of tequila.   7 Fourth category: paragraphs 7–9

Faraway Friends go through phases of intense communication, then may be out of touch for many months. Either way, the connection is always there. A conversation with your Faraway Friend always helps to put your life in perspective: when you feel you've hit a dead end, come to a confusing fork in the road, or gotten lost in some crackerbox subdivision of your life, the advice of the Faraway Friend—who has the big picture, who is so well acquainted with the route that brought you to this place—is indispensable.   8

Another useful function of the Faraway Friend is to help you remember things from a long time ago, like the name of your seventh-grade history teacher, what was in that really good stir-fry, or exactly what happened that night on the boat with the guys from Florida.   9

Ah, the Former Friend. A sad thing. At best a wistful memory, at worst a dangerous enemy who is in possession of many of your deepest secrets. But what was it that drove you apart? A misunderstanding, a betrayed confidence, an unrepaid loan, an ill-conceived flirtation. A poor choice of spouse can do in a friendship just like that. Going into business together can be a serious mistake. Time, money, distance, cult religions: all noted friendship killers. . . .   10 Fifth category

And lest we forget, there are the Friends You Love to Hate. They call at inopportune times. They say stupid things. They butt in, they boss you around, they embarrass you in public. They invite themselves over. They take advantage. You've done the best you can, but they need professional help. On top of all this, they love you to death and are convinced they're your best friend on the planet.   11 Sixth category: paragraphs 11–12

12   So why do you continue to be involved with these people? Why do you tolerate them? On the contrary, the real question is, What would you do without them? Without Friends You Love to Hate, there would be nothing to talk about with your other friends. Their problems and their irritating stunts provide a reliable source of conversation for everyone they know. What's more, Friends You Love to Hate make you feel good about yourself, since you are obviously in so much better shape than they are. No matter what these people do, you will never get rid of them. As much as they need you, you need them too.

Seventh category 13   At the other end of the spectrum are Hero Friends. These people are better than the rest of us, that's all there is to it. Their career is something you wanted to be when you grew up—painter, forest ranger, tireless doer of good. They have beautiful homes filled with special handmade things presented to them by villagers in the remote areas they have visited in their extensive travels. Yet they are modest. They never gossip. They are always helping others, especially those who have suffered a death in the family or an illness. You would think people like this would just make you sick, but somehow they don't.

Eighth category 14   A New Friend is a tonic unlike any other. Say you meet her at a party. In your bowling league. At a Japanese conversation class, perhaps. Wherever, whenever, there's that spark of recognition. The first time you talk, you can't believe how much you have in common. Suddenly, your life story is interesting again, you insights fresh, your opinion valued. Your various short-comings are as yet completely invisible.

Conclusion: memorable observation meshes stylistically with rest of essay 15   It's almost like falling in love.

DISCUSSION QUESTIONS

1. Comment on the effectiveness of Winik's title.
2. Characterize the level of diction that Winik uses in her essay.
3. What elements of Winik's essay interest you the most? What elements interest you the least?

TOWARD KEY INSIGHTS

What traits characterize the various types of friends that you have?
In what ways are these friendships mutually beneficial?

SUGGESTION FOR WRITING

Write an essay classifying the various types of people that you consider undesirable. Choose an appropriate number of categories and support them with appropriate specific details.

Scott Russell Sanders

The Men We Carry in Our Minds

Scott Russell Sanders was born (1945) in Memphis, Tennessee. After earning a B.A. degree from Brown University in 1967 and a Ph.D. from Cambridge University in 1971, he joined the English faculty at Indiana University, where he is a full professor. Sanders is the author of numerous books of fiction and nonfiction. These books span a wide range of genres, including science fiction, historical novels, children's stories, folk tales, biographies, and personal essays. He has contributed to several essay anthologies, and his articles have appeared in literary journals and popular magazines. He has won several awards for his writing. In this essay, Sanders, in light of what he knows about the lives of working men, examines the view that power is rooted in gender.

The first men, besides my father, I remember seeing were black convicts and white guards, in the cottonfield across the road from our farm on the outskirts of Memphis. I must have been three or four. The prisoners wore dingy gray-and-black zebra suits, heavy as canvas, sodden with sweat. Hatless, stooped, they chopped weeds in the fierce heat, row after row, breathing the acrid dust of boll-weevil poison. The overseers wore dazzling white shirts and broad shadowy hats. The oiled barrels of their shotguns flashed in the sunlight. Their faces in memory are utterly blank. Of course those men, white and black, have become for me an emblem of racial hatred. But they have also come to stand for the twin poles of my early vision of manhood—the brute toiling animal and the boss.

When I was a boy, the men I knew labored with their bodies. They were marginal farmers, just scraping by, or welders, steel workers, carpenters; they swept floors, dug ditches, mined coal, or drove trucks, their forearms ropy with muscle; they trained horses, stoked furnaces, built tires, stood on assembly lines wrestling parts onto cars and refrigerators. They got up before light, worked all day long whatever the weather, and when they came home at night they looked as though somebody had been whipping them. In the evenings and on weekends they worked on their own places, tilling gardens that were lumpy with clay, fixing broken-down cars, hammering on houses that were always too drafty, too leaky, too small.

The bodies of the men I knew were twisted and maimed in ways visible and invisible. The nails of their hands were black and split, the hands tattooed with scars. Some had lost fingers. Heavy lifting had given many of them finicky backs and guts weak from hernias. Racing against conveyor belts had given them ulcers. Their ankles and knees ached from years of standing on concrete. Anyone who had worked for long around machines was hard of hearing. They squinted, and the skin of their faces was creased like the leather of old work gloves. There were times, studying them, when I dreaded growing up. Most of them coughed, from dust or cigarettes, and most of them drank cheap wine or whiskey, so their eyes looked bloodshot and bruised. The fathers of my friends always seemed older than the mothers. Men wore out sooner. Only women lived into old age.

As a boy I also knew another sort of men, who did not sweat and break down like mules. They were soldiers, and so far as I could tell they scarcely worked at all. During my early school years we lived on a military base, an arsenal in Ohio, and every day I saw GIs in the guardshacks, on the stoops of barracks, at the wheels of olive drab Chevrolets. The chief fact of their lives was boredom. Long after I left the Arsenal I came to recognize the sour smell the soldiers gave off as that of souls in limbo. They were all waiting—for wars, for transfers, for leaves, for promotions, for the end of their hitch—like so many braves waiting for the hunt to begin. Unlike the warriors of older tribes, however, they would have no say about when the battle would start or how it would be waged. Their waiting was broken only when they practiced for war. They fired guns at targets, drove tanks across the churned-up fields of the military reservation, set off bombs in the wrecks of old fighter planes. I knew this was all play. But I also felt certain that when the hour for killing arrived, they would kill. When the real shooting started, many of them would die. This was what soldiers were *for,* just as a hammer was for driving nails.

5   Warriors and toilers: those seemed, in my boyhood vision, to be the chief destinies for men. They weren't the only destinies, as I learned from having a few male teachers, from reading books, and from watching television. But the men on television—the politicians, the astronauts, the generals, the savvy lawyers, the philosophical doctors, the bosses who gave orders to both soldiers and laborers—seemed as remote and unreal to me as the figures in tapestries. I could no more imagine growing up to become one of these cool, potent creatures than I could imagine becoming a prince.

6   A nearer and more hopeful example was that of my father, who had escaped from a red-dirt farm to a tire factory, and from the assembly line to the front office. Eventually he dressed in a white shirt and tie. He carried himself as if he had been born to work with his mind. But his body, remembering the earlier years of slogging work, began to give out on him in his fifties, and it quit on him entirely before he turned sixty-five. Even such a partial escape from man's fate as he had accomplished did not seem possible for most of the boys I knew. They joined the Army, stood in line for jobs in the smoky plants, helped build highways. They were bound to work as their fathers had worked, killing themselves or preparing to kill others.

7   A scholarship enabled me not only to attend college, a rare enough feat in my circle, but even to study in a university meant for the children of the rich. Here I met for the first time young men who had assumed from birth that they would lead lives of comfort and power. And for the first time I met women who told me that men were guilty of having kept all the joys and privileges of the earth for themselves. I was baffled. What privileges? What joys? I thought about the maimed, dismal lives of most of the men back home. What had they stolen from their wives and daughters? The right to go five days a week, twelve months a year, for thirty or forty years to a steel mill or a coal mine? The right to drop bombs and die in war? The right to feel every leak in the roof, every gap in the fence, every cough in the engine, as a wound they must mend? The right to feel, when the layoff comes or the plant shuts down, not only afraid but ashamed?

8   I was slow to understand the deep grievances of women. This was because, as a boy, I had envied them. Before college, the only people I had ever known who were interested in art or music or literature, the only ones who read books, the only ones who ever seemed to enjoy a sense of ease and grace were the mothers and daughters. Like the menfolk, they fretted about money, they scrimped and made-do. But, when the pay stopped coming in, they were not

the ones who had failed. Nor did they have to go to war, and that seemed to me a blessed fact. By comparison with the narrow, ironclad days of fathers, there was an expansiveness, I thought, in the days of mothers. They went to see neighbors, to shop in town, to run errands at school, at the library, at church. No doubt, had I looked harder at their lives, I would have envied them less. It was not my fate to become a woman, so it was easier for me to see the graces. Few of them held jobs outside the home, and those who did filled thankless roles as clerks and waitresses. I didn't see, then, what a prison a house could be, since houses seemed to me brighter, handsomer places than any factory. I did not realize—because such things were never spoken of—how often women suffered from men's bullying. I did learn about the wretchedness of abandoned wives, single mothers, widows; but I also learned about the wretchedness of lone men. Even then I could see how exhausting it was for a mother to cater all day to the needs of young children. But if I had been asked, as a boy, to choose between tending a baby and tending a machine, I think I would have chosen the baby. (Having now tended both, I know I would choose the baby.)

So I was baffled when the women at college accused me and my sex of having cornered the world's pleasures. I think something like my bafflement has been felt by other boys (and by girls as well) who grew up in dirt-poor farm country, in mining country, in black ghettos, in Hispanic barrios, in the shadows of factories, in Third World nations—any place where the fate of men is as grim and bleak as the fate of women. Toilers and warriors. I realize now how ancient these identities are, how deep the tug they exert on men, the undertow of a thousand generations. The miseries I saw, as a boy, in the lives of nearly all men I continue to see in the lives of many—the body-breaking toil, the tedium, the call to be tough, the humiliating powerlessness, the battle for a living and for territory.   9

When the women I met at college thought about the joys and privileges of men, they did not carry in their minds the sort of men I had known in my childhood. They thought of their fathers, who were bankers, physicians, architects, stockbrokers, the big wheels of the big cities. These fathers rode the train to work or drove cars that cost more than any of my childhood houses. They were attended from morning to night by female helpers, wives and nurses and secretaries. They were never laid off, never short of cash at month's end, never lined up for welfare. These fathers made decisions that mattered. They ran the world.   10

The daughters of such men wanted to share in this power, this glory. So did I. They yearned for a say over their future, for jobs worthy of their abilities, for the right to live at peace, unmolested, whole. Yes, I thought, yes yes. The difference between me and these daughters was that they saw me, because of my sex, as destined from birth to become like their fathers, and therefore as an enemy to their desires. But I knew better. I wasn't an enemy, in fact or in feeling. I was an ally. If I had known, then, how to tell them so, would they have believed me? Would they now?   11

DISCUSSION QUESTIONS

1. Why is the essay titled "The Men *We* Carry in *Our Minds*" rather than "The Men *I* Carry in *My Mind*"?

2. Other than starting the essay, what does paragraph 1 accomplish?

3. What primary categories of men does Sanders discuss? What principle of classification does he use?

4. Sanders uses a number of comparisons, such as "zebra suits, heavy as canvas" in paragraph 1, to enhance his writing. Point out other comparisons and comment on their effectiveness.

5. The last sentence of paragraph 10 and the second, sixth, and eighth sentences of paragraph 11 are short statements. What do you think Sanders accomplishes with these statements?

6. Judging by what Sanders writes in the essay, how do you think he would answer the questions he poses in the final two sentences of paragraph 11?

TOWARD KEY INSIGHTS

To what extent do you believe that the views expressed in the essay by the college women and Sanders reflect the views of today's college women and men? How do you account for any changes you might note?

SUGGESTION FOR WRITING

Write an essay classifying the different grade school or high school teachers that you carry in your mind. Develop your categories with specific, informative details.

Judith Ortiz Cofer

The Myth of the Latin Woman: I Just Met a Girl Named María

Judith Ortiz Cofer is a native of Puerto Rico whose family came to the United States when she was four years old. After earning B.A. and M.A. degrees, she began a teaching career with a strong emphasis on writing. She now teaches English and creative writing at the University of Georgia. Cofer's book-length writings include plays, poetry, fiction, and nonfiction. She is a frequent contributor to anthologies and magazines and has earned numerous awards for her writing. In this selection, Cofer examines the various stereotypes that many Anglo Americans attach to Latinas.

1   On a bus trip to London from Oxford University where I was earning some graduate credits one summer, a young man, obviously fresh from a pub, spotted me and as if struck by inspiration went down on his knees in the aisle. With both hands over his heart he broke into an Irish tenor's rendition of "María" from *West Side Story*. My politely amused fellow passengers gave his lovely voice the round of gentle applause it deserved. Though I was not quite as amused, I managed my version of an English smile: no show of teeth, no extreme contortions of the facial muscles—I was at this time of my life practicing reserve and cool. Oh, that British control, how I coveted it. But María had followed me to London, reminding me of a prime fact of my life: you can leave the Island, mas-

ter the English language, and travel as far as you can, but if you are a Latina, especially one like me who so obviously belongs to Rita Moreno's gene pool, the
Island travels with you.

This is sometimes a very good thing—it may win you that extra minute of
someone's attention. But with some people, the same thing can make *you* an island—not so much a tropical paradise as an Alcatraz, a place nobody wants to
visit. As a Puerto Rican girl growing up in the United States and wanting like
most children to "belong," I resented the stereotype that my Hispanic appearance called forth from many people I met.

Our family lived in a large urban center in New Jersey during the sixties,
where life was designed as a microcosm of my parents' casas on the island. We
spoke in Spanish, we ate Puerto Rican food bought at the bodega, and we practiced strict Catholicism complete with Saturday confession and Sunday mass at
a church where our parents were accommodated into a one-hour Spanish mass
slot, performed by a Chinese priest trained as a missionary for Latin America.

As a girl I was kept under strict surveillance, since virtue and modesty were,
by cultural equation, the same as family honor. As a teenager I was instructed
on how to behave as a proper señorita. But it was a conflicting message girls got,
since the Puerto Rican mothers also encouraged their daughters to look and act
like women and to dress in clothes our Anglo friends and their mothers found
too "mature" for our age. It was, and is, cultural, yet I often felt humiliated
when I appeared at an American friend's party wearing a dress more suitable to
a semiformal than to a playroom birthday celebration. At Puerto Rican festivi-
ties, neither the music nor the colors we wore could be too loud. I still experience a vague sense of letdown when I'm invited to a "party" and it turns out to
be a marathon conversation in hushed tones rather than a fiesta with salsa,
laughter, and dancing—the kind of celebration I remember from my childhood.

I remember Career Day in our high school, when teachers told us to come
dressed as if for a job interview. It quickly became obvious that to the barrio
girls, "dressing up" sometimes meant wearing ornate jewelry and clothing that
would be more appropriate (by mainstream standards) for the company Christmas party than as daily office attire. That morning I had agonized in front of my
closet, trying to figure out what a "career girl" would wear. . . . I knew how to
dress for school: at the Catholic school I attended we all wore uniforms; I knew
how to dress for Sunday mass, and I knew what dresses to wear for parties at my
relatives' homes. Though I do not recall the precise details of my Career Day
outfit, it must have been a composite of the above choices. But I remember a
comment my friend (an Italian-American) made in later years that coalesced
my impressions of that day. She said that at the business school she was attending the Puerto Rican girls always stood out for wearing "everything at once."
She meant, of course, too much jewelry, too many accessories. On that day at
school, we were simply made the negative models by the nuns who were themselves not credible fashion experts to any of us. But it was painfully obvious to
me that to the others, in their tailored skirts and silk blouses, we must have
seemed "hopeless" and "vulgar." Though I now know that most adolescents feel
out of step much of the time, I also know that for the Puerto Rican girls of my
generation that sense was intensified. The way our teachers and classmates
looked at us that day in school was just a taste of the culture clash that awaited
us in the real world, where prospective employers and men on the street would
often misinterpret our tight skirts and jingling bracelets as a come-on.

6   Mixed cultural signals have perpetuated certain stereotypes—for example, that of the Hispanic woman as the "Hot Tamale" or sexual firebrand. It is a one-dimensional view that the media have found easy to promote. In their special vocabulary, advertisers have designated "sizzling" and "smoldering" as the adjectives of choice for describing not only the foods but also the women of Latin America. From conversations in my house, I recall hearing about the harassment that Puerto Rican women endured in factories where the "boss men" talked to them as if sexual innuendo was all they understood and, worse, often gave them the choice of submitting to advances or being fired.

7   It is custom, however, not chromosomes, that leads us to choose scarlet over pale pink. As young girls, we were influenced in our decisions about clothes and colors by the women—older sisters and mothers who had grown up on a tropical island where the natural environment was a riot of primary colors, where showing your skin was one way to keep cool as well as to look sexy. Most important of all, on the island, women perhaps felt freer to dress and move more provocatively, since, in most cases, they were protected by the traditions, mores, and laws of a Spanish/Catholic system of morality and machismo whose main rule was: *You may look at my sister, but if you touch her I will kill you.* The extended family and church structure could provide a young woman with a circle of safety in her small pueblo on the island; if a man "wronged" a girl, everyone would close in to save her family honor.

8   This is what I have gleaned from my discussion as an adult with older Puerto Rican women. They have told me about dressing in their best party clothes on Saturday nights and going to the town's plaza to promenade with their girlfriends in front of the boys they liked. The males were thus given an opportunity to admire the women and to express their admiration in the form of *piropos:* erotically charged street poems they composed on the spot. I have been subjected to a few piropos while visiting the Island, and they can be outrageous, although custom dictates that they must never cross into obscenity. This ritual, as I understand it, also entails a show of studied indifference on the woman's part; if she is "decent," she must not acknowledge the man's impassioned words. So I do understand how things can be lost in translation. When a Puerto Rican girl dressed in her idea of what is attractive meets a man from the mainstream culture who has been trained to react to certain types of clothing as a sexual signal, a clash is likely to take place. The line I first heard based on this aspect of the myth happened when the boy who took me to my first formal dance leaned over to plant a sloppy overeager kiss painfully on my mouth, and when I didn't respond with sufficient passion said in a resentful tone: "I thought you Latin girls were supposed to mature early"—my first instance of being thought of as a fruit or vegetable—I was supposed to *ripen,* not just grow into womanhood like other girls.

9   It is surprising to some of my professional friends that some people, including those who should know better, still put others "in their place." Though rarer, these incidents are still commonplace in my life. It happened to me most recently during a stay at a very classy metropolitan hotel favored by young professional couples for their weddings. Late one evening after the theater, as I walked toward my room with my new colleague (a woman with whom I was co-ordinating an arts program), a middle-aged man in a tuxedo, a young girl in satin and lace on his arm, stepped directly into our path. With his champagne glass extended toward me, he exclaimed, "Evita!"

Our way blocked, my companion and I listened as the man half-recited, half- 10
bellowed "Don't Cry for Me, Argentina." When he finished, the young girl said:
"How about a round of applause for my daddy?" We complied, hoping this would
bring the silly spectacle to a close. I was becoming aware that our little group was
attracting the attention of the other guests. "Daddy" must have perceived this
too, and he once more barred the way as we tried to walk past him. He began to
shout-sing a ditty to the tune of "La Bamba"—except the lyrics where about a girl
named María whose exploits all rhymed with her name and gonorrhea. The girl
kept saying "Oh Daddy" and looking at me with pleading eyes. She wanted me to
laugh along with the others. My companion and I stood silently waiting for the
man to end his offensive song. When he finished, I looked not at him but at his
daughter. I advised her calmly never to ask her father what he had done in the
army. Then I walked between them and to my room. My friend complimented
me on my cool handling of the situation. I confessed to her that I really had
wanted to push the jerk into the swimming pool. I knew that this same man—
probably a corporate executive, well educated, even worldly by most standards—
would not have been likely to regale a white woman with a dirty song in public.
He would perhaps have checked his impulse by assuming that she could be somebody's wife or mother, or at least *somebody* who might take offense. But to him, I
was just an Evita or a María: merely a character in his cartoon-populated universe.

Because of my education and my proficiency with the English language, I 11
have acquired many mechanisms for dealing with the anger I experience. This
was not true for my parents, nor is it true for the many Latin women working at
menial jobs who must put up with stereotypes about our ethnic group such as:
"They make good domestics." This is another facet of the myth of the Latin
woman in the United States. Its origin is simple to deduce. Work as domestics,
waitressing, and factory jobs are all that's available to women with little English
and few skills. The myth of the Hispanic menial has been sustained by the same
media phenomenon that made "Mammy" from *Gone with the Wind* America's
idea of the black woman for generations; María, the housemaid or counter girl,
is now indelibly etched into the national psyche. The big and the little screens
have presented us with the picture of the funny Hispanic maid, mispronounc-
ing words and cooking up a spicy storm in a shiny California kitchen.

This media-engendered image of the Latina in the United States has been 12
documented by feminist Hispanic scholars, who claim that such portrayals are
partially responsible for the denial of opportunities for upward mobility among
Latinas in the professions. I have a Chicana friend working on a Ph.D. in philosophy at a major university. She says her doctor still shakes his head in puzzled
amazement at all the "big words" she uses. Since I do not wear my diplomas
around my neck for all to see, I too have on occasion been sent to that
"kitchen," where some think I obviously belong.

One such incident that has stayed with me, though I recognize it as a minor 13
offense, happened on the day of my first public poetry reading. It took place in
Miami in a boat-restaurant where we were having lunch before the event. I was
nervous and excited as I walked in with my notebook in my hand. An older
woman motioned me to her table. Thinking (foolish me) that she wanted me
to autograph a copy of my brand new slender volume of verse, I went over. She
ordered a cup of coffee from me, assuming that I was the waitress. Easy enough
to mistake my poems for menus, I suppose. I know that it wasn't an intentional
act of cruelty, yet of all the good things that happened that day, I remember

that scene most clearly, because it reminded me of what I had to overcome before anyone would take me seriously. In retrospect I understand that my anger gave my reading fire, that I have almost always taken doubts in my abilities as a challenge—and that the result is, most times, a feeling of satisfaction at having won a convert when I see the cold, appraising eyes warm to my words, the body language change, the smile that indicates that I have opened some avenue for communication. That day I read to that woman and her lowered eyes told me that she was embarrassed at her little faux pas, and when I willed her to look up at me, it was my victory, and she graciously allowed me to punish her with my full attention. We shook hands at the end of the reading, and I never saw her again. She has probably forgotten the whole thing but maybe not.

14   Yet I am one of the lucky ones. My parents made it possible for me to acquire a stronger footing in the mainstream culture by giving me the chance at an education. And books and art have saved me from the harsher forms of ethnic and racial prejudice that many of my Hispanic *compañeras* have had to endure. I travel a lot around the United States, reading from my books of poetry and my novel, and the reception I most often receive is one of positive interest by people who want to know more about my culture. There are, however, thousands of Latinas without the privilege of an education or the entrée into society that I have. For them life is a struggle against the misconceptions perpetuated by the myth of the Latina. . . . We cannot change this situation by legislating the way people look at us. The transformation, as I see it, has to occur at a much more individual level. My personal goal in my public life is to try to replace the old pervasive stereotypes and myths about Latinas with a much more interesting set of realities. Every time I give a reading, I hope the stories I tell, the dreams and fears I examine in my work, can achieve some universal truth which will get my audience past the particulars of my skin color, my accent, or my clothes.

15   I once wrote a poem in which I called us Latinas "God's brown daughters." This poem is really a prayer of sorts, offered upward, but also, through the human-to-human channel of art, outward. It is a prayer for communication, and for respect. In it, Latin women pray "in Spanish to an Anglo God / with a Jewish heritage," and they are "fervently hoping / that if not omnipotent, / at least He be bilingual."

DISCUSSION QUESTIONS

1. Why do you think Cofer uses "María" in the title of the essay?

2. Which paragraphs constitute the introduction? What do these paragraphs accomplish?

3. Identify the essay's thesis statement.

4. Identify the categories that Cofer discusses.

5. Reread the last sentence of paragraph 4 and then explain why Cofer encloses "party" within quotation marks. How does the sentence relate to Cofer's overall message?

6. In paragraph 13 Cofer notes that the woman who assumes she was a waitress "allowed me to punish her with my full attention." Explain what Cofer means.

7. In what ways have you been stereotyped? How did you respond?

What differentiates a truthful portrait from an offensive stereotype?

What do you think causes people to stereotype individuals or groups?

SUGGESTION FOR WRITING *Write an essay classifying stereotyped characteristics of some racial, ethnic, or national group other than Hispanics. Try to account for the existence of the stereotypes and support your categories with appropriate details and examples.*

Ron Geraci

Which Stooge Are You?

Ron Geraci became a Three Stooges *fan while watching TV reruns of their movies as a youngster in southern New Jersey. Now features editor of* Men's Health, *he has written numerous articles on men's physical and emotional health for that magazine. In our selection, Geraci contends that each of the Stooges represents a different universal personality type and that recognizing our own particular type can help us avoid its pitfalls.*

Men spend millions of dollars on psychotherapy trying to figure out why   1
they're unhappy, why their kids don't respect them, why women treat them like idiots. Perhaps shrinks help some men, but for many others, it's money that would have been better spent on popcorn and videotapes. To solve many of life's problems, all you really need to do is watch the *Three Stooges*.

We're all variations of Moe, Larry, or Curly, and our lives are often short   2
subjects filled with cosmic slapstick. When Moe (your boss) hits Curly (your buddy) with a corporate board and then blindsides you when you try to make it all nice, you're living a Stooge moment. Here you'll find the personality type each Stooge represents. Once you determine which Stooge you are, you'll better understand the problems you bring on yourself—and how you can be a generally happier, more successful knucklehead.

Everyone knows more than one Moe. These men are the insufferable know-   3
it-alls who become driving instructors, gym teachers, and divorce attorneys. The coach who had you do pushups in front of the team? He was a Moe. So was that boss who made you carry his golf bag.

In short, Moes are hot-tempered men who intimidate people with verbal   4
slaps and managerial eye pokes, according to Stuart Fischoff, Ph.D., a psychologist at California State University. "Moe has a paternalistic personality, which is pretty common among men," Fischoff says. "He treats everyone like a child and bullies people to keep them off balance." Being a temperamental loudmouth also helps Moe scare off critics who might expose his little secret: He's no smarter than the saps he terrorizes. Moe himself proved that point. Although he served up most of the nose gnashings and belly bonks in 190 shorts, he always ended up back in the mud with Larry and Curly.

5   Even if you've never actually threatened to tear somebody's tonsils out, there are a few other clues that can tag you as a Moe. First, naturally, Moes are explosive hot-heads who storm through life constantly infuriated by other people. "These men suffer from classic low frustration tolerance," says Allen Elkin, Ph.D., a psychologist in New York. "This not only makes them difficult to work with, but it also gives them high blood pressure, high cholesterol, and a much greater risk of heart attack." In fact, Moes often end up seeking counseling to control their anger, usually after it costs them a job, a marriage, or a couple of good pals. "I tell them to just get away from infuriating situations quickly," says Elkin. "Remember, you don't *have* to poke Curly in the eye because he destroyed the plumbing."

6   Second, in the likely event that a Moe manages to foul things up himself, he'll find a way to blame his mistakes on other people, says Fischoff. In *Healthy, Wealthy, and Dumb* (1938), for example, Moe breaks a $5,000 vase with a 2-by-4 and screams at Larry, "Why didn't you bring me a softer board?!"

7   Your habits on the job are the most telling signs. If you're a Moe, you're probably the hardest-driving wise guy at work. "High-strung, bossy men with Moe personalities tend to live at their jobs," says Elkin. To help stop overloading themselves with work they can't possibly finish (a common Moe peccadillo), workaholic Moes should make a list of projects they *won't* do each day—and then make sure they keep their hands off those folders.

8   Moe Howard (1897–1975) had a classic Moe personality. Even offscreen, he was the fiery, short-fused leader of the trio who made all the decisions. Of course, this put a lot of worries on Moe's shoulders. "My father was an anxiety-ridden, nervous man," says Paul Howard, Moe's son. "He didn't have much patience. He always worried about his kid brother Curly, and if Larry flubbed a line, my father could become upset and criticize him almost like a director." Larry probably shaped up fast; Moe could always put some English into the next eye gouge.

9   Now, in fairness to all men with bowl cuts and bad attitudes, there are some big advantages to having a Moe personality. "If I could choose my Stooge, I'd sure as hell be a Moe," says Fischoff. Because they're usually so domineering and assertive, Moes are often able to bark their way into leadership positions quickly. (Kennedy and Nixon were Moes; Carter as a Larry.) If you crammed all the *Fortune*-100 CEOs into one Bennigan's, you'd have Moe Central with a wet bar.

10   Another Moe perk: Women flock to you like geeks to a *Star Trek* premier. Moe is an aggressive, tenacious SOB, and women are genetically programmed to find those traits sexually attractive, says Barbara Keesling, Ph.D., a Southern California sex therapist. That's because prehistoric Moes used their superior eye-poking abilities to scare off those wise-guy tigers. It's why that Moe who gave you noogies in high school went through skirts faster than J. Edgar Hoover—and why he's probably divorced now.

11   "Moes are control freaks," says Keesling. "That can be sexually exciting at first, but women get tired of it very quickly. I know—I've dated examples of all three Stooges. I'm thankful they didn't all try to sleep in my bed at once."

12   Larry is the passive, agreeable fellow who scrapes through life by taking his licks and collecting his paycheck. "Generally, things happen *to* a Larry; he doesn't make them happen," says Alan Entin, Ph.D., a psychologist with the American Psychological Association. Larry is the ubiquitous "nice guy" who commutes to his mediocre job, congenially tries to cover Curly's ass, and spends his day trying to avoid getting whacked in the nose by Moe.

That's right: John Q. Taxpayer is a Larry.   13

A subtle testosterone shift, though, can make all the difference in what   14
kind of life this lovable sap leads. Give the classic Larry a little more testicular-
ity, and you have a good-natured man who isn't a biological doormat. He'll kick
a wino off your lawn but won't fink on your free cable. That makes him a perfect coworker, neighbor, and pal.

But subtract a little gonad power, and a Larry can be an indecisive wimp whose 15
greatest ambition in life is to watch *Everybody Loves Raymond*. These pitiful, wishy-
washy slobs constantly get clobbered for being—as Larry put it—"a victim of
soicumstance," and that typically makes them passive-aggressive, says Fischoff.

"A Larry doesn't have the nerve to be assertive, so he protests by not doing   16
something," Fischoff says: not securing the ladder on the triple-bunk bed, or
not mentioning that the coffee is actually rat poison. Consequently, Larrys are
rarely promoted. If a Larry actually does work up the courage to ask for a raise,
the Moe he works for will usually give a meaningless title upgrade—or say, "Get
outta here before I murder ya."

To determine if you're an overly passive Larry, answer these three questions.   17

What's new? If you're a classic Larry, nothing is new. Your answer will be the 18
latest yarn about the office Curly who once photocopied his own butt. "Larrys
live vicariously through Moes and Curlys," says Fischoff. "They don't really have
a strong identity of their own."

Still dream about writing a screenplay? "Larrys don't have a life plan," says   19
Fischoff. They bumble from one opportunity to the next while awaiting their
"break"; a Moe plots his life like a war and a Curly flatly avoids challenges.

Do you weasel out of big projects? Larrys become good at deflecting responsi- 20
bility. This lets them avoid the risk of failure (and success) without looking like
a bum. In *Idiots Deluxe* (1945), as Curly is being attacked by a giant bear, Moe
screams, "Go out there and help him!" "The bear don't need no help!" Larry
yells back.

The chief bonus in being a Larry, of course, is that almost everyone thinks   21
you're a swell chum. The dames eventually warm up to you, too, although it
might take a few decades. Women reeling from years of turbulent relationships
with Moes and Curlys often settle down with a Larry, says Keesling, because he's
a stable, predictable, okeydokey guy who won't mind heading to the 7-Eleven
for tampons. That makes him husband material. "I'd date Moe and Curly, but
I'd marry Larry," confided several women we asked.

Like most Larrys, Larry Fine (1902–1975) spent his career following Moe   22
and his free time ducking him. "Larry and Moe weren't friends," says Lyla Bud-
nick, Larry's sister. "Their dealings were all business." Like any good Larry, he
found passive-aggressive ways to make Moe fume. "My father would be at an airport hours early," says Joan Maurer, Moe's daughter, "but Larry would show up
5 minutes before the plane took off. This made my dad very upset." For Larry,
making Moe sweat in a crowded airport terminal was probably a tiny payback
for the daily humiliations.

In *The Sweet Pie and Pie* (1941), Curly tries to throw a pie at the usual gang 23
of rich idiots but gets nailed with a pastry each time he cocks his arm. Finally he
bashes himself with the pie to deprive others of the satisfaction. This illustrates
Curly's strategy for life. "These men laugh at themselves so other people can't
ridicule them first," says Elkin. "It comes across as funny, but this kind of defense mechanism really stems from a large reservoir of anger and resentment."

24   Curly had what's called an oral personality, and a particularly self-destructive one. Boisterous, attention-seeking men, especially those who are secretly ashamed of something, like a beer gut or a bald head, often feel that they must perform in order to be liked, says Keesling. "These guys always come in for counseling, because they experience mood swings and addiction problems. It's what killed Curly and his modern-day version, Chris Farley."

25   Men with Curly personalities are almost always fat, says Fischoff, because they live to binge. They overdose on food, booze, gambling, drugs, or sex—and sometimes on all five in one badly soiled hotel bed. Curly, a consummate binger, even outlined his plans for a utopian life in *Healthy, Wealthy, and Dumb:* "Oh boy! Pie à la mode with beer chasers three times a day!"

26   On the job, Curlys pride themselves on providing comedic relief. "A Curly senses he's no leader, so he garners attention by being a fool," says Fischoff. This nets him no respect, but it does defuse criticism. Who can fire a guy when he's down on the carpet running in circles?

27   Just like his two nitwit cohorts, Curly Howard's offscreen personality was pretty similar to that of the Stooge he portrayed. He drank heavily, overate, and smoked several cigars a day. "He would always be out carousing and drinking, and playing the spoons in nightclubs," remembers Paul Howard, his nephew.

28   "I've heard stories that my father sometimes had to pay for the damage Curly caused while drinking," says Joan Maurer, Moe's daughter. If woo-wooing was enough to get Curly belted onscreen, can you imagine what Moe dished out over a real-life antic like this?

29   Curly's lifestyle apparently made him foggy at work, too. When he barked at women or said "nyuk-nyuk-nyuk!" it was often because he had forgotten his lines. After having a series of obvious mini-strokes (he could barely grumble out his woos in 1945's *If a Body Meets a Body*), Curly had a career-ending stroke in 1946 and died in 1952 at age 48.

30   He had a hoot along the way, of course. Everybody loves a clown, so Curlys get plenty of party invites—and nightcaps with attractive women. "If each of the Stooges were to flirt with a woman, Curly would probably take her home, because his humor radiates confidence," Keesling says. (And what woman could resist an opener like "Hiya, Toots"?) But a Curly's neuroses usually shine through within a few dates, which explains why Curlys tend to have few long-term sex partners, says Keesling.

31   Curly Howard was married four times. "With the exception of his fourth marriage, his best relationship was with his dogs," says Paul Howard. Curly expressed his marital outlook pretty clearly in 1941's *An Ache in Every Stake,* as he shaved a lathered block of ice with a razor: "Are you married or happy?"

DISCUSSION QUESTIONS

1. What is Geraci's purpose in writing this essay, and where is it stated?
2. Demonstrate your understanding of coherence by pointing out how paragraphs 3–6 are linked to one another. Refer to the essay when answering.
3. What audience do you think Geraci is trying to reach? Explain your answer.
4. Characterize the level of diction used in this essay. Refer to appropriate passages to support your answer.
5. Do you feel that you are a rather pure version of a Moe, Larry, or Curly, somewhat of a mixture, or that you bear little resemblance to any of them?

TOWARD KEY INSIGHTS

How do you cope with the various personality types that you encounter at school? In your social life? On the job?

Do you think it is an oversimplification to assert that "To solve many of life's problems, all you really need to do is watch the *Three Stooges*" (paragraph 1)? Why or why not?

SUGGESTION FOR WRITING

Write an essay classifying three distinctive personality types. Develop your paper with relevant, specific details and write with a specific audience in mind.

Comparison

Bruce Catton

Grant and Lee: A Study in Contrasts

Bruce Catton (1899–1978) was a nationally recognized expert on the Civil War. Born in Petoskey, Michigan, he attended Oberlin College, then worked as a reporter for several large newspapers. Between 1942 and 1948, he held several positions in the U.S. government and then became an editor of American Heritage *magazine. His first book on the Civil War,* Mr. Lincoln's Army, *appeared in 1951 and was followed by* Glory Road *(1952) and* A Stillness at Appomattox *(1953). This last book won the Pulitzer Prize and the National Book Award and established Catton's reputation as a Civil War historian. In the years that followed, Catton continued to write books on the Civil War. In 1972 he published the autobiographical* Waiting for the Morning Train *and in 1974* Michigan: A Bicentennial History. *In our selection, Catton points out differences as well as similarities in the two foremost adversaries of the Civil War.*

Title sets up differences

Introduction: paragraphs 1–3; background; significance of following contrasts

1 When Ulysses S. Grant and Robert E. Lee met in the parlor of a modest house at Appomattox Court House, Virginia, on April 9, 1865, to work out the terms for the surrender of Lee's Army of Northern Virginia, a great chapter in American life came to a close, and a great new chapter began.

2 These men were bringing the Civil War to its virtual finish. To be sure, other armies had yet to surrender, and for a few days the fugitive Confederate government would struggle desperately and vainly, trying to find some way to go on living now that its chief support was gone. But in effect it was all over when Grant and Lee signed the papers. And the little room where they wrote out the terms was the scene of one of the poignant, dramatic contrasts in American history.

3 They were two strong men these oddly different generals, and they represented the strengths of two conflicting currents that, through them, had come into final collision.

Body: paragraph 4 to first part, paragraph 16; alternating pattern throughout

4 Back of Robert E. Lee was the notion that the old aristocratic concept might somehow survive and be dominant in American life.

5 Lee was tidewater Virginia, and in his background were family, culture, and tradition . . . the age of chivalry transplanted to a New World which was making its own legends and its own myths. He embodied a way of life that had

504

come down through the age of knighthood and the English country squire. America was a land that was beginning all over again, dedicated to nothing much more complicated than the rather hazy belief that all men had equal rights and should have an equal chance in the world. In such a land Lee stood for the feeling that it was somehow of advantage to human society to have a pronounced inequality in the social structure. There should be a leisure class, backed by ownership of land; in turn, society itself should be keyed to the land as the chief source of wealth and influence. It would bring forth (according to this ideal) a class of men with a strong sense of obligation to the community; men who lived not to gain advantage for themselves, but to meet the solemn obligations which had been laid on them by the very fact that they were privileged. From them the country would get its leadership; to them it could look for the higher values—of thought, of conduct, or personal deportment—to give it strength and virtue.

First difference paragraphs
4–6: Lee's background,
character

Lee embodied the noblest elements of this aristocratic ideal. Through him, the landed nobility justified itself. For four years, the Southern states had fought a desperate war to uphold the ideals for which Lee stood. In the end, it almost seemed as if the Confederacy fought for Lee; as if he himself was the Confederacy . . . the best thing that the way of life for which the Confederacy stood could ever have to offer. He had passed into legend before Appomattox. Thousands of tired, underfed, poorly clothed Confederate soldiers, long since past the simple enthusiasm of the early days of the struggle, somehow considered Lee the symbol of everything for which they had been willing to die. But they could not quite put this feeling into words. If the Lost Cause, sanctified by so much heroism and so many deaths, had a living justification, its justification was General Lee.   6

Grant, the son of a tanner on the Western frontier, was everything Lee was not. He had come up the hard way and embodied nothing in particular except the eternal toughness and sinewy fiber of the men who grew up beyond the mountains. He was one of a body of men who owed reverence and obeisance to no one, who were self-reliant to a fault, who cared hardly anything for the past but who had a sharp eye for the future.   7

Paragraphs 7–9: Grant's
background, character

These frontier men were the precise opposites of the tidewater aristocrats. Back of them, in the great surge that had taken people over the Alleghenies and into the opening Western country, there was a deep, implicit dissatisfaction with a past that had settled into grooves. They stood for democracy not from any reasoned conclusion about the proper ordering of human society, but simply because they had grown up in the middle of democracy and knew how it worked. Their society might have privileges, but they would be privileges each man had won for himself. Forms and patterns meant nothing. No man was born to anything, except perhaps to a chance to show how far he could rise. Life was competition.   8

Yet along with this feeling had come a deep sense of belonging to a national community. The Westerner who developed a farm, opened a shop, or set up in business as a trader could hope to prosper only as his own community prospered—and his community ran from the Atlantic to the Pacific and from Canada down to Mexico. If the land was settled, with towns and highways and accessible markets, he could better himself. He saw his fate in terms of the nation's own destiny. As its horizons expanded, so did his. He had, in other words, an acute dollars-and-cents stake in the continued growth and development of his country.   9

And that, perhaps, is where the contrast between Grant and Lee becomes most striking. The Virginia aristocrat, inevitably, saw himself in relation to his own region. He lived in a static society which could endure almost anything   10

Second difference:
Lee's loyalty

except change. Instinctively, first loyalty would go to the locality in which that society existed. He would fight to the limit of endurance to defend it, because in defending it he was defending everything that gave his own life its deepest meaning.

Grant's loyalty 11

The Westerner, on the other hand, would fight with an equal tenacity for the broader concept of society. He fought so because everything he lived by was tied to growth, expansion, and a constantly widening horizon. What he lived by would survive or fall with the nation itself. He could not possibly stand by unmoved in the face of an attempt to destroy the Union. He would combat it with everything he had, because he could only see it as an effort to cut the ground out from under his feet.

Summary of significant 12
differences

So Grant and Lee were in complete contrast, representing two diametrically opposed elements in American life. Grant was the modern man emerging; beyond him, ready to come on the stage, was the great age of steel and machinery, of crowded cities and a restless burgeoning vitality. Lee might have ridden down from the old age of chivalry, lance in hand, silken banner fluttering over his head. Each man was the perfect champion of his cause, drawing both his strengths and his weaknesses from the people he led.

Transition paragraph signals 13
switch to similarities

Yet it was not all contrast, after all. Different as they were—in background, in personality, in underlying aspiration—these two great soldiers had much in common. Under everything else, they were marvelous fighters. Furthermore, their fighting qualities were really very much alike.

First similarity 14

Each man had, to begin with, the great virtue of utter tenacity and fidelity. Grant fought his way down the Mississippi Valley in spite of acute personal discouragement and profound military handicaps. Lee hung on in the trenches at Petersburg after hope itself had died. In each man there was an indomitable quality . . . the born fighter's refusal to give up as long as he can still remain on his feet and lift his two fists.

Second similarity 15

Daring and resourcefulness they had, too; the ability to think faster and move faster than the enemy. These were the qualities which gave Lee the dazzling campaigns of Second Manassas and Chancellorsville and won Vicksburg for Grant.

Third similarity: notes order 16
of climax

Lastly, and perhaps greatest of all, there was the ability, at the end, to turn quickly from war to peace once the fighting was over. Out of the way these two men behaved at Appomattox came the possibility of a peace of reconciliation. It was a possibility not wholly realized, in the years to come, but which did, in the end, help the two sections to become one nation again . . . after a war whose bitterness might have seemed to make such a reunion wholly impossible. No part of either man's life became him more than the part he played in this brief meeting in the McLean house at Appomattox. Their behavior there put all succeeding generations of Americans in their debt. Two great Americans, Grant and Lee—very different, yet under everything very much alike. Their encounter at Appomattox was one of the great moments of American history.

Conclusion: significance of
the meeting

DISCUSSION QUESTIONS

1. Where is Catton's thesis statement?
2. Summarize the way of life that Lee stood for, and then do the same for Grant.
3. Why do the differences between Grant and Lee receive more extended treatment than the similarities? Why are the similarities discussed last?
4. How would you characterize Catton's attitude toward the two men? Refer to specific parts of the essay when answering.

TOWARD KEY INSIGHTS

To what extent does modern society reflect the values embodied by Grant and Lee?

How would you characterize the upper class in the United States today? Does it consist of leisured individuals who own extensive property, as Lee did, or does it have other characteristics? Are its values the same as Lee's? If not, how are they different?

If Grant was typical of the "self-reliant" non-aristocrat, how is his contemporary counterpart similar to and different from him?

SUGGESTION FOR WRITING

Write an essay comparing two past or present political or military figures—perhaps Abraham Lincoln and Jefferson Davis or Dwight Eisenhower and Erwin Rommel. Try for a balanced treatment and select an appropriate organization.

Nancy Masterson Sakamoto

Conversational Ballgames

Nancy Masterson Sakamoto graduated Phi Beta Kappa from UCLA with a degree in English. Married to a Japanese artist and Buddhist priest, she lived in Japan for twenty-four years before moving with her husband and two sons to Honolulu in 1982. While in Japan, she was visiting professor at the University of Osaka. She gave in-service training to Japanese junior and senior high school English teachers and talks on intercultural topics, both in English and in Japanese, to various business, educational, and women's groups. In addition to her book, Polite Fictions: Why Japanese and Americans Seem Rude to Each Other, *still used as a textbook in Japanese universities, she coauthored a research project report sponsored by the Japanese Ministry of Education and wrote various articles for Japanese English-teaching publications. In Hawaii, she has been a speaker and seminar leader for many educational, business, and professional organizations. Her current position is professor of American Studies, Shitennoji Gakuen University (Hawaii branch). In this essay, she discusses the different conversational styles of Americans and Japanese, just one example of the many differences that distinguish different cultures.*

After I was married and had lived in Japan for a while, my Japanese gradually improved to the point where I could take part in simple conversations with my husband and his friends and family. And I began to notice that often, when I joined in, the others would look startled, and the conversational topic would come to a halt. After this happened several times, it became clear to me that I was doing something wrong. But for a long time, I didn't know what it was.

Finally, after listening carefully to many Japanese conversations, I discovered what my problem was. Even though I was speaking Japanese, I was handling the conversation in a western way.

3   Japanese-style conversations develop quite differently from western-style conversations. And the difference isn't only in the languages. I realized that just as I kept trying to hold western-style conversations even when I was speaking Japanese, so my English students kept trying to hold Japanese-style conversations even when they were speaking English. We were unconsciously playing entirely different conversational ballgames.

4   A western-style conversation between two people is like a game of tennis. If I introduce a topic, a conversational ball, I expect you to hit it back. If you agree with me, I don't expect you simply to agree and do nothing more. I expect you to add something—a reason for agreeing, another example, or an elaboration to carry the idea further. But I don't expect you always to agree. I am just as happy if you question me, or challenge me, or completely disagree with me. Whether you agree or disagree, your response will return the ball to me.

5   And then it is my turn again. I don't serve a new ball from my original starting line. I hit your ball back again from where it has bounced. I carry your idea further, or answer your questions or objections, or challenge or question you. And so the ball goes back and forth, with each of us doing our best to give it a new twist, an original spin, or a powerful smash.

6   And the more vigorous the action, the more interesting and exciting the game. Of course, if one of us gets angry, it spoils the conversation, just as it spoils a tennis game. But getting excited is not all the same as getting angry. After all, we are not trying to hit each other. We are trying to hit the ball. So long as we attack only each other's opinions, and do not attack each other personally, we don't expect anyone to get hurt. A good conversation is supposed to be interesting and exciting.

7   If there are more than two people in the conversation, then it is like doubles in tennis, or like volleyball. There's no waiting in line. Whoever is nearest and quickest hits the ball, and if you step back, someone else will hit it. No one stops the game to give you a turn. You're responsible for taking your own turn.

8   But whether it's two players or a group, everyone does his best to keep the ball going, and no one person has the ball for very long.

9   A Japanese-style conversation, however, is not at all like tennis or volleyball. It's like bowling. You wait for your turn. And you always know your place in line. It depends on such things as whether you are older or younger, a close friend or a relative stranger to the previous speaker, in a senior or junior position, and so on.

10   When your turn comes, you step up to the starting line with your bowling ball, and carefully bowl it. Everyone else stands back and watches politely, murmuring encouragement. Everyone waits until the ball has reached the end of the alley, and watches to see if it knocks down all the pins, or only some of them, or none of them. There is a pause, while everyone registers your score.

11   Then, after everyone is sure that you have completely finished your turn, the next person in line steps up to the same starting line, with a different ball. He doesn't return your ball, and he does not begin from where your ball stopped. There is no back and forth at all. All the balls run parallel. And there is always a suitable pause between turns. There is no rush, no excitement, no scramble for the ball.

12   No wonder everyone looked startled when I took part in Japanese conversations. I paid no attention to whose turn it was, and kept snatching the ball halfway down the alley and throwing it back to the bowler. Of course the conversation died. I was playing the wrong game.

This explains why it is almost impossible to get a western-style conversation   13
or discussion going with English students in Japan. I used to think that the
problem was their lack of English language ability. But I finally came to realize
that the biggest problem is that they, too, are playing the wrong game.

Whenever I serve a volleyball, everyone just stands back and watches it fall,   14
with occasional murmurs of encouragement. No one hits it back. Everyone waits
until I call on someone to take a turn. And when that person speaks, he doesn't
hit my ball back. He serves a new ball. Again, everyone just watches it fall.

So I call on someone else. This person does not refer to what the previous   15
speaker has said. He also serves a new ball. Nobody seems to have paid any attention to what anyone else has said. Everyone begins again from the same starting line, and all the balls run parallel. There is never any back and forth. Everyone is trying to bowl with a volleyball.

And if I try a simpler conversation, with only two of us, then the other per-   16
son tries to bowl with my tennis ball. No wonder foreign English teachers in
Japan get discouraged.

Now that you know about the difference in the conversational ballgames,   17
you may think that all your troubles are over. But if you have been trained all your
life to play one game, it is no simple matter to switch to another, even if you know
the rules. Knowing the rules is not at all the same thing as playing the game.

Even now, during a conversation in Japanese I will notice a startled reac-   18
tion, and belatedly realize that once again I have rudely interrupted by instinctively trying to hit back the other person's bowling ball. It is no easier for me to
"just listen" during a conversation, than it is for my Japanese students to "just
relax" when speaking with foreigners. Now I can truly sympathize with how hard
they must find it to try to carry on a Western-style conversation.

If I have not yet learned to do conversational bowling in Japanese, at least   19
I have figured out one thing that puzzled me for a long time. After his first trip
to America, my husband complained that Americans asked him so many questions and made him talk so much at the dinner table that he never had a
chance to eat. When I asked him why he couldn't talk and eat at the same time,
he said that Japanese do not customarily think that dinner, especially on fairly
formal occasions, is a suitable time for extended conversation.

Since westerners think that conversation is an indispensable part of dining,   20
and indeed would consider it impolite not to converse with one's dinner partner, I found this Japanese custom rather strange. Still, I could accept it as a cultural difference even though I didn't really understand it. But when my husband added, in explanation, that Japanese consider it extremely rude to talk
with one's mouth full, I got confused. Talking with one's mouth full is certainly
not an American custom. We think it very rude, too. Yet we still manage to talk
a lot and eat at the same time. How do we do it?

For a long time, I couldn't explain it, and it bothered me. But after I dis-   21
covered the conversational ballgames, I finally found the answer. Of course! In
a western-style conversation, you hit the ball, and while someone else is hitting
it back, you take a bite, chew, and swallow. Then you hit the ball again, and then
eat some more. The more people there are in the conversation, the more
chances you have to eat. But even with only two of you talking, you still have
plenty of chances to eat.

Maybe that's why polite conversation at the dinner table has never been a   22
traditional part of Japanese etiquette. Your turn to talk would last so long without interruption that you'd never get a chance to eat.

DISCUSSION QUESTIONS

1. Sakamoto notes in paragraph 1 that she "had lived in Japan for a while" and in paragraph 2 that she has listened "carefully to many Japanese conversations." Why does she note these facts at the outset of her essay?

2. What purpose is served by the first two sentences of paragraph 3?

3. Why do you think Sakamoto uses various games—tennis, volleyball, bowling—to help explain the differences between American and Japanese conversational styles?

4. Point out specific supporting details that help make this comparison successful.

5. For what audience is Sakamoto writing? Refer to the essay when answering.

6. Sakamoto ends paragraph 17 with the assertion that "Knowing the rules is not at all the same thing as playing the game." Explain what she means.

TOWARD KEY INSIGHTS

In what ways other than conversational style might cultures exhibit pronounced differences?

What problems might these differences create, and how can we best deal with them?

SUGGESTION FOR WRITING   *Write a paper that discusses a problem that arose between you and someone else because of a difference in outlook or lifestyle and explain how you resolved the matter. Use either the block or alternating method of organization.*

Mary Pipher

Then and Now

Mary Pipher was born (1947) in Springfield, Missouri, and attended the University of Nebraska–Lincoln, where she received a Ph.D. in psychology. She now serves on the faculty of her alma mater and of Lincoln Wesleyan University. She also has a private psychology practice in Lincoln. Her books include Hunger Pains *(1987),* Reviving Ophelia *(1994), and* Another Country *(1999). This selection comes from* Reviving Ophelia. *In it, Pipher compares her adolescent years with those of Cassie, a young client who has been sexually assaulted at a party.*

1   Cassie awakened me to an essential truth: In 1993, girls' experiences are different from those of myself and my friends in the 1960s. When I tried to understand them based on my own experience, I failed. There was some common ground, enough to delude me that it was all common ground, but there was much new, uncharted territory. To work with girls in the 1990s I had to understand a new world. I had to let go of my ideas and look at the girls before me with fresh eyes. I had to learn from them before I could help.

During my adolescence, I lived in a town of 400 people where my mother practiced medicine and my father sold seed corn and raised hogs. I spent my days riding my bike, swimming, reading, playing piano and drinking limeades at the drugstore with my friends. I raised all kinds of animals—baby coyotes that we bought from bounty hunters, turtles we picked up on the highway, birds washed from trees in heavy spring rains, mice pulled from their nests by dogs, and snakes and rabbits we caught in the fields on the edge of town.

I knew the names of all the people and most of the cats and dogs. Everyone "doctored" with my mother and bought corn from my father. All the children played at the same places—the swimming pool, the school yard, the swing across Beaver Creek and the fairgrounds. Everyone knew who was related to whom. When people met, the first thing they did was establish a connection. People on the street said hello to someone with whom they had a rich and complicated lifelong relationship. My pottery teacher, Mrs. Van Cleave, was the grandmother of my good friend Patti and the mother of our next-door neighbor. She was my mom's patient, and her husband went fishing with my dad. Her son was the football coach and his children were in my Methodist youth group.

I had eleven aunts and uncles and thirty cousins who showed up for long visits. The women cooked and watched babies, the men played horseshoes and fished. We all played cards in the evening. My grandfather recited limericks and demonstrated card tricks. Conversation was the main entertainment. We cousins would compare stories about our towns and families. The older cousins would impress the younger ones with their worldly wisdom. Children sat and listened as grown-ups told stories and talked politics. My fondest memory is of falling asleep to laughter and talk in the next room.

The word "media" was not in our language. I saw television for the first time when I was six, and I hid behind the couch because the cowboys' guns scared me. I was eight before we had a black-and-white television on which we watched one grainy station that showed a test pattern much of the day.

As a young teenager I watched "The Mickey Mouse Club," "American Bandstand" and "The Ed Sullivan Show." I wasn't allowed to watch "Perry Mason" or "Gunsmoke" because my parents thought these shows were too violent. We had one movie theater with a new movie every other week. The owner of the theater was a family man who selected our town's movies carefully. His wife sold us salty popcorn, Tootsie Rolls and Cokes. Kids went to the movies on Saturday afternoons and spent most of their time spying on other kids or giggling with their friends.

I loved *Tammy, Seven Brides for Seven Brothers, The Chartroose Caboose* and *South Pacific*. I scanned these movies for information about sex. Rock Hudson, Doris Day, Debbie Reynolds and Frank Sinatra fought and flirted until the end of the movie, when they kissed against backdrops of sunsets to the sounds of swelling violins. This was the era of biblical epics. In *The Story of Ruth,* a demure young Ruth lies down on Boaz' pallet for the night and the camera zooms to the stars. I asked myself, What were they doing on that pallet?

Forty-five RPM records were big in the late fifties. I listened to mushy songs by the Everly Brothers, Roy Orbison and Elvis. My favorite song was Elvis' "Surrender," a song whose lyrics gave me goose bumps and filled me with longing for something I couldn't name. My parents forbade me to listen to Bobby Darin's hit "Multiplication" because it was too suggestive. I learned to twist, a dance that was considered daring.

As Garrison Keillor said, "Nobody gets rich in a small town because everybody's watching." Money and conspicuous consumption were downplayed in my community. Some people were wealthier than others, but it was bad taste to flaunt a high income. We all shopped at the Theobald's grocery and the Rexall and ordered our clothes from Sears and JCPenney catalogs. The banker ordered a new Oldsmobile every year, and my family drove to Mexico at Christmas. A rancher's widow with asthma had the only home air-conditioning unit. The only places to spend money foolishly were the Dairy King and the pool hall.

10   Particularly children were outside the money economy. Most of our pleasures were free. Most of us had the same toys—Schwinn bikes, Hula-Hoops, basketballs, Monopoly games and dolls or toy soldiers. We could buy Sugar Babies or licorice at the pool, and makeup, comics and *Mad* magazines at the drugstore.

11   After school I worked for my mother at her clinic. I sterilized syringes and rubber gloves and counted pills. The money I earned went into a college account. By junior high, gifts went into my hope chest—good china, luggage, a dictionary and tatted pillowcases.

12   Elsewhere mass marketing had begun. Women were encouraged to fix up their homes and dress themselves and their children smartly. Via commercials and advertisements, they were fed a distorted image of themselves and their place in society. This image was less focused on their sexuality and more on their femininity. But because of our distance from a city, mass marketing barely touched our town.

13   Our town was a dry town and our state had "blue laws," which kept liquor from being advertised, sold on Sundays or served in restaurants. Even our pool hall served nothing stronger than root beer. My father brought tequila back from Mexico and would open a bottle and share it with other men on a Saturday night. Teenage boys had a difficult time finding alcohol. Once my cousin Roy drove fifty miles, convinced a stranger to buy him a six-pack, returned home and hid the six-pack in a culvert.

14   The Surgeon General had yet to issue his report on smoking, and cigarettes were everywhere, but marijuana and other drugs were unheard of in my town. My father told me that during World War Two a soldier had offered him a marijuana cigarette. He said, "I turned him down and it's a good thing. If I'd said yes, I probably wouldn't be alive today."

15   At Methodist Youth Fellowship we saw films about the deterioration of people who drank or used marijuana. Women in particular were portrayed as degraded and destroyed by contact with chemicals. After these films we signed pledges that we would never drink or smoke. I didn't break mine until I was in college.

16   As Tolstoy knew so well, in all times and places there have been happy and unhappy families. In the fifties, the unhappiness was mostly private. Divorce was uncommon and regarded as shameful. I had no friends whose parents were divorced. All kinds of pain were kept secret. Physical and sexual abuse occurred but were not reported. Children and women who lived in abusive families suffered silently. For those whose lives were going badly, there was nowhere to turn. My friend Sue's father hanged himself in his basement. She missed a week of school, and when she returned we treated her as if nothing had happened. The first time Sue and I spoke of her father's death was at our twenty-fifth-year class reunion.

17   There was cruelty. The town drunk was shamed rather than helped. Retarded and handicapped people were teased. The Green River Ordinance, which kept undesirables—meaning strangers—out of town, was enforced.

18   I was a sheltered child in a sheltered community. Most of the mothers were homemakers who served brownies and milk to their children after school. Many of them may have been miserable and unfulfilled with their lives of service to men, children and community. But, as a child, I didn't notice.

Most of the fathers owned stores downtown and walked home for lunch. Baby-   19
sitters were a rarity. Everyone went to the same chili feeds and county fairs. Adults
were around to keep an eye on things. Once I picked some lilacs from an old lady's
bush. She called my parents before I could make it home with my bouquet.

Teenagers fought less with their parents, mostly because there was less to fight   20
about—designer clothes and R-rated movies didn't exist. There was consensus
about proper behavior. Grown-ups agreed about rules and enforced them.
Teenagers weren't exposed to an alternative value system and they rebelled in
milder ways—with ducktails, tight skirts and rock and roll. Adults joked about how
much trouble teenagers were, but most parents felt proud of their children. They
didn't have the strained faces and the anxious conversations that parents of
teenagers have in the 1990s.

Men had most of the public power. The governor, the state senators, the   21
congressmen, the mayor and city council members were men, and men ran the
stores downtown. My mother was the first "lady doctor" in our town and she suffered some because of this. She wasn't considered quite as feminine and lady-
like as the other women, and she wasn't considered quite as good a doctor as
the male doctor in the next town.

In the fifties women were forced to surrender the independence they'd won   22
during World War Two and return home so as not to threaten men. Women's
work was separate and unequal. Many women had no access to money or transportation. Their husbands controlled the bank accounts and cars. Women's contributions, such as sewing, tending the sick and cooking church dinners, were
undervalued. At its centennial, our town published its history of the last hundred years. In the seventy-five-page book, women are not mentioned.

Language was unself-consciously noninclusive—leaders were "he," hurri-   23
canes and secretaries "she," humanity was mankind. Men made history, wrote
books, won wars, conducted symphonies and created eternal works of art. The
books we read in school were written by men and about men. They were shared
with us by women teachers who didn't comment on their own exclusion.

Schools and churches enforced male power. Men were principals, superin-   24
tendents and ministers; women were teachers. We studied the Bible story of Lot's
wife, who was turned into a pillar of salt because she disobeyed God's orders.
When my female cousins married, they vowed obedience to their husbands.

Kent, Sam and I were the top students. The teachers praised them for   25
being brilliant and creative, while I was praised for being a hard worker. Kent
and Sam were encouraged to go to out-of-state schools to study law or medicine,
while I was encouraged to study at the state university to be a teacher.

There was a pervasive, low-key misogyny. Mothers-in-law, women drivers and   26
ugly women were sources of derisive humor. Men needed to "wear the pants in
the family." Uppity women were quickly chastened and so were their husbands
for allowing themselves to be "henpecked" or "led around by the apron strings."
Women's talk was regarded as inferior to the important talk of men.

Femininity training was strong. We were taught that if we couldn't say any-   27
thing nice about someone, don't say anything. (I remember being delighted
when Alice Roosevelt Longworth was quoted as saying, "If you can't say anything
good about someone, sit right here by me.") We were admonished that "it's not
smart to be smart," and that we should "let boys chase us till we catch them."

By junior high the all-girl activities were different from the all-boy activities.   28
Boys played sports while we walked around the gym with books on our heads so
that we would have good posture. Boy Scouts camped and fished while Girl
Scouts sold cookies and learned to sew, bake and care for children.

29   I read the Cherry Ames student nurse books. In every book Cherry would meet a new young doctor and have an innocent romance in a glorious setting. Thank goodness I also read Nancy Drew and the Dana sisters' mysteries. Those amateur sleuths were competent and confident, brave and adventurous. They gave me role models that were lively and active. They had boyfriends, but they were always ditching them to go solve a robbery.

30   The prettiest girls were the most popular. I read *Teen* magazine with its fashion and beauty tips, and I rolled up my hair at night and combed it out in the morning. I still can feel the pressure of those big spiky rollers on my scalp. I did bust-building and tummy-flattening exercises.

31   Boys preferred dating girls whom they could best in every way. Achievement in girls was valued as long as it didn't interfere with social attractiveness. Too much education or ambition was considered unfeminine. When I received the Bausch & Lomb science award at a school assembly, I almost expired of embarrassment.

32   Sexuality was seen as a powerful force regulated by God Himself. There were rules and euphemisms for everything. "Don't touch your privates except to wash." "Don't kiss a boy on your first date." "Never let a guy go all the way or he won't respect you in the morning."

33   Sex was probably my most confusing problem. I read Pat Boone's *Twixt Twelve and Twenty,* which didn't clarify anything. I wasn't sure how many orifices women had. I knew that something girls did with boys led to babies, but I was unable to picture just what that was. I misunderstood dirty jokes and had no idea that songs were filled with sexual innuendo. Well into junior high, I thought that the word "adultery" meant trying to act like an adult.

34   One of my girlfriends had an older cousin who hid romance magazines under her bed. One day when she was away at a twirling competition, we sneaked up to her room to read them. Beautiful young women were overwhelmed by lust and overpowered by handsome heroes. The details were vague. The couple fell into bed and the woman's blouse was unbuttoned. Her heart would flutter and she would turn pale. The author described a storm outside or petals falling from flowers in a nearby vase. We left the house still uneducated about what really happened. Years later, when I finally heard what the sex act entailed, I was alarmed.

35   I was easily embarrassed. Tony, the town hoodlum, was my particular curse. Tony wore tight jeans and a black leather jacket and oozed sexual evil. In study hall he sketched a naked woman, scribbled my name on her and passed her around the room. Another time he told me to hold out my hand, and when I did, he dropped a screw into it and shouted, "You owe me a screw."

36   There was a scary side of sexuality. One friend's dad told her, "Don't get pregnant, but if you do, come to me and I'll load up my gun." A second cousin had to marry because she was pregnant. She whispered to me that her boyfriend had blackmailed her into having sex. She was a homecoming queen candidate and he said he'd go to homecoming with her only if she gave in. He claimed that he was suffering from "blue balls," a painful and unhealthy condition that only sex would remedy.

37   Lois and Carol taught me my most important lessons. Lois was a pudgy, self-effacing fourteen-year-old whose greatest accomplishment was eight years of perfect attendance at our Sunday school. One Sunday morning she wasn't there, and when I remarked on that fact, the teacher changed the subject. For a time no one would tell me what had happened to Lois. Eventually, however, I was so anxious that Mother told me the story. Lois was pregnant from having sex with a middle-aged man who worked at her father's grocery store. They had

married and were living in a trailer south of town. She was expelled from school and would not be coming to church anymore, at least not until after the baby was born. I never saw her again.

Carol was a wiry, freckled farm girl from a big family. She boarded with our   38
neighbors to attend high school in town. In the evenings, after she had the chores done, Carol came over to play with me. One night we were standing in our front yard when a carload of boys came by and asked her to go for a ride. She hesitated, then agreed. A month later Carol was sent back pregnant to her farm. I worried about her because she'd told me her father used belts and coat hangers on the children. My father told me to learn from Carol's mistake and avoid riding with boys. I took him literally and it was years before I felt comfortable riding in cars with any boys except my cousins.

In my town the rules for boys were clear. They were supposed to like sex and   39
go for it whenever they could. They could expect sex with loose girls, but not with good girls, at least not until they'd dated them a long time. The biggest problem for boys was getting the experience they needed to prove they were men.

The rules for girls were more complicated. We were told that sex would   40
ruin our lives and our reputations. We were encouraged to be sexy, but not sexual. Great scorn was reserved for "cockteasers" and "cold fish." It was tough to find the right balance between seductive and prim.

The rules for both sexes pitted them against their Saturday-night dates.   41
Guys tried to get what they could and girls tried to stop them. That made for a lot of sweaty wrestling matches and ruined prom nights. The biggest danger from rule breaking was pregnancy. This was before birth control pills and legal abortion. Syphilis and gonorrhea were the most common sexually transmitted diseases, and both were treatable with the new miracle drug, penicillin.

Sexual openness and tolerance were not community values. Pregnant   42
teachers had to leave school as soon as they "showed." I had no girlfriends who admitted being sexually active. There was community-wide denial about incest and rape, which undoubtedly occurred in my small town as they did all over America. The official story was kept G-rated.

There was a great deal of hypocrisy. A wealthy man in my town was known   43
for being a pincher. We girls called him "the lobster" among ourselves and knew to avoid him. But because his family was prominent, no one ever told him to stop his behavior.

I didn't know that pornography existed until I was a senior in high school. My   44
parents took me to Kansas City and we stayed near the Time to Read bookstore. It was two bookstores in one: on the left, classics, best-sellers and newspapers from all over the world, and on the right, an eye-popping display of pornography.

In my town male homosexuals were mercilessly scorned. The one known ho-   45
mosexual was the crippled son of a Brethren minister. He made the enormous mistake of asking another boy for a kiss, and forever after he lived a nightmarish life of isolation and teasing. Female homosexuality was never acknowledged.

Outsiders—such as socialists, Native Americans or blacks—were ostracized   46
in small communities. Our town took great pride in having no black or Native American citizens. Restaurant signs that read "We have the right to refuse service to anyone" were used to exclude nonwhites.

Adults told racist jokes and held racist beliefs about ethnic groups they had   47
never even met. My father warned me never to dance with or talk to "Negroes" when I went to college or people would think I was low-class. Terms like "jewing people down" and "Indian giver" were part of the language.

48   Once scorned, a person was out for years. One classmate who broke into a building in the eighth grade was ostracized for years by all the "good" families. We were forbidden to associate with him. He was killed in a car wreck the week after graduation. Only then did I realize how awful his high school years must have been.

49   The town newspaper was full of stories about who attended whose birthday party or fiftieth wedding anniversary. Crime was garbage cans and privies being overturned on Halloween. No one locked their doors. Our town sheriff mostly looked for lost pets and speeders. I could go anywhere before or after dark without my parents' worrying. My most traumatic experiences was reading *The Diary of Anne Frank* and realizing that somewhere people could be incredibly evil.

50   As I recall my childhood, I'm cautioned by Mark Twain's line, "The older I get, the more clearly I remember things that never happened." Remembering is more like taking a Rorschach test than calling up a computer file. It's highly selective and revealing of one's deep character. Of course, others had different experiences, but I recall small-town life as slower, safer and less sexualized. Everyone did know everyone. Sometimes that made the world seem safe and secure and sometimes that made the world seem small and oppressive.

51   Cassie attends a high school with 2,300 students. She doesn't know her teachers' children or her neighbors' cousins. When she meets people she doesn't try to establish their place in a complicated kinship network. When she shops for jeans, she doesn't expect the clerk to ask after her family.

52   Cassie sees her extended family infrequently, particularly since her parents' divorce. They are scattered all over the map. Most of the adults in her neighborhood work. In the evening people no longer sit on their front porches. Instead they prefer the privacy of backyard patios, which keep their doings invisible. Air-conditioning contributes to each family's isolation. On hot summer days and nights people go inside to stay cool. Cassie knows the Cosby family and the people from "Northern Exposure" better than she knows anyone on her block.

53   Cassie fights with her parents in a more aggressive way than the teens of my youth. She yells, swears, accuses and threatens to run away. Her parents tolerate this open anger much more readily than earlier generations would have. I'm confused about whether I was more repressed as a child or just happier. Sometimes I think all this expression of emotion is good, and sometimes, particularly when I see beleaguered mothers, I wonder if we have made progress.

54   Cassie is much more politically aware of the world than I was. By the time she was ten she'd been in a protest march in Washington, D.C. She's demonstrated against the death penalty and the Rodney King trial. She writes letters to her congressmen and to the newspapers. She writes letters for Amnesty International to stop torture all over the world. She is part of a larger world than I was and takes her role as an active participant seriously.

55   Cassie and her friends all tried smoking cigarettes in junior high. Like most teenagers today, Cassie was offered drugs in junior high. She can name more kinds of illegal drugs than the average junkie from the fifties. She knows about local drug-related killings and crack rings. Marijuana, which my father saw once in his lifetime, wafts through the air at her rock concerts and midnight movies.

56   Alcohol is omnipresent—in bowling alleys, gas stations, grocery stores, skating rinks and Laundromats. Alcohol advertising is rampant, and drinking is associated with wealth, travel, romance and fun. At sixteen, Cassie has friends who have been through treatment for drugs or alcohol. The schools attempt alcohol and drug education, but they are no match for the peer pressure to consume.

Cassie knows some Just Say No leaders who get drunk every weekend. By eighth grade, kids who aren't drinking are labeled geeks and left out of the popular scene.

Spending money is a pastime. Cassie wants expensive items—a computer, a   57
racing bike and trips to Costa Rica with her Spanish class and to the ski slopes of Colorado. She takes violin and voice lessons from university professors and attends special camps for musicians.

Cassie's been surrounded by media since birth. Her family owns a VCR, a   58
stereo system, two color televisions and six radios. Cassie wakes to a radio, plays the car stereo on the way to school, sees videos at school and returns home to a choice of stereo, radio, television or videocassettes. She can choose between forty channels twenty-four hours a day. She plays music while she studies and communicates via computer modem with hackers all over the country in her spare time.

Cassie and her friends have been inundated with advertising since birth   59
and are sophisticated about brand names and commercials. While most of her friends can't identify our state flower, the goldenrod, in a ditch along the highway, they can shout out the brand of a can of soda from a hundred yards away. They can sing commercial jingles endlessly.

Cassie's been exposed to years of sophisticated advertising in which she's   60
heard that happiness comes from consuming the right products. She can catch the small lies and knows that adults tell lies to make money. We do not consider that a sin—we call it marketing. But I'm not sure that she catches the big lie, which is that consumer goods are essential to happiness.

Cassie has more access to books than I had. I was limited to a town library the   61
size of a Quick Stop and a weekly bookmobile. She has a six-branch public library system, a school library as big as a gymnasium and three university libraries. But she reads much less than I did. Particularly the classics that I loved, *Jane Eyre, Moby Dick,* and *Return of the Native* bore her with their loopy, ornamental prose. She has more choices about how to spend her time, and like most teens raised in a media-saturated culture, Cassie does not often choose to read books.

There are more magazines for girls now, but they are relatively un-   62
changed in the thirty years since I bought my copies of *Teen.* The content for girls is makeup, acne products, fashion, thinness and attracting boys. Some of the headlines could be the same: TRUE COLORS QUIZ, GET THE LOOK THAT GETS BOYS, TEN COMMANDMENTS OF HAIR, THE BEST PLACES TO MEET AVAILABLE MEN and TEN WAYS TO TRIM DOWN. Some headlines are updated to pay lip service to the themes of the 1990s: TWO MODELS CHILL OUT AT OXFORD UNIVERSITY IN SEASON'S GREATEST GRAY CLOTHES or ECO-INSPIRED LOOKS FOR FALL. A few reflect the greater stress that the 1990s offer the young: REV UP YOUR LOOKS WHEN STRESS HAS YOU DOWN, THE STD OF THE MONTH, GENITAL WARTS and SHOULD I GET TESTED FOR AIDS? Some would never have appeared in the 1950s: WHEN YOU'RE HIGHLY SEXED, IS ONE PARTNER ENOUGH? and ADVICE ON ORGASMS.

Cassie listens to music by The Dead Milkmen, 10,000 Maniacs, Nirvana and   63
They Might Be Giants. She dances to Madonna's song "Erotica," with its sadomasochistic lyrics. The rock-and-roll lyrics by 2 Live Crew that make Tipper Gore cringe don't upset her. Sexist lyrics and the marketing of products with young women's naked bodies are part of the wallpaper of her life.

Cassie's favorite movies are *The Crying Game, Harold and Maude* and *My Own*   64
Private Idaho. None of these movies would have made it past the theater owner of my hometown.

Our culture has changed from one in which it was hard to get information   65
about sexuality to one in which it's impossible to escape information about sexuality. Inhibition has quit the scene. In the 1950s a married couple on TV had

to be shown sleeping in twin beds because a double bed was too suggestive. Now anything—incest, menstruation, crotch itch or vaginal odors—can be discussed on TV. Television shows invite couples to sell their most private moments for a dishwasher.

66   The plot for romance movies is different. In the fifties people met, argued, fell in love, then kissed. By the seventies, people met, argued, fell in love and then had sex. In the nineties people meet, have sex, argue and then, maybe, fall in love. Hollywood lovers don't discuss birth control, past sexual encounters or how a sexual experience will affect the involved parties; they just do it. The Hollywood model of sexual behavior couldn't be more harmful and misleading if it were trying to be.

67   Cassie has seen *Playboys* and *Penthouses* on the racks at local drugstores and Quick Stops. Our city has adult XXX-rated movie theaters and adult bookstores. She's watched the adult channels in hotel rooms while bouncing on "magic fingers" beds. Advertisements that disturb me with their sexual content don't bother her. When I told her that I first heard the word "orgasm" when I was twenty, she looked at me with disbelief.

68   Cassie's world is more tolerant and open about sex. Her friends produced a campy play entitled *Vampire Lesbians of Sodom*. For a joke she displays Kiss of Mint condoms in her room. She's a member of her school's branch of Flag—Friends of Lesbians and Gays—which she joined after one of her male friends "came out" to her. She's nonjudgmental about sexual orientation and outspoken in her defense of gay rights. Her world is a kinder, gentler place for girls who have babies. One-fifth of all babies today are born to single mothers. Some of her schoolmates bring their babies to school.

69   In some ways Cassie is more informed about sex than I was. She's read books on puberty and sexuality and watched films at school. She's seen explicit movies and listened to hours of explicit music. But Cassie still hasn't heard answers to the questions she's most interested in. She hasn't had much help sorting out when to have sex, how to say no or what a good sexual experience would entail.

70   Cassie is as tongue-tied with boys she likes as I was, and she is even more confused about proper behavior. The values she learned at home and at church are at odds with the values broadcast by the media. She's been raised to love and value herself in a society where an enormous pornography industry reduces women to body parts. She's been taught by movies and television that sophisticated people are sexually free and spontaneous, and at the same time she's been warned that casual sex can kill. And she's been raped.

71   Cassie knows girls who had sex with boys they hardly knew. She knows a girl whose reason for having sex was "to get it over with." Another classmate had sex because her two best girlfriends had had sex and she didn't want to feel left out. More touching and sexual harassment happens in the halls of her school than did in the halls of mine. Girls are referred to as bitches, whores and sluts.

72   Cassie has been desensitized to violence. She's watched television specials on incest and sexual assaults and seen thousands of murders on the screen. She's seen *Fatal Attraction* and *Halloween II*. Since Jeffrey Dahmer, she knows what necrophilia is. She wasn't traumatized by *The Diary of Anne Frank*.

73   Cassie can't walk alone after dark. Her family locks doors and bicycles. She carries Mace in her purse and a whistle on her car keys. She doesn't speak to men she doesn't know. When she is late, her parents are immediately alarmed. Of course there were girls who were traumatized in the fifties, and there are girls who lead protected lives in the 1990s, but the proportions have changed significantly. We feel it in our bones.

I am not claiming that our childhoods are representative of the childhoods 74 of all other females in America. In some ways Cassie and I have both had unusual childhoods. I grew up in a rural, isolated area with much less exposure to television than the average child of the times. My mother was a doctor instead of a homemaker. Compared to other girls, Cassie lives in a city that is safer than most and has a family with more money. Even with the rape, Cassie's situation is by no means a worst-case scenario. She lives in a middle-class environment, not an inner city. Her parents aren't psychotic, abusive or drug-addicted.

Also, I am not claiming that I lived in the good old days and that Cassie lives 75 in the wicked present. I don't want to glorify or to "Donna Reedify" the fifties, which were not a golden age. They were the years of Joe McCarthy and Jim Crow. How things looked was more important than how things really were. There was a great deal of sexual, religious and racial intolerance. Many families had shameful secrets, and if revealed, they led to public disgrace rather than community help.

I left my town as soon as I could, and as an adult, I have been much happier in a larger, less structured environment. Many of my friends come from small towns, and particularly the smart women among them have horror stories of not fitting in.

What I am claiming is that our stories have something to say about the way 77 the world has stayed the same and the way it has changed for adolescent girls. We had in common that our bodies changed and those changes caused us anxiety. With puberty, we both struggled to relate to girls and boys in new ways. We struggled to be attractive and to understand our own sexual urges. We were awkward around boys and hurt by girls. As we struggled to grow up and define ourselves as adults, we both distanced ourselves from our parents and felt some loneliness as a result. As we searched for our identities, we grew confused and sad. Both of us had times when we were moody, secretive, inarticulate and introspective.

But while some of our experiences are similar, many are radically different. 78 Cassie's community is a global one, mine was a small town. Her parents were divorcing, mine stayed together. She lives in a society more stratified by money and more driven by addictions. She's been exposed to more television, movies and music. She lives in a more sexualized world.

Things that shocked us in the 1950s make us yawn now. The world has 79 changed from one in which people blushed at the term "chicken breast" to one in which a movie such as *Pretty Woman* is not embarrassing. We've gone from a world with no locks on the doors to one of bolt locks and handguns. The issues that I struggled with as a college student—when I should have sex, should I drink, smoke or hang out with bad company—now must be considered in early adolescence.

Neither the 1950s nor the 1990s offered us environments that totally met 80 our needs. My childhood was structured and safe, but the costs of that security were limited tolerance of diversity, rigid rules about proper behavior and lack of privacy. As one man from a small town said, "I don't need to worry about running my own business because there are so many other people who are minding it for me." Although my community provided many surrogate parents and clear rules about right and wrong, this structure was often used to enforce rigid social and class codes and to keep people in their place.

Cassie lives in a town that's less rigid about roles and more supportive of autonomy, but she has little protected space. Cassie is freer in some ways than I 81 was. She has more options. But ironically, in some ways, she's less free. She cannot move freely in the halls of her school because of security precautions. Everyone she meets is not part of a community of connected people. She can't walk alone looking at the Milky Way on a summer night.

82   The ideal community would somehow be able to combine the sense of belonging that small towns offer with the freedom to be oneself that small towns sometimes inhibit. Utopia for teenage girls would be a place in which they are safe and free, able to grow and develop in an atmosphere of tolerance and diversity and protected by adults who have their best interest at heart.

DISCUSSION QUESTIONS

1. Identify the thesis statement of this selection.
2. Typically, students are advised to use the alternating method of organization for papers that include numerous points of comparison. Why do you think Pipher uses the block method?
3. Point out effective supporting details that Pipher uses to develop her comparison.
4. For what audience do you think Pipher is writing?
5. Explain what Pipher means in paragraph 50 when she says that remembering is "highly selective and revealing of one's deep character." What do the memories of her childhood reveal about her character?
6. Pipher tells us in paragraph 74 that she is not singling out her childhood and Cassie's as representative of all American women's childhoods. What can you learn from this statement that will help you improve your writing?
7. What does Pipher accomplish in the last three paragraphs of this selection?

TOWARD KEY INSIGHTS

What specific attitudes, actions, or policies would be necessary in order to achieve the "ideal community" that Pipher mentions?

SUGGESTION FOR WRITING

Select someone of either sex whom you know well and write an essay comparing how you and the other person, as adolescents, handled such matters as peer pressure, self-image, dating, and relationships with family members. Develop the essay with relevant supporting material.

Richard Rodriguez

Private Language, Public Language

Richard Rodriguez (born 1944) is a native of San Francisco who is of Mexican ancestry. After learning English in the elementary grades, he went on to earn a baccalaureate degree in English at Stanford University (1967) and graduate degrees at Columbia University (1969) and the University of California at Berkeley (1975). Rejecting job offers from several major universities, he spent the next six years writing Hunger of Memory: The Education of Richard Rodriguez *(1982), a book that traces his educational odyssey.* Days of Obligation *was published in 1992, and he is currently (2001) working on a book on race. His articles have appeared in a variety of scholarly magazines. In the following essay, Rodriguez explores his contrasting childhood perceptions concerning English and his native Spanish.*

I remember to start with that day in Sacramento—a California now nearly thirty years past—when I first entered a classroom, able to understand some fifty stray English words. 1

The third of four children, I had been preceded to a neighborhood Roman Catholic school by an older brother and sister. But neither of them had revealed very much about their classroom experiences. Each afternoon they returned, as they left in the morning, always together, speaking in Spanish as they climbed the five steps of the porch. And their mysterious books, wrapped in shopping-bag paper, remained on the table next to the door, closed firmly behind them. 2

An accident of geography sent me to a school where all my classmates were white, many the children of doctors and lawyers and business executives. All my classmates certainly must have been uneasy on that first day of school—as most children are uneasy—to find themselves apart from their families in the first institution of their lives. But I was astonished. 3

The nun said, in a friendly but oddly impersonal voice, "Boys and girls, this is Richard Rodriguez." (I heard her sound out: *Rich-heard Road-ree-guess.*) It was the first time I had heard anyone name me in English. "Richard," the nun repeated more slowly, writing my name down in her black leather book. Quickly I turned to see my mother's face dissolve in a watery blur behind the pebbled glass door. 4

Many years later there is something called bilingual education—a scheme proposed in the late 1960s by Hispanic-American social activists, later endorsed by a congressional vote. It is a program that seeks to permit non-English-speaking children, many from lower-class homes, to use their family language as the language of school. (Such is the goal its supporters announce.) I hear them and am forced to say no: It is not possible for a child—any child—ever to use his family's language in school. Not to understand this is to misunderstand the public uses of schooling and to trivialize the nature of intimate life—a family's "language." 5

Memory teaches me what I know of these matters; the boy reminds the adult. I was a bilingual child, a certain kind—socially disadvantaged—the son of working-class parents, both Mexican immigrants. 6

In the early years of my boyhood, my parents coped very well in America. My father had steady work. My mother managed at home. They were nobody's victims. Optimism and ambition led them to a house (our home) many blocks from the Mexican south side of town. We lived among *gringos* and only a block from the biggest, whitest houses. It never occurred to my parents that they couldn't live wherever they chose. Nor was the Sacramento of the fifties bent on teaching them a contrary lesson. My mother and father were more annoyed than intimidated by those two or three neighbors who tried initially to make us unwelcome. ("Keep your brats away from my sidewalk!") But despite all they achieved, perhaps because they had so much to achieve, any deep feeling of ease, the confidence of "belonging" in public was withheld from them both. They regarded the people at work, the faces in crowds, as very distant from us. They were the others, *los gringos.* That term was interchangeable in their speech with another, even more telling, *los americanos.* 7

I grew up in a house where the only regular guests were my relations. For one day, enormous families of relatives would visit and there would be so many people that the noise and the bodies would spill out to the backyard and front porch. Then, for weeks, no one came by. (It was usually a salesman who rang 8 the doorbell.) Our house stood apart. A gaudy yellow in a row of white bunga-lows. We were the people with the noisy dog. The people who raised pigeons and chickens. We were the foreigners on the block. A few neighbors smiled and waved. We waved back. But no one in the family knew the names of the old cou-ple who lived next door; until I was seven years old, I did not know the names of the kids who lived across the street.

9   In public, my father and mother spoke a hesitant, accented, not always grammatical English. And they would have to strain—their bodies tense—to catch the sense of what was rapidly said by *los gringos*. At home they spoke Span-ish. The language of their Mexican past sounded in counterpoint to the English of public society. The words would come quickly, with ease. Conveyed through those sounds was the pleasing, soothing, consoling reminder of being at home.

10   During those years when I was first conscious of hearing, my mother and fa-ther addressed me only in Spanish; in Spanish I learned to reply. By contrast, English (*inglés*), rarely heard in the house, was the language I came to associate with *gringos*. I learned my first words of English overhearing my parents speak to strangers. At five years of age, I knew just enough English for my mother to trust me on errands to stores one block away. No more.

11   I was a listening child, careful to hear the very different sounds of Spanish and English. Wide-eyed with hearing, I'd listen to sounds more than words. First, there were English (*gringo*) sounds. So many words were still unknown that when the butcher or the lady at the drugstore said something to me, exotic polysyllabic sounds would bloom in the midst of their sentences. Often the speech of people in public seemed to me very loud, booming with confidence. The man behind the counter would literally ask, "What can I do for you?" But by being so firm and so clear, the sound of his voice said that he was a *gringo;* he belonged in public society.

12   I would also hear then the high nasal notes of middle-class American speech. The air stirred with sound. Sometimes, even now, when I have been traveling abroad for several weeks, I will hear what I heard as a boy. In hotel lob-bies or airports, in Turkey or Brazil, some Americans will pass, and suddenly I will hear it again—the high sound of American voices. For a few seconds I will hear it with pleasure, for it is now the sound of *my* society—a reminder of home. But inevitably—already on the flight headed for home—the sound fades with repetition. I will be unable to hear it anymore.

13   When I was a boy, things were different. The accent of *los gringos* was never pleasing nor was it hard to hear. Crowds at Safeway or at bus stops would be noisy with sound. And I would be forced to edge away from the chirping chat-ter above me.

14   I was unable to hear my own sounds, but I knew very well that I spoke En-glish poorly. My words would not stretch far enough to form complete thoughts. And the words I did speak I didn't know well enough to make into distinct sounds. (Listeners would usually lower their heads, better to hear what I was trying to say.) But it was one thing for *me* to speak English with difficulty. It was more troubling for me to hear my parents speak in public: their high-whining vowels and guttural consonants; their sentences that got stuck with "eh" and "ah" sounds; the confused syntax; the hesitant rhythm of sounds so dif-ferent from the way *gringos* spoke. I'd notice, moreover, that my parents' voices were softer than those of *gringos* we'd meet.

15   I am tempted now to say that none of this mattered. In adulthood I am em-barrassed by childhood fears. And, in a way, it didn't matter very much that my par-ents could not speak English with ease. Their linguistic difficulties had no serious consequences. My mother and father made themselves understood at the county

hospital clinic and at government offices. And yet, in another way, it mattered very much—it was unsettling to hear my parents struggle with English. Hearing them, I'd grow nervous, my clutching trust in their protection and power weakened.

There were many times like the night at a brightly lit gasoline station (a blaring white memory) when I stood uneasily, hearing my father. He was talking to a teenaged attendant. I do not recall what they were saying, but I cannot forget the sounds my father made as he spoke. At one point his words slid together to form one word—sounds as confused as the threads of blue and green oil in the puddle next to my shoes. His voice rushed through what he had left to say. And, toward the end, reached falsetto notes, appealing to his listener's understanding. I looked away to the lights of passing automobiles. I tried not to hear anymore. But I heard only too well the calm, easy tones in the attendant's reply. Shortly afterward, walking toward home with my father, I shivered when he put his hand on my shoulder. The very first chance that I got, I evaded his grasp and ran on ahead into the dark, skipping with feigned boyish exuberance.   16

But then there was Spanish. *Español:* my family's language. *Español:* the language that seemed to me a private language. I'd hear strangers on the radio and in the Mexican Catholic church across town speaking in Spanish, but I couldn't really believe that Spanish was a public language, like English. Spanish speakers, rather, seemed related to me, for I sensed that we shared—through our language—the experience of feeling apart from *los gringos.* It was thus a ghetto Spanish that I heard and I spoke. Like those whose lives are bound by a barrio, I was reminded by Spanish of my separateness from *los otros, los gringos* in power. But more intensely than for most barrio children—because I did not live in a barrio—Spanish seemed to me the language of home. (Most days it was only at home that I'd hear it.) It became the language of joyful return.   17

A family member would say something to me and I would feel myself specially recognized. My parents would say something to me and I would feel embraced by the sounds of their words. Those sounds said: *I am speaking with ease in Spanish. I am addressing you in words I never use with* los gringos. *I recognize you as someone special, close, like no one outside. You belong with us. In the family.*   18

(Ricardo.)   19

At the age of five, six, well past the time when most other children no longer easily notice the difference between sounds uttered at home and words spoken in public, I had a different experience. I lived in a world magically compounded of sounds. I remained a child longer than most; I lingered too long, poised at the edge of language—often frightened by the sounds of *los gringos,* delighted by the sounds of Spanish at home. I shared with my family a language that was startlingly different from that used in the great city around us.   20

For me there were none of the gradations between public and private society so normal to a maturing child. Outside the house was public society; inside the house was private. Just opening or closing the screen door behind me was an important experience. I'd rarely leave home all alone or without reluctance. Walking down the sidewalk, under the canopy of tall trees, I'd warily notice the—suddenly—silent neighborhood kids who stood warily watching me. Nervously, I'd arrive at the grocery store to hear there the sounds of the *gringo*—foreign to me— reminding me that in this world so big, I was a foreigner. But then I'd return. Walking back toward our house, climbing the steps from the sidewalk, when the front door was open in summer, I'd hear voices beyond the screen door talking in Spanish. For a second or two, I'd stay, linger there, listening. Smiling, I'd hear my mother call out, saying in Spanish (words): "Is that you, Richard?" All the while her sounds would assure me: *You are home now; come closer; inside. With us.*   21

22   *"Sí,"* I'd reply.

23   Once more inside the house I would resume (assume) my place in the family. The sounds would dim, grow harder to hear. Once more at home, I would grow less aware of that fact. It required, however, no more than the blurt of the doorbell to alert me to listen to sounds all over again. The house would turn instantly still while my mother went to the door. I'd hear her hard English sounds. I'd wait to hear her voice return to soft-sounding Spanish, which assured me, as surely as did the clicking tongue of the lock on the door, that the stranger was gone.

24   Plainly, it is not healthy to hear such sounds so often. It is not healthy to distinguish public words from private words so easily. I remained cloistered by sounds, timid and shy in public, too dependent on voices at home. And yet it needs to be emphasized: I was an extremely happy child at home. I remember many nights when my father would come back from work, and I'd hear him call out to my mother in Spanish, sounding relieved. In Spanish, he'd sound light and free notes he never could manage in English. Some nights I'd jump up just at hearing his voice. With *mis hermanos* I would come running into the room where he was with my mother. Our laughing (so deep was the pleasure!) became screaming. Like others who know the pain of public alienation, we transformed the knowledge of our public separateness and made it consoling—the reminder of intimacy. Excited, we joined our voices in a celebration of sounds. *We are speaking now the way we never speak out in public. We are alone—together,* voices sounded, surrounded to tell me. Some nights, no one seemed willing to loosen the hold sounds had on us. At dinner, we invented new words. (Ours sounded Spanish, but made sense only to us.) We pieced together new words by taking, say, an English verb and giving it Spanish endings. My mother's instructions at bedtime would be lacquered with mock-urgent tones. Or a word like *sí* would become, in several notes, able to convey added measures of feeling. Tongues explored the edges of words, especially the fat vowels. And we happily sounded that military drum roll, the twirling roar of the Spanish *r.* Family language: my family's sounds. The voices of my parents and sisters and brother. Their voices insisting: *You belong here. We are family members. Related. Special to one another. Listen!* Voices singing and sighing, rising, straining, then surging, teeming with pleasure that burst syllables into fragments of laughter. At times it seemed there was steady quiet only when, from another room, the rustling whispers of my parents faded and I moved closer to sleep.

DISCUSSION QUESTIONS

1. What does Rodriguez accomplish in his first four paragraphs? What connection do you see between these paragraphs and later parts of the essay?

2. What is Rodriguez's main point? Where is it stated?

3. Discuss the significance of paragraphs 7–9.

4. Why did his parents' difficulties with English cause Rodriguez such concern?

5. In paragraph 16 Rodriguez tells us that he "looked away to the lights of passing automobiles" and that he "ran on ahead into the dark. . . ." Explain these actions.

6. Rodriguez does not begin to develop his discussion of Spanish—the private language—until paragraph 17. Why do you think this discussion didn't occur earlier in the essay?

7. Explain why the concluding paragraph is effective.

TOWARD KEY INSIGHTS

In what ways other than those noted by Rodriguez do children and their families create or inhabit private worlds that are separate from their public worlds? What are some of the benefits and problems that result from this dichotomy? How important is language to a person's identity and social world?

SUGGESTION FOR WRITING   *Write a comparison essay discussing some noteworthy difference between you, or some group you belong to, and the larger public. The difference may be one of race, ethnic background, religion, or lifestyle. Demonstrate clearly how the difference affects your relationship with that public.*

Marjorie Waters

....

Coming Home

Marjorie Waters was born and educated in upstate New York. A freelance writer who works in Boston, she has authored numerous articles in popular and literary magazines, as well as one longer work, The Victory Garden Kids' Book *(1988). In the essay that follows, Ms. Waters draws an analogy between a house that has weathered a severe winter and an individual who has weathered a period of severe grief.*

After the cruelest of winters, the house still stood. It was pale, washed clean by elements gone wild, and here and there a shutter dangled from a broken hinge. But the structure was sound; the corners had held. I walked around it slowly, studying every detail: the fine edge where window frame met clapboard, the slice of shadow across the roofline, the old wooden railing around the porch. When I climbed the stairs toward the door, I heard the floorboards groan beneath my weight as they had always done. Hello yourself, old friend, I said.

Inside, I made those rooms my own again, drew the curtains back, threw open the window, pulled the covers from the furniture, slapped all the upholstery with my hands. I could feel fresh air move in through open windows, replacing a season's worth of staleness with a smell of moist earth, a hint of flowers. After all the months of darkness light poured again into the house, fell in familiar angled patterns across furniture, walls, and floors. Where light beams passed through moving air, even the dust seemed alive; I watched it swirl, dance, resettle.

I made myself at home, kicked off my shoes so I could feel the floors beneath my feet again. I tilted my head, read the titles on the spines of all my books, I played old songs I hadn't heard in months, felt the summer music move through me as if my muscles were the strings. It carried me from room to room while I swept away the mustiness of winter, shook the rugs, cleaned cobwebs out of corners, hung laundered linens on the line to whip dry in the outdoor air. I pulled closed boxes out of closets and unwrapped all my things, slowly, one by one. I held and turned them in my hands before I put them out again on shelves, in cupboards and drawers. And when I had each room all full of me again, I showered and washed away the last of winter's claims in hot lather and steam.

4   Night fell and brought a chill to the air outside. I built a fire in the stove, drank tea that smelled of oranges and spice. I warmed my fingers round the cup and thought of how my house would look to passers-by, drowsy and content, with soft rectangles of light on the ground below the windows, a breath of smoke from the chimney. She's come back, they would say as they walked through the dark night. She's home again.

5   For me, the end of grief was a homecoming like this one, a returning to myself made sweeter by the long separation. I remember well the months that had followed that most unexpected death, when I felt cut loose, caught in my own cold storm, far away from all that made me feel at home. I wondered if I would ever again belong to any time or place. People spoke to me of sadness and loss, as if they were burdens to carry in my hands. I nodded in agreement, afraid to tell them that I felt no burdens, only weightlessness. I thought the world had pulled itself away from me, that I would drift, beyond reach, forever.

6   But winter ends, and grief does pass. As I had reclaimed my house and made it my own again, so I slowly reclaimed my life. I resumed my small daily rituals: a cup of coffee with a friend, long walks at sunset. I felt like myself again, and when I laughed, it was my own laugh I heard, rich and full. I had feared that, in my absence, the space that I had left behind would close over from disuse, but I returned to find that my house still stood, even after the cruelest of winters.

DISCUSSION QUESTIONS

1. Consider the essay as a whole and then point out the significance of this sentence in paragraph 1: "But the structure was sound; the corners had held."

2. Waters does not introduce her analogy at the start of the essay. Suggest why. Where are we first aware of her analogy?

3. Why do you think Waters, in paragraph 5, doesn't identify the person who died?

4. Reread the "As . . . so . . ." sentence in paragraph 6. What can you learn from its structure that can help you write your own analogy?

5. Does this analogy further explain the familiar by presenting information on the unfamiliar, or does it explain the unfamiliar by likening it to the familiar?

6. What does Waters accomplish by beginning and ending her essay with ". . . the cruelest of winters"?

TOWARD KEY INSIGHTS

What does it mean to say we leave or return to ourselves?

How and under what conditions do we have such experiences?

What is it like to return to oneself, and what allows us to do so?

SUGGESTION FOR WRITING

Write an analogy that helps explain a time of great joy in your life. Feel free either to reveal or conceal the actual joy. Announce your analogy at the point that seems most effective.

Cause and Effect

Richard Tomkins

Old Father Time Becomes a Terror

Richard Tomkins is consumer industries editor of the Financial Times, *where he has been a member of the editorial staff since 1983. He is currently based at the company's London headquarters, where he leads a team of journalists covering the consumer goods sector and writes about consumer trends. Previously, he was the* FT*'s marketing correspondent and, from 1993 to 1999, he was a correspondent in the newspaper's New York bureau, where he covered the consumer goods sector. Earlier positions in London included writing about the transport sector and corporate news. Tomkins was born in Walsall, England, in 1952. His formal education ended at the age of seventeen. Before becoming a journalist, he was a casual laborer, a factory worker, a truck driver, a restaurant cashier, a civil servant, and an assistant private secretary to a government minister. He left government service in 1978 to hitchhike around the world, and on returning to the U.K. in 1979, joined a local newspaper as a trainee reporter. He joined the* FT *as a subeditor four years later. In this selection, Tomkins discusses the time squeeze that many people are experiencing and offers a way of combating the problem.*

It's barely 6:30 A.M. and already your stress levels are rising. You're late for a breakfast meeting. Your cell-phone is ringing and your pager is beeping. You have 35 messages in your e-mail, 10 calls on your Voicemail and one question on your mind.

Why was it never like this for Dick Van Dyke?

Somehow, life seemed much simpler in the 1960s. In *The Dick Van Dyke Show*, the classic American sitcom of the era, Rob Petrie's job as a television scriptwriter was strictly nine-to-five. It was light when he left for work and light when he got home. There was no teleconferencing during his journey from the Westchester suburbs to the TV studio in Manhattan.

At work, deadlines loomed, but there was plenty of time for banter around the office typewriter. There was no internet, no Voicemail, no fax machine, no CNN. The nearest Petrie came to information overload was listening to a stream of wisecracks from his colleague Buddy Sorrell about Mel, the bald producer.

1   Introduction: paragraphs 1–8; compares the leisurely 1960s (paragraphs 1–5) with the time-stressed present

2

3

4

5   Meanwhile, at home, Rob's wife Laura—Mary Tyler Moore—led a life of leisure. After packing little Richie off to school, she had little to do but gossip with Millie, the next-door neighbour, and prepare the evening meal. When Rob came home, the family sat down to dinner: then it was television, and off to bed.

6   Today, this kind of life seems almost unimaginable. The demands on our time seem to grow ever heavier. Technology has made work portable, allowing it to merge with our personal lives. The nine-to-five job is extinct: in the U.S. people now talk about the 24-7 job, meaning one that requires your commitment 24 hours a day, seven days a week.

7   Home life has changed, too. Laura and Millie no longer have time for a gossip: they are vice-presidents at a bank. Richie's after-school hours are spent at karate classes and Chinese lessons. The only person at home any more is Buddy, who went freelance six months ago after being de-layered by Mel.

8   New phrases have entered the language to express the sense that we are losing control of our lives. "Time famine" describes the mismatch between things to do and hours to do them in, and "multi-tasking" the attempt to reconcile the two. If multi-tasking works, we achieve "time deepening," making better use of the time available: but usually it proves inadequate, resulting in "hurry sickness" and an increasingly desperate search for "life balance" as the sufferer moves closer to break-down.

9   It was not supposed to be this way. Technology, we thought, would make our lives easier. Machines were expected to do our work for us, leaving us with ever-increasing quantities of time to fritter away on idleness and pleasure.

Body: paragraphs 10–31

First cause and specific effects of time stress, paragraphs 10–14: technological innovations

10   But instead of liberating us, technology has enslaved us. Innovations are occurring at a bewildering rate: as many now arrive in a year as once arrived in a millennium. And as each invention arrives, it eats further into our time.

11   The motor car, for example, promised unimaginable levels of personal mobility. But now, traffic in cities moves more slowly than it did in the days of the horse-drawn carriage, and we waste our lives immobilized by congestion.

12   The aircraft promised new horizons, too. The trouble is, it delivered them. Its very existence created a demand for time-consuming journeys that we would never previously have dreamed of undertaking—the transatlantic shopping expedition, for example, or the trip to a convention on the other side of the world.

13   In most cases, technology has not saved time, but enabled us to do more things. In the home, washing machines promised to free women from the drudgery of the laundry. In reality, they encouraged us to change our clothes daily instead of weekly, creating seven times as much washing and ironing. Similarly, the weekly bath has been replaced by the daily shower, multiplying the hours spent on personal grooming.

14   Meanwhile, technology has not only allowed work to spread into our leisure time—the laptop-on-the-beach syndrome—but added the new burden of dealing with faxes, e-mails and Voicemails. It has also provided us with the opportunity to spend hours fixing software glitches on our personal computers or filling our heads with useless information from the internet.

Second cause and specific effects, paragraphs 15–18: the information explosion

15   Technology apart, the internet points the way to a second reason why we feel so time-pressed: the information explosion.

16   A couple of centuries ago, nearly all the world's accumulated learning could be contained in the heads of a few philosophers. Today, those heads could not hope to accommodate more than a tiny fraction of the information generated in a single day.

News, facts and opinions pour in from every corner of the world. The television set offers 150 channels. There are millions of internet sites. Magazines, books and CD-Roms proliferate. 17

"In the whole world of scholarship, there were only a handful of scientific journals in the 18th century, and the publication of a book was an event," says Edward Wilson, honorary curator in entymology at Harvard University's museum of comparative zoology. "Now, I find myself subscribing to 60 or 70 journals or magazines just to keep me up with what amounts to a minute proportion of the expanding frontiers of scholarship." 18

There is another reason for our increased stress levels, too: rising prosperity. As ever-larger quantities of goods and services are produced, they have to be consumed. Driven on by advertising, we do our best to oblige: we buy more, travel more and play more, but we struggle to keep up. So we suffer from what Wilson calls discontent with super abundance—the confusion of endless choice. 19

> Third cause and specific effects: rising prosperity

Of course, not everyone is overstressed. "It's a convenient shorthand to say we're all time-starved, but we have to remember that it only applies to, say, half the population," says Michael Willmott, director of the Future Foundation, a London research company. 20

> Distribution of time stress, paragraphs 20–26

"You've got people retiring early, you've got the unemployed, you've got other people maybe only peripherally involved in the economy who don't have this situation at all. If you're unemployed, your problem is that you've got too much time, not too little." 21

Paul Edwards, chairman of the London-based Henley Centre forecasting group, points out that the feeling of pressures can also be exaggerated, or self-imposed. "Everyone talks about it so much that about 50 percent of unemployed or retired people will tell you they never have enough time to get things done," he says. "It's almost got to the point where there's stress envy. If you're not stressed, you're not succeeding. Everyone wants to have a little bit of this stress to show they're an important person." 22

There is another aspect to all of this too. Hour-by-hour logs kept by thousands of volunteers over the decades have shown that, in the U.K., working hours have risen only slightly in the last 10 years, and in the U.S., they have actually fallen—even for those in professional and executive jobs, where the perceptions of stress are highest. 23

In the U.S., John Robinson, professor of sociology at the University of Maryland, and Geoffrey Godbey, professor of leisure studies at Penn State University, both time-use experts, found that, since the mid-1960s, the average American had gained five hours a week in free time—that is, time left after working, sleeping, commuting, caring for children and doing the chores. 24

The gains, however, were unevenly distributed. The people who benefited the most were singles and empty-nesters. Those who gained the least—less than an hour—were working couples with pre-school children, perhaps reflecting the trend for parents to spend more time nurturing their offspring. 25

There is, of course, a gender issue here, too. Advances in household appliances may have encouraged women to take paying jobs: but as we have already noted, technology did not end household chores. As a result, we see appalling inequalities in the distribution of free time between the sexes. According to the Henley Centre, working fathers in the U.K. average 48 hours of free time a week. Working mothers get 14. 26

Inequalities apart, the perception of the time famine is widespread, and has provoked a variety of reactions. One is an attempt to gain the largest possible 27

> First general effect of time stress, paragraphs 27–28: maximizing pleasure in minimum time

amount of satisfaction from the smallest possible investment of time. People today want fast food, sound bytes and instant gratification. And they become upset when time is wasted.

28   "People talk about quality time. They want perfect moments," says the Henley Centre's Edwards. "If you take your kids to a movie and McDonald's and it's not perfect, you've wasted an afternoon, and it's a sense that you've lost something precious. If you lose some money you can earn some more, but if you waste time you can never get it back."

Second general effect: 29   People are also trying to buy time. Anything that helps streamline our lives
buying time   is a growth market. One example is what Americans call concierge services—domestic help, child care, gardening and decorating. And on-line retailers are seeing big increases in sales—though not, as yet, profits.

Third general effect: 30   A third reaction to time famine has been the growth of the work-life debate. You hear more about people taking early retirement or giving up high
re-evaluating jobs, long   pressure jobs in favour of occupations with shorter working hours. And bodies
work hours   such as Britain's National Work-Life Forum have sprung up, urging employers to end the long-hours culture among managers—"presenteeism"—and to adopt family-friendly working policies.

31   The trouble with all these reactions is that liberating time—whether by making better use of it, buying it from others or reducing the amount spent at work—is futile if the hours gained are immediately diverted to other purposes.

Conclusion: paragraphs   32   As Godbey points out, the stress we feel arises not from a shortage of time, but
32–36; sources of time   from the surfeit of things we try to cram into it. "It's the kid in the candy store," he
stress; author's solution   says. "There's just so many good things to do. The array of choices is stunning. Our
to the problem   free time is increasing, but not as fast as our sense of the necessary."

33   A more successful remedy may lie in understanding the problem rather than evading it.

34   Before the industrial revolution, people lived in small communities with limited communications. Within the confines of their village, they could reasonably expect to know everything that was to be known, see everything that was to be seen, and do everything that was to be done.

35   Today, being curious by nature, we are still trying to do the same. But the global village is a world of limitless possibilities, and we can never achieve our aim.

36   It is not more time we need: it is fewer desires. We need to switch off the cell-phone and leave the children to play by themselves. We need to buy less, read less and travel less. We need to set boundaries for ourselves, or be doomed to mounting despair.

DISCUSSION QUESTIONS

1. Identify the thesis statement of this essay and suggest why it is located at this spot.

2. The following sentence appears in paragraph 4: "There is no internet, no Voicemail, no fax machine, no CNN." What does the structure of this sentence accomplish?

3. Reread paragraph 14 and then suggest Tomkins' intention in using the word "opportunity."

4. Explain the meaning of "the confusion of endless choice" at the end of paragraph 19. Then suggest examples that illustrate this idea.

5. Why do you think Tomkins calls attention to groups that are unstressed (paragraph 21) and to studies showing the time gains for average Americans?

TOWARD KEY INSIGHTS

Regarding the essay's final sentence, what type of boundaries do you think time-stressed individuals should set?

How can people establish these boundaries without sacrificing quality of life?

SUGGESTION FOR WRITING

Write an essay discussing the causes and/or effects of some type of stress other than time stress. Possibilities might include academic or financial stress or the stress associated with personal relationships. Develop your paper with appropriate examples.

Deborah Tannen

Gender Gap in Cyberspace[1]

Deborah Tannen (born 1945) earned a B.S. degree from the State University of New York in 1966 and a Ph.D. from the University of California in 1979. She is now a member of the linguistics department of Georgetown University. Tannen has authored a number of books on speaking and writing as well as numerous shorter pieces that have appeared in the New York Times, Newsweek, People, *and the* Harvard Business Review. *In this selection, Tannen investigates the causes and effects of the differing male and female attitudes toward e-mail.*

I was a computer pioneer, but I'm still something of a novice. That paradox is telling. 1

I was the second person on my block to get a computer. The first was my colleague Ralph. It was 1980. Ralph got a Radio Shack TRS-80, I got a used Apple II+. He helped me get started and went on to become a maven, reading computer magazines, hungering for the new technology he read about, and buying and mastering it as quickly as he could afford. I hung on to old equipment far too long because I dislike giving up what I'm used to, fear making the wrong decision about what to buy, and resent the time it takes to install and learn a new system. 2

My first Apple came with videogames; I gave them away. Playing games on the computer didn't interest me. If I had free time I'd spend it talking on the telephone to friends. 3

Ralph got hooked. His wife was often annoyed by the hours he spent at his computer and the money he spent upgrading it. My marriage had no such strains—until I discovered E-mail. Then I got hooked. E-mail draws me the same way the phone does: it's a souped-up conversation. 4

5   E-mail deepened my friendship with Ralph. Though his office was next to mine, we rarely had extended conversations because he is shy. Face to face he mumbled so, I could barely tell he was speaking. But when we both got on E-mail, I started receiving long, self-revealing messages: we poured our hearts out to each other. A friend discovered that E-mail opened up that kind of communication with her father. He would never talk much on the phone (as her mother would), but they have become close since they both got on line.

6   Why, I wondered, would some men find it easier to open up on E-mail? It's a combination of the technology (which they enjoy) and the obliqueness of the written word, just as many men will reveal feelings in dribs and drabs while riding in the car or doing something, which they'd never talk about sitting face to face. It's too intense, too bearing-down on them, and once you start you have to keep going. With a computer in between, it's safer.

7   It was on E-mail, in fact, that I described to Ralph how boys in groups often struggle to get the upper hand whereas girls tend to maintain an appearance of cooperation. And he pointed out that this explained why boys are more likely to be captivated by computers than girls are. Boys are typically motivated by a social structure that says if you don't dominate you will be dominated. Computers, by their nature, balk; you type a perfectly appropriate command and it refuses to do what it should. Many boys and men are incited by this defiance: "I'm going to whip this into line and teach it who's boss! I'll get it to do what I say!" (and if they work hard enough, they always can). Girls and women are more likely to respond, "This thing won't cooperate. Get it away from me!"

8   Although no one wants to think of herself as "typical"—how much nicer to be *sui generis*—my relationship to my computer is—gulp—fairly typical for a woman. Most women (with plenty of exceptions) aren't excited by tinkering with the technology, grappling with the challenge of eliminating bugs or getting the biggest and best computer. These dynamics appeal to many men's interest in making sure they're on the top side of the inevitable who's-up-who's-down struggle that life is for them. E-mail appeals to my view of life as a contest for connections to others. When I see that I have fifteen messages, I feel loved.

9   I once posted a technical question on a computer network for linguists and was flooded with long dispositions, some pages long. I was staggered by the generosity and the expertise, but wondered where these guys found the time—and why all the answers I got were from men.

10   Like coed classrooms and meetings, discussions on E-mail networks tend to be dominated by male voices, unless they're specifically women-only, like single-sex schools. On line, women don't have to worry about getting the floor (you just send a message when you feel like it), but, according to linguists Susan Herring and Laurel Sutton, who have studied this, they have the usual problems of having their messages ignored or attacked. The anonymity of public networks frees a small number of men to send long, vituperative, sarcastic messages that many other men either can tolerate or actually enjoy, but that turn most women off.

11   The anonymity of networks leads to another sad part of the E-mail story: there are men who deluge women with questions about their appearance and invitations to sex. On college campuses, as soon as women students log on, they are bombarded by references to sex, like going to work and finding pornographic posters adorning the walls.

12   Most women want one thing from a computer—to work. This is significant counterevidence to the claim that men want to focus on information while women are interested in rapport. That claim I found was most often true in

casual conversation, in which there is no particular information to be conveyed. But with computers, it is often women who are more focused on information, because they don't respond to the challenge of getting equipment to submit.

Once I had learned the basics, my interest in computers waned. I use it to write books (though I never mastered having it do bibliographies or tables of contents) and write checks (but not balance my checkbook). Much as I'd like to use it to do more, I begrudge the time it would take to learn. 13

Ralph's computer expertise costs him a lot of time. Chivalry requires that he rescue novices in need, and he is called upon by damsel novices far more often than knaves. More men would rather study the instruction booklet than ask directions, as it were, from another person. "When I do help men," Ralph wrote (on E-mail, of course), "they want to be more involved. I once installed a hard drive for a guy, and he wanted to be there with me, wielding the screwdriver and giving his own advice where he could." Women, he finds, usually are not interested in what he's doing; they just want him to get the computer to the point where they can do what they want. 14

Which pretty much explains how I managed to be a pioneer without becoming an expert. 15

DISCUSSION QUESTIONS

1. Does Tannen deal with causes, effects, or both? Refer to the essay when answering.
2. Characterize the level of diction in this essay.
3. Why do you think Tannen cites the two linguists in paragraph 10?
4. Point out the connecting devices that link the paragraphs in this essay.
5. Does your experience in cyberspace bear out Tannen's assertion about a gender gap? Discuss, citing specific examples.

TOWARD KEY INSIGHTS

How do you account for the differences that Tannen describes? Do you believe that they are inborn or stem mainly from cultural patterns?

What steps might be taken to lessen these differences?

SUGGESTION FOR WRITING
Write an essay exploring how gender affects dating done through the Internet. Support your essay with relevant, specific details.

Anne Roiphe

Why Marriages Fail

A native of New York City, Anne Roiphe was born in 1935 and earned a B.A. degree from Sarah Lawrence College in 1957. In a writing career spanning more than three decades, she has produced nearly a dozen works of fiction and nonfiction centering on such matters as alienation, divorce, religious tradition, children's emotional health, and the conflicts arising from the demands of family and the desire for independence. Her many periodical articles reflect these as well as similar concerns. In this essay Roiphe examines the forces leading to marital breakup.

1   These days so many marriages end in divorce that our most sacred vows no longer ring with truth. "Happily ever after" and "Till death do us part" are expressions that seem on the way to becoming obsolete. Why has it become so hard for couples to stay together? What goes wrong? What has happened to us that close to one-half of all marriages are destined for the divorce courts? How could we have created a society in which 42 percent of our children will grow up in single-parent homes? If statistics could only measure loneliness, regret, pain, loss of self-confidence and fear of the future, the numbers would be beyond quantifying.

2   Even though each broken marriage is unique, we can still find the common perils, the common causes for marital despair. Each marriage has crisis points and each marriage tests endurance, the capacity for both intimacy and change. Outside pressures such as job loss, illness, infertility, trouble with a child, care of aging parents and all the other plagues of life hit marriage the way hurricanes blast our shores. Some marriages survive these storms and others don't. Marriages fail, however, not simply because of the outside weather but because the inner climate becomes too hot or too cold, too turbulent or too stupefying.

3   When we look at how we choose our partners and what expectations exist at the tender beginnings of romance, some of the reasons for disaster become quite clear. We all select with unconscious accuracy a mate who will recreate with us the emotional patterns of our first homes. Dr. Carl A. Whitaker, a marital therapist and emeritus professor of psychiatry at the University of Wisconsin, explains, "From early childhood on, each of us carried models for marriage, femininity, masculinity, motherhood, fatherhood and all the other family roles." Each of us falls in love with a mate who has qualities of our parents, who will help us rediscover both the psychological happiness and miseries of our past lives. We may think we have found a man unlike Dad, but then he turns to drink or drugs, or loses his job over and over again or sits silently in front of the TV just the way Dad did. A man may choose a woman who doesn't like kids just like his mother or who gambles away the family savings just like his mother. Or he may choose a slender wife who seems unlike his obese mother but then turns out to have other addictions that destroy their mutual happiness.

4   A man and a woman bring to their marriage bed a blended concoction of conscious and unconscious memories of their parents' lives together. The human way is to compulsively repeat and recreate the patterns of the past. Sigmund Freud so well described the unhappy design that many of us get trapped in: the unmet needs of childhood, the angry feelings left over from frustrations of long ago, the limits of trust and the recurrence of old fears. Once an individual senses this entrapment, there may follow a yearning to escape, and the result could be a broken, splintered marriage.

5   Of course people can overcome the habits and attitudes that developed in childhood. We all have hidden strengths and amazing capacities for growth and creative change. Change, however, requires work—observing your part in a rotten pattern, bringing difficulties out into the open—and work runs counter to the basic myth of marriage: "When I wed this person all my problems will be over. I will have achieved success and I will become the center of life for this other person and this person will be my center, and we will mean everything to each other forever." This myth, which every marriage relies on, is soon exposed.

The coming of children, the pulls and tugs of their demands on affection and time, place a considerable strain on that basic myth of meaning everything to each other, of merging together and solving all of life's problems.

Concern and tension about money take each partner away from the other. 6
Obligations to demanding parents or still-depended-upon parents create further strain. Couples today must also deal with all the cultural changes brought on in recent years by the women's movement and the sexual revolution. The altering of roles and the shifting of responsibilities have been extremely trying for many marriages.

These and other realities of life erode the visions of marital bliss the way 7
sandstorms eat at rock and the ocean nibbles away at the dunes. Those euphoric, grand feelings that accompany romantic love are really self-delusions, self-hypnotic dreams that enable us to forge a relationship. Real life, failure at work, disappointments, exhaustion, bad smells, bad colds and hard times all puncture the dream and leave us stranded with our mate, with our childhood patterns pushing us this way and that, with our unfulfilled expectations.

The struggle to survive in marriage requires adaptability, flexibility, genuine 8
love and kindness and an imagination strong enough to feel what the other is feeling. Many marriages fall apart because either partner cannot imagine what the other wants or cannot communicate what he or she needs or feels. Anger builds until it erupts into a volcanic burst that buries the marriage in ash.

It is not hard to see, therefore, how essential communication is for a good 9
marriage. A man and a woman must be able to tell each other how they feel and why they feel the way they do; otherwise they will impose on each other roles and actions that lead to further unhappiness. In some cases, the communication patterns of childhood—of not talking, of talking too much, of not listening, of distrust and anger, of withdrawal—spill into the marriage and prevent a healthy exchange of thoughts and feelings. The answer is to set up new patterns of communication and intimacy.

At the same time, however, we must see each other as individuals. "To 10
achieve a balance between separateness and closeness is one of the major psychological tasks of all human beings at every stage of life," says Dr. Stuart Bartle, a psychiatrist at the New York University Medical Center.

If we sense from our mate a need for too much intimacy, we tend to push 11
him or her away, fearing that we may lose our identities in the merging of marriage. One partner may suffocate the other partner in a childlike dependency.

A good marriage means growing as a couple but also growing as individuals. 12
This isn't easy. Richard gives up his interest in carpentry because his wife, Helen, is jealous of the time he spends away from her. Karen quits her choir group because her husband dislikes the friends she makes there. Each pair clings to each other and are angry with each other as life closes in on them. This kind of marital balance is easily thrown as one or the other pulls away and divorce follows.

Sometimes people pretend that a new partner will solve the old problems. 13
Most often extramarital sex destroys a marriage because it allows an artificial split between the good and the bad—the good is projected on the new partner and the bad is dumped on the head of the old. Dishonesty, hiding and cheating create walls between men and women. Infidelity is just a symptom of trouble. It is a symbolic complaint, a weapon of revenge, as well as an unraveler of closeness. Infidelity is often that proverbial last straw that sinks the camel to the ground.

All right—marriage has always been difficult. Why then are we seeing so 14
many divorces at this time? Yes, our modern social fabric is thin, and yes the permissiveness of society has created unrealistic expectations and thrown the family

into chaos. But divorce is so common because people today are unwilling to exercise the self-discipline that marriage requires. They expect easy joy, like the entertainment on TV, the thrill of a good party.

15   Marriage takes some kind of sacrifice, not dreadful self-sacrifice of the soul, but some level of compromise. Some of one's fantasies, some of one's legitimate desires have to be given up for the value of the marriage itself. "While all marital partners feel shackled at times it is they who really choose to make the marital ties into confining chains or supporting bonds," says Dr. Whitaker. Marriage requires sexual, financial and emotional discipline. A man and a woman cannot follow every impulse, cannot allow themselves to stop growing or changing.

16   Divorce is not an evil act. Sometimes it provides salvation for people who have grown hopelessly apart or were frozen in patterns of pain or mutual unhappiness. Divorce can be, despite its initial devastation, like the first cut of the surgeon's knife, a step toward new health and a good life. On the other hand, if the partners can stay past the breaking up of the romantic myths into the development of real love and intimacy, they have achieved a work as amazing as the greatest cathedrals of the world. Marriages that do not fail but improve, that persist despite imperfections, are not only rare these days but offer a wondrous shelter in which the face of our mutual humanity can safely show itself.

DISCUSSION QUESTIONS

1. State in your own words what Roiphe means when she remarks at the end of paragraph 1, "If statistics could only measure loneliness, regret, pain, loss of self-confidence and fear of the future, the numbers would be beyond quantifying."

2. In which paragraphs does Roiphe cite expert opinion? Why do you think she includes it?

3. What is accomplished by using the short sentence "This isn't easy" in paragraph 12?

4. What additional reasons can you cite for marriage failure?

TOWARD KEY INSIGHTS

Which of the causes of marital breakdown do you consider most important? Why? What are the most essential things that couples can do to help lower the divorce rate?

SUGGESTION FOR WRITING

Write an essay explaining why certain individuals do well (or poorly) at forming friendships. Develop your causes with relevant specific details.

Brent Staples

Black Men and Public Space

Brent Staples is a journalist whose academic background in psychology and upbringing in the poor and largely black industrial town of Chester, Pennsylvania, have uniquely equipped him to address black problems and concerns. After earning A.B. and M.A. degrees, Staples worked as a college instructor and employee of a management firm while completing his Ph.D. at the University of Chicago in 1982. In 1983, he became a reporter for the Chicago Sun-Times *and three years later accepted a position with the* New York Times, *where he now serves on that paper's editorial board. His latest book,* An American Love Story *(1999), explores the subject of interracial marriage. In our selection, Staples examines the fear and hostility that blacks in public places sometimes arouse.*

My first victim was a woman—white, well dressed, probably in her early twenties. I came upon her late one evening on a deserted street in Hyde Park, a relatively affluent neighborhood in an otherwise mean, impoverished section of Chicago. As I swung onto the avenue behind her, there seemed to be a discreet, uninflammatory distance between us. Not so. She cast back a worried glance. To her, the youngish black man—a broad six feet two inches with a beard and billowing hair, both hands shoved into the pockets of a bulky military jacket—seemed menacingly close. After a few more quick glimpses, she picked up her pace and was soon running in earnest. Within seconds she disappeared into a cross street.   1

That was more than a decade ago. I was twenty-two years old, a graduate   2
student newly arrived at the University of Chicago. It was in the echo of that terrified woman's footfalls that I first began to know the unwieldy inheritance I'd come into—the ability to alter public space in ugly ways. It was clear that she thought herself the quarry of a mugger, a rapist, or worse. Suffering a bout of insomnia, however, I was stalking sleep, not defenseless wayfarers. As a softy who is scarcely able to take a knife to a raw chicken—let alone hold one to a person's throat—I was surprised, embarrassed, and dismayed all at once. Her flight made me feel like an accomplice in tyranny. It also made it clear that I was indistinguishable from the muggers who occasionally seeped into the area from the surrounding ghetto. That first encounter, and those that followed, signified that a vast, unnerving gulf lay between nighttime pedestrians—particularly women—and me. And I soon gathered that being perceived as dangerous is a hazard in itself. I only needed to turn a corner into a dicey situation, or crowd some frightened, armed person in a foyer somewhere, or make an errant move after being pulled over by a policeman. Where fear and weapons meet—and they often do in urban America—there is always the possibility of death.

In that first year, my first away from my hometown, I was to become thor-   3
oughly familiar with the language of fear. At dark, shadowy intersections, I could cross in front of a car stopped at a traffic light and elicit the *thunk, thunk, thunk, thunk* of the driver—black, white, male, or female—hammering down the door locks. On less traveled streets after dark, I grew accustomed to but never comfortable with people crossing to the other side of the street rather than pass me. Then there were the standard unpleasantries with policemen, doormen, bouncers, cabdrivers, and others whose business it is to screen out troublesome individuals *before* there is any nastiness.

I moved to New York nearly two years ago and I have remained an avid   4
night walker. In central Manhattan, the near-constant crowd cover minimizes tense one-on-one street encounters. Elsewhere—in SoHo, for example, where sidewalks are narrow and tightly spaced buildings shut out the sky—things can get very taut indeed.

After dark, on the warrenlike streets of Brooklyn where I live, I often see   5
women who fear the worst from me. They seem to have set their faces on neutral, and with their purse straps strung across their chests bandolier-style, they

forge ahead as though bracing themselves against being tackled. I understand, of course, that the danger they perceive is not a hallucination. Women are particularly vulnerable to street violence, and young black males are drastically overrepresented among the perpetrators of that violence. Yet these truths are no solace against the kind of alienation that comes of being ever the suspect, a fearsome entity with whom pedestrians avoid making eye contact.

6   It is not altogether clear to me how I reached the ripe old age of twenty-two without being conscious of the lethality nighttime pedestrians attributed to me. Perhaps it was because in Chester, Pennsylvania, the small, angry industrial town where I came of age in the 1960s, I was scarcely noticeable against a backdrop of gang warfare, street knifings, and murders. I grew up one of the good boys, had perhaps a half-dozen fistfights. In retrospect, my shyness of combat has clear sources.

7   As a boy, I saw countless tough guys locked away; I have since buried several, too. They were babies, really—a teenage cousin, a brother of twenty-two, a childhood friend in his mid-twenties—all gone down in episodes of bravado played out in the streets. I came to doubt the virtues of intimidation early on. I chose, perhaps unconsciously, to remain a shadow—timid, but a survivor.

8   The fearsomeness mistakenly attributed to me in public places often has a perilous flavor. The most frightening of these confusions occurred in the late 1970's and early 1980's, when I worked as a journalist in Chicago. One day, rushing into the office of a magazine I was writing for with a deadline story in hand, I was mistaken for a burglar. The office manager called security and, with an ad hoc posse, pursued me through the labyrinthine halls, nearly to my editor's door. I had no way of proving who I was. I could only move briskly toward the company of someone who knew me.

9   Another time I was on assignment for a local paper and killing time before an interview. I entered a jewelry store on the city's affluent Near North Side. The proprietor excused herself and returned with an enormous red Doberman pinscher straining at the end of a leash. She stood, the dog extended toward me, silent to my questions, her eyes bulging nearly out of her head. I took a cursory look around, nodded, and bade her good night.

10   Relatively speaking, however, I never fared as badly as another black male journalist. He went to nearby Waukegan, Illinois, a couple of summers ago to work on a story about a murderer who was born there. Mistaking the reporter for the killer, police officers hauled him from his car at gunpoint and but for his press credentials would probably have tried to book him. Such episodes are not uncommon. Black men trade tales like this all the time.

11   Over the years, I learned to smother the rage I felt at so often being taken for a criminal. Not to do so would surely have led to madness. I now take precautions to make myself less threatening. I move about with care, particularly late in the evening. I give a wide berth to nervous people on subway platforms during the wee hours, particularly when I have exchanged business clothes for jeans. If I happen to be entering a building behind some people who appear skittish, I may walk by, letting them clear the lobby before I return, so as not to seem to be following them. I have been calm and extremely congenial on those rare occasions when I've been pulled over by the police.

12   And on late-evening constitutionals I employ what has proved to be an excellent tension-reducing measure: I whistle melodies from Beethoven and Vivaldi and the more popular classical composers. Even steely New Yorkers hunching toward nighttime destinations seem to relax, and occasionally they

even join in the tune. Virtually everybody seems to sense that a mugger wouldn't be warbling bright, sunny selections from Vivaldi's *Four Seasons*. It is my equivalent of the cowbell that hikers wear when they know they are in bear country.

DISCUSSION QUESTIONS

1. Discuss the effectiveness of Staple's opening paragraph.
2. Identify the thesis statement of the essay.
3. Consider the essay as a whole and then point out the significance of the first sentence in paragraph 2.
4. What does Staples accomplish by mentioning at several points in the essay his distaste for violence?
5. Which patterns of causal analysis, discussed on pages 133–34, do you find in this essay?
6. Trace Staples's changing responses to the fear and hostility that he encounters.

TOWARD KEY INSIGHTS

What could and should be done to alleviate some of the racial tension and stereotyping that led to the experiences described in this essay?

SUGGESTION FOR WRITING

Write a cause-and-effect essay exploring your reactions to some actual or perceived threat to you. Possibilities might include engine trouble on a plane flight; a snowstorm that traps you in your car; or recurring head, chest, or stomach pains that send you to your doctor. Include your reactions both at the time and afterward.

Definition

Laurence Shames

The Sweet Smell of Success Isn't All That Sweet

Laurence Shames (born 1951) is a native of Newark, New Jersey, and a graduate of New York University. After completing his education, he began a career as a nonfiction writer contributing to a variety of popular magazines and to the New York Times. *Shames's book-length publicactions include two nonfiction works,* The Harvard Business Schools' Most Successful Class and How It Shaped America *(1986) and* The Hunger for More *(1991), which focuses on the search for values in a world of greed. He has also authored several fictional works, with an emphasis on detective fiction. The latest of these,* The Naked Detective, *appeared in 2000. Shames's concern for values is apparent in this selection, which attacks contemporary attitudes about success.*

<table>
<tr><td>Introduction: paragraphs 1–4; captures attention by ironically attacking high success standards, defending low standards</td><td>1</td><td>John Milton was a failure. In writing "Paradise Lost," his stated aim was to "justify the ways of God to men." Inevitably, he fell short of accomplishing that and only wrote a monumental poem. Beethoven, whose music was conceived to transcend Fate, was a failure, as was Socrates, whose ambition was to make people happy by making them reasonable and just. The inescapable conclusion seems to be that the surest, noblest way to fail is to set one's own standards titanically high.</td></tr>
</table>

1. John Milton was a failure. In writing "Paradise Lost," his stated aim was to "justify the ways of God to men." Inevitably, he fell short of accomplishing that and only wrote a monumental poem. Beethoven, whose music was conceived to transcend Fate, was a failure, as was Socrates, whose ambition was to make people happy by making them reasonable and just. The inescapable conclusion seems to be that the surest, noblest way to fail is to set one's own standards titanically high.

2. The flip-side of that proposition also seems true, and it provides the safe but dreary logic by which most of us live: The surest way to succeed is to keep one's strivings low—or at least to direct them along already charted paths. Don't set yourself the probably thankless task of making the legal system better; just shoot at becoming a partner in the firm. Don't agonize over questions about where your talents and proclivities might most fulfillingly lead you; just do a heads-up job of determining where the educational or business opportunities seem most secure.

3. After all, if "success" itself—rather than the substance of the achievements that make for success—is the criterion by which we measure ourselves and from which we derive our self-esteem, why make things more difficult by reaching for the stars?

4. What is this contemporary version of success really all about?

Body: paragraphs 5–12

According to certain beer commercials, it consists in moving up to a premium brand that costs a dime or so more per bottle. Credit-card companies would have you believe success inheres in owning their particular piece of plastic.

If these examples sound petty, they are. But take those petty privileges, weave them into a fabric that passes for a value system and what you've got is a national mood that has vast motivating power that can shape at least the near future of the entire country.

Under the flag of success, modern-style, liberal arts colleges are withering while business schools are burgeoning—and yet even business schools are having an increasingly hard time finding faculty members, because teaching isn't considered "successful" enough. Amid a broad consensus that there is a glut of lawyers and an epidemic of strangling litigation, record numbers of young people continue to flock to law school because, for the individual practitioner, a law degree is still considered a safe ticket.

The most sobering thought of all is that today's M.B.A.'s and lawyers are tomorrow's M.B.A.'s and lawyers: Having invested so much time and money in their training, only a tiny percentage of them will ever opt out of their early chosen fields. Decisions made in accordance with today's hothouse notions of ambition are locking people into careers that will define and also limit their activities and yearnings for virtually the rest of their lives.

Many, by external standards, will be "successes." They will own homes, eat in better restaurants, dress well and, in some instances, perform socially useful work. Yet there is a deadening and dangerous flaw in their philosophy: It has little room, little sympathy and less respect for the noble failure, for the person who ventures past the limits, who aims gloriously high and falls unashamedly short.

That sort of ambition doesn't have much place in a world where success is proved by worldly reward rather than by accomplishment itself. That sort of ambition is increasingly thought of as the domain of irredeemable eccentrics, of people who haven't quite caught on—and there is great social pressure not to be one of them.

The result is that fewer people are drawn to the cutting edge of noncommercial scientific research. Fewer are taking on the sublime, unwinnable challenges of the arts. Fewer are asking questions that matter—the ones that can't be answered. Fewer are putting themselves on the line, making as much of their minds and talents as they might.

The irony is that today's success-chasers seem obsessed with the idea of *not settling*. They take advanced degrees in business because they won't settle for just a so-so job. They compete for slots at law firms and investment houses because they won't settle for any but the fastest track. They seem to regard it as axiomatic that "success" and "settling" are opposites.

Yet in doggedly pursuing the rather brittle species of success now in fashion, they are restricting themselves to a chokingly narrow swath of turf along the entire range of human possibilities. Does it ever occur to them that, frequently, success is what people settle for when they can't think of something noble enough to be worth failing at?

5	Development by examples and brief definitions
6	Development by effect
7	Development by comparison, examples, and causes
8	Development by effects
9	Development by effects and argument
10	Development by effects
11	Development by effects
12	Development by effect, causes, and comparison
13	Conclusion: argues against contemporary notions of success

DISCUSSION QUESTIONS

1. Shames notes in paragraph 3 that "'success' itself—rather than the substance of the achievements that make for success—" seems to be the touchstone by which

we measure our worth. What do you think he means? Why is the distinction positioned at this point?

2. Why do you think Shames ends his essay with a rhetorical question, that is, one for which no answer is expected?

3. To what extent do you agree with Shames's idea of success? Discuss.

TOWARD KEY INSIGHTS

What evidence do you find that not all people are consumed by the desire for money?

What qualities do you consider crucial to living a "good" life? To happiness?

SUGGESTION FOR WRITING

Write a definition essay explaining how the popular view of responsibility, greed, marriage, single life, friendship, or some other concept needs redefining. Use whatever writing strategies advance your purpose.

Hara Estroff Marano

The Power of Play[1]

Hara Estroff Marano is editor-at-large at Psychology Today *as well as an author of both articles and books on different facets of human relations. Her most recent book,* Why Doesn't Anyone Like Me? *(1999), focuses on strategies for raising socially confident children. In our selection, Marano points out that having fun is essential to our overall well-being.*

1   The beach. Say the words and they conjure the gentle tickle of waves against the shore, the harder kick of surf dashing against rocks, the slap of spray against heated skin. For most of us, the place where earth meets ocean is the very essence of play—antic, full of novelty and joyful abandon.

2   At the beach, we are all children. As we gambol in the shallow surf and toss in the deeper waves, we feel the freedom of helplessness and the satisfaction of improvising defenses. Unburdened by consciousness or self-consciousness, we are caught in the moment. Suffused with pleasure, we exult in the sheer lightness of being.

3   Yet, as welcome and wonderful as those feelings are, play's value among adults is too often vastly underrated. We would all agree that play lifts stress from us. It refreshes us and recharges us. It restores our optimism. It changes our perspective, stimulating creativity. It renews our ability to accomplish the work of the world. By anyone's reckoning, those are remarkably worthy achievements.

---

[1]Hara Estroff Marano, "The Power of Play." Reprinted with permission from *Psychology Today* Magazine. Copyright © (1999) Sussex Publishers, Inc.

But there is also new evidence that play does much more. It may in fact be the highest expression of our humanity, both imitating and advancing the evolutionary process. Play appears to allow our brains to exercise their very flexibility, to maintain and even perhaps renew the neural connections that embody our human potential to adapt, to meet any possible set of environmental conditions.   4

And it may be that playfulness is a force woven through our search for mates. Certainly, playful people are the most fun to be around. But the ability to play may be a strong and appealing signal of something more. Especially among males, playfulness can protect us. It may be a way to indicate to potential partners that a man is not a threat to himself, to his offspring—or to society at large.   5

It can truly be said that we are made for play; after all, humans are among the very few animals that play as adults. What the evidence adds up to is this: we are most human when we play—and just because we play.   6

Like art, play is that quintessential experience that is almost impossible to define—because it encompasses infinite variability—but which we all recognize when we see, or experience. So let us go back to the beach in an attempt to understand all that contributes to such a necessary, and exalted, psychological state.   7

The beach is, above all else, Somewhere Else, far enough away from home, office, and everyday routines in character and distance. That dislocation sets the stage for us to be attuned to the moment, to relax our focus on long-term goals.   8

Being at the beach invariably forces a measure of spontaneity. We bring few of our usual possessions and tools. We are forced to recline, stretch out, relax.   9

If the sand and the water offer their own endless cache of novelty, the sun draws our attention to them. And it cossets us, taking tension out of our bodies with its warmth. Then, too, there is the novelty of (relative) nudity. It renders us all childlike and opens us to the enjoyment of sensations. It renders us ready to play.   10

Despite our readiness to play, at the beach and other places, we Americans have a particularly deep ambivalence toward play. According to Cindy S. Aron, Ph.D., associate professor of history at the University of Virginia, Americans want to get out and play, and we do. But we have also created many ways that keep us connected to work. Partial evidence: the ubiquity of cell phones and laptop computers at the beach.   11

The concept of vacation—time specifically set aside from work for play—grew from the custom of a small elite in the early 19th century, observes Aron in *Working at Play* (Oxford, 1999). Fostered by the growth of the middle class, the creation of a highway system and the changeover from an agricultural to urban society, it expanded to a mass phenomenon by World War II.   12

But at the same time, notes Aron, "Americans have struggled with the notion of taking time off." In fact, she says, we have "a love/hate battle" with our vacations, both wanting to take them and fearing the consequences. Our distrust of leisure is a legacy of our Puritan forebears, who knew that work, not play, was the key to their success and saw labor as a way of glorifying God. Play, according to this view, threatens to undermine both our success and salvation.   13

Freud, too, disregarded play as a powerful force. In his 1930 classic *Civilization and Its Discontents,* he declared that "the communal life of human beings had, therefore, a two-fold foundation: the compulsion to work . . . and the power of love."   14

As a result, today we often use our leisure time not necessarily to play, but in performance of various sorts of work, whether it's time at the health spa or artists' retreats.   15

16   It isn't even clear whether we are playing more or less than we used to. If we're playing more, it doesn't feel like it. Just in the past 30 years, there has been a cultural shift reemphasizing work and getting ahead. "We still play, but much of it seems to lack a playful quality," observes anthropologist Garry Chick, Ph.D., of Penn State University. "Playfulness has been replaced by aggressiveness and the feeling that more needs to be crammed into less time."

17   Scholars themselves debate the state of our leisure time. Many believe that the amount of free time we have to use for play has decreased since about 1970, after having increased steadily since the Industrial Revolution. The increase accompanied a transition from an industrial economy marked by hourly wages to a service economy characterized by salaries. But the globalization of business competition and a general cultural rejection of the ideals of the 1960s in favor of a new materialism have actually eroded our free time since then. Other experts believe we have as much free time today as in 1970—but feel so harried by globalization and intimidated by the speed of things that it seems as if we have less.

18   But the big question is why we bother to play at all. It is a tenet of evolutionary psychology that useless behaviors—and worse, deleterious ones, which play can seem to be since it erodes energy, wastes time that could be spent searching for food, and opens players to both injury and predation—pretty quickly get selected out of behavioral repertoires. Yet in the animal kingdom, play increases, rather than decreases, with increasing complexity of the brain.

19   If Garry Chick is right, we play because it protects us. Chick, who has studied games and sports in a number of cultures, contends that the standard explanations for why we play just don't wash. For example, the belief that play affords practice for skills needed later in life is true—for some animals, and then just for juveniles. "Some animals appear to play at things they will be doing their adult lives," he observes. "Predatory animals play at predation, those that are preyed upon play at escape. Social animals beat each other up to establish rank and hierarchy."

20   Of course, all animals play at sex. "It's essential, something you have to do," Chick notes. "Animals play at mounting. Humans play doctor."

21   But the difficulty is explaining why adults engage in play, activity distinguished by having no goals at all. "Adults really don't have more to learn," says Chick. Which is why in most mammalian species, the adults leave playing to the young.

22   Chick proposes that just as humans have selectively bred the wolf into the dog specifically for playfulness, so we have bred playfulness into our own selves by sexual selection. Males, he argues, can be dangerous. They rape and they kill, especially when one deposes another in a social group. Chick points to evidence that stepfathers are much more likely to kill their stepchildren than fathers are to kill their natural offspring.

23   But one sign that males may not be dangerous either to females or to their children is their willingness to play with them. "So it is possible that females seek out mates who are playful, both for their own protection and for that of their offspring." Men, for their part, are not immune to the pleasures of playfulness in selecting a mate either. Playfulness is an indicator of youthfulness in women.

24   If playfulness is an innate biological quality of higher animals, it is also in part a learned behavior. Chick's studies of preschoolers and their parents demonstrate that younger parents have more playful children than older parents, presumably because they are played with more. And second-borns are more playful than first-borns, because they go through childhood with a near-peer to play with.

25   Through play, contends psychiatrist Lenore Terr, M.D., clinical professor of psychiatry at the University of California at San Francisco, "we get control over

the world. We get to manipulate symbols, control the outcome of events." Terr's own now-classic work with children traumatized by physical and sexual abuse demonstrates how clearly play is necessary to mental health.

In the aftermath of trauma children lose their flexibility. They play, but 26
their play is obsessive; they stay stuck, repeating the traumatic episode endlessly. "Post-traumatic play demonstrates that if we don't find a way out of difficult situations, we will play much of our lives over and over again."

Play is an opening to our very being, Terr observes in *Beyond Love and Work:* 27
Why Adults Need to Play (Scribner, 1999). It permits us emotional discharge, but in a way that carries little risk. In fact, she says, play is not just an activity—it's a state of mind, and "all the mental activity of play comes at you sideways." Therein lies its value: the mental activity is never the direct goal. Terr uses play therapy as a way to allow children—and adults, who often remain frozen in patterns of play originating in fearful experiences in childhood—to create new endings for their experience.

Perhaps for that reason, adults who play appear to live longer than those 28
who don't. Terr cites as evidence the most recent findings of the long-standing Terman study. Begun by Stanford University psychologist Lewis Terman in the 1920s to examine the lives of gifted children, the study has allowed other researchers to track the consequences of high intelligence and other psychological factors to health and longevity. In the Terman group, those still surviving are those who have played the most throughout their lives, Terr told *Psychology Today.*

Play, argues Brian Sutton-Smith, Ph.D., is more than an attitude. And more 29
than an action. While it encompasses development, it's not about that—it's about pure unalloyed enjoyment. Professor emeritus of psychology at the University of Pennsylvania, Sutton-Smith is still the ranking dean of play studies. He considers play an alternative cultural form, like art and music.

"They don't have much to do with immediate working life," says Sutton- 30
Smith, "but that doesn't mean they're a waste of time." He calls play—are you ready?—an autonomous intrinsically motivated activity. We do it spontaneously, just because it's fun.

Like art and music, play has a verbal and body language all its own. Even 31
studies of children at play show that language use is different during play than during normal conversation. For one thing, it takes place mainly in the past tense. A typical exchange between playmates might go: "And then let's say that we went to your place and your mother wouldn't let us in so we had to go home and my mother was out and so we had to make this meal that we are making now. OK? Is that OK?" "OK. And what else did we do?" "We did a poop. Ha-ha!"

Play is also stylized, with regulated ways of behaving. Games have rules. Still, 32
people are very active within its frame. In other words, when you're chased, you run. "Play is always a fantasy, but once you get into the frame it is quite real, and everything you do is real. You put acres and acres of real movement and real action and real belief in it," says Sutton-Smith. So you scream with fear when you're being chased.

Sutton-Smith is betting that neuroimaging studies of the brain will eventu- 33
ally reveal a ludic center in the brain. And he locates it somewhere in the frontal lobes. What play does, he says, is simulate and make more flexible fear responses that are reflexes in the more primitive organism or in more primitive parts of the brain. "What we have in play is a simulation of an anxiety attack," he says.

With one all-important difference. It's anxiety—complete with uncer- 34
tainty—but without the adrenaline and endocrine response. Studies in dogs show that "they're rushing around as if they're in extremity, but adrenaline is

not being pumped into the system. Play looks like an emergency but isn't. It's a simulated emergency. The frontal lobes win out over the reflexive phenomena in the back of the brain."

35   In the simulated explosions and aggressions of play, we get to explore and experiment with feelings. It is one of the few times we are in charge of circumstances. We have much more autonomy than usual, and exchange habit and boredom for novelty and the exercise of our own competencies. And that creates excitement.

36   Somewhere down the line, some creature was untethered from strict necessity and afforded the luxury of an excess action, and then repeated making the move that wasn't strictly necessary. "That animal was in some way turned into a more surviving animal as a result," says Sutton-Smith.

37   We play because it reflects the brains we have and the cultures we live in. By and large, he points out, "the connections in the brain fade away unless used. We know that early stimulation of children leads to higher cognitive scores. Playful stimulation probably hits all kinds of synaptic possibilities. It is all make-believe and all over the map. The potentiality of the synapses and the potentiality of playfulness are a beautiful marriage."

38   When adults play, notes Sutton-Smith, citing a series of Dutch studies of video-game playing, their memory is better. They are cognitively more capable. And they are happier.

39   The same is true for kids. In one study, Austrian children were offered a cache of toys—once they got their work done. As a result, the children were more eager to go to school. The teachers liked being in the classrooms teaching and being with the kids more, and the parents liked the school more. And pointing to a homegrown study of Temple University, children arriving in grade one with a reading background were compared with kids having a more old-fashioned play background. The children who got the reading instruction performed better during the first grade but not by the end of the year. And, Sutton-Smith reports, "they were much more depressed. The opposite of play is not work. It's depression."

40   Although we all need to play, we don't all play the same way. We differ significantly in play style, Penn State's Garry Chick has found. In studies of tic-tac-toe players, Chick observed differences along several dimensions. First there were those he calls high-velocity players; for them, the fewer strokes the better. Low-velocity players, on the other hand, were engaged in the play of play; they simply enjoyed making the moves. Players also differ by strategy. Some people play to win. Others play not to lose; for them, a draw is as pleasurable as a win.

41   Some of us like to play in ways that test physical skill. Some prefer games of pure strategy, like chess. Others of us opt for word games and puzzles at any chance we get. Some of us—the very lucky ones?—get to play in our work. Scientists and writers, for example, regularly play with ideas.

42   How we play is related, in myriad ways, to our core sense of self. Play is an exercise in self-definition; it reveals what we choose to do, not what we have to do. We not only play because we are. We play the way we are. And the ways we could be. Play is our free connection to pure possibility.

43   It is a day at the beach.

DISCUSSION QUESTIONS

1. Which paragraphs constitute the essay's introduction and what purpose, besides starting the essay, do they serve?

2. Identify the thesis statement of the essay.

3. Reread paragraphs 3, 4, and 5 and then construct your own essential definition that includes the major characteristics of play.

4. What writing strategies does Marano use to develop her definition? Refer to specific parts of the essay when answering.

5. Characterize the level of diction of this essay.

6. Suggest why Marano cites quotations from authorities at various points.

7. What does the single sentence that ends the essay accomplish?

TOWARD KEY INSIGHTS

Do activities that involve little direct action, such as chess, puzzles, or video games, qualify as forms of play? Why or why not?

Other than the possibility of injury, what are some possible disadvantages of play?

SUGGESTION FOR WRITING

Write an essay defining the various dimensions of the meaning of work. Develop your essay with an appropriate number of writing strategies and with relevant specific details.

Stephen L. Carter

The Insufficiency of Honesty

Stephen L. Carter (born 1954) earned a B.A. degree from Stanford University in 1976 and a law degree from Yale University in 1979. Between 1979 and 1982, he worked as a law clerk, first for the U.S. Court of Appeals, District of Columbia circuit, and then for Justice Thurgood Marshall of the U.S. Supreme Court. Since 1982, he has served on the faculty of the Yale Law school. Carter's most recent books include God's Name in Vain *(2000),* Civility: Manners, Morals, and the Etiquette of Democracy *(1999), and* The Dissent of the Governed *(1998). Earlier books critique affirmative action policies, attack current political and legal attitudes toward religion, and examine the nature of integrity. In the following selection, Carter examines integrity by distinguishing it from honesty.*

A couple of years ago I began a university commencement address by telling the audience that I was going to talk about integrity. The crowd broke into applause. Applause! Just because they had heard the word "integrity": that's how starved for it they were. They had no idea how I was using the word, or what I was going to say about integrity, or, indeed, whether I was for it or against it. But they knew they liked the idea of talking about it.

Very well, let us consider this word "integrity." Integrity is like the weather: everybody talks about it but nobody knows what to do about it. Integrity is that stuff that we always want more of. Some say that we need to return to the good old days when we had a lot more of it. Others say that we as a nation have never really had enough of it. Hardly anybody stops to explain exactly what we mean by it, or how we know it is a good thing, or why everybody needs to have the same amount of it. Indeed, the only trouble with integrity is that everybody who uses the word seems to mean something slightly different.

3   For instance, when I refer to integrity, do I mean simply "honesty"? The answer is no; although honesty is a virtue of importance, it is a different virtue from integrity. Let us, for simplicity, think of honesty as not lying; and let us further accept Sissela Bok's definition of a lie: "any intentionally deceptive message which is *stated*." Plainly, one cannot have integrity without being honest (although, as we shall see, the matter gets complicated), but one can certainly be honest and yet have little integrity.

4   When I refer to integrity, I have something very specific in mind. Integrity, as I will use the term, requires three steps: discerning what is right and what is wrong; acting on what you have discerned, even at personal cost; and saying openly that you are acting on your understanding of right and wrong. The first criterion captures the idea that integrity requires a degree of moral reflectiveness. The second brings in the ideal of a person of integrity as steadfast, a quality that includes keeping one's commitments. The third reminds us that a person of integrity can be trusted.

5   The first point to understand about the difference between honesty and integrity is that a person may be entirely honest without ever engaging in the hard work of discernment that integrity requires: she may tell us quite truthfully what she believes without ever taking the time to figure out whether what she believes is good and right and true. The problem may be as simple as someone's foolishly saying something that hurts a friend's feelings; a few moments of thought would have revealed the likelihood of the hurt and the lack of necessity for the comment. Or the problem may be more complex, as when a man who was raised from birth in a society that preaches racism states his belief in one race's inferiority as a fact, without ever really considering that perhaps this deeply held view is wrong. Certainly the racist is being honest—he is telling us what he actually thinks—but his honesty does not add up to integrity.

Telling Everything You Know

6   A wonderful epigram sometimes attributed to the filmmaker Sam Goldwyn goes like this: "The most important thing in acting is honesty; once you learn to fake that, you're in." The point is that honesty can be something one *seems* to have. Without integrity, what passes for honesty often is nothing of the kind; it is fake honesty—or it is honest but irrelevant and perhaps even immoral.

7   Consider an example. A man who has been married for fifty years confesses to his wife on his deathbed that he was unfaithful thirty-five years earlier. The dishonesty was killing his spirit, he says. Now he has cleared his conscience and is able to die in peace.

8   The husband has been honest—sort of. He has certainly unburdened himself. And he has probably made his wife (soon to be his widow) quite miserable in the process, because even if she forgives him, she will not be able to remember him with quite the vivid image of love and loyalty that she had hoped for. Arranging his own emotional affairs to ease his transition to death, he has shifted to his wife the burden of confusion and pain, perhaps for the rest of her life. Moreover, he has attempted his honesty at the one time in his life when it carries no risk; acting in accordance with what you think is right and risking no loss in the process is a rather thin and unadmirable form of honesty.

Besides, even though the husband has been honest in a sense, he has now   9
twice been unfaithful to his wife: once thirty-five years ago, when he had his affair, and again when, nearing death, he decided that his own peace of mind was
more important than hers. In trying to be honest he has violated his marriage
vow by acting toward his wife not with love but with naked and perhaps even
cruel self-interest.

As my mother used to say, you don't have to tell people everything you   10
know. Lying and nondisclosure, as the law often recognizes, are not the same
thing. Sometimes it is actually illegal to tell what you know, as, for example, in
the disclosure of certain financial information by market insiders. Or it may be
unethical, as when a lawyer reveals a confidence entrusted to her by a client. It
may be simple bad manners, as in the case of a gratuitous comment to a colleague on his or her attire. And it may be subject to religious punishment, as
when a Roman Catholic priest breaks the seal of the confessional—an offense
that carries automatic excommunication.

In all the cases just mentioned, the problem with telling everything you   11
know is that somebody else is harmed. Harm may not be the intention, but it is
certainly the effect. Honesty is most laudable when we risk harm to ourselves; it
becomes a good deal less so if we instead risk harm to others when there is no
gain to anyone other than ourselves. Integrity may counsel keeping our secrets in
order to spare the feelings of others. Sometimes, as in the example of the way-
ward husband, the reason we want to tell what we know is precisely to shift our
pain onto somebody else—a course of action dictated less by integrity than by
self-interest. Fortunately, integrity and self-interest often coincide, as when a
politician of integrity is rewarded with our votes. But often they do not, and it is
at those moments that our integrity is truly tested.

Error

Another reason that honesty alone is no substitute for integrity is that if   12
forthrightness is not preceded by discernment, it may result in the expression
of an incorrect moral judgment. In other words, I may be honest about what I
believe, but if I have never tested my beliefs, I may be wrong. And here I mean
"wrong" in a particular sense: the proposition in question is wrong if I would
change my mind about it after hard moral reflection.

Consider this example. Having been taught all his life that women are not   13
as smart as men, a manager gives the women on his staff less-challenging assignments than he gives the men. He does this, he believes, for their own
benefit: he does not want them to fail, and he believes that they will if he gives
them tougher assignments. Moreover, when one of the women on his staff does
poor work, he does not berate her as harshly as he would a man, because he expects nothing more. And he claims to be acting with integrity because he is acting according to his own deepest beliefs.

The manager fails the most basic test of integrity. The question is not   14
whether his actions are consistent with what he most deeply believes but
whether he has done the hard work of discerning whether what he most deeply
believes is right. The manager has not taken this harder step.

Moreover, even within the universe that the manager has constructed for   15
himself, he is not acting with integrity. Although he is obviously wrong to think
that the women on his staff are not as good as the men, even were he right, that
would not justify applying different standards to their work. By so doing he be-
trays both his obligation to the institution that employs him and his duty as a
manager to evaluate his employees.

16   The problem that the manager faces is an enormous one in our practical politics, where having the dialogue that makes democracy work can seem impossible because of our tendency to cling to our views even when we have not examined them. As Jean Bethke Elshtain has said, borrowing from John Courtney Murray, our politics are so fractured and contentious that we often cannot even reach *disagreement*. Our refusal to look closely at our own most cherished principles is surely a large part of the reason. Socrates thought the unexamined life not worth living. But the unhappy truth is that few of us actually have the time for constant reflection on our views—on public or private morality. Examine them we must, however, or we will never know whether we might be wrong.

17   None of this should be taken to mean that integrity as I have described it presupposes a single correct truth. If, for example, your integrity-guided search tells you that affirmative action is wrong, and my integrity-guided search tells me that affirmative action is right, we need not conclude that one of us lacks integrity. As it happens, I believe—both as a Christian and as a secular citizen who struggles toward moral understanding—that we *can* find true and sound answers to our moral questions. But I do not pretend to have found very many of them, nor is an exposition of them my purpose here.

18   It is the case not that there aren't any right answers but that, given human fallibility, we need to be careful in assuming that we have found them. However, today's political talk about how it is wrong for the government to impose one person's morality on somebody else is just mindless chatter. *Every* law imposes one person's morality on somebody else, because law has only two functions: to tell people to do what they would rather not or to forbid them to do what they would.

19   And if the surveys can be believed, there is far more moral agreement in America than we sometimes allow ourselves to think. One of the reasons that character education for young people makes so much sense to so many people is precisely that there seems to be a core set of moral understandings—we might call them the American Core—that most of us accept. Some of the virtues in this American Core are, one hopes, relatively noncontroversial. About 500 American communities have signed on to Michael Josephson's program to emphasize the "six pillars" of good character: trustworthiness, respect, responsibility, caring, fairness, and citizenship. These virtues might lead to a similarly noncontroversial set of political values: having an honest regard for ourselves and others, protecting freedom of thought and religious belief, and refusing to steal or murder.

Honesty and Competing Responsibilities

20   A further problem with too great an exaltation of honesty is that it may allow us to escape responsibilities that morality bids us bear. If honesty is substituted for integrity, one might think that if I say I am not planning to fulfill a duty, I need not fulfill it. But it would be a peculiar morality indeed that granted us the right to avoid our moral responsibilities simply by stating our intention to ignore them. Integrity does not permit such an easy escape.

21   Consider an example. Before engaging in sex with a woman, her lover tells her that if she gets pregnant, it is her problem, not his. She says that she understands. In due course she does wind up pregnant. If we believe, as I hope we do, that the man would ordinarily have a moral responsibility toward both the child he will have helped to bring into the world and the child's mother, then his honest statement of what he intends does not spare him that responsibility.

This vision of responsibility assumes that not all moral obligations stem   22
from consent or from a stated intention. The linking of obligations to promises
is a rather modern and perhaps uniquely Western way of looking at life, and
perhaps a luxury that only the well-to-do can afford. As Fred and Shulamit Korn
(a philosopher and an anthropologist) have pointed out, "If one looks at ethno-
graphic accounts of other societies, one finds that, while obligations everywhere
play a crucial role in social life, promising is not preeminent among the sources
of obligation and is not even mentioned by most anthropologists." The Korns
have made a study of Tonga, where promises are virtually unknown but the social order is remarkably stable. If life without any promises seems extreme, we
Americans sometimes go too far the other way, parsing not only our contracts
but even our marriage vows in order to discover the absolute minimum obligation that we have to others as a result of our promises.

That some societies in the world have worked out evidently functional   23
structures of obligation without the need for promise or consent does not tell
us what *we* should do. But it serves as a reminder of the basic proposition that
our existence in civil society creates a set of mutual responsibilities that philosophers used to capture in the fiction of the social contract. Nowadays, here in
America, people seem to spend their time thinking of even cleverer ways to
avoid their obligations, instead of doing what integrity commands and fulfilling
them. And all too often honesty is their excuse.

DISCUSSION QUESTIONS

1. Discuss the effectiveness of Carter's title.
2. Identify the thesis statement of this essay.
3. What writing strategies does Carter use to develop his essay? Refer to specific parts of the essay when answering.
4. In paragraph 8, Carter notes that the husband's deathbed confession "carries no risk." Explain what he means.
5. Point out the linking devices that Carter uses to connect paragraphs.
6. Identify what paragraphs constitute Carter's conclusion and explain why it is effective.
7. Discuss examples of situations you have known when people displayed honesty without integrity and also situations when people displayed honesty with integrity.

TOWARD KEY INSIGHTS

To what extent do you believe that our moral obligations extend beyond our promises and stated intentions?

Do Americans typically try to fulfill their "absolute minimum obligation?" What evidence can you cite to support your answer?

SUGGESTION FOR WRITING

Write an essay defining loyalty. Use appropriate examples and whatever writing strategies will further your purpose.

Nancy Gibbs

When Is It Rape?

A native New Yorker, Nancy Gibbs holds a degree in history from Yale University, from which she graduated with highest honors, and another in politics and philosophy from Oxford University. In 1985 she joined Time *magazine, where she is now a senior editor who writes major stories on national affairs and domestic policy issues. These stories have covered such topics as the right to die, violence in America, welfare reform, the separation of church and state, and the O.J. Simpson case. Several of Gibbs's stories have received awards for excellence. A 1996 book,* Mad Genius, *details the pursuit and capture of the Unabomber. In our selection, Gibbs explores the many dimensions of the term* rape.

1   Be careful of strangers and hurry home, says a mother to her daughter, knowing that the world is a frightful place but not wishing to swaddle a child in fear. Girls grow up scarred by caution and enter adulthood eager to shake free of their parents' worst nightmares. They still know to be wary of strangers. What they don't know is whether they have more to fear from their friends.

2   Most women who get raped are raped by people they already know—like the boy in biology class, or the guy in the office down the hall, or their friend's brother. The familiarity is enough to make them let down their guard, sometimes even enough to make them wonder afterward whether they were "really raped." What people think of as "real rape"—the assault by a monstrous stranger lurking in the shadows—accounts for only 1 out of 5 attacks.

3   So the phrase "acquaintance rape" was coined to describe the rest, all the cases of forced sex between people who already knew each other, however casually. But that was too clinical for headline writers, and so the popular term is the narrower "date rape," which suggests an ugly ending to a raucous night on the town.

4   These are not idle distinctions. Behind the search for labels is the central mythology about rape: that rapists are always strangers, and victims are women who ask for it. The mythology is hard to dispel because the crime is so rarely exposed. The experts guess—that's all they can do under the circumstances—that while 1 in 4 women will be raped in her lifetime, less than 10% will report the assault, and less than 5% of the rapists will go to jail.

5   When a story of the crime lodges in the headlines, the myths have a way of cluttering the search for the truth. The tale of Good Friday in Palm Beach landed in the news because it involved a Kennedy, but it may end up as a watershed case, because all the mysteries and passions surrounding date rape are here to be dissected. William Kennedy Smith met a woman at a bar, invited her back home late at night and apparently had sex with her on the lawn. She says it was rape, and the police believed her story enough to charge him with the crime. Perhaps it was the bruises on her leg; or the instincts of the investigators who found her, panicked and shaking, curled up in the fetal position on a couch; or the lie-detector tests she passed.

6   On the other side, Smith has adamantly protested that he is a man falsely accused. His friends and family testify to his gentle nature and moral fiber and insist that he could not possibly have committed such a crime. Maybe the

truth will come out in court[1]—but regardless of its finale, the case has shoved the debate over date rape into the minds of average men and women. Plant the topic in a conversation, and chances are it will ripen into a bitter argument or a jittery sequence of pale jokes.

Women charge that date rape is the hidden crime; men complain it is hard to prevent a crime they can't define. Women say it isn't taken seriously; men say it is a concept invented by women who like to tease but not take the consequences. Women say the date-rape debate is the first time the nation has talked frankly about sex; men say it is women's unconscious reaction to the excesses of the sexual revolution. Meanwhile, men and women argue among themselves about the "gray area" that surrounds the whole murky arena of sexual relations, and there is no consensus in sight. 7

In court, on campus, in conversation, the issue turns on the elasticity of the word *rape,* one of the few words in the language with the power to summon a shared image of a horrible crime. 8

At one extreme are those who argue that for the word to retain its impact, it must be strictly defined as forced sexual intercourse: a gang of thugs jumping a jogger in Central Park, a psychopath preying on old women in a housing complex, a man with an ice pick in a side street. To stretch the definition of the word risks stripping away its power. In this view, if it happened on a date, it wasn't rape. A romantic encounter is a context in which sex *could* occur, and so what omniscient judge will decide whether there was genuine mutual consent? 9

Others are willing to concede that date rape sometimes occurs, that sometimes a man goes too far on a date without a woman's consent. But this infraction, they say, is not as ghastly a crime as street rape, and it should not be taken as seriously. The *New York Post,* alarmed by the Willy Smith case, wrote in a recent editorial, "If the sexual encounter, *forced or not,* has been preceded by a series of consensual activities—drinking, a trip to the man's home, a walk on a deserted beach at 3 in the morning—the charge that's leveled against the alleged offender should, it seems to us, be different than the one filed against, say, the youths who raped and beat the jogger." 10

This attitude sparks rage among women who carry scars received at the hands of men they knew. It makes no difference if the victim shared a drink or a moonlit walk or even a passionate kiss, they protest, if the encounter ended with her being thrown to the ground and forcibly violated. Date rape is not about a misunderstanding, they say. It is not a communications problem. It is not about a woman's having regrets in the morning for a decision she made the night before. It is not about a "decision" at all. Rape is rape, and any form of forced sex— even between neighbors, co-workers, classmates and casual friends—is a crime. 11

A more extreme form of that view comes from activists who see rape as a metaphor, its definition swelling to cover any kind of oppression of women. Rape, seen in this light, can occur not only on a date but also in a marriage, not only by violent assault but also by psychological pressure. A Swarthmore College training pamphlet once explained that acquaintance rape "spans a spectrum of incidents and behaviors, ranging from crimes legally defined as rape to verbal harassment and inappropriate innuendo." 12

No wonder, then, that the battles become so heated. When innuendo qualifies as rape, the definitions have become so slippery that the entire subject 13

---

[1]Smith, nephew of Senator Edward Kennedy, was acquitted by a jury.

sinks into a political swamp. The only way to capture the hard reality is to tell the story.

14   A 32-year-old woman was on business in Tampa last year for the Florida supreme court. Stranded at the courthouse, she accepted a lift from a lawyer involved in her project. As they chatted on the ride home, she recalls, "he was saying all the right things, so I started to trust him." She agreed to have dinner, and afterward, at her hotel door, he convinced her to let him come in to talk. "I went through the whole thing about being old-fashioned," she says. "I was a virgin until I was 21. So I told him talk was all we were going to do."

15   But as they sat on the couch, she found herself falling asleep. "By now, I'm comfortable with him, and I put my head on his shoulder. He's not tried anything all evening, after all." Which is when the rape came. "I woke up to find him on top of me, forcing himself on me. I didn't scream or run. All I could think about was my business contacts and what if they saw me run out of my room screaming rape."

16   "I thought it was my fault. I felt so filthy, I washed myself over and over in hot water. Did he rape me?, I kept asking myself. I didn't consent. But who's gonna believe me? I had a man in my hotel room after midnight." More than a year later, she still can't tell the story without a visible struggle to maintain her composure. Police referred the case to the state attorney's office in Tampa, but without more evidence it decided not to prosecute. Although her attacker has admitted that he heard her say no, maintains the woman, "he says he didn't know that I meant no. He didn't feel he'd raped me, and he even wanted to see me again."

17   Her story is typical in many ways. The victim herself may not be sure right away that she has been raped, that she had said no and been physically forced into having sex anyway. And the rapist commonly hears but does not heed the protest. "A date rapist will follow through no matter what the woman wants because his agenda is to get laid," says Claire Walsh, a Florida-based consultant on sexual assaults. "First comes the dinner, then a dance, then a drink, then the coercion begins." Gentle persuasion gives way to physical intimidation, with alcohol as the ubiquitous lubricant. "When that fails, force is used," she says. "Real men don't take no for an answer."

18   The Palm Beach case serves to remind women that if they go ahead and press charges, they can expect to go on trial along with their attacker, if not in a courtroom then in the court of public opinion. The *New York Times* caused an uproar on its own staff not only for publishing the victim's name but also for laying out in detail her background, her high school grades, her driving record, along with an unattributed quote from a school official about her "little wild streak." A freshman at Carleton College in Minnesota, who says she was repeatedly raped for four hours by a fellow student, claims that she was asked at an administrative hearing if she performed oral sex on dates. In 1989 a man charged with raping at knife-point a woman he knew was acquitted in Florida because his victim had been wearing lace shorts and no underwear.

19   From a purely legal point of view, if she wants to put her attacker in jail, the survivor had better be beaten as well as raped, since bruises become a badge of credibility. She had better have reported the crime right away, before taking the hours-long shower that she craves, before burning her clothes, before curling up with the blinds down. And she would do well to be a woman of shining character. Otherwise the strict constructionist definitions of rape will prevail in court. "Juries don't have a great deal of sympathy for the victim if she's a willing participant up to the nonconsensual sexual intercourse," says Norman Kinne, a prose-

cutor in Dallas. "They feel that many times the victim has placed herself in the situation." Absent eyewitnesses or broken bones, a case comes down to her word against his, and the mythology of rape rarely lends her the benefit of the doubt.

She should also hope for an all-male jury, preferably composed of fathers   20
with daughters. Prosecutors have found that women tend to be harsh judges of one another—perhaps because to find a defendant guilty is to entertain two grim realities: that anyone might be a rapist, and that every woman could find herself a victim. It may be easier to believe, the experts muse, that at some level the victim asked for it. "But just because a woman makes a bad judgment, does that give the guy a moral right to rape her?" asks Dean Kilpatrick, director of the Crime Victim Research and Treatment Center at the Medical University of South Carolina. "The bottom line is, Why does a woman's having a drink give a man the right to rape her?"

[In 1991,] the Supreme Court waded into the debate with a 7-to-2 ruling that   21
protects victims from being harassed on the witness stand with questions about their sexual history. The Justices, in their first decision on "rape-shield laws," said an accused rapist could not present evidence about a previous sexual relationship with the victim unless he notified the court ahead of time. In her decision, Justice Sandra Day O'Connor wrote that "rape victims deserve heightened protection against surprise, harassment and unnecessary invasions of privacy."

That was welcome news to prosecutors who understand the reluctance of   22
victims to come forward. But there are other impediments to justice as well. An internal investigation of the Oakland police department found that officers ignored a quarter of all reports of sexual assaults or attempts, though 90% actually warranted investigation. Departments are getting better at educating officers in handling rape cases, but the courts remain behind. A New York City task force on women in the courts charged that judges and lawyers were routinely less inclined to believe a woman's testimony than a man's.

The present debate over degrees of rape is nothing new: All through his-   23
tory, rapes have been divided between those that mattered and those that did not. For the first few thousand years, the only rape that was punished was the defiling of a virgin, and that was viewed as a property crime. A girl's virtue was a marketable asset, and so a rapist was often ordered to pay the victim's father the equivalent of her price on the marriage market. In early Babylonian and Hebrew societies, a married woman who was raped suffered the same fate as an adulteress—death by stoning or drowning. Under William the Conqueror, the penalty for raping a virgin was castration and loss of both eyes—unless the violated woman agreed to marry her attacker, as she was often pressured to do. "Stealing an heiress" became a perfectly conventional means of taking—literally—a wife.

It may be easier to prove a rape case now, but not much. Until the 1960s it   24
was virtually impossible without an eyewitness; judges were often required to instruct jurors that "rape is a charge easily made and hard to defend against; so examine the testimony of this witness with caution." But sometimes a rape was taken very seriously, particularly if it involved a black man attacking a white woman—a crime for which black men were often executed or lynched.

Susan Estrich, author of *Real Rape*, considers herself a lucky victim. This is   25
not just because she survived an attack 17 years ago by a stranger with an ice pick, one day before her graduation from Wellesley. It's because police, and her friends, believed her. "The first thing the Boston police asked was whether it was a black guy," recalls Estrich, now a University of Southern California law professor. When she said yes and gave the details of the attack, their reaction

was, "So, you were really raped." It was an instructive lesson, she says, in understanding how racism and sexism are factored into perceptions of the crime.

26   A new twist in society's perception came in 1975, when Susan Brownmiller published her book *Against Our Will: Men, Women and Rape.* In it she attacked the concept that rape was a sex crime, arguing instead that it was a crime of violence and power over women. Throughout history, she wrote, rape has played a critical function. "It is nothing more or less than a conscious process of intimidation, by which *all men* keep *all women* in a state of fear."

27   Out of this contention was born a set of arguments that have become politically correct wisdom on campus and in academic circles. This view holds that rape is a symbol of women's vulnerability to male institutions and attitudes. "It's sociopolitical," insists Gina Rayfield, a New Jersey psychologist. "In our culture men hold the power, politically, economically. They're socialized not to see women as equals."

28   This line of reasoning has led some women, especially radicalized victims, to justify flinging around the term rape as a political weapon, referring to everything from violent sexual assaults to inappropriate innuendos. Ginny, a college senior who was really raped when she was 16, suggests that false accusations of rape can serve a useful purpose. "Penetration is not the only form of violation," she explains. In her view, rape is a subjective term, one that women must use to draw attention to other, nonviolent, even nonsexual forms of oppression. "If a woman did falsely accuse a man of rape, she may have had reasons to," Ginny says, "Maybe she wasn't raped, but he clearly violated her in some way."

29   Catherine Comins, assistant dean of student life at Vassar, also sees some value in this loose use of "rape." She says angry victims of various forms of sexual intimidation cry rape to regain their sense of power. "To use the word carefully would be to be careful for the sake of the violator, and the survivors don't care a hoot about him." Comins argues that men who are unjustly accused can sometimes gain from the experience. "They have a lot of pain, but it is not a pain that I would necessarily have spared them. I think it ideally initiates a process of self-exploration. 'How do I see women?' 'If I didn't violate her, could I have?' 'Do I have the potential to do to her what they say I did?' Those are good questions."

30   Taken to extremes, there is an ugly element of vengeance at work here. Rape is an abuse of power. But so are false accusations of rape, and to suggest that men whose reputations are destroyed might benefit because it will make them more sensitive is an attitude that is sure to backfire on women who are seeking justice for all victims. On campuses where the issue is most inflamed, male students are outraged that their names can be scrawled on a bathroom-wall list of rapists and they have no chance to tell their side of the story.

31   "Rape is what you read about in the *New York Post* about 17 little boys raping a jogger in Central Park," says a male freshman at a liberal-arts college, who learned that he had been branded a rapist after a one-night stand with a friend. He acknowledges that they were both very drunk when she started kissing him at a party and ended up back in his room. Even through his haze, he had some qualms about sleeping with her: "I'm fighting against my hormonal instincts, and my moral instincts are saying, 'This is my friend and if I were sober, I wouldn't be doing this,'" but he went ahead anyway. "When you're drunk, and there are all sorts of ambiguity, and the woman says 'Please, please' and then she says no sometime later, even in the middle of the act, there still may very well be some kind of violation, but it's not the same thing. It's not rape. If you don't hear her

say no, if she doesn't say it, if she's playing around with you—oh, I could get squashed for saying it—there is an element of say no, mean yes."

The morning after their encounter, he recalls, both students woke up 32 hung over and eager to put the memory behind them. Only months later did he learn that she had told a friend that he had torn her clothing and raped her. At this point in the story, the accused man starts using the language of rape. "I felt violated," he says. "I felt like she was taking advantage of me when she was very drunk. I never heard her say 'No!,' 'Stop!,' anything." He is angry and hurt at the charges, worried that they will get around, shatter his reputation and force him to leave the small campus.

So here, of course, is the heart of the debate. If rape is sex without consent, 33 how exactly should consent be defined and communicated, when and by whom? Those who view rape through a political lens tend to place all responsibility on men to make sure that their partners are consenting at every point of a sexual encounter. At the extreme, sexual relations come to resemble major surgery, requiring a signed consent form. Clinical psychologist Mary P. Koss of the University of Arizona in Tucson, who is a leading scholar on the issue, puts it rather bluntly: "It's the man's penis that is doing the raping, and ultimately he's responsible for where he puts it."

Historically, of course, this has never been the case, and there are some 34 who argue that it shouldn't be—that women too must take responsibility for their behavior, and that the whole realm of intimate encounters defies regulation from on high. Anthropologist Lionel Tiger has little patience for trendy sexual politics that make no reference to biology. Since the dawn of time, he argues, men and women have always gone to bed with different goals. In the effort to keep one's genes in the gene pool, "it is to the male advantage to fertilize as many females as possible, as quickly as possible and as efficiently as possible." For the female, however, who looks at the large investment she will have to make in the offspring, the opposite is true. Her concern is to "select" who "will provide the best set up for their offspring." So, in general, "the pressure is on the male to be aggressive and on the female to be coy."

No one defends the use of physical force, but when the coercion involved 35 is purely psychological, it becomes hard to assign blame after the fact. Journalist Stephanie Gutmann is an ardent foe of what she calls the date-rape dogmatists. "How can you make sex completely politically correct and completely safe?" she asks. "What a horribly bland, unerotic thing that would be! Sex is, by nature, a risky endeavor, emotionally. And desire is a violent emotion. These people in the date-rape movement have erected so many rules and regulations that I don't know how people can have erotic or desire-driven sex."

Nonsense, retorts Cornell professor Andrea Parrot, co-author of *Acquaintance* 36 *Rape: The Hidden Crime*. Seduction should not be about lies, manipulation, game playing or coercion of any kind, she says. "Too bad that people think that the only way you can have passion and excitement and sex is if there are miscommunications, and one person is forced to do something he or she doesn't want to do." The very pleasures of sexual encounters should lie in the fact of mutual comfort and consent: "You can hang from the ceiling, you can use fruit, you can go crazy and have really wonderful sensual erotic sex, if both parties are consenting."

It would be easy to accuse feminists of being too quick to classify sex as 37 rape, but feminists are to be found on all sides of the debate, and many protest the idea that all the onus is on the man. It demeans women to suggest that they are so vulnerable to coercion or emotional manipulation that they must always be escorted by the strong arm of the law. "You can't solve society's ills by making everything a crime," says Albuquerque attorney Nancy Hollander. "That comes out of the sense of overprotection of women, and in the long run that is going to be harmful to us."

38   What is lost in the ideological debate over date rape is the fact that men and women, especially when they are young, and drunk, and aroused, are not very good at communicating. "In many cases," says Estrich, "the man thought it was sex, and the woman thought it was rape, and they are both telling the truth." The man may envision a celluloid seduction, in which he is being commanding, she is being coy. A woman may experience the same event as a degrading violation of her will. That some men do not believe a woman's protests is scarcely surprising in a society so drenched with messages that women have rape fantasies and a desire to be overpowered.

39   By the time they reach college, men and women are loaded with cultural baggage, drawn from movies, television, music videos and "bodice ripper" romance novels. Over the years they have watched Rhett sweep Scarlett up the stairs in *Gone With the Wind;* or Errol Flynn, who was charged twice with statutory rape, overpower a protesting heroine who then melts in his arms; or Stanley rape his sister-in-law Blanche du Bois while his wife is in the hospital giving birth to a child in *A Streetcar Named Desire.* Higher up the cultural food chain, young people can read of date rape in Homer or Jane Austen, watch it in *Don Giovanni* or *Rigoletto.*

40   The messages come early and often, and nothing in the feminist revolution has been able to counter them. A recent survey of sixth- to ninth-graders in Rhode Island found that a fourth of the boys and a sixth of the girls said it was acceptable for a man to force a woman to kiss him or have sex if he has spent money on her. A third of the children said it would not be wrong for a man to rape a woman who had had previous sexual experiences.

41   Certainly cases like Palm Beach, movies like *The Accused* and novels like Avery Corman's *Prized Possessions* may force young people to re-examine assumptions they have inherited. The use of new terms, like acquaintance rape and date rape, while controversial, has given men and women the vocabulary they need to express their experiences with both force and precision. This dialogue would be useful if it helps strip away some of the dogmas, old and new, surrounding the issue. Those who hope to raise society's sensitivity to the problem of date rape would do well to concede that it is not precisely the same sort of crime as street rape, that there may be very murky issues of intent and degree involved.

42   On the other hand, those who downplay the problem should come to realize that date rape is a crime of uniquely intimate cruelty. While the body is violated, the spirit is maimed. How long will it take, once the wounds have healed, before it is possible to share a walk on a beach, a drive home from work, or an evening's conversation without always listening for a quiet alarm to start ringing deep in the back of the memory of a terrible crime?

DISCUSSION QUESTIONS

1. What answer, if any, does Gibbs provide to the question posed in her title? Refer to specific parts of the essay when answering.
2. Identify the three brief definitions that Gibbs uses in the first three paragraphs. Consider the essay as a whole and then suggest why she uses them at the beginning of the essay.

3. What writing strategies does Gibbs use to develop the essay? Where does she use them?

4. Where does Gibbs define by negation?

5. What function does paragraph 13 serve in the essay?

6. Why do you think Gibbs uses direct quotations at so many places in the essay?

TOWARD KEY INSIGHTS

Reflect on the case of the male freshman discussed in paragraphs 31–32. Do you think that he was guilty of rape? Why or why not?

Do you agree with the idea of placing "all responsibility on men to make sure that their partners are consenting at every point of a sexual encounter" (paragraph 33)?

Should date rape be considered the same kind of crime as rape by a stranger, or should it be considered a lesser offense? Explain your answer.

Do you agree with the notion that rape is a means by which all men keep all women in a state of fear? Defend your answer.

SUGGESTION FOR WRITING

Write an essay that defines the many dimensions of sexism or racism. Use whatever strategies are appropriate for your purpose.

Argument

Edward I. Koch

Death and Justice

*Edward Koch (born 1924) is a native of New York, a veteran of World War II, and a graduate of New York University, where he earned a law degree in 1948. For some two decades after graduation, he practiced law in New York City, and became active in Democratic party politics. After stints as district leader and a member of the city council, he was elected to the U.S. House of Representatives, serving from 1969 to 1977 and becoming known for his strong liberal stance on social issues. In 1977, he won election as New York mayor, holding the post until 1990. Two books written while he was mayor examine New York City politics and his years as a political fledgling. His latest book—*I'm Not Through Yet! *(2000)—offers his views on politics and a variety of current matters. At present, Koch serves as a TV judge, trying minor cases before a studio audience. The following essay, which criticizes the views of those opposed to capital punishment, reflects Koch's long-held commitment to the death penalty.*

Introduction: paragraphs 1 and 2 Examples	1 Last December a man named Robert Lee Willie, who had been convicted of raping and murdering an 18-year-old woman, was executed in the Louisiana state prison. In a statement issued several minutes before his death, Mr. Willie said; "Killing people is wrong. . . . It makes no difference whether it's citizens, countries, or governments. Killing is wrong." Two weeks later in South Carolina, an admitted killer named Joseph Carl Shaw was put to death for murdering two teenagers. In an appeal to the governor for clemency, Mr. Shaw wrote: "Killing is wrong when I did it. Killing is wrong when you do it. I hope you have the courage and moral strength to stop the killing."
Provides background	2 It is a curiosity of modern life that we find ourselves being lectured on morality by cold-blooded killers. Mr. Willie previously had been convicted of aggravated rape, aggravated kidnapping, and the murders of a Louisiana deputy and a man from Missouri. Mr. Shaw committed another murder a week before the two for which he was executed, and admitted mutilating the body of the 14-year-old girl he killed. I can't help wondering what prompted these murderers to speak out against killing as they entered the death-house door. Did their new-found reverence for life stem from the realization that they were about to lose their own?

Life is indeed precious, and I believe the death penalty helps to affirm this fact. Had the death penalty been a real possibility in the minds of these murderers, they might well have stayed their hand. They might have shown moral awareness before their victims died, and not after. Consider the tragic death of Rosa Velez, who happened to be home when a man named Luis Vera burglarized her apartment in Brooklyn. "Yeah, I shot her," Vera admitted. "She knew me, and I knew I wouldn't go to the chair."

During my 22 years in public service, I have heard the pros and cons of capital punishment expressed with special intensity. As a district leader, councilman, congressman, and mayor, I have represented constituencies generally thought of as liberal. Because I support the death penalty for heinous crimes of murder, I have sometimes been the subject of emotional and outraged attacks by voters who find my position reprehensible or worse. I have listened to their ideas. I have weighed their objections carefully. I still support the death penalty. The reasons I maintained my position can be best understood by examining the arguments most frequently heard in opposition.

1. *The death penalty is "barbaric."* Sometimes opponents of capital punishment horrify with tales of lingering death on the gallows, of faulty electric chairs, or of agony in the gas chamber. Partly in response to such protests, several states such as North Carolina and Texas switched to execution by lethal injection. The condemned person is put to death painlessly, without ropes, voltage, bullets, or gas. Did this answer the objections of death penalty opponents? Of course not. On June 22, 1984, the *New York Times* published an editorial that sarcastically attacked the new "hygienic" method of death by injection, and stated that "execution can never be made humane through science." So it's not the method that really troubles opponents. It's the death itself they consider barbaric.

Admittedly, capital punishment is not a pleasant topic. However, one does not have to like the death penalty in order to support it any more than one must like radical surgery, radiation, or chemotherapy in order to find necessary these attempts at curing cancer. Ultimately we may learn how to cure cancer with a simple pill. Unfortunately, that day has not yet arrived. Today we are faced with the choice of letting the cancer spread or trying to cure it with the methods available, methods that one day will almost certainly be considered barbaric. But to give up and do nothing would be far more barbaric and would certainly delay the discovery of an eventual cure. The analogy between cancer and murder is imperfect, because murder is not the "disease" we are trying to cure. The disease is injustice. We may not like the death penalty, but it must be available to punish crimes of cold-blooded murder, cases in which any other form of punishment would be inadequate and, therefore, unjust. If we create a society in which injustice is not tolerated, incidents of murder—the most flagrant form of injustice—will diminish.

2. *No other major democracy uses the death penalty.* No other major democracy—in fact, few other countries of any description—are plagued by a murder rate such as that in the United States. Fewer and fewer Americans can remember the days when unlocked doors were the norm and murder was a rare and terrible offense. . . . It is not surprising that the laws of each country differ according to differing conditions and traditions. If other countries had our murder problem, the cry for capital punishment would be just as loud as it is here. And I daresay that any other major democracy where 75 percent of the people supported the death penalty would soon enact it into law.

3 Body: paragraphs 3–13
Proposition of fact

Development by example

4 Author's qualifications

Ethical appeal

5 First refutation: rejects emotional appeal

Concedes point
6 Rational appeal: analogy

Ethical appeal: concedes point

7 Second refutation

Third refutation 8	3. *An innocent person might be executed by mistake.* Consider the work of Adam Bedau, one of the most implacable foes of capital punishment in this country. According to Mr. Bedau, it is "false sentimentality to argue that the death penalty should be abolished because of the abstract possibility that an innocent person might be executed." He cites a study of the 7,000 executions in this

country from 1893 to 1971, and concludes that the record fails to show that such cases occur. The main point, however, is this. If government functioned only when the possibility of error didn't exist, government wouldn't function at all. Human life deserves special protection, and one of the best ways to guarantee that protection is to assure that convicted murderers do not kill again. Only the death penalty can accomplish this end. In a recent case in New Jersey, a man named Richard Biegenwald was freed from prison after serving 18 years for murder; since his release he has been convicted of committing four murders. A prisoner named Lemuel Smith, who, while serving four life sentences for murder (plus two life sentences for kidnapping and robbery) in New York's Green Haven Prison, lured a woman corrections officer into the chaplain's office and strangled her. He then mutilated and dismembered her body. An additional life sentence for Smith is meaningless. Because New York has no death penalty statute, Smith has effectively been given a license to kill. . . .

Third refutation   8 (margin)

Evidence: statistics (margin)

Established truth (margin)

Development by examples (margin)

4. *Capital punishment cheapens the value of human life.* On the contrary, it can be easily demonstrated that the death penalty strengthens the value of human life. If the penalty for rape were lowered, clearly it would signal a lessened regard for the victims' suffering, humiliation, and personal integrity. It would cheapen their horrible experience, and expose them to an increased danger of recurrence. When we lower the penalty for murder, it signals a lessened regard for the value of the victim's life. Some critics of capital punishment, such as columnist Jimmy Breslin, have suggested that a life sentence is actually a harsher penalty for murder than death. This is sophistic nonsense. A few killers may decide not to appeal a death sentence, but the overwhelming majority make every effort to stay alive. It is by exacting the highest penalty for the taking of human life that we affirm the highest value of human life.

Emotional appeal (margin)

Fourth refutation   9 (margin)

Rational appeal: analogy (margin)

5. *The death penalty is applied in a discriminatory manner.* This factor no longer seems to be the problem it once was. The appeals process for a condemned prisoner is lengthy and painstaking. Every effort is made to see that the verdict and sentence were fairly arrived at. However, assertions of discrimination are not an argument for ending the death penalty but for extending it. It is not justice to exclude everyone from the penalty of the law if a few are found to be so favored. Justice requires that the law be applied equally to all.

Fifth refutation   10 (margin)

6. *Thou shalt not kill.* The Bible is our greatest source of moral inspiration. Opponents of the death penalty frequently cite the sixth of the Ten Commandments in an attempt to prove that capital punishment is divinely proscribed. In the original Hebrew, however, the Sixth Commandment reads, "Thou Shalt Not Commit Murder," and the Torah specifies capital punishment for a variety of offenses. The biblical viewpoint has been upheld by philosophers throughout history. The greatest thinkers of the 19th century—Kant, Locke, Hobbes, Rousseau, Montesquieu, and Mill—agreed that natural law properly authorizes the sovereign to take life in order to vindicate justice. Only Jeremy Bentham was ambivalent. Washington, Jefferson, and Franklin endorsed it. Abraham Lincoln authorized executions for deserters in wartime. Alexis de Tocqueville, who ex-

Sixth refutation   11 (margin)

Evidence: authoritative opinion (margin)

pressed profound respect for American institutions, believed that the death penalty was indispensable to the support of social order. The United States Constitution, widely admired as one of the seminal achievements in the history of humanity, condemns cruel and inhuman punishment, but does not condemn capital punishment.

7. *The death penalty is state-sanctioned murder.* This is the defense with which Messrs. Willie and Shaw hoped to soften the resolve of those who sentenced them to death. By saying in effect, "You're no better than I am," the murderer seeks to bring his accusers down to his own level. It is also a popular argument among opponents of capital punishment, but a transparently false one. Simply put, the state has rights that the private individual does not. In a democracy, those rights are given to the state by the electorate. The execution of a lawfully condemned killer is no more an act of murder than is legal imprisonment an act of kidnapping. If an individual forces a neighbor to pay him money under threat of punishment, it's called extortion. If the state does it, it's called taxation. Rights and responsibilities surrendered by the individual are what give the state its power to govern. This contract is the foundation of civilization itself.

12 | Seventh refutation

Rational appeal: analogy

Everyone wants his or her rights, and will defend them jealously. Not everyone, however, wants responsibilities, especially the painful responsibilities that come with law enforcement. Twenty-one years ago a woman named Kitty Genovese was assaulted and murdered on a street in New York. Dozens of neighbors heard her cries for help but did nothing to assist her. They didn't even call the police. In such a climate the criminal understandably grows bolder. In the presence of moral cowardice, he lectures us on our supposed failings and tries to equate his crimes with our quest for justice.

13 | Development by example

The death of anyone—even a convicted killer—diminishes us all. But we are diminished even more by a justice system that fails to function. It is an illusion to let ourselves believe that doing away with capital punishment removes the murderer's deed from our conscience. The rights of society are paramount. When we protect guilty lives, we give up innocent lives in exchange. When opponents of capital punishment say to the state: "I will not let you kill in my name," they are also saying to murderers: "You can kill in your *own* name as long as I have an excuse for not getting involved."

14 | Conclusion: paragraphs 14 and 15
Ethical appeal

Rational appeal: deduction

It is hard to imagine anything worse than being murdered while neighbors do nothing. But something worse exists. When those same neighbors shrink back from justly punishing the murderer, the victim dies twice.

15 | Emotional appeal

DISCUSSION QUESTIONS

1. Why do you think Koch ends paragraph 2 with a question rather than a direct statement of his opinion?
2. Why does Koch tell us in paragraph 8 that Bedau is "one of the most implacable foes of capital punishment in this country"?
3. Why do you think Koch devotes most of his essay to refuting opposition arguments?
4. Koch's views on capital punishment differ from those of Anna Quindlen, which are set forth in the following essay. Read Quindlen's essay and evaluate the differences between her attitudes and those expressed by Koch.

| TOWARD KEY INSIGHTS

Do you think the death penalty deters crime? What reasons and evidence lead to your conclusion?

Recently, DNA testing has resulted in *some* people on death row being set free. Does this fact alter your views about the death penalty? Why or why not?

| SUGGESTION FOR WRITING   *Write an essay that argues for a particular strategy for combating the street-crime problem. Possibilities might include a stronger police presence in high-crime areas or the use of neighborhood citizen patrols. Use whatever types of evidence are appropriate.*

Anna Quindlen

Execution

Anna Quindlen (born 1953) attended Barnard College and then began work as a journalist, first at the New York Post *and later at the* New York Times. *In 1994, she left the* Times *to pursue a full-time career as a novelist. Her books include two collections of newspaper columns and four fictional works, the latest of which,* Happily Every After *(1999), is for children. In 1992 she received the Pulitzer Prize for commentary. She is now a contributing editor and columnist for* Newsweek. *Our selection presents Quindlen's thoughts on capital punishment.*

1   Ted Bundy[1] and I go back a long way, to a time when there was a series of unsolved murders in Washington State known only as the Ted murders. Like a lot of reporters, I'm something of a crime buff. But the Washington Ted murders—and the ones that followed in Utah, Colorado, and finally in Florida, where Ted Bundy was convicted and sentenced to die—fascinated me because I could see myself as one of the victims. I looked at the studio photographs of young women with long hair, pierced ears, easy smiles, and I read the descriptions: polite, friendly, quick to help, eager to please. I thought about being approached by a handsome young man asking for help, and I knew if I had been in the wrong place at the wrong time I would have been a goner. By the time Ted finished up in Florida, law enforcement authorities suspected he had murdered dozens of young women. He and the death penalty seemed made for each other.

2   The death penalty and I, on the other hand, seem to have nothing in common. But Ted Bundy has made me think about it all over again, now that the outlines of my sixties liberalism have been filled in with a decade as a reporter covering some of the worst back alleys in New York City and three years as a mother who, like most, would lay down her life for her kids. Simply

---

[1]A serial killer who was executed on January 24, 1989.

put, I am opposed to the death penalty. I would tell that to any judge or lawyer undertaking the *voir dire*[2] of jury candidates in a state in which the death penalty can be imposed. That is why I would be excused from such a jury. In a rational, completely cerebral way, I think the killing of one human being as punishment for the killing of another makes no sense and is inherently immoral.

But whenever my response to an important subject is rational and completely cerebral, I know there is something wrong with it—and so it is here. I have always been governed by my gut, and my gut says I am hypocritical about the death penalty. That is, I do not in theory think that Ted Bundy, or others like him, should be put to death. But if my daughter had been the one clubbed to death as she slept in a Tallahassee sorority house, and if the bite mark left in her buttocks had been one of the prime pieces of evidence against the young man charged with her murder, I would with the greatest pleasure kill him myself.   3

The State of Florida will not permit the parents of Bundy's victims to do that, and, in a way, that is the problem with an emotional response to capital punishment. The only reason for a death penalty is to exact retribution. Is there anyone who really thinks that it is a deterrent, that there are considerable numbers of criminals out there who think twice about committing crimes because of the sentence involved? The ones I have met in my professional duties have either sneered at the justice system, where they can exchange one charge for another with more ease than they could return a shirt to a clothing store, or they have simply believed that it is the other guy who will get caught, get convicted, get the stiffest sentence. Of course, the death penalty would act as a deterrent by eliminating recidivism, but then so would life without parole, albeit at greater taxpayer expense.   4

I don't believe deterrence is what most proponents seek from the death penalty anyhow. Our most profound emotional response is to want criminals to suffer as their victims did. When a man is accused of throwing a child from a high-rise terrace, my emotional—some might say hysterical—response is that he should be given an opportunity to see how endless the seconds are from the thirty-first story to the ground. In a civilized society that will never happen. And so what many people want from the death penalty, they will never get.   5

Death is death, you may say, and you would be right. But anyone who has seen someone die suddenly of a heart attack and someone else slip slowly into the clutches of cancer knows that there are gradations of dying.   6

I watched a television reenactment one night of an execution by lethal injection. It was well done; it was horrible. The methodical approach, people standing around the gurney waiting, made it more awful. One moment there was a man in a prone position; the next moment that man was gone. On another night I watched a television movie about a little boy named Adam Walsh, who disappeared from a shopping center in Florida. There was a reenactment of Adam's parents coming to New York, where they appeared on morning talk shows begging for their son's return, and in their hotel room, where they received a call from the police saying that Adam had just been found: not all of Adam, actually, just his severed head, discovered in the waters of a Florida canal. There is nothing anyone could do that is bad enough for an adult who took a six-year-old boy away from his parents, perhaps tortured, then murdered him and cut off his head. Nothing at all. Lethal injection? The electric chair? Bah.   7

---

[2]The questioning process used to determine the competence of a candidate for jury duty.

8   And so I come back to the position that the death penalty is wrong, not only because it consists of stooping to the level of the killers, but also because it is not what it seems. Just before one of Ted Bundy's execution dates was postponed pending further appeals, the father of his last known victim, a twelve-year-old girl, said what almost every father in his situation must feel. "I wish they'd bring him back to Lake City," said Tom Leach of the town where Kimberly Leach lived and died, "and let us all have at him." But the death penalty does not let us all have at him in the way Mr. Leach seems to mean. What he wants is for something as horrifying as what happened to his child to happen to Ted Bundy. And that is impossible.

DISCUSSION QUESTIONS

1. Discuss the significance of the following sentence in paragraph 1: "But the Washington Ted murders—and the ones that followed . . . fascinated me because I could see myself as one of the victims."
2. Characterize the image of Quindlen that emerges in paragraphs 2 and 3.
3. In paragraph 4, Quindlen says that the justice system allows criminals to "exchange one charge for another with more ease than they could return a shirt to a clothing store. . . ." Does this statement strike you as accurate or as exaggerated?
4. Explain how Quindlen shows awareness of her audience in paragraph 6.
5. Explain what Quindlen means in paragraph 7 when she says, "It was well done; it was horrible."
6. Do you agree with Edward Koch's views on capital punishment (pages 560–63), with Anna Quindlen's, or with a position somewhere between the two, such as reserving the death penalty for serial killers or for persons who murder police officers? Discuss.

TOWARD KEY INSIGHTS

What do you think would be an appropriate punishment for someone convicted of a brutal murder involving mutilation, torture, or the like? How would you defend your answer against the objections of others?

SUGGESTION FOR WRITING

Write an argument favoring or opposing a mandatory failing grade for any student found guilty of plagiarism. Use whatever types of evidence are appropriate.

Marilyn Gaye Piety

Sexual Harassment Is a Serious Problem at Universities

Marilyn Gaye Piety was studying in Denmark on a Fulbright fellowship when she wrote this article, which was published in Christian Social Action. *Piety taught from 1994 to 1998 at*

Denmark's International Study Program, which is affiliated with the University of Copenhagen. In the fall of 1998 she was a visiting professor at Drexel University in Philadelphia, where she is now an assistant professor. In this essay Piety offers evidence that a harassment problem exists, gives reasons for it, and suggests ways of handling the situation.

Shortly after I arrived at a prestigious eastern university to complete the 1 work for my Ph.D., one of the professors in the department began to harass me. This harassment consisted of repeated requests for dates as well as sexually suggestive remarks made to me both in private and in front of other professors in the department. This went on for several weeks.

I made a point of procuring a copy of the university regulations concerning 2 sexual harassment, but I was surprised to discover that there was no university prohibition on sexual relations between professors and students. Students were considered "adults" by the university and, therefore, capable of informed "consent" to such relationships. As long as this professor's repeated requests for dates were phrased politely and involved no overt threat to my situation as a student in the department, they did not fall under the heading of behavior that was prohibited.

Formal Complaint Discouraged.   After several weeks of fending off the advances 3 of this professor (whom I shall refer to as Bill), I turned to the chairman of the department for help. When I explained my situation to him, he seemed sympathetic. But, despite the fact that he admitted I was not the first student Bill had treated this way, he discouraged me from making a *formal* complaint. While he assured me that Bill's behavior was unacceptable, he was certain that it was not maliciously motivated. I would not want, he said, to risk the possibility of doing him any professional injury by making a *formal* complaint against him. He suggested that perhaps the best thing to do would be for him to have a "talk" with Bill.

I was anxious to resolve the problem without harming this person whose actions, for all their damaging nature, may not have been malicious. I did not consider that the chairman must have talked with Bill before, that the talk had clearly been ineffectual, and that there was no reason to believe it would work this time.

After I spoke to the chairman, Bill stopped asking me for dates, so I assumed 5 that my problem had been solved. I was informed, however, by another professor (who could have gotten in considerable trouble with the university for revealing this information to me) that Bill repeatedly made disparaging remarks about my work and intelligence in closed faculty meetings. As a result the faculty was becoming so prejudiced against me that there was a very real chance I would not receive any financial support for the coming academic year, she indicated.

Counselors with No Real Authority.   This university, like many, has counselors 6 specifically appointed to handle complaints of sexual harassment. In desperation, I went to one of these counselors and explained my situation. She was distressed by my story, but I was shocked to discover that she had no real authority to do anything about it. The most she could do was suggest to the department, or to the university, that something should be done, but ultimately either of these authorities had to decide whether and how to act on her suggestion. They never did.

Students who become the objects of romantic attentions of a professor are 7 often caught in a see-saw of emotions. They are sometimes unsure whether their situation would actually be considered "harassment," but they almost always feel exceptionally vulnerable and experience a desire to strike out at the source. . . .

8   It is very difficult to get statistics on the proportion of students harassed by professors because, as one sexual harassment counselor explained, "[m]ost of the cases are handled informally without going to court or to a public forum." Thus, no records of these cases are kept. It is not even possible to get a picture of the average case of harassment because complaints of harassment are usually confidential. This confidentiality is often interpreted by the counselor as meaning that no details concerning these cases may be revealed.

9   One might legitimately wonder why all the secrecy? Surely a counselor could release general information concerning the form most sexual harassment takes without violating the confidentiality of particular cases. The answer behind the secrecy is that many universities simply do not want the pervasiveness of sexual harassment on their campuses to be exposed.

10   Harassment very seldom comes in the form of overt threats or promises and yet that is how it is often defined in university policies. The most common kind of harassment, most commonly based on my research and interviews with both graduate and undergraduate students, as well as established scholars, seldom involves such overt threats. The absence of threats, however, only makes this harassment more, not less, dangerous and destructive. That is, it leaves the student in a vulnerable position, afraid to confide his or her problem for fear of being labeled "paranoid."

11   Often, an investigation of any alleged harassment can only be undertaken "if the complainant agrees to be identified." But imagine an insecure college freshman agreeing to be identified as bringing a complaint of harassment against a professor who has not even overtly threatened him or her! It almost never happens, and universities hope that the absence of such formal complaints will be interpreted by the public as reflecting an absence of harassment.

12   ***Policies Protect Universities and Employees.***   Sexual harassment policies are, more often than not, set up to protect universities and their employees—that is, the *harassers* rather than the *harassees*. This has been allowed to happen because good people have consistently sent the message to universities that they do not care to know what goes on within their walls. The only time most people ever really come to appreciate the inadequacy of most university policies on sexual harassment is when they, or someone they know, have become victims of them and then it is too late. One professor I spoke to, who was also the chairman of his department, explained that few professors in his department were completely free of the stain of such harassment. Thus, when a particularly bad case arose, he was unable to get any of the other professors to support the victim because they were so afraid that the accused would turn around and point the finger at them.

13   There is no formal record anywhere that Bill has ever sexually harassed a student, let alone that he is a chronic harasser. He has now taken a job at another university, but his behavior has not changed. Several months ago I received a letter from the sexual harassment counselor with whom I had spoken at Bill's former university asking if I would be willing to support a woman whom Bill was harassing at this new university. It seemed this woman was considering making a formal complaint against Bill. However, to make a strong case, she needed the testimony of other women he had harassed.

14   Unfortunately, this woman eventually decided *not* to make a formal complaint. She explained that she was afraid of stirring up trouble and possibly prejudicing the rest of the faculty against her by taking such an action. The

difficulty is that her fears were well-founded. Faculties do not like students who make trouble. Even if her complaint was ultimately successful—i.e., even if it eventuated in some censure of Bill—she might never again receive any professional support from anyone on the faculty of her department.

It would appear that the concern of the university is not with the emotional   15 or even professional well-being of its students and graduate students. It is a disappointing thing to realize, but it should not be any great surprise. . . .

Many schools still do not have a formal policy prohibiting the sexual harass-   16 ment of students. Furthermore, many existing policies are inadequate; therefore, it is important to read any information from the schools quite carefully. If the policy in question indicates that harassment must involve *overt* threats or promises of reward, it is inadequate. If it only allows an investigation into reported cases of harassment when the victim agrees to be identified, it is inadequate.

Professors' Rights Are Primary.   No one wants academe to be given over to witch   17 hunts where any anonymous allegation of impropriety can ruin a career. The fact is, however, that under many existing sexual harassment policies, the professors' rights are far more well protected than the students [*sic.*]. One formal complaint of impropriety is far from enough to get a tenured professor dismissed.

However, one instance of such "impropriety" can be enough to injure a stu-   18 dent *substantially*. It can cause a considerable degree of emotional distress and can demoralize the student to the extent that his or her grades will suffer. Perhaps more importantly, it can create a fear and suspicion of authority that may stay with the student for the rest of his or her life.

If the school from which parents have requested information (and they   19 may request this information in person as well as in writing) either does not have a policy concerning sexual harassment or has an inadequate policy, anyone can exert pressure on the school to draft such a policy or to revise existing policy. A person can do this by expressing concern to both the dean of the college or university in question and to local newspapers.

Persons who attended a college or university may exert considerable pres-   20 sure upon the institution by suggesting that they will discontinue support if the school does not adopt a responsible sexual harassment policy and by informing the school that they will encourage other alumni to do the same. Church persons can put similar pressure on church-related colleges and universities. Most colleges and universities are responsive to public concerns—if those concerns are made apparent to them—because so much of their funding comes from the public. So few people, however, really *know* what goes on in most colleges and universities. That is why sexual harassment on college and university campuses is so pervasive.

The best thing for students to do if they find, or even suspect, that they are   21 the object of such harassment (and this is advice every church ought to provide for its young members as well as other individuals in the community) is to make some record of the relevant event or events. This record does not have to be elaborate; a note or two jotted down in a calendar on the date of the event is enough. Such a record will help to lessen the anxiety that the event may have caused. If the student is lucky, there will be no more events to record and the note will simply be forgotten. However, if there is another event, even something as apparently innocent as a professor standing uncomfortably close to the student in a line or in the hall, it should be recorded. In this way it becomes possible to establish whether a pattern is emerging.

22   If such a pattern becomes evident, the student should go to see a university counselor. Again, many universities have counselors who are appointed specifically to talk to students who have complaints about sexual harassment. If a particular university does not have such counselors, it will have counselors appointed to deal with other student problems such as depression and test-anxiety, and the student may speak to one of them.

23   There is no risk involved in seeing a counselor. The counselor will simply listen to the student's story and give advice on how to pursue the matter. It is important to remember, however, that these counselors are often under pressure from their college or university to seek an *informal* solution to the problem and that such informal solutions are often unsatisfactory.

24   ***Students Need Support.***   Apart from exerting pressure upon various colleges and universities to adopt responsible sexual harassment policies, one of the most important things we can do is to encourage young people to be open about such experiences and to support them when they do confide in us. Students need our support because the subtlety of most harassment often leaves them feeling confused, vulnerable, and even guilty.

25   Several students to whom I spoke actually confided to their parents or to other adults that they were being made "uncomfortable" by the behavior of one of their professors. They found, however, that they received little support. Unfortunately, we are sometimes inclined to characterize the vague feelings often expressed by victims of harassment as expressions of paranoia and thus ultimately the problem of the student rather than of the professor or the college or university. We need to assure students that it may not be their fault if they feel "uncomfortable" around a particular professor and that we will support them if they decide to make a formal complaint. . . .

26   It is time we accepted the responsibility for reacting to this pervasive injustice. Although more subtle than other injustices, it is not less devastating to its victims.

DISCUSSION QUESTIONS

1. Why do you think that Piety opens her essay with a six-paragraph illustration of her own experience with sexual harassment?

2. Comment on the effectiveness of the short sentence that ends paragraph 6.

3. What is Piety's proposition and where is it located? Is it one of fact, policy, action, or value?

4. In addition to citing her experience, Piety uses her own findings as evidence. Point out places in the essay where she refers to these findings and indicate why you think she uses them to argue her position.

5. Reread the last sentence of paragraph 17. What is your reaction to the statement it makes?

6. On the basis of your own experience and what you consider reliable information from other students, do you think sexual harassment is a serious problem at your college or university? Discuss.

7. Piety's views on sexual harassment at universities differ markedly from those of Gretchen Morgenson on harassment in the business world (see the following essay). Read Morgenson's essay and then evaluate the differing attitudes of the two authors.

TOWARD KEY INSIGHTS

Do you believe that colleges and universities need to develop official policies regarding sexual harassment? Why or why not?

Assuming the need for such policies, what provisions should be included to protect the rights of both students and faculty?

SUGGESTION FOR WRITING

*Write an essay arguing for a particular solution
to another type of harassment problem. Possibilities might include telephone solicitors who invade one's privacy or automobile salespeople who
are too aggressive in attempting to make a sale.
Develop your topic with appropriate evidence.*

Gretchen Morgenson

Sexual Harassment Is Overestimated

*Gretchen Morgenson is a native of State College, Pennsylva-
nia, and an alumna of Saint Olaf College in Northfield,
Minnesota. Following graduation, she worked as a stockbroker and then as a financial journalist for* Money, Forbes,
and Worth *magazines. She now holds a similar position at
the* New York Times. *In 1992 and again in 1993, the*
Forbes Media Guide *cited a Morgenson business story as one of the ten best of the year.
This selection contends that sexual harassment does not pose a serious problem in the business world.*

On October 11, 1991, in the middle of the Anita Hill/Clarence Thomas
contretemps,[1] the *New York Times* somberly reported that sexual harassment per-
vades the American workplace. The source for this page-one story was a
Times/CBS poll conducted two days earlier in which a handful (294) of women
were interviewed by telephone. Thirty-eight per cent of respondents confirmed
that they had been at one time or another "the object of sexual advances,
propositions, or unwanted sexual discussions from men who supervise you or
can affect your position at work." How many reported the incident at the time
it happened? Four per cent.

Did the *Times* offer any explanation for why so few actually reported the incident? Could it be that these women did not report their "harassment" because
they themselves did not regard a sexual advance as harassment? Some intelligent
speculation on this matter might shed light on a key point: the vague definitions
of harassment that make it easy to allege, hard to identify, and almost impossible
to prosecute. Alas, the *Times* was in no mood to enlighten its readers.

Two Types of Harassment. It has been more than ten years since the Equal Employment Opportunity Commission (EEOC) wrote its guidelines defining sex-

1

2

3

---

[1]Anita Hill charged Clarence Thomas, then a nominee for the Supreme Court, with sexual harassment. Thomas's
appointment was later confirmed.

ual harassment as a form of sexual discrimination and, therefore, illegal under Title VII of the Civil Rights Act of 1964. According to the EEOC there are two different types of harassment: so-called *quid pro quo* harassment, in which career or job advancement is guaranteed in return for sexual favors, and environmental harassment, in which unwelcome sexual conduct "unreasonably interferes" with an individual's working environment or creates an "intimidating, hostile, or offensive working environment."

4   Following the EEOC's lead, an estimated three out of four companies nationwide have instituted strict policies against harassment; millions of dollars are spent each year educating employees in the subtleties of Title VII etiquette. Men are warned to watch their behavior, to jettison the patronizing pat and excise the sexist comment from their vocabularies.

5   Yet, if you believe what you read in the newspapers, we are in the Stone Age where the sexes are concerned. A theme common to the media, plaintiff's lawyers, and employee-relations consultants is that male harassment of women is costing corporations millions each year in lost productivity and low employee morale. "Sexual harassment costs a typical Fortune 500 Service or Manufacturing company $6.7 million a year" says a sexual-harassment survey conducted late in 1988 for *Working Woman* by Klein Associates. This Boston consulting firm is part of a veritable growth industry which has sprung up to dispense sexual-harassment advice to worried companies in the form of seminars, videos, and encounter groups.

6   *Hype and Hysteria.*   But is sexual harassment such a huge problem in business? Or is it largely a product of hype and hysteria? The statistics show that sexual harassment is less prevalent today than it was in 1986. According to the EEOC, federal cases alleging harassment on the job totaled 5,694 in 1990, compared to 6,342 in 1984. Yet today there are 17 per cent more women working than there were then.

7   At that, the EEOC's figures are almost certainly too high. In a good many of those complaints, sexual harassment may be tangential to the case; the complaint may primarily involve another form of discrimination in Title VII territory: race, national origin, or religious discrimination, for example. The EEOC doesn't separate cases involving sexual harassment alone; any case where sexual harassment is mentioned, even in passing, gets lumped into its figures.

8   Many of the stories depicting sexual harassment as a severe problem spring from "consultants" whose livelihoods depend upon exaggerating its extent. In one year, DuPont spent $450,000 on sexual-harassment training programs and materials. Susan Webb, president of Pacific Resources Development Group, a Seattle consultant, says she spends 95 per cent of her time advising on sexual harassment. Like most consultants, Miss Webb acts as an expert witness in harassment cases, conducts investigations for companies and municipalities, and teaches seminars. She charges clients $1,500 for her 35-minute sexual-harassment video program and handbooks.

9   Corporations began to express concern on the issue back in the early Eighties, just after the EEOC published its first guidelines. But it was *Meritor Savings Bank v. Vinson*, a harassment case that made it to the Supreme Court in 1985, that really acted as an employment act for sex-harassment consultants. In *Vinson*, the Court stated that employers could limit their liability to harassment claims by implementing anti-harassment policies and procedures in the workplace. And so, the anti-harassment industry was born.

Harassment Still a Problem.   Naturally, the consultants believe they are filling a   10
need, not creating one. "Harassment is still as big a problem as it has been because
the workplace is not integrated," says Susan Webb. Ergo, dwindling numbers of
cases filed with the EEOC are simply not indicative of a diminution in the problem.

Then what do the figures indicate? Two things, according to the harass-   11
ment industry. First, that more plaintiffs are bringing private lawsuits against
their employers than are suing through the EEOC or state civil-rights commis-
sions. Second, that the number of cases filed is a drop in the bucket compared
to the number of actual, everyday harassment incidents.

It certainly stands to reason that a plaintiff in a sexual-harassment case   12
would prefer bringing a private action against her employer to filing an EEOC
claim. EEOC and state civil-rights cases allow plaintiffs only compensatory damages, such as back pay or legal fees. In order to collect big money—punitive
damages—from an employer, a plaintiff must file a private action.

Yet there's simply no proof that huge or increasing numbers of private actions   13
are being filed today. No data are collected on numbers of private harassment suits
filed, largely because they're brought as tort actions—assault and battery, emotional distress, or breach of contract. During the second half of the Eighties, the
San Francisco law firm of Orrick, Herrington, and Sutcliffe monitored private sexual-harassment cases in California. Its findings: From 1984 to 1989, the number of
sexual-harassment cases in California that were litigated through to a verdict totaled a whopping 15. That's in a state with almost six million working women.

Of course, cases are often settled prior to a verdict. But how many? Orrick,   14
Herrington partner Ralph H. Baxter Jr., management co-chairman of the American Bar Association's Labor Law Committee on Employee Rights and Responsibilities, believes the number of private sexual-harassment cases launched
today is greatly overstated. "Litigation is not as big a problem as it's made out to
be; you're not going to see case after case," says Mr. Baxter. "A high percentage
of matters go to the EEOC and a substantial number of cases get resolved."

Those sexual-harassment actions that do get to a jury are the ones that re-   15
ally grab headlines. A couple of massive awards have been granted in recent
years—five plaintiffs were awarded $3.8 million by a North Carolina jury—but
most mammoth awards are reduced on appeal. In fact, million-dollar sexual-
harassment verdicts are still exceedingly rare. In California, land of the happy
litigator, the median jury verdict for all sexual-harassment cases litigated between 1984 and 1989 was $183,000. The top verdict in the state was just under
$500,000, the lowest was $45,000. And California, known for its sympathetic jurors, probably produces higher awards than most states.

Now to argument number two: that the number of litigated harassment   16
cases is tiny compared to the number of actual incidents that occur. Bringing a
sexual-harassment case is similar to filing a rape case, consultants and lawyers
say; both are nasty proceedings which involve defamation, possible job loss, and
threats to both parties' family harmony.

Unfiled Cases.   It may well be that cases of perceived harassment go unfiled,   17
but is it reasonable to assume that the numbers of these unfiled cases run into
the millions? Consider the numbers of cases filed that are dismissed for "no
probable cause." According to the New York State human-rights commission, almost two-thirds of the complaints filed since 1986 were dismissed for lack of
probable cause. Of the two hundred sexual-harassment cases the commission
receives a year, 38 percent bring benefits to the complainant.

18   What about private actions? No one keeps figures on the percentage of cases nationwide won by the plaintiff versus the percentage that are dismissed. However, the outcomes of private sexual-harassment suits brought in California from 1984 to 1989 mirror the public figures from New York. According to Orrick, Herrington, of the 15 cases litigated to a verdict in California from 1984 to 1989, slightly less than half were dismissed and slightly more than half (53 per cent) were won by the plaintiff.

19   Are California and New York anomalies? Stephen Perlman, a partner in labor law at the Boston firm of Ropes & Gray, who has 15 years' experience litigating sexual-harassment cases, thinks not: "I don't suppose I've had as many as a dozen cases go to litigation. Most of the cases I've seen—the vast majority—get dismissed. They don't even have probable cause to warrant further processing."

20   A major problem is the vague definition of harassment. If "environmental harassment" were clearly defined and specifiable, lawyers would undoubtedly see more winnable cases walk through their doors. Asking a subordinate to perform sexual favors in exchange for a raise is clearly illegal. But a dirty joke? A pin-up? A request for a date?

21   In fact, behavior which one woman may consider harassment could be seen by another as a non-threatening joke. The closest thing to harassment that I have experienced during my 15-year career occurred in the early Eighties when I was a stockbroker-in-training at Dean Witter Reynolds in New York City. I had brought in the largest personal account within Dean Witter's entire retail brokerage system, an account which held roughly $20 million in blue-chip stocks. Having this account under my management meant I had a larger capital responsibility than any of my colleagues, yet I was relatively new to the business. My fellow brokers were curious, but only one was brutish enough to walk right up to me and pop the question: "How did you get that account? Did you sleep with the guy?"

22   Instead of running away in tears, I dealt with him as I would any rude person. "Yeah," I answered. "Eat your heart out." He turned on his heel and never bothered me again. Was my colleague a harasser, or just practicing Wall Street's aggressive humor, which is dished out to men in other ways? Apparently, I am in the minority in thinking the latter. But the question remains. Whose standards should be used to define harassment?

23   Under tort law, the behavior which has resulted in a case—such as an assault or the intent to cause emotional distress—must be considered objectionable by a "reasonable person." The EEOC follows this lead and in its guidelines defines environmental harassment as that which "unreasonably interferes with an individual's job performance."

24   ***Legislating Rude Behavior.***   Yet, sexual-harassment consultants argue that any such behavior—even that which is perceived as harassment only by the most hypersensitive employee—ought to be considered illegal and stamped out. In fact, they say, the subtler hostile-environment cases are the most common and cause the most anguish. Says Frieda Klein, the Boston consultant: "My goal is to create a corporate climate where every employee feels free to object to behavior, where people are clear about their boundaries and can ask that objectionable behavior stop."

25   Sounds great. But rudeness and annoying behavior cannot be legislated out of existence; nor should corporations be forced to live under the tyranny of a hypersensitive employee. No woman should have to run a daily gauntlet of sexual innuendo, but neither is it reasonable for women to expect a pristine work environment free of coarse behavior.

Susan Hartzoge Gray, a labor lawyer at Haworth, Riggs, Kuhn, and Haworth 26
in Raleigh, North Carolina, believes that hostile-environment harassment
shouldn't be actionable under Title VII. "How can the law say one person's lewd
and another's nice?" she asks. "There are so many different taste levels. . . . We
condone sexual jokes and innuendos in the media—a movie might get a PG rating—yet an employer can be called on the carpet because the same thing bothers someone in an office."

But changing demographics may do more to eliminate genuine sexual ha- 27
rassment than all the apparatus of law and consultancy. As women reach a critical mass in the workforce, the problem of sexual harassment tends to go away.
Frieda Klein says the problem practically vanishes once 30 per cent of the workers in a department, an assembly line, or a company are women.

Reaching that critical mass won't take long. According to the Bureau of 28
Labor Statistics, there will be 66 million women to 73 million men in the workplace by 2000. They won't all be running departments or heading companies,
of course, but many will.

So sexual harassment will probably become even less of a problem in the 29
years ahead than it is today. But you are not likely to read that story in a major
newspaper anytime soon. . . .

DISCUSSION QUESTIONS

1. Consider the essay as a whole and then suggest why, in paragraph 3, Morgenson
   names and defines the two types of sexual harassment specified by the EEOC.
2. What is Morgenson's proposition and where is it located? Is it one of fact, policy, action, or value?
3. Point out the different types of evidence that Morgenson uses to develop her
   argument.
4. Explain the quotation marks around "consultants" in paragraph 8.
5. Where does Morgenson refute the opposing position—that is, point out weaknesses or errors in it?
6. Point out three places where Morgenson concedes a point to the opposition.
   Do you think these concessions weaken her argument? Explain your answer.
7. Why do you think Morgenson begins paragraph 19 with "Are California and
   New York anomalies?"
8. Who makes the more convincing case for her position, Piety (pages 567–70) or
   Morgenson? Does your answer stem primarily from the essay's content, manner
   of presentation, or both?

TOWARD KEY INSIGHTS

Do you agree with Morgenson that "sexual harassment will probably become even
   less of a problem in the years ahead than it is today"? (See paragraph 29.) Why
   or why not?

Like many other writers on sexual harassment, Morgenson makes no mention of
   female harassment of males. How do you explain this silence? Under what circumstances might a female harass a male?

What actions might be taken to cope with sexual harassment?

Martin Luther King, Jr.

I Have a Dream

Martin Luther King, Jr. (1929–1968) has earned lasting fame for his part in the civil rights struggles of the 1950s and 1960s. Born in Atlanta, Georgia, he was ordained a Baptist minister in his father's church in 1947. A year later, he graduated from Morehouse College, then went on to take a Bachelor of Divinity degree at Crozier Theological Seminary (1951) and a Ph.D. in philosophy at Boston University (1954), after which he accepted a pastorate in Montgomery, Alabama. King's involvement with civil rights grew when he organized and led a boycott that succeeded in desegregating Montgomery's bus system. In 1957, he founded and became the first president of the Southern Christian Leadership Conference and assumed a leading role in the civil rights movement. King advocated a policy of nonviolent protest based on the beliefs of Thoreau and Gandhi and never veered from it despite many acts of violence directed at him. The success of King's crusade helped bring about the passage of the Civil Rights Act of 1964 and the Voting Rights Act of 1965 and won him the Nobel Peace Prize in 1964. King was assassinated on April 4, 1968, in Memphis. Since then, his birthday, January 15, has been made a national holiday. The speech "I Have a Dream" was delivered August 28, 1963, at the Lincoln Memorial in Washington, D.C., before a crowd of 200,000 people who had gathered to commemorate the centennial of the Emancipation Proclamation and to demonstrate for pending civil rights legislation. It stands as one of the most eloquent pleas ever made for racial justice.

1   I am happy to join with you today in what will go down in history as the greatest demonstration for freedom in the history of our nation.

2   Five score years ago, a great American, in whose symbolic shadow we stand today, signed the Emancipation Proclamation. This momentous decree came as a great beacon light of hope to millions of Negro slaves who had been seared in the flames of withering injustice. It came as a joyous daybreak to end the long night of their captivity.

3   But one hundred years later, the Negro still is not free; one hundred years later, the life of the Negro is still sadly crippled by the manacles of segregation and the chains of discrimination; one hundred years later, the Negro lives on a lonely island of poverty in the midst of a vast ocean of material prosperity; one hundred years later, the Negro is still languishing in the corners of American society and finds himself in exile in his own land.

4   So we've come here today to dramatize a shameful condition. In a sense we've come to our nation's capital to cash a check. When the architects of our

republic wrote the magnificent words of the Constitution and the Declaration of Independence, they were signing a promissory note to which every American was to fall heir. This note was the promise that all men, yes, black men as well as white men, would be guaranteed the unalienable rights of life, liberty, and the pursuit of happiness.

It is obvious today that America has defaulted on this promissory note in so far as her citizens of color are concerned. Instead of honoring this sacred obligation, America has given the Negro people a bad check; a check which has come back marked "insufficient funds." But we refuse to believe that the bank of justice is bankrupt. We refuse to believe that there are insufficient funds in the great vaults of opportunity of this nation. And so we've come to cash this check, a check that will give us upon demand the riches of freedom and the security of justice. 5

We have also come to this hallowed spot to remind America of the fierce urgency of now. This is no time to engage in the luxury of cooling off or to take the tranquilizing drug of gradualism. Now is the time to make real the promises of democracy; now is the time to rise from the dark and desolate valley of segregation to the sunlit path of racial justice; now is the time to lift our nation from the quicksands of racial injustice to the solid rock of brotherhood; now is the time to make justice a reality for all of God's children. It would be fatal for the nation to overlook the urgency of the moment. This sweltering summer of the Negro's legitimate discontent will not pass until there is an invigorating autumn of freedom and equality. 6

Nineteen sixty-three is not an end, but a beginning. And those who hope that the Negro needed to blow off steam and will now be content will have a rude awakening if the nation returns to business as usual. There will be neither rest nor tranquility in America until the Negro is granted his citizenship rights. The whirlwinds of revolt will continue to shake the foundations of our nation until the bright day of justice emerges. 7

But there is something that I must say to my people, who stand on the worn threshold which leads into the palace of justice. In the process of gaining our rightful place, we must not be guilty of wrongful deeds. Let us not seek to satisfy our thirst for freedom by drinking from the cup of bitterness and hatred. We must forever conduct our struggle on the high plain of dignity and discipline. We must not allow our creative protests to degenerate into physical violence. Again and again we must rise to the majestic heights of meeting physical force with soul force. The marvelous new militancy, which has engulfed the Negro community, must not lead us to a distrust of all white people. For many of our white brothers, as evidenced by their presence here today, have come to realize that their destiny is tied up with our destiny. And they have come to realize that their freedom is inextricably bound to our freedom. We cannot walk alone. And as we walk, we must make the pledge that we shall always march ahead. We cannot turn back. 8

There are those who are asking the devotees of Civil Rights, "When will you be satisfied?" We can never be satisfied as long as the Negro is the victim of the unspeakable horrors of police brutality; we can never be satisfied as long as our bodies, heavy with the fatigue of travel, cannot gain lodging in the motels of the highways and the hotels of the cities; we cannot be satisfied as long as the Negro's basic mobility is from a smaller ghetto to a larger one; we can never be satisfied as long as our children are stripped of their selfhood and robbed of their dignity by signs stating "For White Only"; we cannot be satisfied as long as the Negro in 9

Mississippi cannot vote and a Negro in New York believes he has nothing for which to vote. No! No, we are not satisfied, and we will not be satisfied until "justice rolls down like waters and righteousness like a mighty stream."

10   I am not unmindful that some of you have come here out of great trials and tribulations. Some of you have come fresh from narrow jail cells. Some of you have come from areas where your quest for freedom left you battered by the storms of persecution and staggered by the winds of police brutality. You have been the veterans of creative suffering. Continue to work with the faith that unearned suffering is redemptive. Go back to Mississippi. Go back to Alabama. Go back to South Carolina. Go back to Georgia. Go back to Louisiana. Go back to the slums and ghettos of our Northern cities, knowing that somehow this situation can and will be changed. Let us not wallow in the valley of despair.

11   I say to you today, my friends, that even though we face the difficulties of today and tomorrow, I still have a dream. It is a dream deeply rooted in the American dream. I have a dream that one day this nation will rise up and live out the true meaning of its creed, "We hold these truths to be self-evident, that all men are created equal." I have a dream that one day on the red hills of Georgia, sons of former slaves and the sons of former slaves owners will be able to sit down together at the table of brotherhood. I have a dream that one day even the state of Mississippi, a state sweltering with the heat of injustice, sweltering with the heat of oppression, will be transformed into an oasis of freedom and justice. I have a dream that my four little children will one day live in a nation where they will not be judged by the color of their skin, but by the content of their character.

12   I HAVE A DREAM TODAY!

13   I have a dream that one day down in Alabama—with its vicious racists, with its Governor having his lips dripping with the words of interposition and nullification—one day right there in Alabama, little black boys and black girls will be able to join hands with little white boys and white girls as sisters and brothers.

14   I HAVE A DREAM TODAY!

15   I have a dream that one day every valley shall be exalted, every hill and mountain shall be made low. The rough places will be plain and the crooked places will be made straight, "and the glory of the Lord shall be revealed, and all flesh shall see it together."

16   This is our hope. This is the faith that I go back to the South with. With this faith we will be able to hew out of the mountain of despair, a stone of hope. With this faith we will be able to transform the jangling discords of our nation into a beautiful symphony of brotherhood. With this faith we will be able to work together, to pray together, to struggle together, to go to jail together, to stand up for freedom together, knowing that we will be free one day. And this will be the day. This will be the day when all of God's children will be able to sing with new meaning, "My country 'tis of thee, sweet land of liberty, of thee I sing. Land where my fathers died, land of the pilgrim's pride, from every mountain side, let freedom ring." And if America is to be a great nation, this must become true.

17   So let freedom ring from the prodigious hilltops of New Hampshire; let freedom ring from the mighty mountains of New York; let freedom ring from the heightening Alleghenies of Pennsylvania; let freedom ring from the snow-capped Rockies of Colorado; let freedom ring from the curvaceous slopes of California. But not only that. Let freedom ring from Stone Mountain of Georgia; let freedom ring from Lookout Mountain of Tennessee; let freedom ring

from every hill and mole hill of Mississippi. "From every mountainside, let freedom ring."

And when this happens, and when we allow freedom to ring, when we let it   18
ring from every village and every hamlet, from every state and every city, we will
be able to speed up that day when all of God's children, black men and white
men, Jews and Gentiles, Protestants and Catholics, will be able to join hands
and sing in the words of the old Negro spiritual: "Free at last. Free at last.
Thank God Almighty, we are free at last."

DISCUSSION QUESTIONS

1. Why do you think King begins with a reference to Lincoln?
2. Does this speech have a stated or an implied proposition? What is the proposition?
3. What does King hope to accomplish by the speech? How does he go about achieving his aim(s)?
4. What is the audience for the speech?
5. How does King organize his speech? How does this organization advance his purpose?
6. Which type(s) of argumentative appeal does King use? Cite appropriate parts of the speech.
7. What kinds of stylistic devices does King use? Where do they occur? How do they increase the effectiveness of the speech?

TOWARD KEY INSIGHTS

To what extent do people of all races relate to King's message today? Explain your answer.

SUGGESTION FOR WRITING

Write an essay calling for some major social or political change. For example, you might recommend that the country enact national health insurance, institute a peacetime draft, ban smoking in all public places, amend the Constitution to ban or legalize abortions, establish federally funded day-care centers for working parents, or offer all workers a thirty-day leave of absence without pay.

William Raspberry
···

A Journalist's View of Black Economics[1]

William Raspberry (born 1935) grew up in Okolona, Mississippi, and received his education at Indiana Central College, where he earned a Bachelor of Science degree in 1958. In college, he worked as a reporter for the Indianapolis Recorder *and following graduation continued with that publication until he entered the army. In 1962, after his military service, he began working for the* Washington Post, *an association that continues to the present. Raspberry now authors a nationally syndicated column dealing with current issues, such as criminal justice and minority concerns. In this selection Raspberry argues that black Americans should spend less time blaming their problems on racial injustice and more time creating businesses and programs to help solve these problems.*

1   I am intensely interested in the subject of the economics of black America. However, I am neither a businessman, an economist, nor a social scientist. I'm a "newspaper guy."

2   That's not an apology. I like being a newspaper guy, and I like to think I'm a pretty good one. I point it out simply to warn you up front that what you will hear from me is neither economic analysis nor nuts-and-bolt business proposals. I like to think about things in general and my proposal is that we ought to approach this subject in this fashion.

3   ***Myths About Race.***   One of the things I would like us to think about is a myth: a myth that has crippled black America, sent us off on unpromising directions, and left us ill-equipped to deal with either political or economic reality.

4   That myth is that race is of overriding importance, that it is a determinant not just of opportunity but also of potential, a reliable basis for explaining political and economic realities, a reasonable way of talking about geopolitics, and the overwhelming basis on which to deal with the relationships between us.

5   When I refer to race-based explanations of the plight of black America as myth, I do not mean to suggest that all such explanations are false. My reference is to the definition of myth as a "traditional account of unknown authorship, ostensibly with a historical basis, but serving usually to explain some observed phenomenon."

6   The historical basis of our preoccupation with race is easy enough to see. America did not invent slavery. Slavery as an institution predates the Bible. But American slavery was peculiarly race-based. Since slavery is the basis for the very presence of black people in America, small wonder that race has assumed such importance in our mythology.

7   But slavery was more than just involuntary, unpaid servitude. Unlike other populations, to whom enslavement seemed a reasonable way of dealing with conquered enemies, America was never happy with the concept of one group of

human beings holding another group of human beings in bondage. I suppose it was taken as a sin against God. But rather than forgo the economic benefits of slavery, American slaveholders resolved the dilemma by defining blacks not as fellow human beings but more like beasts of burden. There is nothing ungodly about a man requiring unremunerated work of an animal. Didn't God give man dominion over the animals?

Now it may have been that Africans were a special kind of animal: capable 8
of thought, and human language, and even worship. But as long as whites could persuade themselves that blacks were not fully human, they could justify slavery.

Thus was born and reinforced the myth of inherent white superiority, which 9
later became the basis for racial separation, for Jim Crow laws, for unequal opportunity and all sorts of evil. Nor is it just among whites that the myth survives. . . .

The myth that blacks cannot prevail in intellectual competition, that Chi- 10
nese youngsters cannot play basketball, that Jews are specially vulnerable to guilt trips—these are negative myths whose acceptance has led to failure because they feed the assumption that failure is inevitable.

Objective reality is the arena in which we all must perform. But the success 11
or failure of our performance is profoundly influenced by the attitudes—the myths—we bring to that reality.

Two things flow from the racism-is-all myth that we have used to account for 12
our difficulties. The first is that it puts the solution to our difficulties outside our control. If our problems are caused by racism, and their solutions dependent on ending racism, our fate is in the hands of people who, by definition, don't love us.

A Skewed Definition of Civil Rights.   The second outcome of the myth is our incli- 13
nation to think of our problems in terms of a failure of racial justice. "Civil rights," which once referred to those things whose fair distribution was a governmental responsibility, now refers to any discrepancy. Income gaps, education gaps, test-score gaps, infant-mortality gaps, life-expectancy gaps, employment gaps, business-participation gaps—all now are talked about as "civil rights" issues.

The problems indicated by all these gaps are real. But describing them as 14
"civil rights" problems steers us away from possible solutions. The civil rights designation evokes a sort of central justice bank, managed by the government, whose charge is to ladle out equal portions of everything to everybody. It prompts us to think about our problems in terms of inadequate or unfair distribution. It encourages the fallacy that to attack racism as the source of our problems is the same as attacking our problems. As a result, we expend precious resources—time, energy, imagination, political capital—searching (always successfully) for evidence of racism, while our problems grow worse.

Maybe I can make my point clearer by reference to two other minorities. The 15
first group consists of poor whites. There are in America not just individuals but whole pockets of white people whose situation is hardly worse than our own.

And yet these poor whites have their civil rights. They can vote, live where 16
their money permits them to live, eat where their appetites and their pocket-books dictate, work at jobs for which their skills qualify them. And yet they are in desperate straits. It doesn't seem to occur to us that the full grant and enforcement of our civil rights would leave black Americans in about the same situation that poor white people are now in. That isn't good enough for me.

There is another minority whose situations may be more instructive. I 17
refer to recently arrived Asian-Americans. What is the difference between

them and us? Certainly it isn't that they have managed to avoid the effects of racism. Neither the newly arrived Southeast Asians nor the earlier arriving Japanese-Americans, Chinese-Americans, and Korean-Americans are loved by white people. But these groups have spent little of their time and energy proving that white people don't love them.

18 ***Opportunity Knocks: Who Answers?***   The difference between them and us is our operating myths. Our myth is that racism accounts for our shortcomings. Theirs is that their own efforts can make the difference, no matter what white people think.

19   They have looked at America as children with their noses pressed to the window of a candy store: if only I could get in there, boy, could I have a good time. And when they get in there, they work and study and save and create businesses and job opportunities for their people.

20   But we, born inside the candy store, have adopted a myth that leads us to focus only on the maldistribution of the candy. Our myth leads us into becoming a race of consumers, when victories accrue to the producers.

21   Interestingly enough, this is a fairly recent phenomenon. There was a time when we, like the more recent arrivals in this country, sought only the opportunity to be productive, and we grasped that opportunity under circumstances far worse—in law, at least—than those that obtain now.

22   Free blacks and former slaves, though denied many of the rights that we take for granted today, were entrepreneurial spirits. They were artisans and inventors, shopkeepers and industrialists, financiers and bankers. The first female millionaire in America was Madame C. J. Walker. At least two companies founded at the turn of the century are now on the *Black Enterprise* list of the 100 top black firms in the country.

23   Black real estate operatives transformed white Harlem into a haven for blacks. The early 1900s saw the founding of a number of all-black towns: Mound Bayou, Mississippi; Boley, Oklahoma; Nicodemus, Kansas; and others.

24   Boley at one time boasted a bank, twenty-five grocery stores, five hotels, seven restaurants, a waterworks, an electricity plant, four cotton gins, three drug stores, a bottling plant, a laundry, two newspapers, two colleges, a high school, a grade school, four department stores, a jewelry store, two hardware stores, two ice cream parlors, a telephone exchange, five churches, two insurance agencies, two livery stables, an undertaker, a lumber yard, two photography studios, and an ice plant [from J. DeSane, *Analogies and Black History: A Programmed Approach*]. Not bad for an all-black town of 4,000.

25   As Robert L. Woodson observed in his book, *On the Road to Economic Freedom*, "The Harlem and Boley experiences, which matched aggressive black entrepreneurial activity with the self-assertion drive of the black masses, was multiplied nationwide to the point that, in 1913, fifty years after Emancipation, black America had accumulated a personal wealth of $700 million.

26   "As special Emancipation Day festivals and parades were held that year in cities and towns across the country, blacks could take pride in owning 550,000 homes, 40,000 businesses, 40,000 churches, and 937,000 farms. The literacy rate among blacks climbed to a phenomenal 70 percent—up from 5 percent in 1863."

27 ***Over-learning the Civil Rights Lesson.***   What has happened since then? A lot of things, including a good deal of success that we don't talk much about. But among the things that have happened are two that have created problems for us. First is the overemphasis on integration, as opposed to desegregation and in-

creased opportunity. Hundreds of thriving restaurants, hotels, service outlets, and entertainment centers have gone out of business because we preferred integration to supporting our own painstakingly established institutions. Indeed, aside from black churches and black colleges, little remains to show for that entrepreneurial spurt of the early decades of this century.

The other thing that has happened is that we over-learned the lessons of 28 the civil rights movement. That movement, brilliantly conceived and courageously executed, marked a proud moment in our history. The upshot was that black Americans, for the first time in our sojourn here, enjoy the full panoply of our civil rights.

Unfortunately, that period also taught us to see in civil rights terms things 29 that might more properly be addressed in terms of enterprise and exertion rather than in terms of equitable distribution. Even when we speak of business now, our focus is on distribution: on set-asides and affirmative action.

Entrepreneurs and Self-Help.   Our 1960s success in making demands on govern- 30 ment has led us to the mistaken assumption that government can give us what we need for the next major push toward equality. It has produced in us what Charles Tate of the Booker T. Washington Foundation recently described as a virtual antipathy toward capitalism.

Even middle-class blacks seldom talk to their children about going into 31 business. Instead our emphasis is on a fair distribution of jobs in business created and run by others. We ought to have a fair share of those jobs. But the emphasis, I submit, ought to be finding ways to get more of us into business and thereby creating for ourselves the jobs we need.

That is especially true with regard to the so-called black underclass who 32 tend to reside in areas abandoned by white businesses.

In addition to figuring out ways of getting our unemployed to jobs that al- 33 ready exist, we need to look for ways to encourage blacks in those abandoned neighborhoods to create enterprises of their own. What I have in mind are not merely the shops and Mom & Pop stores that we still patronize (but whose owners are far likelier to be Vietnamese or Koreans than blacks), but also an entrepreneurial approach to our social problems.

I am not suggesting that government has no role in attacking these prob- 34 lems. It has a major role. What I am suggesting is that we need to explore ways of creating government-backed programs that instead of merely making our problems more bearable go in the direction of solving those problems. We are forever talking about the lack of day care as an impediment to work for welfare families. But why aren't we lobbying for legislation that would relax some of the anti-entrepreneurial rules and permit some of the money now spent on public welfare to be used to establish child-care centers run by the neighbors of those who need the care? Why aren't we looking for ways to use the funds that are already being expended to create small jitney services to transport job-seekers to distant jobs?

Success is the Goal.   I said at the beginning that I am not a theoretician, but I do 35 have one little theory that may have some relevance to our subject. It is this: When people believe that their problems can be solved, they tend to get busy solving them—partly because it is the natural thing to do and partly because they would like to have the credit. When people believe that their problems are beyond solution, they tend to position themselves so as to avoid blame for their nonsolution.

36   Now none of the black leadership will tell you that they think the problems we face are beyond solution. To do so would be to forfeit their leadership positions. But their behavior, if my theory is correct, suggests their pessimism.

37   Let me offer an example of what I am talking about. Take the woeful inadequacy of education in the predominantly black central cities. Does the black leadership see the ascendancy of black teachers and school administrators and the rise of black politicians to positions of local leadership as assets to be used in improving those dreadful schools? Rarely. What you are more likely to hear are charges of white abandonment, white resistance to integration, white conspiracies to isolate black children even when the schools are officially desegregated. In short, white people are responsible for the problem.

38   But if the youngsters manage to survive those awful school systems and make their way to historically black colleges—that is, if the children begin to show signs that they are going to make it—these same leaders sing a different song. Give our black colleges a fair share of public resources, they say, and we who know and love our children will educate them.

39   The difference, I submit, is that they believe many of our high school students won't succeed, and they conspire to avoid the blame for their failure. But they believe that most of our college youngsters will make it, and they want to be in position to claim credit for their success.

40   I suspect something like that is happening in terms of our economic well-being. Many of us are succeeding, in an astonishing range of fields, and the leadership does not hesitate to point out—with perfect justification—that our success is attributable to the glorious civil rights movement: that black exertion and courage made our success possible.

41   But many of us aren't succeeding. Teenage pregnancy, dope trafficking, lawlessness, and lack of ambition make us doubt that they ever will succeed. But do our leaders suggest that the reasons have to do with the inadequacy of the civil rights movement, or with any lack of exertion and courage on the part of the leadership? No. When we see failure among our people, and have reason to believe that the failure is permanent, our recourse is to our mainstay myth: Racism is the culprit. Mistakenly, we credit black pride for our successes and blame prejudice for our shortfalls.

42   I leave it to others to suggest the specifics by which we will move to increase the economic success of black America. I will tell you only that I believe it can be done—not only because it is being done by an encouraging number of us, but also because it has been done by earlier generations who struggled under circumstances of discrimination, deprivation, and hostility far worse than anything we now face.

43   My simple suggestion is that we stop using the plight of the black underclass as a scourge for beating up on white racists and examine both the black community and the American system for clues to how we can transform ourselves from consumers to producers.

44   I used to play a little game in which I would concede to members of the black leadership the validity of the racism explanation. "Let's say you're exactly right, that racism is the overriding reason for our situation, and that an all-out attack on racism is our most pressing priority," I'd tell them.

45   "Now let us suppose that we eventually win the fight against racism and put ourselves in the position now occupied by poor whites. What would you urge that we do next?"

"Pool our resources? Establish and support black businesses? Insist that our   46
children take advantage of the opportunities that a society free of racism would
offer? What should be our next step?"

"Well, just for the hell of it, why don't we pretend that the racist dragon has   47
been slain already—and take that next step right now?"

DISCUSSION QUESTIONS

1. Explain why Raspberry identifies himself as a "newspaper guy" in paragraph 1.
2. Why do you think Raspberry offers a precise definition of "myth" in paragraph 5?
3. Reread paragraphs 13 and 14 and point out specifically how Raspberry's views differ from those of Martin Luther King Jr. in "I Have a Dream" (pages 576–79).
4. Discuss the effectiveness of the analogy Raspberry uses in paragraphs 19–20.
5. Cite three places in the essay where Raspberry states an idea and uses specific examples to clarify its meaning.
6. What writing strategy does Raspberry use to develop paragraphs 21–29?
7. Paragraphs 44–47 function as Raspberry's conclusion. Indicate why you think the conclusion is or is not effective.
8. Raspberry's and King's arguments were both delivered as speeches, King's in 1963 and Raspberry's in 1989. Which argument seems more effective? Does your answer stem from the content, effectiveness of presentation, or both?

TOWARD KEY INSIGHTS

Raspberry makes an "entrepreneurial approach" seem like a relatively simple solution to widespread black poverty and related problems. What difficulties might such an approach face?

Is Raspberry right in suggesting that black Americans need to spend less time blaming racial injustice for their problems and more time creating businesses and enterprises? Why or why not?

SUGGESTION FOR WRITING

Develop an argument that proposes how a minority group can best enhance its economic prosperity. Use whatever types of evidence seem appropriate.

Daniel James

....

Close the Borders to All Newcomers

Daniel James's opposition to immigration is expressed most fully in Illegal Immigration: An Unfolding Crisis *(1991). In our essay James presents his reasons why the United States should impose a moratorium on all immigration.*

1   Strip the rhetoric from the evolving immigration debate and the bottom line becomes crystal clear: We may desire more and more immigrants, but can we afford so many of them? In his recently published memoirs, *Around the Cragged Hill,* George F. Kennan, perhaps our most eminent statesman, goes to the heart of the matter:

2   "We are already, for better or for worse, very much a polyglot country; and nothing of that is now to be changed. What I have in mind here are sheer numbers. There *is* such a thing as overcrowding. It has its psychic effects as well as its physical ones. There *are* limits to what the environment can stand."

3   The sheer numbers are indeed mind-boggling:

- 10.5 million immigrants, including those arriving illegally, entered the U.S. in the 1980s. That topped the previous record of 8.8 million who came here from 1901 to 1910.

- 15 to 18 million more newcomers, both legal and illegal, are projected to reach America in the 1990s, assuming our present immigration policy remains unchanged. Already, the number arriving in this decade is greater than for the same period in the previous decade. And there were nearly 1.2 million immigrants in 1992, 20 percent more than in 1991.

- 30 million immigrants—perhaps as many as 36 million—are expected to arrive in the first two decades of the next century, according to demographic projections and extrapolation of 1991–92 Census Bureau data.

4   The last two projections indicate that between 45 million and 54 million people—almost equal to the population of Great Britain—will be entering the U.S. in little more than a generation.

5   Add the 20 million immigrants who arrived from 1965 to 1990, and the grand total who will have entered the U.S. in just over a half-century (1965–2020) will be 65 million to 74 million.

6   There is no precedent for these numbers anywhere in the world. They constitute the biggest wave of immigration ever to a single country. Called the "fourth wave" of immigration to the U.S., it is really a tidal wave.

7   Yet the numbers are conservative. Unforeseeable trends in countries that generate immigrants could swell the tidal wave even higher than projected. It is likely, for example, that the demise of Cuba's communist dictatorship would send a flood of refugees to Miami comparable to the 125,000 *Marielitos* who inundated it in 1980.

8   Mexico is an even bigger concern. In the 1980s, it sent the U.S. nearly 4 million immigrants, more than the total for all of Asia. Two great "push" factors will drive ever more of them northward: high population growth—Mexico's

present 90 million inhabitants will become 110 million by 2000—and unemployment/underemployment levels of 40 to 50 percent.

The North American Free Trade Agreement . . . may generate a temporary upsurge in illegal border crossings. It [will] draw more Mexicans to the relatively affluent north and make entering the U.S. affordable. Meanwhile, an expected rise in imports of cheaper U.S. corn [will] bankrupt Mexico's peasant class, the *campesinos,* and drive them to seek work stateside. Only years from now [will] NAFTA create enough jobs to keep Mexicans at home. 9

The cost to U.S. taxpayers of accepting endless numbers of immigrants is intolerable. We learn from a study, "The Costs of Immigration," by economist Donald Huddle, that the net 1992 public assistance cost of the 19.3 million immigrants who have settled here since 1970 was $42.5 billion, after subtracting $20.2 billion they paid in taxes. 10

Huddle examined costs in 22 categories of federal, state and local assistance available to immigrants, including a package of 10 county welfare and health services. The largest net costs for immigrants in 1992 were $16 billion for education (primary, secondary and bilingual), $10.6 billion for health and welfare services and $8.5 billion for Medicaid. 11

Criminal justice and corrections costs for immigrants were found by Huddle to total more than $2 billion in 1992. The social price was greater: A disproportionately large number of illegals were in prison for committing felonies. In California, they made up 11 percent of all inmates. 12

Huddle also found that immigrants in 1992 displaced—probably forever— 2.07 million American workers. This should answer the oft-debated question: Do immigrants take jobs away from Americans? 13

It is true that American workers frequently turn down tasks that immigrants willingly perform, such as picking fruit and vegetables under inhumane conditions or making garments in urban sweatshops. But that hardly explains the virtual elimination of blacks from jobs in entire industries. In Los Angeles, unionized blacks have been displaced by nonunion Hispanics in janitorial services, and in Washington, D.C., by Latino immigrants in hotels and restaurants. 14

The puzzling question is: Why does the U.S. continue to import competition for American workers at a time of high unemployment? The Labor Department reports that 8.5 million Americans, about 6.7 percent of our work force, are unemployed. Our two principal minorities suffer most from joblessness—12.6 percent of blacks and 9.7 percent of Latinos—and they are the most vulnerable to displacement. 15

Immigration costs will rise further in this decade, Huddle forecasts. He projects that from 1993 to 2002, 11.1 million legal and illegal immigrants will be added to the 19.3 million post-1970 immigrants already here, for a total of 30.4 million. Their net cost to taxpayers during the next decade would come to $668.5 billion. . . . 16

Impossible to quantify, but perhaps more devastating in the long run, is the cost of excessive immigration to the environment. As more and more people are added to our population—already excessive at 260 million—the greater the environmental degradation will be. The immigrants will contribute to increasing energy use, toxic waste, smog and urban crowding, all of which affect our mental and emotional health as well as the ecosystem. 17

Our population is increasing by 3 million a year, a rate faster than that of any other advanced country. California provides an example of what can happen to a nearly ideal environment when it is overwhelmed by too many 18 people. Since 1980, its population has zoomed from 23.7 million to more than 31 million, an increase of almost one-third. As a consequence, Los Angeles and its once pristine bay are all but hopelessly polluted, and San Diego and Orange counties are fast becoming sad miniatures of Los Angeles.

19   Equally alarming is the impetus that uncontrolled immigration provides to separatism and its obverse, multiculturalism. Those living in areas where there are many other immigrants, such as Los Angeles and Texas's Rio Grande Valley, see no need to learn English and so live in virtual isolation from the general population. As long as these barrios are constantly replenished with newcomers from Mexico—virtually a stone's throw away—their inhabitants will feel less and less need or desire to assimilate. This process encourages a kind of natural separatism that could lead to political separatism.

20   Richard Estrada, a journalist and scholar, sees an ominous parallel with Quebec: "If Francophone Quebec can bring the Canadian confederation to the brink of disintegration even though France lies an ocean away, should there not at least arise a certain reflectiveness about our Southwest, which lies contiguous to an overpopulated Third World nation?"

21   A growing number of Americans of all classes and ethnic groups share these concerns about immigration and favor reducing it. For at least two decades, a majority of Americans have expressed in various polls their desire to stop or reduce immigration. In January 1992, a Gallup Poll found that 64 percent of registered voters would vote for a presidential candidate who favored tougher laws on immigration. In December, the Latino National Political Survey discovered that Hispanics overwhelmingly believed there is too much immigration.

22   Even politicians who previously shunned immigration as a taboo subject are . . . clamoring to curb illegal immigration. We can hope that they soon will understand that the main problem, as the public generally has perceived, is legal immigration.

23   Serious though illegal immigration is, *legal* immigration poses a much graver problem. We receive more than three times as many legal immigrants, including refugees, as illegal ones. Their numbers are projected to grow exponentially, because under the 1990 Immigration Act they are permitted to bring in an endless procession of family members. In 1992, for example, family-related immigrants totaled 594,000, or 49 percent of the 1.2 million immigrants who entered the U.S. that year.

24   Legal immigrants account for almost three-quarters of the total costs calculated by the Huddle study. Thus, of the $668.5 billion projected net cost to taxpayers for all immigrants from 1993 to 2002, legal immigrants would account for $482 billion. Illegal aliens would cost $186.4 billion.

25   The most effective way to curb illegal immigration is to declare a moratorium on *all* immigration. Why? If the U.S. clamps down on illegals but permits legal immigration to continue uncontrolled, that tells the world we are not serious about solving either problem, for it is easier to reduce or halt the legal flow than to hunt down those who arrive undercover. To do so would require a mere stroke of the pen and wouldn't cost taxpayers extra—Congress could just reform the Immigration Act of 1990, which is directly responsible for the 40 percent increase in immigration. That would send the unequivocal message to anyone who plans to enter the U.S. that we cannot afford to receive them—at least for the time being.

26   The message would ring loud and clear to would-be illegal immigrants that we mean business. It must be backed up, however, by a whole range of law en-

forcement measures that are now on the books but are ignored or not used effectively. In addition, to smoke out illegals and also eliminate the racket in fraudulent documents, Congress should approve a universal ID. . . .

The ID cards would identify those who are legally in the U.S. and entitled   27
to work and receive benefits. Local and state authorities should be directed to share information on illegals with the Immigration and Naturalization Service to aid in apprehending them; at present, authorities deny such information to the INS, in effect protecting illegals.

Instead of sending the National Guard to patrol the border as advocated by   28
some lawmakers, it would be more effective to give the Border Patrol sufficient personnel to do its job. At least 2,000 new agents should be added to the current force of about 4,000, as well as equipment such as better night sensors and new vehicles. . . .

A vital component of any program to curb immigration must be the cooperation of the Mexican government. The White House should take advantage of   29
our cordial relations with Mexico and our growing economic clout to request that our southern neighbor cease its traditional (though unwritten) policy of regarding the U.S. as a safety valve.

A U.S. moratorium on immigration would yield highly positive gains by allowing the 20 million immigrants now within our borders time to assimilate into   30
the mainstream. It would remove the pressure of new millions crowding into inner-city barrios and encourage existing inhabitants to break out of them. This would mitigate the danger of separatism, counter multiculturalist trends, defuse interethnic tensions and reduce crime and violence.

If this prescription sounds like a pipe dream, let us recall that restrictive   31
legislation in 1924 cut immigration to a trickle, allowing enough time for the masses of immigrants the U.S. had then to overcome the obstacles to assimilation. That literally saved America. For when the Japanese struck at Pearl Harbor in 1941 and the U.S. was confronted by their military might plus that of Germany, which already had conquered Europe and had just invaded the Soviet Union, our nation stood united against them. Sadly, one doubts whether today's America, torn by an identity crisis spawned by divisive forces, would be capable of meeting a similar threat.

The United States is headed for a crisis of incalculable magnitude if mass immigration continues unchecked. The argument of those who favor an open border is that immigrants have always contributed to our society, and so they have.   32
But we no longer can afford the world's "huddled masses" when our own are so often homeless and jobless. If we permit immigration to continue uncontrolled, it will explode in a full-blown crisis that will extend beyond the vociferous separatism/multiculturalism debate to engulf us in a violent civil conflict.

America is under siege. It is threatened from without by international terrorism and from within by centrifugal forces that already have revealed their ca-   33
pacity for destruction in bloody riots from Los Angeles to Miami, from Washington to Manhattan.

DISCUSSION QUESTIONS

1. What is James's proposition and where is it located? How do you account for this location? Is the proposition one of fact, policy, action, or value?
2. Why do you think James identifies George F. Kennan as "perhaps our most eminent statesman" in paragraph 1?

3. Point out the different kinds of evidence that James uses to develop his argument. Refer to specific parts of the essay when answering.

4. What types of appeal does James use?

5. Cite two places in the essay where James concedes points to the opposing side.

6. Comment on the effectiveness of the following short sentence in paragraph 31: "That literally saved America."

7. James's views on immigration differ markedly from those of Stephen Moore, which are set forth in the following essay. Read Moore's essay and then evaluate the differing attitudes of the authors.

TOWARD KEY INSIGHTS

Do you believe that "the United States is headed for a crisis of incalculable magnitude" (paragraph 32) if we don't stop immigration? What are the reasons for your position?

SUGGESTION FOR WRITING

Write an essay arguing that children of illegal immigrants should or should not receive public assistance benefits. Develop your topic with appropriate evidence.

Stephen Moore

Give Us Your Best, Your Brightest

Stephen Moore directs fiscal policy at the Cato Institute, a Libertarian think tank. Born (1960) in Chicago, he earned an undergraduate degree at the University of Chicago and a graduate degree in economics at George Mason University. He is the author of Still an Open Door: Immigration Policy and the American Economy *(1994) and* Welfare for the Well-Off *(1997). He contributes regularly to a variety of newspapers and magazines. In this selection, Moore argues for liberalized but carefully targeted immigration.*

1   For many Americans, the word "immigration" immediately conjures up an image of poor Mexicans scrambling across the border near San Diego to find minimum-wage work and perhaps collect government benefits. Recent public opinion polls confirm that the attitude of the American public toward immigration is highly unfavorable. Central Americans are perceived as welfare abusers who stubbornly refuse to learn English, Haitians are seen as AIDS carriers, Russian Jews are considered to be mafiosi, and Asians are seen as international terrorists. The media reinforce these stereotypes by battering the public with negative depictions of immigrants.

2   The conception of immigrants as tired, poor, huddled masses seems permanently sketched into the mind of the public, just as the words are sketched irrevocably at the feet of the Statue of Liberty. But the Emma Lazarus poem simply does not describe the hundreds of thousands of people who are building

new lives here in the 1990s. It would be more appropriate if the words at the base of the statue read: "Give us your best, your brightest, your most energetic and talented." Why? Because in large part those are the people who come to the United States each year.

Before we start slamming shut the golden door, it might be worthwhile to find out who the newcomers are and how they truly affect our lives.   3

Anyone who believes that immigrants are a drain on the U.S. economy has never visited the Silicon Valley in California. Here and in other corridors of high-tech entrepreneurship, immigrants are literally the lifeblood of many of the nation's most prosperous industries. In virtually every field in which the United States asserted global leadership in the 1980s—industries such as computer design and software, pharmaceuticals, bioengineering, electronics, superconductivity, robotics and aerospace engineering—one finds immigrants. In many ways these high-growth industries are the modern version of the American melting pot in action.   4

Consider Intel Corp., ... one of the most prolific and fast-expanding companies in the United States, employing tens of thousands of American workers. It is constantly developing exciting, cutting-edge technologies that will define the computer industry in the 21st century.   5

And it is doing all of this largely with the talents of America's newest immigrants. Three members of Intel's top management, including Chief Executive Officer Andrew S. Grove, from Hungary, are immigrants. Some of its most successful and revolutionary computer technologies were pioneered by immigrants, such as the 8080 microprocessor (an expanded-power computer chip), invented by a Japanese, and polysilicon FET gates (the basic unit of memory storage on modern computer chips), invented by an Italian. Dick Ward, manager of employee information systems at Intel, says: "Our whole business is predicated on inventing the next generation of computer technologies. The engine that drives that quest is brainpower. And here at Intel, much of that brainpower comes from immigrants."   6

Or consider Du Pont-Merck Pharmaceutical Co., an $800 million-a-year health care products company based in Wilmington, Del., which reports that immigrants are responsible for many of its most promising new product innovations. For example, losartan, an antihypertensive drug, was developed by a team of scientists that included two Chinese and a Lithuanian. Joseph Mollica, Chief Executive Officer of Du Pont-Merck, says that bringing together such diverse talent "lets you look at problems and opportunities from a slightly different point of view."   7

Intel and Du Pont-Merck are not alone in relying on immigrants. Robert Kelley Jr., president of SO/CAL/TEN, an association of nearly 200 high-tech California companies, insists: "Without the influx of Asians in the 1980s, we would not have had the entrepreneurial explosion we've seen in California." David N.K. Wang, vice president for worldwide business operations at Applied Materials Inc., a computer-technology company in California, adds that because of immigration, "Silicon Valley is one of the most international business centers in the world."   8

Take away the immigrants, and you take away the talent base that makes such centers operate. Indeed, it is frightening to think what would happen to America's global competitiveness if the immigrants stopped coming. Even scarier is the more realistic prospect that U.S. policymakers will enact laws to prevent them from coming.   9

10   Research has begun to quantify the contributions of immigrants to American industry. The highly respected National Research Council reported in 1988 that "a large fraction of the technological output of the United States [is] dependent upon foreign talent and that such dependency is growing." Noting that well over half of all scientists graduating with doctorate degrees from American universities and one in three engineers working in the United States are immigrants, the report states emphatically: "It is clear . . . that these foreign-born engineers enrich our culture and make substantial contributions to the U.S. economic well-being and competitiveness."

11   The United States' competitive edge over the Japanese, Germans, Koreans and much of Europe is linked closely to its continued ability to attract and retain highly talented workers from other countries. A 1990 study by the National Science Foundation says, "Very significant, positive aspects arise from the presence of foreign-born engineers in our society."

12   For example, superconductivity, a technology that is expected to spawn hundreds of vital new commercial applications in the next century, was discovered by a physicist at the University of Houston, Paul C.W. Chu. He was born in China and came to the U.S. in 1972. His brilliance and inventiveness have made him a top contender for a Nobel Prize.

13   Of course, if Chu does win a Nobel, he will join a long list of winners who were immigrants to America. In the 20th century, between 20 percent and 50 percent of the Nobel Prize winners, depending on the discipline involved, have been immigrants to the United States. Today there are more Russian Nobel Prize winners living in the U.S. than there are living in Russia.

14   Public opinion polls consistently reveal that a major worry is that immigrants take jobs from American workers. The fear is understandable but misplaced. Immigrants don't just take jobs, they create jobs. One way is by starting new businesses. Today, America's immigrants, even those who come with relatively low skill levels, are highly entrepreneurial.

15   Take Koreans, for example. According to sociologists Alendro Portes and Ruben Rumbaut, "In Los Angeles, the propensity for self-employment is three times greater for Koreans than among the population as a whole. Grocery stores, restaurants, gas stations, liquor stores and real estate offices are typical Korean businesses." Cubans also are prodigious creators of new businesses. The number of Cuban-owned businesses in Miami has expanded from 919 in 1967 to 8,000 in 1976 to 28,000 in 1990. On Jefferson Boulevard in Dallas, more than 800 businesses operate, three-quarters of them owned by first- and second-generation Hispanic immigrants. Just 10 years ago, before the influx of Mexicans and other Central Americans, the neighborhood was in decay, with many vacant storefronts displaying "for sale" signs in the windows. Today it is a thriving ethnic neighborhood.

16   To be sure, few immigrant-owned businesses mature into an Intel. In fact, many fail completely. Like most new businesses in America, most immigrant establishments are small and only marginally profitable. The average immigrant business employs two to four workers and records roughly $200,000 in annual sales. However, such small businesses . . . are a significant source of jobs.

17   It should not be too surprising that immigrants are far more likely than average U.S. citizens to take business risks. After all, uprooting oneself, traveling to a foreign culture and making it requires more than the usual amount of courage, ambition, resourcefulness and even bravado. Indeed, this is part of the self-selection process that makes immigrants so particularly desirable. Immi-

grants are not just people—they are a very special group of people. By coming, they impart productive energies on the rest of us.

This is not just romanticism. It is well-grounded in fact. Countless studies have documented that immigrants to the United States tend to be more skilled, more highly educated and wealthier than the average citizen of their native countries. 18

Thomas Sowell, an economist and senior fellow at the Hoover Institution in Stanford, Calif., reports in his seminal study on immigration, "Ethnic America," that black immigrants from the West Indies have far higher skill levels than their countrymen at home. He also finds that the income levels of West Indies immigrants are higher than those of West Indies natives, American blacks and native-born white Americans. 19

Surprisingly, even illegal immigrants are not the poverty-stricken and least skilled from their native countries. Surveys of undocumented immigrants from Mexico to the United States show that only about 5 percent were unemployed in Mexico, whereas the average unemployment rate there was about three times that level, and that a relatively high percentage of them worked in white-collar jobs in Mexico. In addition, surveys have found that illiteracy among undocumented Mexicans in the U.S. is about 10 percent, whereas illiteracy in Mexico is about 22 percent. 20

Perhaps the greatest asset of immigrants is their children, who tend to be remarkably successful in the U.S. Recently, the city of Boston reported that an incredible 13 of the 17 valedictorians in its public high schools were foreign-born—from China, Vietnam, Portugal, El Salvador, France, Italy, Jamaica and the former Czechoslovakia. Many could not speak a word of English when they arrived. Public high schools in Washington, Chicago and Los Angeles also report remarkably disproportionate numbers of immigrant children at the top of the class. Similarly, Westinghouse reports that over the past 12 years, about one-third of its prestigious National Science Talent Search winners have been Asians. Out of this group might emerge America's next Albert Einstein, who himself was an immigrant. 21

So one hidden cost of restricting immigration is the loss of immigrants' talented and motivated children. 22

In the past century, America has admitted roughly 50 million immigrants. This has been one of the largest migrations in the history of the world. Despite this infusion of people—no, because of it—the United States became by the middle of the 20th century the wealthiest nation in the world. Real wages in America have grown more than eightfold over this period. The U.S. economy employed less than 40 million people in 1900; today it employs nearly 120 million people. The U.S. job machine had not the slightest problem expanding and absorbing the 8 million legal immigrants who came to this country in the 1980s. Eighteen million jobs were created. 23

But what about those frightening headlines? "Immigration Bankrupting Nation." "Immigrants Displacing U.S. Workers." "Foreigners Lured to U.S. by Welfare." 24

Here are the facts. The 1990 census reveals that roughly 6 percent of native-born Americans are on public assistance, versus 7 percent of the foreign-born, with less than 5 percent of illegal immigrants collecting welfare. Not much reason for alarm. Because immigrants tend to come to the United States when they are young and working, over their lifetimes they each pay about $20,000 more in taxes than they use in services, according to economist Julian Simon of the University of Maryland. With 1 million immigrants per year, the nation gains about $20 billion more than cost. Rather than fiscal burdens, immigrants are huge bargains. . . . 25

26   We are now witnessing in America what might be described as the return of the nativists. They are selling fear and bigotry. But if any of their allegations against immigrants are accurate, then America could not have emerged as the economic superpower it is today.

27   In fact, most Americans do accept that immigration in the past has contributed greatly to the nation's economic growth. But they are not so sanguine in their assessment of present and future immigrants. It is strangely inconsistent that Americans believe that so long-standing and crucial a benefit is now a source of cultural and economic demise.

28   Shortly before his death, Winston Churchill wrote, "The empires of the future are the empires of the mind." America is confronted with one of the most awesome opportunities in world history to build those empires by attracting highly skilled, highly educated and entrepreneurial people from all over the globe. The Andrew Groves and the Paul Chus of the world do not want to go to Japan, Israel, Germany, France or Canada. Almost universally they want to come to the United States. We can be selective. By expanding immigration but orienting our admission policies toward gaining the best and the brightest, America would enjoy a significant comparative advantage over its geopolitical rivals.

29   By pursuing a liberal and strategic policy on immigration, America can ensure that the 21st century, like the 20th, will be the American century.

DISCUSSION QUESTIONS

1. Why do you think Moore cites popular stereotypes of immigrants in paragraph 1?

2. What is Moore's proposition and where is it located? How do you account for this location? Is the proposition one of fact, policy, action, or value?

3. Point out the different types of evidence that Moore uses to develop his argument. Refer to specific parts of the essay when answering.

4. What type of appeal does Moore use?

5. Cite two places in the essay where Moore refutes errors in the opposing opinion.

6. Explain what you think Moore means by the phrase "the return of the nativists" in paragraph 26.

7. Who makes the more convincing case for his position, James (pages 586–89) or Moore? Does your answer stem primarily from the essay's content, the manner of presentation, or both?

TOWARD KEY INSIGHTS

To what extent do you agree that "a liberal and strategic policy on immigration" will be instrumental in making the twenty-first century "the American century" (paragraph 29)? What reasons underlie your thinking?

SUGGESTION FOR WRITING

Write an essay favoring or opposing a liberal policy on admission to your college or university. Develop your essay with appropriate types of evidence.

Mixing the Writing Strategies

As we noted on page 187, most essays mix various writing strategies for assorted purposes. This section features three examples. Margin notations on the Zimmerman essay point out the interplay of several strategies, and the discussion questions following the Klass and Naylor essays direct your attention to the strategies these writers use as well as other relevant aspects of the essays.

Susan Zimmerman

Blur: Cheetahs. Ranchers. Hope.

Susan Zimmerman is a native of St. Louis, Missouri, and a graduate of the University of Texas in Austin, where she received a bachelor of business administration degree in international business. She has also completed several years of journalism study at St. Louis's Washington University. A freelance writer, she contributes regularly to science, travel, and natural history magazines on various topics. In our selection Zimmerman examines the joint efforts of environmentalists and African ranchers to preserve the local cheetah population—an unlikely alliance offering a possible model for collaborations elsewhere.

Midnight, the Frey ranch, central Namibia—The subcutaneous IV hangs on the back of the kitchen door next to a flyswatter, while test tubes, a centrifuge, and a stethoscope mingle with pots and pans on the counter and the stove. The full moon has long since set and cold desert air chases away any lingering odors of a gulped-down chicken dinner. A four-person crew is bent intently over their two patients, laid out on hastily arranged tables in the middle of the dimly lit kitchen. Their sense of urgency is reflected in their conversation: "Where's the centrifuge? . . . Did anyone bring a stethoscope? . . . Don't label the vials till I draw the blood, it's bad luck!" Veterinary technician Sandy Hurlbut is drawing blood from the thigh of one patient while one of the volunteers takes the temperature. Principal investigator Laurie Marker-Kraus is working on the other, checking the teeth. It could almost pass for a war-time emergency medical station, except for the patients: two adult cheetahs.

1

> Introduction: paragraphs 1–3; illustrates how cheetahs are being helped: Description

> Illustration in narrative form: paragraphs 1–2; examination, tag-and-release of cheetahs

2   The people doing the work are part of Marker-Kraus's organization, the Cheetah Conservation Fund (CCF), the last bastion of hope for the world's last large population of cheetahs. And the work itself is an essential part of this effort, determining the health of the cats and providing vital information on their habits and behavior. The cats' faces are covered with a towel to avoid visual stimulation as they are poked and prodded for measurements, skin analysis, blood tests, and ear tagging. Up close, these exquisite animals seem frail and vulnerable stretched out on the table. Each one's long, slender, spotted body is designed with one exclusive purpose: speed. Its flexible spine, oversized liver, enlarged heart, wide nostrils, and increased lung capacity make for the fastest land mammal on Earth. The two black "tear marks" that run down its face guard against glare and help it focus on its prey while racing at 110 kilometers per hour.

3   The urge to reach out and touch this extraordinary creature steals into my heart. My hand caresses its warm, heaving body, rubs its short, coarse fur, and then I listen to its racing heart beat through a stethoscope. This simple sound brings to life for me the plight of this beleaguered species struggling to survive.

An Earthwatch Primer on How to Save Cheetahs

4   *1. Identify the problem.*   Cheetah numbers overall are anemic—12,500 remain in the world compared to 100,000 at the turn of the century. Ten years ago, there were 25,000, a drop of 50 percent in 10 years. Found mostly in sub-Saharan Africa with a few hundred in Iran, Namibia's 2,500 cats represent the species' largest wild population. But Namibia also represents its greatest threat. Nearly 7,000 cheetahs were removed from Namibia's farmlands from 1980–1991, according to the Convention of International Trade in Endangered Species (CITES, 1992). Ranchers considered them a threat to their livestock and knew this predator was itself easy prey because of its nonaggressive nature. By law, ranchers were allowed to remove cheetahs only if they posed a threat to livestock or to humans. But during this period, ranchers live-trapped over 90 percent in large steel cages at their so-called "playtrees" (socializing areas for cheetahs) and then shot them.

5   To make matters worse, because of their declining populations and some peculiarities of cheetah reproduction, their gene pool is drastically constricted. Marker-Kraus's blood sampling has revealed that whole populations are 10 to 100 times more closely related than human racial groups. One fatal disease could wipe an entire colony. At the same time, scientists are eager to preserve the Namibian cheetah in particular, because it is one of the last populations in Africa free of FIV, the feline version of AIDS, and may offer important clues in AIDS research. The Cheetah Conservation Fund's ambitious goal, then, is to save habitat, rebuild the cheetah's gene pool, and broker a truce with Namibia's ranchers.

6   After 45 minutes of intensive examination, the cheetahs start regaining consciousness. When the towels are removed, they begin slowly blinking their eyes and drowsily scanning the ceiling and the strangers who have abducted them. As one cat begins growling, someone gasps, "Uh-oh, this one wants to wake up." The methodical pace shifts into high gear as three people swiftly lift the 39-kilogram cheetah and race for the recovery cage outside. A wild cheetah pouncing about a kitchen is not desirable.

7   Early the next morning the cheetahs are released. Bewildered from their alien abduction, the cats hesitate a few seconds when the cage door is lifted, then explode into a classic cheetah sprint, leaving a puff of dust. Acceleration

Description

Description

Body: paragraphs 4–29

Step in process

Comparison

Cause and effects

Definition

Causes and effects

Comparison

Definition

Continuation of initial narrative: paragraph 6 to second sentence, paragraph 7

is the cheetahs' specialty. They can't keep up the pace for long, but from a standstill to 110 kph, they are faster than any sports car ever made. They can turn on a dime as well. And that's enough. They have a higher kill rate than any other cat, catching 53 percent of the animals they chase, mostly warthogs, small antelope, and the young of large antelope. For CCF director Laurie Marker-Kraus and her colleagues, this morning's release is cause for celebration. It marks yet another successful tag-and-release for the cheetah and the CCF crew. Marker-Kraus's political savvy and her multipronged, cross-disciplinary approach of conservation, research, and education is earning her the ranchers' respect and cooperation to this end: CCF has examined over 200 cheetahs that would once have been simply shot in the ranchers' traps and discarded as trash.

| Comparison |
| Comparison |

2. Identify the key players.   If one could see the cheetah's future in its huge crystal-ball-like eyes, it would be as a living symbol of conservation. But for this cat to survive, the ranchers must see their future in the cheetah's eyes. Eby Frey, a third-generation Namibian rancher and the son of South African missionaries, has this vision. Clad in a green fatigue jacket, sunglasses, and bush hat, he reflects the changing attitudes of his colleagues. "In the past," he says, "nobody talked about cheetahs, nobody cared about them. They were here and that's it. People shot them and caught them just like they wanted to. I myself had some cheetahs in pens here."   8

| Cause and effect, comparison |
| Step in process |
| Comparison |
| Description |
| Comparison |

Harry Schneider-Waterberg, another third-generation Namibian rancher who lives next to Elands Joy, the farm where CCF is based, echoes those sentiments. "Everybody knew catching cheetahs was easy, and if we took them out we wouldn't have a problem. There was nobody there that really stopped it." Then, five years ago, he and Frey met Marker-Kraus.   9

Today Frey is a professional game guide, out of necessity, having sold off his cattle due to the drought, while Schneider-Waterberg now makes his land available for CCF research and radio-collaring.   10

Frey is an unconventional character—part Dr. Dolittle, James Herriot, and game guide. A sign cautions arriving vehicles to his farm: "Slowly—Disabled Animals." One of his two dogs, Xavier, was crippled in a fight with a baboon. Besides the current residents, which include an orphaned meerkat and a warthog, he used to have a wildebeest, and hartebeests occasionally galloped through the kitchen. His homestead is well-furnished, complete with guest facilities for his game-hunting clients.   11

Without Frey's help, CCF's midnight mission might not have been as triumphant. He drove an hour to a neighboring farm to help CCF retrieve the cheetahs, volunteered his kitchen for tabletop medicine, assisted in the entire operation, provided beds and a barn for his overnight guests, and then offered his land for the cheetahs' release. Ranchers like Frey are the CCF's greatest asset. As a Namibian farmer, he is not an outsider and can go where CCF cannot. "I talk to other farmers about problems with cheetahs," says Frey. As he drives his truck to assist with one last rescue, a CCF car stuck in the sand, Frey says of the successful release, "it feels good to see a cheetah in the open here."   12

3. Add one passionate scientist.   When a farmer calls in a cheetah capture, it is CCF's job to retrieve the animal from a field trap, gather biological information, and then relocate or release it. Normally the work is done in the field and not in a farmer's kitchen. Until last night, there had not been a call in a month—proof that farmers are learning to co-exist with cheetahs rather than to   13

| Step in process |

Description

shoot first and ask questions later. "This is what it's all about," says Marker-Kraus at Elands Joy. Long, brown, wavy hair and large frame glasses eclipse a small face and disguise the tenacity it takes to do her job. Strands of gray are the only hint of the stress on this 42-year-old wildlife specialist, who has dedicated the past five years to establishing and solidifying CCF's place in Namibia's political and cultural landscape.

Narrative

14   Marker-Kraus has made a life-long commitment to protect the cheetah's last stronghold. Her passion for cheetahs began over 20 years ago at a wildlife park in Oregon. "I wanted to know what was so special about this animal that people have raised it for 5,000 years, yet its numbers have continued to decline." In 1991, after several years as director of the Center for New Opportunities for Animal Health Sciences at the U.S. National Zoo, Marker-Kraus became so frustrated by her inability to save the cheetah from afar that she moved to Namibia. Having now achieved residency status, her ultimate goal is to create a reserve for cheetahs in Namibia. She juggles her own self-inflicted demands as administrator, spokesperson, educator, researcher, and fundraiser, wearing whatever hat the situation warrants. "People were seeing the cheetah before through ranchers' eyes," says Marker-Kraus. "Now they are seeing through the eyes of people that love the cheetah."

15   Marker-Kraus's crusade for the cheetahs zeroed in on the ranchers. Opting for a rancher-friendly approach, CCF conducted a three-year survey to first understand the rancher's plight—predation and management problems. "We spent the first couple of years," she says, "going door to door through the ranching community and meeting 240 ranchers. We just put out a book of the findings. This has made us link together with the ranchers in our project."

Step in process

16   ***4. Form an alliance.***   When neighbor rancher Hans Diekmann arrives in his pickup at Elands Joy, we can see that linking clearly. Marker-Kraus invites him into her house, where the two kneel on the kitchen floor papered with telemetry maps. "These are three males, this is a leopard and we just got a brown hyena," she notes as she points out some of CCF's 25 radio-collared cheetahs. The leopard and hyena come from helping out a visiting German student with his research project.

17   CCF's approach is that once ranchers understand how cheetahs live, there is a better chance for the cats' survival. By radio-collaring cheetahs, CCF has shown ranchers that cat movements through their land do not mean problems. With home ranges equivalent to 10 farms averaging 6,000 hectares each, cheetahs are just passersby on any given ranch. Indiscriminate killing is a poor solution, since the cat's territory will simply be taken over by another. "Our problem is trying to find ways cheetahs can live with humans," says Marker-Kraus.

Effect and cause, comparison

18   Livestock losses to predators are definitely an economic factor. The Namibian Department of Veterinary Services estimates that wild predators kill 10 to 15 percent of domestic cattle and 30 to 40 percent of small stock (goats and sheep). But, according to the 1991 CCF survey, cheetahs are responsible for only a third of cattle and a fifth of small livestock predation. Hyenas, jackals, and leopards do the bulk of the damage. The survey noted that ranchers' attitudes toward cheetahs did not reflect cheetahs' small role in predation. CCF's efforts have painstakingly peeled away myths about the cheetah as the arch enemy of livestock. "Cheetahs have been the scapecat so to speak. They are daytime hunters so they are seen more regularly," says Marker-Kraus. "We found that very few cheetahs are livestock-catching animals," she says. "A predator

would much rather have its own game." Cheetahs need the inducement to chase brought on by their prey's "flee" reaction. Though domestic livestock does not act like wild game, all predators are opportunistic. Marker-Kraus explains that if a calf or lamb happens to be at the right place at the right time, a cheetah will go after it.

CCF continues to wage a campaign to show locals there is enough room for everyone to make a living off the land—both cheetah and rancher. "We want ranchers to make a good living and in the process the cheetah will live," Marker-Kraus says. With CCF's help, Namibian ranchers are changing old habits.   19

Simple measures, such as breeding cows within a few days of one another to ensure a short calving season, have helped cut losses from predators. Another successful strategy is protecting the herd with guard donkeys, which, like zebras, aggressively chase cheetahs. One rancher told CCF that in the eight years he had been using donkeys, he had lost only one calf to predators. Before donkeys, he had lost 32 calves in one year. Where cheetah did prey on sheep and goats, CCF has provided free Turkish Anatolian shepherds as guard dogs, and losses in many flocks have since been eliminated. Ranchers are now on a waiting list for these canines, reflecting CCF's progress.   20

> | 20 | Classification of measures, effects that followed |
> | Comparison |

"He belongs to the sheep. He thinks he is a sheep," comments Badie Badenhorst, one of the 28 sheep ranchers with a guard dog. "He is always with them. We have no trouble with any predators." When just two months old, his dog Danie was put out with the sheep to imprint on the flock. He has since had little contact with humans and will faithfully protect his flock to the death, warding off hyenas, jackals, baboons, and the occasional cheetah.   21

> | 21 | Illustration |

After five years, CCF's efforts are paying off. Though ranchers have not packed away their cheetah traps, when they have trapped a cat now, they are more likely to pick up the phone and call CCF rather than kill it. More and more ranchers are becoming participants helping CCF in its fieldwork.   22

> | 22 | Effect |

5. Find a way to make ideals pay off.   One of the brightest hopes for cheetahs is actually the result of adversity. With the growing pains following the country's recent emancipation from South Africa and the stress of a long series of droughts, many ranchers have had to reduce their livestock and reevaluate their livelihoods. Some of them are choosing to test the newest concept of land use in Namibia, called land conservancies.   23

> | 23 | Step in process |
> | Causes and effects |

Conservancies, consisting of adjoining ranches that pool resources to manage livestock and wildlife for maximum sustainability, offer ranchers a way to improve profits through ecotourism and ranching. Schneider-Waterberg and the CCF are partners in such a conservancy, pooling Elands Joy's 7,300 hectares and Schneider-Waterberg's 50,000-plus hectares along with six other farms to create the 130,000-hectare Waterberg Conservancy.   24

> | 24 | Definition |
> | Effect |

"You can use your land without eradicating the predators," says Schneider-Waterberg, "whether consumptive, as in trophy hunting, or nonconsumptive, as in ecotourism." Though the Conservancy's goals do not exactly mirror CCF's, trophy hunting allows ranchers to make some money out of wildlife, so they have a vested interest in preserving the cheetah. "I very much believe in the concept 'if it pays, it stays' in conservation," says this rancher-turned-conservationist. "You want to look at the whole picture, what to preserve, what to cull. That is where research comes in and why I work with CCF, in order to know something more about what is happening on my land."   25

> | 25 | Effect |

26   During a CCF team's tag-and-release of a brown hyena on Schneider-Waterberg's ranch, he accompanies the crew. "Harry and I were dreaming on the drive," says Marker-Kraus as she gets out of his pickup truck. Schneider-Waterberg's plans are big. He sees his farm changing: "The goats will go; the sheep will go; over time the cattle will be reduced if not altogether removed. I have even started a seeding program for waterfowl," says this land baron, whose ranch is big even by Namibian standards. What will be left is basically wildlife and his dream of making a living out of it, a radical change in a country whose beef products are 87 percent of the country's agricultural income.

27   Since 90 percent of cheetahs are found on the 2,500 commercial ranches covering almost half of the country, alliances like the Waterberg Conservancy will play an increasingly important role in wildlife and habitat conservation. More cheetahs are found on commercial ranches than even in national parks, where competition from lions, hyenas, and other predators that eat their cubs and steal their kills keeps cheetah populations in check. "This is the first place for the cheetah and the most important piece of land, because ranchers will allow them to live here," says Marker-Kraus about the Waterberg Conservancy.

Step in process 28   **6. Prime the next generation.**   The idea of conservancies is exciting, and clearly winning over ranchers is critical in conserving cheetahs, but Marker-Kraus knows that if you really want to preserve cheetahs in the long run, you have to win over the ranchers' children. So the CCF team goes into local schools with its "cheetah-in-a-box"—props of skins and pictures. Wearing a spotted cheetah belt, Marker-Kraus and her crew of volunteers enthusiastically explain to rooms full of Namibian schoolchildren that their cheetah is in trouble. So far, the CCF's programs have already reached some 35,000 students.

Cause and effect

29   Marker-Kraus tells the story of one 12-year-old boy who had attended a CCF school assembly program. When a cheetah was caught outside his father's sheep pen, the boy explained to his father that cheetahs are endangered and told him not to kill it and to call CCF. Thanks to that boy, the cheetah was saved. In gratitude, CCF honored the boy and also gave the parents a livestock-guarding dog.

Illustration
Effect

30   "A lot of people say the cheetah is doomed to genetic extinction," says Marker-Kraus. "It is not. It has survived 10,000 years with its genetic problems. It is doomed to humans." This oldest of all the big cats survived the mass extinction that occurred around the Pleistocene Epoch. Having survived the ravages of nature, the cheetah is now poised on the brink of extinction due to human interference. Here in Namibia, CCF is brokering a peace that everyone can live with. After years of animosity and thousands of casualties, this cease-fire holds real promise for the hunted and hunter to co-exist. The cheetah and rancher have more in common than either realizes—they are both dependent on an unforgiving environment and ultimately bonded to one another.

Argument

Conclusion: expresses hope for survival of cheetahs

DISCUSSION QUESTIONS

1. Discuss the effectiveness of Zimmerman's title.
2. Why, in paragraph 1, do you think Zimmerman holds back the identity of the patients until the last three words of the paragraph?
3. Discuss Zimmerman's writing style.
4. What other endangered animals have drawn your attention? What efforts are being made to save them?

TOWARD KEY INSIGHTS

What do you think motivates someone like Marker-Kraus to devote a lifetime to protecting an endangered animal like the cheetah?

Would you devote your life to a similar cause? Why or why not?

SUGGESTION FOR WRITING

Write an essay that explains your own or someone else's efforts to pursue a worthwhile cause. Develop your paper with an appropriate mixture of writing strategies.

Perri Klass

She's Your Basic L.O.L. in N.A.D.

Perri Klass (born 1958) has pursued dual careers as physician and writer. A native of Trinidad, she was brought to the United States by her parents, attended schools in New York and New Jersey, and in 1986 graduated from Harvard Medical School. She is the author of several fiction and non-fiction books and has written numerous short stories for popular magazines. Her essays have appeared in a variety of newspapers and magazines, as well as in a collection entitled A Not Entirely Benign Procedure *(1987). In our essay, Klass examines the gains and losses that result from understanding and using medical jargon.*

1   "Mrs. Tolstoy is your basic L.O.L. in N.A.D., admitted for a soft rule-out M.I.," the intern announces. I scribble that on my patient list. In other words Mrs. Tolstoy is a Little Old Lady in No Apparent Distress who is in the hospital to make sure she hasn't had a heart attack (rule out a myocardial infarction). And we think it's unlikely that she has had a heart attack (a *soft* rule-out).

2   If I learned nothing else during my first three months of working in the hospital as a medical student, I learned endless jargon and abbreviations. I started out in a state of primeval innocence, in which I didn't even know that "s̄ C.P., S.O.B., N/V" meant "without chest pain, shortness of breath, or nausea and vomiting." By the end I took the abbreviations so for granted that I would complain to my mother the English Professor, "And can you believe I had to put down *three* NG tubes last night?"

3   "You'll have to tell me what an NG tube is if you want me to sympathize properly," my mother said. NG, nasogastric—isn't it obvious?

4   I picked up not only the specific expressions but the patterns of speech and the grammatical conventions; for example, you never say that a patient's blood pressure fell or that his cardiac enzymes rose. Instead, the patient is always the subject of the verb: "He dropped his pressure." "He bumped his enzymes." This sort of construction probably reflects the profound irritation of the intern when the nurses come in the middle of the night to say that Mr. Dickinson has disturbingly

low blood pressure. "Oh, he's gonna hurt me bad tonight," the intern may say, inevitably angry at Mr. Dickinson for dropping his pressure and creating a problem.

5   When chemotherapy fails to cure Mrs. Bacon's cancer, what we say is, "Mrs. Bacon failed chemotherapy."

6   "Well, we've already had one hit today, and we're up next, but at least we've got mostly stable players on our team." This means that our team (group of doctors and medical students) has already gotten one new admission today, and it is our turn again, so we'll get whoever is next admitted in emergency, but at least most of the patients we already have are fairly stable, that is, unlikely to drop their pressures or in any other way get suddenly sicker and hurt us bad. Baseball metaphor is pervasive: A no-hitter is a night without any new admissions. A player is always a patient—a nitrate player is a patient on nitrates, a unit player is a patient in the intensive-care unit and so on, until you reach the terminal player.

7   It is interesting to consider what it means to be winning, or doing well, in this perennial baseball game. When the intern hangs up the phone and announces, "I got a hit," that is not cause for congratulations. The team is not scoring points; rather, it is getting hit, being bombarded with new patients. The object of the game from the point of view of the doctors, considering the players for whom they are already responsible, is to get as few new hits as possible.

8   These special languages contribute to a sense of closeness and professional spirit among people who are under a great deal of stress. As a medical student, it was exciting for me to discover that I'd finally cracked the code, that I could understand what doctors said and wrote and could use the same formulations myself. Some people seem to become enamored of the jargon for its own sake, perhaps because they are so deeply thrilled with the idea of medicine, with the idea of themselves as doctors.

9   I knew a medical student who was referred to by the interns on the team as Mr. Eponym because he was so infatuated with eponymous terminology, the more obscure the better. He never said "capillary pulsations" if he could say "Quincke's pulses." He would lovingly tell over the multinamed syndromes—Wolff-Parkinson-White, Lown-Ganong-Levine, Henoch-Schonlein—until the temptation to suggest Schleswig-Holstein or Stevenson-Kefauver or Baskin-Robbins became irresistible to his less reverent colleagues.

10   And there is the jargon that you don't ever want to hear yourself using. You know that your training is changing you, but there are certain changes you think would be going a little too far.

11   The resident was describing a man with devastating terminal pancreatic cancer. "Basically he's C.T.D.," the resident concluded. I reminded myself that I had resolved not to be shy about asking when I didn't understand things. "C.T.D.?" I asked timidly.

12   The resident smirked at me. "Circling The Drain."

13   The images are vivid and terrible. "What happened to Mrs. Melville?"

14   "Oh, she boxed last night." To box is to die, of course.

15   Then there are the more pompous locutions that can make the beginning medical student nervous about the effects of medical training. A friend of mine was told by his resident, "A pregnant woman with sickle-cell represents a failure of genetic counseling."

16   Mr. Eponym, who tried hard to talk like the doctors, once explained to me, "An infant is basically a brainstem preparation." A brainstem preparation, as used in neurological research, is an animal whose higher brain functions have

been destroyed so that only the most primitive reflexes remain, like the sucking reflex, the startle reflex and the rooting reflex.

The more extreme forms aside, one most important function of medical 17 jargon is to help doctors maintain some distance from their patients. By reformulating a patient's pain and problems into a language that the patient doesn't even speak, I suppose we are in some sense taking those pains and problems under our jurisdiction and also reducing their emotional impact. This linguistic separation between doctors and patients allows conversations to go on at the bedside that are unintelligible to the patient. "Naturally, we're worried about adeno-C.A.," the intern can say to the medical student, and lung cancer need never be mentioned.

I learned a new language this past summer. At times it thrills me to hear my- 18 self using it. It enables me to understand my colleagues, to communicate effectively in the hospital. Yet I am uncomfortably aware that I will never again notice the peculiarities and even atrocities of medical language as keenly as I did this summer. There may be specific expressions I manage to avoid, but even as I remark them, promising myself I will never use them, I find that this language is becoming my professional speech. It no longer sounds strange in my ears—or coming from my mouth. And I am afraid that as with any new language, to use it properly you must absorb not only the vocabulary but also the structure, the logic, the attitudes. At first you may notice these new alien assumptions every time you put together a sentence, but with time and increased fluency you stop being aware of them at all. And as you lose that awareness, for better or for worse, you move closer and closer to being a doctor instead of just talking like one.

DISCUSSION QUESTIONS

1. Klass develops her essay by using one primary writing strategy and several secondary ones. Identify her primary strategy and point out where she uses it.
2. Where does she use definition? Cause and/or effect? Narration? Analogy?
3. How does Klass use contrast when she evaluates medical jargon?
4. Klass tells us in paragraph 17 that the use of jargon to describe medical conditions helps in "reducing their emotional impact." Explain what she means.
5. Point out why the last sentence in paragraph 18 is an appropriate ending for the essay.

TOWARD KEY INSIGHTS

To what extent can medical jargon be helpful and to what extent harmful to the medical professional's work? More specifically, how might such jargon affect the doctor's relationship with patients?

What other professions use such abbreviations and jargon, and to what effect?

SUGGESTION FOR WRITING

Write an essay that clarifies the jargon used in some profession or that used by fitness fanatics, computer users, social climbers, dieters, students, or some other people with shared values. Use several writing strategies to make your point.

Gloria Naylor

The Uses of a Word[1]

Gloria Naylor (born 1950) is a native of New York City. After finishing high school she spent several years as a missionary and in hotel service before earning a B.A. from Brooklyn College in 1981 and an M.A. from Yale University in 1983. Since then, she has pursued academic and writing careers and worked in India as a cultural attaché with the United States Information Agency. In 1982 she published her first book-length work, The Women of Brewster Place, *which won the American Book Award as the best first novel of that year. Her shorter writings have appeared in various magazines and in the "Hers" column of the* New York Times, *from which our selection comes. In it, Naylor explores the many uses of the word "nigger."*

1   Language is the subject. It is the written form with which I've managed to keep the wolf away from the door and, in diaries, to keep my sanity. In spite of this, I consider the written word inferior to the spoken, and much of the frustration experienced by novelists is the awareness that whatever we manage to capture in even the most transcendent passages falls far short of the richness of life. Dialogue achieves its power in the dynamics of a fleeting moment of sight, sound, smell, and touch.

2   I'm not going to enter the debate here about whether it is language that shapes reality or vice versa. That battle is doomed to be waged whenever we seek intermittent reprieve from the chicken and egg dispute. I will simply take the position that the spoken word, like the written word, amounts to a nonsensical arrangement of sounds or letters without a consensus that assigns "meaning." And building from the meanings of what we hear, we order reality. Words themselves are innocuous; it is the consensus that gives them true power.

3   I remember the first time I heard the word *nigger.* In my third-grade class, our math tests were being passed down the rows, and as I handed the papers to a little boy in back of me, I remarked that once again he had received a much lower mark than I did. He snatched his test from me and spit out that word. Had he called me a nymphomaniac or a necrophiliac, I couldn't have been more puzzled. I didn't know what a nigger was, but I knew that whatever it meant, it was something he shouldn't have called me. This was verified when I raised my hand, and in a loud voice repeated what he had said and watched the teacher scold him for using a "bad" word. I was later to go home and ask the inevitable question that every black parent must face—"Mommy, what does *nigger* mean?"

4   And what exactly did it mean? Thinking back, I realize that this could not have been the first time the word was used in my presence. I was part of a large extended family that had migrated from the rural South after World War II and formed a close-knit network that gravitated around my maternal grandparents. Their ground-floor apartment in one of the buildings they owned in Harlem was a weekend mecca for my immediate family, along with countless aunts, uncles, and cousins who brought along assorted friends. It was a bustling and open

[1]Editor's title.

house with assorted neighbors and tenants popping in and out to exchange bits of gossip, pick up an old quarrel, or referee the ongoing checkers game in which my grandmother cheated shamelessly. They were all there to let down their hair and put up their feet after a week of labor in the factories, laundries, and shipyards of New York.

Amid the clamor, which could reach deafening proportions—two or three conversations going on simultaneously, punctuated by the sound of a baby's crying somewhere in the back rooms or out on the street—there was still a rigid set of rules about what was said and how. Older children were sent out of the living room when it was time to get into the juicy details about "you-know-who" up on the third floor who had gone and gotten herself "p-r-e-g-n-a-n-t!" But my parents, knowing that I could spell well beyond my years, always demanded that I follow the others out to play. Beyond sexual misconduct and death, everything else was considered harmless for our young ears. And so among the anecdotes of the triumphs and disappointments in the various workings of their lives, the word *nigger* was used in my presence, but it was set within contexts and inflections that caused it to register in my mind as something else. 5

In the singular, the word was always applied to a man who had distinguished himself in some situation that brought their approval for his strength, intelligence, or drive: 6

"Did Johnny *really* do that?" 7

"I'm telling you, that nigger pulled in $6,000 of overtime last year. Said he got enough for a down payment on a house." 8

When used with a possessive adjective by a woman—"my nigger"—it became a term of endearment for her husband or boyfriend. But it could be more than just a term applied to a man. In their mouths it became the pure essence of manhood—a disembodied force that channeled their past history of struggle and present survival against the odds into a victorious statement of being: "Yeah, that old foreman found out quick enough—you don't mess with a nigger." 9

In the plural, it became a description of some group within the community that had overstepped the bounds of decency as my family defined it. Parents who neglected their children, a drunken couple who fought in public, people who simply refused to look for work, those with excessively dirty mouths or unkempt households were all "trifling niggers." This particular circle could forgive hard times, unemployment, the occasional bout of depression—they had gone through all of that themselves—but the unforgivable sin was a lack of self-respect. 10

A woman could never be a "nigger" in the singular, with its connotation of confirming worth. The noun *girl* was its closest equivalent in that sense, but only when used in direct address and regardless of the gender doing the addressing. *Girl* was a token of respect for a woman. The one-syllable word was drawn out to sound like three in recognition of the extra ounce of wit, nerve, or daring that the woman had shown in the situation under discussion. 11

"G-i-r-l, stop. You mean you said that to his face?" 12

But if the word was used in a third-person reference or shortened so that it almost snapped out of the mouth, it always involved some element of communal disapproval. And age became an important factor in these exchanges. It was only between individuals of the same generation, or from any older person to a younger (but never the other way around), that *girl* would be considered a compliment. 13

I don't agree with the argument that use of the word *nigger* at this social stratum of the black community was an internalization of racism. The dynamics 14 were the exact opposite: the people in my grandmother's living room took a word that whites used to signify worthlessness or degradation and rendered it impotent. Gathering there together, they transformed *nigger* to signify the varied and complex human beings they knew themselves to be. If the word was to disappear totally from the mouths of even the most liberal of white society, no one in that room was naive enough to believe it would disappear from white minds. Meeting the word head-on, they proved it had absolutely nothing to do with the way they were determined to live their lives.

15   So there must have been dozens of times that *nigger* was spoken in front of me before I reached the third grade. But I didn't "hear" it until it was said by a small pair of lips that had already learned it could be a way to humiliate me. That was the word I went home and asked my mother about. And since she knew that I had to grow up in America, she took me in her lap and explained.

Discussion Questions

1. Other than starting the essay, what is accomplished in the first paragraph?
2. Explain what Naylor means when she says, in paragraph 2, "Words themselves are innocuous; it is the consensus that gives them true power."
3. In paragraph 14, Naylor tells us that her family "rendered it [the word "nigger"] impotent." Explain how.
4. What writing strategies does Naylor use to develop her essay, and where does she use them?
5. Explain the meaning and significance of "since she knew that I had to grow up in America" in paragraph 15. Where else in the essay does Naylor make a similar comment?
6. Characterize the level of diction in the essay.

Toward Key Insights

Offensive terms like *kike, spic, wop,* or *slant eyes* are included in the everyday language of some people. Why are such terms used? How can the victims best respond to such slurs?

Suggestion for Writing

Write an essay explaining how a particular term—such as fundamentalism, sexual harassment, relationship—means different things to different people. Use a mixture of writing strategies to advance your purpose.

Handbook

Sentence Elements

Learning the parts of English sentences won't in itself improve your writing, but it will equip you to handle errors at the sentence level. Before you can identify and correct unwarranted shifts from past to present time, for example, you need to know about verbs and their tenses. Similarly, recognizing and correcting pronoun case errors require a knowledge of what pronouns are and how they are used. In this section we first cover subjects and predicates, then complements, appositives, and the parts of speech, and finally phrases and clauses.

■ Subjects and Predicates

The subject of a sentence tells who or what it is about. A *simple subject* consists of a noun (that is, a naming word) or a noun substitute. A *complete subject* consists of a simple subject plus any words that limit or describe it.

The predicate tells something about the subject and completes the thought of the sentence. A *simple predicate* consists of one or more verbs (words that show action or existence); a *complete predicate* includes any associated words also. In the following examples the simple subjects are underlined once and the simple predicates twice. The subjects and predicates are separated with slash marks.

William/laughed.

Mary/has moved.

Sarah/painted the kitchen.

The student over there in the corner/is majoring in art.

A sentence can have a compound subject (two or more separate subjects), a compound predicate (two or more separate predicates), or both.

The elephants and their trainer/bowed to the audience and left the ring.

Sentences that ask questions don't follow the usual simple subject–simple predicate order. Instead, the order may be reversed; or if the simple predicate consists of two verbs, the simple subject may come between them.

When <u>is</u>/your/<u>theme</u> due? (Simple subject follows simple predicate.)

<u>Has</u>/Joan/<u>walked</u> her pygmy goat yet? (Simple subject comes between verbs.)

Usage Considerations   Because subjects are such important sentence elements, think carefully about each one you write so that your sentences won't be vague or misleading. Read the example below:

Our government has failed to enact a national value-added tax.

This statement can be expressed more precisely:

Congress has failed to enact a national value-added tax.

The *President* has vetoed the proposed national value-added tax.

Paying close attention to subjects lets you present your ideas more accurately and clearly.

> **EXERCISE**   *Place a slash mark between the complete subject and the complete predicate; then underline the simple subject once and the verb(s) twice. If a subject comes between two verbs, set it off with two slash marks.*

1. My favorite city is Chicago.
2. Sally has sold her car to her best friend.
3. The judge looked sternly at the prisoner.
4. That little girl on the slide is my daughter.
5. The batter hit the ball and streaked toward first base.
6. My best friend is Travis Roberts.
7. Did Mark buy his computer at Virtual World?
8. Copper is a good conductor of electricity.
9. The walls and ceiling shook and cracked in the earthquake.
10. A torque wrench provides even pressure on a bolt.

■ Complements

A complement is a word or word group that forms part of the predicate and helps complete the meaning of the sentence. Complements fall into four categories: direct objects, indirect objects, subject complements, and object complements.

A *direct object* names whatever receives, or results from, the action of a verb.

The millwright repaired the *lathe*. (Direct object receives action of verb *repaired*.)

Hilary painted a *picture*. (Direct object results from action of verb *painted*.)

They took *coffee* and *sandwiches* to the picnic. (Direct objects receive action of verb *took*.)

As the last sentence shows, a sentence may have a compound direct object—two or more separate direct objects.

An *indirect object* identifies someone or something that receives whatever is named by the direct object.

> Doris lent *me* her calculator. (Indirect object *me* receives *calculator*, the direct object.)

> Will and Al bought their *boat* new sails. (Indirect object *boat* receives *sails*, the direct object.)

An indirect object can be converted to a prepositional phrase that begins with *to* or *for* and follows the direct object.

> Doris lent her calculator *to me*.

> Will and Al bought new sails *for their boat*.

A *subject complement* follows a linking verb—one that indicates existence rather than action. It renames or describes the subject.

> Desmond is a *carpenter*. (Complement *carpenter* renames subject *Desmond*.)

> The lights are too *bright* for Percy. (Complement *bright* describes subject *lights*.)

An *object complement* follows a direct object and renames or describes it.

> The council named Donna *treasurer*. (Object complement *treasurer* renames direct object *Donna*.)

> The audience thought the play *silly*. (Object complement *silly* describes direct object *play*.)

Usage Considerations   Like subjects, direct objects can be revised for greater precision, as these examples show:

> John sent *a gift*.

> John sent *a giant coloring book as a birthday gift*.

Often, you can carry the revision one step further by adding an indirect object, subject complement, or other complement to the sentence.

> John sent his *niece* a giant coloring book as a birthday gift. (Indirect object added.)

■ Appositives

An appositive is a noun or word group serving as a noun that follows another noun or noun substitute and expands its meaning. Appositives may be restrictive or nonrestrictive. Restrictive appositives distinguish whatever they modify from other items in the same class. They are written without commas.

noun

My sister *Heidi* is a professional golfer. (Appositive *Heidi* distinguishes her from other sisters.)

I have just read a book by the novelist *Henry James*. (Appositive *Henry James* distinguishes him from other novelists.)

Nonrestrictive appositives provide more information about whatever they modify. This sort of appositive is set off by a pair of commas except at the end of a sentence; then it is preceded by a single comma.

Anatoly Karpov, *the Russian chess player*, was interviewed on TV. (Appositive names *Karpov's* occupation.)

Todd plans to major in paleontology, *the study of fossils*. (Appositive defines *paleontology*.)

Usage Considerations   When a brief definition is necessary, appositives can help you improve your sentences.

John Cage wrote hundreds of pieces for prepared piano.

John Cage, *a twentieth-century avant-garde composer*, wrote hundreds of pieces for prepared pianos, *instruments with odds and ends stuck between their strings to provide unusual effects.*

Don't, however, clutter your writing with appositives that provide unneeded information; the overload will impede and irritate your reader.

EXERCISE   *Identify each italicized item as a direct object (DO), an indirect object (IO), a subject complement (SC), an object complement (OC), or an appositive (AP).*

1. Bill rented a *videotape* for his party.
2. Harriet is the *supervisor* of my department.
3. Everyone thought the race *exciting*.
4. My uncle *Dan* is a computer programmer.
5. Dana Gibbons, my *stockbroker*, recommended buying shares in Microsoft.
6. Al called Joyce *intelligent* and *forceful*.
7. Last evening Jessica visited her *parents*.
8. Father gave *me* skis for Christmas.
9. Elliott was *happy* with the results of his test.
10. Lucille baked *Carrie* a birthday cake.

■ Parts of Speech

Traditional English grammar classifies words into eight parts of speech: *nouns, pronouns, verbs, adjectives, adverbs, prepositions, conjunctions,* and *interjections*. This section discusses these categories as well as verbals, phrases, and clauses, which also serve as parts of speech.

Nouns

Nouns name persons, places, things, conditions, ideas, or qualities. Some nouns, called *proper nouns,* identify one-of-a-kind items like the following:

France	Christmas
Pacific Ocean	North Dakota
George Washington	Mona Lisa
Pulitzer Prize	World Series
Spirit of St. Louis	Wyandotte Corporation
Declaration of Independence	Miami–Dade Junior College

Mount Everest, on the border of *Tibet* and *Nepal,* was named for *Sir George Everest,* an Englishman.

Common nouns name general classes or categories of items and include abstract, concrete, and collective nouns.

Abstract Nouns   An abstract noun names a condition, idea, or quality—something we can't see, feel, or otherwise experience with our five senses.

arrogance	harmony	sickness
envy	liberalism	understanding
fear	love	

His *desire* to win caused him to cheat.

Mary felt great *loyalty* to her family.

Concrete Nouns   A concrete noun identifies something that we can experience with one or more of our senses.

man	desk	pillow	needle
bicycle	lemon	airplane	pan
building	piston	carton	smoke

The *air* was thin at the *peak* of the *mountain.*

The *hammer* had a broken *handle.*

Collective Nouns   A collective noun is singular in form but stands for a group or collection of items.

assembly	committee	crowd	flotilla	herd
bunch	congregation	delegation	gang	tribe
class	convoy	family	group	troop

The *jury* filed into the courtroom to announce its verdict.

The *flock* of geese settled onto the lake.

Usage Considerations   Good writing demands precise, potent nouns. If you carefully select your nouns, you can help sharpen your message. Ill-chosen nouns, on the other hand, suggest poor thinking. Note how the vague word *freedom* robs the following sentence of any specific meaning:

> Our *freedom* needs to be protected.

What did the writer have in mind? Here are a few possibilities:

> Our *right to own guns* needs to be protected.

> Our *private behavior* needs to be protected.

> Our *national sovereignty* needs to be protected.

Even when meaning does not present problems, sentences can be sharpened by careful attention to nouns. Note the greater precision of the second sentence below:

> Our *dog* has a savage bite.

> Our *pit bull* has a savage bite.

EXERCISE   *Identify the nouns in the following sentences:*

1. My mother will bring a casserole to the potluck.
2. The apples from the tree were used for pies and applesauce.
3. Sleet has turned the road into a sheet of ice.
4. Gail told the mechanic about the problem with her brakes.
5. Arnold jumped to his feet, darted to the window, and stared into the yard.
6. Harry, my cousin, has a degree in physics.
7. My last job was in Spokane, Washington.
8. It was a hot, sunny day, and the beach was crowded with fugitives from the city.
9. The suddenness of her anger made her companion gasp with surprise.
10. Her friendliness and humor make her a favorite with everyone.

Pronouns

Pronouns, which take the place of nouns in sentences, help you avoid the awkward repetition of nouns.

> If Brad doesn't like the *book*, take *it* back to the library.

There are eight categories of pronouns: *personal, relative, interrogative, demonstrative, reflexive, intensive, indefinite,* and *reciprocal.*

Personal Pronouns   Personal pronouns refer to one or more clearly identified persons, places, or things.

Subjective	Objective	Possessive
I	me	my, mine
you	you	your, yours

he	him	his
she	her	her, hers
it	it	its
we	us	our, ours
you	you	your, yours
they	them	their, theirs

Subjective pronouns serve as the subjects of sentences or clauses, objective pronouns serve as direct and indirect objects, and possessive pronouns show possession or ownership. *My, your, our,* and *their* always precede nouns and thus function as possessive adjectives. *His* and *its* may or may not precede nouns.

He bought a sport shirt. (pronoun as subject)

Donald saw *them.* (pronoun as direct object)

Simon lent *her* ten dollars. (pronoun as indirect object)

That car is *theirs.* (pronoun showing ownership)

Relative Pronouns   A relative pronoun relates a subordinate clause—a word group that has a subject and a predicate but does not express a complete idea— to a noun or pronoun, called an antecedent, in the main part of the sentence. The relative pronouns include the following:

who	whose	what	whoever	whichever
whom	which	that	whomever	whatever

Who in its various forms refers to people, *which* to things, and *that* to either people or things.

Mary Beth Cartwright, *who* was arrested last week for fraud, was Evansville's "Model Citizen" two years ago. (The antecedent of *who* is *Mary Beth Cartwright.*)

He took the electric razor, *which* needed a new cutting head, to the repair shop. (The antecedent of *which* is *electric razor.*)

David Bullock is someone *whom* we should definitely hire. (The antecedent of *whom* is *someone.*)

Montreal is a city *that* I've always wanted to visit. (The antecedent of *that* is *city.*)

Which typically introduces nonrestrictive clauses, that is, clauses that provide more information about whatever they modify (see pages 674–75).

The palace, *which* was in bad condition a century ago, is finally going to be restored. (Clause adds information about palace.)

That is typically used in other situations, especially to introduce restrictive clauses: those that distinguish the things they modify from others in the same class (see page 675).

pro

The used car *that* I bought last week at Honest Bill's has already broken down twice. (Clause distinguishes writer's used car from others.)

Page 656 explains the use of *who* and *whom*.

Interrogative Pronouns Interrogative pronouns introduce questions. All of the relative pronouns except *that* also function as interrogative pronouns.

who	which	whoever	whichever
whom	what	whomever	whatever
whose			

What is the matter?

Who asked you?

Whatever do you mean?

When *what, which* and *whose* are followed by nouns, they act as adjectives, not pronouns.

Which movie should we see?

Demonstrative Pronouns As their name suggests, demonstrative pronouns point things out. There are four such pronouns.

this	these
that	those

This and its plural *these* identify recent or nearby things.

This is the play to see.

These are the times that try men's souls.

That and its plural *those* identify less recent or more distant things.

That is Mary's house across the road.

Those were very good peaches you had for sale last week.

Reflexive and Intensive Pronouns A reflexive pronoun reverses the action of a verb, making the doer and the receiver of the action the same. An intensive pronoun lends emphasis to a noun or pronoun. The two sets of pronouns are identical.

myself	herself	ourselves
yourself	itself	yourselves
himself	oneself	themselves

My father cut *himself* while shaving. (reflexive pronoun)

The President *himself* has asked me to undertake this mission. (intensive pronoun)

Don't substitute a reflexive pronoun for a personal pronoun.

Faulty	Jill and *myself* are going to a movie.
Revision	Jill and *I* are going to a movie.
Faulty	Give the tickets to John and *myself*.
Revision	Give the tickets to John and *me*.

Sometimes you'll hear people say things like "He made it *hisself*," "They're only fooling *theirself*," or "They bought *theirselves* sodas." Such forms are non-standard. Say "himself" and "themselves" instead.

Indefinite Pronouns   These pronouns refer to unidentified persons, places, or things. One group of indefinite pronouns consistently acts as pronouns.

anybody	everything	one
anyone	nobody	somebody
anything	no one	someone
everybody	nothing	something
everyone		

A second group may function as either pronouns or adjectives.

all	any	most	few	much
another	each	either	many	neither

Here are some examples:

Everyone is welcome. (indefinite pronoun)

Many are called, but *few* are chosen. (indefinite pronouns)

Many men but only a *few* women attend the Air Force Academy. (adjectives)

Pages 648–49 discuss indefinite pronouns as antecedents.

Reciprocal Pronouns   The two reciprocal pronouns show an interchange of action between two or more parties. *Each other* is used when two parties interact, *one another* when three or more do.

Pam and Patty accidentally gave *each other* the same thing for Christmas. (two persons)

The members of the football team joyfully embraced *one another* after their victory. (more than two persons)

Usage Considerations   Many students handle pronouns carelessly, damaging the clarity of their writing. Problems include letting the same pronoun stand for different nouns or using a pronoun where detailed, vivid language would be more effective. The following passage illustrates poor pronoun usage:

My brother loves fly fishing. He thinks *it* is the only way to spend a summer weekend. In fact, whenever he's off work, he'll do *it*.

Rewritten as follows, the passage has been notably improved:

> My brother loves fly fishing. He thinks that *wading a stream and casting leisurely for trout* is the only way to spend a summer weekend. In fact, whenever he's off work, he *can be found up to his hips in water, offering his hand-tied flies to the waiting rainbows.*

EXERCISE   *Identify each pronoun in the following sentences and indicate its type:*

1. Which of these cars do you want to borrow, Jill's or mine?
2. If you can't handle the job, I myself will do it.
3. What made you decide that the children wouldn't play with one another?
4. Everyone whom he met thought him charismatic.
5. This is the sort of humor that I especially dislike.
6. Everybody who is anybody dines at Chez Snobbisme.
7. That is an unusual house; I wonder who lives there.
8. Everyone commented on the new car he had bought.
9. Whenever Seth bought a Lotto ticket, he imagined himself living in a castle.
10. The two drivers blamed each other for the accident.

Verbs

A verb indicates action or existence: what something is, was, or will be. Verbs fall into three classes: *action verbs, linking verbs,* and *helping* (or *auxiliary*) *verbs.*

Action Verbs   As its name suggests, an action verb expresses action. Some action verbs are transitive, others intransitive. A *transitive* verb has a direct object that receives or results from the action and rounds out the meaning of the sentence.

> The photographer *took* the picture.

Without the direct object, this sentence would not express a complete thought. In contrast, an *intransitive* verb requires no direct object to complete the meaning of the sentence.

> Lee Ann *gasped* loudly.

> Little Tommy Tucker *sings* for his supper.

Many action verbs can play both transitive or intransitive roles, depending on the sentences they are used in.

> Kari *rode* her bicycle into town. (transitive verb)

> Karl *rode* in the front seat of the car. (intransitive verb)

Linking Verbs   A linking verb shows existence—what something is, was, or will be—rather than action. Linking verbs are intransitive and tie their subjects to subject complements. Some subject complements are nouns or noun substitutes that rename their subjects. Others are adjectives that describe their subjects.

Ms. Davis *is* our new director. (Complement *director* renames subject *Ms. Davis.*)

The soup *was* lukewarm. (Complement *lukewarm* describes subject *soup.*)

The most common linking verbs are forms of the verb *to be (is, are, am, was, were, be, being, been.)* Likewise, verbs such as *seem, become, appear, remain, feel, look, smell, sound,* and *taste* function as linking verbs when they do not indicate actual physical action. In such cases, they are followed by adjectives (see pages 626–28). Here is an example:

Harry looked *angry.*

When such verbs do indicate physical action, they function as action verbs and are followed by adverbs (see pages 628–30).

Harry looked *angrily* at the referee.

Helping Verbs   Helping verbs accompany action or linking verbs, allowing them to express with great precision matters such as possibility, obligation, and time. Common helping verbs include the following:

has	been	had (to)
have	do	shall
had	does	will
am	did	going (to)
is	used (to)	about (to)
are	may	would
was	might	should
were	must	ought (to)
be	have (to)	can
being	has (to)	could

I *should ask* my parents. (helping verb *should* with action verb *ask*)

The driver *was being lifted* onto a stretcher. (helping verbs *was* and *being* with action verb *lifted*)

You *have been* good. (helping verb *have* with linking verb *been*)

The patient *will feel* better soon. (helping verb *will* with linking verb *feel*)

We *might go* to Corvallis next weekend. (helping verb *might* with action verb *go*)

Helping verbs usually appear next to the main verbs, but they don't have to.

Ellen *will* undoubtedly *resign.*

Combinations of two or more verbs are called verb phrases.

Usage Considerations Energetic writing requires precise verbs. Don't take verbs for granted; revise them as necessary in order to strengthen a sentence. Note the improved precision of the second example sentence:

I *gave* the maître d' a ten-dollar bill.

I *slipped* the maître d' a ten-dollar bill.

EXERCISE *Identify each verb in the following sentences and indicate its type:*

1. Whenever I want exercise, I walk in the park.
2. Your comments on this proposal have been very helpful.
3. The pianist played beautifully, but the listeners were unimpressed.
4. This float will surely be awarded first prize in the parade.
5. Myra has donated over one hundred books to the local library.
6. Lenore has been using her computer for over three hours.
7. The director had been watching the players rehearse all afternoon.
8. Don't call after 7 P.M.; I will be having out-of-town visitors.
9. Will you hand me that hammer over there?
10. He should have been an actor.

Principal Parts Verbs change in form to show time (tense) distinctions. For every action verb, tenses are built from three principal parts: *present, past,* and *past participle.* The present is the principal part you would look up in the dictionary (*win, skip, go,* and so on). If the subject of a verb is a singular pronoun *(he, she, it)* or a singular noun, add an *s* or *es* to the dictionary form *(wins, skips, goes).* Most verbs have identical past and past participles.

	Present	**Past**	**Past Participle**
I, you, we, they	talk	talked	talked
He, she, it, Henry	talks	talked	talked
I, you, we, they	stand	stood	stood
He, she, it, the decision	stands	stood	stood

Some verbs have different past and past participles.

	Present	**Past**	**Past Participle**
I, you, we, they	swim	swam	swum
He, she, it, the boy	swims	swam	swum
I, you, we, they	bite	bit	bitten
He, she, it, the dog	bites	bit	bitten

With a few verbs, the past and past participles are identical to the dictionary form.

	Present	**Past**	**Past Participle**
I, you, we, they	set	set	set
He, she, it	sets	set	set

If you're uncertain about the principal parts of a verb, check your dictionary.

Tense English has six basic tenses: present, past, future, present perfect, past perfect, future perfect. They are formed from the principal parts of action and linking verbs, either alone or combined with helping verbs.

The *present tense* is formed from the present principal part of the main verb. It shows present condition and general or habitual action, indicates permanent truths, tells about past events in the historical present, and sometimes denotes action at some definite future time.

Helen *looks* beautiful in her new gown. (present condition)

John *works* on the eighteenth floor. (general action)

I *brush* my teeth each morning. (habitual action)

The earth *rotates* on its axis. (permanent truth)

On November 11, 1918, the guns *fall* silent, and World War I *comes* to an end. (historical present)

Monday, I *begin* my new job. (future action)

The *past tense* is based on the past principal part of the verb. The past tense shows that a condition existed or an action was completed in the past. The verb tense leaves the time indefinite, but surrounding words may specify it.

Paul *was* angry with his noisy neighbors. (past condition, time indefinite)

Sandy *received* a long letter yesterday. (past action, time specified by *yesterday*)

The *future tense* combines *shall* or *will* and the present principal part of the main verb. It indicates that a condition will exist or an action will take place in the future.

You *will feel* better after a good night's sleep. (future condition)

I *shall attend* the concert next week. (future action)

The *present perfect* tense is formed with *has* or *have* and the past participle of the main verb. It shows that a past condition or action, or its effect, continues until the present time.

The players *have been* irritable since they lost the homecoming game. (Condition continues until present.)

Juanita *has driven* a United Parcel Service truck for five years. (Action continues until present.)

William *has repaired* the snow blower. (Effect of action continues until present although the action itself was completed in the past.)

The *past perfect* tense combines *had* and the past participle of the main verb. It refers to a past condition or action that was completed before another past condition or action.

vbs

He *had been* in the army two years when the war ended. (Past perfect condition occurred first.)

Vivian moved into the house that she *had built* the summer before. (Past perfect action occurred first.)

The *future perfect* tense is formed from the verbs *shall have* or *will have* plus the past participle of the main verb. It shows that a condition or an action will have been completed at some time in the future. Surrounding words specify time.

Our sales manager *will have been* with the company ten years next July. (Condition will end.)

By the end of this year, I *shall have written* the great American novel. (Action will be completed.)

Each of these basic tenses has a *progressive tense* that indicates action in progress. The progressive tense always includes some form of the verb *to be* followed by a present participle, a verb that ends in *-ing*.

Present progressive	I am running.
Past progressive	I was running.
Future progressive	I will be running.
Present perfect progressive	I have been running.
Past perfect progressive	I had been running.
Future perfect progressive	I will have been running.

Pages 658–91 discuss unwarranted shifts in tense and their correction.

Voice   Transitive verbs have two voices: active and passive. A verb is in the *active voice* when the subject carries out the action named by the verb.

Barry *planned* a picnic. (Subject *Barry* performs action.)

A verb is in the *passive voice* when the subject receives the action. The performer may be identified in an accompanying phrase or go unmentioned.

A picnic *was planned* by Barry. (The phrase *by Barry* identifies the performer.)

The picnic *was canceled*. (The performer goes unmentioned.)

A passive construction always uses a form of *to be* and the past participle of an action verb. Like other constructions, the passive may show past, present, or future time.

Amy *is paid* handsomely for her investment advice. (present tense)

I *was warned* by a sound truck that a tornado was nearby. (past tense)

I *will be sent* to Ghana soon by the Peace Corps. (future tense)

I *have been awarded* a sizable research grant. (present perfect tense)

The city *had been shelled* heavily before the infantry moved in. (past perfect tense)

By the end of this month, the site for our second factory *will have been cho-sen.* (future perfect tense)

To convert a sentence from the passive to the active voice, make the performer the subject, the original subject the direct object, and drop the form of *to be.*

The treaty *was signed* by the general. (passive)

The general *signed* the treaty. (active)

Technical and scientific writing commonly uses the passive voice to explain processes since its flat, impersonal tone adds an air of scientific objectivity and authority. Other kinds of writing, however, avoid the passive voice except when it is desirable to conceal the one performing the action or when the action is more significant than the actor. See pages 228–29 for more information on usage.

EXERCISE   *Identify each verb in the following sentences, indicate its tense, and note any use of the passive voice:*

1. Helen baked a peach pie for the church social.
2. Sheila has worked here for six years.
3. The Wilsons will have left France by tomorrow.
4. After the meeting, John was praised for his speech.
5. Everyone cheered as the flag was carried into the arena.
6. Last year my parents bought the house that we had rented for a decade.
7. We have been told that our car needs new piston rings.
8. Jeffrey will graduate from Yale with honors.
9. The museum is located at the corner of Fifth and Dreyfus Streets.
10. Our school playground will be repaved in about two weeks.
11. The rioters had been warned twice before the police moved in.
12. We believe the strike will have been settled by Monday evening.

Mood   The mood of a verb shows whether the writer regards a statement as a

1. fact
2. command or request
3. wish, possibility, condition contrary to fact, or the like.

English has three moods: the indicative, imperative, and subjunctive.

A sentence in the *indicative mood* states a real or supposed fact or asks a question.

Nancy *graduates* from high school tomorrow.

We *lived* in Oakmont when Rachel was born.

He *had been* a sailor during the war.

Has Joe *asked* anyone to the prom yet?

vbs

Most verbs are used in the indicative mood.

A sentence in the *imperative mood* delivers a command or makes a request.

Leave the room immediately! (command)

Please *turn* the CD player down. (request)

The subject of a sentence in the imperative mood is always *you*. Although ordinarily unstated, the subject sometimes appears in the sentence.

You leave the room immediately!

The *subjunctive mood* is used

1. in *if, as if,* and *as though* clauses to express a wish, a possibility, or an action or a condition contrary to fact
2. in *that* clauses expressing orders, demands, requests, resolutions, proposals, or motions
3. with modal auxiliaries to express wishes, probability, possibility, permission, requirements, recommendations, suggestions, and conditions contrary to fact.

To express a present or future wish, possibility, condition or action in an *if, as if,* or *as though* clause, use *were* with any personal pronoun or noun serving as the subject of the clause.

If only Stan *were* less gullible! (present wish contrary to fact)

Even if Kay *were* to explain, Mary wouldn't believe her. (future possibility)

Arthur is behaving as if he *were* a millionaire (present condition contrary to fact)

To express a wish, possibility, or condition contrary to past facts, use *had been* or *had* plus the past participle of an action verb.

If the engine *had been lubricated,* the bearing wouldn't have burned out. (past condition contrary to fact)

Alice looked as if she *had lost* her best friend. (condition expressed in clause occurs before action of verb *looked*)

When writing *that* clauses expressing orders, demands, requests, resolutions, proposals, or motions, use *be* or the present plural form of an action verb.

I move that they *be* rewarded for their bravery.

The group proposed that Margaret *go* to the scene of the accident and *inspect* it personally.

In other *that* clauses, use the appropriate indicative form of the verb.

I know that they *were* rewarded for their bravery.

The group believed that Margaret *had gone* to the scene of the accident and *inspected* it personally.

The modal auxiliaries include the helping verbs *can, could, may, might, must, shall, will, would, should,* and *ought to.* The examples below illustrate the meanings they can express.

1. Wishes *(could, would)*

   I wish I *could* shimmy like my sister Kate.

   The Republicans wish the Democrats *would* go away and vice versa.

2. Probability *(should)*

   Because I've studied diligently, I *should* do better on my next chemistry test.

3. Possibility *(may, might, can, could)*

   Low inflation *could* cause our stock market to soar.

   I *might* stay up to watch the eclipse of the moon tonight.

4. Permission *(can, may)*

   The public *can* use these tennis courts every afternoon.

   You *may* leave as soon as you've finished filing these folders.

5. Requirements *(must)*

   The landlord has raised our rent again; we *must* find another apartment.

6. Recommendations, suggestions *(should, ought to)*

   Randy *should* see a doctor about his chest pains.

   All of us *ought to* exercise regularly.

7. Conditions contrary to fact *(could)*

   If only I *could* live my life over!

EXERCISE *For each of the following sentences, identify the mood as indicative (IND), imperative (IMP), or subjunctive (SUB):*

1. See your doctor before starting a strenuous exercise program.
2. The tired runner staggered across the finish line.
3. These new cell phones should prove very popular.
4. Let me know what you think of this novel.
5. Hang gliding is a great sport for anyone unafraid of heights.
6. If you practiced more, you could become an outstanding pianist.
7. The latest unemployment figures should help calm inflation fears.
8. Stop talking right now or leave the class.
9. This movie could have been shortened by fifteen minutes without harming the story.
10. Who wants to play Scrabble this evening?

Adjectives

An adjective *modifies* a noun or pronoun by describing it, limiting it, or otherwise making its meaning more exact.

> The *brass* candlestick stood next to the *fragile* vase. (*Brass* modifies *candlestick*, and *fragile* modifies *vase*.)

> The cat is *long-haired* and *sleek*. (*Long-haired* and *sleek* modify *cat*.)

There are three general categories of adjectives: limiting, descriptive, and proper.

Limiting Adjectives   A limiting adjective identifies or points out the noun or pronoun it modifies. It may indicate number or quantity. Several categories of pronouns can serve as limiting adjectives, as can numbers and nouns.

> *Whose* briefcase is on the table? (interrogative adjective)

> The couple *whose* car was stolen called the police. (relative adjective)

> *This* restaurant has the best reputation for gourmet food. (demonstrative adjective)

> *Some* people have no social tact at all. (indefinite adjective)

> Sally swerved *her* car suddenly to avoid an oncoming truck. (possessive adjective)

> *Three* people entered the lecture hall late. (number as adjective)

> The *schoolgirl* look is fashionable this year. (noun as adjective)

Descriptive Adjectives   A descriptive adjective names a quality, characteristic, or condition of a noun or pronoun. Two or more of these adjectives, members of the largest category of adjectives, may modify the same noun or pronoun.

> The *yellow* submarine belongs to the Beatles.

> He applied *clear* lacquer to the tabletop.

> The *slim, sophisticated* model glided onto the runway.

> The child was *active, happy,* and *polite*.

Proper Adjectives   A proper adjective is derived from a proper noun and is always capitalized.

> Harwell is a *Shakespearean* actor.

Articles as Adjectives   Articles appear immediately before nouns and can therefore be considered adjectives. There are three articles in English: *a, an,* and *the*. *The* points to a specific item; *a* and *an* do not. *A* precedes words beginning with consonant sounds; *an* precedes words with vowel sounds, making pronunciation easier.

The right word at *the* right moment can save a friendship. (Definite articles suggest there is one right word and one right moment.)

A right word can save a friendship. (Indefinite article suggests there are several right words.)

I think I'd like *an* apple with my lunch. (No particular apple is specified.)

Sometimes the definite article refers to a class of items.

The tiger is fast becoming an endangered species.

Context shows whether such a sentence refers to particular items or entire classes.

Comparison with Adjectives Adjectives may be used to show comparison. When two things are compared, shorter adjectives usually add *-er* and longer adjectives add *more*. When three or more things are compared, shorter adjectives usually add *-est* and longer ones add *most*.

John is *taller* than Pete. (short adjective comparing two things)

Sandra seems *more cheerful* than Jill today. (long adjective comparing two things)

John is the *tallest* of the three brothers. (short adjective comparing three things)

Sandra is the *most cheerful* girl in the class. (longer adjective comparing more than three things)

Some adjectives, like the examples below, have irregular forms for comparisons.

good—better—best

bad—worse—worst

Don't use the *-est* form of the shorter adjective for comparing just two things.

Faulty   This is the *smallest* of the two castles.

Instead, use the *-er* form.

Revision   This is the *smaller* of the two castles.

Position of Adjectives Most adjectives come immediately before the words they modify. In a few set expressions (for example, heir *apparent*), the adjective immediately follows the word it modifies. Similarly, adjective pairs sometimes appear in a follow-up position for added emphasis (The rapids, *swift* and *dangerous*, soon capsized the raft). Sometimes adjectives also serve as subject complements and follow their subjects (The puppy was *friendly*).

Usage Considerations Some students overuse adjectives, especially in descriptions, but most underuse them. Review your sentences carefully to see where adding or cutting adjectives can increase the impact of your writing.

My Buick is the talk of my friends.

My *old, dilapidated, rusty, fenderless 1970* Buick is the talk of my friends.

My *rusty, fenderless 1970* Buick is the talk of my friends.

The first sentence lacks adjectives that show why the car is discussed. The second sentence overcorrects this fault by including two adjectives that repeat the information provided by the others. The final sentence strikes the proper balance.

> **EXERCISE**   *Identify the adjectives in the following sentences:*
>
> 1. The shaggy dog chased the small kitten up a tree.
> 2. Stephanie bought a tall mahogany sideboard for the dining room.
> 3. We bought a dozen red roses at the flower shop.
> 4. The wind is so fierce and cold that walking is nearly impossible.
> 5. Shirley sang the song in a high, clear soprano voice.
> 6. Clarence is the most intelligent student in this class.
> 7. The large man ate five hamburgers at one sitting.
> 8. In the evening the meadow was misty.
> 9. The leadoff batter hit a fastball into the outfield.
> 10. Tammy is taller than Janice.

Adverbs

An adverb modifies a verb, an adjective, another adverb, or a whole sentence. Adverbs generally answer questions such as "How?" "When?" "Where?" "How often?" and "To what extent?"

The floodwaters receded *very* slowly. (Adverb modifies adverb and answers the question "How?")

My sister will visit me *tomorrow.* (Adverb modifies verb and answers the question "When?")

The coach walked *away* from the bench. (Adverb modifies verb and answers the question "Where?")

The tire is *too* worn to be safe. (Adverb modifies adjective and answers the question "To what extent?")

The teller is *frequently* late for work. (Adverb modifies adjective and answers the question "How often?")

Unfortunately, the game was canceled because of rain. (The adverb modifies the whole sentence but does not answer any question.)

Formation of Adverbs   Most adverbs are formed by adding *-ly* to adjectives.

The wind is *restless*. (*Restless* is an adjective modifying *wind*.)

He walked *restlessly* around the room. (*Restlessly* is an adverb modifying *walked*.)

Many common adverbs, however (*almost, never, quite, soon, then, there,* and *too*), lack *-ly* endings.

I *soon* realized that pleasing my boss was impossible.

This movie is *too* gruesome for my taste.

Furthermore, some words such as *better, early, late, hard, little, near, only, straight,* and *wrong* do double duty as either adjectives or adverbs.

We must have taken a *wrong* turn. (*Wrong* is an adjective modifying the noun *turn*.)

Where did I go *wrong*? (*Wrong* is an adverb modifying the verb *go*.)

Comparison with Adverbs Like adjectives, adverbs can show comparison. When two things are compared, adverbs add *more*. When three or more things are compared, *most* is used.

Harold works *more* efficiently than Don. (adverb comparing two people)

Of all the people in the shop, Harold works the *most* efficiently. (adverb comparing more than two people)

Some adverbs, like some adjectives, use irregular forms for comparisons.

well—better—best

much—more—most

Position of Adverbs Adverbs are more movable than any other part of speech. Usually, adverbs that modify adjectives and other adverbs appear next to them to avoid confusion.

Her *especially* fine tact makes her a welcome guest at any party. (Adverb *especially* modifies adjective *fine*.)

The novel was *very* badly written. (Adverb *very* modifies adverb *badly*.)

Adverbs that modify verbs, however, can often be shifted around in their sentences without causing changes in meaning.

Quickly, he slipped through the doorway.

He slipped *quickly* through the doorway.

He slipped through the doorway *quickly*.

Usage Considerations You can often sharpen the meaning of a sentence by adding a well-chosen adverb.

The student squirmed in his chair.

The student squirmed *anxiously* in his chair.

Including the adverb *anxiously* in the second sentence shows the mental state of the student.

Be careful, however, not to overuse adverbs as they can bog down your writing.

EXERCISE *Identify the adverbs in the following sentences:*

1. The men walked silently outside and whispered indistinctly.
2. Liz is seldom in a cheerful mood.
3. The movie, while quite entertaining, did poorly at the box office.
4. The storm struck very suddenly and completely destroyed the house.
5. If you play fair with me, you'll not regret it.
6. Unfortunately, Jeff was too tired to go skiing yesterday.
7. Slowly, cautiously, the cat approached the unsuspecting mouse.
8. I never forget a face, but sometimes I wish I could.
9. I've never known anyone to work more rapidly than Larry.
10. These directions are too complicated for most people to follow easily.

Prepositions

A preposition links its object—a noun or noun substitute—to some other word in the sentence and shows a relationship between them. The relationship is often one of location, time, means, or reason or purpose. The word group containing the preposition and its object makes up a prepositional phrase.

The new insulation *in* the attic keeps my house much warmer now. (Preposition *in* links object *attic* to *insulation* and shows location.)

We have postponed the meeting *until* tomorrow. (Preposition *until* links object *tomorrow* to *postponed* and shows time.)

The tourists traveled *by* automobile. (Preposition *by* links object *automobile* to *traveled* and shows means.)

Warren swims *for* exercise. (Preposition *for* links object *exercise* to *swims* and shows reason or purpose.)

The following list includes the most common prepositions, some of which consist of two or more words:

above	among	below	down
about	around	beside	during
across	at	between	except
after	because of	by	for
against	before	by reason of	from
along with	behind	contrary to	in

instead of	of	over	toward
into	on	since	under
like	onto	through	with
near	out of	to	without
next to			

Many of these combine to form additional prepositions: *except for, in front of, by way of, on top of,* and the like.

Certain prepositions sometimes occur in close association with certain verbs, forming verb units with altered meanings. When this happens, we call the prepositions verb particles. Here is an example:

The instructor let Jeff make *up* the test.

Note the great difference between the meaning of the foregoing sentence and "The instructor let Jeff make the test."

Usage Considerations   It is easy to use a small group of prepositions over and over in your writing. This habit often results in imprecise or misleading sentences. To avoid this problem, think carefully about your choice of prepositions as you revise. Read the following example:

He walked *by* the railroad tracks on his way home.

Note that two interpretations are possible.

He walked *along* the railroad tracks on his way home.

He walked *past* the railroad tracks on his way home.

Clearly you would use the preposition that conveys your intended meaning.

EXERCISE   *Identify the prepositions and their objects in the following sentences:*

1. Annette went to the store for a box of cereal.
2. The excursion to Lake Archer is scheduled for Friday.
3. Because of a headache, Courtney felt edgy and out of sorts.
4. After lunch, Dick rested for an hour and then went to a movie.
5. Contrary to expectation, Dave majored in English instead of history.
6. In a moment of panic, a person can behave very foolishly.
7. During the war, Barry served in the infantry.
8. The stretch of river below the dam is an excellent spot for a swim.
9. Linda voted against Ken Conwell in this election.
10. Most people expect guests to be on time for dinner.

Conjunctions

Conjunctions serve as connectors, linking parts of sentences or whole sentences. These connectors fall into three groups: coordinating conjunctions, subordinating conjunctions, and conjunctive adverbs.

Coordinating Conjunctions   Coordinating conjunctions connect terms of equal grammatical importance: words, word groups, and simple sentences. These conjunctions can occur singly *(and, but, or, nor, for, yet, so)* or in pairs called correlative conjunctions *(either—or, neither—nor, both—and,* and *not only— but also).* The elements that follow correlative conjunctions must be parallel, that is, have the same grammatical form.

> Tom *and* his cousin are opening a video arcade. (Coordinating conjunction connects nouns.)

> Shall I serve the tea in the living room *or* on the veranda? (Coordinating conjunction connects phrases.)

> I am going to Europe this summer, *but* Marjorie is staying home. (Coordinating conjunction connects simple sentences.)

> Amy *not only* teaches English *but also* writes novels. (Correlative conjunctions connect parallel predicates.)

> You can study nursing *either* at Ferris State University *or* at DeWitt College. (Correlative conjunctions connect parallel phrases.)

> Friendship is *both* pleasure *and* pain. (Correlative conjunctions connect parallel nouns.)

Subordinating Conjunctions   Like relative pronouns, subordinating conjunctions introduce subordinate clauses, relating them to independent clauses, which can stand alone as complete sentences. Examples of subordinating conjunctions include *because, as if, even though, since, so that, whereas,* and *whenever* (see page 639 for a more complete list).

> I enjoyed the TV program *because* it was so well acted. (Conjunction connects *it was so well acted* to rest of sentence.)

> *Whenever* you're ready, we can begin dinner. (Conjunction connects *you're ready* to rest of sentence.)

Conjunctive Adverbs   These connectors resemble both conjunctions and adverbs. Like conjunctions, they serve as linking devices between elements of equal rank. Like adverbs, they function as modifiers, showing such things as similarity, contrast, result or effect, addition, emphasis, time, and example. The following list groups the most common conjunctive adverbs according to function:

Similarity: likewise, similarly
Contrast: however, nevertheless, on the contrary, on the other hand, otherwise
Result or effect: accordingly, as a result, consequently, hence, therefore, thus
Addition: also, furthermore, in addition, in the first place, moreover
Emphasis or clarity: in fact, in other words, indeed, that is
Time: afterward, later, meanwhile, subsequently
Example: for example, for instance, to illustrate

The job will require you to travel a great deal; *however,* the salary is excellent.

Sean cares nothing for clothes; *in fact,* all of his socks have holes in their toes.

Usage Considerations You can add variety and precision to your writing by varying the conjunctions you use. If you consistently rely on the conjunction *because,* try substituting *as* or *since.* Likewise, you may periodically replace *if* with *provided that.* The right conjunction shows the realtionship among ideas.

When you have choppy sentences, try combining them by using a conjunction.

You can buy smoked salmon at Sally's Seafoods. You can buy it at Daane's Thriftland as well.

You can buy smoked salmon *either* at Sally's Seafoods *or* at Daane's Thriftland.

The revision is much smoother than the original sentence pair.

Interjections

An interjection is an exclamatory word used to gain attention or to express strong feeling. It has no grammatical connection to the rest of the sentence. An interjection is followed by an exclamation point or a comma.

Hey! Watch how you're driving! (strong interjection)

Oh, is the party over already? (mild interjection)

EXERCISE *Identify the coordinating conjunctions (CC), subordinating conjunctions (SC), conjunctive adverbs (CA), and interjections (I) in the following sentences:*

1. Neither Fred nor his father could solve the algebra problem.
2. I've bought Lotto tickets for years even though I've never won.
3. Our dog and cat co-exist without showing real friendship.
4. The speaker's views were unpopular; nevertheless, the audience listened politely.
5. Mark didn't wear a bicycle helmet; therefore, he hurt his head when he fell.
6. Help! I think I've broken my leg!
7. Karen's not a basketball fan; in fact, she's never seen a game.
8. I attended yesterday's seminar on Web page design, but Sue didn't.
9. Ah, that lemonade really hit the spot.
10. I expect either Jack or Steve to buy my fishing boat.
11. Marcy looked as if she were about to be ill.
12. We can leave whenever you finish packing the picnic basket.

■ Phrases and Clauses

Phrases

A phrase is a group of words that lacks a subject and a predicate and serves as a single part of speech. This section discusses four basic kinds of phrases: *prepositional phrases, participial phrases, gerund phrases,* and *infinitive phrases.* The last three are based on participles, gerunds, and infinitives, verb forms known as verbals. A fifth type of phrase, the verb phrase, consists of sets of two or more verbs (*has fixed, had been sick, will have been selected,* and the like).

Prepositional Phrases   A prepositional phrase consists of a preposition, one or more objects, and any associated words. These phrases serve as adjectives or adverbs.

> The picture *over the mantel* was my mother's. (prepositional phrase as adjective)

> He bought ice skates *for himself.* (prepositional phrase as adverb modifying verb)

> The toddler was afraid *of the dog.* (prepositional phrase as adverb modifying adjective)

> Our visitors arrived late *in the day.* (prepositional phrase as adverb modifying another adverb)

Frequently, prepositional phrases occur in series. Sometimes they form chains in which each phrase modifies the object of the preceding phrase. At other times some or all of the phrases may modify the verb or verb phrase.

> John works *in a clothing store / on Main Street / during the summer.*

Here the first and third phrases serve as adverbs modifying the verb *works* and answering the questions "Where?" and "When?" while the second phrase serves as an adjective modifying *store* and answering the question "Where?"

On occasion, especially in questions, a preposition may be separated from its object, making the phrase difficult to find.

> Dr. Perry is the person *whom* I've been looking *for.*

> *What* are you shouting *about?*

Participial Phrases   A participial phrase consists of a participle plus associated words. Participles are verb forms that, when used in participial phrases, function as adjectives or adverbs. A present participle ends in *-ing* and indicates an action currently being carried out. A past participle ends in *-ed, -en, -e, -n, -d,* or *-t* and indicates some past action.

> The chef *preparing dinner* trained in France. (present participial phrase as adjective)

The background, *sketched in lightly,* accented the features of the woman in the painting. (past participial phrase as adjective)

She left *whistling a jolly melody.* (present participial phrase as adverb)

A perfect participial phrase consists of *having* or *having been* plus a past participle and any associated words. Like a past participial phrase, it indicates a past action.

Having alerted the townspeople about the tornado, the sound truck returned to the city garage. (perfect participial phrase)

Having been alerted to the tornado, the townspeople sought shelter in their basements. (perfect participial phrase)

Some participial phrases that modify persons or things distinguish them from others in the same class. These phrases are written without commas. Other phrases provide more information about the persons or things they modify and are set off with commas. For a further discussion of these usages, see pages 674–75.

The man *fixing my car* is a master mechanic. (Phrase distinguishes man fixing car from others.)

Mr. Welsh, *fatigued by the tennis game,* rested in the shade. (Phrase provides more information about Mr. Welsh.)

Gerund Phrases   A gerund phrase consists of a gerund and the words associated with it. Like present participles, gerunds are verb forms that end in *-ing.* Unlike participles, though, they function as nouns rather than as adjectives or adverbs.

Kathryn's hobby is *collecting stamps.* (gerund phrase as subject complement)

Kathryn's hobby, *collecting stamps,* has made her many friends. (gerund phrase as appositive)

He devoted every spare moment to *overhauling the car.* (gerund phrase as object of preposition.)

Infinitive Phrases   An infinitive phrase consists of the present principal part of a verb preceded by *to (to fix, to eat),* together with any accompanying words. These phrases serve as adjectives, adverbs, and nouns.

This looks like a good place *to plant the shrub.* (infinitive phrase as adjective)

Lenore worked *to earn money for college.* (infinitive phrase as adverb)

My goal is *to have my own business some day.* (infinitive phrase as noun)

Gerunds can often be substituted for infinitives and vice versa.

To repair this fender will cost two hundred dollars. (infinitive phrase as subject)

Repairing this fender will cost two hundred dollars. (gerund phrase as subject)

At times the *to* in an infinitive may be omitted following verbs such as *make, dare, let,* and *help.*

Kristin didn't dare *(to) move* a muscle.

The psychiatrist helped me *(to) overcome* my fear of flying.

Verbals Not in Phrases   Participles, gerunds, and infinitives can function as nouns, adjectives, or adverbs, even when they are not parts of phrases.

That *sunbathing* woman is a well-known model. (participle as adjective)

Dancing is fine exercise. (gerund)

The children want *to play.* (infinitive as noun)

If you're looking for a job, Sally is the person *to see.* (infinitive as adjective)

I'm prepared *to resign.* (infinitive as adverb)

Usage Considerations   Phrases can often help clarify or develop the information in a sentence or combine choppy sentences.

Original	My brother is fishing.
Revision	My brother is fishing *for trout just below Barnes Dam on Sidewinder Creek.* (prepositional phrases added)
Original	The boat barely made shore.
Revision	The boat, *listing heavily and leaking badly,* barely made shore. (participial phrases added)

To avoid ponderous sentences, don't, however, weigh them down with phrases, as in the following example:

My brother is fishing for trout just below Barnes Dam on Sidewinder Creek *near Perry Pass in the mountains of Central Colorado.*

EXERCISE   *Identify the italicized phrases as prepositional, participial, gerund, or infinitive and tell whether each is used as a noun, an adjective, or an adverb.*

1. *Waiting tables this summer* will help me buy this fall's textbooks.
2. Growling savagely, the dog went *for the intruder's leg.*
3. *To reduce expenses by ten percent* is our aim.
4. *Hurrying down the sidewalk,* Janice stubbed her toe.
5. The town band will be here *for the groundbreaking ceremony.*
6. The committee rejected Brandon's plan *to rewrite the club's bylaws.*
7. *Wanting to get to the party on time,* we took a shortcut through the woods.
8. The refrigerant used *to cool our food* was ordinary ice.
9. We desire happiness *for everyone.*
10. I dread *meeting my fiancee's parents.*
11. My long-held dream, *visiting France,* will be realized this summer.

12. Sally bought stain *to refinish her dining room table.*

13. *Burdened by debt,* the company filed for bankrupcy.

14. Debbie wants *to become a computer software designer.*

15. The picture *over the mantel* was painted by Andy Warhol.

Clauses

A clause is a word group that includes a subject and a predicate. An *independent clause,* sometimes called a main clause, expresses a complete thought and can function as a simple sentence. A *subordinate clause,* or dependent clause, cannot stand by itself. Subordinate clauses may serve as nouns, adjectives, or adverbs.

Noun Clauses   A noun clause can serve in any of the ways that ordinary nouns can.

> *What the neighbor told John* proved to be incorrect. (noun clause as subject)

> The woman asked *when the bus left for Spokane.* (noun clause as direct object)

> I'll give a reward to *whoever returns my billfold.* (noun clause as object of preposition *to*)

Noun clauses normally begin with one of the following words:

Relative Pronouns		Subordinating Conjunctions
who	whoever	when
whom	whomever	why
whose	that	where
what	whatever	how
which	whichever	whether

The relative pronoun *that* is sometimes omitted from the beginning of a clause that acts as a direct object.

> Dr. Kant thinks *(that) he knows everything.*

If a clause is serving as a noun, you can replace it with the word *something* or *someone,* and the sentence will still make sense.

> Dr. Kant thinks *something.*

If the clause is serving as an adjective or an adverb, making the substitution turns the sentence into nonsense.

> The person *who wins the lottery* will receive two million dollars.

> The person *someone* will receive two million dollars.

Adjective Clauses   Like ordinary adjectives, adjective clauses modify nouns and noun substitutes.

cl

Give me one reason *why you feel the way you do.* (Adjective clause modifies noun.)

I'll hire anyone *that Dr. Stone recommends.* (Adjective clause modifies pronoun.)

Generally, adjective clauses begin with one of the following words:

Relative Pronouns	Subordinating Conjunctions
who	when
whom	where
whose	why
what	after
which	before
that	

Sometimes the word that introduces the clause can be omitted.

The chair *(that) we ordered last month* has just arrived. (pronoun *that* omitted but understood)

The man *(whom) we were talking to* is a movie producer. (pronoun *whom* omitted but understood)

Sometimes, too, a preposition comes ahead of the introductory pronoun.

The grace *with which Nelson danced* made the onlookers envious.

An adjective clause may be restrictive and distinguish whatever it modifies from others in the same class, or it may be nonrestrictive and provide more information about whatever it modifies.

Flora wiped up the cereal *that the baby had spilled.* (restrictive clause)

Harriet Thomas, *who was born in Alaska,* now lives in Hawaii. (nonrestrictive clause)

As these examples show, restrictive clauses are not set off with commas, but nonrestrictive clauses are. See pages 674–75 for further information.

Adverb Clauses   These clauses modify verbs, adjectives, adverbs, and sentences, answering the same questions that ordinary adverbs do.

You may go *whenever you wish.* (Adverb clause modifies verb.)

Sandra looked paler *than I had ever seen her look before.* (Adverb clause modifies adjective.)

Darryl shouted loudly *so that the rescue party could hear him.* (Adverb clause modifies adverb.)

Unless everyone cooperates, this plan will never succeed. (Adverb clause modifies whole sentence.)

The word or word group that introduces an adverb clause is always a subordinating conjunction. Here are the most common of these conjunctions, grouped according to the questions they answer.

When? after, as, as soon as, before, since, until, when, whenever, while
Where? where, wherever
How? as if, as though
Why? as, because, now that, since, so that
Under what conditions? although, if, once, provided that, though, unless
To what extent? than

Occasionally in an adverb clause, the omission of one or more words won't hurt its meaning. Such a construction is called an *elliptical clause.*

While (he was) making a sandwich, Garth hummed softly. (*he was* omitted but understood)

Unlike noun and adjective clauses, adverb clauses can often be moved about in their sentences.

Garth hummed *softly while (he was) making a sandwich.*

Usage Considerations　　Like phrases, clauses can help develop sentences as well as smooth out choppiness.

Original	The old grandfather clock ticked loudly through the night.
Revision	The old grandfather clock *that my great-aunt gave me before she died* ticked loudly through the night. (Clause adds information.)
Original	The chemistry professor insisted on lab safety. He had been hurt in a lab explosion the previous year.
Revision	The chemistry professor, *who had been hurt in a lab explosion the previous year,* insisted on lab safety. (Clause adds smoothness.)

To avoid clumsiness, avoid overloaded sentences like the one below:

The old grandfather clock that my great-aunt gave me before she died *and that I took with me to England when my company transferred me there for two years* ticked loudly through the night.

EXERCISE　　*Identify the italicized clauses as noun, adjective, or adverb.*

1. The used car *Sam bought last week* has already broken down.
2. Maria forgot *that the road was closed for repairs.*
3. My dog, *which is a beagle,* is seven years old.
4. Zeke hit his thumb with a hammer *while repairing his deck.*
5. We are much happier *since we moved into our new house.*

cl

6. The golfer finally won the fame *for which he'd struggled so long.*

7. The fact of the matter is *that I don't like Allen very much.*

8. Mr. Evans will be very disturbed *if the speaker arrives late.*

9. *Whoever wrote this brochure* has a great sense of humor.

10. Brad is clearly pleased with the watch *that he received for Christmas.*

11. *While watching the movie,* Jennifer ate popcorn.

12. *Why Chris dropped out of school* is a mystery to me.

Editing to Correct Sentence Errors

Accepted usage improves the smoothness of your prose, makes your writing easier to understand, and demonstrates that you are a careful communicator. These assets, in turn, increase the likelihood that the reader will accept your ideas.

When you've finished revising the first draft of a piece of writing, edit it with a critic's eye to ensure that you eliminate all errors. Circle sentences or parts of them that are faulty or suspect. Then check your circled items against this section of the Handbook, which deals with the most common errors in college writing.

■ Sentence Fragments

A sentence fragment is a group of words that fails to qualify as a sentence but is capitalized and punctuated as if it were a sentence. To be a sentence, a word group must (1) have a subject and a verb and (2) make sense by itself. The first of the following examples has a subject and a verb; the second does not. Neither makes sense by itself.

If you want to remain.

His answer to the question.

Methods of Revision   Eliminating a sentence fragment is not hard. Careful reading often shows that the fragment goes with the sentence that comes just before or just after it. And sometimes two successive fragments can be joined. Note how we've corrected the fragments (italicized) in the following pairs:

Faulty	*Having been warned about the storm.* We decided to stay home.
Revision	Having been warned about the storm, we decided to stay home.
Faulty	*After eating.* The dog took a nap.
Revision	After eating, the dog took a nap.
Faulty	Sally went to work. *Although she felt sick.*
Revision	Sally went to work although she felt sick.

Faulty	Dave bought a new suit. *Over at Bentley's.*
Revision	Dave bought a new suit over at Bentley's.
Faulty	*That bronze clock on the mantel. Once belonged to my grandmother.*
Revision	That bronze clock on the mantel once belonged to my grand-mother.

frag

Joining a fragment to a sentence or to another fragment works only if the problem is simply one of mispunctuation. If the fragment stems from an improperly developed thought, revise the thought into correct sentence form.

Punctuating Your Corrections   When you join a fragment to the following sentence, you need not place a comma between the two unless the fragment has six or more words or if omitting a comma might cause a misreading. When joining a fragment to the preceding sentence, omit a comma unless there is a distinct pause between the two items. The preceding examples illustrate these points.

Intentional Fragments   Fragments are commonly used in conversation and the writing that reproduces it. Professional writers also use fragments to gain special emphasis or create special effects. Pages 230–31 discuss these applications.

CONNECTED DISCOURSE EXERCISE   *Identify and correct the sentence fragments in the following letter:*

Dear Phone Company:

Recently I received a phone bill for over $500. While I do use the phone fairly extensively. Most of the calls I make are local ones. In this case, many of the calls on my bill were to other countries. Including a phone call to New Delhi, India. I can hardly be held responsible for these calls. Especially since I don't know anyone who lives overseas. Since the only long-distance call I made was to Kalamazoo, Michigan. I have deducted the charges for all the other long-distance calls from my bill and am sending you the balance. In order to prevent this type of error from happening again. Would you please have a representative determine why these charges appeared on my bill?

Sincerely,

Desperate

EXERCISE   *Ten main clauses paired with fragments are shown below. In each case identify the sentence (S) and the fragment (F) and then eliminate the fragment.*

1. I would like you to meet Janine Lee. One of my good friends from high school.

2. Jason and Steve bought several posters. To spruce up their dorm room walls.

3. In order to get tickets to the concert. We had to stand in line for hours.

4. After we finish studying for our math test. We plan to go out for pizza.

5. The road to Cedar Lake will be closed for months. Because the flood has washed away the bridge over the Rouge River.

6. Carol bought the new computer. That she had wanted for months.

7. If the debate team lives up to its potential. We are sure to win the state finals.

8. There are several ways for companies to save on energy costs. One of them energy recycling.

9. Kristen first searched the library for information for her report. And then turned to the Internet for additional material.

10. Pleased by the amount of the painting he had already completed. John allowed himself a two-hour break to watch the football game.

ro cs

■ Run-On Sentences and Comma Splices

A run-on, or fused, sentence occurs when one sentence runs into another without anything to mark their junction. A comma splice occurs when only a comma marks the junction. These errors lead your readers to think that you are hasty or careless. Here are several examples:

Run-on sentence	Laura failed to set her alarm she was late for work.
Comma splice	Violets are blooming now, my lawn is covered with them.
Run-on sentence	Rick refused to attend the movie he said he hated horror shows.
Comma splice	Perry watched the road carefully, he still missed his turn.
Run-on sentence	Janet worked on her term paper her friend studied for a calculus test.
Comma splice	Janet worked on her term paper, her friend studied for a calculus test.

Testing for Errors   To check out a possible comma splice or fused sentence, read what precedes and follows the comma or suspected junction and see whether the two parts can stand alone as sentences. If *both parts* can stand alone, there is an error. Otherwise, there is not.

Darryl is a real troublemaker, someday he'll find himself in serious difficulty.

Examination of the parts preceding and following the comma shows that each is a complete sentence:

ro cs

Darryl is a real troublemaker.
Someday he'll find himself in serious difficulty.

The writer has therefore committed a comma splice that needs correction.

Methods of Revision   You can correct run-on sentences and comma splices in several ways.

1. Create two separate sentences.

   Revision   Violets are blooming now. My lawn is covered with them.

   Revision   Rick refused to attend the movie. He said he hated horror shows.

2. Join the sentences with a semicolon.

   Revision   Violets are blooming now; my yard is covered with them.

   Revision   Rick refused to attend the movie; he said he hated horror shows.

3. Join the sentences with a comma and a coordinating conjunction *(and, but, or, nor, for, yet, so)*.

   Revision   Laura failed to set her alarm, *so* she was late for work.

   Revision   Perry watched the road carefully, *but* he still missed his turn.

4. Join the sentences with a semicolon and a conjunctive adverb (see pages 632–33).

   Revision   Laura failed to set her alarm; *consequently,* she was late for work.

   Revision   Violets are blooming now; *in fact,* my yard is covered with them.

5. Introduce one of the sentences with a subordinating conjunction (see pages 635, 639).

   Revision   *Because* Laura failed to set her alarm, she was late for work.

   Revision   Janet worked on her term paper *while* her friend studied for a calculus test.

As our examples show, you can often correct an error in several ways.

CONNECTED DISCOURSE EXERCISE   *Identify and correct the comma splices and run-on sentences in the following letter:*

Dear Desperate:
We are sorry to hear that you are having difficulty paying your bill, it is, however, your responsibility. Unfortunately we

have no way to prevent you from making overseas calls, you have to curb your own tendency to reach out and touch your friends. Following your instructions, we are sending a technician to remove your phone. Please be home this Friday morning he will arrive then. Even though we will remove your phone, you are still responsible for the unpaid portion of your bill, it is your financial obligation. We would dislike referring this matter to a collection agency, it could ruin your credit rating.

Sincerely,

Your friendly phone representative

sv agr

EXERCISE *Indicate whether each item is correct (C), is a run-on sentence (RO), or contains a comma splice (CS) and then correct the faulty items.*

1. Our company's Internet-based sales are up twenty percent; however, our store sales are down thirty percent.

2. Our computer assistants have only had three weeks of training, you cannot expect them to know the answer to every technical question.

3. Ellen worked very hard on her report she really earned her A.

4. The research on the effect of T.V. violence on children remains inconclusive, but still most of us would think that excessive exposure to images of violence would be harmful.

5. Alternative forms of punishment such as home incarceration have proven very effective, nevertheless prison is still the standard punishment for most nonviolent crimes.

6. The photographer accidentally exposed his film to the light as a result all our wedding pictures were ruined.

7. Jason got a terrific tan, he spent the winter break in Florida.

8. While tuberculosis is a terrible disease, it is rare and usually can be treated with antibiotics.

9. Many doctors' offices want to decrease costs they increasingly use physician assistants.

10. We have carefully reviewed your proposal for flexible work hours, we think it would improve employee satisfaction.

■ Subject–Verb Agreement

A verb should agree in number with its subject. Singular verbs should have singular subjects, and plural verbs should have plural subjects.

Correct   My *boss is* a grouch. (singular subject and verb)

Correct   The *apartments have* two bedrooms. (plural subject and verb)

Ordinarily, matching subjects and verbs causes no problems. The following special situations, however, can create difficulties.

Subject and Verb Separated by a Word Group   Sometimes a word group that includes one or more nouns comes between the subject and the verb. When this happens, match the verb with its subject, not a noun in the word group.

Correct   Our *basket* of sandwiches *is* missing.

Correct   Several *books* required for my paper *are* not in the library.

Correct   *Mr. Schmidt,* along with his daughters, *runs* a furniture store.

Correct   The old *bus,* crammed with passengers, *was* unable to reach the top of the hill.

Two Singular Subjects   Most singular subjects joined by *and* take a plural verb.

Correct   The *couch* and *chair were* upholstered in blue velvet.

Sentences like the one above almost never cause problems. With subjects like *restoring cars* and *racing motorcycles,* however, singular verbs are often mistakenly used.

Faulty   *Restoring cars* and *racing motorcycles consumes* most of Frank's time.

Revision   *Restoring cars* and *racing motorcycles consume* most of Frank's time.

When *each* or *every* precedes the subjects, use a *singular* verb in place of a plural.

Correct   Every *book* and *magazine was* badly water-stained.

Singular subjects joined by *or, either—or,* or *neither—nor* also take singular verbs.

Correct   A *pear* or an *apple is* a good afternoon snack.

Correct   Neither *rain* nor *snow slows* our letter carrier.

Finally, use a singular verb when two singular subjects joined by *and* name the same person, place, or thing.

Correct   My *cousin* and business *partner is* retiring next month.

Cousin and *partner* refer to the same person.

One Singular and One Plural Subject   When one singular subject and one plural subject are joined by *or, either—or,* or *neither—nor,* match the verb with the closer of the two.

Correct   Neither *John* nor his *parents were* at home.

Correct   Neither his *parents* nor *John was* at home.

As these examples show, the sentences are usually smoother when the plural subject follows the singular.

Collective Nouns as Subjects   Collective nouns (*assembly, class, committee, family, herd, majority, tribe,* and the like) are singular in form but stand for groups or collections of people or things. Ordinarily, collective nouns are considered to be singular and therefore take singular verbs.

Correct   The *class is* writing a test.

Correct   The *herd was* clustered around the water hole.

Sometimes, though, a collective noun refers to the separate individuals making up the grouping, and then it requires a plural verb.

Correct   The *jury are* in dispute about the verdict.

Sentences in Which the Verb Comes Ahead of the Subject   Sentences that begin with words such as *here, there, how, what,* and *where* fall into this category. With such sentences, the verb must agree with the subject that follows it.

Correct   Here *is* my *house.*

Correct   Where *are* my *shoes?*

Correct   There *is* just one *way* to solve this problem.

Correct   There *go* my *chances* for a promotion.

sv agr

CONNECTED DISCOURSE EXERCISE   *Identify and correct the subject–verb agreement errors in the following letter:*

Regional Accounts Manager:

One of your area phone representatives have seriously misread a letter I submitted with my bill. I refused to pay for long-distance overseas calls since neither I nor my roommate know anyone who lives overseas. Instead of deducting the calls from my bill, she sent someone to remove my phone. Now my phone, along with many of my valuable possessions, have been removed. Unfortunately the technician, whom I allowed into my apartment only after carefully checking his credentials, were a thief. He locked me in a closet and cleared out the apartment. I have called the police, but I also expect the phone company to reimburse me for my losses. There is only two choices. Either the stolen items or a check covering the loss need to be sent to me immediately. Otherwise I am afraid I will be forced to sue. A jury are sure to rule in my favor. In addition, I expect to find that those overseas calls has been deducted from my bill.

Sincerely,

Desparately Desperate

pa agr

> **EXERCISE**   *Choose the correct verb form from the pair in parentheses.*
>
> 1. The library, along with many of the books, (*was, were*) severely damaged by the storm.
> 2. Congress (*retains, retain*) the right to control the country's purse strings.
> 3. A house with two baths and four bedrooms (*is, are*) for sale in my neighborhood.
> 4. What (*does, do*) these new printers cost?
> 5. A van or three cars (*is, are*) needed to drive the wrestling team to the meet.
> 6. Each of these suggestions (*has, have*) a lot of merit.
> 7. John Finch and his assistant (*plans, plan*) to review the contract with you next Friday.
> 8. There (*is, are*) a few advantages to carefully planning your work schedule.
> 9. Every piece of clothing and bedding (*has, have*) to be washed in scalding water.
> 10. Each of our employees (*knows, know*) the answer to the most common questions about our product.

■ Pronoun–Antecedent Agreement

The antecedent of a pronoun is the noun or pronoun to which it refers. Just as subjects should agree with their verbs, pronouns should agree with their antecedents: singular antecedents require singular pronouns, and plural antecedents require plural pronouns. Ordinarily, you will have no trouble matching antecedents and pronouns. The situations below, however, can cause problems.

Indefinite Pronouns as Antecedents   Indefinite pronouns include words like *each, either, neither, any, everybody, somebody,* and *nobody.* Whenever an indefinite pronoun is used as an antecedent, the pronoun that refers to it should be singular.

> *Faulty*   *Neither* of the actors had learned *their* lines.
>
> *Revision*   *Neither* of the actors had learned *his* lines.

As the revised example shows, this rule applies even when the pronoun is followed by a plural noun.

When the gender of the antecedent is unknown, you may follow it with *his or her,* or if this results in awkwardness, rewrite the sentence in the plural.

> *Correct*   *Anyone* who has studied *his or her* assignments properly should do well on the test.
>
> *Correct*   *Those* who have studied *their* assignments properly should do well on the test.

Occasionally, a ridiculous result occurs when a singular pronoun refers to an indefinite pronoun that is obviously plural in meaning. When this happens, rewrite the sentence to eliminate the problem.

> *Faulty*   *Everybody* complained that the graduation ceremony had lasted too long, but I didn't believe *him.*

Revision   Everybody complained that the graduation ceremony had lasted too long, but I didn't agree.

Two Singular Antecedents   Two or more antecedents joined by *and* ordinarily call for a plural pronoun.

Correct   Her briefcase and umbrella were missing from *their* usual place on the hall table.

When *each* or *every* precedes the antecedent, use a singular pronoun.

Incorrect   Every college and university must do *their* best to provide adequate student counseling.

Correct   Every college and university must do *its* best to provide adequate student counseling.

Singular antecedents joined by *or, either–or,* or *neither–nor* call for singular pronouns.

Correct   Neither Carol nor Irene had paid *her* rent for the month.

Applying this rule can sometimes yield an awkward or foolish sentence. When this happens, rewrite the sentence to avoid the problem.

Faulty   Neither James nor Sally has finished *his or her* term project.

Revision   James and Sally have not finished *their* term projects.

Singular antecedents joined by *and* that refer to the same person, place, or thing use a singular pronoun.

Correct   My *cousin* and business *partner* is retiring to *his* condo in Florida next month.

Singular and Plural Antecedents   If one singular and one plural antecedent are joined by *or, either—or,* or *neither—nor,* the pronoun agrees with the closer one.

Correct   Either Terrence James or the Parkinsons will let us use *their* lawn mower.

Correct   Either the Parkinsons or Terrence James will let us use *his* lawn mower.

Sentences of this sort are generally smoother when the plural subject follows the singular.

Collective Nouns as Antecedents   When a collective noun is considered a single unit, the pronoun that refers to it should be singular.

Correct   The *troop* of scouts made *its* way slowly through the woods.

When the collective noun refers to the separate individuals in the group, use a plural pronoun.

Correct   The *staff* lost *their* jobs when the factory closed.

pa agr

pa agr

CONNECTED DISCOURSE EXERCISE   *Identify and correct the pronoun—antecedent agreement errors in the following letter:*

Dear Desperately Desperate:

We were sorry to hear about the theft from your apartment. Apparently a gang of con artists recently had their base of operations in your city. It posed as repair technicians and presented false credentials to anyone expecting their phone to be repaired. Someone also must have intercepted your mail and written their own response since we have no record of any previous letter from you. Clearly neither the representative you mentioned nor the phony phone technician could have held their position with our company. Every one of our technicians must provide us with their fingerprints and take periodic lie detector tests. Further, none of our representatives will answer correspondence since it is not a part of their job description. For these reasons, we do not believe we are responsible for your losses. However, a review of our records shows that you owe $500; we have included a copy of the bill in case you have misplaced the original.

Sincerely,

Accounts Manager

EXERCISE   *Choose the right pronoun from the pair in parentheses.*

1. Company rules require every memo and letter to receive (*its, their*) correct authorization number.
2. Neither the Grangers nor Tom Cauldwell knew (*his, their*) lines by opening night.
3. After weeks of deliberation, the jury finally reached (*its, their*) decision.
4. Maria and Tim completed (*his or her, their*) project by the deadline.
5. Either Roderick or Shannon will present (*his or her, their*) personalized invitation to our special sale.
6. Either Sally or the Randalls will lend us (*her, their*) punch bowl for our party.
7. The class rushed into the computer room and took (*his or her, their*) seats.
8. Everybody has been assigned (*his or her, their*) own log-on name and password.
9. Every one of the women in our police force has proved that (*she, they*) can handle the duties of a officer.
10. Either Richard or Frank will be able to offer you (*his, their*) help in planning the science fiction film festival.

■ Avoiding Faulty Pronoun Reference

Any pronoun except an indefinite pronoun should refer to just one noun or noun substitute—its antecedent. Reference problems result when the pronoun has two or more antecedents, a hidden antecedent, or no antecedent. These errors can cause mixups in meaning as well as ridiculous sentences.

More Than One Antecedent   The following sentences lack clarity because their pronouns have two possible antecedents rather than just one:

> *Faulty*   Take the screens off the windows and wash *them*.

> *Faulty*   Harry told Will that *he* was putting on weight.

The reader can't tell whether the screens or the windows should be washed or who is putting on weight.
Sometimes we see a sentence like this one:

> *Faulty*   If the boys don't eat all the Popsicles, put *them* in the freezer.

In this case, we know it's the Popsicles that should be stored, but the use of *them* creates an amusing sentence.
  Correct these faults by replacing the pronoun with a noun or by rephrasing the sentence.

> *Revision*   Wash the windows after you have taken off the screens.

> *Revision*   Take off the screens so that you can wash the windows.

> *Revision*   Harry told Will, "I am (you are) putting on weight."

> *Revision*   Put any uneaten Popsicles in the freezer.

Hidden Antecedent   An antecedent is hidden if it takes the form of an adjective rather than a noun.

> *Faulty*   The movie theater is closed today, so we can't see *one*.

> *Faulty*   As I passed the tiger's cage, *it* lunged at me.

To correct this fault, replace the pronoun with the noun used as an adjective or switch the positions of the pronoun and the noun and make any needed changes in their forms.

> *Revision*   The theater is closed today, so we can't see a movie.

> *Revision*   As I passed its cage, the tiger lunged at me.

No Antecedent   A no-antecedent sentence lacks any noun to which the pronoun can refer. Sentences of this sort occur frequently in everyday conversation but should be avoided in formal writing. The examples below illustrate this error:

> *Faulty*   The lecture was boring, but *they* took notes anyway.

> *Faulty*   On the news program, *it* told about a new crisis in the Persian Gulf.

pr ref

To set matters right, substitute a suitable noun for the pronoun or reword the sentence.

> *Revision*   The lecture was boring, but the students took notes anyway.

> *Revision*   The news program told about a new crisis in the Persian Gulf.

Sometimes a *this, that, it,* or *which* will refer to a whole idea rather than a single noun. This usage is acceptable provided the writer's meaning is obvious, as in this example:

> *Correct*   The instructor spoke very softly, *which* meant we had difficulty hearing him.

Problems occur, however, when the reader can't figure out which of two or more ideas the pronoun refers to.

> *Faulty*   Ginny called Sally two hours after the agreed-upon time and postponed their shopping trip one day. *This* irritated Sally very much.

What caused Sally to be irritated—the late call, the postponement of the trip, or both? Again, rewording or adding a clarifying word will correct the problem.

> *Revision*   Ginny called Sally two hours after the agreed-upon time and postponed their shopping trip one day. This *tardiness* irritated Sally very much.

> *Revision*   Ginny called Sally two hours after the agreed-upon time and postponed their shopping trip one day. Ginny's *change of plans* irritated Sally very much.

The first of these examples illustrates the addition of a clarifying word; the second illustrates rewriting.

CONNECTED DISCOURSE EXERCISE   *Identify and correct any faulty pronoun references in the following memorandum:*

> TO: Director of Food Services, Groan University
> FROM: Vice-President of College Services
> DATE: February 19, 20__ __
> SUBJECT: Student Complaints about Cafeteria
> Complaints about food quality and cafeteria hours are common
> but easily resolved. They can be extended by simply installing
> vending machines. It might not make for a nutritious meal, but
> it certainly will undercut some of the dissatisfaction. Of
> course, no matter how good the food, they will complain. Still,
> you can partially defuse those complaints by having students
> list their major concerns and then meeting them. Of course, you

can always increase student satisfaction by purchasing a soft
ice cream machine and offering it for dessert.

EXERCISE *Indicate whether each sentence is correct (C) or contains a faulty pronoun reference (F) and then correct any faulty sentences.*

1. When Al accidentally slammed down on his car's accelerator instead of the
   brake, it roared forward into the intersection.
2. They have informed me that we have seen a 15 percent increase in sales this
   month.
3. When the supervisor walked by the water cooler, they stopped talking.
4. I like trout fishing because it is very relaxing.
5. Since I knew that our employees found their chairs uncomfortable, I replaced
   them with new ones.
6. In the report, it suggested that we needed to be more attentive to employee
   suggestions.
7. Because the batting cap hurt his head, Fred removed it.
8. Frank told his best friend that his wife wanted to spend more time with him.
9. At Electronic City, they sell many different brands of computers.
10. Janine asked Caroline if she could rewrite her paper for her English class.

shft

■ Avoiding Unwarranted Shifts in Person

Pronouns can be in the first person, second person, or third person. *First-
person* pronouns identify people who are talking or writing about themselves, *second-person* pronouns identify people being addressed directly, and
third-person pronouns identify persons or things that are being written or
spoken about. The following table sorts pronouns according to person:

First Person	Second Person	Third Person
I	you	he
me	your	she
my	yours	it
mine	yourself	his
we	yourselves	her
us		hers
our		its
ours		one
ourselves		they
		their
		theirs
		indefinite pronouns

All nouns are in the third person. As you revise, be alert for unwarranted shifts
from one person to another.

Faulty   I liked *my* British vacation better than *my* vacation in France and Italy because *you* didn't have language problems.

Revision   I liked *my* British vacation better than *my* vacation in France and Italy because *I* didn't have language problems.

Faulty   Holidays are important to *everyone*. They boost *your* spirits and provide a break from *our* daily routine.

Revision   Holidays are important to *everyone*. They boost *one's* spirits and provide a break from *one's* daily routine.

Faulty   The taller the *golfer,* the more club speed *you* will have with a normally paced swing.

Revision   The taller the *golfer,* the more club speed *he* or *she* will have with a normally paced swing.

As these examples show, the shift can occur within a single sentence or when the writer moves from one sentence to another.

Some shifts in person, however, are warranted. Read the following correct sentence:

Correct   *I* want *you* to deliver these flowers to Ms. Willoughby by three o'clock. *She* needs them for a party.

Here the speaker identifies himself or herself (*I*) while speaking directly to a listener (*you*) about someone else (*she*). In this case, shifts are needed to get the message across.

CONNECTED DISCOURSE EXERCISE   *Identify and correct the unwarranted shifts in person in the following paragraph:*

> Good health is clearly important to you. But it is one's responsibility to ensure our own good health. You can start with simple exercises. We would like to provide you with a low-impact aerobics videotape for only $9. We guarantee that the more out of shape the customer, the quicker you will notice the benefits. The way our bodies feel affects the quality of one's lives. Let our tape help you to a better life.

EXERCISE   *Indicate whether the sentence is correct (C) or contains an unwarranted shift in person (S). Correct faulty sentences.*

1. After the teacher collected our essays, she told the students that she would return the graded papers on Wednesday.

2. For someone to be successful in today's marketplace, you need to have adequate technical skills.

3. If you each will bring the results of your assigned research to the next meeting, we will be ready to begin working on our collaborative report.

4. Because our tickets were in the nosebleed section of the stadium, many of the fans felt they would have been off watching the football game on TV.

5. If you want theater tickets, I will be glad to purchase them on my way home from work.

6. Anyone who would like to purchase the discounted Caribbean cruise tickets should place your order by May 15.

7. We enjoy living in the Grand Rapids area very much; you have access to theater, sporting events, and fine dining.

8. On major holidays, most Americans travel long distances, often at great inconvenience, to visit our relatives.

9. If you would like to learn to kayak, novices can usually get free lessons from the people who sell kayaks.

10. In our attempt to determine whether there has been an increase in tornado activity over the last twenty years, the researchers collected data on storm sightings and damage reports.

case

■ Using the Right Pronoun Case

Case means the changes in form that a personal pronoun (see pages 614–15) undergoes to show its function in a sentence. English has three cases: the *subjective*, the *nonsubjective* (objective), and the *possessive*. The following chart shows the different forms:

Subjective Form	Nonsubjective Form	Possessive Form
I	me	my, mine
he	him	his
she	her	her, hers
we	us	our, ours
you	you	your, yours
they	them	their, theirs
who	whom	whose

The subjective case is used for subjects and subject complements, the nonsubjective for direct objects, indirect objects, and objects of prepositions. The possessive case shows ownership and is also used with gerunds.

The following pointers will help you select the proper pronoun as you revise.

We and Us Preceding Nouns   Nouns that serve as subjects take the pronoun *we*. Other nouns take the pronoun *us*.

Correct   *We* tourists will fly home tomorrow. (*We* accompanies the subject.)

Correct   The guide showed *us* tourists through the cathedral. (*Us* accompanies a nonsubject.)

If you can't decide which pronoun is right, mentally omit the noun and read the sentence to yourself, first with one pronoun and then with the other. Your ear will indicate the correct form.

My mother made (*we, us*) children vanilla pudding for dessert.

Omitting *children* shows immediately that *us* is the right choice.

> *Correct*   My mother made *us* children vanilla pudding for dessert.

Pronouns Paired with Nouns   When such a combination serves as the subject of a sentence or accompanies the subject, use the subject form of the pronoun. When the combination plays a nonsubject role, use the nonsubject form of the pronoun.

> *Correct*   Arlene and *I* plan to join the Peace Corps. (*I* is part of the compound subject.)

> *Correct*   Two people, Mary and *I*, will represent our school at the meeting. (*I* is part of a compound element accompanying the subject.)

> *Correct*   The superintendent told Kevin and *him* that they would be promoted soon. (*Him* is part of a compound nonsubject.)

> *Correct*   The project was difficult for Jeffrey and *him* to complete. (*Him* is part of a compound nonsubject.)

Again, mentally omitting the noun from the combination will tell you which pronoun is correct.

Who and Whom in Dependent Clauses   Use *who* for the subjects of dependent clauses; otherwise use *whom*.

> *Correct*   The Mallarys prefer friends *who are interested in the theater.* (*Who* is the subject of the clause.)

> *Correct*   Barton is a man *whom very few people like.* (*Whom* is not the subject of the clause.)

A simple test will help you decide between *who* and *whom*. First, mentally isolate the dependent clause. Next, block out the pronoun in question and then insert *he* (or *she*) and *him* (or *her*) at the appropriate spot in the remaining part of the clause. If *he* (or *she*) sounds better, *who* is right. If *him* (or *her*) sounds better, *whom* is right. Let's use this test on the sentence below:

> The woman *who(m) Scott is dating* works as a mechanical engineer.
> Scott is dating (she, her.)

Clearly *her* is correct; therefore, *whom* is the proper form.

> *Correct*   The woman *whom Scott is dating* works as a mechanical engineer.

Pronouns as Subject Complements   In formal writing, pronouns that serve as subject complements (see page 611) always take the subject form.

> *Correct*   It is *I*.

> *Correct*   It was *she* who bought the old Parker mansion.

case

This rule, however, is often ignored in informal writing.

It's *her.*

That's *him* standing over by the door.

Comparisons Using *than* or *as . . . as*   Comparisons of this kind often make no direct statement about the second item of comparison. When the second naming word is a pronoun, you may have trouble choosing the right one.

Harriet is less outgoing than *(they, them).*

My parents' divorce saddened my sister as much as *(I, me).*

Not to worry. Expand the sentence by mentally supplying the missing material. Then try the sentence with each pronoun and see which sounds right.

Harriet is less outgoing than *(they, them)* are.

My parents' divorce saddened my sister as much as it did *(I, me).*

Obviously *they* is the right choice for the first sentence, and *me* is the right choice for the second one.

Correct   Harriet is less outgoing than *they* are.

Correct   My parents' divorce saddened my sister as much as it did *me.*

Pronouns Preceding Gerunds   Use the possessive form of a pronoun that precedes a gerund (see page 635).

I dislike *their* leaving without saying goodbye.

Ted can't understand *her* quitting such a good job.

This usage emphasizes the action named by the gerund instead of the person or persons performing it. Thus, in the above sentences, the possessive form of the pronoun signals that it's the *leaving* the writer dislikes and the *quitting* that Ted can't understand. The persons involved are secondary.

When the pronoun precedes a participle (see pages 634–35), it should be in the nonsubject case. The emphasis is then on the actor rather than the action.

Jennifer caught *them* listening to records instead of studying.

In this example, Jennifer caught the listeners, not the listening.

If you have trouble deciding between the nonsubject and possessive forms of a pronoun, ask yourself whether you want to emphasize the action or the actor; then proceed accordingly.

CONNECTED DISCOURSE EXERCISE   *Identify and correct the pronoun case errors in the following paragraph:*

Between my brother and I, we are always able to pull at
least five good-sized trout a day from the creek behind our
house. Us rural trout fishermen just seem to have the knack. Of

course, those city fishermen whom insist on employing artificial
flies won't appreciate our methods even if they can't do as well
as us. We just let our bait, usually a juicy worm, float downstream to the waiting trout. Of course, my brother won't let the
fishing interfere with him sleeping. In fact, it was him that
developed the idea of looping the line around his toe so that he
would wake up when a trout took the bait. Others have told my
brother and I that this method is dangerous, but neither of us
has lost a toe yet. Of course, the people who we invite to dinner don't complain about our methods, and they seem to enjoy the
fish.

EXERCISE *Choose the right form of the pronoun for each of the following sentences. For the purpose of this exercise, assume that there would have been the appropriate pronoun antecedent in the sentence preceding the one that is shown.*

1. No one is as pleased as (*I, me*) by John's recent promotion to assistant vice-president.
2. There is no excuse for (*him, his*) yelling at us in public.
3. The newspaper's editor praised Marge and (*I, me*) for our co-authored article on women in the military.
4. Randy has a better grasp of European history than (*I, me*).
5. Megan is one student (*who, whom*) I believe really understands the importance of writing well.
6. (*We, Us*) Americans pride ourselves on our individuality.
7. The conductor decided that Marie and (*I, me*) should sing a duet at the next recital.
8. Rilke is the poet (*who, whom*) I like best.
9. The judge told (*we, us*) contestants that we would be called when it was our turn.
10. The manager of the movie theater gave Tom and (*I, me*) four free passes.

■ Avoiding Inconsistency in Showing Time

Inconsistencies occur when a writer shifts from the past tense to the present or vice versa without a corresponding shift in the time of the events being described. The following paragraph contains an uncalled-for shift from the present tense to the past:

As *The Most Dangerous Game* opens, Sanger Rainsford, a famous hunter and author, and his old friend Whitney are standing on the deck of a yacht and discussing a mysterious island as the ship passes near it. Then, after everyone else has gone to bed, Rainsford manages to fall overboard. He swims to the island and ends up at a chateau owned by General Zaroff, a refugee from the Communist takeover in Russia. Zaroff, bored with hunting animals, has turned to hunting humans on his desert island. Inevitably, Rainsford is turned out into the jungle to be hunted down. There were [shift to past tense] actually four hunts over a three-day period, and at the end of the last one, Rainsford jumped into the sea, swam across a cove to the chateau, and killed Zaroff in the general's own bedroom. Afterward he sleeps [shift back to present tense] and decides "he had never slept in a better bed."

The sentence with the unwarranted shift in tense should read as follows:

There are actually four hunts over a three-day period, and at the end of the last one, Rainsford jumps into the sea, swims across a cove to the chateau, and kills Zaroff in the general's own bedroom.

time

The time shift in the quotation part of the final sentence is justified because the sleeping has occurred before Rainsford's thoughts about it.

A second kind of inconsistency results when a writer fails to distinguish the immediate past from the less immediate past. The following sentence illustrates this error:

Faulty   Mary *answered* all thirty test questions when the class ended.

This sentence indicates that Mary completed all thirty test questions during the final instant of the class, an impossibility. When you detect this type of error in your writing, determine which action occurred first and then correct the error by adding *had* to the verb. In this case, the first verb needs correcting:

Revision   Mary *had answered* all thirty test questions when the class ended.

Besides adding *had,* you may sometimes need to alter the verb form.

Faulty   Before he turned twenty, John *wrote* two novels.

Revision   Before he turned twenty, John *had written* two novels.

CONNECTED DISCOURSE EXERCISE   *Identify and correct any inconsistencies in showing time in the following passage:*

```
    There is no better time to go swimming than at night. The
summer after I had graduated from high school, I worked for a
landscaping company. After a sweaty day mowing lawns and dig-
ging up gardens, all of us who worked there would jump into the
back of Dick's old pickup and rattle out to Woods Lake. It is
just dark as we arrive. The moon is beautiful, reflected in that
black mirror set in a frame of hills. We stumble down a small,
sandy hill to the beach, where we strip off our dusty jeans and
sweaty shirts before plunging into the cool reflection of
stars.
```

EXERCISE   *Indicate whether each sentence is correct (C) or contains an unwarranted shift (S) in tense. Then correct the faulty sentences.*

1. A thin wisp of smoke drifts from under the hood, and then the engine burst into flames.

2. After Kyra finishes checking the computers for viruses, she will load the new software.

3. Jason took on many projects but finishes few of them.

4. After I finished preparing dinner, I went for a long walk.

5. As Charlie laid pieces of the model on the table, his wife picks them up.

6. As soon as the snow falls, we break out our cross-country skis.

7. David is building his own house but found it harder work than he anticipated.

8. While Robert applies the adhesive, David carefully positioned the floor tiles.

9. Tonya stood in line for the movie tickets while Doug searches for a parking space.

10. Although it started to rain heavily, Debbie continues to mow the lawn.

■ Avoiding Misuse of Adjectives and Adverbs

Inexperienced writers often use adjectives when they should use adverbs and also confuse the comparative and superlative forms of these parts of speech when making comparisons.

Misusing Adjectives for Adverbs   Although most adjectives can be misused as adverbs, the following seven, listed with the corresponding adverbs, cause the most difficulty.

Adjectives	Adverbs
awful	awfully
bad	badly
considerable	considerably
good	well
most	almost
real	really
sure	surely

The following sentences show typical errors:

Faulty   Bryan did *good* in his first golf lesson. (*good* mistakenly used to modify verb *did*)

Faulty   *Most* every graduate from our auto service program receives several job offers. (*Most* mistakenly used to modify adjective *every*)

Faulty   The speech was delivered *real* well. (*real* mistakenly used to modify adverb *well*)

Because adverbs modify verbs, adjectives, and other adverbs (see page 628), and adjectives modify nouns and noun substitutes (see page 626), the above sentences clearly require adverbs.

Revision	Bryan did *well* in his first golf lesson.
Revision	*Almost* every graduate from our auto service program receives several job offers.
Revision	The speech was delivered *really* well.

In one notable case, an adverb is commonly misused as an adjective.

Faulty	I feel *badly* about providing the wrong phone number. (*Badly* is mistakenly used as a subject complement.)
Revision	I feel *bad* about providing the wrong phone number.

If you can't decide whether a sentence requires an adjective or an adverb, determine the part of speech of the word being modified and proceed accordingly.

Confusing the Comparative and Superlative Forms in Comparisons   The comparative form of adjectives and adverbs is used to compare two things, the superlative form to compare three or more things. Adjectives with fewer than three syllables generally add *-er* to make the comparative form and *-est* to make the superlative form (tall, tall*er,* tall*est*). Adjectives with three or more syllables generally add *more* to make the comparative and *most* to make the superlative (enchanting, *more* enchanting, *most* enchanting), as do most adverbs of two or more syllables (loudly, *more* loudly, *most* loudly).

When making comparisons, beginning writers sometimes mistakenly use double comparatives or double superlatives.

Faulty	Harry is *more taller* than James. (double comparative)
Faulty	The Chrysler Building has the *most splendidest* lobby I've ever seen. (double superlative)

The correct versions read as follows:

Revision	Harry is *taller* than James.
Revision	The Chrysler Building has the *most splendid* lobby I've ever seen.

In addition, writers may erroneously use the superlative form, rather than the comparative form, to compare two things.

Faulty	Barry is the *richest* of the two brothers.
Faulty	Jeremy is the *most talented* of those two singers.

Here are the sentences correctly written:

Revision	Barry is the *richer* of the two brothers.
Revision	Jeremy is the *more talented* of those two singers.

Reserve the superlative form for comparing three or more items.

Correct	Barry is the *richest* of the three brothers.
Correct	Jeremy is the *most talented* of those four singers.

CONNECTED DISCOURSE EXERCISE   *Identify and correct the adjective–adverb errors in the following paragraph:*

mis
adj/adv

mm

> This year our football team is outstanding. Spike Jones, our quarterback, has been playing real good this past season. Stan Blunder, the most talented of our two ends, hasn't dropped a pass all season. The team can most always count on Stan to catch the crucial first-down pass. Of course, the team wouldn't be where it is today without John Schoolyard's good coaching. He has made this team much more better than it was even a year ago. Only the kicking team has done bad this season. Of course, with this most wonderfulest offense, the defensive players haven't gotten much practice. The good news is, then, that we can sure expect to watch some terrific college football for years to come.

EXERCISE   *For each of the following sentences, choose the proper word from the pair in parentheses:*

1. The milk in the refrigerator tastes (*bad, badly*).
2. Old science fiction movies can be (*real, really*) funny to watch because of the clumsy special effects and stilted dialogue.
3. Steve did (*good, well*) on his history project.
4. The Vandorns have the (*prettiest, most prettiest*) house in the development.
5. Dana is the (*quieter, quietest*) of our three children.
6. Terry hurt his knees (*bad, badly*) playing football.
7. The Mustang is the (*less, least*) expensive of the two sports cars you are considering.
8. (*Most, Almost*) all of our employees make use of the day care facility we provide on the premises.
9. It is (*real, really*) important to read the entire manual.
10. The Powermax is the (*stronger, strongest*) of the three kinds of garage door openers we sell.

■ Avoiding Misplaced Modifiers

A misplaced modifier is a word or word group that is improperly separated from the word it modifies. When separation of this type occurs, the sentence often sounds awkward, ridiculous, or confusing.

Usually, you can correct this error by moving the modifier next to the word it is intended to modify. Occasionally, you'll also need to alter some of the phrasing.

Faulty   There is a bicycle in the basement *with chrome fenders*. (The basement appears to have chrome fenders.)

Faulty   David received a phone call from his uncle *that infuriated him*. (The uncle appears to have infuriated David.)

Revision   There is a bicycle *with chrome fenders* in the basement.

Revision   David received an *infuriating* phone call from his uncle. (Note the change in wording.)

In shifting the modifier, don't inadvertently create another faulty sentence.

Faulty   Fritz bought a magazine with an article about Michael Jackson *at the corner newsstand.* (The article appears to tell about Jackson's visit to the corner newsstand.)

Faulty   Fritz bought a magazine *at the corner newsstand* with an article about Michael Jackson. (The corner newsstand appears to have an article about Jackson.)

Revision   *At the corner newsstand,* Fritz bought a magazine with an article about Michael Jackson.

mm

As you revise, watch also for *squinting modifiers*—that is, modifiers positioned so that the reader doesn't know whether they are supposed to modify what comes ahead of them or what follows them.

Faulty   The man who was rowing the boat *frantically* waved toward the onlookers on the beach.

Is the man rowing frantically or waving frantically? Correct this kind of error by repositioning the modifier so that the ambiguity disappears.

Revision   The man who was *frantically* rowing the boat waved toward the onlookers on the beach.

Revision   The man who was rowing the boat waved *frantically* toward the onlookers on the beach.

EXERCISE   *Indicate whether each sentence is correct (C) or contains a misplaced modifier (MM). Correct faulty sentences.*

1. Jason handed his report to his teacher neatly tucked into a binder.
2. The girl driving past the school wildly waved at her friends.
3. The dancers practiced Swan Lake for a month before the performance.
4. I tossed the rainbow trout to my brother still hooked firmly in the mouth.
5. Most companies do not like placing managers in charge of employees who are inexperienced.
6. There is a computer in our classroom that beeps loudly at the most unexpected times.
7. You can learn about recent volcanic eruptions at your local library.
8. Steve devoured greasy barbecued spareribs wearing a new suit.
9. The instructor reminded students on the last day of classes to turn in their twenty-page paper.
10. Stacey found beautiful and inexpensive macramé wall hangings for her dorm room in the Bahamas.

■ Avoiding Dangling Modifiers

A dangling modifier is a phrase or clause that lacks clear connection to the word or words it is intended to modify. As a result, sentences are inaccurate, often comical. Typically, the modifier leads off the sentence, although it can also come at the end.

Sometimes the error occurs because the sentence fails to specify who or what is modified. At other times, the separation is too great between the modifier and what it modifies.

dm

Faulty	*Walking in the meadow,* wildflowers surrounded us. (The wildflowers appear to be walking in the meadow.)
Faulty	Dinner was served *after saying grace.* (The dinner appears to have said grace.)
Faulty	*Fatigued by the violent exercise,* the cool shower was very relaxing. (The cool shower appears to have been fatigued.)

The first of these sentences is faulty because the modifier is positioned too far away from *us.* The other two are faulty because they do not identify who said grace or found the shower relaxing.

You can correct dangling modifiers in two basic ways. First, leave the modifier unchanged and rewrite the main part of the sentence so that it begins with the term actually modified. Second, rewrite the modifier so that it has its own subject and verb, thereby eliminating the inaccuracy.

Revision	*Walking in the meadow,* we were surrounded by wildflowers. (The main part of the sentence has been rewritten.)
Revision	*As we walked in the meadow,* wildflowers surrounded us. (The modifier has been rewritten.)
Revision	Dinner was served *after we had said grace.* (The modifier has been rewritten.)
Revision	*Fatigued by the violent exercise,* Ted found the cool shower very relaxing. (The main part of the sentence has been rewritten.)
Revision	*Because Ted was fatigued by the violent exercise,* the cool shower was very relaxing. (The modifier has been rewritten.)

Ordinarily, either part of the sentence can be rewritten, but sometimes only one part can.

EXERCISE   *Indicate whether each sentence is correct (C) or contains a dangling modifier (DM). Correct faulty sentences.*

1. After listening to a tape of Orson Wells' radio broadcast of *The War of the Worlds,* I understood why many who tuned into the middle of the broadcast panicked.
2. The baseball game will start after singing *The Star-Spangled Banner.*

3. Looking at the night sky, a million stars seemed to smile down on us.

4. Driving with his emergency brake on, Matt wore down the brake pads.

5. Having scored 100 percent on the pre-test, the teacher placed two students in the next level math class.

6. Picasso was known to leave customers waiting for several days, painting furiously.

7. John cataloged his CD collection, listing each CD in a database.

8. Sitting on the back porch, a black bear shuffled across the lawn to raid our garbage cans.

9. Please send an e-mail to the project head listing your concerns.

10. Rushing over the banks, Main Street was soon under three feet of water.

■ Avoiding Nonparallelism

Nonparallelism results when equivalent ideas follow different grammatical forms. One common kind of nonparallelism occurs with words or word groups in pairs or in a series.

| *Faulty* | Althea enjoys *jogging, to bike,* and *to swim.* |

| *Faulty* | The superintendent praised the workers *for their productivity* and *because they had an excellent safety record.* |

| *Faulty* | The banner was *old, faded,* and *it had a rip.* |

Note how rewriting the sentences in parallel form improves their smoothness.

| *Revision* | Althea enjoys *jogging, biking,* and *swimming.* |

| *Revision* | The superintendent praised the workers for *their productivity* and *their excellent safety record.* |

| *Revision* | The banner was *old, faded,* and *ripped.* |

Nonparallelism also occurs when correlative conjunctions *(either—or, neither—nor, both—and,* and *not only—but also)* are followed by unlike elements.

| *Faulty* | That sound *either* was a thunderclap *or* an explosion. |

| *Faulty* | The basement was *not only* poorly lighted *but also* it had a foul smell. |

Ordinarily, repositioning one of the correlative conjunctions will solve the problem. Sometimes, however, one of the grammatical elements must be rewritten.

| *Revision* | That sound was *either* a thunderclap *or* an explosion. (*Either* has been repositioned.) |

| *Revision* | The basement was *not only* poorly lighted *but also* foul smelling. (The element following *but also* has been rewritten.) |

> **EXERCISE**   *Indicate whether each sentence is correct (C) or nonparallel (NP). Correct faulty sentences.*
>
>   1. The cause of the fire either was faulty wiring or an overloaded outlet.
>
>   2. After graduation, Marci will be moving to Chicago and work for a large public relations firm.
>
>   3. For spring break, Steve and his friends plan to visit either New Orleans or Orlando.
>
>   4. A good candidate for social work enjoys talking with people, helps solve problems, and seeing projects through to their conclusion.
>
>   5. This course will involve reading a number of short stories, and you will need to turn in weekly journal responses.
>
>   6. Although he was an excellent auto mechanic, Andy could neither repair air conditioning units nor car stereos.
>
>   7. Canton chicken balls are sweet, tangy, and satisfying.
>
>   8. In my spare time, I enjoy reading, canoeing, and to play the piano.
>
>   9. As stage manger, Susan had to design, construct, and maintain the set for the school play.
>
>   10. As a reference librarian, Colin is responsible for instructing students in how to perform database searches, helping researchers find the material they need, maintaining the reference section, and he also manages the patent collection.

■ Avoiding Faulty Comparisons

A faulty comparison results if you (1) mention one of the items being compared but not the other, (2) omit words needed to clarify the relationship, or (3) compare different sorts of items. Advertisers often offend in the first way.

> *Faulty*   Irish tape has better adhesion.

With what other tape is Irish tape being compared? Scotch tape? All other transparent tape? Mentioning the second term of a comparison eliminates reader guesswork.

> *Revision*   Irish tape has better adhesion than any other transparent tape.

Two clarifying words, *other* and *else,* are frequently omitted from comparisons, creating illogical sentences.

> *Faulty*   Sergeant McNabb is more conscientious than any officer in his precinct.
>
> *Faulty*   Stretch French is taller than anyone on his basketball team.

The first sentence is illogical because McNabb is one of the officers in his precinct and therefore cannot be more conscientious than any officer in the precinct. Similarly, because French is a member of his basketball team, he can't be taller than anyone on his team. Adding *other* to the first sentence and *else* to the second corrects matters.

Revision	Sergeant McNabb is more conscientious than any *other* officer in his precinct.
Revision	Stretch French is taller than anyone *else* on his basketball team.

Comparing unlike items is perhaps the most common kind of comparison error. Here are two examples:

Faulty	The cities in California are larger than North Dakota.
Faulty	The cover of this book is much more durable than the other book.

comp

The first sentence compares the cities of California with a state, while the second compares the cover of a book with a whole book. Correction consists of rewriting each sentence so that it compares like items.

Revision	The cities in California are larger than *those in* North Dakota.
Revision	The cover of this book is much more durable than *that of* the other book.

CONNECTED DISCOURSE EXERCISE   *Identify and correct the misplaced modifiers, dangling modifiers, nonparallelism, and faulty comparisons in the following memorandum:*

```
TO: All Residency Hall Advisors in Knuckles Hall
FROM: John Knells, Residency Hall Director
DATE: March 13, 20_ _
SUBJECT: Noise in Residence Hall
Recently I received a report from a student that deeply dis-
turbed me. Apparently, after quiet hours students still have
visitors in their rooms, are playing their stereos loudly, and
are even staging boxing matches in the halls. The student who
wrote me desperately tries to study. However, he is often forced
to leave his room disturbed by the noise. He was not the only one
to complain. You should know that we have had more complaints
about Knuckles Hall than any dorm on campus. Since discussing
this problem with you at the last staff meeting, things haven't
seemed to get any better. The rules are not only poorly enforced
but also they are completely ignored. Your job performance is
```

worse than the students. If you don't improve immediately, I
will be forced to dismiss you.

EXERCISE   *Indicate whether each sentence is correct (C) or contains a faulty comparison (FC). Correct any faulty comparison.*

1. *Death of a Salesman* is performed more often than any American play.
2. The power of today's laptop computers is much greater than the large defense department mainframes of the 1950s.
3. This quarter's earning report shows significantly greater net profits.
4. The Sunday brunch at the 1913 room is much more elegant than the Eatery.
5. Of the two quarterbacks, Allen has a stronger throwing arm than Tom.
6. In contrast to your car, I usually get 40 miles to the gallon.
7. The winters in North Dakota are much worse than Maine.
8. Our new ice cream shop offers many more flavors.
9. The paint on the front of the house is much lighter than the back.
10. Professor Hinkley has published many more articles than the other members of his department.

comp

Editing to Correct Faulty Punctuation and Mechanics

Punctuation marks indicate relationships among different sentence elements. As a result, these marks help clarify the meaning of written material. Similarly, a knowledge of mechanics—capitalization, abbreviations, numbers, and italics—helps you avoid distracting inconsistencies.

This part of the Handbook covers the fundamentals of punctuation and mechanics. Review it carefully when you edit your final draft.

■ Apostrophes

Apostrophes (') show possession, mark contractions, and indicate plurals that are singled out for special attention.

Possession   Possessive apostrophes usually show ownership *(Mary's cat)*. Sometimes, though, they identify the works of creative people *(Hemingway's novels)* or indicate an extent of time or distance *(one hour's time, one mile's distance)*.

Possessive apostrophes are used with nouns and with pronouns like *someone, no one, everybody, each other,* and *one another.* The possessive form is easily recognized because it can be converted to a prepositional phrase beginning with *of.*

The collar of the dog

The whistle of the wind

The intention of the corporation

The birthday of Scott

To show possession with pronouns like those above, singular nouns, and plural nouns that do not end in an *s,* add an apostrophe followed by an *s.*

669

Someone's car is blocking our drive. (possessive of pronoun *someone*)

The *manager's* reorganization plan will take effect next week. (possessive of singular noun *manager*)

The *women's* lounge is being redecorated. (possessive of plural noun *women*)

Sentences that make comparisons sometimes include two possessives, the second coming at the very end. In such cases, be sure to use an apostrophe with the second possessive.

Birmingham's football team is much better than *Central's.*

With singular nouns that end in *s,* the possessive is sometimes formed by merely adding an apostrophe at the end (*James' helmet*). The preferred usage, however, is *'s* (*James's helmet*) unless the addition of the *s* would make it awkward to pronounce the word.

Moses's followers entered the Promised Land. (awkward pronunciation of *Moses's*)

Moses' followers entered the Promised Land. (nonawkward pronunciation of *Moses'*)

Plural nouns ending in *s* form the possessive by adding only an apostrophe at the end.

All the *ladies'* coats are on sale today. (possessive of plural noun *ladies*)

The *workers'* lockers were moved. (possessive of plural noun *workers*)

To show joint ownership by two or more persons, use the possessive form for the last-named person only. To show individual ownership, use the possessive form for each person's name.

Ronald and *Joan's* boat badly needed overhauling. (joint ownership)

Laura's and *Alice's* term projects are almost completed. (individual owner-ship)

Hyphenated nouns form the possessive by adding *'s* to the last word.

My *mother-in-law's* house is next to mine.

Never use an apostrophe with the possessive pronouns *his, hers, whose, its, ours, yours, theirs.*

This desk is *his;* the other one is *hers.* (no apostrophes needed)

Contractions Contractions of words or numbers omit one or more letters or numerals. An apostrophe shows exactly where the omission occurs.

Wasn't that a disappointing concert? (contraction of *was not*)

Around here, people still talk about the blizzard of *'79.* (contraction of *1979*)

Don't confuse the contraction *it's*, meaning *it is* or *it has*, with the possessive pronoun *its*, which should never have an apostrophe. If you're puzzled by an *its* that you've written, try this test. Expand the *its* to *it is* or *it has* and see whether the sentence still makes sense. If it does, the *its* is a contraction and needs the apostrophe. If the result is nonsense, the *its* is a possessive pronoun and does not get an apostrophe. Here are some examples:

Its awfully muggy today.

Its been an exciting trip.

Every dog has *its* day.

The first example makes sense when the *its* is expanded to *it is*.

It is awfully muggy today.

The second makes sense when the *its* is expanded to *it has*.

It has been an exciting trip.

Both of these sentences therefore require apostrophes.

It's awfully muggy today.

It's been an exciting trip.

The last sentence, however, turns into nonsense when the *its* is expanded.

Every dog has *it is* day.

Every dog has *it has* day.

In this case, the *its* is a possessive pronoun and requires no apostrophe.

Every dog has *its* day.

Plurals   To improve clarity, the plurals of letters, numbers, symbols, and words being singled out for special attention are written with apostrophes.

Mind your *p*'s and *q*'s. (plurals of letters)

Your *5*'s and *6*'s are hard to tell apart. (plurals of numbers)

The formula was sprinkled with *Π*'s and *Σ*'s. (plurals of symbols)

Don't use so many *however*'s and *therefore*'s in your writing. (plurals of words)

Apostrophes can be used, though they are not needed, to form the plurals of abbreviations.

How many *CD*'s (or *CDs*) do you own? (plurals of abbreviation for *compact discs*)

When no danger of confusion exists, an *s* alone will suffice.

During the late *1960s*, many university students demanded changes in academic life.

CONNECTED DISCOURSE EXERCISE   *Supply, delete, or relocate apostrophes as necessary in the following memorandum:*

TO: The Records Office Staff

FROM: The Assistant Registrar

DATE: January 27, 20__ __

SUBJECT: Faulty Student Transcripts

Recently, we have had too many student complaints' about hand-written transcripts. Apparently its hard to tell the *B*s and *D*s apart. One staff members' handwriting is totally illegible. This staffs carelessness is unacceptable. Someones even gone so far as to write grade change's in pencil, which allows students to make changes. This cant continue. In a short time, John and Marys student assistants will be typing the past transcripts into our new computer system. Once grades are entered, the computers ability to generate grade reports will solve this problem. Until that time, lets make an effort to produce clear and professional-looking transcripts.

EXERCISE   *Supply apostrophes where necessary to correct the following sentences:*

1. This years winter promises to be significantly more severe than last years.
2. Everyones office will be furnished with the newest ergonomic chairs and work spaces.
3. Were attempting to determine how our students needs can best be met.
4. When writing numbers quickly by hand, its very important to keep your *7*s and *1*s very distinct.
5. Somebodys purse was left in Dean Smiths office.
6. Once everybodys research has been presented, well be better able to reach a decision.
7. Cindys computer program was much more efficient than her peers programs.
8. There are two *R*s and two *S*s in the word "embarrassment."
9. Lets determine what caused the schools mainframe computer to fail before we panic.
10. Every city has its own charms that are available for the informed visitors delight.

■ Commas

Since commas (,) occur more frequently than any other mark of punctuation, it's vital that you learn to use them correctly. When you do, your sentence structure is clearer, and your reader grasps your meaning without having to reread.

Commas separate or set off independent clauses, items in a series, coordinate adjectives, introductory elements, places and dates, nonrestrictive expressions, and parenthetical expressions.

Independent Clauses   When you link two independent clauses with a coordinating conjunction (*and, but, or, nor, for, yet,* or *so*), put a comma in front of the conjunction.

Arthur is majoring in engineering, *but* he has decided to work for a clothing store following graduation.

The water looked inviting, *so* Darlene decided to go for a swim.

Don't confuse a sentence that has a compound predicate (see page 609) with a sentence that consists of two independent clauses.

Tom watered the garden and mowed the lawn. (single sentence with compound predicate)

Tom watered the garden, *and* Betty mowed the lawn. (sentence with two independent clauses)

Here's a simple test. Read what follows the comma. Unless that part can stand alone as a sentence, don't use a comma.

Items in a Series   A series consists of three or more words, phrases, or clauses following on one another's heels. Whenever you write a series, separate its items with commas.

Sarah, Paul, and *Mary* are earning *A's* in advanced algebra. (words in a series)

Nancy strode *across the parking lot, through the revolving door,* and *into the elevator.* (phrases in a series)

The stockholders' report said *that the company had enjoyed record profits during the last year, that it had expanded its work force by 20 percent,* and *that it would soon start marketing several new products.* (clauses in a series)

Coordinate Adjectives   Use commas to separate coordinate adjectives—those that modify the same noun or noun substitute and can be reversed without altering the meaning of the sentence.

Andrea proved to be an efficient, cooperative employee.

Andrea proved to be a cooperative, efficient employee.

When reversing the word order wrecks the meaning of the sentence, the adjectives are not coordinate and should be written without a comma.

Many new brands of videocassette recorders have come on the market lately.

Reversing the adjectives *many* and *new* would turn this sentence into nonsense. Therefore, no comma should be used.

Introductory Elements   Use commas to separate introductory elements—words, phrases, and clauses—from the rest of the sentence. When an introductory element is short and the sentence will not be misread, you can omit the comma.

Correct   After bathing, Jack felt refreshed.

Correct   Soon I will be changing jobs.

Correct   Soon, I will be changing jobs.

Correct   When Sarah smiles her ears wiggle.

Correct   When Sarah smiles, her ears wiggle.

The first example needs a comma; otherwise, the reader might become temporarily confused.

After bathing Jack . . .

Always use commas after introductory elements of six or more words.

Correct   Whenever I hear the opening measure of Beethoven's *Fifth Symphony,* I get goose bumps.

Places and Dates   Places include mailing addresses and geographical locations. The following sentences show where commas are used:

Sherry Delaney lives at 651 Daniel Street, Memphis, Tennessee 38118.

I will go to Calais, France, next week.

Morristown, Oklahoma, is my birthplace.

Note that commas appear after the street designation and the names of cities, countries, and states, except when the name of the state is followed by a zip code.
Dates are punctuated as shown in the following example:

On Sunday, June 9, 1991, Elaine received a degree in environmental science.

Here, commas follow the day of the week, the day of the month, and the year.
With dates that include only the month and the year, commas are optional.

Correct   In July 1989 James played chess for the first time.

Correct   In July, 1989, James played chess for the first time.

Nonrestrictive Expressions   A nonrestrictive expression supplies added information about whatever it modifies. This information, however, is *nonessential* and does not affect the basic meaning of the sentence. The two sentences below include nonrestrictive expressions:

Senator Conwell, *the senior senator from this state,* faces a tough campaign for re-election.

My dog, *frightened by the thunder,* hid under my bed while the storm raged.

If we delete the phrase *the senior senator from this state* from the first sentence, we still know that Senator Conwell faces a tough re-election battle. Likewise, if we delete *frightened by the thunder* from the second sentence, we still know that the dog hid during the storm.

Restrictive expressions, which are written *without commas,* distinguish whatever they modify from other persons, places, or things in the same category. Unlike nonrestrictive expressions, they are almost always *essential* sentence elements. Omitting a restrictive expression alters the meaning of the sentence, and the result is often nonsense.

Any person *caught stealing from this store* will be prosecuted.

Dropping the italicized part of this sentence leaves us with the absurd statement that any person, not just those caught stealing, faces prosecution.

Parenthetical Expressions A parenthetical expression is a word or a word group that links one sentence to another or adds information or emphasis to the sentence in which it appears. Parenthetical expressions include the following:

Clarifying phrases
Names and titles of people being addressed directly
Abbreviations of degree titles
Echo questions
"Not" phrases
Adjectives that come after, rather than before, the words they modify

The examples that follow show the uses of commas:

All of Joe's spare time seems to center around reading. Kevin, *on the other hand,* enjoys a variety of activities. (phrase linking two sentences together)

Myra Hobbes, *our representative in Seattle,* is being transferred to Spokane next month. (clarifying phrase)

I think, *Jill,* that you'd make a wonderful teacher. (name of person addressed directly)

Tell me, *Captain,* when the cruise ship is scheduled to sail. (title of person addressed directly)

Harley Kendall, *Ph.D.,* will be this year's commencement speaker. (degree title following name)

Alvin realizes, *doesn't he,* that he stands almost no chance of being accepted at West Point? (echo question)

Mathematics, *not home economics,* was Tammy's favorite high school subject. ("not" phrase)

The road, *muddy and rutted,* proved impassable. (adjectives following word they modify)

CONNECTED DISCOURSE EXERCISE *Add or delete commas as necessary in the following letter:*

Dear Loy Norrix Knight:

While we know you will be busy this summer we hope you will take time to join us for the twenty-five-year reunion of the graduating class of 1977. The reunion will include a cocktail hour a buffet dinner and a dance. For your entertainment we are going to bring in a professional band and a band starring some of your good, old high school chums. John Mcleary who is now a well-known professional nightclub performer will serve as the emcee. Do you remember him hosting our senior-year assemblies?

Yes many of your former, hardworking teachers will be at the reunion. You can thank them for the difference they made in your life or you can tell them what you've thought of them all these years. This reunion will also be your opportunity to catch up on the lives of your former friends find out what that old flame now looks like and brag a little about your own successes. And if you are really lucky you might even be able to sneak a dance with your high school prom partner.

We hope you will make plans, to join us here at the Kalamazoo Hilton on July 28, 2002, at 7 P.M. Wear your best 1970s-style clothes. Remember revisiting the past, can be fun.

> Sincerely,
>
> The Reunion Committee

EXERCISE *Supply commas as necessary to correct the following sentences:*

1. Let us know Ms. Granger when you would like to enjoy your free stay at Rolling Hills Resort.
2. The landscapers killed the existing grass rototilled the ground added new topsoil and sprayed the prepared ground with hydroseed.
3. If you are interested in making a tax-deductible donation to the Stratford Festival please write Carla Darma treasurer at 165 University Avenue Suite 700 Toronto Ontario Canada M5H 3B8.
4. The day was unusually beautiful so Mr. Collins decided to hold his class on the Romantic poets outside.
5. Standing in the long winding line for hours on a hot muggy New York summer day Tom was able to get discount tickets to one of the most popular musicals.

6. Mr. Carlin was hired by our New York office on March 25 1997 and was supposed to report to work in our Nome Alaska office three months after his hiring date.

7. Before eating raccoons carefully wash their paws.

8. Despite the many kinds of electronic entertainment available today many people continue to prefer to read a good book.

9. Your fireplace which is cracked in several places will need to be repaired before you can use it.

10. When it is performed well *Waiting for Godot* considered by many to be a masterpiece of existential theater is actually quite humorous.

■ Semicolons

The main use of the semicolon (;) is to separate independent clauses, which may or may not be connected with a conjunctive adverb (see pages 632–33). Other uses include separating

two or more of a series of items
items containing commas in a single series
independent clauses that contain commas and are connected with a coordinating conjunction.

Independent Clauses   The examples that follow show the use of semicolons to separate independent clauses.

The fabric in this dress is terrible; its designer must have been asleep at the swatch. (no conjunctive adverb)

Steve refused to write a term paper; *therefore,* he failed the course. (conjunctive adverb *therefore* joining independent clauses)

Conjunctive adverbs can occur within, rather than between, independent clauses. When they do, set them off with commas.

Marsha felt very confident. Jane, *on the other hand,* was nervous and uncertain. (conjunctive adverb within independent clause)

To determine whether a pair of commas or a semicolon and comma are required, read what comes before and after the conjunctive adverb. Unless both sets of words can stand alone as sentences, use commas.

Two or More Series of Items   With sentences that have two or more series of items, writers often separate the series with semicolons in order to lessen the chances of misreading.

My duties as secretary include typing letters, memos, and purchase orders; sorting, opening, and delivering mail; and making plane and hotel reservations for traveling executives.

The semicolons provide greater clarity than commas would.

Comma-Containing Items within a Series   When commas accompany one or more of the items in a series, it's often better to separate the items with semicolons instead of commas.

> The meal included veal, which was cooked to perfection; asparagus, my favorite vegetable; and brown rice, prepared with a touch of curry.

Once again, semicolons provide greater clarity than additional commas.

Independent Clauses with Commas and a Coordinating Conjunction
Ordinarily, a comma is used to separate independent clauses joined by a coordinating conjunction. When one or more of the clauses have commas, however, a semicolon provides clearer separation.

> The long black limousine pulled up to the curb; and Jerry, shaking with excitement, watched the President alight from it.

The semicolon makes it easier to see the two main clauses.

CONNECTED DISCOURSE EXERCISE   *Add and delete semicolons as appropriate in the following letter. You may have to substitute semicolons for commas.*

> Dear Student:
>
> Our college, as you are well aware, has been going through a number of changes, and these developments, both in the registration system and the curriculum, will continue next year. In the end these improvements will only benefit you; but we know that many of you have been anxious about the exact nature of the changes. To answer your questions, we have arranged an open forum with Linda Peters, president of the college, Drake Stevens, the registrar, and Jerry Mash, vice-president of academic affairs. The meeting will be held in Johnston Hall; 2 P.M.; March 23. Please come with your questions, this is your opportunity to put your fears to rest.
>
> Sincerely,
>
> John X. Pelle
>
> Dean of Students

EXERCISE   *Supply semicolons wherever they are necessary or desirable in the following sentences. You may have to substitute semicolons for commas. If a sentence is correct, write C.*

1. When he visits the main office, Mr. Harmon would like to meet with the vice-president of marketing, Carol Chaffe, the personnel director, Carl Hart, and the vice-president of finance, Mary Angelo.

2. Donald Nathanson, a clinical psychologist, has written an insightful book on shame, and other psychologists, who at first were very critical of his work, have begun to use his ideas in their practice.

3. E-mail is a crucial part of most businesses; in fact, some companies have replaced all memos with electronic communication.

4. This year a number of new musicals have opened on Broadway, it promises to be an exciting theater season.

5. The reading for the course was eclectic, including *The Invisible Man*, a science fiction novel, *Shane*, a western, and *Antigone*, a classic Greek play.

6. Computers can crash at any time, therefore, it is important to back up your data frequently.

7. Sales have decreased significantly this past year, we are likely to see an equivalent drop in our profits.

8. The landscaper planted carpet juniper, canby pachistima, and English ivy for ground cover, rhododendron, pyracantha, and pieris for shrubs, and a blue spruce, a Japanese black pine, and a maple for trees.

9. Chess, a game played by millions, can sharpen your mind, and now there are computer programs, most very inexpensive, that can help you learn the game.

10. We will offer sales training this summer in Lansing, Michigan, Ames, Iowa, and Minneapolis, Minnesota.

Periods, Question Marks, and Exclamation Points

Since periods, question marks, and exclamation points signal the ends of sentences, they are sometimes called *end marks*. In addition, periods and question marks function in several other ways.

Periods Periods (.) end sentences that state facts or opinions, give instructions, make requests that are not in the form of questions, and ask indirect questions—those that have been rephrased in the form of a statement.

Linda works as a hotel manager. (Sentence states fact.)

Dean Harris is a competent administrator. (Sentence states opinion.)

Clean off your lab bench before you leave. (Sentence gives instruction.)

Please move away from the door. (Sentence makes request.)

I wonder whether Ruthie will be at the theater tonight. (Sentence asks indirect question.)

Periods also follow common abbreviations as well as a person's initials.

Mr.	Sr.	P.M.
Mrs.	B.C.	lb.
Jr.	A.D.	St.
Dr.	A.M.	Corp.

Mark J. Valentini, Ph.D., has consented to head the new commission on traffic safety.

Writers today often omit periods after abbreviations for the names of organizations or government agencies, as the following examples show:

ABC	FBI	IRS
ACLU	FHA	NAM
AFL-CIO	GM	USAF

An up-to-date college dictionary will indicate whether a certain abbreviation should be written without periods.

Periods also precede decimal fractions and separate numerals standing for dollars and cents.

0.81 percent	$5.29
3.79 percent	$0.88

Question Marks   A question mark (?) ends a whole or a partial sentence that asks a direct question (one that repeats the exact words of the person who asked it).

Do you know how to operate this movie projector? (whole sentence asking a direct question)

Has Cinderella scrubbed the floor? Swept the hearth? Washed the dishes? (sentence and sentence parts asking direct questions)

Dr. Baker—wasn't she your boss once?—has just received a promotion to sales manager. (interrupting element asking a direct question)

The minister inquired, "Do you take this woman to be your lawful wedded wife?" (quotation asking a direct question)

A question mark may be used to indicate uncertainty.

Jane Seymour (1509?–1537), third wife of Henry VIII, was a lady in waiting to his first two wives.

Exclamation Points   Exclamation points (!) are used to express strong emotion or especially forceful commands.

Darcy! I never expected to see you again!

Sam! Turn that radio down immediately!

Help! Save me!

Use exclamation points sparingly; otherwise, they will quickly lose their force.

CONNECTED DISCOURSE EXERCISE   *Add, change, or remove end marks as necessary. You may want to do some slight recording.*

It was horrifying, the mob of screaming fans grabbed Jack Slitherhips as he left the concert hall. Soon all I could see were his arms reaching for help. But it never came. Why do fans act this way. I am left wondering whether they love or hate their idols? They tore the clothes off Slitherhips, they tore out patches of his hair, someone even snatched his false teeth. Is this any way to treat a fading rock star. Jack is now in the hospital in a complete body cast; when I finally got to see him, he mumbled that he was giving up show business, he plans to settle down on a small farm. Who can blame him?

EXERCISE *Supply periods, question marks, or exclamation points wherever they are necessary. You may have to change existing punctuation marks. If a sentence is correct, write C.*

1. Be sure to proofread your paper before you submit it for a grade.

2. Sigmund Freud—isn't he now generally dismissed by many psychologists—really established the concept of the unconscious.

3. The sales tax in our state was raised to 65 percent.

4. Great we will have to buy another candle.

5. Carla used to study until 2 AM every night.

6. When you shopped for a new computer, did you consider what programs you wanted to run, set a budget for yourself, check the reliability of the different brands.

7. The engineer wanted to know how much stress would be placed on the beams.

8. Has Dr Stevens read the research on the most recent anti-clotting medication.

9. Run for your life, the tiger has escaped from the zoo.

10. Be sure to check your e-mail as soon as you start work.

■ Colons, Dashes, Parentheses, and Brackets

Colons, dashes, parentheses, and brackets separate and enclose, thereby clarifying relationships among the various parts of a sentence.

Colon Colons (:) introduce explanations and anticipated lists following words that could stand alone as a complete sentence.

His aim in life is grandiose: to corner the market in wheat. (explanation)

Three students have been selected to attend the conference: Lucille Perkins, Dan Blakely, and Frank Napolis. (list)

Three factors can cause financial problems for farmers: (1) high interest rates, (2) falling land values, and (3) a strong dollar, which makes it difficult to sell crops abroad. (numbered list)

The first of the following sentences is incorrect because the words preceding the colon can't stand alone as a sentence:

> *Faulty*   The tools needed for this job include: a hacksaw, a file, and a drill.

> *Revision*   The tools needed for this job include a hacksaw, a file, and a drill.

Colons also frequently introduce formal quotations that extend beyond a single sentence.

> The speaker stepped to the lectern and said: "I am here to ask for your assistance. Today several African nations face a food crisis because drought has ruined their harvests. Unless we provide help quickly, thousands of people will die of starvation."

In such situations, the material preceding the quotation need not be a complete sentence.

Colons also separate hours from minutes (8:20 A.M.), salutations of business letters from the body of the letters (Dear Ms. Stanley:), titles of publications from subtitles (*The Careful Writer: A Guide to English Usage*), numbers indicating ratios (a 3:2:2 ratio), and chapter from verse in biblical references (Luke 6:20–49).

Dashes   Like colons, dashes (—) set off appositives, lists, and explanations but are used in less formal writing. A dash emphasizes the material it sets off.

> Only one candidate showed up at the political rally—Jerry Manders. (appositive)

> The closet held only three garments—an out-at-the-elbows sports coat, a pair of blue jeans, and a tattered shirt. (list)

> I know what little Billy's problem is—a soiled diaper. (explanation)

Dashes set off material that interrupts the flow of thought within a sentence.

> Her new car—didn't she get it just three months ago?— has broken down twice.

Similarly, dashes are used to mark an interrupted segment of dialogue.

> "I'd like to live in England when I retire."

> "In England? But what will your wife—?"

> "My wife likes the idea and can hardly wait for us to make the move."

Dashes set off parenthetical elements containing commas, and a dash can set off comments that follow a list.

> The comedian—short, fat, and squeaky-voiced—soon had everyone roaring with laughter. (parenthetical element with commas)

> A brag, a blow, a tank of air—that's what Senator Conwell is. (comment following a list)

Type a dash as two unspaced hyphens and leave no space between it and the words on either side of it.

Parentheses   Parentheses ( ) are used to enclose numbers or letters that designate the items in a formal list and to set off incidental material within sentences. Except in the kind of list shown in the first example below, a comma does not usually precede a parenthesis.

> Each paper should contain (1) an introduction, (2) several paragraphs developing the thesis statement, and (3) a conclusion.

> Some occupations (computer programming, for example) may be overcrowded in ten years.

If the material in parentheses appears within a sentence, don't use a capital letter or period, even if the material is itself a complete sentence.

> The growth of genetic engineering (one cannot forsee its consequences) worries some people today.

If the material in parentheses is written as a separate sentence, however, then punctuate it as you would a separate sentence.

> Paula's angry outburst surprised everyone. (She had seemed such a placid person.)

If the material in parentheses comes at the end of a sentence, put the final punctuation after the closing parenthesis.

> This company was founded by Willard Manley (1876–1951).

> In contrast to dashes, parentheses de-emphasize the material they enclose.

Brackets   In quoted material, brackets [ ] enclose words or phrases that have been added to make the message clearer. They are also used with the word *sic* (Latin for "thus") to point out errors in quoted material.

> "This particular company [Zorn Enterprises, Inc.] pioneered in the safe disposal of toxic wastes," the report noted. (The bracketed name is added to the original.)

> "[John Chafin's] expertise in science has made him a popular figure on the lecture circuit," his friend stated. (The bracketed name replaces *his* in the original.)

> "The principle [sic] cause of lung cancer is cigarette smoking," the article declared. (the word *principal* is misspelled "principle" in the original.)

To call attention to an error, follow it immediately with the bracketed *sic*. The reader will then know that the blame rests with the original writer, not with you.

CONNECTED DISCOURSE EXERCISE   *Supply any necessary or appropriate colons, dashes, parentheses, and brackets in the following letter:*

Wayout Auto Company

We at Oldfield Sales a subsidiary of Jip, Inc., have had a serious problem with the cars we ordered from your company for leas-
ing to our customers who will probably never return to us again.
Two major parts fell off while the cars were sitting in the customers' driveways the exhaust system and the transmission. If
this had happened while they were driving thank goodness it
didn't, our customers could have been killed. Just imagine what
that especially once it got into the newspapers would have done
to our business. We must hold you to your claim that "while our
cars are the cheepest sic on the market, we garuntee sic every
car we sell." We expect immediate reimbursement for all the cars
we purchased from you plus one million dollars to cover the damage to our reputation. A menace, a rip-off, a bad business deal,
that's what your cars are. If you don't issue a formal recall
for all your vehicles by 530 P.M., Friday, July 23, we will be
forced to forward this matter to the federal government.

                              Sincerely,

                              Ken Swindelle

                              Service Manager

EXERCISE *Supply colons, dashes, parentheses, and brackets wherever they are neces-*
sary.

1. Many former Presidents Millard Fillmore, for example have been largely forgotten by most Americans.
2. Our international sales have outperformed domestic sales by an 83 ratio.
3. The newspaper headline read, "Piece sic deal broken."
4. Among our social ills, one condition seems to be the source of many other
   problems poverty.
5. The new library better considered an information center will have over fifty
   computers with full Internet capability.
6. Our city area offers many advantages to businesses a skilled workforce, a well-
   developed infrastructure, and low taxes.
7. His Friedrich Nietzsche's *Thus Spoke Zarathustra* should be very familiar to anyone interested in the history of ideas.
8. In early June every elementary school student's thoughts turn to one thing
   summer vacation.
9. Mozart, Miles Davis, The Talking Heads his tastes certainly are eclectic.
10. The activities at the Pine Tree Resort include horseback riding, kayaking, swim-
    ming, water skiing, and much more.

[]

■ Quotation Marks

Quotation marks (" ") set off direct quotations, titles of short written or broadcast works, subdivisions of books, and expressions singled out for special attention.

Direct Quotations A direct quotation repeats a speaker's or writer's exact words.

> "Tell me about the movie," said Debbie. "If you liked it, I may go myself."

> The placement director said, "The recruiter for Procter and Gamble will be on campus next Thursday to interview students for marketing jobs." (spoken comment)

> "The U.S. trade deficit is expected to reach record levels this year," the *Wall Street Journal* noted. (written comment)

> Jackie said the party was "a total flop."

As these sentences show, a comma or period that follows a direct quotation goes inside the quotation marks. When a quotation is a sentence fragment, the comma preceding it is omitted.

When an expression like "he said" interrupts a quoted sentence, use commas to set off the expression. When the expression comes between two complete quoted sentences, use a period after the expression and capitalize the first word of the second sentence.

> "Hop in," said Jim. "Let me give you a ride to school."

> "Thank you," replied Kelly, opening the car door and sliding into the front seat.

> "I can't remember," said Jim, "when we've had a worse winter."

Titles of Short Works and Subdivisions of Books These short works include magazine articles, essays, short stories, chapters of books, one-act plays, short poems, songs, and television and radio episodes.

> The article was titled "The Real Conservatism." (article)

> Last night I read John Cheever's "The Enormous Radio," "Torch Song," and "The Swimmer." (short stories)

> Many John Denver fans consider "Take Me Home, Country Roads" to be his greatest piece of music. (song)

> The unsuccessful TV show *Pursued* ended its brief run with a segment titled "Checkmate." (TV episode)

Here, as with direct quotations, a comma or period that follows a title goes inside the quotation marks.

Expressions Singled Out for Special Attention Writers who wish to call the reader's attention to a word or symbol sometimes put it within quotation marks.

" "

The algebraic formula included a "π," a "Θ," and a "Δ."

"Bonnets" and "lifts" are British terms for car hoods and elevators.

More frequently, however, these expressions are printed in italics (page 696).

Again, any commas and periods that follow expressions set off by quotation marks go inside the marks.

Quotation Marks Within Quotation Marks   When a direct quotation or the title of a shorter work appears within a direct quotation, use single quotation marks (' ').

"I heard the boss telling the foreman, 'Everyone will receive a Christmas bonus,'" John said.

The instructor told the class, "For tomorrow, read Ernest Hemingway's 'The Killers.' "

Note that the period goes inside of both the single and double quotation marks.

Positioning of Semicolons, Colons, and Question Marks   Position semicolons and colons that come at the end of quoted material after, not before, the quotation marks.

Marcia calls Francine "that greasy grind"; however, I think Marcia is simply jealous of Francine's abilities.

There are two reasons why I like "Babylon Revisited": the characters are interesting and the writing is excellent.

When a question mark accompanies a quotation, put it outside the quotation marks if the whole sentence rather than the quotation asks the question.

Why did Cedric suddenly shout, "This party is a big bore"?

Put the question mark inside the quotation marks if the quotation, but not the whole sentence, asks a question or if the quotation asks one question and the whole sentence asks another.

Marie asked, "What college is your brother planning to attend?" (The quoted material, not the whole sentence, asks the question.)

Whatever possessed him to ask, "What is the most shameful thing you ever did?" (The whole sentence and the quoted material ask separate questions.)

CONNECTED DISCOURSE EXERCISE   *Use quotation marks correctly in the following paragraph:*

Mr. Silver recently lectured our class on Stephen Crane's The Bride Comes to Yellow Sky. One thing we shouldn't forget, Mr. Silver insisted, is that the town is deliberately named Yellow Sky. What is the significance of Crane's choice of the words Yellow Sky? Mr. Silver pointed out a number of possible associations, including cowardice, the setting sun, the open expanse of the West, freedom, the sand in the concluding passage. The story, Mr. Silver stated, is drenched in color words. For example, he pointed out, in the first three paragraphs alone Crane mentions vast flats of green grass, brick-colored hands, new black clothes, and a dress of blue cashmere.

EXERCISE *Supply properly positioned quotation marks wherever they are necessary.*

1. Some linguists think that the quintessential American ok may have come from the African waka.

2. My favorite piece of jazz music is St. James Infirmary.

3. What did Yeats mean by the line in his famous poem The Second Coming, Things fall apart, the center cannot hold?

4. Carl Thomas described the performance as extremely intense.

5. I managed to read Faulkner's short story The Bear, Jennifer sighed, but I don't really know what I want to say about it in my paper for English.

6. Why do so many student writers consistently confuse effect with affect?

7. In response to the Great Depression, Franklin Roosevelt declared The only thing we have to fear is fear itself; however, many families who had lost their homes and couldn't even earn enough for food really did have something to fear.

8. Yiddish words like mishugana and kibitz have come to be used outside the Jewish community.

9. In his closing argument, the defense attorney asked the jury, How would any one of us act if accused of a crime we knew we didn't commit?

10. Henry Ford supposedly called history bunk.

■ Hyphens

Hyphens (-) are used to join compound adjectives and nouns, compound numbers and word-number combinations, and certain prefixes and suffixes to the words with which they appear. In addition, hyphens help prevent misreadings and awkward combinations of letters or syllables and are used to split words between two lines.

Compound Adjectives Hyphens are often used to join separate words that function as single adjectives and come before nouns. Typical examples follow:

Howard is a very *self-contained* person.

The *greenish-yellow* cloud of chlorine gas drifted toward the village.

Betty's *devil-may-care* attitude will land her in trouble someday.

When the first word of the compound is an adverb ending in *-ly* or when the compound adjective follows the noun it modifies, no hyphen is used.

The *badly* burned crash victim was rushed to the hospital.

The color of the chlorine gas was *greenish yellow.*

When two or more compound adjectives modify the same last term, the sentence will flow more smoothly if that term appears just once, after the last item in the series. The hyphens accompanying the earlier terms in the series are kept, however.

Many seventeenth-, eighteenth-, and nineteenth-century costumes are on display in this museum.

Compound Nouns   Hyphenated nouns include such expressions as the following:

secretary-treasurer   good-for-nothing
sister-in-law   man-about-town

Here is a sentence with hyphenated nouns:

Denton is *editor-in-chief* of the largest newspaper in this state.

Compound Numbers and Word–Number Combinations   Hyphens are used to separate two-word numbers from twenty-one to ninety-nine and fractions that have been written out.

Marcy has worked *twenty-one* years for this company.

One-fourth of my income goes for rent.

Similarly, hyphens are used to separate numerals from units of measurement that follow them.

This chemical is shipped in *50-gallon* drums.

Prefixes and Suffixes   A prefix is a word or set of letters that precedes a word and alters its meaning. A suffix is similar but comes at the end of the word. Although most prefixes are not hyphenated, the prefixes *self-* and *all-* do get hyphens, as does the suffix *-elect.* Also the prefix *ex-* is hyphenated when it accompanies a noun.

This stove has a *self-cleaning* oven.

Let Claire Voyant, the *all-knowing* soothsayer, read your future in her crystal ball.

Ethel is the *chairperson-elect* of the club.

Several *ex-teachers* work in this department.

A prefix used before a capitalized term is always hyphenated.

The *ex-FBI* agent gave an interesting talk on the operations of that agency.

Preventing Misreadings and Awkward Combinations of Letters and Syllables Hyphens help prevent misreadings of certain words and also break up awkward combinations of letters and syllables between certain prefixes and suffixes and their core words.

> The doctor *re-treated* the wound with a new antibiotic. (The hyphen prevents the misreading *retreated*.)

> The company plans to *de-emphasize* sales of agricultural chemicals. (The hyphen prevents the awkward repetition of the letter *e* in *deemphasize*.)

Between Syllables Whenever you have to split a word between two lines, place a hyphen at the end of the first line to show the division. The word is always broken, and the hyphen inserted, between syllables. (Any good dictionary shows the syllable divisions of each word it includes.) Never divide a one-syllable word or leave two letters to be placed on the second line, even if those two letters constitute a syllable.

> **EXERCISE** *Supply hyphens wherever they are necessary. If the sentence is correct, write C.*

> 1. The piece of music ended with bird like sounds made by the entire woodwind section.
> 2. In this brokerage firm we follow sound investment strategies rather than chase after will o' the wisp schemes.
> 3. It can be sobering for the president elect to learn the full requirements of the job.
> 4. The union negotiators were forced to retreat from their initial demands.
> 5. One fifth of the shipment of fresh tomatoes turned out to be spoiled.
> 6. The classical radio station can be received by anyone within a 100 mile radius of its broadcasting tower.
> 7. In this class, we will study nineteenth and twentieth century American authors.
> 8. Emerson thought that it was important for people to be self reliant.
> 9. Once the power came back on, I had to recreate the file.
> 10. The Gundersons have been married for thirty five years.

■ Capitalization

cap

Capitalize the first word in any sentence, the pronoun *I*, proper nouns and adjectives, titles used with names, and the significant words in literary and artistic titles.

Proper Nouns A proper noun names one particular person, group of persons, place, or thing. Such nouns include the following:

Persons
Organizations
Racial, political, and religious groups

Countries, states, cities, and streets
Companies and buildings
Geographical locations and features
Days, months, and holidays
Trademarks
Languages
Ships and aircraft
Abbreviations for academic degrees
Sacred writings and pronouns standing for God and Jesus
Titles used in place of names

The sentences below show the capitalization of proper nouns:

Sigmund works for the *National Psychoanalytical Institute,* an organization that has done much to advance the science of psychiatry.

How much does this roll of *Saran Wrap* cost?

Gwen Greene moved to *Paris, France,* when her father became the consul there.

On *Friday, December* 10, 1993, *Michael Jordan* visited our city.

Larry has a master of arts degree, and his sister has a *Ph.D.*

My father works for the *Ford Motor Company,* but I work for *Diamler Chrysler.*

cap

Do not capitalize words like *institute, college, company,* or *avenue* unless they form part of a proper name. Likewise, do not capitalize the names of courses unless they start a sentence, are accompanied by a course number, or designate a language.

I have a 95 average in *Economics* 112 but only a 73 average in sociology.

Harry plans to take intermediate *German* in his junior year.

Do you plan to attend *Drew College* or some other college?

Proper Adjectives   Adjectives created from proper nouns are called proper adjectives. Like the nouns themselves, they should be capitalized.

Lolita Martinez, our class valedictorian, is of *Mexican* ancestry. (*Mexican* is derived from the proper noun *Mexico.*)

Abbreviations   As a general rule, capitalize abbreviations only if the words they stand for are capitalized.

Milton DeWitt works for the *IRS.* (*IRS* is capitalized because *Internal Revenue Service* would be.)

The flask holds 1,500 *ml* of liquid. (The abbreviation *ml* is not capitalized because *milliliters* would not be.)

A few abbreviations are capitalized even though all or some of the words they stand for aren't. Examples include TV (television) and VCR (videocassette recorder). Others are shown on page 680.

Personal Titles   Capitalize a personal title if it precedes a name or is used in place of a name. Otherwise, do not capitalize.

The division is under the command of *General* Arnold Schafer.

Tell me, *Doctor,* do I need an operation?

The *dean* of our engineering division is Dr. Alma Haskins.

Many writers capitalize titles of high rank when they are used in place of names.

The *President* will sign this bill tomorrow.

The *president* will sign this bill tomorrow.

Either usage is acceptable.

Titles of Literary and Artistic Works   When citing the titles of publications, pieces of writing, movies, television programs, paintings, sculptures, and the like, capitalize the first and last words and all other words except *a, an, the,* co-ordinating conjunctions, and one-syllable prepositions.

Last week I played *Gone with the Wind* on my VCR and read Christopher Isherwood's *Goodbye to Berlin.* (the preposition *with,* the article *the,* and the preposition *to* are not capitalized.)

John is reading a book called *The Movies of Abbott and Costello.* (The preposition *of* and the coordinating conjunction *and* are not capitalized.)

Although I'm no TV addict, I used to watch every episode of *Murder, She Wrote.* (All of the words in the title are capitalized.)

Note that the titles of literary and artistic works are italicized. If you don't have access to italic print on your computer program, underline the titles.

EXERCISE   *Identify any word or abbreviation that should be capitalized in the following sentences:*

1. Every friday at 1:00 P.M. the computer support team meets to review the problems that occurred during the previous week.

2. Any student of mexican history will soon see how radically different that history has been from american history.

3. Though many consider it a liberal organization, the aclu has actually protected the right to free speech of many extremely conservative groups.

4. Many students in the rotc choose to take history 321: american military history to satisfy their humanities requirement.

5. A student has a right to be proud upon earning an a.a.s. or a b.s. degree.

6. All requests for sabbatical leave must be submitted to dean Styron by october 1.

7. Though many consider latin a dead language, others continue to study it since so many great classical works were written in that language.

8. Your request for a leave of absence cannot be approved by professor Murphy.

cap

9. Students of roman literature should be familiar with ovid's *metamorphoses.*

10. During World War II, dr. Johnson served on the u.s. submarine eel.

■ Abbreviations

Items that are abbreviated include certain personal titles, names of organizations and agencies, Latin terms, and specific and technical terms.

Personal Titles   Abbreviate *Mister, Doctor,* and similar titles when they come just ahead of a name, and *Junior, Senior,* and degree titles when they follow names.

Will *Mr.* Harry Babbitt please come to the front desk?

Arthur Compton, *Sr.,* is a well-known historian; his son, Arthur Compton, *Jr.,* is a television producer.

This article on marital discord was written by Irma Quarles, *Ph.D.*

Names of Organizations and Agencies   Many organizations and agencies are known primarily by their initials rather than their full names. Several examples follow:

AAA	FBI	NBC
CARE	FHA	NATO
CIA	IBM	UNESCO

Latin Terms   Certain Latin terms are always abbreviated; others are abbreviated when used with dates or times.

e.g. (*exempli gratia:* for example)
i.e. (*id est:* that is)
etc. (*et cetera:* and [the] others)
vs. or v. (*versus:* against)
A.D. (*anno Domini:* in the year of our Lord)
A.M. or a.m. (*ante meridiem:* before noon)
P.M. or p.m. (*post meridiem:* after noon)

The play starts at 8 P.M.

Many writers (*e.g.,* Dylan Thomas and Truman Capote) have had serious problems with alcohol.

For consistency with A.D., the term "before Christ" is abbreviated as B.C.

Scientific and Technical Terms   For brevity's sake, scientists and technicians abbreviate terms of measurement that repeatedly occur. Terms that the reader would not know are written out the first time they are used, and they are accompanied by their abbreviation in parentheses. Unfamiliar organizations and agencies that are mentioned repeatedly are handled in like manner.

The viscosity of the fluid measured 15 centistokes (cs) at room temperature.

ab

Common practice calls for writing such abbreviations without periods unless they duplicate the spelling of some word.

Standard dictionaries list common abbreviations. When you don't recognize one, look it up. Use abbreviations sparingly in essays. If you're unsure about what is appropriate, don't abbreviate.

EXERCISE *Supply abbreviations wherever they are necessary or are customarily used.*

1. Despite extensive competition, International Business Machines continues to be a major player in the computer industry.
2. We are pleased that Mister Jones has decided to join our firm.
3. Dissolve 1 gram of NaCl in 20 milliliters of water.
4. The freezing point of water at sea level is 32° Fahrenheit (0° Celsius).
5. Since its start, the National Broadcasting Company has been strongly committed to its news programming.
6. Doctor Baxter has been doing extensive research on nanotechnology, supported by a National Science Foundation grant.
7. Carl Thorton, Junior, will offer a workshop on how to save for retirement.
8. Many composers who are now seen as giants of classical music (*exempli gratia*, Mozart and Beethoven) died paupers.
9. After Friday's performance of Shakespeare's *Midsummer Night's Dream*, Carol Brice, Doctor of Philosophy, will discuss the use of nature imagery in the play.
10. Crimes that cross state boundaries are often investigated by the Federal Bureau of Investigation.

num

■ Numbers

Some instructors ask their students to use figures for numbers larger than ninety-nine and to spell out smaller numbers.

Boise is *100* miles from here.

Boise is *ninety-nine* miles from here.

Other instructors prefer that students switch to figures beginning with the number ten.

My son will be *nine* years old on his next birthday.

My son will be *10* years old on his next birthday.

With either practice, the following exceptions apply.

Numbers in a Series Write all numbers in a series the same way regardless of their size.

Gatsby has *64* suits, *110* shirts, and *214* ties.

In just one hour the emergency room personnel handled *two* stabbings, *five* shootings, and *sixteen* fractures.

We have *150* salespeople, *51* engineers, and *7* laboratory technicians.

Dates   Use figures for dates that include the year.

> February *14, 1985* (not February 14th, 1985)

When the date includes the day but not the year, you may use figures or spell out the number.

> June 9
> June ninth
> the ninth of June

Page Numbers and Addresses   Use figures for page numbers and street numbers in addresses.

> Check the graph on page *415*.

> I live at *111* Cornelia Street, and my office is at *620* Fifth Avenue.

Numbers Beginning Sentences   Spell out any number that begins a sentence. If this requires three or more words, rephrase the sentence so that the number comes after the opening and numerals can be used.

> The year *1989* was a good year for this wine.

> *Sixty thousand* fans jammed the stadium.

> An army of *265,000* troops assaulted the city. (If this number began the sentence, five words—an excessive number—would be needed to write it out.)

Decimals, Percentages, Times   Use figures for decimals and percentages as well as for expressions of time that are accompanied by A.M. or P.M.

> The shaft has a *0.37*-inch diameter.

> Last year the value of my house jumped *25* percent.

> The plane leaves here at *9:50* A.M. and reaches New Orleans at *2:30* P.M.

One Number Following Another   When a number-containing term that denotes a unit of weight or measurement comes immediately after another number, spell out the first number, if smaller than 100, and use numerals for the second one. If the first number is larger than 100, use numerals for it and spell out the second one.

> We ordered *six 30*-gallon drums of solvent for the project.

> The supplier shipped us *600 thirty*-gallon drums by mistake.

> **EXERCISE**   *Identify any miswriting of numbers in the following sentences and rewrite these numbers correctly:*
>
> 1. The supermarket ordered five hundred five-pound bags of sugar.
> 2. The Whitney Museum of American Art is at Nine Hundred and Forty-Five Madison Avenue, New York City.

3. The holes that the automated system drilled in the brackets were off by two hundredths of an inch.

4. The first memo warning the company of the problem was dated May fifteenth, 1993.

5. There will be a meeting at three-thirty P.M., May fifth, to discuss our new marketing plan.

6. Our local library has 658 CDs, 132 videocassettes, and sixty-three computer programs.

7. 8,000 people usually subscribe to our symphony orchestra series.

8. There are a number of serious editing errors on page thirty-nine of the report.

9. Over the last year, sales have increased by twenty-three percent.

10. We found that only 3 computers needed to be upgraded.

■ Italics

Italics are used for the titles of longer publications, the names of vehicles and vessels, foreign words and phrases, and expressions singled out for special attention. Unless your computer program allows you access to italic print, use underlining to represent italics when writing or typing papers.

ital

Titles of Longer Publications and Artistic Works These items may include the following:

books	record albums	long musical works and poems
magazines	paintings	plays
newspapers	movies	sculptures

As noted on page 685, quotation marks are used for the titles of articles, short stories, short poems, one-act plays, and other brief pieces of writing.

Last night I finished F. Scott Fitzgerald's *The Great Gatsby* and read two articles in *The New Yorker.* (book, magazine)

Michelangelo's *David* is surely one of the world's greatest sculptures. (sculpture)

The *Detroit Free Press* had praise for the revival of Tennessee William's play *The Glass Menagerie.* (newspaper, play)

Stephen Vincent Benét's poem *John Brown's Body* won a Pulitzer Prize in 1929. (book-length poem)

Do not use italics when naming the Bible and its parts or other religious works such as the Torah and Koran.

Joanna's favorite book of the Bible is the Book of Ecclesiastes, part of the Old Testament.

Names of Vehicles and Vessels Names of particular airplanes, ships, trains, and spacecraft are italicized.

The plane in which Charles Lindbergh flew over the Atlantic Ocean was named *The Spirit of St. Louis.*

Foreign Expressions   Use italics to identify foreign words and phrases that have not yet made their way into the English language.

The writer has a terribly pessimistic *weltanschauung.* (philosophy of life)

This season, long skirts are the *dernier cri.* (the latest thing)

When such expressions become completely assimilated, the italics are dropped. Most dictionaries use an asterisk (*), a dagger (†), or other symbol to identify expressions that need italicizing.

Expressions Singled Out for Special Attention   These include words, letters, numerals, and symbols.

The Greek letter *pi* is written Π.

I can't tell whether this letter is meant to be an *a* or an *o* or this number a *7* or a *9.*

In England, the word *lorry* means truck.

As noted on pages 685–86, quotation marks sometimes replace italics for this purpose.

CONNECTED DISCOURSE EXERCISE   *Use hyphens, capitalization, abbreviations, numbers, and italics properly in the following passage:*

Because I can speak Russian fluently, I was recruited by the central intelligence agency while still at Boston college. I suspected that it was professor Hogsbottom, a Political Science teacher, who had suggested that they consider me. After all, he had been a General during World War II and still had connections with the intelligence community. It turned out that my brother in law was responsible; he was an ex FBI agent. Soon I was an american spy located, of all places, in England. Who would suspect that we had to spy on the english? For 3 years I posed as a british aristocrat who was a general bon vivant and man about town. I went by the alias of Mister Henry Higgins, Junior. Everyone, of course, wanted to know if I had seen My Fair Lady. Personally I thought the whole thing was a monty python type of joke until I found a position in the british secret service. Who could have believed the british kept so many secrets from their american allies? For twenty one years I spied on the british

ital

without anyone suspecting that I was an all american boy. I did
find out recently, however, that because of my fluent russian
they had suspected me of being a russian spy and had been feeding me false information all along.

EXERCISE *Supply italics wherever they are necessary.*

1. The British often use the word lift to refer to an elevator.
2. Arthur Miller's Death of a Salesman is considered by many critics to be the great American tragedy.
3. Linguists consider b to be voiced and p to be unvoiced.
4. Given the quality of the movie version, it takes a considerable amount of courage to produce a stage version of the musical West Side Story.
5. The delight many people take in the discomfort of characters in situation comedies suggests that all of us may be subject to some schadenfreude.
6. The USS Enterprise was the first nuclear aircraft carrier.
7. I have always fantasized about taking a ride on the Orient Express, which fig- ured so prominently in a mystery by Agatha Christie.
8. There are few artistic statements against war that are stronger than Picasso's Guernica.
9. There has been a very conscious effort to make Scientific American available to a larger segment of the reading public.
10. It is a shame that so few students read Dostoevsky's Crime and Punishment as part of their education.

ital

Spelling

"Why the big deal about accurate spelling?"
"Does it really make that much difference if I have an *i* and an *e* turned around or if I omit a letter when spelling a word?"

Students frequently question the importance of proper spelling. Perhaps the answer is suggested by the following sentence, taken from a student essay:

I spent over seven hours *studing* one day last week.

The omission of a *y* in *studing* changes the person from one who is studious to one who is a dreamer. Not only does inaccurate spelling smack of carelessness, but also it sometimes drastically alters meaning.

Although there is no sure-fire way of becoming a good speller, you can minimize the difficulties by learning basic spelling rules, applying helpful spelling tips, and memorizing the proper spelling of troublesome words.

sp

■ Spelling Rules

The following four rules should ease spelling pains.

Rule 1 If a word has the double vowels* *ie* or *ei* and the combination has a long *e* sound (as in *me*), use *ie* except after *c*. If the combination has an *a* sound, use *ei*.

ie (as long *e*)	*ei* after *c*	*ei* (as *a*)
relieve	deceive	freight
belief	receive	neighbor
grieve	receipt	reign
piece	perceive	weigh

The main exceptions to this rule include *either, financier, leisure, neither, seize, species,* and *weird.*

---

*The vowels are *a, e, i, o,* and *u.* The consonants are the remaining letters of the alphabet.

Rule 2 If a one-syllable word (example: *sin*) ends in a single consonant preceded by a single vowel, double the consonant before adding a suffix (see page
688) that starts with a vowel. Apply the same rule with a word of two or more syllables (example: *admit*) if the final syllable is accented and ends with a single
consonant preceded by a vowel.

"Dear Mom. Wud you belive I lost my job at the offise today? I gess sumwun
thair doesnt like me."

From *Recess Time,* The Best Cartoons from *The Kappan,* edited by Kristin Herzog, 1983.

Words with Single Syllables	**Words with Two or More Syllables**
rig—rigged	admit—admittance
sin—sinned	control—controller
stop—stopping	equip—equipped

If the accent does not fall on the last syllable, do not double the final consonant.

audit—audited	chatter—chattered
counsel—counselor	simmer—simmering

Rule 3 If a word ends in *y* preceded by a single consonant, change the *y* to an
i unless you are adding the suffix *-ing.*

y changed to *i*	**y retained**
beauty—beautiful	copy—copying
fury—furious	defy—defying
easy—easily	dry—drying
vary—various	vary—varying

Rule 4 If a word ends in a silent *e*, the *e* is usually dropped when a suffix starting with a vowel is added.

blue—bluish	fame—famous
dense—density	grieve—grievous

In a few cases, the *e* is retained to avoid pronunciation difficulties or confusion with other words.

dye—dyeing (not dying)	singe—singeing (not singing)
shoe—shoeing (not shoing)	

The *e* is also retained when it is preceded by a soft *c* sound (pronounced like the letter *s*) or a soft *g* sound (pronounced like the letter *j*) and the suffix being added starts with an *a* or an *o*.

peace—peaceable	courage—courageous
change—changeable	manage—manageable

■ Helpful Spelling Tips

Here are some tips that can further improve your spelling:

1. Examine each problem word carefully, especially prefixes (*au*dience, *au*dible), suffixes (superintend*ent*, descend*ant*), and double consonants (sate*ll*ite, roo*mm*ate, and co*ll*apsible).

2. Sound out each syllable carefully, noting its pronunciation. Words like *height, governor,* and *candidate* are often misspelled because of improper pronunciation.

3. Make a list of your problem words and review them periodically. Concentrate on each syllable and any unusual features (ar*c*tic, ambig*uous*).

4. Use any crutches that will help: there is *gain* in *bargain;* to *breakfast* is to *break a fast;* a disease causes *dis-ease.*

5. When you copy anything from the blackboard or a textbook, copy it carefully. Writing a word correctly helps you to spell it correctly the next time.

6. Buy a good collegiate dictionary and look up the words you don't know how to spell. (See pages 238–40 for more information on dictionaries.)

7. If you have a word processor that has a spell checker, use it. But a word of caution: Don't rely exclusively on this tool. Your spell checker may not distinguish between *to* and *too, their* and *there,* and similar sound-alike words. The ultimate spell checker is you.

■ List of Troublesome Words

Students frequently misspell the words in the following list. Study these words carefully until the correct spelling becomes automatic. Then have a friend read them to you while you write them down. Tag the ones you misspell and whenever you revise a paper, check especially for these words.

abandoned	allowed	beggar	committee
abbreviate	all right	believe	committing
absence	already	beneficial	comparatively
absorb	although	benefit	competent
absorption	altogether	benefited	competition
absurd	always	biscuit	concede
academy	amateur	boundary	conceive
accelerate	ambiguous	bourgeois	condemn
accept	among	breathe	condescend
access	analysis (analyses)	Britain	confident
accessible	analyze	bulletin	congratulations
accident	anonymous	bureau	connoisseur
accidentally	anxiety	bureaucracy	conqueror
accommodate	apartment	business	conscience
accomplish	apparent	cafeteria	conscientious
accumulate	appearance	calendar	conscious
accustom	appreciate	camouflage	consistency
achieve	appropriate	campaign	consistent
achievement	architecture	candidate	conspicuous
acknowledge	arctic	carburetor	contemptible
acknowledgment	argue	carriage	continuous
acquaintance	arguing	carrying	controversy
acquire	argument	casual	convenience
acquit	arithmetic	category	convenient
acquitted	ascent	causal	coolly
address	assassin	ceiling	cooperate
advice	assent	cellar	corollary
advise	assistance	cemetery	corps
aerial	assistant	changeable	corpse
aggravate	athlete	changing	correlate
aggravated	athletics	characteristic	counterfeit
aggression	attempt	chauffeur	courteous
aggressive	attendance	chief	criticism
aging	average	colloquial	criticize
alcohol	bachelor	colonel	cruelty
allege	balance	column	curiosity
alleviate	balloon	commission	curriculum
alley(s)	barbarous	commit	dealt
allot	barbiturate	commitment	deceit
allotted	beautiful	committed	deceive

sp

sp

decent
decision
defendant
defense
definite
definitely
dependent
descendant
descent
describe
description
desert
desirable
despair
desperate
dessert
develop
development
difference
dilemma
disappear
disastrous
discernible
disciple
discipline
discussion
disease
dissatisfied
dissipate
dominant
drunkenness
echoes
ecstasy
efficiency
efficient
eighth
eligible
eliminate
embarrass
emphasis
employee
engineer
enthusiastic
environment
equal
equip

equipment
equipped
equivalent
especially
exaggerate
exceed
excellent
except
excerpt
excess
excitement
exercise
existence
experience
extraordinary
extremely
fallacy
familiar
fascinate
fascist
February
fiery
finally
financier
foreign
foreword
forfeit
forward
friend
fulfill
gaiety
gases
gauge or gage
genius
genuine
government
grammar
guarantee
guard
handkerchief
harass
height
heroes
hindrance
hygiene
hypocrisy

hysterical
illiterate
illogical
illusion
immediate
implement
impromptu
inadequate
incident
incidentally
independent
indict
indispensable
individual
inevitable
infinitely
ingenious
ingenuous
innocent
intelligent
interest
interfere
irresistible
irresponsible
jeopardy
judgment
judicial
knowledge
knowledgeable
laboratory
legitimate
leisure
library
license
lightning
loneliness
loose
lose
magnificent
maintain
maintenance
maneuver
manual
marriage
mathematics
mattress

meant
medicine
medieval
mediocre
melancholy
miniature
minute
miscellaneous
mischievous
misspell
modifies
modify
modifying
moral
morale
mortgage
mosquitoes
muscle
mysterious
necessary
neither
nevertheless
niece
noticeable
obedience
occasion
occasionally
occur
occurred
occurrence
occurring
official
omission
omit
omitted
omitting
opinion
opponent
opportunity
optimistic
original
outrageous
pamphlet
parallel
paralysis
parliament

particularly
pastime
patent
peaceable
perceive
perfectible
perform
permanent
permissible
perseverance
persuade
physical
physician
picnic
picnicked
playwright
pleasant
pleasurable
politician
possess
possession
possible
potatoes
practice
precede
precedent
precious
predominant
preference
preferred
prejudice
preparation
privilege
probably
procedure
proceed
professor
prominent
pronounce
pronunciation
propaganda
propagate
propeller
prophecy
prophesy
prostate

prostrate
protein
psychiatry
psychology
pursue
pursuit
quantity
questionnaire
quiet
quite
quiz
quizzes
realize
receipt
receive
recipe
recognizable
recommend
refer
reference
referring
reign
relevant
relieve
religious
remembrance
reminisce
reminiscence
reminiscent
rendezvous
repellent
repentance
repetition
representative
resemblance
resistance
restaurant
rhetoric
rhyme
rhythm
roommate
sacrifice
sacrilege
sacrilegious
safety
salary

sandwich
scarcely
scene
scenic
schedule
science
secretary
seize
sensible
separate
sergeant
severely
siege
similar
simultaneous
sincerely
skeptical
skiing
skillful
skis
society
sophomore
source
specifically
specimen
sponsor
spontaneous
statistics
steely
strategy
studying
subtle
subtlety
subtly
succeed
success
successful
succinct
suffrage
superintendent
supersede
suppose
suppress
surprise
syllable
symmetry

sympathize
synonym
synonymous
tangible
tariff
technical
technique
temperament
temperature
temporary
tenant
tendency
thorough
thought
through
traffic
trafficking
tragedy
tranquillity
  or tranquility
transcendent
transcendental
transfer
transferred
transferring
translate
tries
truly
twelfth
tyrannical
tyranny
unanimous
unconscious
undoubtedly
unmistakable
unnecessary
until
unwieldy
urban
urbane
usage
useful
using
usual
usually
vacancy

sp

vacillate
vacuum
valuable
vegetable
vengeance
victorious
village

villain
waive
warrant
warring
weather
Wednesday
weird

whether
whole
wholly
wield
wintry
wiry
worshiped

or worshipped
wreak
wreck
writing
written
yield

sp

Glossary of Word Usage

The English language has many words and expressions that confuse writers and thereby lessen the precision and effectiveness of their writing. These troublesome items include the following:

Word pairs that sound alike or almost alike but are spelled differently and have different meanings

Word pairs that do not sound alike but still are often confused

Words or phrases that are unacceptable in formal writing

The following glossary identifies the most common of these troublemakers. Familiarize yourself with its contents. Then consult it as you revise your writing if you have even the slightest doubt about the proper use of a word, phrase, or expression.

a, an   Use *a* with words beginning with a consonant sound (even if the first written letter is a vowel); use *an* with words beginning with a vowel or a vowel sound.

a brush, *a* student, *a* wheel, *a* risky situation, *a* once-in-a-lifetime opportunity

an architect, *an* apple, *an* unworthy participant, *an* interesting proposal, *an* honest politician

accept, except   *Accept* is a verb meaning "to receive" or "to approve." *Except* is used as a verb or a preposition. As a verb, *except* means "to take out, exclude, or omit." As a preposition, it means "excluding," "other than," or "but not."

She *accepted* the bouquet of flowers.

Linda *excepted* Sally from the list of guests. (verb)

All of Linda's friends *except* Sally came to the party. (preposition)

access, excess   *Access* is a noun meaning "means or right to enter, approach, or use." In the computer field it is a verb meaning "gain entrance to." *Excess* is an adjective meaning "too much; more than needed; lack of moderation."

I have *access* to a summer cottage this weekend.

The code permits users to *access* the computer.

The airline booked an *excess* number of passengers on that flight.

adapt, adopt   To *adapt* is "to adjust," often by modification. To *adopt* is "to take as one's own."

He *adapted* to the higher elevations of the Rocky Mountains.

She *adopted* the new doctrine expounded by the prophet.

adverse, averse   *Adverse* is an adjective meaning "unfavorable." *Averse* is an adjective meaning "disinclined" or "feeling distaste for."

Adverse circumstances caused the ceremony to be postponed.

Martha was *averse* to naming all the guilty children.

advice, advise   *Advice* is a noun meaning "a recommendation about how to deal with a situation or problem." *Advise* is a verb meaning "to recommend or warn."

The young man followed his sister's *advice*.

Mr. Smith *advised* John to buy 10,000 shares of the stock.

affect, effect   Although both words may function as nouns and verbs, usually *affect* is a verb and *effect* is a noun. The verb *affect* means "to influence, cause a change in, or arouse the emotions of." The noun *affect* is a technical term in psychology and refers to feeling. The noun *effect* means "result or outcome." The verb *effect* means "to bring about or achieve."

His speech *affected* me greatly. (verb)

The *effect* of the announcement was felt immediately. (noun)

The doctor was soon able to *effect* a cure. (verb)

aggravate   *Aggravate* is a verb meaning "to intensify or make worse" an existing situation. The use of *aggravate* to mean "annoy" or "anger" is colloquial.

Colloquial	Susan's behavior at the dance really *aggravated* me.
Standard	Marcy's interference only *aggravated* the conflict between Bill and Nadine.

ain't   This nonstandard term for *isn't, aren't, hasn't,* or *haven't* is unacceptable in college writing.

all ready, already   *All ready* means "completely prepared" or "everyone is ready." *Already* means "previously, even now, even then."

The scouts are *all ready* for the camp out.

When we arrived we found he had *already* gone.

The report is *already* a week overdue.

all right, alright   *Alright* is a nonstandard spelling of *all right* and is not acceptable in college writing.

all together, altogether   *All together* means "all in one place" or "in unison." *Altogether* is an adverb meaning "completely, entirely."

The family was *all together* at the wedding.

All together, men, push!

Mr. Doe is *altogether* at fault for writing the letter.

allusion, delusion, illusion An *allusion* is an indirect reference. A *delusion* is a mistaken belief, often part of a psychological condition. An *illusion* is a deceptive appearance presented to the sight or created by the imagination.

In his sermon, the minister made many *allusions* to the New Testament.

He suffers from the *delusion* that he is a millionaire.

They wore makeup to give the *illusion* of beauty.

a lot, alot *Alot* is an erroneous spelling of the two words *a lot.* The phrase *a lot* is usually colloquial; in formal writing replace it with "many."

already See *all ready, already.*

alright See *all right, alright.*

alternately, alternatively *Alternately* means "occurring by turns, one after the other." *Alternatively* means "providing a choice between two items."

The U.S. flag has seven red and six white stripes, arranged *alternately.*

Highway 44 offers the most direct route to Junction City. *Alternatively,*

Highway 88 is much more scenic.

altogether See *all together, altogether.*

among, between Use *between* when referring to two things and *among* when referring to more than two.

He divided the candy *between* Allan and Stephanie.

He divided the candy *among* the five children.

amoral, immoral *Amoral* means "neither moral nor immoral; morally neutral." *Immoral* means "contrary to the moral code."

The movie, which takes no clear position on the behavior it depicts, seems curiously *amoral.*

Murder is an *immoral* act.

amount, number *Amount* refers to total quantities, things in bulk, or weight. *Number* refers to countable things. Never use *amount* when referring to people.

Cassandra inherited a large *amount* of money.

Cassandra now has a large *number* of friends.

an, a See *a, an.*

and/or Although often used in commercial and legal documents, this combination should be avoided in other writing.

angry, mad *Mad* means "insane," although it is often used colloquially to mean "annoyed" or "angry." To be precise, use *mad* only to mean insane.

usage

> *Colloquial*   I was *mad* at Debbie.
>
> *Standard*   I was *angry* with Debbie.

any, any other   Do not use *any* when you mean *any other*. Using *any* in the following example would mean that Theresa is more qualified than herself:

> Theresa is more qualified than *any other* candidate.

anyone, any one   *Anyone* means "any person." *Any one* means "any single person or thing."

> I can whip *anyone* in this room.

> I saw three movies last week but didn't like *any one* of them.

appraise, apprise   *Appraise* means "to determine the value of something." *Apprise* means "to notify" or "to tell."

> The jeweler *appraised* the gold brooch at $1,500.

> Having been *apprised* of the situation, the family priest was able to reconcile the parents and the children.

apt, liable, likely   Both *apt* and *liable* express a tendency or inclination. *Liable* suggests something unpleasant or likely to result in legal action. It should be used only when the event may have unpleasant consequences.

> We are *liable* to miss the train.

> My lawyer said that I was *liable* for the damage my car had caused.

If the probable consequences are not unpleasant, *apt* is the better word.

> I am *apt* to buy books if we go to the shopping center.

Likely merely implies strong probability.

> Sandra is *likely* to pass this course without any difficulty.

around   *Around* is colloquial use for "approximately" or "about."

> *Colloquial*   She arrived *around* 10:00 P.M.
>   The blouse cost *around* $15.
>
> *Standard*   She arrived at *approximately* 10:00 P.M.
>   The blouse cost *about* $15.

as   *As* is frequently used as a weak substitute for *because, since, when,* and *while.*

> *Weak*   She ran out of the house *as* it was on fire.
>
> *Better*   She ran out of the house *because* it was on fire.

As should not be used in place of *whether* or *that.*

> *Nonstandard*   I don't know *as* I like her.
>
> *Standard*   I don't know *that* I like her.
>   I don't know *whether* I like her.

usage

as, like   *As* may be used as a conjunction that introduces an adverb clause, but *like* should not be used this way.

> Unacceptable   *Like* my father always said, "You can fool some of the people all of the time."
>
> Standard   *As* my father always said, "You can fool some of the people all of the time."

Like may, however, be used as a preposition.

In times *like* this, it's hard not to despair.

Any woman *like* Sally can expect a successful career in business.

assure, ensure, insure   To *assure* is "to make safe from risk, to guarantee" or "to convince." *Ensure* and *insure* can be variant spellings meaning "to make certain." *Insure,* however, is now generally associated with the business of insurance.

The counselor tried to *assure* the students that they had made a wise choice.

The captain *assured* them that they would be rescued.

The father, wanting to *ensure* his son's college education, applied for a federally *insured* loan.

averse   See *adverse, averse.*

awful, awfully   In everyday speech, *awful* is used to describe things disagreeable or objectionable: "an *awful* movie," "an *awful* character." *Awfully* is used colloquially as an intensifier: "*awfully* nice," "*awfully* bad." Unless they are used to mean "solemnly impressive," however, both words should be avoided in formal writing.

The *awful* majesty of the cathedral silenced the chattering tourists.

awhile, a while   *A while,* consisting of the noun *while* and the article *a,* means "a period of time." *Awhile* is an adverb meaning "for a short time."

Dinner will be served in *a while.*

Sit *awhile* and tell me the latest gossip.

bad, badly   *Bad* is an adjective. *Badly* is an adverb. *Badly* is colloquial when used to mean "very much."

> Unacceptable   She feels *badly* about her mistake.
> Tom behaved *bad* at the circus.
>
> Colloquial   I want a new car *badly.*
>
> Standard   She feels *bad* about her mistake. (adjective as subject complement)
> Tom behaved *badly* at the circus. (adverb)
> I want a new car *very much.*

being as, being that   When used as substitutes for *because* or *since,* these expressions are nonstandard.

usage

> *Nonstandard*   *Being that* I was the first in line, I was able to purchase choice tickets.

> *Standard*   *Because* I was first in line, I was able to purchase choice tickets.

beside, besides   Both words are prepositions, but they have different meanings. *Beside* means "at the side of," and *besides* means "in addition to."

Sheila and Bill sat *beside* the trailer to eat their lunch.

Besides Harvey, Seymour is coming to dinner.

between   See *among, between.*

breath, breathe   *Breath* is a noun and *breathe* is its verb counterpart.

Nicole stepped outside the stuffy cabin for a *breath* of fresh air.

The cabin was so stuffy that Nicole could hardly *breathe.*

broke   *Broke,* when used to mean "without money," is colloquial.

> *Colloquial*   Because Shelley was *broke,* she had to miss the movie.

> *Standard*   Because Shelley *had no money,* she had to miss the movie.

can, may   *Can* refers both to permission and to the ability to do something, while *may* refers to permission only.

I think I *can* pass the exam on Friday. (ability)

My mother says I *can* go to the movies. (permission)

May I take the test next Monday? (permission)

When used to denote permission, *can* lends a less formal air to writing than does *may.*

cannot, can not   The use of *cannot* is preferred unless the writer wishes to italicize the *not* for emphasis.

You *cannot* expect a raise this year.

No, you can *not* expect a raise this year.

can't hardly   This nonstandard form for *cannot, can't,* or *can hardly* is unacceptable in college writing.

can't help but   In college writing, this colloquial phrase should be revised to the simpler *I can't help* or *I cannot help.*

> *Colloquial*   I *can't help but* wish that I were going to the concert.

> *Standard*   I *can't help* wishing that I were going to the concert.

capital, capitol   *Capital* means "a city that serves as a seat of government." *Capitol* means "a building in which a state legislature meets" or "the building in which Congress meets."

Dover is the *capital* of Delaware.

The *capitol* in Dover is popular with visitors.

Capital can also refer to wealth or assets, to an offense punishable by death, or to something excellent or first-rate.

My *capital* consists entirely of stocks and bonds.

Murder is a *capital* crime in this state.

That's a *capital* suggestion!

censor, censure   To *censor* is "to judge"—literature, movies, letters, and the like—and to decide what material is unfit to be read or seen. To *censure* is "to judge harshly" or "find fault with."

The warden *censored* all the prisoners' mail.

The judge *censured* Clyde's criminal behavior.

childish, childlike   Both of these terms mean "like a child." *Childish*, however, has a negative connotation.

He is fifty-two years old, but he behaves in a *childish* manner.

Jon's face has a *childlike* quality that everyone likes immediately.

cite, sight, site   *Cite* means "to mention or quote as an example," *sight* means "to see" or "a view," and *site* means "a location."

Cheryl *cited* Abraham Lincoln's Emancipation Proclamation in her talk.

He was able to *sight* the enemy destroyers through the periscope.

The building *site* is a woody area south of town.

climactic, climatic   *Climactic* is an adjective that means "of, being, or relating to a climax." *Climatic* is an adjective meaning "of or relating to a climate."

Riding the roller coaster was the *climactic* event of Alice's day.

The *climatic* features of Arizona are desirable to many people.

complement, compliment   Both words can act as nouns or verbs. As a noun, *complement* means "something that completes or makes up the whole." As a verb, it means "to complete or perfect." As a noun, *compliment* means "a flattering or praising remark." As a verb, it means "to flatter or praise."

A *complement* of navy personnel boarded the foreign freighter. (noun)

This fruit will *complement* the meal nicely. (verb)

Scott paid Sara Jane a lovely *compliment* at the time of her graduation. (noun)

Mother *complimented* me for cleaning my room. (verb)

conscience, conscious   *Conscience* refers to the sense of moral right or wrong. *Conscious* refers to the awareness of one's feelings or thoughts.

Edgar's *conscience* forced him to return the money.

Basil was not *conscious* of his angry feelings.

usage

Do not confuse *conscious* with *aware;* although these words are similar in meaning, one is *conscious* of feelings or actions but *aware* of events.

contemptible, contemptuous   *Contemptible* means "deserving of contempt." *Contemptuous* means "displaying contempt."

     Peter's drunkenness is *contemptible.*

     Mary is *contemptuous* of Peter's drunkenness.

continual, continuous   *Continual* means "frequently or regularly repeated." *Continuous* means "uninterrupted."

     The telephone's *continual* ringing made the morning a nightmare.

     His wound caused him *continuous* pain for a week.

could have, could of   *Could of* is an unacceptable substitute for *could have* because a preposition cannot substitute for a verb.

     Nonstandard   I *could of* gone with my parents to Portugal.

     Standard   I *could have* gone with my parents to Portugal.

council, counsel   A *council* is a group of people that governs or advises. *Counsel* can be used as both a noun and a verb. The noun means "advice," and the verb means "to advise."

     The city *council* meets on the second Tuesday of every month.

     The lawyer's *counsel* was sound. (noun)

     The psychologist *counsels* many abused children. (verb)

couple   *Couple* denotes two things and should not be used to refer to more than that number.

criteria, criterion   *Criterion* is always singular, *criteria* always plural.

     The primary *criterion* for performing this job is manual dexterity.

     Manual dexterity is but one of many *criteria* on which you will be judged.

cute   *Cute,* an overused colloquialism, should be avoided; it has too many connotations to be used precisely in writing.

data   *Data* is the plural of *datum.* Although *data* is sometimes used with a singular verb, this use is considered incorrect.

     Standard   These *data* are incorrect.

     Unacceptable   This *data* is incorrect.

definite, very definite   Since *definite* means "precise" or "unmistakable," *very definite* is repetitive. One really cannot be more definite than *definite.*

delusion   See *allusion, delusion, illusion.*

desert, deserts, dessert   *Desert* is land that is arid. With the accent on the last syllable, it is a verb meaning "to abandon." *Deserts* means "that which is deserved." *Dessert* is food served after dinner.

The Sonoran *desert* is full of plant life.

You'll get your just *deserts* if you *desert* me now.

They had cheesecake for *dessert* every Thursday night.

device, devise   *Device* is a noun meaning "a mechanical contrivance, gadget, or tool." *Devise* is a verb meaning "to plan or invent."

This new *device* gives us better gas mileage.

We must *devise* a new approach to our problem.

different from, different than   *Different from* is preferred over *different than.*

His ideas on marriage were *different from* those of his wife.

Different than is accepted, however, when a clause follows and the *from* construction would be wordy.

> *Acceptable*   Susan looks *different than* she did last summer.

> *Wordy*   Susan looks *different from* the way she looked last summer.

discreet, discrete   To be *discreet* means to be "prudent, tactful, or careful of one's actions." *Discrete* means "distinct or separate."

Jack was always *discreet* when he talked to his grandparents.

When two atoms of hydrogen combine with one atom of oxygen, they are no longer *discrete* entities.

disinterested, uninterested   A person who is *disinterested* is impartial or unbiased. A person who is *uninterested* is indifferent or not interested.

We need a *disinterested* judge to settle the dispute.

Joe is completely *uninterested* in sports.

don't   This contraction for *do not* should never be used with singular subjects such as *he, she,* or *it.* Instead, use *doesn't,* the contraction for *does not,* with singular subjects.

> *Nonstandard*   *Don't* he know how to spell?
> She *don't* think of anyone except herself.
> That mistake *don't* help your image.

> *Standard*   *Doesn't* he know how to spell?
> She *doesn't* think of anyone except herself.
> That mistake *doesn't* help your image.

due to   *Due to* has always been acceptable following a linking verb.

Her success was *due to* hard work.

Purists, however, object to *due to* when it is used in other situations, especially in introductory phrases.

> *Due to* the many requests we have had, not everyone who wishes tickets will receive them.

usage

In such cases, you may wish to recast the sentence.

> *Because* we have had so many requests, not everyone who wishes tickets will receive them.

effect   See *affect, effect.*

e.g.   This abbreviation, from the Latin *exempli gratia,* means "for example." Avoid using it except in comments in parentheses and in footnotes, and always follow it with a comma.

elicit, illicit   *Elicit* is a verb that means "to draw forth." *Illicit* is an adjective meaning "not permitted."

> A good professor can always *elicit* responses from students.

> He was engaged in many types of *illicit* activities.

emigrate, immigrate   When people *emigrate,* they move out of a country. When people *immigrate,* they move into a country.

> The family *emigrated* from Poland.

> Many Russians *immigrated* to America.

eminent, imminent   *Eminent* means "prominent," whereas *imminent* means "about to happen."

> Niels Bohr was an *eminent* physicist.

> Our instruments show that an earthquake is *imminent.*

ensure   See *assure, ensure, insure.*

enthused, enthusiastic   *Enthused* is a colloquial word and should not be used in place of *enthusiastic.*

> *Colloquial*   John was *enthused* about the prospects for jobs in his hometown.

> *Standard*   John was *enthusiastic* about the prospects for jobs in his hometown.

especially, specially   The term *especially* means "particularly, notably." *Specially* means "for a specific purpose."

> He is an *especially* talented pianist.

> He was *specially* chosen to represent his group.

et al.   This expression, from the Latin *et alia,* means "and others," referring to people. Ordinarily, the abbreviation should be used only in footnotes and bibliographic entries.

etc.   This abbreviation, from the Latin *et cetera,* means "and other things" and is used in reference to objects rather than people. It should be avoided except in comments in parentheses or in footnotes. It should never be preceded by *and.*

everyone, every one   *Everyone* means "every person." *Every one* means "every particular person or thing."

> *Everyone* who wants to go to the ball game should let me know today.

> If you carefully check *every one* of your paragraphs, you can improve your writing.

except   See *accept, except.*

excess   See *access, excess.*

explicit, implicit   *Explicit* means "clearly expressed" or "straightforward." *Implicit* means "implied" or "understood without direct statement."

You must state your needs *explicitly* if you want them fulfilled.

When I took on the project, I made an *implicit* commitment to see it through.

extant, extent   *Extant* is an adjective meaning "still existing." *Extent* is a noun meaning "scope, size, range, limit."

The dodo bird is no longer *extant.*

From Nevada to Colorado is the *extent* of my travels.

farther, further   The traditional distinction is that *farther* refers to physical distance and *further* to distance in time. Only *further* should be used to mean "additional" or "additionally."

In the race for the Muscular Dystrophy Association, Janet ran *farther* than Cindy.

If you think *further* on the matter, I am certain we can reach an agreement.

Let me make one *further* point.

fewer, less   *Fewer* refers to countable items. *Less* refers to quantity or degree.

Mrs. Smith has *fewer* dogs than cats.

There is *less* money in Joan's checking account than in Stanley's.

Jack was *less* ambitious in his later years.

Never use *less* to refer to people.

> *Nonstandard*   *Less* people were there than I expected.
>
> *Standard*   *Fewer* people were there than I expected.

flaunt, flout   To *flaunt* is "to display in a showy way." To *flout* is "to express contempt" or "to show scorn."

Jay *flaunted* his handsome physique before all his friends.

Jerrold *flouted* the convention of dressing for dinner by arriving in tennis shoes.

formally, formerly   *Formally* means "according to established forms, conventions, and rules; ceremoniously." *Formerly* means "in the past."

The ambassador *formally* greeted his dinner guests.

Formerly, smallpox was one of our most serious diseases.

funny   *Funny* refers to something that is amusing. In college writing it should not be used to mean "odd" or "unusual."

> *Colloquial*   I felt *funny* visiting my old fourth-grade classroom.
>
> *Standard*   I felt *odd* visiting my old fourth-grade classroom.

usage

further   See *farther, further.*

get   *Get,* in any of its many colloquial senses, should not be used in writing.

> *Colloquial*   Her way of looking at a man really *gets* me.
> I'll *get* him if it's the last thing I do.
>
> *Standard*   Beth will *get* at least a *B* in this course.

good and   Replace this colloquial phrase with *very.*

> *Colloquial*   She is *good and* tired of the cafeteria food.
>
> *Standard*   She is *very* tired of the cafeteria food.

good, well   Do not mistakenly use *good* as an adverb when an adjective is required.

> *Unacceptable*   John did *good* on his first test.
>
> *Standard*   John is making *good* progress on his report.
> John is a *good* student.

Well can be used as an adjective meaning "in good health." Otherwise it should always be used as an adverb.

> Last week I had a bad cold, but now I am *well.* (adjective)

> John did *well* on his first test. (adverb)

got, gotten   Both are acceptable past-participle forms of the verb *to get.*

had ought, hadn't ought   Both are incorrect in formal writing. The correct forms are *ought* and *ought not.*

> I *ought* to start studying.

> You *ought not* to cut class again.

hanged, hung   People may be *hanged.* Objects may be *hung.*

> The prisoner was *hanged* at noon.

> Mavis *hung* the picture in the dining room.

hisself, theirself, theirselves   These are nonstandard forms of *himself* and *themselves.*

hopefully   *Hopefully* means "in a hopeful manner." In informal speaking, it is used to mean "it is hoped" or "I hope," but this usage is not correct in formal writing. (Compare this with *carefully,* which means "in a careful manner"; no one uses *carefully* to mean "it is cared.")

> *Colloquial*   *Hopefully,* it will not rain during the class picnic.
>
> *Standard*   Sally walked *hopefully* into the boss's office to ask for a raise.

hung   See *hanged, hung.*

i.e.   This abbreviation, meaning "that is," comes from the Latin *id est.* Avoid using it except in comments in parentheses or footnotes, and always follow it with a comma.

if, whether   *If* is used to introduce adverb clauses, where it means "assuming that."

If I finish my report on time, I'll attend the concert with you.

If and *whether* are often used interchangeably to introduce noun clauses that follow verbs such as *ask, say, doubt, know,* and *wonder.* In formal writing, however, *whether* is preferred.

> *Less Desirable*   I don't know *if* we'll be able to see the North Star tonight.
>
> *More Desirable*   I don't know *whether* we'll be able to see the North Star tonight.

illicit   See *elicit, illicit.*

illusion   See *allusion, delusion, illusion.*

immigrate   See *emigrate, immigrate.*

imminent   See *eminent, imminent.*

immoral   See *amoral, immoral.*

impact   Although *impact* is sometimes used in colloquial speech as a verb meaning "affect," this use is unacceptable in college writing.

> *Colloquial*   This new law will greatly *impact* political campaigning.
>
> *Standard*   This new law will greatly *affect* political campaigning.

implicit   See *explicit, implicit.*

imply, infer   To *imply* is "to indicate indirectly or give implication." To *infer* is "to conclude from facts, evidence, or indirect suggestions."

Jack *implied* that he wanted a divorce.

Doris *inferred* that Jack wanted a divorce.

As these examples indicate, speakers and writers imply; listeners and readers infer.

incidence, incidents   *Incidents* are separate, countable experiences. *Incidence* refers to the rate at which something occurs.

Two *incidents* during childhood led to her reclusiveness.

The *incidence* of cancer in Japan is less than that in the United States.

incredible, incredulous   *Incredible* means "fantastic, unbelievable." *Incredulous* means "skeptical, disbelieving."

That she could run so fast seemed *incredible.*

Why is Bill wearing that *incredulous* look?

infer   See *imply, infer.*

ingenious, ingenuous   *Ingenious* means "clever and inventive." *Ingenuous* means "unsophisticated and innocent."

usage

Sue presented an *ingenious* solution to our problem.

Mary's *ingenuous* comments amused everyone in the room.

in regards to   This is an incorrect use of *in regard to.*

insure   See *assure, ensure, insure.*

inter-, intra-   *Inter-* means "between or among." *Intra-* means "within."

From Chicago to Milwaukee is an *interstate* drive of approximately ninety miles.

From San Francisco to Los Angeles is an *intrastate* drive of about 400 miles.

in terms of   Avoid this vague, overused expression.

Vague	*In terms of* the price he is asking, I would not recommend purchasing Tom's car.
Preferred	*Because* of the price he is asking, I would not recommend purchasing Tom's car.

irregardless   This nonstandard form of *regardless* includes the repetitive elements of *ir* and *less,* both of which mean "without."

is when, is where   *Is when* properly refers only to time.

April *is when* our lilac bush blooms.

Is where properly refers only to place.

Athens *is where* I met him.

The following sentences are *faulty* because of poorly phrased predicates which indicate that muckraking is a place and an abscess is a time:

Muckraking *is where* someone investigates corporate or governmental abuses of power.

An abscess *is when* some spot in body tissue fills with pus.

These sentences should be rephrased to eliminate the faulty assertion.

Muckraking is the investigation of corporate or governmental abuses of power.

An abscess occurs when some spot in body tissue fills with pus.

its, it's, its'   *Its* is a possessive pronoun. *It's* is a contraction of *it is* or *it has.*

The gold chair was ruined, for someone had torn *its* seat.

It's all I have to offer. (It is all I have to offer.)

It's been a difficult day. (It has been a difficult day.)

There is no correct use for *its'.*

kind of, sort of   In college writing, these are unacceptable substitutes for *somewhat, rather,* or *slightly.*

| *Colloquial* | She is *sort of* angry. |
| | I am *kind of* glad she went away. |

| *Standard* | She is *somewhat* angry. |
| | I am *rather* glad she went away. |

When *kind* and *sort* refer to a type, use them with singular nouns and verbs. With their plural forms, *kinds* and *sorts,* use plural nouns and verbs.

| *Unacceptable* | These *kind* of exams are difficult. |

| *Standard* | This *kind* of exam is difficult. |
| | These *kinds* of exams are difficult. |

In such constructions, be certain that *kind of* or *sort of* is essential to your meaning. Otherwise, these phrases are unnecessary.

later, latter   *Later* refers to time; *latter* points out the second of two items. If more than two items are listed, use *last* to refer to the final one.

He arrived at the party *later* than he was expected.

Although Professors Stein and Patterson both lectured during the course, only the *latter* graded the final exam.

Of my three cats, Sheba, Tiger, and Spot, only the *last* still needs the vaccination.

lay, lie   *Lie* means "to recline" or "to remain in a particular position." It never takes a direct object. *Lay* means "to place" and always takes a direct object. These verbs are often confused, in part because the past tense of *lie* is *lay.* (The past tense of *lay* is *laid.*)

If I *lie* here a minute, I shall feel better.

Lay the book on the table, please.

As I *lay* asleep, a robber entered my apartment and stole my stereo.

He *laid* a hand on her shoulder.

leave, let   *Leave* means "to depart," and *let* means "to allow." Never use *leave* when *let* is meant.

| *Nonstandard* | *Leave* him figure it out alone. |

| *Standard* | *Let* him figure it out alone. |

lend, loan   Traditionally, *loan* has been classed as a noun and *lend* as a verb. Today, the use of *loan* as a verb is so commonplace that it is accepted as colloquial English.

| *Standard* | I have applied for a *loan* so that I can buy a car. (noun) |
| | Please *lend* me your class notes. (verb) |

| *Colloquial* | Please *loan* me your class notes. (verb) |

less   See *fewer, less.*

let   See *leave, let.*

usage

liable   See *apt, liable, likely.*

lie   See *lay, lie.*

like   See *as, like.*

likely   See *apt, liable, likely.*

literally   The word *literally* means "restricted to the exact, stated meaning." In formal writing, use *literally* only to designate factual statements.

> *Colloquial*   It was 65°, but I was *literally* freezing.
>
> *Standard*   Our dog was *literally* foaming at the mouth.
> It was 65°, but I was *very* cold.

loan   See *lend, loan.*

loose, loosen, lose   *Loose* can be used as both a verb and an adjective. As a verb, it means "untie or unfasten"; as an adjective, it means "unattached, unrestrained, not confined." *Loosen* is a verb meaning "undo or ease." *Lose* can be used only as a verb meaning "mislay, fail to win, unable to maintain."

> He *loosed* the restraints on the tiger. (verb)
>
> One should wear *loose* clothing when bowling. (adjective)
>
> When will Mrs. Brady *loosen* her control over young Tom? (verb)
>
> You would *lose* your nose if it were not attached to your face. (verb)

lots, lots of   *Lots* and *lots of* colloquially mean "many, much, a large amount, or a great amount." Avoid these expressions in college writing.

> *Colloquial*   I've spent *lots of* money in my life.
>
> *Standard*   I have spent *much* money in my life.

mad   See *angry, mad.*

many, much   *Many* is used when referring to countable items; *much* is used when referring to an indefinite amount or to abstract concepts.

> There are *many* students in the biology class.
>
> How did Betty learn so *much* in so little time?

may   See *can, may.*

may be, maybe   *May be* is always used as a verb phrase. *Maybe* is an adverb meaning "perhaps."

> I *may be* chairman of the board by next June.
>
> *Maybe* we will see Jim at home.

medium, media   *Medium* is the singular form of this word; *media* is the plural.

> Television is the *medium* I use most to get the news.

usage

The *media* have given extensive coverage to the brain transplant story.

much   See *many, much.*

myself   *Myself* is an intensive and a reflexive pronoun; it cannot substitute for a personal pronoun such as *I* or *me.*

> *Unacceptable*   Four other students and *myself* founded the club.

> *Standard*   Four other students and *I* founded the club.

nice   *Nice* is an adjective suggesting delicacy, precision, subtlety, accuracy, the ability to discriminate, or the need for great care.

These two seemingly identical proposals actually have several *nice* differences.

This author's short stories have a *nice* touch.

Nice as a term of approval meaning "pleasing, enjoyable, attractive" is too generalized for use in college writing.

not hardly   This is a nonstandard variation of *hardly* and is inappropriate in college writing.

number   See *amount, number.*

of between, of from, off of   Eliminate the unnecessary *of* from these colloquial phrases.

> *Colloquial*   There was a crowd *of between* three and four thousand people at the contest.
> Get *off of* my property!

> *Standard*   The crowd at the contest numbered *between* three and four thousand people.
> Get *off* my property!

on account of   When used to begin an adverb clause (see pages 638–39), this is a nonstandard substitute for *because.*

> *Nonstandard*   The team was unable to practice *on account of* everyone was still upset over Tuesday's loss.

> *Standard*   The team was unable to practice *because* everyone was still upset over Tuesday's loss.

When *on account of* precedes a single word or a phrase, it is considered colloquial.

> *Colloquial*   The game was called *on account of* rain.

passed, past   *Passed* is a verb designating activity that has taken place. *Past* is a noun or an adjective designating a former time.

The parade *passed* the reviewing stand at 10:30 A.M.

In the *past*, few people were concerned about the environmental effects of pesticides.

This *past* summer, I visited France.

usage

patience, patients   *Patience* means "the ability to wait or endure without complaining." *Patients* are "people being treated by health-care professionals."

> Thad's *patience* was exhausted by the slow service in the restaurant.

> Following the tornado, doctors in the emergency room treated over sixty *patients.*

persecute, prosecute   *Persecute* means "to harass persistently because of race, religion, or belief." *Prosecute* means "to bring legal suit against."

> Ethnic groups are often *persecuted.*

> The company will *prosecute* anyone caught stealing.

personal, personnel   *Personal* is an adjective meaning "private, individual." *Personnel* are the people working in an organization.

> Religious preference is a *personal* matter that you do not have to reveal during a job interview.

> The *personnel* of the sanitation department will not be involved in the city workers' strike.

plenty   When used as an adverb, *plenty* should be replaced by *very.*

> *Colloquial*   That geology exam was *plenty* hard.

> *Standard*   That geology exam was *very* hard.

precede, proceed   *Precede* means "to go before or ahead of." *Proceed* means "to go on" or "to go forward."

> The ritual of sharpening his pencils always *preceded* doing his homework.

> The guide then said, "If you will *proceed,* I will show you the paintings by da Vinci."

predominant, predominate   *Predominant* is an adjective meaning "chief, main, most frequent." *Predominate* is a verb meaning "to have authority over others."

> The *predominant* European influence on South American culture was Spanish.

> In America, the will of the people should *predominate.*

presently   *Presently* means "soon" rather than "at the present time." *Currently* is correct for the second meaning.

> I will be there *presently.*

> *Currently,* I am otherwise engaged.

principal, principle   *Principal,* which means "chief," "most important," or "the amount of money on which interest is computed," is used as both a noun and an adjective. *Principle* is used only as a noun and means "truths, beliefs, or rules generally dealing with moral conduct."

> The *principal* suspect in the case was arrested last Friday by the police.

> The *principal* of Lewiston High School is Alison Cooperstein.

> At this interest rate, your *principal* will double in ten years.

His *principles* are unconventional.

proceed   See *precede, proceed.*

prosecute   See *persecute, prosecute.*

quiet, quite   *Quiet* is an adjective meaning "silent, motionless, calm." *Quite* is an adverb meaning "entirely" or "to a considerable extent or degree."

The class grew *quiet* when the teacher walked in.

He is *quite* wrong.

The movie was *quite* good.

raise, rise   *Raise* is a transitive verb and therefore requires a direct object. *Rise,* its intransitive counterpart, takes no direct object.

We plan to *raise* horses on our new farm.

The temperature is expected to *rise* to 75°F tomorrow.

Raise can also be a noun meaning "an increase in pay."

Tammy received a 25 percent *raise* last week.

real, really   *Real* is an adjective; *really* is an adverb.

She had *real* plants decorating the bedroom.

When used as an adverb, *real* is a colloquialism and should be replaced with *really.*

Colloquial   We had a *real* good time at the party.

Standard   We had a *really* good time at the party.

reason is because, reason is that   The *reason is because* is colloquial and unacceptable in formal writing; the *reason is that* is the correct usage.

Colloquial   The *reason is because* I love her.

Standard   The *reason is that* I love her.

respectfully, respectively   *Respectfully* means "with respect." *Respectively* indicates that the items in one series are related to those in a second series in the order given.

Joseph should treat his parents *respectfully.*

Tom, Anna, and Susan were assigned *Bleak House, Great Expectations,* and *Dombey and Son, respectively,* for their reports.

rise   See *raise, rise.*

sensual, sensuous   *Sensual* refers to bodily or sexual sensations. *Sensuous* refers to impressions experienced through the five senses.

Singles bars offered *sensual* pleasures without emotional commitments.

The Tivoli Garden provides many *sensuous* delights for visitors.

usage

set, sit   Generally, *set* means "to place" and takes a direct object. *Sit* means "to be seated" and does not take a direct object.

> Alice *set* her glass on the mantel.

> May I *sit* in this chair?

When it refers to the sun, however, *set* is used without a direct object.

> As the sun *set*, we turned homeward.

shall, will   *Shall* is used in first-person (see page 653) questions and in specialized forms of writing such as military orders and laws. Otherwise, *will* is generally used.

> *Shall* we go to the movies tonight?

> The company *shall* fall into formation at precisely twelve noon.

> No family home *shall* be assessed at more than 50 percent of its actual value.

should have, should of   *Should of* is an unacceptable substitute for *should have* because a preposition cannot substitute for a verb.

> *Nonstandard*   I *should of* gone to the lake.

> *Standard*   I *should have* gone to the lake.

[sic]   This Latin word, always enclosed in brackets, follows quoted errors in grammar, spelling, or information. Inclusion of [sic] indicates that the error appeared in the original, which is being quoted exactly.

sight   See *cite, sight, site*.

sit   See *set, sit*.

site   See *cite, sight, site*.

so   *So* is an acceptable coordinating conjunction but tends to add an informal effect to writing and should therefore be used sparingly. For example, "Tom said he was divorcing me, *so* I began to cry" would be more effective if restated as follows: "When Tom said he was divorcing me, I began to cry." Do not use *so* as a substitute for *extremely* or *very* except with adverb clauses beginning with *that*.

> *Colloquial*   You are *so* careless in what you say.
> The discussion was *so* informative that I took many notes.

> *Standard*   You are *very* careless in what you say.
> The discussion was *extremely* informative.

some   *Some* is colloquial and unacceptable in writing when used as an intensifier (We had *some* time of it!) or an adverb (He'll probably pout *some* after you leave).

sometime, some time, sometimes   *Sometime* means "at a future unspecified time," *some time* means "a span of time," and *sometimes* means "occasionally."

> We should get together *sometime* and play bridge.

> The weather has been hot for *some time*.

Sometimes I go to dinner with Ethel.

sort of   See *kind of, sort of.*

specially   See *especially, specially.*

stationary, stationery   *Stationary* means "not moving" or "fixed." *Stationery* means "paper for writing letters."

The circular part in the center must remain *stationary,* or the machine will not function.

Sue always writes on scented *stationery.*

such, such . . . that   The use of *such* when it means "very" or "extremely" is unacceptable unless it is followed by a *that* clause completing the thought.

Colloquial	They were *such* good cookies.
Standard	They were *such* good cookies *that* I asked Steve for his recipe.

suppose to, supposed to   *Suppose to* is the nonstandard form of *supposed to.* In speech, it is difficult to hear the final *d* on *supposed,* and one may say *suppose to* without being detected; however, the correct written form is always *supposed to.*

sure, surely   *Sure* is colloquial for the adverb *surely.*

Colloquial	You *sure* know how to make good coffee, Mrs. Olsen.
Standard	You *surely* know how to make good coffee, Mrs. Olsen.

Although *surely* is correct, it may sound too formal and insincere. Therefore, *certainly* is often a better word to use.

take and, try and   Avoid these expressions. Simply eliminate them from the sentence or substitute *try to* for *try and.*

Unacceptable	If you *take and* cover the tomato plants, they probably won't freeze.
	I think you should *try and* settle your differences.
Standard	If you cover the tomato plants, they probably won't freeze.
	I think you should *try to* settle your differences.

than, then   *Than* is used to make comparisons; *then* means "at that time, in that case," or "after that."

Jill is taller *than* her brother.

First we will eat, and *then* we will discuss business.

that, which   These two words have the same meaning. *That* may refer both to things and groups of people; *which,* only to things. When referring to things, *that* is generally used with clauses that distinguish the things they modify from others in the same class (restrictive clauses). *Which* is generally used with clauses that add information about the things they modify (nonrestrictive clauses). Note that clauses starting with *which,* unlike those starting with *that,* are generally preceded by a comma.

Any book *that* she likes is certain to be trashy. (restrictive clause)

The Winthrop Building, *which* cost two million dollars to construct, could not now be duplicated for ten times that much. (nonrestrictive clause)

usage

See pages 674–75 of the Handbook for a more complete explanation of restrictive and nonrestrictive expressions.

their, there, they're   These three separate words are often confused because they sound alike. *Their* is the possessive form of *they*. *There* is an expletive that appears at the beginning of a sentence and introduces the real subject, or it is an adverb meaning "in or at that place, at that point." *They're* is a contraction of *they are*.

> It is *their* basketball.

> *There* are many reasons why I cannot come.

> Put the sofa down *there*.

> *They're* going to be here soon.

theirself, theirselves   See *hisself, theirself, theirselves*.

then   See *than, then*.

there   See *their, there, they're*.

thorough, through   *Thorough* means "careful, complete, exact, painstaking." *Through* means "in one side and out the other, from end to end, from start to finish, over the whole extent of, finished."

> Brenda has done a *thorough* job.

> Let's run *through* the plan again.

thusly   *Thusly* is a nonstandard form of *thus*.

to, too, two   *To* is a preposition meaning "as far as, toward, until, onto." *Too* is an adverb meaning "excessively" or "also." *Two* is a number.

> I'm going *to* the store.

> Are you going *too*?

> This car is *too* expensive for me.

> There are *two* characters in the play.

toward, towards   Both forms are correct. *Toward* generally is used in the United States and *towards* in England.

try and   See *take and, try and*.

two   See *to, too, two*.

uninterested   See *disinterested, uninterested*.

unique   *Unique* means "without an equal" or "extremely unusual" and thus should not be modified by an adverb such as *very*.

use to, used to   *Use to* is the nonstandard form of *used to*. In speech it is difficult to hear the *d* on *used*, and one may say *use to* without being detected; however, the correct written form is always *used to*.

used to could   This phrase is nonstandard for *used to be able to.*

> *Nonstandard*   I *used to could* run ten miles.

> *Standard*   I *used to be able to* run ten miles.

very definite   See *definite, very definite.*

wander, wonder   *Wander* is a verb meaning "to move about without a plan or set destination." *Wonder* is a noun meaning "something causing surprise, admiration, or awe" or a verb meaning "to be curious about."

> Some people like to *wander* through shopping malls for recreation.

> That child is a *wonder* at mathematics.

> I *wonder* whether I have received an *A* on that test.

way, ways   *Ways* may be used to refer to two or more means or methods but not to time or distance.

> *Unacceptable*   Timbuktu is a long *ways* from the United States.

> *Standard*   There are two *ways* of thinking about that issue.
> Timbuktu is a long *way* from the United States.

well   See *good, well.*

were, where   *Were* is the past form of the verb *to be. Where* is an adverb or a pronoun meaning "in, at, to, from a particular place or situation" or "which or what place."

> I'm sorry that you *were* ill yesterday.

> Mr. Morris will show you *where* to register.

where . . . at, to   *At* and *to* are unnecessary after *where.*

> *Wordy*   *Where* are you taking the car *to?*
> *Where* does she live *at?*

> *Standard*   *Where* are you taking the car?
> *Where* does she live?

whether   See *if, whether.*

which   See *that, which.*

usage

who, whom   In formal writing, *who* should be used only as a subject in clauses and sentences and *whom* only as an object.

> *Unacceptable*   *Who* are you taking to dinner on Friday?
> I know *who* the boss will promote.
> John is the candidate *whom* I think will be elected.

> *Standard*   *Whom* are you taking to dinner on Friday?
> I know *whom* the boss will promote.
> John is the candidate *who* I think will be elected.

See page 656 of the Handbook for a fuller discussion of *who* and *whom.*

who's, whose   *Who's* is a contraction of *who is* or *who has,* and *whose* is the possessive form of *who.*

> *Who's* coming to see us tonight?

> I would like to know *who's* been dumping trash in my yard.

> *Whose* book is that?

will   See *shall, will.*

wise   Do not randomly add *wise* to the ends of nouns. Such word coinings are ineffective.

> *Ineffective*   Personality*wise,* Sheila is ideal for the job.

> *Standard*   Sheila has an *ideal personality* for the job.

wonder   See *wander, wonder.*

would have, would of   *Would of* is an unacceptable substitute for *would have.* A preposition cannot substitute for a verb.

> *Nonstandard*   I *would of* enjoyed seeing the Picasso exhibit.

> *Standard*   I *would have* enjoyed seeing the Picasso exhibit.

would have been, had been   When *would* occurs in the main part of a sentence, use *had been* (not *would have been*) in an "if" clause.

> *Nonstandard*   If the engine *would have been* lubricated, the bearing *would not have* burned out.

> *Standard*   If the engine *had been* lubricated, the bearing *would not have* burned out.

your, you're   *Your* is a possessive form of *you; you're* is a contraction of *you are.*

> Where is *your* history book?

> Tell me when *you're* ready to leave.

usage

Acknowledgments (Continued from page iv)

R. T. Allen, "The Porcupine," from *Children, Wives, and Other Wildlife* by Robert Thomas Allen. Copyright © 1970 by Robert Thomas Allen (New York: Doubleday, 1970).

Bonnie Angelo, "Those Good Ole Boys," *Time,* Sept. 27, 1976, p. 47.

Maya Angelou, "Mamma's Encounter," from *I Know Why the Caged Bird Sings.* Copyright © 1969 by Maya Angelou. Used by permission of Random House, Inc.

"Antigen," *Encyclopaedia Britannica,* 1974, I, 417.

Carl Becker, *Freedom and Responsibility in the American Way of Life* (New York: Vintage-Knopf, 1945).

Bruno Bettelheim, "Joey: A 'Mechanical Boy,'" *Scientific American,* March 1959, p. 122.

Ray Allen Billington, "The Frontier Disappears," *The American Story,* ed. Earl Schenck Miers (Great Neck, NY: Channel, 1956).

"The Brink of a Disaster," *America,* March 31, 1979, p. 247.

Claude Brown, *Manchild in the Promised Land* (New York: Macmillan, 1965), p. 304.

James L. Buckley, "Three Cheers for the Snail Darter," *National Review,* September 14, 1979, pp. 1144–45.

Gladys Hasty Carroll, *Sing Out the Glory* (Boston: Little Brown, and Co., 1958).

Rachel Carson, *Silent Spring* (Boston: Houghton Mifflin, 1962).

Stephen L. Carter, "The Insufficiency of Honesty." Copyright © 1996. Reprinted by author's permission.

Bruce Catton, "Grant and Lee: A Study in Contrasts," from *The American Story,* ed. Earl Schenck Miers. Reprinted by permission of U.S. Capital Historical Society.

Lorna Dee Cervantes, "Cannery Town in August" is from *Emplumada* by Lorna Dee Cervantes, © 1981. Reprinted by permission of the University of Pittsburgh Press.

John Ciardi, "What Is Happiness?" in *Manner of Speaking* (New Brunswick, NJ: Rutgers University Press, 1972).

Robert Claiborne, "Future Schlock," *The Nation,* January 25, 1971, p. 117.

Cecil Clutton and John Stanford, *The Vintage Motor-car* (New York: Charles Scribner's Sons, 1955), p. 135.

Judith Ortiz Cofer, "The Myth of the Latin Woman," from *The Latin Deli: Prose and Poetry* by Judith Ortiz Cofer. Copyright © 1993 by Judith Ortiz Cofer. Used by permission of the University of Georgia Press. All rights reserved.

Joseph Conrad, *Lord Jim* (New York: Holt, Rinehart and Winston, 1957), p. 13.

"Controlling Phobias Through Behavior Modification," *USA Today,* August 1978.

Countee Cullen, "Yet Do I Marvel" Copyrights held by the Amistad Research Center, Tulane University, New Orleans, Louisiana. Administered by JJKR Associates, New York, NY.

Kelly Davis, "Health and High Voltage: 765 KV Lines," *Sierra,* July-August 1978.

Vine Deloria, Jr. "Custer Died for Your Sins," *Playboy,* Aug. 1969.

Lester del Ray, *The Mysterious Sky* (New York: Chilton Book Company, 1964).

Magda Denes, *In Necessity and Sorrow: Life and Death in an Abortion Hospital* (New York: Basic Books, 1976), p. xiv.

Robert Dick-Read, *Sanamu: Adventures in Search of African Art* (New York: E.P. Dutton, 1964), pp. 228–29.

Joan Didion, "On Self-Respect," in *Slouching Toward Bethlehem* (New York: Farrar, Straus and Giroux, 1968), pp. 143–44.

Annie Dillard, "In the Jungle" from *Teaching a Stone to Talk* by Annie Dillard. Copyright © 1982 by Annie Dillard. Reprinted by permission of HarperCollins Publishers, Inc.

Michael Dorris, excerpt from *A Yellow Raft in Blue Water,* New York, Henry Holt and Co., Inc., 1987.

Ian Dunbar, "Fast Track to Perfection." *Dog Fancy,* April, 1999, reprinted by permission of the author.

Leo Durocher, *Nice Guys Finish Last* (New York: Simon & Schuster, 1975), p. 54.

Wayne Dyer, *What Do You Really Want for Your Children?* (New York: William Morrow, Inc., 1985).

Loren Eiseley, *The Unexpected Universe* (New York: Harcourt Brace Jovanovich, 1969) p. 88.

Loren Eiseley, "The Judgment of the Birds," in *The Immense Journey* (New York: Random House, 1956), pp. 174–75.

Marian Engle, review of *The Goddess and Other Women*, by Joyce Carol Oates, *New York Times Book Review*, Nov. 24, 1974, p. 7.

Sabrina Rubin Erdely, "Binge Drinking, A Campus Killer." Reprinted from the November 1998 *Reader's Digest*, with permission from the author.

Howard Ensign Evans, *Life on a Little-Known Planet* (New York: E.P. Dutton, 1968), pp. 107–8.

Henry Fairlie, "A Victim Fights Back," *The Washington Post*, April 30, 1978.

David Finkelstein, "When the Snow Thaws," *The New Yorker*, Sept. 10, 1979, p. 127.

"Formlessness" from *Roget's International Thesaurus*, 5th edition by Peter Mark Roget, Copyright © 1992 by HarperCollins Publishers, Inc. Reprinted by permission of HarperCollins Publishers, Inc.

Adam Frank, excerpts from "Winds of Change," in *Discover*, June 1994, pp. 100–4.

Bruce Jay Friedman, "Eating Alone in Restaurants." From *The Lonely Guy's Book to Life*, copyright © 1978 by McGraw-Hill, Inc. Reprinted by permission of the McGraw-Hill Companies.

Otto Friedrich, "There are 00 Trees in Russia," *Harper's Magazine*, Oct. 1964.

Ron Geraci, "Which Stooge Are You?" From *Men's Health* Magazine, Sept., 1999. Reprinted by permission of *Men's Health* Magazine. Copyright © 1999 Rodale Press, Inc. All rights reserved.

Nancy Gibbs, "When Is It Rape?" Copyright © 1991 Time Inc. Reprinted by permission.

Matea Gold and David Ferrell, "Going for Broke." Excerpt from the December 13, 1998, *Los Angeles Times*. Copyright, 1998, *Los Angeles Times*. Reprinted with permission.

Ellen Goodman, "The Company Man." Reprinted with the permission of Simon & Schuster from *Close to Home* by Ellen Goodman. Copyright © 1979 by The Washington Post Company.

Martin Gottfried, "Rambos of the Road," *Newsweek*, Sept. 8, 1986. Reprinted by permission of the author.

Dan Greenburg, "Sound and Fury." Reprinted by permission of the author. All rights reserved.

Amy Gross, "The Appeal of the Androgynous Man." *Mademoiselle*. Copyright © 1976 by The Condé Nast Publications, Inc. Reprinted by permission of Amy Gross.

L.D. Hamilton, "Antibodies and Antigens," *The New Book of Knowledge* 1967, I, 317.

S.I. Hayakawa, *Language in Thought and Action*, 3rd ed. (New York: Harcourt Brace Jovanovich, 1972), p. 50.

Lesley Hazleton, "Assembly Line Adventure." Reprinted with the permission of The Free Press, a division of Simon & Schuster, Inc., from *Driving to Detroit: An Automotive Odyssey* by Lesley Hazleton. Copyright © 1998 by Lesley Hazleton.

John Hersey, *Hiroshima* (New York: Modern Library, 1946), p. 4.

Nancy K. Hill, "Scaling the Heights: The Teacher as Mountaineer," *The Chronicle of Higher Education*, June 16, 1980, p. 48.

Thomas Henry Huxley, "A Liberal Education and Where to Find It," *Macmillan's Magazine*, March 17, 1868.

Dina Ingber, "Computer Addicts," *Science Digest*, July 1981.

Washington Irving, "The Spectre Bridegroom," in *Selected Writings of Washington Irving*, ed. Saxe Commins (New York: Modern Library, 1945), p. 53.

Bruce Jackson, "Who Goes to Prison: Caste and Careerism in Crime," *Atlantic Monthly*, Jan. 1966, p. 52.

Daniel James, "Close the Borders to All Newcomers." Reprinted with permission from *Insight*. Copyright 1997 News World Communications, Inc. All rights reserved.

Robert Jastrow, *Until the Sun Dies* (New York: Norton, 1977).

Ellen Herbert Jordan, "My Affair with the One-Armed Bandit," *Modern Maturity*, July-August 1995: 37, 86+.

Vernon E. Jordan, Jr., "The New Negativism," *Newsweek*, Aug. 14, 1978, p. 13. Copyright © 1978, Newsweek, Inc.

Doris Kearns, "Who Was Lyndon Baines Johnson?" from *Lyndon Johnson and the American Dream* (New York: Harper & Row, 1976).

Helen Keller, "Three Days to See," *Atlantic Monthly*, Jan. 1933, p. 35.

John F. Kennedy, "Inaugural Address," Washington, D.C., Jan. 20, 1961.

Martin Luther King, Jr., "I Have a Dream." Reprinted by arrangement with the heirs to the Estate of Martin Luther King, Jr., c/o Writers House, Inc., as agent for the proprietor. Copyright 1963 by Martin Luther King, Jr., copyright renewed 1991 by Coretta Scott King.

Martin Luther King, Jr., "Pilgrimage to Nonviolence," in *Stride Toward Freedom* (New York: Harper & Row, 1958), p. 84.

Perri Klass, "She's Your Basic L.O.L. in N.A.D." Reprinted by permission of the Putnam Publishing Group from *A Not Entirely Benign Procedure* by Perri Klass. Copyright © 1987 by Perri Klass. Used by permission of G. P. Putnam's Sons, a division of Penguin Putnam, Inc.

Marilyn Kluger, "A Time of Plenty," *Gourmet,* Nov. 1976, p. 22.

Edward I. Koch, "Death and Justice." Reprinted by permission of *The New Republic,* copyright © 1985, The New Republic, Inc.

Kenneth Labich, "The Scandal of Killer Trucks," *Fortune,* March 30, 1987.

John Lovesey, "A Myth is as Good as a Mile," *Sports Illustrated,* Nov. 9, 1964.

Marilyn Machlowitz, "Workaholism: What's Wrong with Being Married to Your Work?" *Working Woman,* May 1978, p. 51.

Malcolm X, *The Autobiography of Malcolm X* (New York: Ballantine Books, 1964), p. 171.

Marshall Mandell, "Are You Allergic to Your House?" *Prevention,* Sept. 1979, p. 101.

Marya Mannes, "Wasteland," in *More in Anger* (Philadelphia: J. B. Lippincott, 1958), p. 40.

Hara Estroff Marano, "The Power of Play." Reprinted with permission from *Psychology Today* Magazine. Copyright © 1999 Sussex Publishers, Inc.

Margaret Mead, "New Superstitions for Old," from *A Way of Seeing* by Margaret Mead and Rhoda Metraux. Copyright © 1966 by Margaret Mead and Rhoda Metraux.

L. David Mech, "Where Can the Wolves Survive?" *National Geographic,* Oct. 1977, p. 536.

H. L. Mencken, "The Libido for the Ugly," Copyright 1927 by Alfred A. Knopf, Inc., and renewed 1955 by H. L. Mencken. Reprinted from *A Mencken Chrestomathy,* edited and annotated by H. L. Mencken, by permission of the publisher.

Thomas H. Middleton, "The Magic Power of Words," *Saturday Review,* Dec. 11, 1976, p. 90.

Don Ethan Miller, "A State of Grace: Understanding the Martial Arts," *Atlantic Monthly,* Sept. 1980. Copyright © 1980 by Don Ethan Miller.

Gretchen Morgenson, "Sexual Harassment Is Overestimated," © 1991 by *National Review,* Inc., 150 East 35th Street, New York, NY, 10016. Reprinted by permission.

Stephen Moore, "Give Us Your Best, Your Brightest." Reprinted with permission from *Insight.* Copyright 1997 News World Communications, Inc. All rights reserved.

Gloria Naylor, "The Uses of a Word." Reprinted by permission of Sterling Lord Literistic, Inc. Copyright © 1986 by Gloria Naylor.

George Orwell, excerpt from "Shooting an Elephant," in *Shooting an Elephant and Other Essays,* copyright 1950 by Sonia Brownell Orwell; renewed 1978 by Sonia Pitt-Rivers. Reprinted by permission of Harcourt, Inc.

Jo Goodwin Parker, "What Is Poverty?" in George Henderson, *America's Other Children:Public Schools Outside Suburbia* (University of Oklahoma Press, 1971).

Nancy Perry, "Saving the Schools: How Business Can Help," from *Fortune,* Nov. 7, 1988.

Alexander Petrunkevitch, from "The Spider and the Wasp," *Scientific American,* August, 1952. Copyright © 1952 by Scientific American, Inc. All rights reserved.

Marilyn Gaye Piety, "Sexual Harassment Is a Serious Problem at Universities," from *Christian Social Action,* July/August 1991. Reprinted by permission.

Mary Pipher, "Then and Now." Reprinted by permission of The Putnam Publishing Group from *Reviving Ophelia* by Mary Pipher, Ph.D. Copyright © 1994 by Mary Pipher, Ph.D.

J. Winston Porter, "We'll Trash *U.S.A. Today* Too," from *U.S.A. Today,* July 11, 1988. All rights reserved.

Anna Quindlen, "Execution," from *Living Out Loud* by Anna Quindlen. Copyright © 1987 by Anna Quindlen. Used by permission of Random House, Inc.

William Raspberry, "A Journalist's View of Black Economics," © 1990, Washington Post Writers Group. Reprinted with permission.

Lord Richie-Calder, "The Doctor's Dilemma," *The Center Magazine,* Sept./Oct. 1971.

Edwin Arlington Robinson, "The Miller's Wife," *The Three Taverns,* Charles Scribner's Sons, 1920.

Richard Rodriguez, "Private Language, Public Language." From *Aria: A Memoir of a Bilingual Childhood* by Richard Rodriguez. Copyright © 1980 by Richard Rodriguez. Reprinted by permission of Georges Borchardt, Inc., for the author. Originally appeared in *American Scholar.*

Anne Roiphe, "Why Marriages Fail," from *Family Weekly,* Feb. 27, 1983. Permission granted by International Creative Management, Inc. Copyright © 1983 by Anne Roiphe.

Bertrand Russell, *The ABC of Relativity* (London: Allen and Unwin, 1965), pp. 46–47.

Bertrand Russell, "Respect for Law," *San Francisco Review,* Winter, 1958, pp. 63–65. Reprinted by permission of June Oppen Degnan.

Nancy Masterson Sakamoto, "Conversational Ballgames." From Kinsiedo, Ltd., 1982. Reprinted by permission of Nancy Masterson Sakamoto. All rights reserved.

Robert J. Samuelson, "Getting Serious," *Newsweek,* September 18, 1995: 40–44.

Scott Russell Sanders, "The Men We Carry in Our Minds," copyright © 1984 by Scott Russell Sanders; first appeared in *Milkweed Chronicle;* reprinted by permission of the author and Virginia Kidd Agency, Inc.

Lewis Sawaquat, "For My Indian Daughter," *Newsweek,* Sept. 5, 1983. Reprinted by permission of the author.

Mark Schapiro, "Children of a Lesser God," *Harper's Bazaar,* April, 1996: 205–18.

Richard Selzer, "The Knife," from *Mortal Lessons.* Copyright © 1974, 1975, 1976 by Richard Selzer. Reprinted by permission of Georges Borchardt, Inc., for the author.

Laurence Shames, "The Sweet Smell of Success Isn't All That Sweet." Copyright © 1986 by The New York Times Company. Reprinted by permission.

Gideon Sjoberg, "The Origin and Development of Cities," *Scientific American,* Sept. 1965, p. 55.

Elliott L. Smith and Andrew W. Hart, *The Short Story: A Contemporary Looking Glass* (New York: Random House, 1981).

Brent Staples, "Black Men and Public Space," *Harper's,* Dec. 1986. Reprinted by permission.

Joyce Susskind, "Surprises in a Woman's Life," *Vogue,* Feb. 1979, p. 252.

Amy Tan, excerpt from *The Joy Luck Club,* New York, G. P. Putnam's Sons, 1989.

Deborah Tannen, "Gender Gap in Cyberspace." From *Newsweek,* April 16, 1994. Newsweek, Inc. All rights reserved. Reprinted by permission.

Deems Taylor, "The Monster" in *Of Mice and Music* (New York: Simon & Schuster, 1965).

James Alexander Thom, "The Perfect Picture." Reprinted with permission from the August 1976 *Reader's Digest.* Copyright © 1976 by The Reader's Digest Ass'n., Inc.

Lewis Thomas, excerpt from "Societies As Organisms," in *The Lives of a Cell* by Lewis Thomas. Copyright © 1971 by The Massachusetts Medical Society.

Richard Tomkins, "Old Father Time Becomes a Terror." From *Financial Times* March 21, 1999. Copyright © 1999 by *Financial Times.* All rights reserved.

Beth Wald, "Let's Get Vertical!" from *Listen: Journal of Better Living.* June 1989. Reprinted by permission.

Marjorie Waters, "Coming Home." Copyright © 1982 by Marjorie Waters. Originally published in the *Bedford Reader* (Bedford Books of St. Martin's Press, 1982). Reprinted by permission of the author.

Eudora Welty, "A Visit of Charity," from *A Curtain of Green and Other Stories* (New York: Harcourt, 1941, 1969).

E. B. White, "Once More to the Lake," from *One Man's Meat,* text copyright © 1941 by E. B. White. Reprinted by permission of Tilbury House, Publishers, Gardiner, Maine.

Marion Winik, "What Are Friends For?" From *Telling* by Marion Winik, copyright © 1994 by Marion Winik. Used by permission of Villard Books, a division of Random House, Inc.

Tom Wolfe, *The Pump House Gang* (New York: World Journal Tribune, 1966), p. 293.

Orvill Wyss and Curtis Eklund, *Microorganisms and Man* (New York: John Wiley and Sons, 1971), pp. 232–33.

Rafael Yglesias, excerpt from *Fearless,* New York, Warner Books, 1993.

John V. Young, "When the Full Moon Shines Its Magic over Monument Valley," *New York Times,* March 16, 1969. Section 10, p. 1. Copyright © 1969 by the New York Times Company. Reprinted by permission.

David Zimmerman, "Are Test-Tube Babies the Answer for the Childless?" *Woman's Day,* May 1979, p. 26.

Susan Zimmerman, "Blur: Cheetahs. Ranchers. Hope." This article originally appeared in the November/December 1996 issue of *Earthwatch Magazine.* Copyright Susan Zimmerman.

Photos: p. 190, Rob Kinmonth; p. 434, S.R. Watkins/Betsy Flagler; p. 436, L. Romero/NYT Pictures; p. 439, AP/Wide World Photos; p. 446, Alexander Lowry; p. 448, AP/Wide World Photos; p. 452, Watkins/Loomis Agency; p. 461, Dr. Ian Dunbar; p. 465, TimePix; p. 467, Daniel Corrigan; p. 470, Donald Cousey/AP/Wide World Photos; p. 474, Sabrina Rubin Erdely; p. 478, Amy Meadow/Martin Gottfried; p. 481, Los Angeles Times Syndicate; p. 481, Los Angeles Times Syndicate; p. 485, Kimberley Arrington-Oster/The Washington Post; p. 488, Todd V. Wolfson; p. 491, Eve Sanders/Scott Russell Sanders; p. 494, The University of Georgia Press; p. 499, Ron Geraci; p. 504, AP/Wide World Photos; p. 507, Nancy Masterson Sakamoto; p. 510, Randy Barger/Riverside Literary Agency; p. 520, Brit Thurston/Georges Borchardt, Inc.; p. 525, Marjorie Waters; p. 527, Financial Times, London; p. 531, Deborah Tannen; p. 533, Lorin Klaris Photography; p. 536, Brent Staples; p. 540, Marilyn Shames; p. 542, Hara Estroff Marano; p. 547, Gale Zucker Photography; p. 552, Doug Goodman/Time Inc., NJ; p. 560, AP/Wide World Photos; p. 564, Joyce Ravid/Corbis/Outline; p. 566, Marilyn Gaye Piety; p. 571, Roger Ressmeyer © 1999 Corbis/Starlight Division, a Division of Corbis; p. 576, UPI/Corbis; p. 580, © 1998, The Washington Post Writers Group, reprinted by permission; p. 590, Chas Geer Photography/Stephen Moore; p. 595, © Randall Hyman; p. 601, Frank Curran; p. 604, Marion Ettinger.

Subject Index